EC COMPETITION LAW

EUROPEAN LAW SERIES

Series Editor: Professor John A. Usher

EC COMPETITION LAW

ROBERT LANE

An imprint of Pearson Education

Harlow, England · London · New York · Reading, Massachusetts · San Francisco
Toronto · Don Mills, Ontario · Sydney · Tokyo · Singapore · Hong Kong · Seoul
Taipei · Cape Town · Madrid · Mexico City · Amsterdam · Munich · Paris · Milan

TO MY FATHER AND IN MEMORY OF MY MOTHER

Pearson Education Limited
Edinburgh Gate
Harlow
Essex CM20 2JE
England

and Associated Companies throughout the world

Visit us on the World Wide Web at:
www.pearsoneduc.com

———————————

First published 2000

© Pearson Education Limited 2000

ISBN 0-582-28976-9

British Library Cataloguing-in-Publication Data
A catalogue record for this book is available from the British Library.

10 9 8 7 6 5 4 3 2 1
05 04 03 02 01 00

Set by 7 in 10/13 pt Sabon.
Printed in Great Britain by Henry Ling Ltd, at the Dorset Press, Dorchester, Dorset

CONTENTS

12 The Competition Act 1998   344

SERIES PREFACE

The Longman European Law Series is the first comprehensive series of topic-based books on EC law aimed primarily at a student readership, though I have no doubt that they will also be found useful by academic colleagues and interested practitioners. It has become more and more difficult for a single course or a single book to deal comprehensively with all the major topics of Community law, and the intention of this series is to enable students and teachers to 'mix and match' topics which they find to be of interest: it may also be hoped that the publication of this Series will encourage the study of areas of Community law which have historically been neglected in degree courses. However, while the Series may have a student readership in mind, the authors have been encouraged to take an academic and critical approach, placing each topic in its overall Community context, and also in its socio-economic and political context where relevant.

It gives me particular pleasure to welcome this volume on EC Competition Law by my colleague Bob Lane. Dr Lane has taught the subject to advanced students in the University of Edinburgh for many years, and is well known as a writer in the area. The topic itself is perhaps the most widely-studied area of substantive EC law, and it is one where the volume of material has grown exponentially. Dr Lane has nevertheless presented the full range of EC competition law in a manageable and readable format, while drawing attention to the many contentious issues which arise. It is particularly appropriate that a new book on this topic should be published now, when changes have occurred in the EC legislation (and in views on how it should be administered) and when UK competition legislation has been reformed so as to reflect the principles of the EC legislation.

John A. Usher

AUTHOR'S PREFACE

Twenty years ago, a legal practitioner or academic might be asked whether he or she had a specialisation. If the response was 'EC law', the normal supplementary question was 'yes, and what else?' If the same exchange occurs today, the supplementary question is now 'yes, but which area?' This is one mark of the vast growth of all aspects of Community law, both into new areas unforeseen by the framers of the Treaty (human rights, environmental law, consumer protection, for example) – 'broadening', to transpose Community jargon – but also the profound 'deepening' of those in existence from the beginning.

Into the latter category falls competition law. Competition law was addressed in the Treaty in a handful of, at first blush, apparently innocuous articles. From this modest beginning it has evolved, and continues to evolve, into a substantial, complex and hugely important aspect of Community endeavour. It is also the area in which the legal practitioner, excepting perhaps the specialists in agricultural or employment law, is most likely to encounter Community law. And it has a further importance in that the law and principles developed within the Community have now haemorrhaged into national law: virtually unknown in Europe 40 years ago, the Community rules have inspired the adoption of substantial competition law regimes in all member states, in most cases lifted directly from the Treaty approach.

The complexity of Community competition law can be measured (roughly) by the fact that most books in the field run into many hundreds of pages. Whilst this is by no means disproportionate, the Longman series seeks a gentler approach: to make the field accessible, as it ought to be, without substantial cost to both comprehensiveness and comprehension. Students of various fields of law sometimes say of their required reading 'it's a very good book; I didn't understand a word of it'. It is the intention, and hope, of the author that the latter sentiment at least might not be said often of this book.

The law is stated as at 1 June 2000.

Robert Lane
Culross, Scotland
Victoria Day 2000

TABLE OF CASES

EFTA Court

European Court of Human Rights

TABLE OF LEGISLATION

National Legislation

INTRODUCTION

Competition law is about state intervention in the marketplace. More precisely, it is about regulation not *of* the marketplace but of the conduct of firms within it in order that the benefits of their economic activity be maximised for the public good.

A simple proposition – but it is laden with ambiguities and, if accepted, admits of a host of variations. Put simply, there is a contradiction and tension in economic systems, such as those of the European Community and the member states which make it up, so devoutly (and vocally) wedded to the unfettered play of market forces which at the same time countenance, let alone encourage, intervention and regulation of those forces. To some the very term 'market regulation' is Orwellian Newspeak – however deft its touch, competition law is an affront to the freedom of commerce and the freedom of contract which are the defining components of the free market. But to the liberal economist, the free market posits a system which recognises that it is first and foremost for the market to be left to its own devices for it is its own best regulator, yet it sometimes falters and requires a moderating hand when it does so. This is the concern of competition law. It is the competition law of the European Community that this book is about.

Competition law is a variant of economic law and a relative newcomer to legal science, developments in Europe other than the rudimentary occurring only in the latter half of the century just past. When the European Economic Community came into being in 1958 only one member state, Germany, had anything approaching comprehensive competition law on the statute book. It is in fact so new that there is no agreement even as to what to call it. Modern competition law is generally recognised to spring originally from the United States where it is, for historical reasons, 'antitrust' law. In half the present member states of the Community it is the law of 'concurrence', which at first sight suggests exactly the opposite of that which it addresses; in others it is the law of competition (*Wettbewerb*; *competencia*; *mededinging*; *kilpailu*) and cartel law (*Kartellrecht*), and

1

owing to the statutory framework until very recently in force, it was in the United Kingdom sometimes called restrictive trade practices law. Closest to the mark seems to be two of the less widely spoken Treaty languages in which it is the law of rivalry (*iomaíocht*) and the law of antagonism (αvταγωvισμός).

Novelty notwithstanding, it is a field of law which is growing by leaps and bounds, both broadening and deepening. This is a direct result of Community development and in part a response to the huge complexity of modern commerce and as a function of which the law is developing a complexity of its own to match. And as it is new, so it is catching: since 1958 all member states have seen fit to adopt their own comprehensive competition legislation, in most cases modelled very closely upon the Community approach. The entry into force in March 2000 of the Competition Act 1998, marking a coming of age in the United Kingdom, is only the latest in the queue. For good or ill the policy argument for competition law has been won, and firms, and legal practitioners, now ignore it at their peril.

The plan of any book on EC competition law confronts difficulties because the substantive rules are so closely intertwined with their administration, and the one cannot be properly understood without reference to the other. The question is, simply, where to start. Uncontentious perhaps is an introduction to the discipline of competition law generally (Chapter 1) and its Community context and the common principles of the Treaty approach (Chapter 2). There then follows consideration of the core substantive provisions of the Treaty (Chapters 3–5), then their enforcement (Chapter 6). Both elements having then been digested, consideration is given to more nuanced issues (Chapters 7–11). Finally, this being a British book, there will be brief consideration of the Competition Act 1998 (Chapter 12) which was born of EC competition law. But for the British and non-British reader alike, it should bring home (along with reference to it from time to time throughout the book) the fact that with competition law in the Community, there may be slight variations in the melody which are the products of national law and regulation.

Caveat lector

There are two points of which the reader ought constantly to be aware in the course of reading the book. The first is that it is about European competition law, and because it is about competition law it is about the law of the European Community. The reader will not be confronted with, and need not worry about, aspects of the law of the European Union and their tangency with EC law. Where the reader will require to be on guard is in being aware that, as a result of the Amsterdam Treaty which entered into force in 1999, articles of the EC Treaty (and of the Treaty on European

Union) were renumbered from scratch. This was, apparently, a response to a perception that various amendments made to it since it first came into force had created a sense of clutter, which could be swept away with the application of a numerical new broom. The decision to do so has gone largely unremarked – except amongst lawyers (and the Court of Justice was not consulted until the deal was done), to whom it was one of crass, casual stupidity. Not only must the judge, the practitioner and the academic already familiar with the old numbers now adjust to the new, not only will the Court of Justice face formidable transitional difficulties in dealing intelligibly with cases raised by reference to the old numbers but decided under the new, and not only will computer searches be rendered chaotic, but anyone new to the study of Community law will be required to rely for the foreseeable future upon 40 years of essential and defining case law which, without constant cross referencing to a table of equivalence, will make no apparent sense. It is a recipe for muddle and confusion, all the more galling for being wholly unnecessary. To overcome (or at least to mitigate) the problem, the Court of Justice has now settled upon a style whereby pre-Amsterdam Treaty articles are cited as articles 'of the EC Treaty' whilst the post-Amsterdam numeration is indicated with the suffix 'EC'. So, 'Article 85 of the EC Treaty' and 'Article 81 EC' are one and the same article. However, this solution was adopted in part because of the necessity facing the Court to refer not only to the EC Treaty but also to other Treaty texts. It is unwieldy, it brings its own confusion, for the Court has in the past sometimes used the new formulation to refer to the old numbers, and it is unnecessary if concentrating almost exclusively upon the one (the EC) Treaty. The style will therefore not be adopted in this book. Instead, Treaty articles will generally be cited by their new number but with an indication of their pre-Amsterdam number thus: Article 81 (ex Article 85). Where the immediate context requires it, first reference will be to the old number with an indication of the new: Article 85 (now Article 81). However, as the book is concerned pre-eminently with two Treaty articles – that is, Articles 81 and 82 (ex Articles 85 and 86) – and the text and case law cited refers to them copiously, it would add clutter far greater than that of the pre-Amsterdam Treaty were this formula to be applied religiously. Following a gentle introduction in each chapter, the reader will be assumed thereafter to be aware that the new Articles 81 and 82 are the erstwhile Articles 85 and 86, and ought to take note that passages taken from virtually all case law (that is, that decided prior to May 1999) refer to Articles 85 and 86, will be unencumbered by '[now Article 81 and/or 82]', but are to be read as reference to Articles 81 and 82. Where the old numbers are cited formally in a legislative or related act which predates the entry into force of the Amsterdam Treaty, the latter provides (Article

12(3)) that they 'shall be understood' as references to the Treaty as renumbered, but as the diktat is merely that they be understood or deemed to be, and not amended as, the new numbers (so generating further confusion), the old numbers will be retained in any formal citation in the text.

The second point is that the reader is also presumed to have a basic familiarity with Community law. The revolutionary and evolutionary nature of Community law and the constitutional principles which the Court of Justice has developed to give it flesh and ensure its effectiveness are subjects eminently worthy of inquiry, and are canvassed in a number of other books in this series; they will be referred to but not directly considered here. Likewise an understanding of the structure and workings of the institutions, the nature and force of Community legislation – and in particular the jurisdiction and role of the Court of Justice as final arbiter of the meaning of the Treaty (including also that of its 'little brother' the Court of First Instance, which since its inception in 1989 has played a significant part in the field of competition law, and the role and authority of the Advocates-General, a number of whom are cited in the text) – are important in order to understand the context, but not the substance, of this book, and the reader is presumed to be literate with them. One point worth bearing in mind throughout is that the Court encounters competition law by means of two distinct heads of jurisdiction: first, actions raised under Article 230 (ex Article 173) of the Treaty, which is essentially a judicial review procedure, here review of the Commission as it discharges the substantial delegated powers by which it enforces the competition rules; and second, requests from national courts for a preliminary ruling under Article 234 (ex Article 177) in order to assist those courts in the interpretation of the Community rules raised in litigation before them, in which context the jurisdiction of the Court is limited to interpretation of the law and not its application, and always within the framework of the questions framed by the referring court. In reading a judgment of the Court it is important to differentiate between the two distinct types of jurisdiction in order properly to understand its context and limitations. A related consideration, and one the importance of which is often overlooked, is that the Community legal system is one which exists in 12 (the Treaties) and 11 (Community legislation) equally authentic language versions, no one of which has pre-eminence. This sometimes colours the interpretative techniques of the Court of Justice which must take all languages into account, and explains in part its emphasis upon purposive rather than textual (or literal) interpretation. But it also means that the official English language version, and that of all languages, of legislation and of judgments of the Court is sometimes (happily, rarely) misleading. Where this is so in a passage cited from the Court, reference will be made also to the terms used in the language of the case (the only authentic language version) and in the French, *de facto* the most reliable version as it is the internal working language of the Court.

CHAPTER 1

On the nature of competition and competition law

Competition is about the struggle by firms to achieve superiority over other firms in the marketplace; competition law is about the rules limiting the freedom by which they may do so. Since there is now abroad a general adherence to the liberal economic predisposition that it is the free market which best delivers the benefits of economic activity, this is of course inherently a contradiction – for why should the free market require (or countenance) regulation in order to make it free? There exist still champions of the free market wielding the crusader's sword against any fetters to unreconstructed market capitalism, although in some cases the conviction falters even amongst its most stalwart champions when things, in their lights, go awry. Many are, however, in principle less certain, and take the view that given an unfettered free hand the market in some circumstances breaks down, fails to deliver on its promise, and therefore requires a degree of regulation.

It is the acceptance of this proposition that is the justification for competition law. In order to understand why this is so, some familiarity with basic economic concepts and models is necessary. If, for example, competition law seeks to prevent 'restrictions' or 'distortions' to competition it necessarily posits an alternative outcome, or model, of 'non-restricted' or 'non-distorted' competition. Some concepts are intuitive and require no close analysis, others are less so. What follows is a brief and much simplified consideration of the economics and terminology of competition, or the economic environment in which competition operates, and the preliminary considerations which go to the creation of a set of rules to regulate it.

1.1 Competition

According to neo-classical economic theory a system of open competition within free markets maximises consumer welfare. Consumer welfare ought not to be confused with the wellbeing or the protection of the consumer which the term may suggest, welfare economics being that branch of microeconomics concerned with the efficiency of the firm, the market and/or the economy. The market is an allocative device. To liberal economists it is the free choice of market participants, which are assumed always to act in their own and not in the public interest, which leads to optimal overall wealth. It generally maximises efficiency in terms both of resource allocation (allocative efficiency) and in the lowest overall cost in the production of goods or services (productive or cost efficiency). It is also presumed (for it is difficult to quantify) to foster innovation (dynamic efficiency), the rapid adjustment to technological advance and to change and discrimination in consumer preference. Where such a system obtains it is the play of supply and demand – Adam Smith's 'invisible hand'[1] – which regulates and disciplines the market and maximises consumer welfare. Anything that diminishes free choice lessens the utility of the market, producing a sub-optimal net system.

As competition is about superiority in the marketplace, at the core of any economic analysis of competition lies the concept of market power. To the economist market power is the ability of a producer or supplier to raise prices – price being of course in the first rank of the means by which competition is waged – whilst limiting the production or supply of goods or services (shown to be necessary by even cursory reference to a demand curve) above competitive levels and still increase net profits. Where the invisible hand obtains, no producer or supplier ought to be able to charge supracompetitive prices. But if a firm is able to do so, either in the short term (prices above marginal cost – the production cost of the last unit produced) or the longer term (prices above average total cost), it has market power. Market power may therefore be said to describe a situation in which the constraints of competitive forces which would normally ensure that firms behave in a competitive manner are not working effectively.[2] A purpose of competition law may in turn be said to be the identification of circumstances in which market power is or may be exercised and the prevention of it.

1.1.1 The relevant market

Since competition rules are all about the play of the market, it is necessary to define, in any particular case, the market under consideration, or the 'relevant market'. Competition and competition law do not exist in a vac-

---

[1] A. Smith, *An Inquiry into the Nature and Sources of the Wealth of Nations* (1776), *passim.*
[2] *Assessment of Market Power*, OFT 415, para 1.2.

uum. If competition is to be distorted, it is necessary to ascertain how it is distorted, and for that it is necessary to ascertain the market in which it is distorted in order to assess market power within it. As the Court of First Instance has noted, 'the appropriate definition of the market in question is a necessary precondition of any judgment concerning allegedly anti-competitive behaviour'.[3]

The identification of a relevant market consists implicitly in identification of a product or service or group of products or services in which a hypothetical single producer or supplier could exercise market power. Put another way, a relevant market is a market worth monopolising.[4] It has two essential elements: the product or service market in issue and the geographic market in issue. These will be considered in greater detail below, especially in the context of the rules governing monopoly behaviour and mergers, in which areas market definition is of clinical importance. For present, introductory, purposes it will suffice to consider a 1997 Commission notice which defines relevant markets 'for the purposes of Community competition law',[5] according to which

> [a] relevant product market comprises all those products and/or services which are regarded as interchangeable or substitutable by the consumer, by reason of the products' characteristics, their price and their intended use ....[6]

The primary tests to be applied are those of product/service substitutability or interchangeability and cross-elasticity of demand, that is the identification of a product or products or service(s) for which no other product(s) or service(s) can satisfactorily be substituted. If products or services can be differentiated by various criteria but nonetheless satisfy the same essential consumer demand it is the wider market, comprising all products or services that are interchangeable with or substitutable for one another, which constitutes the relevant market for purposes of determining competition within it. If they do not the market is accordingly narrower. It is sufficient that there be an identifiable market in which the substitution of one product or service for another is more burdensome or less attractive, for whatever reason, to the consumer. Put another way, a relevant market is defined by all products or services which generate a competitive restraint

---

[3] Cases T–66, 77 & 78/89 *Società Italiano Vetro* v *Commission* (Flat Glass) [1992] ECR II–1403 at 1463.

[4] See S. Bishop and M. Walker, *The Economics of EC Competition Law* (Sweet & Maxwell, London, 1999), pp 49 *et seq.*

[5] Notice of definition of the relevant market for the purposes of Community competition law, OJ 1997 C372/5.

[6] para 7.

and so (ought to) prevent the exercise of market power. A test of substitutability may in the first instance be intuitive or one of common sense: there is, for example, clearly a market for single malt whisky distinct from that of blended whisky, for the latter retails in the United Kingdom for half the price of the former yet single malt still commands a loyal (and growing) following. The question becomes more difficult the narrower the market(s) – whether, say, there is cross-elasticity of demand between Speyside and Islay malts. In any event intuition and common sense do not pass muster as operationalising tools of market analysis. The methodology by which an economist would normally measure elasticity is the 'small but significant non-transitory increase in price' (SSNIP) test, that is identification of the narrowest range of products or services for which a hypothetical monopolist could permanently and profitably raise relative prices by a small but significant amount (say 5 to 10 per cent; hence also sometimes called the '5 per cent test').[7] It can be illustrated as follows: if an increase, of extended duration, of 5 to 10 per cent in the price of draught beer would lead a sufficient number of draught beer drinkers to switch allegiance to lager such that the price increase would not be profitable to beer producers owing to loss of sales, then draught beer and lager taken together constitute a single product market. If a similar increase in the price of both were to convert the draught beer/lager drinker to wine, the relevant market is draught beer, lager and wine. If a similar increase in the price of all three were to drive the beer/lager/wine drinker from the pub to take his refreshment at home, the relevant market is draught beer, lager, wine and off licence sales of each. And so on. The test does not require a large shift in allegiance, only that of the marginal, not discriminating, consumer to the extent that it would cancel out any profits of the price increase. Yet it normally yields a definition of product market which is narrow rather than broad.

To take some actual examples from Community case law, bananas constitute their own, distinct product market because of special characteristics – 'appearance, taste, softness, seedlessness, easy handling, a constant level of production which enable [them] to satisfy the constant needs of an important section of the population consisting of the very young, the old and the sick' – which distinguish them from fresh fruit generally.[8] Bottled

---

7 The SSNIP test is considered in the 1997 notice, para 17.
8 Case 27/76 *United Brands* v *Commission* [1978] ECR 207 at 273. For other Treaty purposes – the prohibition of discriminatory indirect taxation under Art 90 (ex Art 95) – bananas do compete with other fresh fruit; Case 193/85 *Cooperativa Co-Frutta* v *Amministrazione delle Finanze dello Stato* [1987] ECR 2085.

water is a product market distinct from soft drinks[9] and cola drinks are distinct from other soft drinks;[10] roses are distinct from other ornamental cut flowers;[11] new replacement tyres for lorries, buses and other heavy vehicles are products distinct from retreaded tyres and tyres for motorcars and vans.[12] The rail services market constitutes a sub-market distinct from the rail transport market in general, for it offers a specific range of services – the provision of locomotives, traction and access to the railway infrastructure – which, although provided by the railway transport operators, is not interchangeable or in competition with their services.[13] Equally flights between Luton and Brussels airports[14] or between Heathrow and Dublin airports[15] form distinct service markets owing to the inconvenience for a number of passengers of using other airline routes and certainly other means of transportation. A single product can be subdivided into different product markets depending upon user demand: white granulated sugar, for example, may be divided into two product markets, industrial sugar (sold in bulk or large bags to, primarily, the food and drink industry and to packers) and retail sugar (sold in smaller quantities to, primarily, the individual consumer and the catering trade);[16] and ice cream into four or three product markets applying similar criteria to the peculiarities of the market: in Germany industrial ice cream, multipack ice cream, craft trade ice cream and impulse ice cream,[17] and in Ireland catering ice cream, take-home ice cream and impulse ice cream.[18]

Whilst the above considerations address the principal test of demand

---

[9] Decision 92/553 (*Nestlé/Perrier*) OJ 1992 L356/1.

[10] Decision 97/540 (*Coca-Cola/Amalgamated Beverages GB*) OJ 1997 L218/15.

[11] Decision 85/561 (*Breeders' Rights: Roses*) OJ 1985 L369/9.

[12] Case 322/81 *Michelin* v *Commission* [1983] ECR 3461.

[13] Case T-229/94 *Deutsche Bahn* v *Commission* [1997] ECR II-1689, upheld on appeal as Case C-436/97P *Deutsche Bahn* v *Commission* [1999] ECR I-2387.

[14] Decision 88/589 (*London European/Sabena*) OJ 1988 L317/47.

[15] Decision 92/213 (*British Midland/Aer Lingus*) OJ 1992 L96/34.

[16] Decision 97/624 (*Irish Sugar*) OJ 1997 L258/32, upheld on review as Case T-228/97 *Irish Sugar* v *Commission* [1999] ECR II-2969 (under appeal as Case C-497/99P *Irish Sugar* v *Commission*, pending), but the decision was not challenged on the ground of misdefinition of the product market; Decision 1999/210 (*British Sugar/Tate & Lyle/Napier Brown/James Budgett*) OJ 1999 L76/1 (under review as Cases T-202 & 207/98 *Tate & Lyle and Napier Brown* v *Commission*, pending).

[17] Decisions 93/405 (*Schöller*) OJ 1992 L183/1 and 93/406 (*Langnese-Iglo*) OJ 1992 L183/19, upheld in Case T-7/93 *Langnese-Iglo* v *Commission* [1995] ECR II-1533 and Case T-9/93 *Schöller* v *Commission* [1995] ECR II-1611, and on appeal as Case C-279/95P *Langnese-Iglo* v *Commission* [1998] ECR I-5609.

[18] Decision 98/531 (*van den Bergh Foods*) OJ 1998 L246/1 (under review as Case T-65/98 *van den Bergh Foods* v *Commission*, pending).

side substitutability, there may also be considerations of supply side substitutability (or 'latent competition') – that is the ease with which a producer which does not produce a given product or service (applying a demand side test) could alter production methods in order to do so in the face of a price increase of that product, so increasing supply and rendering the price increase unprofitable.[19] Generally, and in practice in the Community,[20] supply side substitutability is accorded an importance secondary to demand side in determination of the relevant market.

The second limb of the tests to be applied in identifying a relevant market is that of the geographic market. This addresses that homogenous territory in which the product in question moves or the service in question is available. According to the Court of Justice the relevant geographic market is

> a clearly defined geographic area in which [the product or service] is marketed and where the conditions of competition are sufficiently homogenous for the effect of ... economic power ... to be able to be evaluated.[21]

According to the 1997 notice it is a territory involving the supply and demand of products or services

> in which the conditions of competition are sufficiently homogenous and which can be distinguished from neighbouring areas because the conditions of competition are appreciably different in those area [*sic*].[22]

The relevant geographic market therefore turns on questions of market homogeneity, identification of a geographic territory in which the objective conditions of competition are similar or sufficiently homogenous that it can be said to constitute a coherent but discrete territory in which competitive forces apply – in other words, a territory sufficiently isolated so that market power could be deployed insufficiently disturbed by the moderating influence of competitors from elsewhere. It does not require the objective conditions of competition to be perfectly homogenous; it is sufficient that they are 'similar' or 'sufficiently homogenous', and only those territories in which the objective conditions of competition are 'heterogenous' may not be considered to constitute a uniform market.[23] In the

---

[19] 1997 notice, paras 20–24; see eg Case T-65/96 *Kish Glass* v *Commission*, judgment of 30 March 2000, not yet reported.

[20] 1997 notice, para 20.

[21] Case 27/76 *United Brands* v *Commission* [1978] ECR 207 at 270.

[22] 1997 notice, para 8.

[23] Case 27/76 *United Brands* v *Commission* [1978] ECR 207; Case T-83/91 *Tetra Pak* v *Commission* [1994] ECR II-755; Case T-229/94 *Deutsche Bahn* v *Commission* [1997] ECR II-1689.

Community the gradual integration of markets ought to lead to the growth in size of geographic markets as conditions of homogeneity increase. Yet for a variety of reasons and in a variety of circumstances the relevant geographic market for purposes of the application of the competition rules remains that of a member state. It may be smaller in specific circumstances.[24]

1.1.2 Market structures

Production or supply in any given market may be described by a spectrum across a linear plane ranging from monopoly at one end to perfect (or pure or 'atomistic') competition at the other. Perfect competition is a construct particularly favoured by the Chicago (or 'freshwater') school of economists (as opposed to the Harvard or 'saltwater' school)[25] as the optimal structure for competitive markets. It posits a very large number of firms each producing a good or service for a very large number of consumers, a market existing for all goods and services, present and to come, all consumers having complete and perfect information about their availability and no barriers to entry (or to exit) excepting those created by regulation: where a niche in the market opens up it may be filled by a new market entrant without difficulty. Where a situation of perfect competition obtains the play of supply and demand regulates market conduct and ensures both productive and allocative efficiency – productive efficiency because firms which do not produce or supply at the lowest possible cost will exit the market leaving no repercussions in their wake, allocative efficiency because price and marginal cost are equal. So, no firm has or can have market power, alteration of a single firm's conduct has no perceptible influence upon market price, prices remain competitive at no more than the marginal cost of production, profits cover the opportunity costs of the necessary capital and no more, and consumer welfare is maximised and cannot be improved upon by intervention.

At the other end of the spectrum is monopoly. Monopoly is a gross affront to perfect competition, complete or maximum market power. It has long and universally been recognised to be the fly in the ointment to the play of competitive forces, for it brings with it the power to exclude competition; it therefore constitutes a 'deadweight loss', the cost of a market

---

[24] See pp 144–6 *infra*.

[25] The Chicago analysis is stated in its most orthodox formulations in R. Bork, *The Antitrust Paradox: A Policy at War with Itself* (Basic Books, New York, 1978) and Y. Brozen (ed) *The Competitive Economy: Selected Readings* (General Learning Press, Morristown, 1975); the classic formulation of the Harvard school is C. Kaysen and D. Turner, *Antitrust Policy: An Economic and Legal Analysis* (Harvard UP, Cambridge, 1959).

not operating efficiently. Monopolies exist, either because of statutory privileges conferred upon them (so state intervention), ownership of intellectual property rights (another form of state intervention) or the nature of a given market being such that there is a natural tendency towards monopolisation ('natural monopoly'), a function of the cost of market entry and/or efficient use of economies of scale. But perfect competition exists essentially only in the economist's laboratory. Real markets do not behave that way: demand may be inelastic; producers may be few; brand loyalty may be high (and exploitable); entry barriers (the threat of new market entrant(s), or 'potential competition', normally being a powerful constraint to the exercise of market power) may be prohibitive in terms of cost (primarily sunk costs, those necessary for market entry but irrecoverable upon exit) or otherwise, or at least prohibitive absent the most egregious abuse of the market power of the players already in the market. In some markets the requirements of capital investment mean that there is profit only if a firm can occupy a significant share (say plus 25 per cent) of the market; there is therefore a natural tendency towards the monopoly end of the spectrum. In others the full rigours of competitive forces are thought to be inappropriate for social or political reasons – agricultural production and provision of basic utilities being the most obvious examples. And there are other externalities in state regulation of markets ensuring, for example, safety and, latterly, environmental standards. Close on that end of the spectrum but closer to the real world are markets which approximate the conditions of perfect competition but are flawed (they have 'market imperfections'), in which case the optimal goal for which to strive is a stable market in which there is 'workable' or 'effective' competition,[26] or a system which prevents 'significant' market power.

Where there is monopoly in a market there is by definition no competition. But where a market is stable (but not in a state of perfect competition, which would exclude the possibility) producers or providers may see net gains to be had from collusion in suspension of market forces, from, for example, fixing prices, adopting production quotas (so artificially stimulating demand) or sharing out markets – in other words, the cartel, which can be defined as a joint exercise in achieving market power where individually firms cannot do so. It brings benefits not for consumer welfare, but for the producers. Nor is it a new phenomenon. Adam Smith wrote over 200 years ago:

---

[26] First developed in J.M. Clark, 'Towards a Concept of Workable Competition' [1940] *American Economic Review* 241.

The interest of the dealers ... in any particular branch of trade or manufactures, is always in some respects different from, and even opposite to, that of the public. To widen the market and to narrow the competition, is always in the interest of the dealers. To widen the market may frequently be agreeable enough to the interest of the public; but to narrow the competition must always be against it, and can serve only to enable the dealers, by raising their profits above what they naturally would be, to levy, for their own benefit, an absurd tax upon the rest of their fellow-citizens.[27]

And so

[p]eople of the same trade seldom meet together, even for merriment and diversion, but the conversation ends in a conspiracy against the public, or in some contrivance to raise prices.[28]

Cartels are therefore brought into play, and unless they can be hindered by regulation they thrive, because producers can make supracompetitive profits. There are costs even for them to be factored into the equation. Producers or suppliers party to a cartel must satisfy themselves that losses generated by lower volume of sales (higher prices, production quotas) or loss of markets (market sharing) are offset by those same higher prices and by lower costs and so result in overall net higher profits ('net high price outcome') for all participants. There are additional costs in establishing and running the cartel, for the optimal state of affairs, at least in the short term, for an individual producer may be the existence of a cartel with which it breaks ranks. The maintenance of cartel stability and discipline is therefore an important consideration and cost; it is easier to achieve the narrower (more oligopolistic) the market for it is marked by fewer players and greater transparency. And producers or suppliers must take account of potential losses from detection and fines, should that sanction exist, and loss of reputation for straight dealing.

1.2 Competition law

The basic proposition that control of market power is a justification for competition law having been accepted, it then admits of a host of policy and procedural variations. At the outset there is general agreement that the two primary flaws of the market are monopoly (single market power) and cartels (joint market power), and they are (and must be) addressed by any

---

[27] A. Smith, *An Inquiry into the Nature and Sources of the Wealth of Nations* (1776), Book I, Chapter XI, conclusions.
[28] Book I, Chapter X, Part II.

system of competition regulation. More recent economic consideration has added two more to the list: the first is the oligopoly, a market marked by a small number of producers or suppliers no one of which has a monopoly, but between or amongst them they may exhibit some of the characteristics thereof. Oligopoly is close to the monopoly end of the spectrum, falls uncomfortably between the two stools of monopoly and workable competition, and brings with it its own particular problems. The second, which is the most recent concern of welfare economists, is mergers and takeovers.

This is, however, only the beginning. General agreement upon what to address is not agreement upon how to address it. The goal of competition policy and regulation is frequently said to be the existence of a 'level playing field'; but in the real world the playing field is not level: firms use market power to their advantage whenever they are able, and this is in itself a spur to competition, and regulatory inhibition to their doing so makes the market less free. If competition is about survival of the fittest then, like Marx's capitalism, it surely contains the seeds of its own destruction, for the entrepreneur who competes best may do so with such success that he grows above the fray and threatens the collapse of the system which put him there. But if the purpose of competition law is to draw the claws of the powerful and protect and nurture the smaller players, is it not a penalty for market success and inimical to competition, for why should the weak(er) survive (and the stronger be penalised) when their efforts could be more efficiently directed elsewhither? Ought, then, the concern of competition law to be purely that of consumer welfare – to some, especially those of the Chicago school, its only legitimate concern – or ought other socio-political considerations be admitted to the equation? To many, competition law cannot be divorced from industrial, regional and social policies, the dispersal/plurality of economic power (or 'economic democracy'), protection of employment and against the effects of labour dislocation, and the 'national champions' question, for ensuring the rigours of competition amongst firms in the home market may cripple them in competition in the broader, global market.

Once (or if) these issues are settled, there come procedural/enforcement questions. Ought competition rules to be permissive (everything is permitted except that which is proscribed) or proscriptive (everything is proscribed except that which is permitted)? If proscription, how rigidly should it be drawn? The economics of competition is not an exact science, which reasonably favours a wider degree of discretion in the application of competition rules – that anticompetitive conduct be censured because it is simply 'not on'. But this verges upon the arbitrary and runs counter to the legal certainty which firms in the conduct of their business, equally reasonably, crave. Should anticompetitive conduct be subject to an absolute prohibition or should there be the means of permitting it by reference to other considerations, and if so, how, by whom and upon what grounds? Should competition rules be enforced by administrative authorities only or also by civil process before the courts? And if the latter, is it an area given to justiciability, and if so do judges trained in the law have the economic literacy to deal with it? All of these are considerations which are required to go into the pot.

Competition law in its modern incarnation finds its *fons et origo* in the Sherman Act 1890 in the United States.[29] The Sherman Act was a response to the vast agglomeration of a number of sectors of American industry (the 'trusts'; hence, 'antitrust law') in the latter half of the 1800s. So necessary was it perceived to be that it was adopted unanimously by the House of Representatives and suffered only one vote against in the Senate. Section 1 of the Act provides:

> Every contract, combinations in the form of trust or otherwise, in restraint of trade or commerce among the several States, or with foreign nations, is declared to be illegal .... Every person who shall make any contract or engage in any combination or conspiracy hereby declared to be illegal shall be deemed guilty of a felony ....

Section 2 provides:

> Every person who shall monopolize, or attempt to monopolize or combine or conspire with any other person or persons, to monopolize any part of the trade or commerce among the several States, or with foreign nations shall be deemed guilty of a felony.

It will be observed therefore that the Sherman Act addresses cartels ('trusts') (section 1) and monopolies (section 2). Whilst breach of either section was made a felony, the civil teeth came subsequently with the Clayton Act 1914 which prohibited (but did not criminalise) four types of conduct (price discrimination, tying and exclusive dealing contracts, mergers and acquisitions, and interlocking directorates) which 'substantially' lessened competition, but also provided the effective/draconian civil remedy of treble damages to any person who could show injury by breach of either Act.[30] This has proved a potent lure (compounded by the system of contingency fees) to litigation and has provided to the Sherman Act a profound influence in the American market regulation – what Jean Monnet called 'la législation antitrust que les États-Unis appliquaient chez eux aussi rigoureusement que les règles morales'.[31]

---

[29] Sherman Act 15 USC §§ 1–7.
[30] § 4 Clayton Act 15 USC § 15.
[31] J. Monnet, *Mémoires* (Fayard, Paris, 1976), p 412.

In Europe, aspects of what we now call competition law surfaced only sporadically. In Britain rules developed piecemeal in the common law of restraint of trade and conspiracy and there was occasional statutory intervention,[32] but generally governments remained wedded to *laissez faire* capitalism. At the time of the entry into force of the EC Treaty in 1958 only one member state, Germany, had a comprehensive competition law on the statute book.[33] It was largely unknown elsewhere.[34] For Germany it was a product of economic history: the self-regulation and cartellisation of German industry at the end of the 1800s which was tolerated (in effect given a green light) by the Reichsgericht as economically necessary and

---

32 Ironically, one of the first interventions from the British Parliament was the passing of the Combinations Acts 1799 and 1800 which prohibited 'all contracts, covenants and agreements' amongst workers aimed at securing an advance of wages, limitation of working time or improvement in working conditions. For certainty any such contract was 'illegal, null, and void, to all Intents and Purposes whatsoever', was made an offence punishable by a fine of up to £10 and by forced labour, and a right in damages for injury (treble costs in the 1799 Act) was expressly granted third parties. This is language which the draftsmen of the Competition Act 1998 might usefully have studied; see Chap 12.

33 Gesetz gegen Wettbewerbsbeschränkungen vom 27. Juli 1957, 1957 BGBl. I, S. 1081 (hereinafter 'GWB'). The GWB has been amended substantially on six occasions, the most recent (and most extensive) coming into force in 1999; see now the 'new version' of the GWB, 1998 BGBl. I, S. 2546. In fact 'competition law' in Germany falls into two discrete strands. The first finds its origins in legislation pre-dating 1900 and its present form in a law of 1909 (Gesetz gegen den unlauteren Wettbewerb vom 7. Juni 1909, 1909 RGBl., S. 499; hereinafter 'UWG') which prohibits 'unfair competition', addressing business conduct contrary to 'good morals' (*gute Sitten*', or *boni mores*; § 1 UWG); a clearer indication of what is meant may be rendered by a prohibition of sharp practices, such as passing off, deceptive, misleading or 'sensational' (*blickfangmäsig*) advertising and sales, rubbishing (*Anschwärzung*) a competitor, bribery or poaching of employees and disclosure, or inducement of disclosure, of trade secrets, conduct which in the United Kingdom would fall, if at all, within the common law, the Trade Descriptions Act 1968, the Consumer Credit Act 1974, the Unfair Contract Terms Act 1977 and the Consumer Protection Act 1987. The second strand, embodied in the GWB, addresses 'restraints of competition' and the regulation of market conduct more widely recognised as competition law. The GWB is for that reason also sometimes referred to as the Kartellgesetz – which is also the formal name of the equivalent Austrian law (Kartellgesetz, BGBl. 1988/600, hereinafter 'ÖKG').

34 France introduced legislation prohibiting price fixing and certain restrictions to competition in 1953 – ironically embedded in legislation which otherwise authorised public price controls; l'ordonnance nº 45–1483 du 30 juin 1945 relative aux prix, JORF du 8 juillet 1945, arts 37, 59 bis. British and Dutch legislation was adopted in 1956 (the Restrictive Trade Practices Act 1956; wet van 28 juni 1956 (the Wet Economische Mededinging), stb. 1956, 401, entering into force in November 1958), which permitted administrative control of market abuses. All three were rudimentary compared to the GWB and the subsequent French, Dutch and UK laws which came to amend or replace them.

legitimate at the time[35] and which increased up to and during the Great War, and, notwithstanding the 'Cartel Regulation' of 1923[36] designed to prevent it but which served only to regularise it, the massive concentration of industry which followed into (and abetted) the period of National Socialism – and, not least, the gentle hand of the western occupying powers (but primarily the Americans) in the restructuring (for which read 'decartellisation') of the economy of the nascent Federal Republic.[37] But if the Germans had been won (or forced) over to the *Soziale Marktwirtschaft*, it was not a sentiment universally held. French industry had been highly cartellised before the war and the state remained wedded to *dirigisme*, whilst important sectors of British industry had recently been nationalised. European governments generally did not recoil from collectivism, and rather winked at the existence and practices of cartels. However, considerations of competition regulation were recognised by the Spaak Report[38] to be a necessary component of the process of economic integration launched in Europe in the 1950s, and Spaak, and the Germans armed with the righteousness of the convert, carried the day. According to one (American) commentator,

> EEC competition law was born in 1958 of transatlantic parents. Its European mother was the basic Treaty goal of market integration. Its father (or godfather) was US anti-trust law and theory which influenced the drafting of Articles 85 and 86 through German law and thought.[39]

This (rightly) notes not only the original inspiration of the Sherman Act but also (and equally rightly) the influence of German thinking and practice which has informed not only the Treaty but also the manner in which Community competition rules have come to be developed. But if the new

---

[35] Urteil vom 4. Februar 1897, RGZE 38, 155 (*Sächsischen Holzstoff-Fabrikanten-Verband*).

[36] Verordnung gegen den Mißbrauch wirtschaftlicher Machtstellungen vom 2. November 1923, 1923 RGBl. II, S. 1067.

[37] All three western occupying powers adopted measures in 1947 (Law No 56 of 1947 of the American Zone of Control, *Military Government Gazette* Issue C at 2; Ordinance No 78 of 1947 of the British Zone of Control, 16 *Military Government Gazette* 412; l'ordonnance n° 96 du 9 juin 1947, 2 *Journal Officiel du Commandement en Chef Français en Allemagne* 784) designed to dismantle the cartels and restructure German industry. The American and British laws were virtually identical and based upon American antitrust legislation and procedure, the French less detailed. Notwithstanding the adoption of the Grundgesetz and the creation of the Federal Republic in 1949 they remained law until the entry into force of the GWB in 1958.

[38] Comité Intergouvernemental Créé par la Conférence de Messine, Rapport des Chefs de Délégation aux Ministres des Affaires Etrangères (1956), pp 53 *et seq.*

[39] B. Hawk, 'The American (Anti-Trust) Revolution: Lessons for the EEC?' (1988) 9 ECLR 53 at 53.

rules were necessary they were not necessarily welcome: the introduction of a 'culture of competition' and inclusion of competition provisions in the 1957 Treaty of Rome were, according to Jean Monnet, 'une innovation fondamentale en Europe'.[40] The distaste for this new culture is put most gloriously by a subsequent Dutch commentator who regarded it as a violation of a fundamental law of ethics:

> I hope ... that the 1980s will bring to light that Adam Smith's *Homo Economicus*, who has stood as the example for anti-cartel law, is a degrading reduction of man ... and that it is unethical to take him as an example for the purpose of legislation. For any one unscrupulous businessman who tries to undo the working of the invisible hand in order to deviate wealth into his own pockets, I can show you three, maybe more, managers whose first care is not profit at the expense of the community at large but the continuation of their enterprise, the protection of loss of investment, which is nothing else than blood, sweat and tears, and the preservation of their employment ....
>
> And now I expect, but I sincerely do not hope, that this second time that Western civilization is seriously endangered since the eighth century when Rome crumbled under the victorious Islam, that the second time will bring to light that the Sherman Act and Article 85 are luxuries, the fundamental errors of which are not felt in a fast-growing economy but that they are an obstacle to a society which should be based on solidarity and regard for others.
>
> In my country, before the 85 men on horseback came galloping in, we did not speak about competitors; we spoke about 'colleagues'. I feel we shall have to face the oncoming economic war not with *competitor competitori lupus*, but with the concepts I just evoked – solidarity and regard for others.[41]

Why this 'innovation fondamentale' was seen to be a necessary part of the Community experiment, and the considerations of Community competition law other than consumer welfare which are considered to be equally legitimate in their context, is considered in the following chapter. What has been wrought by the 85 men on horseback (reduced to 81 by Amsterdam) will follow.

---

[40] J. Monnet, *Mémoires* (Fayard, 1976), p 413.

[41] F. Salomonson, in F.M. Rowe, F.G. Jacobs and M.R. Joelson (eds) *Enterprise Law of the 80's: European and American Perspectives on Competition and Industrial Organization* (ABA Press, Chicago, 1980), pp 69–70.

CHAPTER 2

Community competition law: general considerations and common principles

A proper understanding of EC competition law is not possible without at the least a basic familiarity with the economic context of the Community in which it operates and the goals of which it promotes. Whilst all competition law regimes share general characteristics, they are also all purpose designed and built to address particular issues and problems unique to each system. For the Community these are of course primarily those which adhere to the process of the progressive economic integration of 15 erstwhile individual and protected national markets. The purpose of this chapter is therefore to consider, very cursorily, the economic law of the Treaty and the nature of the integration it sets out to achieve, and also the place in the scheme of the competition rules, the scheme of the competition rules themselves, and the general considerations which apply across the board to them.

2.1 The Community context

The European Economic Community (EEC) came into being on 1 January 1958 by virtue of a Treaty (the 'Treaty of Rome') signed and duly ratified by the then six contracting parties of Belgium, Germany, France, Italy, Luxembourg and the Netherlands ('the original six'). The new Community took its place alongside the already existing European Coal and Steel Community (ECSC), which came into being in 1952 by virtue of another Treaty (the 'Treaty of Paris') signed by the original six, and the European Atomic Energy Community (EAEC, or Euratom) which was founded at the same time as the EEC by the second, and frequently forgotten, Treaty of Rome. Thus from 1958 there were – and continue to be – three distinct

Communities.[1] They are governed by the same institutions,[2] but the powers of the institutions vary depending upon which of the three Treaties under which they are acting. The original six were joined subsequently, by means of a series of accession Treaties, by Denmark, Ireland and the United Kingdom (1973), Greece (1981), Spain and Portugal (1986) and Austria, Finland and Sweden (1995), bringing the number of member states to the present 15. A number of middle and Eastern European countries are waiting in the wings to join.

By far and away the pre-eminent of the three Communities was the EEC. The EEC Treaty has political ambitions woven into it, given expression in the preambular Treaty recital 'RESOLVED to lay the foundations of an ever closer union among the peoples of Europe', but the immediate 'task' (*mission*; *Aufgabe*) of the EEC was

> by establishing a common market and progressively approximating the economic policies of Member States, to promote throughout the Community a harmonious development of economic activities, a continuous and balanced expansion, an increase in stability, an accelerated raising of the standard of living and closer relations between the States belonging to it.[3]

To this end it was to pursue a number of 'activities', *inter alia* the elimination of customs duties, quantitative restrictions and all other measures having equivalent effect in trade between member states, the abolition of

---

1 Whilst the EEC and Euratom Treaties were concluded for 'an unlimited period' (EEC Treaty, Art 240 (now EC Treaty, Art 312), Euratom Treaty, Art 208), the ECSC Treaty was concluded for a period of 50 years (Art 97). The ECSC is therefore scheduled to come to an end in 2002. The option now considered (although there seems to be little sense of urgency in addressing it) is that, rather than renewing it, the ECSC ought to be allowed to die a natural death, all coal and steel activity thereafter to be subsumed within the EC Treaty, either as it stands or with special new provisions. The competition rules of the EC (ex EEC; see *infra*) apply across the activities of all three Communities except where they are pre-empted or moderated by express *lex specialis* provisions of the other two Treaties.

2 Each of the Treaties established four institutions: a Commission (a High Authority in the case of the ECSC), a Council, a Common Assembly (now the Parliament) and a Court of Justice. Under a convention signed at the same time as the Treaties of Rome, a single Assembly and a single Court of Justice served all three Communities from the start, whilst the three Councils and the two Commissions and the High Authority were fused into a single Council and a single Commission by a subsequent Treaty (the 'Merger Treaty') in 1967. As a result of amendments made in 1993 by the Maastricht Treaty (see *infra*), the status of the Court of Auditors was elevated to that of an institution: EC Treaty, Art 7 (ex Art 4). The 1957 Convention and the Merger Treaty were both repealed by the Treaty of Amsterdam (Art 9) but their legal effects were retained (Art 10), a peculiar state of affairs.

3 EEC Treaty, Art 2.

obstacles to the movement of persons, services and capital, the adoption of common policies in the spheres of agriculture and transport, the approximation of national laws to the extent necessary for the proper functioning of the common market, and activities in a number of areas ancillary and complementary to these fields.[4] Of especial importance to the concerns of this book, one of the activities of the Community was, and is, 'the institution of a system ensuring that competition in the common market is not distorted'.[5]

Central to Community endeavour was therefore the creation of the common market – the economic integration of the member states, addressing all forms of economic activity (excepting those within the subject matter of the ECSC and Euratom) across four broad fields: the free movement of goods, persons, services and capital (the 'four freedoms'). There was, and is, no definition of a common market in the Treaty, but according to the Court of Justice

> [t]he concept of a common market ... involves the elimination of all obstacles to intra-Community trade in order to merge the national markets into a single market bringing about conditions as close as possible to those of a genuine internal market.[6]

It was to be achieved, in accordance with more detailed rules laid down in what was then Part Two of the Treaty ('Foundations of the Community'), by the elimination by the end of a 12-year transitional period, and thereafter prohibition, of any and all obstacles to the four freedoms. The free movement of goods entailed the creation of a customs union (the abolition and prohibition, as between member states, of customs duties on imports and exports[7] and the creation of a common customs tariff[8]), the abolition and prohibition of quantitative restrictions and measures having equivalent effect (so including technical barriers to trade) on imports and exports,[9] and the prohibition of national taxation which conferred direct or indirect benefit upon domestic production to the disadvantage of imported goods;[10] the free movement of persons and services was to be achieved across three Treaty chapters addressing the free movement of

---

[4] Art 3.
[5] Art 3(f).
[6] Case 15/81 *Gaston Schul* v *Inspecteur voor Invoerrechten en Accijnzen* [1982] ECR 1409 at 1431–2.
[7] EEC Treaty, Arts 9–17 (see now EC Treaty, Arts 9–25).
[8] Arts 9, 18–29 (Arts 23, 26).
[9] Arts 30–36 (Arts 28–30).
[10] Art 95 (Art 90).

workers,[11] the right of establishment[12] and the freedom to provide services,[13] the latter two conferring Treaty rights upon juristic as well as natural persons; capital merited a distinct chapter.[14] Many of the rules governing the four freedoms were laid down in sufficient detail in the Treaty that they were, from the end of the transitional period, self-standing provisions which were complete in themselves and so capable of producing 'direct effect' – that is, they produce rights and obligations which are enforceable in national courts;[15] others were less detailed, and would require flesh to be supplied subsequently by legislation adopted by the Community institutions in accordance with the powers conferred upon them so to do, which legislation may in turn be directly effective.

The EEC Treaty has been substantially amended – an onerous undertaking[16] – on three occasions, by the Single European Act (1986, in force 1987), the Treaty on European Union, or Maastricht Treaty (1992, in force 1993) and the Treaty of Amsterdam (1997, in force 1999). The original competition provisions of the EEC Treaty have remained virtually unchanged since the start, but the following should be noted in order better to understand their context.

---

[11] Arts 48–51 (Arts 39–42).

[12] Arts 52–58 (Arts 43–48).

[13] Arts 59–66 (Arts 49–55).

[14] Arts 67–73 (Arts 56–60).

[15] The development of the direct effect of Community law through the case law of the Court of Justice forms the cornerstone of the Community legal order, but any proper discussion of it is outwith the scope and purpose of this book. As to direct effect generally, see L. Collins, *European Community Law in the United Kingdom* (Butterworths, London, 2000); H.G. Schermers and D.F. Waelbroeck, *Judicial Protection in the European Communities* (Kluwer, Deventer, 1992), Chap 1; J.A. Winter, 'Direct Applicability and Direct Effect: Two Distinct and Different Concepts in Community Law' (1972) 9 CMLRev 425; P. Pescatore, 'The Doctrine of "Direct Effect": An Infant Disease of Community Law' (1983) 8 ELRev 155.

[16] Treaty amendment requires the convening of an intergovernmental conference of representatives of all member states following consultation with the Parliament, the Commission and the European Central Bank (if in the monetary area), unanimous approval of an amending text by all delegations and subsequently ratification by all member states in accordance with their own constitutional rules (Treaty on European Union, Art 48 (ex Art N)). The Treaty has been amended on nine occasions by recourse to what is now Art 48 of the TEU, most of the amendments being technical. It may also be, and has been, amended by authority of Art 49 (ex Art O) of TEU in order to make adjustments necessitated by the accession of new member states; in a few minor 'housekeeping' matters – for example increasing the number of judges (Art 221(4) (ex Art 165(4)) and Advocates-General (Art 222(3) (ex Art 166(3)) in the Court – it may be amended by the Council.

■ *The Single European Act* was in part a response to the log jam in the legislative programme necessary to bring about the completion of the common market. The work remaining to be done, and the remaining physical, fiscal and technical barriers to the common market, were identified in a 1985 Commission White Paper (the 'Cockfield White Paper')[17] and the Treaty was amended in a number of respects designed to do away with them and so bring about the achievement by the end of 1992 of the 'internal market', a definition of which was inserted into the EEC Treaty as

> an area without internal frontiers in which the free movement of goods, persons, services and capital is ensured in accordance with the provisions of this Treaty.[18]

As will be evident from the Court's definition of 'common market' and the new Treaty definition of 'internal market', the latter is a subset of the former and there may be lacunae between the two, but they are of no deep concern to competition law. In the event, the internal market was not fully achieved by 1993, the setting of the date for its completion has been declared by the Court of Justice not to be of itself directly effective,[19] and some work, particularly in the fields of fiscal harmonisation and the free movement of persons, remains still to be completed.

■ *The Maastricht Treaty* created the European Union, which is a constitutional superstructure which embraces the existing Communities at its core (the first of its three 'pillars') but includes also provisions on areas in which member states undertake to cooperate outwith Community fields, that is in the areas, distinct from but complementary to Community activities, of defence and foreign policy (the second pillar) and justice and home affairs (the third pillar). The institutions originally established by the Community Treaties were given authority to pursue action under the non-Community pillars of the Union, but their activities thereunder are conducted in a manner wholly intergovernmental in character, and the measures they produce are generally not legally binding. The 'supranational' character of Community law and legislation, the effects and quasi-constitutional principles which adhere to it, and the democratic and judicial control the Parliament and the Court of Justice exert over it, remain unique to the Community, and not the wider Union. Maastricht also changed the name of the European Economic Community to the European Community (EC) in recognition of its pre-eminence amongst the

---

[17] *Completing the Internal Market,* White Paper from the Commission to the European Council, COM(85) 310.
[18] EC Treaty, Art 14 (ex Art 7a).
[19] Case C-378/97 *Criminal proceedings against Florus Wijsenbeek* [1999] ECR I-6209.

three Communities and the conferral upon it by Maastricht of new competences in areas which are not primarily economic; it repealed the provisions in each Community Treaty addressing accession, so barring *à la carte* accession, which is possible now only to the European Union and not to any or all of the Communities;[20] it amended significantly the Treaty provisions on the free movement of capital,[21] achievement of which had thitherto lagged behind the other of the four freedoms but is as a result of Maastricht amendments now perhaps the one most fully achieved; it laid down (in the EC Treaty) the rules governing the nascent Economic and Monetary Union and the single currency, which came blinking into the light in January 1999 and, with Greece joining in January 2001, is binding for all member states except Denmark, Sweden and the United Kingdom; and finally (for present purposes), as an afterthought better suited to the Single European Act, it amended Article 3(f), which had provided as a core activity of the Community 'the institution of a system ensuring that competition in the common market is not distorted', to read 'internal market'. The subsequent operative provisions of the Treaty in the competition field continue to refer to 'common market', but not too much ought to be read into this.

■ *The Amsterdam Treaty* made a number of changes to the constitutional and institutional structure of the European Union and of the Community. It amended substantially the provisions regulating third pillar matters and at the same time will bring about a significant diminution of its direct importance, as much of what has or is to be agreed in the area of justice and home affairs will over a five-year period be drawn into the first (Community) pillar. However, it did nothing new which is of relevance to competition law, other than bequeathing general confusion by the renumeration of Treaty articles.

2.2 The competition rules

The preamble to the EC Treaty recognises that the creation of the common market 'calls for concerted action in order to guarantee ... fair competition'.[22] For 'fair' other language versions use words (*loyauté*; *lealtà*; *Redlichkeit*; *eerlijkheid*) which mean honest or upright, and it refers more

---

[20] Treaty on European Union, Art 49 (ex Art O); Austria, Sweden and Finland therefore acceded in 1995 to the EU, not the EC.
[21] EC Treaty, Arts 56–60 (ex Arts 73b–73g).
[22] 4th recital.

accurately to the type of unfair competition addressed in Germany by the UWG.[23] The provision is in any event exhortatory only, and there have been limited Community inroads in this particular strand of competition law.[24] Of far greater significance is the inclusion amongst the activities of the Community of 'the institution of a system ensuring that competition in the internal market is not distorted',[25] and *this* addresses competition law as it is more generally understood. Its purpose, and necessity, require consideration.

The Community competition rules have two fundamental purposes and roles to play. First, for all the reasons discussed in Chapter 1 they are seen to be good things in themselves, to maximise the benefits of economic activity, in free market economies. Distortions to competition are to be avoided as inherently of benefit to the internal market and consumer welfare within it. This was given a Treaty base by amendments made by the Maastricht Treaty, prior to which the EEC Treaty envisaged approximation of economic policies but was silent as to the direction they ought to take. After the Maastricht blueprint for economic and monetary union this was no longer possible, and a new provision was added to Part I of the Treaty, comprising the 'Principles' in the light of which the remainder of the Treaty is to be interpreted and applied:

> [T]he activities of the Member States and the Community shall include ... the adoption of an economic policy which is based on the close coordination of the Member States' economic policies, on the internal market and on the definition of common objectives, and *conducted in accordance with the principle of an open market economy with free competition.*[26]

The free market is therefore now a constitutional imperative. But even before Maastricht (with the exception of the agricultural and transport sectors which were to be *dirigiste*) the Treaty betrayed its faith in neo-classical liberal economics and the mechanism of the market:

> The competition rules of the EC Treaty ... are based on the fundamental liberal belief that that market forces should be the principal regulating factor in the

---

[23] See Chap 1, n 33.

[24] Examples include Council (or post-Maastricht, Parliament/Council) Directives harmonising national legislation on misleading advertising (Directive 84/450, OJ 1984 L250/17), 'doorstep' (Directive 85/577, OJ 1985 L372/31) and 'distance' (Directive 97/7, OJ 1997 L144/19) selling, package travel (Directive 90/314, OJ 1990 L158/59), unfair terms in consumer contracts (Directive 93/13, OJ 1993 L95/29) and the availability of injunctive relief for the protection of consumers' interests (Directive 98/27, OJ 1998 L166/51).

[25] EC Treaty, Art 3(1)(g) (ex Art 3(g), pre-Maastricht Art 3(f)).

[26] Art 4 (ex Art 3a); emphasis added.

economy and must be protected from improper interference: optimal economic efficiency is achieved when economic decisionmaking is left to businesses competing with one another in the marketplace, so that available resources are allocated to the most productive sectors and firms are stimulated to undertake risk, innovate, stimulate technical progress and develop active market strategies.[27]

In even more extravagant language, the competition provisions of the Treaty and the manner in which they have been construed by the Court of Justice

> reinforce the free-market thrust of the EEC Treaty .... Bearing in mind that fact that all these provisions involve Community constitutional law, it would seem clear that the Community has the most strongly free-market oriented constitution in the world.[28]

These may be termed the 'economic goals' of the competition rules. The rigours of international liberalism, it must be noted, are kept at bay, the domestic (Community) market continuing to be protected by stout import barriers of various types (hence concerns of 'Fortress Europe'), although these have been and are being whittled away slowly by multilateral advances under the General Agreement on Tariffs and Trade (GATT) and latterly (and notwithstanding Seattle setbacks) the World Trade Organisation (WTO).

However, the competition rules have a second, equally important, purpose, commonly termed 'integration goals' or their 'integration function'. The Treaty provisions indicated above – those addressing the four freedoms – are wholly necessary in the dismantling of national barriers to the movement of goods, persons, services and capital and so the attainment of the common/internal market. But they are not the whole story. They are mandatory prohibitions addressed to the member states, that they not deploy any of the measures by which states habitually regulate, and so impede, such movement – tariff barriers, non-tariff barriers, tax advantages, control of immigration, residence and access to the labour market, regulation of business and commerce and of capital movements. But they are addressed to and impose obligations upon the member states only, and *not* to and upon private persons. It does limited good if the Treaty dismantles and prohibits public barriers to trade whilst at the same time doing nothing to ensure that private industry does not deploy private law – con-

---

[27] M. Siragusa, 'Privatization and EU Competition Law', in B. Hawk (ed) *International Antitrust Law and Policy* (1995), p 375.

[28] C.-D. Ehlermann, 'The Contribution of EC Competition Policy to the Single Market' (1992) 29 CMLRev 257 at 273.

tractual – barriers to trade or simply market power to take their place. National markets and competition therein have long sheltered behind the protection of tariff and other barriers of the state's fashioning, resulting in many cases in a degree of economic lethargy and inefficiency. In the Community these are now gone. But if merriment and diversion amongst competitors lead to conspiracies against the public even in a long homogenised market, they are all the more likely to do so amongst markets once protected but now laid bare to new competition by the rules of the common/internal market. The competition rules are therefore the private law flip side of the coin, reinforcing and complementing other Treaty provisions. This was recognised and stressed in the Spaak Report, underpinned much of the thinking behind the Treaty and has been stressed consistently by the Court of Justice:

> [A]n agreement ... which might tend to restore the national divisions in trade between Member States might be such as to frustrate the most fundamental objections [sic] of the Community. The Treaty, whose preamble and content aim at abolishing the barriers between States, and which in several provisions gives evidence of a stern attitude with regard to their reappearance, could not allow undertakings to reconstruct such barriers. Article 85(1) is designed to pursue this aim ....[29]

It said subsequently that the requirement set out in Article 3(1)(g) that competition within the Community is not distorted or eliminated is 'so essential that without it numerous provisions of the Treaty would be pointless';[30] and most recently:

> [A]ccording to [conformément à; in overeenstemming met] Article 3[(1)(g)] of the EC Treaty ..., Article 81 ... constitutes a fundamental provision which is essential to the accomplishment of the tasks entrusted to the Community and, in particular, the functioning of the internal market.[31]

So important are the integration goals of the competition rules that it is sometimes observed that they are deployed in a manner as much, if not more, to assist free movement as they are to address the economic goals of competition. They are the 'first goal' of Community rules; 'the basic sin in Europe is not so much restricting competition but creating an obstacle to

---

[29] Cases 56 & 58/64 *Consten & Grundig* v *EEC Commission* [1966] ECR 299 at 340.

[30] Case 6/72 *Europembellage & Continental Can* v *Commission* [1973] ECR 215 at 244.

[31] Case C-126/97 *Eco Swiss China Time* v *Benetton International* [1999] ECR I-3055 at 3092.

integration'.[32] And the twin purposes of the competition rules, consumer welfare and Community integration, are not necessarily entirely harmonious. In some circumstances, for example, territorial limitations to economic activity may improve economic efficiency and so be pro-competitive in the context of economic goals, yet are likely to run counter to the integration goals. Alternatively, some forms of horizontal cooperation – for example, joint ventures and specialisation agreements between small and medium-sized firms – may be inimical to competition goals but may be tolerated, or encouraged, within the Community if they interlock firms from various member states. Where economic and integration goals collide the Community rules have generally been deployed hitherto in a manner which gives preference to the latter. As the aims of the Treaty come to fruition and the internal market nears completion they may progressively be allowed a back seat and emphasis redirected to the economic goals of competition, although it is not suggested this stage has been reached. Further, the competition rules may serve integration goals not only passively but also actively. Notwithstanding the achievements of the Treaty it remains that national markets continue to show some of the characteristics thereof; the Community market is not (yet) entirely homogenised. This may be a function of residual public barriers, of tradition, habit, tastes, inertia or simple geography. (It may also be a function of anticompetitive practices.) In this context the competition rules may be deployed not merely to prevent the frustration of integration goals by economic operators, but in a manner actively to encourage them, to assist in market interpenetration and so the attainment of the internal market.

The competition rules apply across the full spectrum of Community activities. They were applied first and with greatest vigour to anticompetitive practices or conduct in the manufacture, distribution and sale of goods. Latterly and increasingly they have been applied to impediments in the services sectors, and recently they have seen preliminary action in the area of the free movement of persons.

2.2.1 The Treaty Scheme

The 'rules on competition' (or in most language versions, the rules *of* competition) which provide the flesh to Article 3(1)(g) are contained in Chapter 1 of Title VI (ex Title V) of Part III ('Community Policies') of the

---

[32] A. Deringer, in F.M. Rowe, F.G. Jacobs and M.R. Joelson (eds) *Enterprise Law of the 80's: European and American Perspectives on Competition and Industrial Organization* (ABA Press, Chicago, 1980), p 64.

EC Treaty, comprising Articles 81 to 89 (ex Articles 85 to 94) of the Treaty. The layout of these provisions is as follows.

Articles 81 and 82 (ex Articles 85 and 86)

Articles 81 and 82 are the very core of the competition rules of the Treaty. Indeed, they comprise the substance of the overriding concern of this, or any, book on EC competition law.

Article 81 addresses anticompetitive accommodation between or amongst economic operators which compete, or ought to be competing, with each other. In a free market economy they are required and presumed to be in a state of competition. But all too often, for the reasons considered in Chapter 1, there is a tendency to recoil from competition: that the interests of producers, if not consumers, are best served if competition between or amongst them is curtailed in an effort to build and profit from market power. The threat (in terms of both economic and integration goals) is greatest where accommodation is reached amongst operators which (ought to) compete on the horizontal plane, that is, those in direct competition for the same markets (cartels). But competition may also be diminished by an accommodation reached on the vertical plane – for example, by contracts between producers and distributors which contain various restrictive provisions. Article 81 strikes primarily at cartels, but they are not its only target.

Article 82 on the other hand addresses essentially the unilateral conduct of single operators which alone enjoy such market power that they are not subject to the normal forces of competition. There is a presumption that it is the motive force of competition between or amongst economic operators which will make them efficient. But some will be so powerful, through either statutory privilege or some other advantage, legal or economic, that they are above the fray and can pursue strategies, policies and conduct irrespective of the moderating behaviour of their competitors (if any). This is the concern of Article 82. And whilst it addresses first and foremost the conduct of monopolies, it applies also to other operators which enjoy substantial, but not monopolistic, market strength.

This approach addressing, distinctly, (a) accommodation between or amongst economic operators which ought to be competing with one another but by which they elect not to do so, and primarily, but not exclusively, cartels, and (b) the unilateral conduct of dominant operators with such market strength that they need not trouble themselves with competition and primarily, but not exclusively, monopolies, derives originally from sections 1 and 2 of the Sherman Act and was championed during Treaty negotiation by the recently converted Germans. The Treaty approach is now the standard in the formulation of rules intended to regulate competition, and has been copied, virtually *verbatim* from Articles 81 and 82, by a number of member states in order to regulate competition law internally – for example, in the past decade alone the competition laws adopted in Italy,[33] Ireland,[34] Belgium,[35] Portugal,[36] Sweden,[37] the Netherlands,[38] Denmark,[39] and finally, the United Kingdom.[40] In 1999 amendments to the GWB – which predates the Community – came into force which aligned German law more closely to the Treaty.[41] The approach has also been adopted by a number of states waiting in the wings for accession to the Community as part of the strategy and process of 'accession partnership' or pre-accession adaptation to Community norms.[42]

Both Articles 81 and 82 address the conduct or behaviour of economic operators. They are concerned primarily not with the structure of markets and the anticompetitive forces which may be a direct or indirect result of those structures, but with the manner in which operators conduct themselves in the market. The Treaty presumes an environment of stable markets and so workable competition:

> The requirement contained in Articles 3 and 85 of the EEC Treaty that competition shall not be distorted implies the existence on the market of workable competition, that is to say the degree of competition necessary to ensure the observance of the basic requirements and the attainment of the objectives of the Treaty, in particular the creation of a single market achieving conditions similar to those of a domestic market.[43]

Where competition is hindered not because market participants elect to make it so but because the very structure of the market is inimical to competition, Articles 81 and 82 are in ways ill suited to it. This is especially so in addressing the problems of oligopolistic markets and mergers.[44]

---

[33] Legge N° 287 del 10 ottobre 1990, GURI del 13 ottobre 1990, N° 240.

[34] Competition Act, 1991 (Act No 24 of 1991); also the Competition (Amendment) Act, 1996 (Act No 19 of 1996).

[35] Loi du 5 août 1991 sur la protection de la concurrence économique, *Moniteur Belge* du 11 octobre 1991.

[36] Decreto-Lei n.° 371/93 de 29 de Outubro 1993, D.R. n.° 254, p 6069.

[37] Konkurrenslaget, Svensk Författningssamling 1993:20.

[38] Wet van 22 mei 1997 houdende nieuwe regels omtrent de economische mededinging, stb. 1997, 242; hereinafter 'the Mededingingswet'.

[39] Lov nr. 384 af 10. juni 1997; hereinafter 'the Konkurrenceloven'.

[40] Competition Act 1998; see Chap 12.

[41] Sechste Gesetz zür Änderung des GWB vom 26. August 1998, 1998 BGBl. I, S. 2521. See now the 'new version' of the GWB, 1998 BGBl. I, S. 2546.

[42] eg, in Estonia, Konkurentsiseadus, RT I 1998, 30, 410.

[43] Case 26/76 *Metro-SB-Großmärkte v Commission (No 1)* [1977] ECR 1875 at 1904.

[44] See Chap 8.

Articles 83–85 (ex Articles 87–89)

Articles 83 to 85 address the enforcement of the competition rules. Under Article 83, the Community institutions may 'adopt any appropriate regulations or directives to give effect to the principles set out in Articles 81 and 82'.[45] Article 83 is therefore the Treaty authority (the 'legal base') for Community legislation in the field of competition, although should ambitious Community legislation go beyond what is necessary to give effect to Articles 81 and 82, a supplementary legal base may be required.[46] Measures adopted under Article 83 ought in particular to (a) ensure compliance with the prohibitions of Articles 81 and 82 by means of financial penalties; (b) lay down detailed rules for the provision of exemption from the prohibition of Article 81; (c) define the scope of Articles 81 and 82 to various economic sectors; (d) define the functions of the Commission and the Court of Justice in the enforcement of the competition rules; and (e) determine the relationship between national competition rules and Community competition rules.[47] As we shall see, the Council has adopted a number of measures under Article 83 designed and intended to give effect to the enforcement of the Community rules.

Articles 84 and 85 provide provisionally for the enforcement of the competition rules by, respectively, national competition authorities and the Commission. They were intended to be transitional measures pending the adoption of implementing legislation under Article 83. Whilst measures now in force occupy much of the field, the application of Articles 84 and 85 is not entirely spent; indeed, proposals are afoot to give Article 84 a new lease of life.[48]

Article 86 (ex Article 90)

Article 86 is a *lex specialis* provision. It addresses entities in public ownership and those to which member states 'grant special or exclusive rights' in order to ensure that they comply with the competition rules (Article 86(1)) and provides a degree of immunity from the full vigour of Articles 81 and 82 to entities (essentially state monopolies) which operate services 'of gen-

---

[45] EC Treaty, Art 83(1). Such legislation is adopted by qualified majority vote in the Council following a proposal from the Commission and consultation with the Parliament. Prior to 1961 (when in fact no legislation was adopted) unanimity in the Council was required: EEC Treaty, Art 87(1).

[46] This was the case, for example, for Community legislation in the field of merger control, for which recourse to both Arts 87 (now Art 83) and 235 (now Art 308) was necessary: see Chap 8.

[47] EC Treaty, Art 83(2).

[48] See pp 134–6 and pp 219–23 *infra*.

eral economic interest' (Article 86(2)). For some time Article 86 lay dormant and its meaning and breadth were rarely tested. Latterly, and owing in part to the raft of privatisation of public utilities throughout a number of member states, it has come into its own.[49]

Dumping

The Treaty pre-Amsterdam identified as an anticompetitive practice and addressed in Article 91 the dumping of goods or services between member states, that is the sale of goods or services in a member state at a price lower than that which obtains in the state where it is produced. As dumping is economically impossible within the internal market, it was to apply only during the transitional period, both as amongst the original six member states and during the transitional periods provided the 'accession' member states. As accession for future members follows a different strategy of transition and harmonisation during the lead up to accession so that the Treaty may apply in its entirety immediately upon accession, Article 91 was thought no longer to be necessary, and, as part of the Amsterdam process of Spring cleaning (or 'simplification')[50] of the Treaty, it was repealed. Dumping from third countries is a different matter, and is a (highly complex) facet of the Community's common commercial policy, regulated under Article 133 (ex Article 113) of the Treaty.

Articles 87–89 (ex Articles 92–94)

Articles 87 to 89 address state aids. They are therefore concerned directly not with the commercial conduct of economic operators but with distortions through the competitive advantage to be had from the allocation of public funds. There has now developed a significant body of case law on and distinct to Articles 87 to 89, which will be discussed below.[51]

2.2.2 Common principles
Undertakings

Articles 81 and 82 are addressed to 'undertakings'. The peculiar term is lifted from the equivalent and more commonly used German (*Unternehmen*) and Dutch (*ondernemingen*) – compare the French *entreprises* – and its use is in part a function of the need to avoid other terminology with established meanings in English which might distort the (autonomous) meaning the term is to bear in Community law.

---

[49] See Chap 7.
[50] Amsterdam Treaty, Art 6.
[51] See Chap 11.

'Undertaking' is defined neither in the Treaty nor in Community legislation. It is construed very broadly, embracing, according to the case law of the Court of Justice, 'every entity engaged in an economic activity, regardless of the legal status of the entity and the way in which it is financed'.[52] Bearing in mind that any activity consisting in offering goods or services on a given market is an economic activity,[53] the term therefore applies to any natural or juristic person insofar as he or it carries out economic or commercial activities of some sort. The fact that the activity is one primarily of cultural,[54] social[55] or sporting[56] pursuits, that it may be non-profit-making,[57] or that the undertaking may be incorporated and/or situated outwith the territory of the Community[58] is immaterial. Articles 81 and 82 have therefore been held to apply not only to companies (in all their various corporate forms, which notwithstanding some harmonisation of company law vary significantly amongst the member states) but to trade associations,[59] to mutual associations,[60] to private associations issuing

---

[52] Case C-41/90 *Höfner v Macrotron* [1991] ECR I-1979 at 2016; Case C-244/94 *Fédération Française des Sociétés d'Assurance v Ministère de l'Agriculture et de la Pêche* [1995] ECR I-4013 at 4028; Case C-55/96 *Job Centre Coop* [1997] ECR I-7119 at 7147; Case C-67/76 *Albany International v Stichting Bedrijfspensioenfonds Textielindustrie* [1999] ECR I-5751 at 5886 (two very similar cases (Cases C-115–17/97 *Brentjens' Handelsonderneming v Stichting Bedrijfspensioenfonds voor de Handel in Bouwmaterialen* [1999] ECR I-5983 and Case C-219/97 *Maatschappij Drijvende Bokken v Stichting Pensioenfonds voor de Vervoer- en Havenbedrijven* [1999] ECR I-6121) were decided the same day, but hereinafter reference will be made only to *Albany International*).

[53] Case 118/85 *Commission v Italy* [1987] ECR 2599.

[54] Cases 43 & 63/82 *Vereniging ter Bevordering van het Vlaamse Boekwezen v Commission* [1984] ECR 19.

[55] Case C-70/95 *Sodemare v Regione Lombardia* [1997] ECR I-3395; Case C-67/96 *Albany International v Stichting Bedrijfspensioenfonds Textielindustrie* [1999] ECR I-5751.

[56] Case C-415/93 *Union Royale Belge des Sociétés de Football Association v Bosman* [1995] ECR I-4921, *per* A-G Lenz; see also Cases C-51/96 & 191/97 *Deliège v Asbl Ligue Francophone de Judo*, judgment of 11 April 2000, not yet reported, *per* A-G Cosmas; Case C-176/96 *Lehtonen v Fédération Royale Belge des Sociétés de Basketball*, judgment of 13 April 2000, not yet reported, *per* A-G Alber.

[57] Cases 209–15 & 218/78 *van Landewyck v Commission* (FEDETAB) [1980] ECR 3125; Case C-244/94 *Fédération Française des Sociétés d'Assurances v Ministère de l'Agriculture et de la Pêche* [1995] ECR I-4013; Case C-70/95 *Sodemare v Regione Lombardia* [1997] ECR I-3395; Case C-67/96 *Albany International v Stichting Bedrijfspensioenfonds Textielindustrie* [1999] ECR I-5751.

[58] Cases 89 etc/85 *Åhlström v Commission* (Woodpulp) [1988] ECR 5193; see Chap 9.

[59] Case 71/74 *Frubo v Commission* [1975] ECR 563.

[60] Decision 1999/329 (*P & I Clubs*) OJ 1999 L125/12.

quality and safety certification to which affiliation is optional,[61] to agricultural cooperatives,[62] to performing rights societies,[63] to public television broadcasting organisations,[64] to supplementary pension funds,[65] to association football clubs,[66] to the World Cup organising committee,[67] to Lloyd's 'names',[68] to individuals engaged in the liberal professions of intellectual property agents,[69] customs agents[70] and patent agents,[71] to judoka (individual practitioners of that martial art),[72] and to opera singers.[73] Medical specialists,[74] architects[75] and advocates[76] are next in the queue for consideration. Indeed, it may be said that the sale of a pint of beer in a public house transmutes both publican[77] and customer into undertakings. There is a view abroad, stemming from analogous rules in national legislation, that an individual buying a product or service for personal consumption is not an undertaking[78] – which would exclude from the competition rules, for example, consumer boycotts – but this does not seem to square with the Court's construction of 'every entity engaged in an economic activity'; there is in any event no authority yet from the Court on the point. Nor is

---

[61] Cases T-213/95 & 18/96 *Stichting Certificatie Kraanverhuurbedrijf* v *Commission* [1997] ECR II-1739.

[62] Case 61/80 *Coöperatieve Stremsel- en Kleurselfabriek* v *Commission* [1981] ECR 851; Case C-250/92 *Gøttrup-Klim* v *Dansk Landbrugs Grovvarselskab* [1994] ECR I-5641.

[63] Case 127/73 *Belgische Radio en Televisie* v *SABAM* [1974] ECR 313.

[64] Case 155/73 *Guiseppe Sacchi* [1974] ECR 409; Case C-260/89 *Elliniki Radiophonia Tileorassi* v *Dimotiki Etairia Pliroforissis* [1991] ECR I-2925.

[65] Case C-67/96 *Albany International* v *Stichting Bedrijfspensioenfonds Textielindustrie* [1999] ECR I-5751.

[66] Case C-415/93 *Union Royale Belge des Sociétés de Football Association* v *Bosman* [1995] ECR I-4921, *per* A-G Lenz.

[67] Decision 2000/12 (*Comité Français d'Organisation de la Coupe du Monde*) OJ 2000 L5/55.

[68] *Society of Lloyd's* v *Clementson* [1995] 1 CMLR 693 (CA).

[69] Decision 95/188 (*Coapi*) OJ 1995 L122/37.

[70] Decision 93/438 (*CNSD*) OJ 1993 L203/27, upheld on review in Case T-513/93 *CNSD* v *Commission*, judgment of 30 March 2000, not yet reported; Case C-35/96 *Commission* v *Italy* [1998] ECR I-3851.

[71] Decision 1999/267 (*EPI Code of Conduct*) OJ 1999 L106/14 (under review as Case T-144/99 *EPI* v *Commission*, pending).

[72] Cases C-51/96 & 191/97 *Deliège* v *Asbl Ligue Francophone de Judo*, judgment of 11 April 2000, not yet reported, *per* A-G Cosmas.

[73] Decision 78/516 (*RAI/Unitel*) OJ 1978 L157/39.

[74] Cases C-180–4/98 *Pavlov* v *Stichting Pensioenfonds Medische Specialisten*, pending.

[75] Case C-221/99 *Conte* v *Rossi*, pending.

[76] Case C-309/99 *Wouters* v *Algemene Raad van de Nederlandse Orde van Advocaten*, pending.

[77] Decisions 1999/230 (*Whitbread*), 1999/473 (*Bass*) and 1999/474 (*Scottish & Newcastle*) OJ 1999 L88/26, L186/1 and L186/28 (lessees to a tied public house are undertakings).

[78] eg, Bundeskartellamt, *Jahresbericht* 1961, S. 61.

there yet any authority on whether trusts and partnerships,[79] which have no legal personality in English (*cf.* Scots) law, are undertakings, but it is submitted that they clearly are. The question of whether individual shareholders may be undertakings has been considered by the Commission but expressly left open.[80] Employees acting as such are not undertakings, even taken collectively, for they form an 'economic unit' with their employer undertaking;[81] according to Advocate-General Jacobs nor are they undertakings in their economic relationships *vis-à-vis* their employers (ie, in matters of their contracts of employment) and nor are trade unions undertakings (or associations of undertakings) insofar as they represent those interests, but the question was not addressed by the Court in the judgment.[82] The question of whether the functions of a Bar Council in representing the interests of its members (and so is an association of undertakings) can be severed from those which it discharges in accordance with statutory powers in the public interest (and so is not) is currently before the Court of Justice.[83] 'Undertaking' has the same meaning for both Article 81 and Article 82.[84]

The question which then arises is, if the competition rules are addressed to persons in private law, whether the state, acting in any of its many guises, is an undertaking and so subject to them. The state discharges various functions, many of which are purely public and regulatory, and many of which are addressed by other provisions of the Treaty. But it also engages in various aspects of commercial activity, and insofar as it does, it is 'an entity engaged in an economic activity' and so an undertaking.

> [T]he State may act either by exercising public powers or by carrying on economic activities of an industrial or commercial nature by offering goods and

---

[79] A *Kommanditgesellschaft* (KG), a type of limited partnership in German law and a popular form of association for small and medium-sized firms, is an undertaking (eg Decision 73/323 (*William Prym-Werke KG*) OJ 1973 L296/24), as is a *société en nom collectif* (SNC), a type of partnership in French law (Decision 85/561 (*Breeders' Rights: Roses*) OJ 1985 L369/9).

[80] Case M.1169 (*EDFI/Graninge*), decision of 25 May 1998, unpublished.

[81] Cases 40 etc/73 *Coöperatieve Vereniging 'Suiker Unie'* v *Commission* [1975] ECR 1663; Case C-22/98 *Criminal Proceedings against Jean Claude Becu* [1999] ECR I-5665.

[82] Case C-67/96 *Albany International* v *Stichting Bedrijfspensioenfonds Textielindustrie* [1999] ECR I-5751. See also Cases C-180 & 184/98 *Pavlov* v *Stichting Pensioenfonds Medische Specialisten*, pending, opinion of A-G Jacobs of 23 March 2000; Case C-222/98 *van der Woude* v *Stichting Beatrixoord*, pending.

[83] Case C-309/99 *Wouters* v *Algemene Raad van de Nederlandse Orde van Advocaten*, pending; *cf.* similar (and unsuccessful) arguments in Decision 95/188 (*Coapi*) OJ 1995 L122/37.

[84] Cases T-66, 77 & 78/89 *Società Italiano Vetro* v *Commission* (Flat Glass) [1992] ECR II-1403.

services on the market. In order to make such a distinction, it is therefore necessary in each case, to consider the activities exercised by the State and to determine the category to which those activities belong ....

[T]he fact that a body has or has not, under national law, legal personality separate from that of the State is irrelevant in deciding whether it may be regarded as a[n] ... undertaking.[85]

So national post offices,[86] a body forming part of the financial administration of the Italian state (which has in Italian constitutional law a single legal personality) which is charged with carrying out various administrative activities as well as enjoying certain monopoly rights,[87] an office of the German federal government charged with promoting employment and, to that end, securing employment,[88] a public employment office acting within the Italian Ministry of Labour and supplying its services free of charge,[89] a non-profit-making French public body charged with the management of an optional old age insurance scheme[90] and a non-profit-making Dutch sectoral pension fund,[91] for both operate according to the principles of capitalisation and compete with life assurance companies, a French governmental corporation charged with planning, administering and developing airports in the Paris region[92] and the Finnish civil aviation authority[93] are all undertakings. Even the Eastern bloc foreign trade organisations, which in then Soviet law were indistinguishable from the state, were undertakings, notwithstanding pleas of sovereign immunity.[94] It follows that the Community itself, or its organs, are undertakings when discharging various of their economic activities, although it must be said that the Commission has not used its enforcement powers to pursue anti-

---

[85] Case 118/85 *Commission v Italy* [1987] ECR 2599 at 2621, 2622. The case was concerned with the definition of 'public undertaking' within the meaning of a Directive (Directive 80/723, OJ 1980 L195/35) for purposes of Arts 86 and 87–89 (see Chaps 7 and 11), but it applies equally to the definition of undertaking generally.

[86] Case C-320/91 *Criminal Proceedings against Paul Corbeau* [1993] ECR I-2533; Decision 1999/695 (*REIMS II*) OJ 1999 L275/17.

[87] Case 118/85 *Commission v Italy* [1987] ECR 2599; Decision 98/538 (*Amministrazione Autonoma dei Monopoli di Stato*) OJ 1998 L252/47 (under review as Case T-139/98 *Amministrazione Autonoma dei Monopoli di Stato v Commission*, pending).

[88] Case C-41/90 *Höfner v Macrotron* [1991] ECR I-1979.

[89] Case C-55/96 *Job Centre Coop* [1997] ECR I-7119.

[90] Case C244/94 *Fédération Française des Sociétés d'Assurance v Ministère de l'Agriculture et de la Pêche* [1995] ECR I-4013.

[91] Case C-67/96 *Albany International v Stichting Bedrijfspensioenfonds Textielindustrie* [1999] ECR I-5751.

[92] Decision 98/513 (*Alpha Flight Services/Aéroports de Paris*) OJ 1998 L230/10.

[93] Decision 1999/198 (*Ilmailulaitos/Luftfartsverket*) OJ 1999 L69/24 (under review as Case T-116/99 *Ilmailulaitos v Commission*, pending).

[94] Decision 85/206 (*Aluminium Imports from Eastern Europe*) OJ 1985 L92/1.

competitive Community conduct with vigour. There is very little case law in the United Kingdom as to when an arm of government may constitute an undertaking. The Post Office is an undertaking[95] and the Keeper of the Registers of Scotland, although an officer of the Crown created by statute and charged with public duties,[96] was held provisionally to be an undertaking in a petition for interim interdict,[97] although the matter was abandoned before proof. However, it is well to note at this point that the state *qua* undertaking, its emanations, and public utilities and services, even if they are in private ownership, may enjoy a (small) degree of privilege from the full vigour of the competition rules.[98]

The state in any of its guises is caught directly by the competition rules only insofar as it is an undertaking; it is not an undertaking, and so not a subject of those rules, where it discharges public functions in its legislative or administrative capacity. So, for example, neither French municipalities acting in their capacity as public authorities in the regulation of public concessions,[99] nor French regional social security offices operating a compulsory social security scheme,[100] nor an international body (Eurocontrol) charged with tasks in the public interest pursuing maintenance and improvement of safety in air navigation, even though (ancillary) route charges are exigible,[101] nor an Italian port's anti-pollution surveillance authority, even where port users must pay dues to finance its activities,[102] are undertakings. The dividing line may sometimes be a thin one, but the case law of the Court seems to indicate that bodies which are the instruments of public policy and which enjoy prerogatives typical of a public authority, not merely traditional *ius imperii* but also welfare state activities, are not undertakings. If there are economic aspects relating to the discharge of their functions they are merely incidental.

But this does not mean that the competition rules have no relevance to the state in its public functions. The Court of Justice has said that Articles 81 and 82, in conjunction with the principle *pacta sunt servanda* articu-

---

[95] Decision 82/861 (*British Telecommunications*) OJ 1982 L360/36; Decision 1999/695 (*REIMS II*) OJ 1999 L275/17.

[96] ie, the maintenance of the Register of Inhibitions and Adjudications: see the Public Registers and Records (Scotland) Act 1948.

[97] *Millar & Bryce v Keeper of the Registers of Scotland* 1997 SLT 1000 (OH).

[98] See Chap 7.

[99] Case 30/87 *Bodson v Pompes Funèbres des Régions Libérées* [1988] ECR 2479.

[100] Cases C-159–60/91 *Poucet v Assurance Générales de France* [1993] ECR I-637.

[101] Case C-362/92 *SAT Fluggesellschaft v Eurocontrol* [1994] ECR I-43.

[102] Case C-343/95 *Diego Calì & Figli v Servizi Ecologici Porto di Genova* [1997] ECR I-1547.

lated in Article 10 (ex Article 5),[103] and sometimes with Article 3(1)(g), impose upon the member states a duty not to adopt or maintain in force any measure which would deprive the competition rules of their effectiveness. As for Article 81:

> In interpreting Article 3[(1)(g)], the second paragraph of Article 5 and Article 85 of the Treaty it should be noted that Article 85, read in isolation, relates only to the conduct of undertakings and does not cover measures adopted by Member States by legislation or regulations. However, the Court has consistently held that Article 85, read in conjunction with Article 5 of the Treaty, requires the Member States not to introduce or maintain in force measures, even of a legislative or regulatory nature, which may render ineffective the competition rules applicable to undertakings .... [S]uch is the case where a Member State requires or favours the adoption of agreements, decisions or concerted practices contrary to Article 85 or reinforces their effects or deprives its own legislation of its official character by delegating to private traders responsibility for taking economic decisions affecting the economic sphere.[104]

And as for Article 82:

> Whilst it is true that Article 86 concerns undertakings ..., the fact nevertheless remains that the Treaty requires the Member States not to take or maintain in force measures which could destroy the effectiveness of that provision ....

---

[103] Art 10 is contained in Part I of the Treaty ('Principles') and lays down a principle of general application into which the Court of Justice has read a number of duties borne by the member states in order to ensure the effectiveness of Treaty rights. It reads:

Member States shall take all appropriate measures, whether general or particular, to ensure fulfilment of the obligations arising out of this Treaty .... They shall facilitate the achievement of the Community's tasks.

They shall abstain from any measure which could jeopardize the attainment of the objectives of this Treaty.

[104] Case C-2/91 *Criminal Proceedings against Wolf Meng* [1993] ECR I-5751 at 5797; for similar, and latterly virtually identical, *dicta* applied in various contexts in which the state may through legislation or regulation distort competition, see Case 229/83 *Leclerc v Au Blé Vert* [1985] ECR 1 at 31; Cases 209–13/84 *Ministère Public v Asjes (Nouvelles Frontières)* [1986] ECR 1425 at 1471; Case 311/85 *Vereniging van Vlaamse Reisebureaus v Sociale Dienst van de Plaatselijke en Gewestelijke Overheidsdiesten* [1987] ECR 3801 at 3826; Case 267/86 *van Eycke v ASPA* [1988] ECR 4769 at 4791; Case C-185/91 *Bundesanstalt für den Güterfernverkehr v Gebrüder Reiff* [1993] ECR I-5801 at 5847; Case C-245/91 *Criminal Proceedings against Ohra Schadeverzekeringen* [1993] ECR I-5851 at 5878; Case C-35/96 *Commission v Italy* [1998] ECR I-3851 at 3899–900; Case C-67/96 *Albany International v Stichting Bedrijfspensioenfonds Textielindustrie* [1999] ECR I-5751 at 5883. For 'favours' in the final sentence the French texts use *favoriser* but other language versions use words (*agevolare, erleichtern, begunstigen*) which are closer in meaning to promote, facilitate or make easier. The inclusion of 'depriv[ing] its own legislation of its official character by delegating to private traders responsibility for taking economic decisions affecting the economic sphere' addresses a practice more common on the continent than in the UK.

Consequently any measure adopted by a Member State which maintains in force a statutory provision that creates a situation in which a[n undertaking] cannot avoid infringing Article 86 is incompatible with the rules of the Treaty.[105]

There is no recognition (or not yet at any rate) of a general public interest objective which may excuse a breach of Article 10.

A member state may adopt legislation or administrative rules which may impede free competition in a number of ways. First and foremost are rules of public law which create and govern publicly owned undertakings and statutory monopolies.[106] But they may also do so in a host of other ways by means of legislation of general application: public law regulating public procurement,[107] price controls (resale price maintenance, discounting, loss leaders), marketing, packaging, retail, zoning and licensing, taxation, transport tariffs, building and construction, advertising, employment and health and safety law, pension funds, regulation of service industries and of the professions, environmental legislation and of course national rules directly regulating competition law itself, may all require, encourage, favour, facilitate and/or induce practices contrary to EC competition rules. Indeed, it can be argued that *any* regulation will necessarily produce a knock-on effect in the market and so distort competition. This is *a fortiori* the case with regulation which varies from member state to member state, which served as the justification for the adoption of Community legislation in the environmental sphere before there was any Treaty authority (ie, pre-Single European Act) to do so, and was the thinking behind the last British government's efforts to trumpet the attractions of the United Kingdom for direct foreign investment, UK employers not (then) bearing the costs of the social agreement adopted by Maastricht. The Community rules presume and prescribe to undertakings freedom of action, conduct a function of 'their own initiative'.[108] If national legislation encourages or favours on the

---

[105] Case C-41/90 *Höfner* v *Macrotron* [1991] ECR I-1979 at 2017. Most of the Art 82 cases arise in the context of state monopolies, as to which see Chap 7.

[106] See Chap 7.

[107] Public procurement is recognised to be a special area justifying the intervention of Community legislation so as to ensure the fairness of the award of public works and public services contracts. The main legislation is Directive 71/305, JO 1971 L185/5 (public works); Directive 77/62, OJ 1977 L13/1 (public services); Directive 90/531, OJ 1990 L297/1 (utilities); Directive 89/665, OJ 1989 L395/33 (compliance).

[108] Case 202/88 *France* v *Commission* (Telelcommunications Terminal Equipment) [1991] ECR I-1223 at 1272; Case 18/88 *Régie des Télégraphes et des Téléphones* v *GB-Inno-BM* [1991] ECR I-5941 at 5980.

part of undertakings conduct proscribed by the competition rules, the member state is in breach of its Treaty obligations. So long as the rules do not compel anticompetitive conduct – if they allow a 'residual field for the operation of the rules of competition',[109] a 'sufficient margin within which [undertakings] could compete with one another'[110] or a 'margin to allow effective competition',[111] or if national law 'merely exempts ... but does not require'[112] anticompetitive conduct – undertakings are subject to the prohibitions of Articles 81 and 82. But if anticompetitive conduct is required of undertakings by national legislation, or if the latter creates a legal framework which eliminates any possibility of competitive activity, so that undertakings are deprived of their freedom of action, the 'restriction of competition is not attributable, as [the competition rules] implicitly require, to the autonomous conduct of the undertakings', and Articles 81 and 82 do not apply.[113] According to the Court of First Instance, this is also the case where undertakings are subjected by public authorities to the force not only of legislation or regulation but to 'irresistible pressures' such as threats to adopt measures likely to generate substantial loss to the undertaking.[114] Presumably it applies also to compliance with an order of a court, although this has yet to be tested.[115] There is an argument, which the Court of Justice seemed at one time to support,[116] that the requirements of the primacy of Community law ought to override any duty of undertakings to comply with compulsory national legislation which compelled infringement of the competition rules, but presumably because of the vacuum and so chaos such a result could produce, the Court has abandoned it. Where such a situation obtains, the remedies available to cure it are therefore two: first, the Commission may adopt a decision ordering the

---

[109] Cases 40 etc/73 *Coöperatieve Vereniging 'Suiker Unie' v Commission* [1975] ECR 1663 at 1924.

[110] Decision 82/506 (*Stichting Sigarettenindustrie*) OJ 1982 L232/1 at para 100, upheld on review as Cases 240 etc/82 *Stichting Sigarettenindustrie v Commission* [1985] ECR 3831.

[111] Case C-219/95P *Ferriere Nord v Commission* [1997] ECR I-4411 at 4438.

[112] Cases 89 etc/85 *Åhlström v Commission* (Woodpulp) [1988] ECR 5193 at 5244.

[113] Cases C-359 & 379/95P *Commission & France v Ladbroke Racing* [1997] ECR I-6265 at 6312.

[114] Case T-387/94 *Asia Motor France v Commission* [1996] ECR II-961 at 991, upheld implicitly on appeal as Case C-401/96P *Somaco v Commission* [1998] ECR I-2587.

[115] It may come to be tested should the judgment of the Court of Justice in Case C-344/98 *Masterfoods v HB Ice Cream*, pending, lead to a question of the award of damages; see pp 209–11 *infra*.

[116] Cases 43 & 63/82 *Vereniging ter Berfordering van het Vlaamse Boekwezen v Commission* [1984] ECR 19.

breach to be rectified, but only in the context of publicly owned undertakings or undertakings granted special rights by public law;[117] otherwise it may raise enforcement proceedings against the member state under Article 226 (ex Article 169) seeking a declaratory judgment from the Court of Justice that it, the member state, has failed in its obligations under the Treaty – that is, for breach of Articles 81 and/or 82 in combination with Article 10. In this context the Commission is surprisingly reluctant to resort to Article 226: the first such case came to judgment only in 1998.[118] Second, because Articles 81 and 82 are directly effective,[119] an action seeking an analogous declaratory judgment,[120] or a petition for judicial review, could competently be raised before a national court (which would have the advantage, if successful, of setting aside the offending national rules, which power the Court of Justice does not have in the context of Article 226 proceedings); and in light of the series of judgments which have now established a right in reparation from a member state which has deprived a natural or legal person of a Community law right,[121] it is likely that an undertaking injured by the obligatory anticompetitive conduct of a competitor would have a remedy in damages against the state. Where anticompetitive conduct is a product of mandatory Community legislation – of particular (but not exclusive) resonance in the coal and steel sectors owing to the powers of intervention enjoyed by the Commission under the ECSC Treaty[122] – the same principles apply *mutatis mutandis*, but there is no individual access to the Court of Justice for a declaratory judgment and a challenge would require to be orchestrated before a national court and come to the Court of Justice via an Article 234 (ex Article 177) refer-

---

[117] EC Treaty, Art 86(3) (ex Art 90(3)); see Chap 7.

[118] Case C-35/96 *Commission v Italy* [1998] ECR I-3851.

[119] See Chap 6.

[120] On the availability of declaratory relief in order to protect a Community law right in English law, see *R v Secretary of State for Employment, ex parte Equal Opportunities Commission* [1995] 1 AC 1 (HL).

[121] Cases C-6 & 9/90 *Francovich and Bonifaci v Italy* [1991] ECR I-5357; Cases C-46 & 48/93 *Brasserie du Pêcheur v Germany* and *R v Secretary of State for Transport, ex parte Factortame (No 3)* [1996] ECR I-1029; Case C-392/93 *R v HM Treasury, ex parte British Telecommunications* [1996] ECR I-1631; Case C-5/94 *R v Ministry of Agriculture, Fisheries and Food, ex parte Hedley Lomas* [1996] ECR I-2553; Cases C-178 etc/94 *Dillenkofer v Germany* [1996] ECR I-4845; Cases C-283 & 291–92/94 *Denkavit Internationaal v Bundesamt für Finanzen* [1996] ECR I-5063; Case C-140/97 *Rechberger v Austria* [1999] ECR I-3499.

[122] See, eg, Case T-141/94 *Thyssen Stahl v Commission* [1999] ECR II-347 at 522–9 (under appeal as Case C-194/99P *Thyssen Stahl v Commission*, pending).

ence.[123] An action for damages for injury caused would competently lie under Articles 235 and 288(2) (ex Articles 178 and 215(2)).

The economic entity doctrine

The freedom of action, the conduct of undertakings acting 'on their own initiative', has another relevance in Community competition law. An undertaking is, in principle, any person with distinct legal capacity engaged in economic activity. However, where a company or other similar person has such personality, but has no real freedom to determine its own course of conduct – as is the case with a wholly owned and directly controlled subsidiary – Community law will view the group, independent legal personality of its component companies notwithstanding, as a single undertaking. Indeed, this may be one reason for adopting the amorphous term 'undertaking' in the Treaty. So, where the Treaty proscribes anticompetitive conduct *between* undertakings (Article 81) it is addressing conduct between undertakings which are capable of and presumed to be competing with one another,[124] and the prohibition therefore does not, and cannot, apply to agreements between parent and subsidiary or between or amongst subsidiaries that are part of the same corporate group:

> [I]n competition law the term 'undertaking' must be understood as designating an economic unit for the purposes of the subject-matter of the agreement in question even if in law the economic unit consists of several persons, natural or legal.[125]

And

> for the purposes of the application of the competition rules, the unified conduct on the market of the parent company and its subsidiaries takes precedence over the formal separation between those companies as a result of their separate legal personalities.

It follows that, where there is no agreement between economically independent entities, relations within an economic unit cannot amount to an agreement or concerted practice between undertakings within the meaning of Article 85(1) of

---

[123] This is an area which remains wholly unexplored. A reference under Art 234 would probably be necessary, for it is established that a question arising in a national court involving the *validity* of a Community act must be referred (Case 314/85 *Foto-Frost* v *Hauptzollamt Lübeck-Ost* [1987] ECR 4199), and a question of its *compatibility* with Arts 81 and 82 may go to its validity as an infringement of the Treaty (Art 230(2) (ex Art 173(2)). Doubtless in practice a national court would be inclined to refer the question in any event.

[124] Cases T-66, 77 & 78 *Società Italiano Vetro* v *Commission* (Flat Glass) [1992] ECR II-1403.

[125] Case 170/83 *Hydrotherm* v *Compact* [1984] ECR 2999 at 3016.

the Treaty. Where ... the subsidiary, although having a separate legal personality, does not freely determine its conduct on the market but carries out the instructions given to it directly or indirectly by the parent company by which it is wholly controlled, Article 85(1) does not apply to the relationship between the subsidiary and the parent company with which it forms an economic unit.[126]

But on the flip side of the same coin, where the Treaty proscribes unilateral conduct of a single, dominant undertaking (Article 82), or where considerations of market share are relevant for determining whether anticompetitive practices between parent/subsidiary on the one hand and a third party on the other (and so falling within Article 81) produce 'appreciable' effects,[127] the entire corporate family is taken into account in assessing its market strength and market share. Whether there is control, and so the economic entity (or 'single entity') doctrine applies, is a matter of fact, taking into account criteria such as links between various undertakings as a result of share ownership and overlapping management which deprive the members of the group of the autonomy to determine its course of action on the market.[128] According to the Commission,

> [t]he subject of Community competition rules is the 'undertaking', which is not the same concept as that of the incorporated company possessing separate legal personality. The term 'undertaking' is not defined in the Treaty. It may however refer to any entity engaged in a commercial activity. In the context of large corporate groups, any of the following may, depending upon the circumstances, be treated as an 'undertaking'.
> – the parent or holding company of the group,
> – the whole group consisting of the parent and its direct and indirect subsidiaries,
> – intermediate holding companies,
> – the subgroups or divisions formed by the subholding companies and their subsidiaries,
> – the individual subsidiary companies.[129]

Problems, however, arise in the case of partly owned subsidiaries (ie, joint

---

[126] Case T-102/92 *Viho Europe* v *Commission* [1995] ECR II-17 at 35, upheld on appeal as Case C-73/95P *Viho Europe* v *Commission* [1996] ECR I-5457.

[127] See pp 71–5 *infra*.

[128] Case 22/71 *Béguelin* v *GL Import Export* [1971] ECR 949; Case 48/69 *ICI* v *Commission* (Dyestuffs) [1972] ECR 619; Case 15/74 *Centrafarm* v *Sterling Drug* [1974] ECR 1147; Case 107/82 *AEG-Telefunken* v *Commission* [1983] ECR 3151; Case 30/87 *Bodson* v *Pompes Funèbres des Régions Libérées* [1988] ECR 2479; Case T-65/89 *BPB Industries & British Gypsum* v *Commission* [1993] ECR II-389.

[129] Decision 94/601 (*Cartonboard*) OJ 1994 L243/1 at para 140.

ventures)[130] and the appropriate legal person against whom enforcement action may be directed.[131] Generally the economic entity doctrine applies also to an agency agreement, for the agent is deemed to be acting as an adjunct of the principal,[132] and so a true agency contract is not an agreement within the meaning of Article 81.[133]

The relevant market

As indicated in Chapter 1, identification and definition of the relevant market is a key component of the application of competition rules; it is 'a necessary precondition of any judgment concerning allegedly anti-competitive behaviour'.[134] The relevant tests are discussed above[135] and their outcome will be considered in greater detail below.[136] However, it is appropriate to note here that the determination of the relevant market serves a different purpose depending upon whether Article 81 or 82 is at issue[137] and generally requires much greater precision under the latter than under the former. Indeed it may be said that the Commission and the Court of Justice pay mere lip service to the concept under Article 81 and view it with astringency only under Article 82; having identified a practice which has an element of restriction of trade between member states (and so going to the integration goals of the competition rules) the Commission may find a breach of Article 81 without careful consideration of geographic markets. This may change as a result of the judgment in *European Night Services*,[138] an Article 81 case, in which the Court of First Instance

---

[130] See pp 89–91 *infra*.

[131] See pp 182–4 *infra*.

[132] EC Commission, Guidelines on vertical restraints attached to the draft Commission regulation on the application of Article 81(3) to categories of vertical agreements and concerted practices, OJ 1999 C270/12, Chap II.2; this replaces a 1962 notice on exclusive dealing contracts with commercial agents, JO 1962, 2921.

[133] Cases 56 & 58/64 *Consten & Grundig* v *EEC Commission* [1966] ECR 299 at 340. However, the agent must be tightly integrated into the organisation of the principal. As to shadings between true agency and an independent trader, which is a function of risk undertaken by the latter, see Decision 72/403 (*Pittsburgh Corning Europe*) JO 1972 L272/35; Cases 40 etc/73 *Coöperatieve Vereniging 'Suiker Unie'* v *Commission* [1975] ECR 1663; Case 311/85 *Vereniging van Vlaamse Reisebureaus* v *Sociale Dienst van de Plaatselijke en Geswestelijke Overheidsdiensten* [1987] ECR 3801; Case C-266/93 *Bundeskartellamt* v *Volkswagen* [1995] ECR I-3508; Guidelines on vertical restraints, *ibid*.

[134] Cases T-66, 77 & 78/89 *Società Italiano Vetro* v *Commission* (Flat Glass) [1992] ECR II-1403 at 1463.

[135] At pp 7–12.

[136] At pp 142–7.

[137] Case T-29/92 *Vereniging van Samenwerkende Prijsregelende Organisaties in de Bouwnijverheid* v *Commission* [1995] ECR II-289.

[138] Cases T-374 etc/94 *European Night Services* v *Commission* [1998] ECR II-3141.

annulled a Commission decision granting an exemption to a complex rail passenger agreement[139] and censured the Commission in robust language for failure to include proper market definition and analysis of the position of the parties within it. However, it should be noted that this was a case involving 'appreciability' of the effects of an (allegedly) anticompetitive agreement[140] in which considerations of market share (and so necessarily prior definition of product or service market) are uncommonly acute in the context of Article 81. In any event identification of relevant market is necessary and pivotal to the application of a growing number of instruments which exempt certain agreements from the prohibition of Article 81 upon just such a criterion as market share.

The role of the Commission

One of the various hats worn by the Commission is that of 'guardian' of the Treaty, for it has a general responsibility to 'ensure that the provisions of [the] Treaty and the measures taken by the institutions pursuant thereto are applied'.[141] Whilst most Community law is administered through the medium of competent national authorities, the regulation and administration of the competition rules come to a much greater degree under direct Community control, and, as we shall see, 'hands on' Community authority has been delegated by the Council to the Commission. Two important points are required to be borne in mind.

First, in the field of competition, the Commission has been authorised to adopt regulations and decisions within the meaning of Article 249 (ex Article 189) of the Treaty, instruments of, respectively, a legislative and an administrative/quasi-judicial nature. Decisions in this sense are legal acts addressed to undertakings[142] which create legal obligations for their addressee(s), and are the means by which the Commission identifies and condemns breaches of the competition rules. Throughout the book they are cited as sources of law, for they are key instruments in establishing the meaning and the breadth of Articles 81 and 82. But it is important to note that if a decision is not taken on review to the Court of First Instance or the Court of Justice under Article 230 (ex Article 173), it is, except for the addressee, not the final word. The Commission is not innocent of seeking

---

[139] As to exemption, see Chap 4.

[140] As to appreciability, see pp 71–5 *infra*.

[141] EC Treaty, Art 211 (ex Art 155).

[142] Decisions generally may also be addressed to member states, but in the field of competition this is restricted to the areas of public undertakings or undertakings enjoying special rights (Art 86(3), ex Art 90(3)) and state aids (Art 88, ex Art 93); see Chaps 7 and 11.

to stretch the law to, and sometimes beyond, its limits. Whilst a Commission decision is authoritative as to the meaning of the law, it is not definitive.

Second, where the Council authorises it to adopt formal acts the Commission must in principle do so as the 'college' of Commissioners,[143] although authority may, only exceptionally, only in matters of management or administration and only under closely circumscribed conditions, be delegated to a single Commissioner.[144] Having said that, much of the work of the Commission is performed by its 'services', the *fonctionnaires* who comprise its civil service. In the field of competition the work is carried out by the Directorate-General for Competition (prior to restructuring of the Prodi Commission in 1999 known as Directorate-General IV, or D-G IV). But given the responsibilities it is required to discharge, and the close economic and legal analysis which attends all competition matters, the Competition D-G is, like the Commission generally, seriously understaffed: in 1998 the number of officials in D-G IV actually responsible for investigating cases involving restrictive practices, abuse of a dominant position and mergers – and so charged with overseeing competition in a market of 380 million people across 15 states and 15 different regulatory systems – numbered 153;[145] compare an equivalent staff of 372 in the Australian Competition and Consumer Commission (population 18 million) and of 385 in the Canadian Competition Bureau (population 28 million) and, an administrative bottleneck not to be downplayed, the number of languages in which each must work – one in Canberra, two in Ottawa and eleven in Brussels. This is, according to a former Commissioner responsible for competition, 'self-evidently grossly inade-

---

[143] EC Treaty, Art 219 (ex Art 163); Commission Rules of Procedure (OJ 1999 L252/41), Art 1; Case C-137/92P *Commission v BASF* (PVC) [1994] ECR I-2555; Cases T-80 etc/89 *BASF v Commission* (LdPE) [1994] ECR II-729; Cases T-31 & 32/91 *Solvay v Commission* (Soda Ash) [1995] ECR II-1821 and 1825, upheld on appeal in Cases C-287 & 288/95P *Commission v Solvay*, judgment of 6 April 2000, not yet reported; Case T-37/91 *ICI v Commission* (Soda Ash) [1995] ECR II-1901, upheld on appeal in Case C-286/95P *Commission v ICI*, judgment of 6 April 2000, not yet reported; Case C-199/92P *Hüls v Commission* (Polypropylene) [1999] ECR I-4287. There is a presumption that a Community act has been validly adopted, and it is for the party alleging that a decision has not been adopted by the college of Commissioners to show that this was the case; Cases T-305 etc/94 *Limburgse Vinyl Maatschappij v Commission* (PVC) [1999] ECR II-931 (under appeal as Cases C-238 etc/99P *Limburgse Vinyl Maatschappij v Commission*, pending).

[144] Case 5/85 *AKZO v Commission* [1986] ECR 2585; Cases 97–9/87 *Dow Chemical Ibérica v Commission* [1989] ECR 3165; Case T-442/93 *Association des Amidonneries de Céréales v Commission* [1995] ECR II-1329.

[145] European Commission, White Paper on Modernisation of the Rules Implementing Articles 85 and 86 of the EC Treaty, Programme No 99/027, n 44.

quate'.[146] As a result the Commission is reeling under the burdens it is required to discharge and so has turned to various soft law devices as a means of encouraging devolution to national authorities of enforcement powers. As economic operators crave legal certainty these devices are sometimes to be treated warily and, if they are found to cut corners, increase the necessity for vigilance on the part of the Court of Justice. It has also led the Commission now to 'capitulate', according to the president of the *Bundeskartellamt*, and to propose fundamental change to enforcement of the system which may, or may not, come to pass.[147]

---

[146] *Staffing of Community Institutions*, House of Lords Select Committee on the European Communities, Session 1987–88, HL Paper 66, Q 298 (Mr Sutherland).

[147] See pp 134–6 and pp 219–23 *infra*.

CHAPTER 3

Article 81(1)

Articles 81 and 82 (ex Articles 85 and 86) are the cornerstone of EC competition law. Article 81 is the first operative provision of the Treaty giving flesh to the core Community activity prescribed by Article 3(1)(g) of creating 'a system ensuring that competition in the internal market is not distorted'. And it is pivotal thereto, constituting according to the Court of Justice 'a fundamental provision which is essential for the accomplishment of the tasks entrusted to the Community and, in particular, the functioning of the internal market'.[1]

Article 81 reads:

1. The following shall be prohibited as incompatible with the common market: all agreements between undertakings, decisions by associations of undertakings and concerted practices which may affect trade between Member States and which have as their object or effect the prevention, restriction or distortion of competition within the common market, and in particular those which:

    (a) directly or indirectly fix purchase or selling prices or any other trading conditions;
    (b) limit or control production, markets, technical development, or investment;
    (c) share markets or sources of supply;
    (d) apply dissimilar conditions to equivalent transactions with other trading parties, thereby placing them at a competitive disadvantage;
    (e) make the conclusion of contracts subject to acceptance by other parties of supplementary obligations which, by their nature or according to commercial usage, have no connection with the subject of such contracts.

---

[1] Case C-126/97 *Eco Swiss China Time* v *Benetton International* [1999] ECR I-3055 at 3092.

2. Any agreement or decision prohibited pursuant to this Article shall be automatically void.

3. The provisions of paragraph 1 may, however, be declared inapplicable in the case of:

    – any agreement or category of agreements between undertakings;
    – any decision or category of decisions by associations of undertakings;
    – any concerted practice or category of concerted practices;

    which contributes to improving the production or distribution of goods or to promoting technical or economic progress, while allowing consumers a fair share of the resulting benefits, and which does not:

    (a) impose on the undertakings concerned restrictions which are not indispensable to the attainment of those objectives;
    (b) afford such undertakings the possibility of eliminating competition in respect of a substantial part of the products in question.

The first point to be noted is that, in order to be joined, Article 81 requires accommodation between or amongst two or more undertakings. A grossly anticompetitive course of action pursued unilaterally by an undertaking absent any agreement or coordinated action with another undertaking does not and cannot infringe Article 81 – although conduct which is 'unilateral' for these purposes requires a degree of circumspection.[2] Article 81, unlike Article 82, is concerned with distortions to competition which are the fruit of collaboration between or amongst undertakings – first and foremost those which are, or ought to be, in direct competition with one another but, as we shall see, also those which do not compete (indeed cannot compete for their points of tangency are on the vertical plane alone) but may nevertheless pursue arrangements which frustrate competition.

It will be observed that Article 81 is, like Gaul, divided into three parts. Article 81(1) sets out the general prohibition: the types of anticompetitive, collusive conduct between or amongst undertakings which is 'incompatible with the common market' and therefore prohibited. Article 81(2) lays down the civil consequences of engaging in such prohibited conduct: an agreement or decision which contravenes Article 81(1) is automatically void, and cannot be enforced or given effect. But Article 81(3) represents a recognition that some agreements or practices which fall within the prohibition of Article 81(1) may nevertheless produce beneficial effects either in terms of competition itself or, perhaps, in other respects which may outweigh their anticompetitive effects, and so provides authority for setting

---

[2] See *infra.*

aside ('declaring inapplicable'), or exempting them from, the prohibition. Article 81(3) provides neither who is to be competent to wield this authority nor the manner in which it is to be wielded. As we shall see in the following chapter, the power is one which has been conferred exclusively upon the Commission. But the manner of its use, and the very exclusivity of Commission authority, is one not without its difficulties and detractors.

Article 81 is a complete, coherent package, or 'indivisible whole'. Article 81(3) in particular is part and parcel, and a necessary component, of the package.[3] Difficulties in exposition therefore arise, for understanding of the prohibition cannot be complete without appreciation of the possibility of exemption and the manner in which it is granted. Article 81(3) will be considered in detail in the following chapter; Article 81(2), which addresses effectively questions of enforcement of Article 81(1), in Chapter 6. Both ought to be borne in mind throughout. Equally, Article 81(1) is itself a web of some complexity, with the very heart of the prohibition, 'the prevention, restriction or distortion of competition', falling towards the end of the operative part. The whole requires to be parsed very carefully, and it is probably clearest to begin with the preceding considerations of the article and hold fire on the core of it until these preliminaries are settled.

3.1 'Agreements, decisions of associations of undertakings and concerted practices'

According to Article 81(1), the prohibition applies to anticompetitive 'agreements between undertakings, decisions by associations of undertakings and concerted practices'. The term 'restrictive practices' is sometimes used as shorthand to cover all three. Of the three, agreements and concerted practices merit equal, and closest, consideration.

3.1.1 Agreements and concerted practices

Neither 'agreement' nor 'concerted practice' is defined in the Treaty or in Community legislation. The choice of the word 'agreement' (*accord*; *Vereinbarung*) was deliberate so as to allow the concept a very wide latitude. It is *not* synonymous with a contract formed in accordance with, and recognised and enforced by, the law of a member state. It requires, as with much of Community terminology, its own autonomous meaning independent of national law, and the proper law of a contract is irrelevant to the formation of an agreement for the purposes of Article 81. An agreement

---

[3] Cases 209 etc/84 *Ministère Public* v *Asjes* (Nouvelles Frontières) [1986] ECR 1425; Case 66/86 *Ahmed Saeed Flugreisen* v *Zentrale zur Bekämpfung unlauteren Wettbewerbs* [1989] ECR 803.

requires *consensus ad idem* but in a sense much wider and looser than that normally accorded by the law of contract. In most cases it will therefore certainly embrace any contract recognised in national law. It is not always so: a gratuitous promise, for example, is capable of forming a contract in a number of national legal systems, but is not an agreement within the meaning of Article 81. In order for an agreement to exist 'it is sufficient if the undertakings in question have expressed their joint intention to conduct themselves on the market in a specific way.'[4] It need not involve an otherwise valid and legally binding contract (a contract which infringes Article 81(1) cannot be said to be a valid contract owing to the automatic nullity provided in Article 81(2)[5]) but merely an 'expression of the intention of the parties';[6] it is unnecessary that provision be made for constraints or penalties.[7] The fact that a party reneges on an agreement, or can show that it never intended to comply with it, is immaterial.[8] It need not be reduced to written form[9] and may be merely a gentlemen's agreement.[10] The fact it may be tainted with illegality and so voidable as a matter of its proper law – for example, that it was secured under duress – does not deprive it of its character as an agreement.[11] It may be inferred from all the surrounding circumstances and terms may be implied by subsequent practice of the parties with significantly greater ease than in national law.[12] Thus was the Commission recently able to say:

> An agreement can be said to exist ... when the parties adhere to a common plan which limits or is likely to limit their individual commercial conduct by determining the lines [*Richtung; lignes*] of their mutual action or abstention from action in the market. While it involves joint decision-making and commitment to

---

[4] Case T-1/89 *Rhône-Poulenc* v *Commission* (Polypropylene) [1991] ECR II-867 at 1073.

[5] See Chap 6.

[6] Cases 209 etc/78 *van Landewyck* v *Commission* (FEDETAB) [1980] ECR 3125; Case 277/87 *Sandoz Prodotti Farmaceutici* v *Commission* [1990] ECR I-45.

[7] Decision 94/815 (*Cement*) OJ 1994 L343/1 at para 45(6).

[8] Cases 209 etc/78 *van Landewyck* v *Commission* (FEDETAB) [1980] ECR 3125; Decision 86/399 (*Belgian Roofing Felt*) OJ 1986 L232/15, upheld on review as Case 246/86 *Balasco* v *Commission* [1989] ECR 2117.

[9] Case 28/77 *Tepea* v *Commission* [1978] ECR 1391.

[10] Case 41/69 *ACF Chemiefarma* v *Commission* [1970] ECR 661; Case T-141/89 *Tréfileurope Sales* v *Commission* [1995] ECR II-791.

[11] Case T-141/89 *Tréfileurope Sales*, *ibid*; Decision 96/478 (*Bayer/Adalat*) OJ 1996 L201/1 (under review as Case T-41/96 *Bayer* v *Commission*, pending); Decision 98/273 (*Volkswagen*) OJ 1998 L124/60 (under review as Case T-62/98 *Volkswagen* v *Commission*, pending).

[12] See *infra*.

a common scheme, it does not have to be made in writing; no formalities are necessary, and no contractual sanctions or enforcement measures are required. The fact of agreement may be express or implicit in the behaviour of the parties.[13]

A concerted practice, on the other hand, is

a form of coordination between undertakings which, without having reached the stage where an agreement properly so-called has been concluded, knowingly substitutes practical cooperation between them for the risks of competition [which leads to conditions of competition which do not correspond to the normal conditions of the market ....].[14]

It

in no way require[s] the working out of an actual plan, [but] must be understood in the light of the concept inherent in the provisions of the Treaty relating to competition that each economic operator must determine independently the policy which he intends to adopt on the common market ....

Although it is correct to say that this requirement of independence does not deprive economic operators of the right to adapt themselves intelligently to the existing and anticipated conduct of their competitors, it does however strictly preclude any direct or indirect contact between such operators, the object or effect whereof is either to influence the conduct on the market of an actual or potential competitor or to disclose to such a competitor the course of conduct which they themselves have decided to adopt or contemplate adopting on the market.[15]

Alternatively,

conduct may fall under Article 85(1) as a concerted practice where the parties have not agreed or decided in advance among themselves what each will do in

---

13 Decision 1999/60 (*Pre-Insulated Pipes*) OJ 1999 L24/1 at para 129 (under review as Cases T-9 etc/99 *HFB Holding für Fernwärmetechnik Beteiligungsgesellschaft* v *Commission*, pending). For similar constructions see Decision 94/815 (*Cement*) OJ 1994 L343/1, partially annulled on appeal in Cases T–25 etc/95 *Cimenteries CBR* v *Commission*, judgment of 15 March 2000, not yet reported; Decision 94/601 (*Cartonboard*) OJ 1994 L243/1, upheld essentially on review in a series of judgments the first of which is Case T-295/94 *Buchmann* v *Commission* [1998] ECR II-813; Decision 1999/210 (*British Sugar/Tate & Lyle/Napier Brown/James Budgett*) OJ 1999 L76/1 (under review as Cases T-202 & 207/98 *Tate & Lyle and Napier Brown* v *Commission*, pending).

14 Case 48/69 *ICI* v *Commission* (Dyestuffs) [1972] ECR 619 at 655; Cases 40 etc/73 *Coöperatieve Vereniging 'Suiker Unie'* v *Commission* [1975] ECR 1663 at 1916; Case 172/80 *Zückner* v *Bayerische Vereinsbank* [1980] ECR 2021 at 2031. The words in square parentheses appear only in the *Suiker Unie* judgment.

15 Cases 40 etc/73 *Suiker Unie*, *ibid* at 1942; also Cases T-305 etc/94 *Limburgse Vinyl Maatschappij* v *Commission* [1999] ECR II-931 at 1133 (under review as Cases C-328 etc/99, *Limburgse Vinyl Maatschappij* v *Commission*, pending).

the market, but knowingly adopt or adhere to some collusive device which encourages or facilitates the co-ordination of their commercial activity.[16]

The object of the Treaty in creating the concept of concerted practice 'was to forestall the possibility of undertakings evading the application of competition rules by colluding in an anti-competitive manner falling short of a definite agreement'.[17] It is clearly intended to catch collusive conduct between or amongst undertakings which is a product not of an agreement, however generously defined, but of a nod and a wink: not *consensus ad idem*, but informal accommodation or an understanding.[18] And such conduct is legion. However, concerted practice is not a 'subset' of agreement, or a device simply to lessen the evidential burden where the existence of an agreement cannot be shown or adduced, but a construct of independent scope and application. Having said that, it is one which resists precise definition.

A simple but singularly useful illustration can be had by adopting a football metaphor and considering the infamous (West) Germany–Austria match in the 1982 World Cup. That, it may be recalled, was the last match of the opening round. At half time, with the score 1–0 in Germany's favour, the result from the other match in the group came in, and the arithmetic of the table was such that if the Germany–Austria match finished with the score unchanged both sides would go through to the next round; if either scored, the other would be out. There then ensued the dreariest 45 minutes of football in World Cup history, effectively the two sides kicking the ball back and forth across the centre line. Presumably there was no agreement to do so, but both sides appeared to see mutual advantage in this course of conduct at the expense of the consumer/spectator/other competitors in the group. Applying (if adapting) the *Suiker Unie* test, did they 'knowingly substitute practical cooperation between them for the risks of competition which led to conditions of competition which do not correspond to the normal conditions of [football]'? If so, it is (the football equivalent of) a concerted practice.

---

[16] Decision 1999/210 (*British Sugar/Tate & Lyle/Napier Brown/James Budgett*) OJ 1999 L76/1 at para 69 (under review as Cases T-202 & 207/98 *Tate & Lyle and Napier Brown v Commission*, pending).

[17] Decision 94/601 (*Cartonboard*) OJ 1994 L243/1 at para 126.

[18] In a 1982 decision (Decision 82/506 (*Stichting Sigarettenindustrie*) OJ 1982 L232/1 at para 106, upheld on review as Cases 240 etc/82 *Stichting Sigarettenindustrie v Commission* [1985] ECR 3831) the Commission went so far as to characterise an 'understanding' between undertakings to be an agreement, and this is sometimes cited as extending the breadth of 'agreement', but it is more accurately attributable to a bad translation of the (authentic) Dutch term used (*overeenstemming*).

The problem is, of course, one of proof. Undertakings consciously engaged in anticompetitive conduct, be it by medium of agreement or of concerted practice, may go to great lengths to cover their tracks. Where there is no agreement it is much easier to do. In either case, it is the reason behind the adoption by the Commission of a policy of not imposing or of mitigating fines for cartel whistleblowers.[19] But assuming no breaking of ranks, how is a party seeking to show the existence of a concerted practice and bearing the onus of proof – which must in all events be based upon concrete evidence and not mere hypothesis[20] – to do so? The prime indicator, although not necessarily in itself constitutive of a concerted practice,[21] is parallel conduct – suspiciously uniform and contemporaneous price rises (price parallelism being in the first rank of concerted practices) or refusal to deal outwith established markets, for example. But this is inherently risky, as there may be a fine line between independent 'intelligent adaptation to market conditions', or 'innocent parallel behaviour', which is not objectionable, and the 'knowing substitution of practical cooperation', 'conscious parallelism', 'artificial certainty' or most commonly 'concertation', which is. It is an especially fine line in oligopolistic markets in which the 'normal conditions of the market' are marked by price parallelism.[22] The Court of Justice has said that the allegation must be considered as a whole, account being taken of the specific nature and features of the products or services at issue, the size and number of undertakings in the market, the volume of the market and conduct within it.[23] Evidence such consideration yields must then be 'sufficiently precise and coherent ... to justify the view that the parallel behaviour ... was the result of concerted action'[24] and that '[i]n the absence of a firm, precise and consistent body of evidence, it must be held that concertation ... has not been established'.[25] According to Advocate-General Darmon this means that 'it is necessary to establish a degree of certainty that goes beyond any reasonable doubt',[26] which, at least to English ears, is perhaps overegging the pudding. A better formulation is simply whether the existence of concertation is necessarily

---

[19] Notice on the non-imposition or the mitigation of fines in cartel cases, OJ 1996 C207/4, especially Part A which lays out the rationale behind it; on the notice see pp 180–1 *infra*.

[20] Cases T-374 etc/94 *European Night Services* v *Commission* [1998] ECR II-3141.

[21] Case 48/69 *ICI* v *Commission* (Dyestuffs) [1972] ECR 619.

[22] See Chap 8.

[23] Case 48/69 *ICI* v *Commission* (Dyestuffs) [1972] ECR 619.

[24] Cases 29–30/83 *Compagnie Royale Asturienne des Mines* v *Commission* [1984] ECR 1679 at 1702.

[25] Cases 89 etc/85 *Åhlström* v *Commission* (Woodpulp) [1993] ECR I-1307 at 1614.

[26] Cases 89 etc/85 *Woodpulp*, *ibid* at 1493.

to be inferred. To revert to Teutonic football, given the fixture, its timing, the information available to both sides at half time, the arithmetic of the table and the rules on progression to the next round, is concertation between the two sides necessarily to be inferred from their conduct in the second half? Put another way, if parties alleged to be engaged in a concerted practice can show any one reason why their conduct can be attributable to other than concertation, a concerted practice cannot be found.

Of course undertakings accused of concertation will put forward all manner of reasons otherwise to justify their conduct. To escape Article 81(1) it must be plausible. So, for example, in *Compagnie Royale Asturienne des Mines*[27] the Commission libelled a concerted practice in a refusal to sell to certain buyers. On review the Court of Justice said:

> It is sufficient for the applicants to prove circumstances which cast the facts established by the Commission in a different light and which thus allow another explanation of the facts to be substituted for the one adopted by the contested decision.[28]

In this case they could show a poor payment record of the buyers which was a reasonable explanation not to sell, and a concerted practice was therefore not proven. The Court seems to suggest, following the establishment of *prima facie* parallel conduct, a reversal of the normal burden of proof. This would be (partially) consistent with the view of Advocate-General Slynn enunciated in *Pioneer*:

> Once a finding has been made that a concerted practice exists, since it is the applicant who is claiming that the Commission's decision should be annulled, the burden of proving the illegality of the decision falls, in general and in the first instance, upon the applicant ....
>
> On the other hand, the allegations of fact made by the Commission in its Decision must be such as to warrant the conclusion drawn from them. If they do not warrant that conclusion, the Decision may be annulled, even in the absence of any evidence adduced by the applicants.[29]

But in its subsequent formulation in *Woodpulp*, in which the Commission found concertation in parallel price rises,[30] the Court seems to suggest otherwise:

---

[27] Decision 82/866 OJ 1982 L362/40.

[28] Cases 29–30/83 *Compagnie Royale Asturienne des Mines* v *Commission* [1984] ECR 1679 at 1702.

[29] Cases 100–103/80 *Musique Diffusion Française* v *Commission* [1983] ECR 1825 at 1930–1.

[30] Decision 85/202 OJ 1985 L85/1.

[P]arallel conduct cannot be regarded as furnishing proof of concertation unless concertation is the only plausible explanation for such conduct ....

Accordingly, it is necessary ... to ascertain whether the parallel conduct alleged by the Commission cannot ... be explained otherwise than by concertation.[31]

And in order to do so it had recourse to two 'experts' reports' which it itself had commissioned[32] and which, by finding a plausible alternative explanation (the oligopolistic nature of the market) to the conduct upon which the Commission had relied, holed its reasoning below the waterline. *Woodpulp* was the Court of Justice's swansong in competition law, the last case following the establishment of the Court of First Instance in which it exercised sole jurisdiction on consideration of matters both of fact and of law, and it marks a significant increase in the degree of rigour required in the economic analysis necessary to show concertation. The Court of First Instance at first took up the baton in much the same manner.[33] Nevertheless it (re)confirmed subsequently that where the Commission's allegations are based upon more than mere parallel conduct the burden lies with the undertaking(s) to supply an alternative explanation and to challenge the existence of the facts put forward by the Commission.[34] Most recently the Court of Justice confirmed that where the Commission can show concertation which is manifestly anticompetitive in nature it is for the parties to show otherwise, and this not- withstanding a presumption of innocence which is a fundamental right recognised in and protected by Community law.[35]

A concerted practice may be inferred from parallel conduct following contact between or amongst the parties. Although it is not impossible to have concertation absent any contact, in no case to date has the Commission libelled it. The *Suiker Unie* construct that Article 81(1) 'strictly preclude[s] any direct or indirect contact between ... operators, the

---

[31] Cases 89 etc/85 *Åhlström* v *Commission* (Woodpulp) [1993] ECR I-1307 at 1601.

[32] Summarised in the Report for the Hearing at pp 1428–44.

[33] So in this context it said in Case T-145/89 *Baustahlgewebe* v *Commission* [1995] ECR II-987 at 1022, following *Woodpulp*, that where an undertaking put forward an alternative explanation for apparently concertative conduct 'the Court must verify whether the matters raised by the Commission can be accounted for by anything other than [concertation]'. But it said subsequently that the Commission is under no burden to seek out alternative explanations; Cases T-25 etc/95 *Cimenteries CBR* v *Commission* (Cement), judgment of 15 March 2000, not yet reported, at paras 498 and 3922 *et seq*.

[34] Cases T-305 etc/94 *Limburgse Vinyl Maatschappij* v *Commission* [1999] ECR II-931 (under review as Cases T-328 etc/99 *Limburgse Vinyl Maatschappij* v *Commission*, pending).

[35] Case C-199/92P *Hüls* v *Commission* (Polypropylene) [1999] ECR I-4287.

object or effect whereof [is concertation]' therefore requires consideration. The object is to bring within the scope of a concerted practice the exchange of commercially confidential information which may lead to the creation or continuation of a (tacit at least) cartel. In response to the decision in *Polypropylene*[36] in which the Commission had libelled the existence of a concerted practice evidenced by, *inter alia*, an extensive series of meetings amongst participants in an (alleged) cartel, a number of undertakings argued that a concerted practice (in contradistinction to an agreement) required an overt act, the adoption of coordinated conduct which actually and concretely had the effect of altering the conditions of competition, which proposition had the implied support of the Advocates-General in two earlier concerted practices cases;[37] otherwise it could be found in any contact between or amongst undertakings, even that which did not have the slightest effect upon commercial conduct and which the undertakings had no intention of allowing to have that effect. The Commission was wholesomely afraid that if the Court of First Instance agreed, it would drive a coach and four through a prime indicator of concerted practice. But it did not. If sensitive information was exchanged at a meeting, it could not but inform those taking part as to the future conduct of its competitors, which is of itself anticompetitive even if it cannot be shown that market conduct was as a result of this information adjusted in any way:

> Not only did the applicant pursue the aim of eliminating in advance uncertainty about the future conduct of its competitors but also, in determining the policy which it intended to follow on the market, it could not fail to take account, directly or indirectly, of the information obtained during the course of those meetings. Similarly, in determining the policy which they intended to follow, its competitors were bound to take into account, directly or indirectly, the information disclosed to them by the applicant about the course of conduct which the applicant itself had decided upon or which it contemplated adopting on the market.[38]

On appeal the Court of Justice upheld the Court of First Instance, but by the imputation of an object to a concerted practice:

> It follows, first, that the concept of a concerted practice, as it results from the actual terms of Article 81(1) EC, implies, besides undertakings' concerting with

---

[36] Decision 86/398 OJ 1986 L230/1.

[37] Case 41/69 ACF *Chemiefarma* v *Commission* [1970] ECR 661 *per* A–G Gand at 715; Case 48/69 *ICI* v *Commission* (Dyestuffs) [1972] ECR 619 *per* A–G Mayras at 671.

[38] Case T-1/89 *Rhône-Poulenc* v *Commission* [1991] ECR II-867 at 1074.

each other [*sic*], subsequent conduct on the market, and a relationship of cause and effect between the two.

However, subject to proof to the contrary ... the presumption must be that the undertakings taking part in the concerted action and remaining active on the market take account of the information exchanged with their competitors for the purposes of determining their conduct on the market. This is all the more true where the undertakings concert together on a regular basis over a long period ....

Secondly ... a concerted practice as defined above is caught by Article 81(1) EC, even in the absence of anti-competitive effects on the market.

First, it follows from the actual text of the provision that, as in the case of agreements between undertakings and decisions of associations of undertakings, concerted practices are prohibited, regardless of their effect, when they have an anti-competitive object.

Next, although the very concept of concerted practice presupposes conduct by the participating undertakings on the market, it does not necessarily mean that that conduct should produce the specific effect of restricting, preventing or distorting competition ....

[S]ince the Commission had established to the requisite legal standard that [the parties] had taken part in polypropylene producers' concerting together [*sic*] for the purpose of restricting competition, it did not have to adduce evidence that their concerting together had manifested itself in conduct on the market or that it had effects restrictive of competition.[39]

This underscores a key component of competition: the importance of uncertainty of the conduct of competitors. A producer unsure of a competitor's future price structure may be tempted to cut margins in order to offer lower prices. This is the motive force of competition. But if the former learns of the latter's intentions it is less likely to do so. In this context, not to act may be to act. The irony is that undertakings will expend great time and effort divining the intentions of the competition, and if they do so accurately, market success may follow: reward for, in part, the risk undertaken and won. But if they do so by exchanging the very information each is seeking they remove the uncertainty, or create 'the necessary atmosphere of mutual certainty' or 'mutual assurance' as to their respective strategies and policies,[40] and it is concertation. Of course some information exchange is unobjectionable, and may indeed be beneficial to competition: information on regulation, market conditions, volume of demand, capacity and so on may lead to increased more rational decision making and cost

---

[39] Case C-199/92P *Hüls* v *Commission* (Polypropylene) [1999] ECR I-4287 at 4386–7.
[40] Decision 1999/210 (*British Sugar/Tate & Lyle/Napier Brown/James Budgett*) OJ 1999 L76/1 at para 72 (under review as Cases T-202 & 207/98 *Tate & Lyle and Napier Brown* v *Commission*, pending).

reduction. In any event, it cannot be prevented. What is pivotal is what is discussed; and the narrower (more oligopolistic) the market the greater the sensitivity and value of information exchanged.[41] If, as was argued by one party in *Cartonboard*, meetings amongst competitors were mere 'social occasions' the attractions of which were 'conviviality and pleasant location' at which its representative could not follow any discussion because he could not understand the language,[42] no harm can come thereby. But if confidential information is discussed, especially that involving, but not restricted to, pricing policies – for example, that involving respective sales figures,[43] orders and/or deliveries[44] which facilitates cartel monitoring – undertakings are presumed to react thereto. An almost total absence of minutes of such a meeting creates a presumption that participating undertakings attempted to hide its true nature, and it is then for them to show that the meeting had a lawful object.[45] Even where an undertaking can show that, following participation in meetings, it instructed its representatives to avoid any collusive practices, it will not be saved.[46] The only escape, indicated *obiter* by the Court of First Instance, appears to be if an undertaking cannot be shown to have responded to information disclosed *and* it has publicly distanced itself from it[47] or, according to the Court of Justice, where it can produce evidence to establish that its participation had no anticompetitive intention by showing that it had indicated to its competitors that that participation was in a spirit different from theirs.[48]

Most concerted practices involve cartels, but they may exist in vertical arrangements as well, such as an understanding reached between a manufacturer and its various distributors by which through regular meetings supplies and sales are coordinated and, implicitly, markets allocated.[49] It

---

[41] Case T-34/92 *Fiatagri & New Holland Ford* v *Commission* [1994] ECR II-905, upheld on appeal in Case C-8/95P *New Holland Ford* v *Commission* [1998] ECR I-3175; Case T-35/92 *John Deere* v *Commission* [1994] ECR II-957, upheld on appeal in Case C-7/95P *John Deere* v *Commission* [1998] ECR I-3111.

[42] Decision 94/601 OJ 1994 L243/1 at para 109.

[43] Case T-43/92 *Fiatagri & New Holland Ford* v *Commission* [1994] ECR II-905.

[44] Case T-148/89 *Tréfilunion* v *Commission* [1995] ECR II-1063; Case T-141/94 *Thyssen Stahl* v *Commission* [1999] ECR II-347 (under appeal as Case C-194/99P *Thyssen Stahl* v *Commission*, pending).

[45] Case T-334/94 *Sarrió* v *Commission* (Cartonboard) [1998] ECR II-1439.

[46] Case T-141/89 *Tréfileurope Sales* v *Commission* [1995] ECR II-791; Decision 1999/271 (*Greek Ferries*) OJ 1999 L109/24 (under review as Cases T-56 etc/99 *Marlines* v *Commission*, pending).

[47] Case T-145/89 *Baustahlgewebe* v *Commission* [1995] ECR II-987; Case T-334/94 *Sarrió* v *Commission* (Cartonboard) [1998] ECR II-1439.

[48] Case C-199/92P *Hüls* v *Commission* (Polypropylene) [1999] ECR I-4287.

[49] Cases 100–103/80 *Musique Diffusion Française* v *Commission* (Pioneer) [1983] ECR 1825.

may be inferred from conduct attendant upon an agreement – where, for example, a distribution contract expressly permits solicited sales outwith the contract territory (and so generally is exempted from the prohibition of Article 81(1))[50] but a tacit understanding can be shown to exist that such orders are to be rebuffed.[51] It may also consist in cooperation in order to identify, and so to eliminate, parallel imports[52] and simple test purchases by the manufacturer for the same purpose followed by requests to its distributors to cease supplying.[53]

Whilst agreement and concerted practice are independent and distinct concepts, there is no rigid dividing line between the two and they are not mutually exclusive to a given situation. Especially where there is a complex of cartel relationships amongst undertakings which contains elements of both and extends over a period of time and so where

> it may not even be feasible or realistic to make any such distinction as the infringement may present simultaneously characteristics of both types of prohibited conduct [and it would] be artificial to subdivide what is clearly a continuing common enterprise having one and the same overall objective into several discrete infringements,[54]

the Commission has turned latterly to finding a single infringement of Article 81(1),[55] and in this it has been supported by the Court of First Instance:

> The Commission was ... entitled to characterize that single infringement as 'an agreement and a concerted practice' since the infringement involved at one and the same time factual elements to be characterized as 'agreements' and factual elements to be characterized as 'concerted practices'. Given such a complex infringement, the dual characterization ... must be understood not as requiring, simultaneously and cumulatively, proof that each of those factual elements represents the constituent elements both of an agreement and of a concerted practice, but rather as referring to a complex whole comprising a number of factual elements some of which were characterized as agreements and others as concerted

---

[50] See *infra*.
[51] Case T-43/92 *Dunlop Slazenger* v *Commission* [1994] ECR II-441.
[52] Case 28/77 *Tepea* v *Commission* [1978] ECR 1391.
[53] Case 86/82 *Hasselblad* v *Commission* [1984] ECR 883; also Case C-349/95 *Frits Loendersloot* v *Ballantine and Son* [1997] ECR I-6227.
[54] Decision 94/601 (*Cartonboard*) OJ 1994 L243/1 at para 128.
[55] eg, Decision 86/398 (*Polypropylene*) OJ 1986 L230/1; Decision 94/215 (*Steel Beams*) OJ 1994 L116/1; Decision 94/599 (*PVC II*) OJ 1994 L349/14; Decision 94/815 (*Cement*) OJ 1994 L343/1; Decision 94/601 (*Cartonboard*), *ibid*; Decision 1999/210 (*British Sugar/Tate & Lyle/Napier Brown/James Budgett*) OJ 1999 L76/1.

practices for the purposes of Article 85(1) of the EEC Treaty, which lays down no specific category for a complex infringement of this type.[56]

3.1.2 'Unilateral' agreements

As indicated above, a course of action pursued unilaterally by an undertaking does not and cannot fall within the prohibition of Article 81(1); an agreement or concertation between or amongst undertakings is a *sine qua non* of Article 81. There are, however, a small number of cases in which what appears to be unilateral action on the part of a producer is deemed to have the quality of an agreement, so falling within Article 81. This has its origins in the Commission asserting that in certain circumstances unilateral conduct on the part of a manufacturer forms part of the complex of contractual arrangements between it and its distributors or dealers, and hitherto the Court of Justice has generally agreed. Recently the Commission has become more ambitious and it may find the Court parting company with it.

The relevant cases all involve alleged export bans which if they form part of a agreement between manufacturer and distributor are in most circumstances a *per se* infringement of Article 81(1).[57] The starting point was the recognition by the Court of Justice that admission to a selective distribution system is based upon an acceptance, tacit or express, of the policies pursued by the manufacturer.[58] Proceeding therefrom, in *Ford Werke* a motor manufacturer (Ford) had become concerned that its official distribution system in the United Kingdom was being undercut by parallel imports from the continent of (much cheaper) motorcars. Ford AG therefore sent a circular to its German dealers indicating that it would henceforward refuse to fill orders from them for right-hand drive motorcars, so seeking to isolate the British and Irish markets. The Commission asserted[59] that the circular was not a unilateral act but formed part of the contractual relations between manufacturer and dealer and so became in effect an implied term of those contracts, and the Court of Justice, whilst confirming that 'a unilateral act cannot be included among the agreements, decisions and concerted practices prohibited by Article 85 of the Treaty', accepted the Commission's reasoning.[60] Essentially the same tale recurred in

---

[56] Case T-1/89 *Rhône-Poulenc* v *Commission* (Polypropylene) [1991] ECR II-867 at 1075, upheld on appeal in a number of cases, the first of which is Case C-49/92P *Commission* v *Anic Partecipazione* [1999] ECR I-4125.

[57] See *infra*.

[58] Case 107/82 *AEG-Telefunken* v *Commission* [1983] ECR 3151.

[59] Decision 83/560, OJ 1983 L327/31.

[60] Cases 25 & 26/84 *Ford Werke* v *Commission* [1985] ECR 2725 at 2741.

BMW.[61] Most recently, the Commission found an agreement to exist in an export ban imposed by a manufacturer by a system of preventive and monitoring measures and penalties given effect by circulars and word of mouth in *Volkswagen*.[62] Pressure to comply brought to bear by the manufacturer upon its dealers was irrelevant to the existence of an agreement.

Beyond motorcars and selective dealerships, in *Sandoz*[63] the Commission found that an export ban existed by virtue of the words 'export prohibited' appearing systematically on invoices, that this formed an integral part of the continuous commercial relations between Sandoz, an Italian pharmaceutical supplier, and its customers, it showed the existence of the consent of the former and the tacit acceptance of the latter, and so constituted not unilateral conduct but an agreement within the meaning of Article 81(1). The Court of Justice upheld the Commission, finding that

> the Commission was justified in considering that the set of continuous commercial relations, of which the 'export prohibited' clause formed an integral part, established between Sandoz PF and its customers was governed by a pre-established general agreement applicable to innumerable individual orders for Sandoz products. Such an agreement is covered by the provisions of Article 85(1) of the EEC Treaty.[64]

Prior to *Sandoz* the Commission had identified an export ban being incorporated into continuous commercial relations and imposed not by express words but by a monitoring system and threats to suspend or delay supplies, and characterised it as an agreement;[65] but this decision was not taken to, and so was never tested before, the Court of Justice. Judicial support for this line of argument may be had from *Dunlop Slazenger*,[66] but the Court of First Instance implied that the offending conduct may have been a concerted practice, not an agreement, which would be consistent with the earlier judgment of the Court of Justice in *Hasselblad*.[67]

The most ambitious (or brazen) example of 'unilateral' agreement is that

---

[61] Case C-70/93 *Bayerische Motorenwerke* v *ALD Auto-Leasing* [1995] ECR I-3439.

[62] Decision 98/273, OJ 1998 L124/60 (under review as Case T-62/98 *Volkswagen* v *Commission*, pending).

[63] Decision 87/409, OJ 1987 L222/28. See also, to much the same effect, Decision 91/335 (*Vincent Gosme/Distribution Martell Piper*) OJ 1991 L185/23, which was never taken to the Court of First Instance.

[64] Case 277/87 *Sandoz Prodotti Farmaceutici* v *Commission* [1990] ECR I-45, para 12. The passage is taken and translated from the original judgment which is reported in ECR only in (now happily abandoned) summary judgment form.

[65] Decision 80/1283 (*Johnson & Johnson*) OJ 1980 L377/16.

[66] Case T-43/92 *Dunlop Slazenger* v *Commission* [1994] ECR II-441.

[67] Case 86/82 *Hasselblad* v *Commission* [1984] ECR 883.

of *Bayer/Adalat*.[68] There the Commission found that a German pharmaceutical manufacturer (Bayer), which through its wholly owned subsidiaries in France and Spain had enjoyed longstanding sales to wholesalers in those markets, withheld from the wholesalers supplies of a range of medicinal products used in the treatment of cardiovascular disease (Adalat) which were likely to be destined, by re-export, for the (much dearer) British market. The Commission found that the Bayer subsidiaries in France and in Spain

> have committed an infringement of Article 85(1) by imposing an export ban as part of their continuous commercial relations with their customers. The agreement [*sic*] constitutes an appreciable restriction of competition and has an appreciable effect on trade between Member States.[69]

The export ban was deduced from a system of identifying exporting wholesalers and, notwithstanding persistent orders from them, successive reductions of supplies to levels which were appropriate to supplying their respective markets.[70] In all its aspects, claimed the Commission, the conduct of the Bayer subsidiaries indicated that they subjected their wholesalers to a permanent threat of reducing quantities supplied, a threat which was carried out if they did not comply with the export ban, and the conduct had been incorporated into longstanding commercial relations systematically and consistently.

Bayer/Adalat goes significantly beyond existing precedents. First, it involves significant assumptions of fact: that wholesalers interpreted Bayer's conduct as a threat to discontinue supply, that they believed this threat would be carried out, that they moderated their own conduct in response to it, and that this, as a matter of fact and law, formed tacit consent to an export prohibition and so constituted an agreement. But was it consent, or at least the expression of a joint intention? Does it meet the *Sandoz* test of 'clear and unequivocal conduct' spanning innumerable individual orders? If merely continuing to place orders with Bayer is sufficient to constitute a prohibited agreement, the only safe alternative would seem to be to cease doing so, which surely cannot be right. The key question is whether a refusal to sell, even in the context of continuing commercial relations, is or can be a function of an agreement. Whilst an obligation to

---

[68] Decision 96/478, OJ 1996 L201/1.

[69] at para 155.

[70] This was of course no guarantee that those supplies would not be re-exported in parallel trade, which gives rise to the potential problem, and a serious one for pharmaceutical products, of shortage of supplies in low price member states.

supply is a common enough burden for a dominant undertaking, as a price of that dominance, under Article 82,[71] in the context of Article 81 freedom of contract must remain the general rule.[72] If *Bayer/Adalat* is accepted, a supplier adopting such unilateral measures would be unable to prevent an 'agreement' from coming into being, even against its wishes, as a function of the conduct of its customers in relation to its orders. This is arguably an abuse of Article 81 and a significant limitation to contractual and commercial freedom to impose upon an undertaking in a competitive market.

Bayer/Adalat is clearly designed by the Commission to be a test case to explore the limits of Article 81(1) – evident, if in nothing else, in the fact that the Commission cleaved exclusively to the finding of an agreement, and made no allegation of a concerted practice. The decision was adopted in 1996. Bayer responded immediately with an action before the Court of First Instance under Article 173 (now Article 230) of the Treaty seeking its annulment,[73] and the judgment, still awaited, will be an important one whichever way the Court (or more accurately the Court of Justice on the inevitable appeal) goes. The better argument seems to be that, even accepting that Bayer's conduct had the object or effect of inhibiting parallel trade, it is not enough that the Commission does not much care for a particular course of behaviour: it must be conduct which is proscribed. In another context, arising from the economic entity doctrine and an instance of a parent undertaking instructing its subsidiaries in other member states not to distribute outwith their contract territory, the Court of First Instance accepted that this may well result in a partitioning of the market contrary to the principles of the competition rules, but that

> [i]t is not for the Court, on the pretext that certain conduct … may fall outside the competition rules, to apply Article 85 to circumstances for which it is not intended in order to fill a gap which may exist in the system of regulation laid down by the Treaty.[74]

Or, to borrow from Advocate-General Jacobs in a slightly different context,

> [t]he Court cannot in my view be expected to stand legislation on its head in order to achieve an objective, even were it to be considered desirable. If [legisla-

---

[71] See Chap 5.

[72] Case T-24/90 *Automec* v *Commission* [1992] ECR II-2223.

[73] Case T-41/96 *Bayer* v *Commission*, pending. Bayer also sought, and was granted, interim suspension (as to which see p 194 *infra*) of the operative part of the decision pending judgment: Case T-41/96R *Bayer* v *Commission* [1996] ECR II-381.

[74] Case T-102/92 *Viho Europe* v *Commission* [1995] ECR II-17 at 36, upheld on appeal as Case C-73/95P *Viho Europe* v *Commission* [1996] ECR I-5457.

tion] is found to have effects which are unacceptable, the correct remedy is to amend [it].[75]

It is suggested that *Bayer/Adalat* may well suffer the same fate.

3.1.3 Decisions of associations of undertakings

An association of undertakings is normally a trade association which is made up of separate undertakings or, on a grander scale, separate associations of undertakings[76] or a hybrid thereof, the purpose of which is to represent and defend the interests of its constituent members. However, the term embraces other forms of association, commonly in the Community agricultural cooperatives[77] but extending to liner conferences,[78] to national football,[79] basketball[80] and judo[81] associations and probably to Bar Councils.[82] A trade union appears not to be an association of undertakings because its members are not undertakings.[83] Often they discharge blameless functions: useful liaison with public authorities and regulators, legal advice and representation, organisation, product and market research, technical and standards development, promotion and information and education. But they might also, in the interests of their members, and intentionally or otherwise, be the author of anticompetitive conduct. The more inclusive they are – they may represent all producers in a member

---

[75] Case C-173/98 *Sebago* v *GB-Unic* [1999] ECR I-4103 at 4112.

[76] Although Art 81(1) refers only to 'associations of undertakings' the terms have been held to encompass also associations of associations of undertakings, otherwise the competition rules could be too easily sidestepped: Case 123/83 *Bureau National Interprofessionnel du Cognac* v *Clair* [1985] ECR 391 *per* A-G Slynn at 396; see also Decision 94/815 (*Cement*) OJ 1994 L343/1.

[77] Case 61/80 *Coöperatieve Stremsel- en Kleurselfabriek* v *Commission* [1981] ECR 851; Case C-250/92 *Gøttrup-Klim* v *Dansk Landbrugs Grovvarselskab* [1994] ECR I-5641.

[78] Cases C-395 & 396/96P *Compagnie Maritime Belge* v *Commission*, judgment of 16 March 2000, not yet reported.

[79] Case C-415/93 *Union Royale Belge des Sociétés de Football Association* v *Bosman* [1995] ECR I-4921 *per* A-G Lenz at 5026.

[80] Case C-196/96 *Lehtonen* v *Fédération Royale Belge des Sociétés de Basketball*, judgment of 13 April 2000, not yet reported, *per* A-G Alber at para 103 of his opinion.

[81] Cases C-51/96 & 191/97 *Deliège* v *Asbl Ligue Francophone de Judo*, judgment of 11 April 2000, not yet reported, *per* A-G Cosmas at para 104 of his opinion.

[82] Case C-309/99 *Wouters* v *Algemene Raad van de Nederlandse Orde van Advocaten*, pending.

[83] Case C-67/96 *Albany International* v *Stichting Bedrijfspensioenfonds Textielindustrie* [1999] ECR I-5751. This was put more forcefully in the opinion of A–G Jacobs, the Court to an extent sidestepping the issue.

state or have an even wider affiliation[84] – the more likely this is to be. The inclusion amongst the three classes of restrictive practices of 'decisions of associations of undertakings' was intended to catch anticompetitive conduct which might otherwise fall uncomfortably between the two stools of coordination between or amongst undertakings (Article 81) and the unilateral conduct of a single undertaking (Article 82).

In a few cases the very articles of association will compel anticompetitive conduct and so themselves offend Article 81(1);[85] but in most cases it is the activities of the association which come into question. Any attempt to impose 'order' or 'discipline' in the market in a manner which leads to price fixing, the imposition of quotas amongst its members or the allocation of markets will breach Article 81(1). An association may also engage in activities – exchange of information, collection of statistical and other data for example – which lead all too easily to a concerted practice amongst its members[86] and for which the association may act, perhaps inadvertently, as a front or screen for concertation. Nor is it uncommon for meetings to take place in back rooms on the occasion and under cover of an otherwise legitimate trade association meeting,[87] although the association bears no direct responsibility for this. As a general rule, membership of an association necessarily means acceptance of its rules and conduct and implies awareness of its activities; so where an association issues instructions for a proposed course of action, whether or not all members are expected to take part, and the results of implementation of the instructions are subsequently communicated to all, an agreement involving all members exists even if they took no positive action.[88] It is of no consequence that the association has no legal personality,[89] that it does not engage in commercial activities (and so is not itself an undertaking)[90] or that it is

---

[84] The association at issue in Decision 94/815 (*Cement*) OJ 1994 L343/1 (the European Cement Association (Cembureau)), for example, was made up of national associations from each Community member state, each EFTA state and Turkey.

[85] eg, Decision 80/917 (*National Sulphuric Acid Association*) OJ 1980 L260/25 (compulsory joint buying pool of an association representing almost the total manufacturing capacity for the end product in the UK and Ireland).

[86] Case T-29/92 *Vereniging van Samenwerkende Prijsregelende Organisaties in de Bouwnijverheid* v *Commission* [1995] ECR II-289; Decision 94/815 (*Cement*) OJ 1994 L343/1.

[87] eg, Decision 1999/60 (*Pre-Insulated Pipes*) OJ 1999 L24/48.

[88] Decision 94/815 (*Cement*) OJ 1994 L343/1 at para 45(8).

[89] Cases C-395 & 396/96P *Compagnie Maritime Belge* v *Commission*, judgment of 16 March 2000, not yet reported.

[90] Case 123/83 *Bureau National Interprofessionnel du Cognac* v *Clair* [1985] ECR 391; Cases T-39–40/92 *Groupement des Cartes Bancaires* v *Commission* [1992] ECR II-49; Cases T-25 etc/95 *Cimenteries CBR* v *Commission* (Cement), judgment of 15 March

governed by public law and/or has public functions;[91] it is enough that anticompetitive conduct stems from its activities or those of their members. The fact (or argument) that, in accordance with the rules of the association, its decisions (or recommendations) are non-binding does not circumvent the application of Article 81(1);[92] this is consistent with the breadth accorded the definition of 'agreement'. Agreements within the framework of an association may fall for consideration, in the application of Article 81(1), both under decisions of the association and agreements amongst its members.[93]

3.2 'Which may affect trade between member states'

In order that Article 81(1) be joined, an anticompetitive agreement, decision or concerted practice must affect, or be capable of affecting, trade between member states. So a restrictive practice, even a gross cartel, will not fall within the prohibition if its effects are limited to the territory of a single member state, and it will be governed, if at all, by the national competition rules there in force. This is entirely consistent with the principle of subsidiarity, enshrined in the Treaty since Maastricht.[94] Equally, a restrictive practice which affects trade between a member state and one or more non-member states will also escape the prohibition, for it does not affect trade *between* member states. The effect upon trade between member states is required also to be an 'appreciable' one. These points will be discussed in sequence.

The test for a restrictive practice which may affect trade between member states was first set out by the Court of Justice in *Société Technique Minière*:

> It is in fact to the extent that the agreement may affect trade between Member States that the interference with competition caused by that agreement is caught by the prohibitions of ... Article 85, while in the converse case it escapes those prohibitions. For this requirement to be fulfilled it must be possible to foresee with a sufficient degree of probability on the basis of a set of objective factors of

---

2000, not yet reported. If an association *is* an undertaking it may itself be capable of entering into agreements which infringe Art 81(1).

[91] Case 123/83 *BNIC, ibid*; Decision 95/188 (*Coapi*) OJ 1995 L122/37; Decision 1999/267 (*EPI Code of Conduct*) OJ 1999 L106/14 (under review as Case T-144/99 *EPI v Commission*, pending).

[92] Case 8/72 *Vereniging van Cementhandelaren v Commission* [1972] ECR 977; Cases 209 etc/78 *van Landewyck v Commission* (FEDETAB) [1980] ECR 3125; Cases 96 etc/82 *IAZ International Belgium v Commission* [1983] ECR 3369; Case 45/85 *Verband der Sachversicherer v Commission* [1987] ECR 405.

[93] Case 123/83 *Bureau National Interprofessionnel du Cognac v Clair* [1985] ECR 391.

[94] EC Treaty, Art 5, 2nd para (ex Art 3b, 2nd para).

law or of fact that the agreement in question may have an influence, direct or indirect, actual or potential, on the pattern of trade between Member States.[95]

This formula has been repeated many times, sometimes adding as a coda 'the influence foreseeable must give rise to a fear that the realization of a single market between Member States might be impeded',[96] which draws attention to the integration goals of Article 81 but otherwise seems to add nothing material to the test. Accordingly, the effect upon intra-Community trade is normally the result of a combination of a number of factors which, taken separately, are not necessarily decisive.[97] The normal test is consideration of the nature of the relevant market(s), supply, demand, cost and price structures, the place of the parties in the market (and in related markets) and assessment of the competition in question as it would occur in the absence of the agreement or practice in dispute.[98] It is not necessary to examine each clause individually in order to show an effect upon trade; it is enough if an agreement viewed in the round does so.[99] As is clear from the *Société Technique Minière* formulation which includes 'potential' effect, Article 81(1) does not require that agreements or practices have actually affected trade between member states, only that they are capable of having that effect.[100] Nor, notwithstanding the original language texts which suggest otherwise, need trade be affected adversely or injuriously;[101] it need only be 'affected'.[102] The agreement or practice must be shown to have the requisite effect or potential effect; it is not enough simply to aver

---

[95] Case 56/65 *Société Technique Minière v Maschinenbau Ulm* [1966] ECR 235 at 249.

[96] eg, Cases 209 etc/78 *van Landewycke v Commission* (FEDETAB) [1980] ECR 3125 at 3274; Case 42/84 *Remia e Nutricia v Commission* [1985] ECR I-2545 at 2572; Case C-250/92 *Gøttrup-Klim v Dansk Landbrugs Grovvarselskab* [1994] ECR I-5641 at 5692; Case T-148/89 *Tréfilunion v Commission* [1995] ECR II-1063 at 1105; Case T-7/93 *Langnese Iglo v Commission* [1995] ECR II-1533 at 1578; Cases T-24 etc/93 *Compagnie Maritime Belge v Commission* [1996] ECR II-1201 at 1266.

[97] Case C-250/92 *Gøttrup-Klim, ibid.*

[98] Case 56/65 *Société Technique Minière v Maschinenbau Ulm* [1966] ECR 235; Cases 209 etc/78 *van Landewycke v Commission* (FEDETAB) [1980] ECR 3125; Case 61/80 *Coöperatieve Stremsel- en Kleurselfabriek v Commission* [1981] ECR 851; Case T-34/92 *Fiatagri & New Holland Ford v Commission* [1994] ECR II-905.

[99] Cases 25 & 26/84 *Ford Werke v Commission* [1985] ECR 2725; Case 193/83 *Windsurfing International v Commission* [1986] ECR 611.

[100] Case 19/77 *Miller v Commission* [1978] ECR 131; Case T-29/92 *Vereniging van Samenwerkende Prijsregelende Organisatie in de Bouwnijverheid v Commission* [1995] ECR II-289; Case C-219/95P *Ferriere Nord v Commission* [1997] ECR I-4411.

[101] This is especially so in the Dutch (*ongungstig kunnen beïvloeden*) but also in the German (*beeinträchtigen geeignet sind*) and the Italian (*pregiudicare*); the French (*affecter*) is neutral, like the English, but even it conveys a pejorative connotation.

[102] Cases 56 & 58/64 *Consten & Grundig v EEC Commission* [1966] ECR 299; see *infra*.

by rote that it does so.[103] Having said that, it is not of itself a burdensome test to meet. It requires little effort where the parties are domiciled in more than one member state; even if they are not, especially where an agreement or practice extends throughout the territory of a single member state and so on its face produces effects which are restricted to that state, it is particularly likely (but not necessarily)[104] to have a tendency to inhibit real or potential competitors in other member states from entering or establishing themselves in the market and so

> by its very nature has the effect of reinforcing the compartmentalization of markets on a national basis, thereby holding up the economic interpenetration which the Treaty is designed to bring about and protecting domestic production.[105]

Alternatively,

> [a]n infringement of Article 85(1) does not presuppose that the object or effect of the restriction of competition concerns a market which in terms of geography or product goes beyond the borders of one Member State, so long as the pattern of trade between Member States may have been affected, either negatively or positively.[106]

By the same token, Article 81(1) is not joined if on the facts the relevant trade is confined to trade between one member state and a third country or a number of third countries.[107] However, an agreement between or amongst Community undertakings, Community and non-Community undertakings or even wholly non-Community undertakings which nominally affect only one member state (or none at all) but which may reduce the supply within the Community of goods or services originating in third countries may be capable, at least potentially, of affecting trade between member states and so falling foul of Article 81(1).[108] This raises issues of

---

[103] eg, Case 73/74 *Groupement des Fabricants des Papiers Peints de Belgique* v *Commission* [1975] ECR 1491.

[104] Decision 1999/687 (*Nederlandse Vereniging van Banken*) OJ 1999 L271/28.

[105] Case 8/72 *Vereeniging van Cementhandelaren* v *Commission* [1972] ECR 977 at 991; Case 42/84 *Remia & Nutricia* v *Commission* [1985] ECR 2545 at 2572; Case C-35/96 *Commission* v *Italy* [1998] ECR I-3851 at 3898.

[106] Decision 1999/210 (*British Sugar/Tate & Lyle/Napier Brown/James Budgett*) OJ 1999 L76/1 at para 155 (under review as Cases T-202 & 207/98 *Tate & Lyle and Napier Brown* v *Commission*, pending).

[107] Case 28/77 *Tepea* v *Commission* [1978] ECR 1391; Case 22/78 *Hugin* v *Commission* [1979] ECR 1869; Case 174/84 *Bulk Oil* v *Sun International* [1986] ECR 559.

[108] eg, Case 22/71 *Béguelin* v *GL Import/Export* [1971] ECR 949; Case 71/74 *Frubo* v *Commission* [1975] ECR 563; Case 51/75 *EMI* v *CBS* [1976] ECR 811; Cases T-24 etc/93 *Compagnie Maritime Belge* v *Commission* [1996] ECR II-1201, upheld essentially on appeal in Cases C-395 & 396/96P *Compagnie Maritime Belge* v *Commission*, judg-

limitation of exports (or re-exports) to Community markets and the territorial application of Article 81, which are discussed in Chapter 9. Of
course even the most remote of overseas contracts – a distribution agreement between, say, a Korean manufacturer and a Mongolian distributor –
could have a *potential* effect upon intra-Community trade because it may
restrict re-sale of the contract goods outwith the contract territory and so
in the Community market. The relevant question in this context is the next
test to be applied to an effect upon trade between member states, and that
is whether trade is affected appreciably.

3.2.1 *De minimis*

The Court of Justice said early on that not only must trade be affected
between member states, it must be affected to an 'appreciable' extent.[109]
Care must be taken with this appreciability test in two particulars: first,
'appreciable' is a rendering of other language versions which use terminology (*de façon sensible*; *spürbar*) which is closer in meaning to 'perceptible'
and so a lower threshold than that suggested by 'appreciable'; the Court
has also used the (negative) formulations 'only an insignificant effect' upon
trade in the market,[110] affecting the market 'only to an insignificant
extent'[111] and 'that effect must not be insignificant'.[112] Second, appreciability is measured generally as a function of relevant market and market
share and *not* of raw trade. An anticompetitive agreement cannot have an
appreciable effect upon trade between member states if there is no trade in
the relevant product: a cartel amongst Scottish manufacturers of shinty
sticks cannot on its face affect intra-Community trade and so cannot be
caught by Article 81(1) if no one elsewhere buys them or wants to buy
them (and assuming they comprise a product market distinct from that of
hurling or hockey sticks). The existence of a Brussels Camanacht Club
made up of a dozen homesick expatriates would create a tiny Belgian market which would not alter trade flows significantly; but it would have a

---

ment of 16 March 2000, not yet reported; Decision 94/815 (*Cement*) OJ L343/1, upheld
in this particular in Cases T-25 etc/95 *Cimenteries CBR* v *Commission*, judgment of 15
March 2000, not yet reported, paras 3868 *et seq*.

[109] First considered by the Commission in its first formal decision under Art 81, Decision
64/344 (*Grosfillex/Fillistorf*) JO 1964, 1426; first recognised by the Court *obiter* in Case
56/65 *Société Technique Minière* v *Maschinenbau Ulm* [1966] ECR 235 at 249, applied
subsequently in Case 5/69 *Völk* v *Vervaecke* [1969] ECR 295; Case 22/71 *Béguelin* v *GL
Import Export* [1971] ECR 949.

[110] Case 5/69 Völk, ibid, at 302.

[111] Case 30/78 *Distillers* v *Commission* [1980] ECR 2229 at 2265.

[112] Case C-306/96 *Javico International* v *Yves Saint Laurent Parfums* [1998] ECR I-1983 at
2003.

bearing upon trade in shinty sticks. Few products, even traditional cultural products, are quite so market specific: consumers throughout Europe now play golf, drink whisky and even eat haggis. But even for shinty sticks the Commission view would be, given a goal of market interpenetration, that a cartel may inhibit the growth of a market elsewhere where shinty could or should advantageously be played, and, more important, that it may create barriers to market entry in inhibiting sporting goods producers in other member states from manufacturing shinty sticks in order to supply the Scottish market.

Two further points ought also to be noted: first, even if there is no appreciable trade in a particular product, Article 81(1) applies if that product is caught up in an agreement with other, similar products in which there is appreciable trade;[113] and second, in the event of a cartel, even if the conduct of an individual party to an agreement does not itself appreciably affect trade between member states, the small scale of its participation in the agreement will not exculpate it if the effect of the agreement as a whole is appreciable.[114]

3.2.2 The notice on agreements of minor importance

The difficult question is, of course, when trade is affected appreciably (or perceptibly). The test was first clearly enunciated by the Court of Justice in *Völk* v *Vervaecke*[115] in which a distribution contract between a German manufacturer of washing machines and a Belgian distributor was in all other respects a blatant breach of Article 81(1) but was saved because the manufacturer was a small one, responsible annually for only 0.08 per cent of Community production and 0.2 per cent of German production and representing only 0.6 per cent of sales in the Belgium/Luxembourg market (the contract territory). By most conceivable standards this is an inappreciable market share. But where does the threshold lie? The relevant case law of the Court indicates a degree of fluidity, appreciability hovering around the 5 per cent market share mark, and the larger the undertakings

---

[113] Case 30/78 *Distillers* v *Commission* [1980] ECR 2229 (distribution contracts for a number of spirituous drinks, including Pimm's, for which there was no appreciable market outwith the UK).

[114] Case T-13/89 *ICI* v *Commission* (Polypropylene) [1992] ECR II-1021; Case T-143/89 *Ferriere Nord* v *Commission* [1995] ECR II-917, upheld on appeal as Case C-219/95P *Ferriere Nord* v *Commission* [1997] ECR I-4411; Decision 85/206 (*Aluminium Imports from Eastern Europe*) OJ 1985 L92/1; Decision 89/515 (*Welded Steel Mesh*) OJ 1989 L260/1; Decision 1999/271 (*Greek Ferries*) OJ 1999 L109/24 (under review as Cases T-56 etc/99 *Marlines* v *Commission*, pending).

[115] Case 5/69 [1969] ECR 295.

involved the lower the threshold.[116] In order to assist, the Commission has adopted a series of notices on agreements 'of minor importance'. The present notice was adopted in 1997,[117] replacing previous notices adopted in their turn in 1970, 1977 and 1986.[118] According to the 1997 notice, an agreement does not affect trade appreciably, and so falls outwith the prohibition of Article 81(1), if the aggregate market share of all parties to it does not exceed 5 per cent of the relevant market for horizontal agreements and 10 per cent for vertical agreements; for mixed horizontal/vertical agreements the 5 per cent ceiling applies.[119] This applies also where these thresholds are exceeded but by no more than one-tenth over two successive financial years.[120]

Agreements between small and medium-sized enterprises (SMEs) as defined by Community law[121] are 'rarely capable' of producing an appreciable effect upon trade, and the Commission will intervene, even where the thresholds are exceeded, only exceptionally.[122] However, an SME caught up in a cartel involving larger players will not be exculpated by its size.[123] Guidance is provided as to the definition of 'participating undertakings' and definition of relevant market for purposes of calculating market share.[124]

The notice is of general application. *De minimis* considerations also appear in other instruments – for example, a notice accompanying and complementing the (now repealed) block exemptions on exclusive distribution and exclusive purchasing[125] which indicates *inter alia* quantitative

---

[116] Case 19/77 *Miller* v *Commission* [1978] ECR 131; Case 30/78 *Distillers* v *Commission* [1980] ECR 2229; Cases 100–103/80 *Musique Diffusion Française* v *Commission* (Pioneer) [1983] ECR 1825; Case 107/82 *AEG-Telefunken* v *Commission* [1983] ECR 3151; Case 319/82 *Société de Vente de Ciments et Bétons de l'Est* v *Kerpen & Kerpen* [1983] ECR 4173.

[117] Notice on agreements of minor importance which do not fall within the meaning of [*sic*; *cf.* qui ne sont pas visés par] Article 85(1) of the Treaty establishing the European Community, OJ 1997 C372/13.

[118] JO 1970 C84/1, OJ 1977 C313/3 and OJ 1986 C231/2 respectively.

[119] 1997 notice, para 9.

[120] *Ibid.*, para 10.

[121] Recommendation 96/280 OJ 1996 L107/4, according to which SMEs are undertakings of which the annual turnover or the balance sheet do not exceed €40 million and €27 million respectively and which have fewer than 250 employees.

[122] 1997 notice, paras 19–20.

[123] Decision 1999/271 (*Greek Ferries*) OJ 1999 L109/24 (under review as Cases T-56 etc/99 *Marlines* v *Commission*, pending).

[124] 1997 notice, paras 12–18.

[125] Notice concerning Commission Regulations 1983/83 and 1984/83, OJ 1984 C101/2. On block exemption see Chap 4.

criteria by which agreements specific to those fields fall outwith Article 81(1), and in various block exemptions themselves.[126]

A number of observations are called for. First, the notice is a soft law device. The Commission is turning ever more frequently to such notices as part of its policy of decentralisation of enforcement, but their reliability is not absolute. The notice's purpose is to create a degree of legal certainty as to whether an agreement escapes the prohibition of Article 81(1) by virtue of its lack of appreciable effect upon competition. But it comprises simply the view of the Commission as to whether or not this is so. Since it is the Court of Justice and not the Commission which authoritatively interprets the breadth of Article 81(1), a mere notice from the Commission must be approached with a degree of circumspection. In fact, the notice is shot through with disclaimers: a quantitative definition of appreciability 'serves only as a guideline';[127] the notice is 'without prejudice' to the competence of national courts to apply Article 81, although it constitutes a 'factor' which they may take into account when deciding cases before them;[128] and the applicability of Article 81(1) 'cannot be ruled out' to certain, especially anticompetitive, agreements even where the parties fall below the thresholds.[129] Equally, an agreement amongst parties the combined market share of which exceeds the ceilings does not necessarily mean its effect is appreciable.[130] And should an agreement fall within the notice yet nevertheless infringe Article 81(1), the Commission 'will not consider imposing fines' upon undertakings party to it if they believed in good faith that the agreement was covered by the notice,[131] and is probably estopped thereby from so doing; but this has no bearing upon any civil consequences of an unlawful agreement, which is a matter exclusively for the courts.[132]

Second, the 1997 notice marks a departure from the previous notices, which embraced both market share and turnover criteria in their definition of minor importance. So, under the 1986 notice agreements produced no appreciable effect if the market share of the parties to it fell below a 5 per

---

[126] eg, Reg 417/85 OJ 1985, L53/1 (specialisation agreements) and Reg 418/85, OJ 1985 L53/5 (research and development agreements). This of course is an indication not that the agreements fall outwith Art 81(1) but that they are exempted from it.

[127] 1997 notice, para 3.

[128] para 7.

[129] para 11; see eg Decision 91/301 (*Ansac*) OJ 1991 L152/54.

[130] Case T-7/93 *Langnese-Iglo* v *Commission* [1995] ECR II-1533, upheld on appeal as Case C-279/95P *Langnese-Iglo* v *Commission* [1998] ECR I-5609; Case T-9/93 *Schöller* v *Commission* [1995] ECR II-1611; Cases T-374 etc/94 *European Night Services* v *Commission* [1998] ECR II-3141.

[131] 1997 notice, para 5; on the Commission's power to impose fines, see Chap 6.

[132] See Chap 6.

cent threshold *and* their combined aggregate turnover did not exceed 200 million ECUs[133] (updated in 1994 to 300 million ECUs[134]). With no intervention from authorities competent actually to alter the meaning of the law, quite what happened on 9 December 1997 (the date of publication of the 1997 notice) which meant that turnover was not relevant to the calculation of appreciability, whereas the day before it had been, is by no means clear. The 1997 changes are a function of a new, general, Commission approach which is more economic, of which the best example is the new block exemption on vertical restraints.[135] There is a degree of legal certainty provided in that there are no moving goalposts. But in order to gain the benefit of *de minimis* implicitly the market share of parties to an agreement must remain below the thresholds throughout its duration (subject to the temporary 'plus one-tenth' rule); this means that an agreement could by its very success evolve over time into appreciability.

3.2.3 Networks of agreements

There is a particular problem with agreements which taken singly will benefit from the *de minimis* defence but form part of a larger whole which may not do so. For example, a tied lease between a brewer and a publican is an agreement within the meaning of Article 81. It normally stipulates the beer which the publican may or must stock. If the publican is obliged to stock only the brewer's beer this will prevent him from stocking other, perhaps imported, beer. The lease may therefore inhibit imports and so breach Article 81(1), *except* that any restrictive provisions of a single lease over one public house cannot possibly exert an appreciable effect upon intra-Community trade. But a large number of like leases with a major brewer taken cumulatively (and so a 'network' or 'bundle' of agreements) could do so. Beer has been a particular issue in the United Kingdom owing to the oligopolistic nature of the market, the prominence of the tied house system and other vagaries.[136] It has attracted remedial action from the British government acting under the Fair Trading Act 1973 (the duty of brewers with more than 2000 tied houses to divest control of half of the surplus and the

---

[133] 1986 notice, para 7.

[134] OJ 1994 C368/20.

[135] See pp 128–30 *infra*.

[136] See the 1989 report of the Monopolies and Mergers Commission on the UK beer market, Cmnd 651. Other vagaries include generally the perishability of the product and the slow shrinking of a mature market and, in the UK, the strict licensing laws and the lack of independent wholesaling. In fact, in the UK most 'foreign' beer is not imported at all but produced in the UK under licence; it is difficult to resist the observation that whilst this eases access to an established distribution network and increases the number of brands available, the UK product is often a pale shadow of its home namesake.

'guest beer' rule)[137] but it is also a live Community issue, and has hitherto formed the subject matter of a large proportion of Treaty related competition litigation in the English courts. It is also a particularly apt context in which to consider the problem owing to the partitioning of national markets a product of the fierce consumer loyalty, in some member states, to national brands, but the issues to which it gives have been applied elsewhere – for example in the ice cream market[138] in and sectoral obligatory pension schemes.[139]

The issue first arose prior to British accession. In *Brasserie de Haecht (No 1)*[140] the Court of Justice first established the principle that it is necessary to consider agreements not in isolation but in the broader context of the general body of contracts of which they form part. But the template was laid down subsequently in *Delimitis*, in which the Court developed a two-fold and cumulative test: first, will a network of agreements taken cumulatively and in their context foreclose the market or hinder significantly the access of producers in other member states to it? The effects of such agreements must

> be assessed in the context in which they occur and where they might combine with others to have a cumulative effect on competition .... The cumulative effect of several similar agreements constitutes one factor amongst others in ascertaining whether, by way of a possible alteration of competition, trade between Member States is capable of being affected.[141]

Other factors are the availability of access to the market and the conditions under which competitive forces operate in the relevant market. If the first test is satisfied, second, does a particular bundle of agreements contribute significantly to that foreclosure?

> If ... examination reveals that it is difficult to gain access to the relevant market, it is necessary to assess the extent to which the agreements entered into by the brewery in question contribute to the cumulative effect produced in that respect by the totality of the similar contracts found on that market. Under the Community rules on competition, responsibility for such an effect of closing off the market must be attributed to the brewers which make an appreciable contri-

---

[137] Supply of Beer (Tied Estates) Order 1989, SI 1989/2390.

[138] Case T-7/93 *Langnese Iglo* v *Commission* [1995] ECR II-1539; Case T-9/93 *Schöller* v *Commission* [1995] ECR II-1611; Decision 98/531 (*van den Bergh Foods*) OJ 1998 L246/1 (under review as Case T-65/98 *van den Bergh Foods* v *Commission*, pending).

[139] Case C-67/96 *Albany International* v *Stichting Bedrijfspensioenfonds Textielindustrie* [1999] ECR I-5751.

[140] Case 23/67 *Brasserie de Haecht* v *Wilkin* [1967] ECR 407.

[141] Case C-234/89 *Delimitis* v *Henninger Bräu* [1991] ECR I-935 at 984.

bution thereto. Beer supply agreements entered into by breweries whose contribution to the cumulative effect is insignificant do not therefore fall under the prohibition under Article 85(1).[142]

In order to assess whether this is so account must be had to market share, the number of tied outlets as a proportion of the total and the duration of the agreements. Applying all these tests, the Commission recently underwent a conversion (having previously been minded to consider tied leases (given the guest beer rule) to fall outwith Article 81(1)) and found the standard lease networks of Whitbread,[143] Bass[144] and Scottish & Newcastle[145] to breach Article 81(1), although it granted exemptions in each case;[146] and in each case the decision has been challenged by disgruntled tenants.[147] A similar decision for Allied Domecq is in the pipeline.[148] *Delimitis* also inspired the Commission to adopt, for greater certainty, a 'beer *de minimis* notice' in 1992.[149] Of course, much of this will be unnecessary to attract the application of the Competition Act 1998 and the 'big 6' UK brewers may now find various terms of their tied leases under serious attack from that quarter.

3.3 'Which have as their object or effect'

An agreement, decision or concerted practice may fall foul of Article 81(1) if its object *or* effect is to distort competition.[150] An agreement which is not intended to distort competition, but nevertheless does so, is caught. This was established early on by the Court of Justice:

> The fact that these are not cumulative but alternative conditions, indicated by the conjunction 'or', suggests first the need to consider the very object of the agreement, in the light of the economic context in which it is to be applied. The alterations in the play of competition envisaged by Article 85(1) should result

---

[142] at 986–7.
[143] Decision 1999/230, OJ 1999 L88/26.
[144] Decision 1999/473, OJ 1999 L186/1.
[145] Decision 1999/474, OJ 1999 L186/28.
[146] On exemption see Chap 4.
[147] Case T-131/99 *Shaw* v *Commission* (Whitbread), Case T-231/99 *Joynson* v *Commission* (Bass) and Case T-232/99 *McKenzie Campbell* v *Commission* (Scottish & Newcastle), all pending.
[148] See the Reg 17, art 19(3) notice in OJ 1999 C82/5.
[149] OJ 1992 C121/2, amending the notice concerning Commission Regulations 1983/83 and 1984/83, OJ 1984 C101/2.
[150] The Italian text unequivocally lays down a cumulative test (*per oggetto e per effeto*) but this has been ignored as inconsistent with all other language versions: Case C-219/95P *Ferriere Nord* v *Commission* [1997] ECR I-4411.

from all or part of the clauses of the agreement itself. Where, however, an analysis of the said clauses does not reveal a sufficient degree of harmfulness with regard to competition, examination should then be made of the effects of the agreement ....[151]

And subsequently:

Although the contested provisions of those agreements [at issue] do not, by their very nature, have as their object the prevention, restriction or distortion of competition within the common market within the meaning of Article 85(1), it is, however, [necessary] to determine whether they have that effect.[152]

Conversely, an agreement the purpose of which is to distort competition (tested objectively, not subjectively) but fails to produce the intended result is also caught. Put another way, if the object of an agreement can be shown to be anticompetitive, it is unnecessary to show that it produces that effect.[153]

In any case, for Article 85(1) to be applicable, it is sufficient for there to have been the intention to restrict competition; it is not necessary for the intention to have been carried out, in full or only in part, that is to say, for the restriction of competition to have been put into effect.[154]

This applies inevitably to a cartel, where the Commission will identify its existence and look no further for the effects it produces. But it applies also to a less blatantly objectionable anticompetitive agreement (or part of an agreement) which was never put into force,[155] or one which has been suspended or is formally no longer in force, in which case it is sufficient to show that it continues to produce its effects after formal suspension or termination.[156] The fact that the object of the agreement cannot be achieved

---

[151] Case 56/65 *Société Technique Minière* v *Maschinenbau Ulm* [1966] ECR 235 at 249; the text cited is taken from the CMLR report of the judgment ([1966] CMLR 357 at 375) as the ECR report in English (the language of the case was French) is seriously misleading in this particular.

[152] Case C-306/96 *Javico International* v *Yves Saint Laurent Parfums* [1998] ECR I-1983 at 2004–05.

[153] Cases 56 & 58/64 *Consten & Grundig* v *EEC Commission* [1966] ECR 299; Case 277/87 *Sandoz Prodotti Farmaceutici* v *Commission* [1990] ECR I-45; Case C-219/95P *Ferriere Nord* v *Commission* [1997] ECR I-4411; Case C-199/92P *Hüls* v *Commission* (Polypropylene) [1999] ECR I-4287.

[154] Decision 84/405 (*Zinc Producer Group*) OJ 1984 L220/27 at para 71.

[155] Case T-43/92 *Dunlop Slazenger* v *Commission* [1994] ECR II-441; Case T-77/92 *Parker Pen* v *Commission* [1994] ECR II-549.

[156] Case 51/75 *EMI* v *CBS* [1976] ECR 811; Case 243/83 *Binon* v *Agence et Messageries de la Presse* [1985] ECR 2015.

is irrelevant.[157] The existence of a spent contract may also legitimately be a factor in inferring the existence of a concerted practice relative to the subject matter of the agreement and producing similar effects following termination,[158] and this is reflected in the Commission's recent practice of blurring the distinction between agreement and concerted practice. The question of whether an object may subsist in a concerted practice in the absence of any apparent effect is discussed above.[159]

3.4 'The prevention, restriction or distortion of competition within the common market'

3.4.1 Preliminary issues

The prevention, restriction or distortion of competition (or in some other language versions, 'of the play of competition') is of course the very heart of Article 81. There is nothing legally to be distinguished amongst the three terms. A price fixing cartel may normally be said to restrict competition simply because it is the term which first springs to mind to describe that state of affairs, whilst the majority of vertical agreements probably distort it more than they restrict it. Any conduct which prevents, restricts or distorts competition is equally prohibited, and the three taken together admit of a very wide ambit. Given the ingenuity with which undertakings will seek to play the market to their best advantage, it is prudent that this is so.

There is a tension inherent in the very structure of Article 81. That is, Article 81(1) lays down the prohibition of the prevention, restriction or distortion of competition, but Article 81(3) provides authority for the prohibition to be set aside. From the outset there therefore arise key questions as to the very meaning of Article 81(1) both in isolation and by virtue of its relationship with Article 81(3). It is axiomatic that every commercial contract is a restraint of trade. Mr Justice Brandeis said in the American Supreme Court:

> [T]he legality of an agreement ... cannot be determined by so simple a test as whether it restrains competition. Every agreement concerning trade ... restrains. To bind, to restrain, is of their very essence.[160]

---

[157] Decision 89/515 (*Welded Steel Mesh*) OJ 1989 L260/1, upheld on review as Case T-148/89 *Tréfilunion* v *Commission* [1995] ECR II-1063.

[158] Case 51/75 *EMI* v *CBS* [1976] ECR 811; Case 243/83 *Binon* v *Agence et Messageries de la Presse* [1985] ECR 2015; Case T-1/89 *Rhône-Poulenc* v *Commission* (Polypropylene) [1991] ECR II-867.

[159] at pp 57–60.

[160] *Chicago Board of Trade* v *United States* 246 US 231 (1918) at 238.

Given the language and potential breadth of the prohibition, the question is whether it ought it to be interpreted strictly so that it applies as far as that breadth will permit, the only means of escape then being Article 81(3), or whether it ought it to be interpreted with a gentler touch so that agreements or practices which it may be straining to say restrain or distort competition fall outwith the prohibition altogether. The context is one in which it is useful to take notice of two principles of American antitrust law which have come to inform/infect Community competition law. There the Sherman Act prohibits '[e]very contract ... in restraint of trade or commerce ...'[161] without the possibility enshrined in Article 81(3) of the Treaty of the prohibition being set aside where it may be appropriate and expedient to do so. The American courts therefore came quickly to develop a 'rule of reason' doctrine that the prohibition applied not to 'every contract in restraint of trade' but only to contracts which restrain trade unreasonably or to an unreasonable degree,[162] so necessitating a balancing test of their anticompetitive and pro-competitive aspects and qualities. However, the rule of reason is not applied across the board: some cartel agreements are so nakedly inimical to competition that they are *per se* anticompetitive (the '*per se* rule'),[163] and in order to fall foul of the Sherman Act it is necessary only to show that the agreement exists, not that it produces anticompetitive effects.[164] It is only if the agreement is not *per se* anticompetitive that the balancing test, and possible salvation, of the rule of reason is brought into play. The closest (but not identical) equivalent in Community law to the *per se* rule is an agreement or concerted practice which has as its very object the prevention, restriction or distortion of competition, in which case it is unnecessary to consider whether it produces that effect.[165] But it remained (and remains) a live issue the extent to which Article 81(1) ought if at all to incorporate a rule of reason approach to agreements or practices the effects of which are only (remotely) anticompetitive. The Commission generally favours the strict view, that Article 81(1) is all embracing and admits of little if any of a rule of reason. This is only to be expected, for the greater the breadth of the prohibition of Article 81(1) the greater the influence and authority of he to whom is reserved the power of exemption under Article 81(3). As we shall see, the

---

[161] § 1 Sherman Act 15 USC § 1.
[162] First deployed in *Standard Oil of New Jersey v United States* 221 US 1 (1911); see also *Chicago Board of Trade v United States*, n 160 *supra*.
[163] *United States v Socony-Vacuum Oil Co* 310 US 658 (1940).
[164] *United States v Addyson Pipe and Steel Co* 85 F 271 (6th Cir 1898).
[165] See pp 77–9 *supra*.

Court of Justice has taken a more lenient view. It is also of course danger-
ous to seek to transplant principles from one legal system to another:[166]
for example, given that the Community rules are a means not only of promoting competition but also a tool of the Treaty goal of integration, an
agreement which may be relatively innocuous and so not *per se* anticompetitive in the American context might be a cardinal sin in the Community
context. Even the use of the terms *per se* and rule of reason can be misleading: express reference to *per se* anticompetitive agreements crops up from
time to time in judgments of the Court of Justice, but the Commission has
taken recently to referring instead to 'hardcore' restraints to competition;
and 'rule of reason', a term not used by the Court, is especially misleading
as it has another common application in another context in Community
law, that of the mandatory requirements, or *'Cassis de Dijon'*, doctrine
applied to measures having effect equivalent to a quantitative restriction
under Article 28 (ex Article 30).[167] Having said that, their nature ought to
be borne in mind as an existing prism through which the ambit and application of Article 81(1) might be determined.

Agreements and concerted practices which may prevent, restrict or distort competition can be divided into two broad subsets: horizontal and
vertical arrangements. Whilst the law of some member states formally dis-
tinguishes between the two,[168] Article 81(1) does not. A horizontal
agreement or practice is an agreement or practice between or amongst two
or more undertakings at the same level of supply, at its most basic an
agreement between direct competitors to fix prices or to share out markets.
In other words, the classic cartel. That horizontal cartel arrangements are
the main target of Article 81 is clear from the first three examples provided
in Article 81(1) which 'in particular' prevent, restrict or distort competition: price fixing, production quotas and market sharing. These may be
elements present in and given effect by vertical arrangements as well, but
they are barest and most grievous in a cartel. In fact the application of
Article 81(1) to horizontal agreements is fairly straightforward, and
becomes difficult only in the context of vertical agreements where the
application is much more nuanced. At the same time, the two most instructive cases for getting under the skin of Article 81(1) – *Consten &*

---

[166] For particular consideration of transplantation of the rule of reason see the discussion of
A–G Cosmas in Case C-235/92P *Montecatini* v *Commission* [1998] ECR I-4539 at
4560–2.

[167] First developed in Case 120/78 *Rewe-Zentral* v *Bundesmonopolverwaltung für
Branntwein* (Cassis de Dijon) [1979] ECR 649.

[168] eg §§ 14–18 GWB; §§ 30a–e ÖKG.

Grundig[169] and *Société Technique Minière*[170] – were cases involving vertical restraints. They will be considered below.

3.4.2 Horizontal agreements

Cartel agreements or practices are, through the initiative of undertakings, common enough in a homogenous market; but are especially so in the Community, in which producers long enjoyed the protection of state intervention in their national markets and may be in no great hurry to surrender the advantages accruing thereto. In this they are abetted by residual barriers to intra-Community trade, but also of course by any accommodation they may reach with like inclined (actual or potential) competitors in other member states. It is in order to combat this tendency that the competition rules are a tool of assisting the goal of integration.

Price fixing agreements

The clearest and most transparent medium of competition is that of price. Agreements or practices aimed at restricting price competition are therefore a matter of 'indisputable gravity'.[171] There have been a large number of cases involving price-fixing cartels, pre-eminent amongst which are *Woodpulp*,[172] *Polypropylene*,[173] *PVC* (*I*[174] and *II*[175]) and *LdPE*[176] (the 'thermoplastics' cases), *Welded Steel Mesh*,[177] *Cewal*,[178] *Steel*

---

[169] Cases 56 & 58/64 *Consten & Grundig v EEC Commission* [1996] ECR 299.

[170] Case 56/65 *Société Technique Minière v Maschinenbau Ulm* [1966] ECR 235.

[171] Decision 94/210 (*HOV SVZ/MCN*) OJ 1994 L104/34 at para 259; Decision 1999/243 (*Transatlantic Conference Agreement*) OJ 1999 L95/1 at para 591.

[172] Decision 85/202, OJ 1985 L85/1, annulled for the most part as Cases 89 etc/85 *Åhlström v Commission* [1993] ECR I-1307.

[173] Decision 86/398, OJ 1986 L230/1, upheld on review in a series of judgments the first of which is Case T-1/89 *Rhône-Poulenc v Commission* [1991] ECR II-867, appeal (and cross-appeal) on a single plea of the 'non-existence' of the Decision rejected in a series of cases the first of which is Case C-49/92P *Commission v Anic Partecipazioni* [1999] ECR I-4125.

[174] Decision 89/190, OJ 1989 L74/1, annulled on procedural grounds in Case C-137/92P *Commission v BASF* [1994] ECR I-2555.

[175] Decision 94/599, OJ 1994 L349/14, upheld on review in Cases T-305 etc/94 *Limburgse Vinyl Maatschappij v Commission* [1999] ECR II-931 (under appeal as Cases C-328 etc/99P *Limburgse Vinyl Maatschappij v Commission*, pending).

[176] Decision 89/191, OJ 1989 L74/21, annulled on procedural grounds in Cases T-80 etc/89 *BASF v Commission* [1995] ECR II-729.

[177] Decision 89/515, OJ 1989 L260/1, upheld on review in most cases in a number of judgments, the first of which is Case T-141/89 *Tréfileurope Sales v Commission* [1995] ECR II-791.

[178] Decision 93/82 (*Central West Africa Lines*) OJ 1993 L34/20, upheld on review in Cases T-24 etc/93 *Compagnie Maritime Belge v Commission* [1996] ECR II-1201 and on appeal as Cases C-395 & 396/96P *Compagnie Maritime Belge v Commission*, judgment of 16 March 2000, not yet reported.

Beams,[179] Cartonboard,[180] Cement,[181] Pre-Insulated Pipes,[182] British Sugar[183] and TACA,[184] some of which involved not only price fixing but also production quotas and market sharing. Price-fixing elements may also be present in vertical agreements.[185] Whilst most of the cases have involved agreements amongst producers of goods the prohibition applies equally to agreements amongst suppliers of services, although with services the Commission may be more equably disposed (which it is not for producer cartels) to granting exemption under Article 81(3) if it is sought.

Instances of price fixing agreements, decisions or concerted practices have included: setting prices at specific levels;[186] adopting a common price list;[187] setting[188] and/or observing[189] 'list' or 'official' prices; setting target prices;[190] setting minimum[191] or maximum[192] prices, or maximum discounts;[193] setting or jointly publishing recommended, 'acceptable' or 'reasonable' prices;[194] agreeing the amount, rate and/or timing of price

---

[179] Decision 94/215, OJ 1994 L116/1, upheld essentially on review in a number of judgments, the principal of which is Case T-141/94 *Thyssen Stahl* v *Commission* [1999] ECR II-347 (under appeal as Case C-194/99P *Thyssen Stahl* v *Commission*, pending).

[180] Decision 94/601, OJ 1994 L243/1, upheld essentially on review in a number of cases, the first of which is Case T-295/94 *Buchmann* v *Commission* [1998] ECR II-813 (under appeal in a number of cases, the first of which is Case C-248/98P *Koninklijke KNP BT* v *Commission*, pending).

[181] Decision 94/815, OJ 1994 L343/1, partly annulled in Cases T-25 etc/95 *Cimenteries CBR* v *Commission*, judgment of 15 March 2000, not yet reported.

[182] Decision 1999/60, OJ 1999 L24/1 (under review as Cases T-9 etc/99 *HFB Holding für Fernwärmetechnik Beteiligungsgesellschaft* v *Commission*, pending).

[183] Decision 1999/210 (*British Sugar/Tate & Lyle/Napier Brown/James Budgett*) OJ 1999 L76/1 (under review as Cases T-202 & 207/98 *Tate & Lyle and Napier Brown* v *Commission*, pending).

[184] Decision 1999/243 (*Transatlantic Conference Agreement*) OJ 1999 L95/1 (under review as Cases T-191 etc/98 *Atlantic Container Line* v *Commission*, pending).

[185] See *infra*.

[186] Case 48/69 *ICI* v *Commission* (Dyestuffs) [1972] ECR 619; Cases T-68, 77 & 78/89 *Società Italiano Vetro* v *Commission* (Flat Glass) [1992] ECR II-1403; Decision 85/202 (*Woodpulp*); Decision 94/601 (*Cartonboard*).

[187] Decision 86/398 (*Polypropylene*), n 173 *supra*; Decision 1999/60 (*Pre-Insulated Pipes*), n 182 *supra*.

[188] Decision 86/398 (*Polypropylene*), n 173 *supra*.

[189] Decision 1999/60 (*Pre-Insulated Pipes*), n 182 *supra*.

[190] Case 72/22 *Vereniging van Cementhandeleren* v *Commission* [1972] ECR 977; Decision 86/398 (*Polypropylene*), n 173 *supra*; Decisions 89/190 and 94/599 (*PVC I and II*), nn 174 and 175 *supra*; Decision 94/215 (*Steel Beams*), n 179 *supra*.

[191] Case 123/83 *Bureau National Interprofessionnel du Cognac* v *Clair* [1985] ECR 391; Decision 89/44 (*Net Book Agreement*) OJ 1989 L22/12; Decision 92/444 (*Scottish Salmon Board*) OJ 1992 L246/37.

[192] Decision 94/815 (*Cement*), n 181 *supra*; Decision 1999/243 (*TACA*), n 184 *supra*.

[193] Decision 83/361 (*Vimpoltu*) OJ 1983 L200/44.

[194] Cases T-213/95 & 18/96 *Stichting Certificatie Kraanverhuurbedrijf* v *Commission* [1997] ECR II-1739; Decision 1999/60 (*Pre-Insulated Pipes*), n 182 *supra*.

increases[195] or announcement thereof;[196] agreeing to refrain from price cutting;[197] agreeing not to make public any deviation from published prices or to announce rebates;[198] appointing a price leader for individual buyers;[199] agreeing to maintain price differentials amongst various buyers;[200] and collective resale price maintenance.[201] Joint conduct ancillary to a price fixing agreement (or to any cartel) such as intimidation of or retaliation against an undertaking which refuses to join the cartel is prohibited.[202] Article 81(1) applies, however, not only to outright price fixing but equally[203] to any agreement or practice the effect of which is to suppress price competition or to distort the normal formation of prices on the market. So, arrangements for pooling profits or indemnifying losses,[204] intervention buying,[205] joint prohibition of discounts or rebates,[206] joint setting of terms and conditions of sale and related services such as delivery prices, payment and handling charges[207] are all caught. Indeed, given the nature of a concerted practice an exchange of price information may in itself be a breach of Article 81(1).[208] It is quite irrelevant that prices agreed or concerted upon cannot be achieved,[209] that a party or parties to them had no intention of adhering to any accommodation made[210] or that it leads to an increase or decrease in price.[211] They are all hardcore breaches

---

[195] Case 48/69 *ICI* v *Commission* (Dyestuffs) [1972] ECR 619; Decision 94/601 (*Cartonboard*), n 180 *supra*; Decision 1999/60 (*Pre-Insulated Pipes*), n 182 *supra*; Decision 1999/210 (*British Sugar*), n 183 *supra*.

[196] Decision 86/398 (*Polypropylene*), n 173 *supra*; Decision 1999/60 (*Pre-Insulated Pipes*), n 182 *supra*.

[197] Decision 1999/210 (*British Sugar*), n 183 *supra*.

[198] Case 73/74 *Groupement des Fabricants des Papiers Peints de Belgique* v *Commission* [1975] ECR 1491.

[199] Decision 86/398 (*Polypropylene*), n 173 *supra*; Decision 94/815 (*Cement*), n 181 *supra*.

[200] Decision 1999/210 (*British Sugar*), n 183 *supra*.

[201] See pp 109–10 *infra*.

[202] Decision 1999/60 (*Pre-Insulated Pipes*), n 182 *supra*.

[203] Art 81(1)(a).

[204] Decision 91/299 (*Soda Ash*) OJ 1991 L152/21; Decision 93/82 (*Cewal*), n 178 *supra*; Cases T-213/95 & 18/96 *Stichting Certificatie Kraanverhuurbedrijf* v *Commission* [1997] ECR II-1739; Decision 1999/60 (*Pre-Insulated Pipes*), n 182 *supra*.

[205] Decision 84/405 (*Zinc Producer Group*) OJ 1984 L220/27.

[206] Cases 209 etc/78 *van Landewyck* v *Commission* (FEDETAB) [1980] ECR 3125; Cases T-68, 77 & 78/89 *Società Italiano Vetro* v *Commission* (Flat Glass) [1992] ECR II-1403.

[207] Case 73/74 *Groupement des Fabricants des Papiers Peints de Belgique* v *Commission* [1975] ECR 1491; Cases 209 etc/78 *FEDETAB*, *ibid*; Decision 94/815 (*Cement*), n 181 *supra*; Decision 1999/243 (*TACA*), n 184 *supra*.

[208] See pp 57–60 *supra*.

[209] Decision 89/515 (*Welded Steel Mesh*), n 177 *supra*.

[210] Decision 86/399 (*Belgian Roofing Felt*) OJ 1986 L232/15, upheld on review in Case 246/86 *Belasco* v *Commission* [1989] ECR 2117.

[211] Decision 86/398 (*Polypropylene*), n 173 *supra*; Cases T-213/95 & 18/96 *Stichting Certificatie Kraanverhuurbedrijf* v *Commission* [1997] ECR II-1739.

of Article 81(1) and if rumbled by the Commission will attract high fines.[212]

Article 81(1) applies equally to price fixing on the demand side. There have been few cases of this except for instances of collusive tendering or bid rigging. According to the Commission invitation to tender is 'an ideal way of generating competition',[213] and

[a] system of allocations by tender is an area par excellence where competition must be capable of operating. In a system of tendering, competition is of the essence. If the tender submitted by those taking part are not the result of individual economic calculation, but of knowledge of the tenders by other participants or of concertation with them, competition is prevented, or at least distorted and restricted.[214]

In this it has the support of the Court of First Instance:

[C]oncertation by contractors regarding the manner in which they intend responding to an invitation to tender is incompatible with Article 85(1) of the Treaty, even where the invitation sets unreasonable conditions. It is for each contractor to determine independently what he regards as reasonable or unreasonable and to conduct himself accordingly.[215]

Bid rigging may well also attract the application of the criminal law in a number of member states.

Production quotas

A quota agreement is a type of market sharing whereby competitors fix or limit the quantity of goods (or less commonly services) they each produce and/or market. It is an indirect means of, and goes hand in hand with, price fixing, its purpose being artificially to adjust supply to demand. As price is closely a function of supply, production quotas may directly, certainly indirectly, affect price competition.[216] Quota arrangements are frequently an ancillary to, and buttress, price-fixing agreements or practices.[217] It is a classic form of market sharing and a hardcore breach of

---

[212] See Chap 6.
[213] Decision 92/204 (*Vereniging van Samenwerkende Prijsregelende Organisaties in de Bouwnijverheid*) OJ 1992 L92/1 at para 73.
[214] Decision 73/109 (*European Sugar Cartel*) OJ 1973 L140/17 at para II F, upheld on review as Cases 40 etc/73 *Coöperatieve Vereniging 'Suiker Unie' v Commission* [1975] ECR 1663.
[215] Case T-29/92 *Vereniging van Samenwerkende Prijsregelende Organisaties in de Bouwnijverheid v Commission* [1995] ECR II-289 at 331–2.
[216] Decision 94/599 (*PVC II*), n 175 *supra*, at para 35.
[217] eg, Decision 89/515 (*Welded Steel Mesh*), n 177 *supra*; Decision 94/601 (*Cartonboard*), n 180 *supra*; Decision 94/815 (*Cement*), n 181 *supra*; Decision 1999/60 (*Pre-Insulated Pipes*), n 182 *supra*.

Article 81(1), being expressly prohibited as a 'limit[ation] or control [of] production ...'.[218] However, it is not an easy cartel to engineer: it may be difficult to allocate quotas and it is difficult to police. Of the classic cartels it is the least transparent and so the easiest upon which to cheat.

In exceptional circumstances – those of excessive overcapacity in a declining industry – the Commission may by way of exemption take a kindly view of anticompetitive 'crisis cartel' agreements designed to achieve capacity reduction,[219] but only where they are short term and likely to return the sector to rude, or at least tolerable, health, and never to the extent of permitting price fixing or production quotas.[220]

Market sharing

Like price fixing, market sharing is normally a horizontal accommodation which has the same effect, if prosecuted successfully, of eliminating or at least moderating price competition. Of the classic cartels it is the easiest to engineer: the difficulties of actually agreeing on prices or quotas is avoided, and policing of cartel loyalty is more efficient. It is also less transparent a cartel than is price fixing, for it can be disguised by vertical selling arrangements and the allocation and exercise of intellectual property rights. It is seriously anticompetitive in itself – 'by [its] very nature restrict[s] competition within the meaning of Article 85(1)'[221] – but particularly so in the Community context because it may reinforce the isolation of national markets.

Market sharing may consist in the 'allocation' to producers or suppliers of agreed buyers,[222] either specifically or by volume sales, or even in the proportion of sales to a single (large) customer.[223] But more obvious, and more natural and common in the Community context is the allocation of territories, particularly along the lines of traditional home market(s) (the 'home market' rule). The most blatant examples are *Quinine*,[224] *Sugar*

---

[218] Art 81(1)(b).

[219] eg, Decision 84/380 (*Synthetic Fibres II*) OJ 1984 L207/17; Decision 94/296 (*Stichting Baksteen*) OJ 1994 L131/15.

[220] Decision 89/515 (*Welded Steel Mesh*), n 177 *supra*. The exception is the steel sector, in which the Commission has not been shy in using its powers under Art 58 of the ECSC Treaty to order production quotas in the event of a 'manifest crisis' in the industry.

[221] Decision 1999/60 (*Pre-Insulated Pipes*), n 182 *supra*, at para 147.

[222] Cases 40 etc/73 Coöperatieve Vereniging 'Suiker Unie' v Commission [1975] ECR 1663; Case 246/86 Belasco v Commission [1989] ECR 2117.

[223] Cases T-68, 77 & 78/89 *Società Italiano Vetro* v Commission (Flat Glass) [1992] ECR II-1403.

[224] Decision 69/240, JO 1969 L192/5, partially annulled on review in Case 41/69 *ACF Chemiefarma* v Commission [1970] ECR 661.

Cartel,[225] *Peroxygen Cartel*,[226] *Polypropylene*,[227] *Welded Steel Mesh*,[228] *Soda Ash*,[229] *Steel Beams*[230] and *Pre-Insulated Pipes*.[231]

Other horizontal arrangements

Cooperation agreements

There are a number of forms of horizontal cooperation amongst undertakings which constitute no threat (or do so only remotely) to competition. They may bring economic benefits to the producers at no cost to the consumer – indeed, to the advantage of the consumer owing to cost reductions. They may be particularly advantageous to small and medium-sized undertakings. In order that they not be deterred from pursuing them through fear of Article 81, in 1968 the Commission adopted a notice on 'cooperation agreements'[232] which in the normal course of events fall outwith Article 81(1). They are:

- exchanges of information and joint information gathering (market research, studies of industry, statistics, calculation models) provided they do *not* lead to coordination of market behaviour;
- financial cooperation (accountancy, credit guarantees, debt collection, tax consultancy);
- joint research and development up to the stage of industrial application provided there is no restriction upon independent research and development or exploitation of the fruits of joint efforts;
- sharing of production, storage and transport facilities;
- cooperation in execution of orders where the parties are not in competition with one other;
- joint selling and after sales service where the parties are not in competition with one other;

---

[225] Decision 73/109, OJ 1973 L140/17, upheld on review as Cases 40 etc/73 *Coöperatieve Vereniging 'Suiker Unie'* v *Commission* [1975] ECR 1663.

[226] Decision 85/74, OJ 1985 L35/1.

[227] Decision 86/398, n 173 *supra*.

[228] Decision 89/515, n 177 *supra*.

[229] Decisions 91/297 and 91/298, OJ 1991 L152/1 and 16, annulled on procedural grounds in Cases T-30 & 31/91 *Solvay* v *Commission* [1995] ECR 1775 and 1821 and Case T-36/91 *ICI* v *Commission* [1995] ECR II-1847, upheld on appeal in Cases C-287 & 288/95P *Commission* v *Solvay* and Case C-286/95P *Commission* v *ICI*, judgments of 6 April 2000, not yet reported.

[230] Decision 94/215, n 179 *supra*.

[231] Decision 1999/60, n 182 *supra*.

[232] Notice on agreements, decisions and concerted practices in the field of co-operation between enterprises (*sic*), JO 1968 C75/3. For the draft of an amended version see OJ 2000 C118/4.

- joint advertising, provided there is no limit placed upon individual advertising; and
- use of common quality labels available to all upon the same conditions.

Like all notices, the 1968 notice is to be treated with a degree of caution.

There are other horizontal agreements which are less benign, yet at the same time less offensive than the gross cartel, which require a lighter touch under Article 81. They are as follows.

Specialisation agreements

An agreement between competitors whereby a party or parties mutually refrain(s) from producing certain products or supplying certain services in deference to a competitor is tantamount to a market sharing agreement. The pre-eminent example is *Welded Steel Mesh*, which the Court of First Instance condemned as an infringement of Article 81(1) capable of 'intrinsic gravity and obviousness'.[233] However, Community law takes a relatively benign approach to specialisation agreements, recognising that they can contribute to cost efficiencies, increased output and consumer benefits. As a result the Commission has been known to grant exemption from Article 81(1),[234] and has adopted a block exemption in the field by virtue of which a specialisation agreement is exempted from the prohibition where the parties to it represent not more than 20 per cent (joint production) or 10 per cent (joint production and distribution) of the relevant market and the parties have an annual aggregate turnover of no more than €1000 million.[235]

Research and development agreements

Equally, the Commission adopts a positive attitude towards joint research and development agreements. Generally they promote technical progress, avoid the inefficiency of duplication of research and rationalise means of production. But they may in certain circumstances (those of agreements between or amongst powerful competitors) achieve the opposite and facilitate price coordination. They are now the subject of a block exemption

---

[233] Case T-141/89 *Tréfileurope Sales v Commission* [1995] ECR II-791 at 831.

[234] eg, Decision 69/242 (*Jaz/Peter*) JO 1969 L195/5; Decision 76/172 (*Bayer/Gist-Brocades*) OJ 1976 L30/13; Decision 83/668 (*VW/MAN*) OJ 1983 L376/11.

[235] Reg 417/85, OJ 1985 L53/1; on exemption and block exemption see Chap 4. An association agreement is also amongst the (rare) category of horizontal agreements which may be exempted by the Commission without notification provided the products its subject do not represent more than 15 per cent of the volume of business within the relevant market and the total annual turnover of the parties does not exceed €200 million: Reg 17/62, JO 1962, 204, art 4(2), (3)(c); see pp 121–2 *infra*.

regulation adopted alongside that on specialisation agreements.[236] They also raise questions for the exercise of intellectual property rights, which are considered below.[237]

Joint ventures

A particular form of horizontal cooperation is the joint venture. A joint venture is an exercise whereby two or more (but frequently two only) undertakings pool their existing capacity, or more commonly their potential capacity, in the production or distribution of goods or services through the creation of a distinct entity which may, but need not, have corporate form. The key determining indicator of a joint venture is therefore the partial integration of operations combined with the preservation of the independence of the undertakings party to it (the parent undertakings). It is related to but distinct from mergers. Community law therefore draws a distinction between 'concentrative' joint ventures and 'cooperative' joint ventures (or more precisely, 'cooperative non-full-function' joint ventures); concentrative joint ventures fall to be considered under the terms of the Merger Regulation[238] and cooperative joint ventures fall solely within the ambit of Article 81 (and Article 82 if one of the parties enjoys a dominant position).

Joint ventures are an attractive option in a number of contexts. They are particularly common in third country markets (and in some countries in Eastern Europe were, if less so now, required by law): the Community party gains access to a protected market, the non-Community party (and its country) gains technology and expertise. The staple of joint ventures are activities ancillary to the parents' interests such as distribution, specialisation, research and development and the licensing (and working) of intellectual property rights, but may extend to taxation and business consultancy, planning and financing of investment, the supply of raw materials or semifinished products, the manufacture of goods and the provision of services, advertising and customer service.[239]

Joint ventures may have a variety of pro-competitive aspects. They may generate efficiencies and their knock-on economic benefits, they may lead to technological development, and new products, which the parents could

---

[236] Reg 418/85, OJ 1985 L53/5. The additional possibility of exemption without notification which applies to specialisation agreements (*ibid*) applies also to R & D agreements: Reg 17/62, art 4(2), (3)(b).

[237] See Chap 10.

[238] For the difference between concentrative and cooperative joint ventures and for discussion of the former see pp 270–3 *infra*.

[239] Notice on the assessment of cooperative joint ventures, OJ 1993 C43/2, para 2.

not achieve individually, or they may allow the parents to enter new markets producing the benefits of competition therein. Yet they necessarily unite to some degree the economic interests of the parents and so a diminution of competition between them. They will normally include non-compete clauses and, even if they do not, create a framework which is all too prone to collusion, both between the parents *inter se* and between the parents and the joint venture. This may apply even to future ('potential') competition, where there is no market (yet) because there is not yet the product which the joint venture is set up to produce. In order to assist in assessment of the application of Article 81, in 1993 the Commission adopted a notice on the assessment of the compatibility of cooperative joint ventures with Article 81.[240]

Joint ventures between non-competitors will offend Article 81 only if they restrict the access of third parties to the market.[241] If the joint venture involves competitors, it is the relationship between the activities of the joint venture and those of its parents which is decisive. According to the Commission, the following considerations apply:

- a research and development joint venture restricts competition only exceptionally, that is where it excludes individual activity in the area by the parents or restricts competition between them in the market for the resulting product(s) or service(s); this will normally be so where the joint venture is responsible for their exploitation;[242]

- a sales joint venture belongs to the category of classic horizontal cartels which have as a rule the object and effect of coordinating the sales policy of competing manufacturers;[243] it is a clear breach of Article 81(1);

- a purchasing joint venture may rationalise ordering and the more efficient use of infrastructure (transport, storage) but it may also create advantages on the demand side, reduce the choice of suppliers and lead to weakening of price competition between the parents;[244]

- a production joint venture which manufactures primary or intermediate products for competing parents raises similar questions; if the joint venture processes materials supplied by the parents and resupplies finished (or partly finished) products to the latter, and particularly where the

---

[240] *Ibid.*
[241] *Ibid*, paras 32–35.
[242] *Ibid*, para 37.
[243] *Ibid*, paras 38, 60.
[244] *Ibid*, paras 39, 61.

parents' entire production activity is concentrated in the joint venture, competition is considerably weakened.[245]

As a general rule a joint venture which has as its main purpose the coordination of actual or potential competition between the parents (and the joint venture), especially if it is one of joint price fixing, reduction of production and sales, the division of markets or prohibition or restriction of investment is prohibited by Article 81(1) and will attract no Commission sympathy.[246] However, the Commission stresses that joint ventures can be exceptionally complex beasts, and each must be considered on its merits upon a case by case basis both for compatibility with Article 81(1) and the appropriateness of granting an exemption under Article 81(3). In order to assist, and mindful of the time constraints which may adhere to joint ventures, in 1993 the Commission introduced a 'fast track' procedure for exemption of cooperative joint ventures, undertaking to respond with an initial analysis within two months of notification and provide a timetable within which a formal decision may be expected.[247]

Mergers and takeovers
Mergers and takeovers may be characterised as horizontal agreements when they are concerned with the fusion, or 'concentration', of competitors. The same may be said of concentrative joint ventures, to which the rules on mergers apply. They are discussed in Chapter 8.

Exclusionary practices
It is not uncommon for a dominant undertaking to seek to engineer the exclusion of a competitor from the market. If it does so, Article 82 will apply.[248] Although it is more difficult a course of action successfully to prosecute, Article 81 will apply where undertakings seek jointly to achieve the same result. The situation arises most frequently with trade associations (of undertakings) seeking to exclude non-members from the market or disciplining errant members. Examples include: certification for heavy hire equipment made compulsory and certification refused to non-members, even if they could provide guarantees equivalent to those of the certification system;[249] collective refusal to supply retailers or distributors

---

[245] *Ibid*, para 40.
[246] *Ibid*, para 56.
[247] Reg 3385/94, OJ 1994 L377/28, Annex, Chap D and Operational Part, Chap III.
[248] See Chap 5.
[249] Cases T-213/95 & 18/96 *Stichting Certificatie Kraanenverhuurbedrijf* v *Commission* [1997] ECR II-1739.

which undercut fixed prices or did not stock a minimum range of products;[250] a collective boycott of or blacklisting certain suppliers, even if enforced only intermittently;[251] collective predatory pricing;[252] collective aggregate rebates;[253] and exclusion of would-be competitors from a trade fair.[254]

3.4.3 Vertical agreements

Vertical agreements are those between undertakings at different levels on the economic chain, such as, for example, between producer of raw materials and manufacturer, manufacturer and distributor, distributor and retailer, retailer and customer or any variation within these distinctions. Primarily they address the contractual chain(s) between the original producer of a good or service and its eventual consumer. Their prime advantage is that they allow for net economic efficiency: they enable the producer to concentrate upon production and relieve it of the obligation of shifting the goods on the market, for that will be the concern of the (specialist) distributor who is better suited to the task. The consumer in turn is better served as the marketing of goods and services is devolved from their production and distinct efficiencies may thereby be produced at that level.

Consten & Grundig; Société Technique Minière

The pre-eminent case in EC competition law, and the basic exposition of much of the Court's thinking on Article 81(1), is *Consten & Grundig*,[255] which therefore merits close consideration. At the same time its defining importance can be fully understood only by comparing it with *Société Technique Minière*,[256] a case decided a fortnight earlier which involved similar facts and considerations but produced a diametrically opposite result.

---

[250] Respectively Case 73/74 *Groupement des Fabricants des Papiers Peints de Belgique* v *Commission* [1975] ECR 1491; Cases 209 etc/78 *van Landewyck* v *Commission* (FEDETAB) [1980] ECR 3125.

[251] Decision 73/431 (*Papiers Peints de Belgique*) OJ 1974 L237/3, annulled on review in Case 73/74 *Groupement des Fabricants des Papiers Peints de Belgique* v *Commission* [1975] ECR 1491 but not on that ground; Decision 1999/60 (*Pre-Insulated Pipes*), n 182 *supra*.

[252] Case 246/86 *Belasco* v *Commission* [1989] ECR 2117; Decision 1999/210 (*British Sugar*), n 183 *supra*; Decision 1999/243 (*TACA*), n 184 *supra*.

[253] Case 260/82 *Nederlandse Sigarenwinkeliers Organisatie* v *Commission* [1985] ECR 3801.

[254] Decision 88/447 (*British Dental Trade Association*) OJ 1988 L233/15.

[255] Cases 56 & 58/64 *Consten & Grundig* v *EEC Commission* [1966] ECR 299.

[256] Case 56/65 *Société Technique Minière* v *Maschinenbau Ulm* [1966] ECR 235.

In *Consten & Grundig* a German manufacturer of radiophonic equipment (Grundig) had entered into a contract (which pre-dated the entry into force of the Treaty) of indefinite duration with a French distributor of electrical goods (Consten), appointing Consten the 'sole representative' (*représentant exclusif*) of Grundig for metropolitan France, the Saar and Corsica. It was a fairly standard exclusive distribution contract, Consten undertaking to buy minimum quantities of the contract goods, to make advance orders, to advertise, to stock sufficient spare parts and to provide after-sales service. It also undertook not to sell competing goods produced by other manufacturers and not to sell Grundig goods outwith the contract territory. A similar prohibition had already been imposed by Grundig upon its distributors in other member states and upon its German wholesalers. Grundig undertook to confer upon Consten the whole of distribution sales rights within the contract territory and not to deliver directly or indirectly contract goods there to any other distributor. It also assigned to Consten exclusive use of its French trade mark.

In the early 1960s Consten found itself undercut by parallel traders which secured supplies of the contract goods on the German market and re-sold them in France. Consten brought actions against them in the French courts for unfair competition (*concurrence déloyale*), a tort/delict[257] (and a criminal offence)[258] in French law, and for infringement of Consten's trade mark. In the meanwhile, one of the parallel traders had lodged a complaint with the Commission regarding the anticompetitive effects of the contract[259] and Consten notified the contract to the Commission seeking an exemption from the prohibition of Article 81(1) in accordance with Article 81(3).[260] The French court seised of the action for unfair competition stayed proceedings pending the Commission decision in order to determine whether the contract was void as a matter of Article 81, and so also of French law.[261] In the event the Commission refused the exemption and declared the contract to be a breach of Article 81(1).[262]

---

[257] L'ordonnance n° 45–1483 du 30 juin 1945 relative aux prix, JORF du 8 juillet 1945; now repealed and replaced by l'ordonnance n° 86–1243 du 1 décembre 1986 relative à la liberté des prix et de la concurrence, JORF du 9 décembre 1986.

[258] L'ordonnance n° 45–1484 du 30 juin 1945 relative à la constatation, la poursuite et la répression des infractions à la législation économique, JORF du 8 juillet 1945; repealed by l'ordonnance n° 86–1243, art 57 and replaced by arts 17 *et seq* thereof.

[259] As to the complaints procedure see Chap 6.

[260] As to exemption see Chap 4.

[261] Cour d'Appel, Paris, arrêt du 26 janvier 1963 (*UNEF v Consten*), Dalloz Jur, p. 189.

[262] Directive (*sic*) 64/566 JO 1964, 2545. The French text in the Official Journal reads '*La Commission ... a arrêté la présente directive ...*'; the German (the other authentic language of the decision) reads, correctly, *Entscheidung*. The Commission has power under

Both Consten and Grundig sought review of the decision under Article 173 (now Article 230) of the Treaty.

Before addressing the Court's response it is appropriate to consider the nature of distribution. A basic Treaty goal is market integration, which means that manufacturers or producers throughout the Community are allowed unrestricted access to markets hitherto closed to them – or if not closed, more difficult to penetrate. So a manufacturer now has access to new untried markets. The question then arises of how best to shift its goods there. There are a number of options. It could attempt to sell directly to retailers or even to consumers from its home base; this presents few legal difficulties but is not very efficient. It could establish a subsidiary in another member state (as it is entitled to do under Treaty rules on the right of establishment[263]) for purposes of distributing the goods, or it could appoint an agent there. Both of these latter options (the first especially for larger undertakings) are common enough. But in light of the economic entity doctrine, neither involves an agreement within the meaning of Article 81(1). A fourth, frequently preferred option – a contract with an established distributor – does so. The attractions of this option are obvious: a distributor controls a distribution system; it enjoys an infrastructure of warehousing and transport; it knows the vagaries of the market, and the national and regional regulation of it; it understands the capital and tax systems and how to use them to best advantage; it speaks the language; it has the contacts; it greases the appropriate palms. It is 'home produced' with all the advantages that may bring and it 'knows the territory'; and the business of shifting goods on the market within the territory is, after all, its very *raison d'être*. So in many situations, a distribution contract is (seen to be) the optimal means of getting the goods into the shops.

But manufacturer and distributor will of course strike a deal only if there is mutual financial advantage to be had from it. For the former, this means that the latter will use best endeavours to sell as many of the contract goods as possible in and throughout the contract territory, including minimum orders, forward orders, demand forecasting, stocking, advertising, servicing and the like; it will also want (but may not get) a promise to distribute its goods to the exclusion of other competing goods lest the

---

Reg 17 (as to which see Chap 6) to adopt decisions and not directives, which cannot in any event be addressed to natural or legal persons (EC Treaty, Art 249 (ex Art 189)). This was one ground of review (at least for Consten) but the Court dismissed it peremptorily, finding the text actually notified (and which is authentic) to have read '*décision*'.

[263] EC Treaty, Arts 43–48 (ex Arts 52–58).

distributor's vigour be diluted by its interest in the competing goods. For the distributor, the main concern is that, having expended time, resources and money in order to establish and maintain a market for the goods, it will not be undercut by parallel traders or 'free riders', competing traders who, not having borne the setting up costs, including sunk costs, can cherry pick markets and sell the same goods within the contract territory at lower prices. It is the business of parallel traders to take advantage of price disparities which still exist from member state to member state (which are a product of currency movements, differing tax systems, price regulation, technical regulation, administrative formalities and market demand and, of course, restrictive practices), buy up goods where they are cheapest and, if they can, on the 'grey market' (outwith official distribution systems) and resell them where the price is highest. A parallel trader is therefore a serious irritant to official distribution channels for it is his job to subvert those channels; but this of course produces a wider beneficial effect in keeping them efficient. Parallel trade is not necessarily contrary to the interests of the manufacturer, and may in fact work to its advantage, but it is a state of affairs the distributor will wish to counter. It will therefore insist (and require to insist in order to make the risk viable) upon a degree of exclusivity – that it, and as much as possible only it, enjoys an exclusive right to sell the contract goods within the contract territory, and that that right will be secured and protected by contract.

Such was the nature of the contract in *Consten & Grundig*. The judgment of the Court goes to the heart of Article 81(1): whether the Commission had properly construed the meaning of 'the prevention, restriction or distortion of competition'. According to Consten the contract did no such thing: it actually encouraged competition, and market interpenetration, by securing for the French consumer access to goods which he would not otherwise enjoy, or would not enjoy as efficiently. Whilst not an unreasonable reading of the original language texts of Article 81(1),[264] the Court gave it short shrift: 'the fact that an agreement encourages an increase, even a large one, in the volume of trade between States is not sufficient to exclude the possibility that the agreement may "affect" such trade' in a manner contrary to Article 81(1);[265] the fact that an agreement does not prevent – or indeed, promotes – an increase in the volume of trade does not mean there is no restriction or distortion of competition, for such trade could have developed under other conditions and in other ways had there been no restrictive agreement. It may improve competition; it does not necessarily optimise it.

---

[264] See n 101 *supra*.
[265] Cases 56 & 58/64 *Consten & Grundig* at 341.

Second, Consten and Grundig argued that Article 81 did not apply to a vertical agreement at all, or at least not to a distribution agreement such as that at issue. The purpose of Article 81 was to prohibit restraints between competitors by which they limit the competition in which they ought to be engaged. Consten and Grundig were not in competition with one another. Therefore Article 81 did not apply. To this the Court was equally short:

> The principle of freedom of competition concerns the various stages and manifestations of competition. Although competition between producers is generally more noticeable than that between distributors of products of the same make, it does not thereby follow that an agreement tending to restrict the latter kind of competition should escape the prohibition of Article 85(1) merely because it might increase the former.[266]
>
> [T]he possible application of Article 85 to a sole distributorship contract cannot be excluded merely because the grantor and the concessionnaire [sic] are not competitors *inter se* and not on a footing of equality. Competition may be distorted within the meaning of Article 85(1) not only by agreements which limit it as between the parties, but also by agreements which restrict or prevent the competition which might take place between one of them and third parties .... [B]y such an agreement, the parties might seek, by preventing or limiting the competition of third parties in respect of their products, to create or guarantee for their benefit an unjustified advantage at the expense of the consumer or user, contrary to the general aims of Article 85.[267]

This is the first enunciation from the Court of Justice of the integration goals of the competition rules and is what cracks Article 81 wide open. It is concerned not only with horizontal agreements which limit competition between competitors but also with vertical agreements which may encourage but nonetheless distort it. The distribution contract awarded Consten sole distribution rights in France, Grundig agreed not to sell there directly and Grundig's other distribution contracts prohibited its other distributors from selling there: because of this the object and effect of the agreement were hermetically to seal the French market, to ensure for Consten 'absolute territorial protection' in the sale of Grundig products and re-create a partitioning of the market along national lines which the Treaty sets out to eliminate.

> The applicants thus wished to eliminate any possibility of competition at the wholesale level in Grundig products in the territory specified in the contract ....
>
> The situation ... results in the isolation of the French market and makes it

---

[266] at 342.
[267] at 339.

possible to charge for the products in question prices which are sheltered from all effective competition.[268]

Thus Article 81 addresses both 'inter-brand' and 'intra-brand' competition. It is not enough that producers compete (inter-brand competition); there ought also to be competition in the market for distribution of an individual producer's goods (intra-brand competition). Looking at the economics, it is not surprising: the factory gate value of goods is sometimes a fraction of their shop value, the rest subsumed in transport, warehousing, retail costs and VAT. In 1994 distribution costs accounted for about 13 per cent of value added to all goods sold within the Community.[269] It also represented 22 million jobs (16 per cent of total employment) and was the mainstay of 4.5 million undertakings.[270] It is only if there is competition in this substantial sector of the market that benefits for the consumer will be maximised.

For sake of completeness, it should be added, finally, that the Court found that the Commission had not acted unlawfully in refusing to grant an exemption.

What, then, of its sister case, *Société Technique Minière*, which appears on all fours with *Consten & Grundig* but produced the opposite result? There a French company (Société Technique Minière) engaged in selling public works heavy equipment had entered into a contract denominated an 'export agreement' (*accord d'exportation*) with a German manufacturer (Maschinenbau Ulm) for the purchase of a number of graders over a period of two years (but tacitly renewable subject to termination with six months' notice). By the terms of the contract the former undertook to buy a certain number of machines, to further the interests of Maschinenbau Ulm, to maintain stocks and repairs and to meet market demand, in exchange for which it was awarded 'the exclusive right to sell' the contract goods in France and its overseas territories. A contractual dispute arose out of a failure to meet payments and Maschinenbau Ulm brought an action in a French commercial court for rescission and damages which were duly awarded. Technique Minière appealed to the Cour d'Appel, Paris on grounds of unfair competition and that the contract was void for breach of Article 81(1). The Cour d'Appel referred the latter question to the Court of Justice under Article 177 (now Article 234) of the Treaty.

On its face it is not much different from *Consten & Grundig*. But the Court said:

---

[268] at 342–3.
[269] EC Commission, Green Paper on vertical restraints in EC competition policy, COM (96) 721 final, para 15.
[270] *Ibid.*

[A]n agreement whereby a producer entrusts the sale of his products in a given area to a sole distributor cannot automatically fall under the prohibition of Article 85(1). But such an agreement may contain the elements set out in that provision by reason of a particular factual situation or of the severity of the clauses protecting the exclusive dealership ....

The competition in question must be understood within the actual context in which it would occur in the absence of the agreement in dispute. In particular it may be doubted whether there is an interference with [*altération de*] competition if the said agreement seems really necessary for the penetration of a new area by an undertaking. Therefore, in order to decide whether an agreement containing a clause 'granting an exclusive right of sale' is to be considered as prohibited by reason of its object or of its effect, it is appropriate to take into account ... the severity of the clauses intended to protect the exclusive dealership or ... the opportunities allowed for other commercial competitors in the same products by way of parallel re-exportation and importation.[271]

The importance of *Société Technique Minière* lies in a number of respects. Implicit in the judgment is that Community competition law recognises market imperfections and its goal is therefore effective or work-able, not perfect, competition. Advocate-General Roemer advised several times that it is necessary to proceed upon the basis of a 'realistic look at the market',[272] and the goal of workable competition was expressly con-firmed by the Court subsequently in *Metro I*:

The requirement contained in ... the EEC Treaty that competition shall not be distorted implies the existence on the market of workable competition ....

[T]he requirements for the maintenance of workable competition may be rec-onciled with ... certain restrictions on competition ....[273]

Adopting this realistic look at the market, if *some* degree of exclusivity is 'really necessary' (*précisément nécessaire*) to penetrate a new market (an object consistent with Treaty aims and so to be encouraged and sup-ported), and without it a party would not be induced into the contract and the relevant trade would not take place at all, the agreement may fall out-with the prohibition of Article 81(1) entirely.

---

[271] Case 56/65 *Société Technique Minière* v *Maschinenbau Ulm* [1966] ECR 235 at 248, 250.

[272] at 258.

[273] Case 26/76 *Metro-SB-Großmärkte* v *Commission (No 1)* [1977] ECR 1875 at 1904–05; see *infra*. The target of the maintenance of workable or effective competition was con-firmed subsequently in the Merger Regulation (as to which see Chap 8), in which compatibility with the common market is appraised as a function of 'the need to maintain and develop effective competition ...': Art 2(1)(a).

The difference between *Consten & Grundig* and *Société Technique Minière* therefore lies simply in the degree of exclusivity. Consten was afforded absolute territorial protection. Because of the Treaty aim of market integration there is in Community competition law a particular antipathy, not found in other competition law regimes, to agreements which strike at cross-border trade; the agreement therefore had as its very object the distortion of competition within the meaning of Article 81(1), and was a *per se* infringement. But Technique Minière was afforded only partial exclusivity: Maschinenbau Ulm could not itself sell in France (except through Technique Minière) but there was no prohibition imposed upon its other distributors in other member states from doing so.[274] This goes to 'the severity of the clauses intended to protect the exclusive dealership or … the opportunities allowed for other commercial competitors in the same products by way of parallel re-exportation and importation'. Consten was ring fenced, enjoying absolute protection from inter-brand competition from other suppliers. Technique Minière was not. It would have the cost advantages stemming from direct importation from Germany, but would be kept on its toes by the possibility, should it become greedy or inefficient, of being undercut by parallel imports into France of the contract goods from other member states in which the goods were distributed and sold. Taking account of market conditions, the partial exclusivity was (objectively) 'really necessary' to induce Technique Minière to enter into the agreement. The agreement therefore fell outwith Article 81(1).[275]

A rule of reason?
Article 81(1) is therefore not joined where an agreement can be said to restrain competition but does so only in certain contexts and minimally and justifiably. This is sometimes called the rule of reason, but the term ought to be treated with care both because of its foreign provenance[276] and because it is on any view of much narrower scope and application than its American progenitor. The term has never appeared in a judgment of the Court of Justice except to cite submissions of parties arguing it,[277] although it was used by Advocate-General Roemer in *Société Technique*

---

[274] The Commission is always sensitive here to the possibility of, and will look for, a concerted practice tacitly corrupting what is otherwise an unobjectionable agreement.

[275] This was of course a question to be determined by the Cour d'Appel in the context of the Article 234 (ex Article 177) procedure, but the determination of the law by the Court of Justice made clear what the outcome ought to be.

[276] See pp 80–81 *supra*.

[277] Cases 56 & 58/64 *Consten & Grundig* v *EEC Commission* [1966] ECR 299 at 342.

Minière[278] and it has been used by the Court of First Instance (in a manner which betrays its origins) in a horizontal cartel case but only in order to set it aside:

> The fact that the infringement of Article 85(1) of the Treaty ... is a clear one necessarily precludes the application of a rule of reason, assuming such a rule to be applicable in Community competition law, since in that case it must be regarded as an infringement *per se* of the competition rules.[279]

Indeed the Court of First Instance appears to favour the American construction, saying that where an agreement contains no *per se* (or hardcore) restrictions its anticompetitive effects must be weighed against the claimed pro-competitive effects necessary to formulate the agreement, taking account of the conditions in which it functions and in particular the economic context in which the undertakings operate, the product or service covered by the agreement and the actual structure of the market at issue, noting always both existing and potential competition.[280] But the Court of Justice has never done so, characterising it otherwise as simply restraints proportionate, objectively justifiable and ancillary to a legitimate commercial venture which is not hardcore anticompetitive. Whatever it is styled, it is an integral, if elusive, variable of the breadth of the prohibition of Article 81(1). It has been applied hitherto in the context of various distribution arrangements and joint ventures. Thus, restrictive elements inherent in, or ancillary to, partial exclusivity in a distribution agreement (*Société Technique Minière*),[281] protection of the legitimate interests of the consumer (*Metro I* and *Metro II*)[282] and of the producer (*Binon*)[283] in selective distribution networks, restrictive covenants on the transfer of an undertaking necessary to protect goodwill (*Nutricia*),[284] ancillary restraints to protect know-how in a franchising agreement (*Pronuptia*),[285] limited restriction of plant breeders' licensees in order to encourage investment in and protect against improper handling of seed varieties (*Maize Seeds*),[286]

---

[278] Case 56/65 *Société Technique Minière* v *Maschinenbau Ulm* [1966] ECR 235 at 257: '... the introduction of such a rule of reason (let us give it this name) ...'.

[279] Case T-148/89 *Tréfilunion* v *Commission* [1995] ECR II-1063 at 1108.

[280] Cases T-374 etc/94 *European Night Services* v *Commission* [1998] ECR II-3141 at 3195–6.

[281] Case 56/65 *Société Technique Minière* v *Maschinenbau Ulm* [1966] ECR 235.

[282] Case 26/76 *Metro-SB-Großmärkte* v *Commission* (No 1) [1977] ECR 1875; Case 75/84 *Metro-SB-Großmärkte* v *Commission* (No 2) [1986] ECR 3021; see *infra*.

[283] Case 243/83 *Binon* v *Agence et Messageries de la Presse* [1985] ECR 2015.

[284] Case 42/84 *Remia & Nutricia* v *Commission* [1985] ECR 2545.

[285] Case 161/84 *Pronuptia de Paris* v *Schillgalis* [1986] ECR 353.

[286] Case 258/78 *Nungesser* v *Commission* [1982] ECR 2015.

even to the extent, given the exceptional nature of the goods, of an export ban (*Erauw-Jacquery*),[287] generally the protection of the 'specific subject matter' of an intellectual property right (*Maize Seeds; Coditel II*),[288] non-compete and exclusive supply clauses in a joint venture agreement operative during the launch phase of a high risk venture requiring significant investment[289] and a prohibition of cross control of or interest in association football clubs (in order to protect the integrity of club competitions)[290] might all be argued to restrain competition, but as they are proportionate, ancillary to a legitimate commercial venture and 'really necessary', they fall outwith the prohibition of Article 81(1). It is more a product of the case law of the Court of Justice that it is of Commission largesse, of whom the acceptance and recognition of a rule of reason has generally been grudging;[291] indeed, the Commission claims it is 'a concept which the Court of Justice has hitherto declined to embrace'.[292]

The two are often confused, so it is important to note that the rule of reason (and, as Advocate-General Roemer says, let us give it this name) is to be contrasted with the *de minimis* defence. Both produce the same practical result, that the agreement in issue falls outwith the prohibition of Article 81(1), but they do so for distinct reasons: the rule of reason because the restraints are minimal, proportionate and ancillary, *de minimis* because their effects are inappreciable. Therefore even an agreement which is *per se* anticompetitive can escape the prohibition under *de minimis* (as in *Völk*)[293] but may never do so under the rule of reason (as in *Tréfilunion*),[294] although under the latter there is always the (remote) possibility of exemption under Article 81(3).[295]

[287] Case 27/87 *Erauw-Jacquery* v *La Hesbignonne* [1988] ECR 1818.

[288] Case 258/78 *Nungesser*, n 286 *supra*; Case 262/81 *Coditel* v *Ciné Vog Films* (*No 2*) [1982] ECR 3381. On the specific subject matter of intellectual property rights see Chap 10.

[289] Decision 1999/242 (*Télévision par Satellite*) OJ 1999 L90/6; Decision 1999/573 (*Cégétel + 4*) OJ 1999 L218/14; Decision 1999/574 (*Télécom Développement*) OJ 1999 L218/24.

[290] See the Reg 17, art 19(3) notice of the Commission on UEFA rules on the independence of clubs: OJ 1999 C363/2.

[291] For examples see Decision 87/407 (*Computerland*) OJ 1987 L222/12; Decision 90/410 (*Elopak/Metal Box-Odin*) OJ 1990 L209/15; Decision 90/446 (*Konsortium ECR 900*) OJ 1990 L228/31; Decisions 1999/242, 573 and 574, n 289 *supra*.

[292] Cases T-374 etc/94 *European Night Services* v *Commission* [1998] ECR II-3141 at 3196.

[293] Case 5/69 *Völk* v *Vervaecke* [1969] ECR 295; see *supra*.

[294] Case T-148/89 *Tréfilunion* v *Commission* [1995] ECR II-1063; see n 279 *supra* and accompanying text.

[295] Cases T-374 etc/94 *European Night Services* v *Commission* [1998] ECR II-3141 at 3197.

Exemption
Both *de minimis* and rule of reason are also to be contrasted in turn with agreements which are exempted, which offend Article 81(1) but escape the prohibition only because they are adjudged to meet the beneficial criteria provided in Article 81(3) and so are expressly permitted to do so. It is well to bear in mind that this applies to a number of aspects of vertical agreements, which the Commission may exempt from Article 81(1) upon an individual basis ('individual exemption') or with blanket effect across a category of agreements ('block exemption'). Exemption and block exemption are discussed in the following chapter. But reference will be made to relevant block exemptions in considering the following types of vertical agreements.

Common types of vertical agreements

Exclusive distribution agreements
The nature and anticompetitive elements of distribution agreements and their relevance for intra-brand competition are discussed above. Given the policy goal of market integration, key in the Community context is the degree of territorial protection afforded the distributor. An 'open' exclusive distribution agreement such as that at issue in *Société Technique Minière* may escape the prohibition entirely by application of the rule of reason.[296] An agreement which confers upon the distributor exclusive territorial protection will not; it is in Community law a hardcore restraint of competition. So, an export ban outwith the contract territory is a blatant and unsalvageable breach of Article 81(1);[297] but so is a ban on export to the Community from a third country contract territory,[298] and even a ban upon export from the Community, for that precludes the possibility of export and (cheaper) re-importation,[299] provided both meet the appreciability test. A contractual term which requires a distributor to redirect orders from outwith contract territory to the distributor therein is tantamount to an export ban;[300] if not part of the contract but a tacit understanding between manufacturer and distributor, it is a concerted

---

[296] The distinction between an 'open' exclusive distribution agreement and a closed exclusive distribution agreement was drawn subsequently in Case 258/78 *Nungesser* v *Commission* (Maize Seeds) [1982] ECR 2015.

[297] Cases 56 & 58/64 *Consten & Grundig* v *EEC Commission* [1966] ECR 299; Case T-77/92 *Parker Pen* v *Commission* [1994] ECR II-549; Case C-70/93 *Bayerische Motorenwerke* v *ALD Auto-Leasing* [1995] ECR I-3439.

[298] Case C-306/96 *Javico International* v *Yves St Laurent Parfums* [1998] ECR I-1983.

[299] Decision 78/163 (*Distillers*) OJ 1978 L50/16, upheld on review in Case 30/78 *Distillers* v *Commission* [1980] ECR 2229.

[300] Case T-175/95 *BASF Coatings* v *Commission* [1999] ECR II-1581.

practice achieving the same result and equally prohibited.[301] Even an agreed monitoring system or any cooperation between producer and distributor intended to identify and so eliminate parallel trade is a breach.[302] The gravity with which the Commission views export bans is well illustrated in *Volkswagen*,[303] in which it found Volkswagen to have sealed off the German and Austrian markets from (cheaper) imports of its own motorcars from the Italian market by requiring its authorised Italian dealers to obtain its consent before selling outwith their contract territory, restricting bonus payments to sales within that territory, reducing margins for sales outwith it, prohibiting cross-deliveries between authorised dealers and threatening termination of dealership contracts in the event of breach of the terms, and fined Volkswagen a record 102 million ECUs – even though a vertical agreement and not a function of a classic cartel, the highest fine ever imposed upon a single undertaking.[304]

Exclusive purchasing agreements

Exclusive purchasing agreements are the mirror image on the demand side of exclusive distribution agreements. Generally they improve distribution. They enable the supplier to plan sales with greater precision, ensure the requirements of the buyer (usually a retailer) will be met upon a regular basis and allow both to limit risk owing to disruption to market conditions. They also assist market interpenetration (especially for small and medium-sized undertakings) and so greater consumer choice, and indirectly improve distribution systems and promotion of the contract product(s) at little or no cost to the retailer. However, as with any contract exclusivity they limit (voluntarily) the buyer's freedom of choice and run the risk of restricting competition and so breaching Article 81(1).

Having said that, they are generally less offensive to Article 81(1) than are exclusive distribution agreements, for they do not confer upon the buyer/retailer an exclusive sales territory, and intra-brand competition is therefore not appreciably diminished. Whether or not an exclusive purchasing agreement can appreciably affect trade within the meaning of Article 81(1) turns largely upon considerations of the cumulative fore-

---

[301] Case T-43/92 *Dunlop Slazenger* v *Commission* [1994] ECR II-441.

[302] Case 28/77 *Tepea* v *Commission* [1978] ECR 1391; Case 86/82 *Hasselblad* v *Commission* [1984] ECR 883; Case C-349/95 *Frits Loendersloot* v *Ballantine and Son* [1997] ECR I-6227; Decision 96/478 (*Bayer/Adalat*) OJ 1996 L201/1 (under review as Case T-41/96 *Bayer* v *Commission*, pending).

[303] Decision 98/273, OJ 1998 L124/60 (under review as Case T-62/98 *Volkswagen* v *Commission*, pending).

[304] On the Commission power to impose fines see Chap 6.

closure effect of a supplier's network or bundle of similar agreements. This is discussed above.[305]

Hitherto the Commission has thought it appropriate to adopt special rules for exclusive purchasing in the beer and petrol markets,[306] but these have now been abandoned.[307]

Franchising

Franchising agreements are a specific type of distribution agreement marked by the additional element of licensing of the franchisor's know-how. Generally they are beneficial to competition, for they allow the franchisor to penetrate new markets without set-up costs and allow the franchisee immediate start up upon the basis of the franchisor's methods and reputation. Franchising agreements may be of the nature of a service franchise, a production or manufacturing franchise, or a distribution franchise. The application of Article 81(1) to them is set out principally in the judgment of the Court of Justice in *Pronuptia*.[308]

Contractual provisions which go to the transfer of know-how between franchisor and franchisee and protection of the franchisor's identity and reputation (an obligation to apply commercial methods and know-how, to sell contract goods only in premises arranged in accordance with specifications, not to relocate the franchise without approval, not to assign it without approval, to accept control over selection of goods offered in the premises and to submit all advertising for approval) are either not anti-competitive at all or are saved by application of the 'rule of reason'. Further, and unnecessary, ancillary restraints (terms which partition the market between franchisor and franchisee or between franchisees *inter se* or which fix the franchisee's prices) are not, and breach Article 81(1).

Regulation 2790/1999

It is appropriate here to consider the block exemption system for the three types of agreement just described (exclusive distribution, exclusive purchasing, franchising). In 1967 the Commission adopted a block exemption – the first and for many years the only block exemption – which exempted from the prohibition of Article 81(1) certain additional restraints common

---

[305] See pp 76–7.
[306] Reg 1984/83, OJ 1983 L173/5, Title II (beer supply agreements) and Title III (service-station agreements).
[307] See *infra*.
[308] Case 161/84 *Pronuptia de Paris* v *Schillgalis* [1986] ECR 353.

to exclusive distribution and exclusive purchasing agreements.[309] It was replaced by two separate block exemptions (exclusive distribution[310] and exclusive purchasing[311]) in 1983, and in 1988 a third block exemption was adopted on franchising,[312] which codified much of the Court's thinking in *Pronuptia*.

As part of a comprehensive reconsideration of its policy on vertical restraints, in 1997 the Commission published a Green Paper[313] which was followed by a 'follow-up paper' in 1998.[314] Both signalled a more 'economic' approach to vertical restraints, that is, closer scrutiny of vertical arrangements in which substantial market power is in issue and a concomitant relaxation of proscriptive and prescriptive rules where it is not. The primary fruit of the green and follow-up papers is a new, single block exemption which replaced the three on distribution, purchasing and franchising and which came into force in June 2000.[315] It will be discussed more fully in Chapter 4, but it can be noted here that the following restraints in a vertical agreement (provided the parties do not exceed the market share and turnover thresholds set by the regulation) are now permitted:

- the restriction of active sales into the exclusive territory or to an exclusive customer group allocated to another supplier/buyer, and provided no such restriction is passed on to subsequent buyers;
- the restriction of sales to end users by a wholesaler;
- the restriction of sales to authorised distributors by the members of a selective distribution system; and
- the restriction of the buyer's ability to sell components, supplied for the purposes of incorporation, to customers which would use them to manufacture the same type of goods produced by the supplier.[316]

Selective distribution

A selective distribution system is one in which a producer wishes to ensure that its goods are sold at retail only in outlets which meet certain criteria laid down by the producer ('authorised dealers') and so sells only to them or imposes upon its distributors and/or wholesalers an obligation to do

---

[309] Reg 1967/67, JO 1967, 849; on exemption and block exemption see Chap 4.
[310] Reg 1983/83, OJ 1983 L173/1.
[311] Reg 1984/83, OJ 1983 L173/5.
[312] Reg 4087/88, OJ 1988 L359/46.
[313] COM (96) 721 fin.
[314] Follow-up to the Green Paper on vertical restraints: Communication on the application of the Community competition rules to vertical restraints, OJ 1998 C365/3.
[315] Reg 2790/1999, OJ 1999 L336/21.
[316] art 4(b).

likewise and ensure the obligation is passed on in re-sale. The system is used normally for branded goods and found most commonly in the sale of technical equipment (computers, electronic and electrical goods, cameras and the like), luxury items (jewellery, watches, perfumes and beauty products) and musical recordings (cassettes, compact discs), but it may be found elsewhere, in clothing for example: well-known trenchcoats or cashmere available only in upmarket shops, branded jeans only in those which assault the buyer with loud popular music. It is also an inherent characteristic of the specialist motor trade. The selective nature of the system ensures on its face that the customer will have the advantage of, for example, knowledgeable sales staff and easy performance of a manufacturer's guarantee. But it also has the effect of limiting sales of goods to technical or 'posh' outlets when they could be sold more cheaply by less prepossessing retailers. By their nature they therefore restrict price competition. Uniquely amongst the principal types of vertical selling arrangements, selective distribution (except for motor vehicle distribution and servicing) has never expressly been the subject of a Commission block exemption (although some provisions of the new block exemption on vertical restraints apply). Given the nature and price ranges of the products, it is also that in which parallel imports from grey markets, especially those outwith the Community, have generally been most rewarding; however, much of this has been put in jeopardy by the judgment of the Court of Justice in *Silhouette*.[317]

The question first arose in *Metro I*.[318] The Commission had adopted a decision which was part negative clearance (a declaration that an agreement falls outwith Article 81(1))[319] and part exemption under Article 81(3) to the selective distribution system deployed by a German manufacturer of consumer electronic goods (radio, television, tape recorders).[320] By the terms of the system, the German manufacturer would sell to any retailer in the Community which was a specialist electronics concern and agreed to a reasonable turnover and to take part in an after sales servicing system. Its distributors and wholesalers were bound by contract to supply no other buyer. Owing to these terms Metro, a large 'cash and carry' warehouse operation blighting many German cities, could secure no supplies of

---

[317] Case C-355/96 *Silhouette International Schmied* v *Hartlauer* [1998] ECR I-4799; see Chap 10.

[318] Case 26/76 *Metro-SB-Großmärkte* v *Commission* (*No 1*) [1977] ECR 1875.

[319] See Chap 4.

[320] Decision 76/159 (*Schwartzwälder Apparate-Bau-Anstalt August Schwer und Söhne*) OJ 1976 L28/19.

the contract goods. Metro therefore raised an action under Article 173 (now Article 230) challenging the Commission decision. The Court of Justice responded with a recognition that a selective distribution system does inhibit price competition for it excludes from the network (lower cost) retailers which have not borne the cost of establishing and maintaining a specialist outlet, but that whilst competition on price is pre-eminent, there are other effective forms of competition to which it must sometimes give way, or at least be modulated.

> [T]he requirements for the maintenance of workable competition may be reconciled with the safeguarding of objectives of a different nature and that to this end certain restrictions on competition are permissible, provided that they are essential to the attainment of those objectives and that they do not result in the elimination of competition for a substantial part of the Common Market.
>
> For specialist wholesalers and retailers the desire to maintain a certain price level, which corresponds to the desire to preserve, in the interests of consumers, the possibility of the continued existence of this channel of distribution in conjunction with new methods of distribution based on a different type of competition policy, forms one of the objectives which may be pursued without necessarily falling under the prohibition contained in Article 85(1) ....[321]

The Court therefore recognised a second rule of reason criterion, that of consumer interest. It went on subsequently to describe the manner in which an exclusive distribution system network falls outwith the prohibition of Article 81(1) thus:

> [A]greements constituting a selective system necessarily affect competition in the common market. However, ... systems of selective distribution, in so far as they aim at the attainment of a legitimate goal capable of improving competition in relation to factors other than price, therefore constitute an element of competition which is in conformity with Article 85(1) ....
>
> [T]he Court specified in [Metro I] that such systems are permissible, provided that resellers are chosen on the basis of objective criteria of a qualitative nature related to the technical qualifications of the reseller and his staff and the suitability of his trading premises and that such conditions are laid down uniformly for all potential resellers and are not applied in a discriminatory manner.[322]

So a selective distribution system escapes Article 81(1) entirely if outlets are selected upon qualitative criteria alone, such as staff training and technical and operational requirements of the outlet, which are related to and objectively justifiable given the nature of the goods (the 'principle of neces-

---

[321] Case 26/76 *Metro I* at 1905. See also Metro's second and equally abortive bite at the cherry in Case 75/84 *Metro-SB-Großmärkte* v *Commission (No 2)* [1986] ECR 3021.
[322] Case 107/82 *AEG-Telefunken* v *Commission* [1983] ECR 3151 at 3194–5.

sity'), proportionate and non-discriminatory (in which case it is a 'simple selective distribution' system), and assuming all the while that there remains a reasonable level of inter-brand competition.[323]

The key question lies in the justification of necessity. Motorcars and electronic and electrical equipment are the staple of selective distribution and generally unobjectionable. The principle has been extended to micro-computers,[324] to luxury watches,[325] to perfumes,[326] to luxury beauty care products[327] and to high quality ceramic tableware,[328] but not to plumbing fixtures and fittings.[329] The Commission therefore seems to adopt a fairly generous line on necessity, although it has been firm that specialist sections of department stores which otherwise meet the technical criteria be eligible.[330] Of course manufacturer and retailer are trading to an extent upon the cachet of a luxury item. It is not immediately apparent why 'luxurious ambience' is necessary and/or legitimate for the sale of unguents and soaps, but buyers seem prepared to accept it. It is even less apparent for the sale of a pair of jeans, and manufacturers are finding selective distribution thereof increasingly porous through grey market sales.

If an exclusive distribution agreement extends beyond a 'simple' agreement – for example, requiring wholesalers to establish a retail network[331] or requiring after sales service or the display of a wide range of the product(s) and their promotion[332] – it is likely to be caught by Article 81(1) but may well qualify for an exemption under Article 81(3). But any criteria for admission to the network which are quantitative rather than qualitative will breach Article 81(1) and the Commission is not sympathetic to requests for exemption.[333] Certainly, should a producer attempt to deploy a selective distribution system in a manner which reduces the contractual

---

[323] On the latter point see Case 75/84 *Metro-SB-Großmärkte* v *Commission* (No 2) [1986] ECR 3021.

[324] Decision 84/233 (*IBM Personal Computers*) OJ 1984 L118/24; Decision 87/407 (*Computerland*) OJ 1987 L222/12.

[325] Case C-376/92 *Metro-SB-Großmärkte* v *Cartier* [1994] ECR I-15.

[326] Decision 92/33 (*Yves Saint Laurent Parfums*) OJ 1992 L12/24; Decision 92/428 (*Parfums Givenchy*) OJ 1992 L236/11.

[327] However, it is not objectively justified to restrict retail sale of luxury beauty products to chemists/pharmacies: Case T-19/91 *Société d'Hygiène Dermatologique de Vichy* v *Commission* [1992] ECR II-415.

[328] Decision 85/616 (*Villeroy & Boch*) OJ 1985 L376/15.

[329] Decision 85/45 (*Ideal Standard*) OJ 1985 L20/38.

[330] Case 26/76 *Metro-SB-Großmärkte* v *Commission* (No 1) [1977] ECR 1875; Decision 77/100 (*Gebrüder Junghans*) OJ 1977 L30/10.

[331] Case 26/76 *Metro I*, *ibid*.

[332] Case 26/76 *Metro I*, *ibid*; Case 75/84 *Metro-SB-Großmärkte* v *Commission* (No 2) [1986] ECR 3021; Decision 94/29 (*Grundig*) OJ 1994 L20/15.

[333] eg Case 86/82 *Hasselblad* v *Commission* [1984] ECR 883.

freedom or economic independence of the dealer or is in truth a means of controlling prices or inhibiting exports, it is a breach of Article 81(1).[334] The restriction of active *and* passive sales to end users by members of a retail selective distribution system and restrictions of cross-supplies between distributors at any level within a selective distribution system fall expressly outwith the block exemption on vertical restraints.[335] If a selective distribution system falls outwith (or is exempted from) Article 81(1) it is ancillary to that system, and so permissible, for any manufacturer's guarantee to be limited to products sold by authorised dealers.[336]

Licensing

A common and commonly vertical arrangement (although it may also be addressed in specialisation and research and development agreements and joint ventures) is licensing. Licensing falls under a specific block exemption,[337] and will be discussed in Chapter 10.

Resale price maintenance

A potential component of any vertical agreement is resale price maintenance. Depriving a buyer of the freedom to sell at a price of his choosing is an obvious restraint of competition, expressly prohibited by Article 81(1) ('directly or indirectly fix[ing] ... selling prices').[338] The prohibition applies not only at the retail level but throughout the producer–consumer chain.[339] It applies equally to setting minimum profit margins[340] or (maximum) discounts[341] which would produce the same result. Fixing prices not by agreement but by inducement (bonuses or rebates) or by threat is equally prohibited; this is particularly an issue for intra-brand competition within selective distribution systems wherein price-conscious dealers may attract the manufacturer's displeasure. Perhaps surprisingly, an agreement fixing resale prices was eligible for exemption without notification provided there were only two parties to it,[342] but this anomaly was withdrawn in 1999.[343]

---

[334] Case 107/82 *AEG-Telefunken* v *Commission* [1983] ECR 3151; Case 86/82 *Hasselblad*, *ibid*; Decision 98/273 (*Volkswagen*) OJ 1998 L124/60 (under review as Case T-62/98 *Volkswagen* v *Commission*, pending).

[335] Reg 2790/1999 OJ 1999, L336/21, art 4(c) and (d).

[336] Case C-376/92 *Metro-SB-Großmärkte* v *Cartier* [1994] ECR I-15.

[337] Reg 240/96 OJ 1996, L31/2 on technology transfer.

[338] EC Treaty, Art 81(1)(a).

[339] eg, Cases 209 etc/78 *van Landewyck* v *Commission* (FEDETAB) [1980] ECR 3125.

[340] Decision 78/59 (*Centraal Bureau voor de Rijwielhandel*) OJ 1978 L20/18.

[341] Case 311/85 *Vereniging van Vlaamse Reisbureaus* v *Sociale Dienst van de Plaatselijke en Gewestelijke Overheidsdiensten* [1987] ECR 3801.

[342] Reg 17/62, JO 1962, 204, art 4(2)(2)(a) prior to 1999; see pp 121–2 *infra*.

[343] Reg 1216/1999, OJ 1999 L148/5, amending art 4(2) of Reg 17.

The new block exemption on vertical restraints expressly discounts (minimum) resale price maintenance.[344] The setting of maximum retail prices or recommended retail prices appears to fall outwith the prohibition unless it amounts to a fixed resale price[345] or leads to concerted action.[346]

Collective resale price maintenance (that is, a horizontal agreement amongst dealers, or a decision of their association of undertakings) is a clear breach of Article 81(1).[347]

It was (if less so now) not uncommon for resale price maintenance to be a legal requirement in a number of member states. Where such legislation obtains the Commission generally recognises that there may be a legitimate social aim pursued and will intervene only where there is a significant breach of Article 81. If compliance with legislation is mandatory undertakings are absolved from compliance with Article 81, but the legislation itself may constitute a breach of the competition rules.[348] The most sensitive area is resale price maintenance for books, which for reasons of cultural policy is compulsory in some member states[349] and common in others. The Commission has hitherto disregarded resale price maintenance imposed both by law and by agreement amongst publishers/booksellers as a measure which does not appreciably affect trade between member states except for books in those languages which are officially used in more than one member state (that is, French, German, Dutch, English and Swedish), and even then it has intervened only with kid gloves.[350] The Court sustained the Commission in *VBBB/VBVB*[351] and condemned aspects of the French

---

[344] Reg 2790/1999, OJ 1999 L336/21, art 4(a).

[345] Follow-up to the Green Paper on vertical restraints, OJ 1998 C365/3, section III.2.1; Reg 2790/1999, art 4(a).

[346] Case 161/84 *Pronuptia de Paris* v *Schillgalis* [1986] ECR 353; Decision 85/616 (*Villeroy & Boch*) OJ 1985 L376/15; Decision 87/14 (*Yves Rocher*) OJ 1987 L8/49.

[347] Cases 209 etc/78 *van Landewyck* v *Commission* (FEDETAB) [1980] ECR 3125; Cases 43 & 63/82 *Vereniging ter Bevordering van het Vlaamse Boekwezen* v *Commission* [1984] ECR 19; Cases 240 etc/82 *Stichting Sigarettenindustrie* v *Commission* [1985] ECR 3831; Case 45/85 *Verband der Sachversicherer* v *Commission* [1987] ECR 405.

[348] See pp 38–43 *supra*.

[349] eg, loi n° 81-766 du 10 août 1981, JORF du relative au prix du livre du 11 août 1981.

[350] See Decision 82/123 (*VBBB/VBVB*) OJ 1982 L54/36; Decision 89/44 (*Net Book Agreements*) OJ 1989 L22/12. In 1998 the Commission initiated an investigation into the fixed book price system in the Netherlands, but following abolition by the KVB (the Dutch association of publishers and booksellers) of resale price maintenance on imported books the Commission closed the file: see IP/99/668.

[351] Cases 43 & 63/82 *Vereniging ter Bevordering van het Vlaamse Boekwezen* v *Commission* [1984] ECR 19.

system,[352] but annulled the Commission decision in *Net Book Agreements* on grounds of insufficient reasoning,[353] which may suggest an uncommon tolerance of resale price maintenance in the book trade.

---

[352] Case 229/83 *Leclerc* v *Au Blé Vert* [1985] ECR 1. See also Case C-9/99. *Échirolles Distribution* v *Association du Dauphiné*, pending.

[353] Case 360/92P *Publishers Association* v *Commission* [1995] ECR I-23.

CHAPTER 4

Exemption from Article 81(1)

4.1 Exemption

Whilst Article 81(1) (ex Article 85(1)) lays down a prohibition of restrictive agreements, decisions and concerted practices, it was recognised in the Treaty that certain of these, although caught by the prohibition, might actually be beneficial in terms of competition or, alternatively, might produce benefits in other spheres which outweigh their anticompetitive effects. Article 81(3) (ex Article 85(3)) therefore provides for the possibility of setting aside ('declaring inapplicable'), or exemption from, the prohibition provided a number of criteria are met. If exempted, an agreement or practice becomes valid and enforceable notwithstanding any breach of Article 81(1). It is a benefit which applies only in the context of Article 81, and not of Article 82 (ex Article 86), conduct prohibited by which is always illegal without possibility of exemption.[1] Exemption is available across all three categories of anticompetitive devices recognised by Article 81 (agreements, decisions of associations of undertakings and concerted practices), but is sought in the majority of cases for agreements, and virtually never for concerted practices, for that would amount to an admission of their existence. Reference will therefore be made in this chapter primarily to exemption for restrictive agreements, but it ought to be remembered that it is equally applicable to anticompetitive decisions of associations of undertakings and, *in extremis*, to concerted practices.

The Treaty laid down mechanisms for the provisional enforcement of Articles 81 and 82 by national competition authorities[2] and by the Commission[3] pending the (compulsory) adoption under Article 83 (ex

---

[1] See Case T-51/89 *Tetrapak* v *Commission* (Tetrapak I) [1990] ECR II-309. There is one exception to this rule provided in Art 86(2) (ex Art 90(2)); see Chap 7. It might also be argued that Art 82 has an implied exemption provision analogous to Art 81(3) in that conduct of a dominant undertaking (to which Art 82 applies; see Chap 5) which might benefit from a power of exemption because of the economic benefits it brings may thereby cease to be abusive and so is not caught by Art 82.

[2] EC Treaty, Art 84 (ex Art 88).

[3] Art 85 (ex Art 89).

Article 87) of 'appropriate regulations or directives to give effect to the principles' set out therein, which were to include *inter alia* 'detailed rules for the application of Article 81(3)'.[4] The provisional regime included the power conferred upon national competition authorities by Article 84 (ex Article 88) to 'rule on the admissibility' of agreements, decisions and concerted practices in accordance with 'the provisions of Article 81, in particular paragraph 3'. Therefore pending the adoption of Community legislation under Article 83 (ex Article 87), the power of exemption envisaged by Article 81(3) fell exclusively to national competition authorities. The Commission enjoyed no equivalent power under Article 85 (ex Article 89).[5]

The legislation required by Article 83 was adopted by the Council in 1962 in the form of Regulation 17,[6] the principal regulation implementing Articles 81 and 82. Regulation 17 is of general application; analogous measures in the coal and steel sectors derive directly from the ECSC Treaty, and other, equivalent regulations apply in the specific sectors of agriculture and transport.[7] Regulation 17 in fact does much more than provide the mechanism for exemption; its other provisions will be considered in Chapter 6.

It was not absolutely clear from the text of Article 81(3) the means by

---

[4] Art 83(1) and (2)(b).

[5] Cases 209 etc/84 *Ministère Public* v *Asjes* (Nouvelles Frontières) [1986] ECR 1425.

[6] Reg 17/62, JO 1962, 204.

[7] Reg 17 applies except to:

- *coal and steel*: competition rules for coal and steel derive directly from provisions of the ECSC Treaty and from specific legislation giving effect to them; with the lapse of the ECSC Treaty in 2002 (see Chap 2, n 1) they will be absorbed into Arts 81 and 82 and Reg 17;

- *agriculture*: the competition rules are applied to the agricultural sector by Reg 26/62, JO 1962, 993 (in accordance with Art 36 (ex Art 42) of the Treaty); however, Reg 26 serves merely to provide derogation from Art 81(1) for anticompetitive conduct involving agricultural products, without which much of the CAP would fall foul of Art 81(1), and Reg 17 remains the operative instrument for the application of Arts 81 and 82 in the sector; it should be noted that 'agricultural products' are primary products or products of first stage processing (EC Treaty, Art 32(1) (ex Art 8(1)) which alone enjoy derogation from the full vigour of Arts 81 and 82;

- *transport*: Reg 141/62, JO 1962, 2751 expressly precludes the application of Reg 17 to transport; specific implementing regulations were subsequently adopted for rail, road and inland waterways transport (Reg 1017/68, JO 1968 L175/1), maritime transport (Reg 4056/86, OJ 1986 L378/4), and air transport (Reg 3975/87, OJ 1987 L374/1); the three cover all transport except tramp shipping, cabotage and air transport between a member state and a third country, which are excluded from Reg 4056/86 and Reg 3975/87; the Commission has proposed a regulation governing air transport with third countries (COM (97) 218 final) but the Council has not adopted it; in its 1999 White Paper (see pp 134–6 *infra*) the Commission envisages the scrapping of these regulations, leaving transport matters to fall within Reg 17;

which exemption would be secured. This was a product of disagreement between the German and French delegations during the drafting stages: the former supported an authorisation scheme such as their own (and such as that provided clearly by the ECSC Treaty[8]) whereby anticompetitive agreements were prohibited unless expressly exempted (so favouring an earlier draft which provided that 'restrictive agreements may be declared valid'), the latter a scheme such as *their* own whereby such agreements were valid from their formation if they met certain conditions defined by law (*exception légale*). The upshot was a final text – 'the provisions of paragraph 1 may ... be declared inapplicable' – which fudged the issue but, in concert with Article 81(2), implied support for the German camp. Regulation 17 confirmed it: agreements, decisions and concerted practices falling within Article 81(1) are 'prohibited, no prior decision to that effect being required',[9] and the prohibition could be lifted only by *ex post* authorisation (exemption), the power of which passed exclusively to the Commission.[10] Whilst it is suggested from time to time and from various quarters that the Commission is, owing to workload and the size of its staff, unable efficiently, or even competently, to discharge this exclusive power,[11] and it ought therefore to be shared with or delegated to other authorities – for example, an independent (that is, free of the political considerations and the broader Community responsibilities which inform the Commission) administrative European Cartel Office modelled upon the *Bundeskartellamt*,[12] or existing national competition authorities – the

---

- *mergers*: Reg 4064/89, OJ 1990 L257/13 expressly precludes the application of Reg 17 to the control of mergers and takeovers (as it defines them) and occupies the field; see Chap 8.
[8] ECSC Treaty, Art 65(2).
[9] Reg 17, art 1.
[10] *Ibid*, art 9(1). National authorities may therefore still grant exemption only in those (very few) fields not yet regulated by Reg 17 or the equivalent transport regulations. Exemptions granted by national authorities prior to the entry into force of Reg 17 (a power which in the event was used only by the *Bundeskartellamt*) were homologated: art 23.
[11] The Commission receives an average of 250 requests for exemption and adopts on average 25 formal decisions (including all decisions, not just exemption decisions) per year: EC Commission, *XXVIIIth Report on Competition Policy, 1998*, p 59. Broadsides are frequently directed at the Commission for its inability to cope with its workload; for the most recent see 'Perspektiven des Europäischen Kartellrechts', a position paper delivered by Dr Dieter Wolf, president of the *Bundeskartellamt* to the Frankfurter Institut – Stiftung Marktwirtschaft und Politik on 8 July 1999.
[12] The existence of a European Cartel Office was envisaged as long ago as the 1960s (see eg Art 3(2) of the Decision of the Representatives of the Governments of the Member States on the Provisional Location of Certain Institutions and Departments of the Communities attached to the 1965 Merger Treaty), and its establishment was seriously championed by the German delegation during the 1996/97 intergovernmental conference which led to the Treaty of Amsterdam, but exhortation fell upon deaf ears. The lack of enthusiasm is a

Commission has until recently shown no enthusiasm to relinquish its monopoly. Change is now in the offing.[13] British legislation purports to authorise the Secretary of State to exempt an agreement under Article 81(3) in certain circumstances,[14] but this power is *ultra vires* owing to the exclusive authority conferred by Regulation 17 upon the Commission in most if not all circumstances and, pending amendment to Regulation 17, is unlikely in practice to arise at all.[15]

The basic procedure for applying for and obtaining exemption is laid down in Regulation 17.[16] It may be granted only if the agreement meets the conditions for exemption set out in Article 81(3) which are both positive and negative, two of each. The agreement must:

- positively, (1) contribute to 'improving the production or distribution of goods or to promoting technical or economic progress, while (2) allowing consumers a fair share of the resulting benefit'; and
- negatively, (3) neither 'impose on the undertakings concerned restrictions which are not indispensable to the attainment of these objectives' nor (4) 'afford such undertakings the possibility of eliminating competition in respect of a substantial part of the products in question'.

It is primarily for the undertaking(s) seeking exemption to show that the agreement fulfils the four conditions;[17] the Commission is under no duty to suggest alternative solutions or to indicate the respects in which it would regard the grant of exemption justified.[18] Undertakings seeking exemption and third parties that can show 'sufficient interest' have a right

---

function essentially of the perception outwith Germany that competition policy is legitimately an instrument intertwined with other policy areas. It is shared by the European Parliament (see Resolution on the Twenty-Fifth Competition Report of the European Commission, OJ 1996 C362/135, point 10) and the Economic and Social Committee (see Opinion on the Twenty-Fifth Report on Competition, OJ 1997 C75/22, points 6.1–6.5). For the most recent arguments for a European Cartel Office see M.J. Nordmann, 'The Case for a European Cartel Office' [1997] *European Public Law* 223; B. Selinger, 'Ein unabhängiges Kartellamt für Europa – ordnungs- und wettbewerbspolitische Aspekte' (1997) 11 *Wirtschaft und Wettbewerb* 874.

[13] See pp 134–6. *infra.*

[14] EC Competition Law (Articles 88 and 89) Enforcement Regulations 1996 (SI 1996/2199), regs 4, 19.

[15] See pp 194–7. *infra.*

[16] Reg 17, arts 4–9, 19, 21.

[17] Cases 43 & 63/82 *Vereniging ter Bervordering van het Vlaamse Boekwezen* v *Commission* [1984] ECR 19; Case T-66/89 *Publishers Association* v *Commission* [1992] ECR II-1995, set aside on appeal as Case C-360/92P *Publishers Association* v *Commission* [1995] ECR I-23 but not on that point; Case T-7/93 *Langnese-Iglo* v *Commission* [1995] ECR II-1533 and Case T-9/93 *Schöller* v *Commission* [1995] ECR II-1611; Cases T-213/95 & 18/96 *Stichting Certificatie Kraanverhuurbedrijf* v *Commission* [1997] ECR II-1739.

[18] Cases 43 & 63/82 *VBVB, ibid*; Case T-29/92 *Vereniging van Samenwerkende Prijsregelende Organisatie in de Bouwnijverheid* v *Commission* [1995] ECR II-289.

to be heard, and there is a procedure for exercising it, prior to a final decision being adopted.[19] The Advisory Committee on Restrictive Practices and Monopolies, the composition and function of which is established by Regulation 17, is also required to be consulted.[20]

It will be observed that the four conditions are purely economic in character. There is no provision for, and the Commission has never deployed, consideration of other criteria, such as cultural or social benefits or requirements.[21] The four are cumulative and each must be met before exemption can be granted; if any one of the four is not satisfied exemption may be,[22] and latterly must be,[23] refused. Nevertheless, if the four are fulfilled exemption ought to be granted; the size of the undertakings involved, and so for example a risk that they might by the agreement achieve collective dominance in the relevant market, cannot of itself justify a refusal,[24] although it may increase the burden of meeting the Article 81(3) tests.[25] It is important to bear in mind that an exemption granted to some undertakings may confer upon them an (unfair?) advantage over their competitors, so the Commission ought closely to examine the criteria of Article 81(3) and the circumstances in which they arise in order to ensure that they are fairly met. The discretion enjoyed by the Commission requires that

respect of the rights guaranteed by the Community legal order in administrative procedures is of even more fundamental importance; those guarantees include, in particular, the duty of the [Commission] to examine carefully and impartially all the relevant aspects in the individual case.[26]

---

[19] Reg 17, art 19; Reg 2842/98, OJ 1998 L354/18 (repealing and replacing Reg 99/63, JO 1963, 2268).

[20] art 10(3)–(6).

[21] Although such considerations do not appear in Art 81(3) they do appear elsewhere in the Treaty. The Treaty provides six instances of 'integration' or 'comprehensive' clauses (*Querschnittsklausel*) whereby, in varying terms, the subject areas in question ought to form part of Community policy throughout its activities. There are integration clauses in the areas of environmental protection (Art 6 (ex Art 130r(2))), culture (Art 151(4) (ex Art 128(4))), public health (Art 152(1) (ex Art 129(1))), industry (Art 157(3) (ex Art 130(3))), economic and social cohesion (Art 159 (ex Art 130b)) and development cooperation (Art 178 (ex Art 130v)). The Commission could presumably incorporate these concerns into Art 81(3) reasoning, but it has never done so, at least expressly. The Court has, however, taken notice of Treaty adherence to social justice in order to determine whether collective bargaining falls within the scope of Art 81(1) – which it does not: Case C-67/96 *Albany International* v *Stichting Bedrijfspensioenfonds Textielindustrie* [1999] ECR I-5751.

[22] Cases 43 & 63/82 *Vereniging ter Bervordering van het Vlaamse Boekwezen* v *Commission* [1984] ECR 19.

[23] Case T-7/93 *Langnese-Iglo* v *Commission* [1995] ECR II-1533 and Case T-9/93 *Schöller* v *Commission* [1995] ECR II-1611; Cases T-213/95 & 18/96 *Stichting Certificatie Kraanverhuurbedrijf* v *Commission* [1997] ECR II-1739.

[24] Case T-17/93 *Matra Hachette* v *Commission* [1994] ECR II-595.

[25] Decision 1999/485 (*Europe Asia Trades Agreement*) OJ 1999 L193/23 at para 188.

[26] Cases T-528 etc/93 *Métropole Télévision* v *Commission* [1996] ECR II-649 at 683 (under appeal as Case C-320/96P *European Broadcasting Union* v *Commission*, pending).

It is nevertheless a wide discretion, and it must be said that the reasoning by which it finds the conditions satisfied is sometimes paper thin. In the light of a failure properly to justify it, the Court of First Instance annulled a decision granting exemption for the first time in 1996.[27]

Exemption, if granted, is for a specified period of time,[28] which must be sufficient to enable the beneficiaries to achieve the benefits justifying the exemption and make a proper return on investment.[29] It may provide for conditions and obligations,[30] and is renewable.[31] Exemption decisions must be published in the *Official Journal*.[32] The Commission may revoke exemption where there has been a material change in circumstances or, with retroactive effect, a party breaches a condition imposed upon it, the decision was based upon incorrect information or was induced by deceit, or the parties abuse the exemption granted.[33] In a recent decision the Commission granted an exemption with an extensive series of conditions attached and intimated ('considers') that a material (but not 'trivial') breach thereof would enable a national court to set the exemption aside;[34] it is not clear that the Commission has authority to make such provision or that a national court has the jurisdiction ostensibly recognised by it. An exemption allows an exception to the prohibition laid down in Article 81(1), so it must be interpreted restrictively to ensure that its effects are not extended to situations it is not intended to cover.[35]

4.2 Notification

Exemption from the prohibition of Article 81(1) can be granted only if the agreement has been 'notified' to the Commission.[36] This is not a mere formality but an 'indispensable condition' of exemption.[37] Thus, the Commission has said, for example, 'the absence of notification is in any

---

[27] Cases T-528 etc/93 *Métropole Télévision*, *ibid*; on judicial control of the Commission see pp 132–4 *infra*.

[28] Reg 17, art 8(1).

[29] Cases T-374 etc/94 *European Night Services* v *Commission* [1998] ECR II-3141.

[30] Reg 17, art 8(1).

[31] art 8(2). A request for renewal of an existing exemption need not comply with the formal requirements of notification, but may be made simply by letter: Case 75/84 *Metro-SB-Großmärkte* v *Commission* (*No 2*) [1986] ECR 3021.

[32] art 21.

[33] art 8(3).

[34] Decision 1999/781 (*British Interactive Broadcasting/Open*) OJ 1999 L312/1, para 192 and art 3.

[35] Cases T-70-1/92 *Florimex* v *Commission* [1997] ECR II-693; Case C-306/96 *Javico International* v *Yves Saint Laurent Parfums* [1998] ECR I-1983.

[36] Reg 17, art 4(1).

[37] Cases 100–103/80 *Musique Diffusion Française* v *Commission* (Pioneer) [1983] ECR 1825 at 1902.

event fatal and the case [for exemption] cannot be considered';[38] '[t]he ... agreement ... was not notified to the Commission .... For this reason alone individual exemption cannot be granted';[39] and '[t]he agreement and/or concerted practice ... has not been notified. By virtue of Article 4(1) of Regulation No 17, therefore, on procedural grounds alone no exemption can be granted',[40] and the Court of First Instance has confirmed the competence of a national court to strike down an agreement which might be eligible for exemption but which had not been notified.[41] The procedure for notification, the forms ('Form A/B') and guidance as to their use are laid down by regulations.[42] Use of Form A/B, which was modified in 1994[43] (and arguably made overly complex), is obligatory.[44] Notification may be made by any undertaking and any association of undertakings being a party to agreements or to concerted practices, and any association of undertakings adopting decisions or engaging in practices, which may fall within the scope of Article 81(1).[45] Any party to such an agreement or practice may notify it; other parties must be or ought to be informed.[46] Notification must be complete and proper in all respects, otherwise the agreement is deemed not to have been notified;[47] providing misleading or incorrect information intentionally or negligently can result in a fine of up to €5,000.[48] In the interests of legal certainty and adequate judicial protection the Commission must respond to a notification within a 'reasonable' period of time, reasonable to be determined in relation to the particular circumstances of the case.[49] Before granting an exemption the Commission

---

[38] Decision 84/405 (*Zinc Producer Group*) OJ 1984 L220/27 at para 87.

[39] Decision 95/477 (*BASF Lacke + Farben/Accinauto*) OJ 1995 L272/16 at para 98.

[40] Decision 1999/210 (*British Sugar/Tate & Lyle/Napier Brown/James Budgett*) OJ 1999 L76/1 at para 184.

[41] Case T-573/93 *Koelman* v *Commission* [1996] ECR II-1, upheld on appeal as Case C-59/96P *Koelman* v *Commission* [1997] ECR I-4809.

[42] Reg 17, arts 4, 5; Reg 3385/94, OJ 1994 L377/28 (repealing and replacing Reg 27/62, JO 1962, 1118). A different form ('Form TR') is used under the transport regulations: Reg 2843/98, OJ 1998 L354/22.

[43] Reg 3385/94, Annex.

[44] art 2(1); Cases 209–15 & 218/78 *van Landewyck* v *Commission* (FEDETAB) [1980] ECR 3125.

[45] art 1(1).

[46] The texts are ambiguous: Reg 3385/94, art 1(1) provides that a referring party 'shall give notice' to the other parties, but Form A/B, heading G provides that it 'should inform' them.

[47] Case 30/78 *Distillers* v *Commission* [1980] ECR 2229; Decision 85/206 (*Aluminium Imports from Eastern Europe*) OJ 1985 L92/1.

[48] Reg 17, art 15(1)(a); see eg Case 28/77 *Tepea* v *Commission* [1978] ECR 1391. It is proposed by the 1999 Commission White Paper (see pp 219–23 *infra*) that this sum be increased to €50,000.

[49] Cases T-213/95 & 18/96 *Stichting Certificatie Kraanverhuurbedrijf* v *Commission* [1997] ECR II-1739.

is required to publish a summary of the relevant notification in the *Official Journal* and allow 'interested third parties' to comment.[50] Even though not expressly provided in Regulation 17, information provided in notification enjoys a limited degree of privilege; it cannot be used for purposes other than those of the notification procedure, and cannot be used in national proceedings as evidence of infringement of national competition rules[51] – an important defence to national proceedings, as the Commission transmits (and is required to do so)[52] a copy of each notification to the competition authorities of each member state.

It is important to note that there is no legal obligation to notify an agreement to the Commission. Failure to notify does not of itself attract any penalty. The advantages of notification are essentially two: first, without it there can be no exemption (with two exceptions),[53] and without exemption an agreement is laid bare to the application of Article 81(1), both through Commission enforcement and in civil proceedings;[54] second, the Commission has the power to impose fines upon undertakings engaged in practices prohibited by Article 81(1),[55] but notification provides immunity from fines in respect of any act occurring after notification, the immunity being operative from the date of notification until the Commission adopts a formal decision refusing to grant exemption or, following a preliminary examination, issues a preliminary notice withdrawing immunity.[56] It is therefore not uncommon for an agreement to be notified when Commission enforcement proceedings are looming. But this may be bolting the door too late, as the parties are still liable to fines for conduct prior to the date of notification – although parties entertaining a short-term anti-competitive agreement might well elect to notify in order to insulate themselves from Commission fines during the period it takes the Commission to act upon the notification. In any event, notification of itself has no suspensory effect as to the enforceability of an agreement in civil proceedings: unless and until exempted, a notified agreement is liable to be struck down by a national court under Article 81(2).[57] It is also well to point out the risks of proceeding with a contract whilst its validity is in

---

[50] Reg 17, art 19(3).

[51] Case C-67/91 *Dirección General de Defensa de la Competencia* v *Asociación Española de Banca Privada* [1992] ECR I-4785. This does not prevent national authorities from initiating their own autonomous procedures in the light of information brought to their attention.

[52] Reg 17, art 10(1).

[53] ie, art 4(2) agreements and agreements benefiting from block exemption; see *infra*.

[54] See Chap 6.

[55] See Chap 6.

[56] Reg 17, art 15(5)(a) and (6).

[57] But see pp 211–12 *infra*.

(sometimes lengthy) limbo pending a Commission decision. To give but one illustration: in *ARD/Nefico*[58] a German television consortium (ARD) bought exclusive television rights to a 'library' of American films for a sizeable sum ($80 million) and notified the agreement to the Commission. It then sunk appreciable costs into the project (the fee, trawling the library, dubbing, sub-titling), only to be told by the Commission that it, the Commission, objected to the duration of exclusivity and the lack of access for third parties to the films. The American proprietors were unwilling to renegotiate and the Commission granted an exemption only upon unilateral undertakings given by ARD not to exercise some of the rights conferred by the agreement.[59] The consortium was left with an enforceable contract, but one which brought significantly fewer benefits than those originally negotiated, and doubtless one worth less than $80 million.

The disadvantage of notification is that it brings to the attention of the Commission, of national competition authorities, and of competitors conduct which undertakings might prefer to remain undisturbed by publicity, formal scrutiny and possibly censure. Nor may they be enthusiastic to answer detailed questions not only on matters under investigation but also on related activities. The Commission has also asserted the authority, having been notified of a proposed course of action and having refused exemption, to order the parties not to put it into effect;[60] whilst the Court of First Instance found that since Article 81(1) is binding as a matter of public policy upon undertakings irrespective of any Commission intervention and so such an order is declaratory only,[61] there seem few courses of conduct more likely to attract the Commission's interest and inclination to bring to bear its enforcement powers. And a final, if perhaps relatively minor, consideration is that, given the detailed information now required by Form A/B to be produced, including information not only about the agreement itself but also on the structure of the market, notification may be costly to a smaller undertaking in terms simply of the time and resources necessary to complete it. A decision to notify an agreement therefore falls to be considered from both legal and commercial standpoints by the various parties to it.

---

[58] Decision 89/536, OJ 1989 L284/36.

[59] To add insult to injury, the Americans challenged the exemption decision on the ground that it ought not to have been granted under any circumstances, but withdrew the action prior to judgment: Cases T-157 & 168/89 *Nefico & MGM/UA v Commission*, removed from the register by order of 5 May 1993, unreported.

[60] Decision 91/301 (*Ansac*) OJ 1991 L152/54; Decision 92/157 (*UK Agricultural Tractor Registration Exchange*) OJ 1992 L68/19; Decision 1999/485 (*Europe Asia Trades Agreement*) OJ 1999 L193/23.

[61] Case T-34/92 *Fiatagri UK & New Holland Ford v Commission* [1994] ECR II-905, upheld tacitly on appeal as Case C-8/95P *New Holland Ford v Commission* [1995] ECR I-3175.

4.3 Article 4(2) agreements

Article 4(2) of Regulation 17 relaxes the requirement to notify certain types of agreement, which may but need not be notified. These are agreements where:

(a) the parties are all domiciled in one member state and the agreement does not 'relate either to imports or to exports' between member states;

(b) the agreement is between two parties only, and does no more than impose restrictions upon (i) resale price maintenance or conditions of sale of the contract goods or (ii) the process(es) to be used in the exercise of the rights (ie, the specific subject matter)[62] of the assignee or licensee to an intellectual property right; or

(c) the sole object of the agreement is the development of uniform standards or types, joint research into improvement of production techniques, or specialisation where the parties enjoy less than 15 per cent of the relevant market and their combined annual turnover does not exceed €200 million.

However, in line with the Commission's new benevolence regarding vertical restraints,[63] in 1999 Article 4(2) was amended in order to extend its application to all vertical agreements regulating conditions of sale or resale, even if more than two undertakings are party to them (provided each is at a different level in the production or distribution chain), and including the marketing of services.[64] This has brought a great raft of agreements within the ambit of Article 4(2) and so increases appreciably its practical significance.

The exact status of Article 4(2) agreements remains unclear. An agreement which falls within Article 4(2) is *not* by that fact exempted from the prohibition of Article 81(1) – although given its nature, an agreement meeting the original Article 4(2) criteria may well fall outwith the prohibition because it does not affect trade between member states or, if it does, by application of the *de minimis* rule or the rule of reason,[65] and an agreement meeting the new Article 4(2) criteria may fall within a block exemption on vertical restraints.[66] Nor, notwithstanding the general principle of legitimate expectation, are they immune from Commission fines

---

[62] See Chap 10.

[63] See p 105 *supra*.

[64] Reg 17, art 4(2)(2)(a) as amended by Reg 1216/1999, OJ 1999, L148/5. The amendments also (necessarily) delete the provision indicated in (b) as far as (ii) above but leave the rest intact.

[65] See pp 71–5 and pp 99–101 *supra*.

[66] See *infra*.

under Regulation 17.[67] However, if the Commission carries out an investigation of an Article 4(2) agreement, it may grant exemption with effect retroactive to the date of the agreement, even though it was not notified;[68] and, if notified subsequently, exemption may be granted backdated to the date of the agreement.[69] A national court ought not therefore to strike down an Article 4(2) agreement in certain circumstances without first consulting the Commission.[70] Bearing all this in mind, any reliance upon Article 4(2) ought to be circumspect. The signal advantage of Article 4(2) is that it provides for retroactive exemption, so recasting the automatic nullity of Article 81(2) and increasing the reliability of unnotified contracts. Changes now proposed would render it otiose.[71]

4.4 Provisional validity

There is one exception to the rule that notification has no suspensory effect. The entry into force of the competition rules called into question the legality and enforceability of a great raft of existing agreements, decisions or practices, some of great venerability, so creating problems both of legal certainty and of swamping the Commission with the burden of determining whether exemption ought to be granted. Regulation 17 therefore provides that agreements, decisions and practices in force prior to the adoption of the Regulation (that is, March 1962) ought to have been notified to the Commission before November 1962.[72] From this the Court of Justice fashioned the concept of 'provisional validity', whereby if (and only if) so notified, the interests of legal certainty exempt the agreement or practice from the prohibition of Article 81(1), so rendering the agreement valid and the terms enforceable, until such time as the Commission responds to the notification.[73] Such agreements are commonly called 'old'

---

[67] Case 240/82 *Stichting Sigarettenindustrie* v *Commission* [1985] ECR 3831.

[68] Reg 17, art 6(2).

[69] See eg Decision 1999/230 (*Whitbread*) OJ 1999 L88/26; Decision 1999/473 (*Bass*) OJ 1999 L186/1; Decision 1999/474 (*Scottish & Newcastle*) OJ 1999 L186/28. There is no indication in the 1999 amendments as to whether they are intended to enable backdating of exemption prior to their entry into force, so it is possible that an older agreement meeting the new criteria may be exempted only from that date (18 June 1999).

[70] Case C-234/89 *Delimitis* v *Henninger Bräu* [1991] ECR I-935; see pp 211–12 *infra*.

[71] See pp 134–6 *infra*.

[72] Reg 17, art 5. Or, if a bilateral contract, before February 1963.

[73] eg, Case 13/61 *de Geus* v *Bosch* [1962] ECR 45; Case 10/69 *Portelange* v *Smith Corona Marchant* [1969] ECR 309; Case 48/72 *Brasserie de Haecht* v *Wilkin-Janssen (No 2)* [1973] ECR 77; Case 59/77 *de Bloos* v *Bouyer* [1977] ECR 2359. An art 4(2) agreement or practice, and so not required to be notified, existing in 1962 also enjoys provisional validity: Case 43/69 *Bilger* v *Jehle* [1970] ECR 127.

agreements.[74] Similar rules apply following accession of a new member state, so that agreements which are brought within the purview of Article 81 by virtue of accession may be notified to the Commission within six months of accession, and they too ('accession agreements') will enjoy provisional validity thereafter in the manner of old agreements.[75]

There are many thousands of notified old and accession agreements still gathering dust in the Commission's in-tray. So long as the Commission has not acted, provisional validity survives; there is no prescription.[76] The exact renewal of a standard contract enjoying provisional validity keeps the provisional validity alive.[77] Likewise, amendment to a contract enjoying provisional validity which renders the agreement *less* restrictive of competition will not affect its validity.[78] But where amendments reinforce or extend the restrictions, even minimally, or *a fortiori* introduce new restrictions, the agreement is deemed to have terminated and a new agreement, not enjoying provisional validity, has taken its place, unless the new or amended provisions can be severed.[79] Provisional validity terminates if and when the Commission adopts a decision on the application of Article 81(3). If the Commission refuses an exemption, the agreement is rendered void with retroactive effect.[80] It also terminates, bizarrely, in cases where the Commission closes the file or issues a comfort letter.[81] Thereafter national courts may apply the prohibition of Article 81(1) in accordance with Article 81(2).

4.5 Negative clearance

Application may also be made, in a like manner and on the same forms as exemption, for 'negative clearance'.[82] Negative clearance is *not* exemption; rather it is a declaration by the Commission that the agreement or practice

---

[74] Case 48/72 *Brasserie de Haecht (No 2)*, *ibid.*

[75] Reg 17, art 25. It is likely, but not yet certain, that unnotified accession agreements falling within art 4(2) also enjoy provisional validity.

[76] Case C-39/96 *Koninklijke Vereeniging ter Berevordering van de Belangen des Boekhandels* v *Free Record Shop* [1997] ECR I-2303.

[77] Case 1/70 *Marcel Rochas* v *Bitsch* [1970] ECR 515.

[78] Case 106/79 *Vereniging ter Bevordering van de Balangen der Boekhandels* v *Eldi Records* [1980] ECR 1137.

[79] Case C-39/96 *Koninklijke Vereeniging ter Berevordering van de Belangen des Boekhandels* v *Free Record Shop* [1997] ECR I-2303.

[80] Case 48/72 *Brasserie de Haecht* v *Wilkin-Janssen (No 2)* [1973] ECR 77.

[81] Case 99/79 *Lancôme* v *Etos* (Perfume) [1980] ECR 2511. As to comfort letters see *infra*.

[82] Reg 17, art 2. There is no provision for negative clearance under Reg 1017/68, JO 1968 L175/1 (rail, road and inland waterway transport) and Reg 4056/86, OJ 1986 L378/4 (maritime transport).

in question falls outwith the prohibition of Article 81(1) altogether.[83] It is appropriate to seek negative clearance where an agreement may (but may not) escape the prohibition as a result of *de minimis*[84] or rule of reason considerations, where an agreement ventures into new, untested fields, or where undertakings enter into complicated contractual arrangements and there are genuine questions as to the very application of Article 81. Frequently a notification will seek negative clearance and/or, in the alternative, exemption; and it is not uncommon for certain aspects of a complex agreement to be declared to fall outwith Article 81(1) (negative clearance), whilst others are then considered on their merits for the grant of exemption.[85] The duty of the Commission to respond within a reasonable period of time, to notify national competition authorities, to publish a summary of notification, to allow third parties to comment, to respect the rights of defence, to consult the Advisory Committee on Restrictive Practices and Monopolies and to publish final decisions in the *Official Journal* which applies to the granting of an exemption applies equally to the granting of negative clearance.[86]

Two points ought to be observed. First, whilst there can be no exemption from conduct infringing Article 82 – that is, abuse by an undertaking of a dominant position[87] – there may be serious questions as to whether an undertaking is, or may be, in a dominant position and whether a proposed course of conduct would constitute an abuse of that (possible) dominance. Negative clearance may therefore, unlike exemption, be sought within the context of Article 82. Second, negative clearance – which is a creation of Regulation 17, and is not provided for in the Treaty – is a declaration that, 'on the basis of the facts in its possession',[88] and *in the view of the Commission*, the agreement or conduct falls outwith the prohibitions of Articles 81 and 82. The declaration does not in the same way as exemption bind a national court,[89] which may, and is entitled to, take a different view

---

[83] *cf.* the different phrasing of a decision granting exemption ('the provisions of Article 81(1) of the Treaty are hereby declared inapplicable' to the agreement) with that of a decision granting negative clearance ('the Commission has no grounds for action under Article 81(1)' as regards the agreement).

[84] See pp 73–5 *supra*. In its 1997 notice on agreements of minor importance OJ 1997 C372/13 (see pp 73–5 *supra*) the Commission indicated (at para 4) that the tests it lays down 'should eliminate the need to have the legal status of agreements covered by it established through individual Commission decisions [for negative clearance, and] notification for this purpose will no longer be necessary'.

[85] eg Decision 1999/242 (*Télévision par Satellite*) OJ 1999 L90/6; Decision 1999/329 (*P & I Clubs*) OJ 1999 L125/12.

[86] Reg 17, arts 10, 19(3), 21; Reg 2842/98, OJ 1998 L354/18.

[87] See Chap 5.

[88] Reg 17, art 2.

[89] Case T-51/89 *Tetra Pak Rausing v Commission* (Tetra Pak I) [1990] ECR II-309 *per* acting A-G Kirschner at 324, 343.

as to whether an agreement or conduct falls within Article 81 or 82. A national court would of course be likely to accord significant weight to the Commission view; in England the Court of Appeal has said, in the context of a decision granting negative clearance, 'it is plain the court is bound to give very great weight to the decisions of the Commission',[90] and with the entry into force of the Competition Act 1998 British courts are under a statutory duty to 'have regard to any relevant decision or statement of the Commission' in determining a question of competition law.[91] However, whilst exemption is granted for a fixed period and is immutable during that period (unless revoked by the Commission or annulled by the Court of Justice), negative clearance is more of the nature of a 'snapshot'. The passage of time and any evolution of events – for example, growth of market share, new competitors entering the market, new or unforeseen barriers to market entry or other change in market conditions[92] – may therefore erode its reliability. In light of this, in a recent decision the Commission granted negative clearance but for a fixed period of time only.[93]

4.6 Block exemption

Article 81(3) envisages exemption granted not only to individual agreements, decisions or concerted practices but also to 'categories' thereof. Enabling authority to grant these 'block exemptions' was first conferred upon the Commission in 1965 by Regulation 19,[94] and it constitutes an important mechanism for the implementation of Commission policy in the competition field. The Council has authorised the adoption of block exemptions (if by different regulations and upon slightly differing conditions) which apply (a) to vertical agreements, that is, the parties to them operate at different levels of the production or distribution chain on the production, sale or resale of goods and services,[95] (b) to horizontal agreements addressing the application of standards or types, research and development or specialisation,[96] (c) to various aspects of transport[97] and (d) to agreements in the insurance sector.[98] The exemptions are set out in

---

[90] *Gibbs Mew* v *Gemmell* [1998] EuLR 588 *per* Peter Gibson LJ at 600.

[91] Competition Act 1998, s 60(3).

[92] See eg Decision 93/406 (*Langnese-Iglo*) OJ 1993 L183/19; upheld in Case T-7/93 *Langnese-Iglo* v *Commission* [1995] ECR II-1533 and on appeal as Case C-279/95P *Langnese-Iglo* v *Commission* [1998] ECR I-5609.

[93] Decision 1999/242 (*Télévision par Satellite*) OJ 1999 L90/6 (under review as Case T-112/99 *Métropole Télévision* v *Commission*, pending).

[94] Reg 19/65, JO 1965, 533.

[95] art 1(1).

[96] Reg 2821/71, JO 1971 L285/46.

[97] Reg 4056/86, OJ 1986 L378/4 (maritime transport); Reg 3976/87, OJ 1987 L374/9 (commercial air transport); Reg 479/92, OJ 1992 L55/3 (liner conferences).

[98] Reg 1534/91, OJ 1991 L143/1.

Commission regulations which for the most part lay down expressly permitted ('white list') and expressly prohibited ('black list') criteria for exemption.[99] The white list criteria vary from block exemption to block exemption depending upon their subject matter, but the black list criteria are fairly standard, embracing the 'hardcore restrictions' of retail price maintenance, tying/non-compete clauses, restrictions on resale (excepting active sales in other contract territories and legitimate selective distribution), after-market sales restrictions and any combination of clauses which produce absolute territorial protection. An agreement which falls within the white list criteria and offends none of the black list criteria is, without need for notification, automatically exempt from the prohibition of Article 81(1). Undertakings remain free of course to notify an agreement which they fear might fall outwith a block exemption, in effect for a declaration that it does fall within the block exemption, but if not, for individual exemption. Some block exemption regulations further provide that elements of an agreement ('grey' in character) which do not fall entirely within the stated criteria may be notified to the Commission in accordance with the block exemption and will be automatically exempt unless the Commission objects (starts 'opposition procedure') within, normally, six months.[100] Otherwise, agreements are exempt only if they fall wholly within the four corners of the relevant regulation; a national court may not sever provisions in order to bring it within the block exemption.[101] As with individual exemption, because block exemptions constitute a derogation from the general prohibition laid down in Article 81(1) their terms must be strictly construed.[102] Where an agreement falls within a block exemption but nevertheless produces effects incompatible with the criteria of Article 81(3) the exemption may be withdrawn by the Commission[103] or, since 1999, by a national competition authority which can show the characteristics of a distinct market within its jurisdiction[104] with retroactive effect. It is also important to note that whilst an agreement falling within a block

---

[99] This was a requirement of Reg 19/65, art 1(2) and is a requirement of Reg 2821/71, art 1(2). By amendments made to art 1(2) in 1999 (see *infra*) it is no longer necessary to provide a white list in Reg 19 block exemptions.

[100] Reg 240/96 (technology transfer; n 114 *infra*) provides for four months, the transport regulations (nn 110 and 112 *infra*) 90 days.

[101] Case C-234/89 *Delimitis* v *Henninger Bräu* [1991] ECR I-935; Case C-230/96 *Cabour* v *Arnor 'SOCO'* [1998] ECR I-2055; applied by the Court of Appeal in England in *Byrne* v *Tibisco*, judgment of 27 May 1999, not yet reported.

[102] Case T-9/92 *Peugeot* v *Commission* [1993] ECR II-493; Case C-70/93 *Bayerische Motorenwerke* v *ALD Auto-Leasing* [1995] ECR I-3439; Case C-266/93 *Bundeskartellamt* v *Volkswagen* [1995] ECR I-3477; Cases T-24 etc/93 *Compagnie Maritime Belge* v *Commission* [1996] ECR II-1201.

[103] Reg 19/65, art 7(1).

[104] art 7(2); as this is a product of amendments made to Reg 19 in 1999 (see *infra*) it applies only to block exemption regulations adopted by authority of Reg 19.

exemption will escape the prohibition of Article 81(1), it may still be subject to the discipline of Article 82 if one or more of the parties is in a dominant position and the agreement could be construed as abusive, which is far less likely to be so in the case of an individual exemption.[105] Two block exemption regulations in fact provide expressly that the Commission may withdraw the benefit of block exemption if conduct within its parameters falls foul of Article 82,[106] and a number of them provide in a preambular recital that exemption by it is without prejudice to/does not preclude/exclude the application of Article 82.[107]

As at 1 June 2000 block exemptions are in force regulating the following fields:

- specialisation agreements;[108]
- research and development agreements;[109]
- maritime transport;[110]
- agreements in the insurance sector;[111]
- commercial air transport agreements;[112]
- motor vehicle distribution and servicing agreements;[113]
- technology transfer;[114]

---

[105] In Case T-51/89 *Tetra Pak Rausing* v *Commission* (Tetra Pak I) [1990] ECR II-309, an undertaking in a dominant position (and so subject to Art 82) had acquired an exclusive licence to work a patent. The licensing agreement fell within block exemption Reg 2349/84 (n 114 *infra*), and it was argued that this automatic exemption from Art 81(1) must logically set aside the prohibition of Art 82. The Court of First Instance distinguished between agreements benefiting from block exemption and those benefiting from individual exemption. The former was, effectively, fortuitous, but the latter required active consideration by the Commission of the circumstances and benefits of the agreement, the characteristics of which relevant to Art 82 'may be taken to have been established', and so would implicitly amount to negative clearance of the Art 82 aspects of the agreement.

[106] Reg 4056/86 (maritime transport; n 110 *infra*) and Reg 823/2000 (liner shipping consortia; n 116 *infra*), arts 8(2) and 12(c) respectively.

[107] eg, Reg 2790/1999 (vertical agreements; n 115 *infra*), recital 16.

[108] Reg 417/85, OJ 1985 L53/1. For the draft of an amended version see OJ 2000 C118/10.

[109] Reg 418/85, OJ 1985 L53/5. For the draft of an amended version see OJ 2000 C118/4.

[110] Reg 4056/86, OJ 1986 L378/4. This regulation applies arts 81 and 82 to maritime transport generally, but also contains elements of block exemption in arts 3 and 6.

[111] Reg 3932/92, OJ 1992 L398/7.

[112] Reg 1617/93, OJ 1993 L155/18 (schedules, joint operation, tariff consultation and slot allocation at airports; subsequently amended by Reg 1523/96, OJ 1996 L190/11); Reg 3652/93, OJ 1993 L333/37 (computer reservation systems; replacing Reg 83/91, OJ 1991 L10/9). Both regulations apply with retroactive effect.

[113] Reg 1475/95, OJ 1995 L145/25 (replacing Reg 123/85, OJ 1985 L15/16).

[114] Reg 240/96, OJ 1996 L31/2 (replacing both Reg 2349/84, OJ 1984 L219/15 on patent licensing agreements and Reg 556/89, OJ 1989 L61/1 on know-how agreements).

- vertical agreements;[115] and
- agreements within liner shipping consortia.[116]

The block exemptions are sometimes criticised for lacking suppleness in that, generally,[117] they take no account of the market strength of the parties (except insofar as their benefits may be expressly withdrawn in a particular case, a cumbersome procedure). The counterbalance is that they allow for a (relatively) high degree of legal certainty. However, because of both the narrowness of their strictures and the tendency of undertakings, craving legal certainty, to adhere conservatively within them they are sometimes also criticised for discouraging innovation in commercial dealing. Whilst block exemptions do not oblige contracting parties to align to them the contents of their agreements – rather merely laying down conditions which, if satisfied, exclude the application of Article 81(1)[118] – the attraction of so doing means that they have developed into types of standard form contracts.

By far and away the most commonly deployed of the block exemptions is the (new) block exemption on vertical restraints, which calls for particular comment. The original Regulation 19 restricted block exemption to agreements to which only two undertakings were party and which addressed the purchase and sale of goods for resale.[119] The fruit of this power was the first, and for many years only, block exemption adopted in 1967 on exclusive dealing.[120] In 1983 it was split into two block exemptions governing exclusive distribution[121] and exclusive purchasing.[122] A specialist block exemption, on franchising, was adopted subsequently in 1988.[123] However, the 1997 Commission Green Paper on vertical restraints in competition policy[124] and the 1998 follow-up draft paper to it[125] recommended the adoption of a more 'economic' approach to vertical restraints. As a result, in 1999 Regulation 19 was amended by the Council so as to authorise the Commission to adopt a block exemption regulation applying to vertical agreements (each party operating at different levels of

---

[115] Reg 2790/1999, OJ 1999 L336/21 (replacing Reg 1983/83 OJ 1983, L173/1 on exclusive distribution agreements, Reg 1984/83, OJ 1983 L173/5 on exclusive purchasing agreements and Reg 4087/88, OJ 1988 L359/46 on franchising agreements).

[116] Reg 823/2000, OJ 2000 L100/24 (replacing Reg 870/95, OJ 1995 L89/7).

[117] An important exception is Reg 2790/1999 (vertical agreements); see *infra*.

[118] Case 10/86 *VAG France v Magne* [1986] ECR 4071; Case C-230/96 *Cabour v Arnor 'SOCO'* [1998] ECR I-2055.

[119] Reg 19/65, art 1(1) prior to 1999.

[120] Reg 67/67, JO 1967, 849.

[121] Reg 1983/83, OJ 1983 L173/1.

[122] Reg 1984/83, OJ 1983 L173/5.

[123] Reg 4087/88, OJ 1988 L359/46.

[124] COM (96) 721 final; see p 105 *supra*.

[125] COM (98) 544 final.

the chain of production, distribution or sale) to which any number of undertakings are party and extending to the provision of services.[126] Using this new power the Commission adopted a single block exemption regulation on vertical restraints[127] which applies from 1 June 2000[128] and replaces the three previous vertical block exemptions (exclusive distribution, exclusive purchasing and franchising) which, having been renewed several times beyond their originally intended shelf life, expired at the end of May 2000.[129] It applies to

> agreements or concerted practices entered into between two or more undertakings each of which operates, for the purposes of the agreement, at a different level of the production or distribution chain, and relating to the conditions under which the parties may purchase, sell or resell certain goods or services ('vertical agreements')[130]

except those involving (a) a supplier or a buyer which enjoys a market share exceeding 30 per cent of the relevant market,[131] (b) an association of distributors with a combined annual turnover exceeding €50 million[132] and (c) competing undertakings (entering into a non-reciprocal vertical agreement) where the buyer is a manufacturer (and not merely a distributor) with an annual turnover exceeding €100 million.[133] The regulation provides a black list excluding certain hardcore restraints, principally the imposition of fixed or minimum resale prices,[134] certain resale conditions and forms of territorial protection (including passive (but not active) sales outwith the contract territory),[135] 'non-compete' clauses except of short duration,[136] restraints following termination of the agreement[137] and cer-

---

[126] Reg 19 as amended by Reg 1215/1999, OJ 1999 L148/1, art 1(1).

[127] Reg 2790/1999, OJ 1999 L336/21.

[128] art 13.

[129] art 12(1). An 18-month grace period is provided for agreements concluded before 1 June 2000 which fall within any of the three existing block exemptions but not within the new block exemption: art 12(2). The new regulation does not apply to vertical restraints which fall within other block exemption regulations: art 2(5). The block exemption on motor vehicle distribution (Reg 1475/95) is not scheduled to expire until 2002, when the Commission will re-examine it.

[130] art 2(1).

[131] art 3. Market share is to be calculated in accordance with criteria provided in art 9.

[132] art 2(2). Annual turnover is to be calculated in accordance with criteria provided in art 10.

[133] art 1(4). The Commission had proposed that this be written into Reg 19 (Commission proposal for a Council Regulation amending Regulation No 19/65, COM (98) 546 final) but on it the regulation remained silent.

[134] art 4(a).

[135] art 4(b), (c).

[136] art 5(a).

[137] art 5(b).

tain sales restrictions within a selective distribution system,[138] but sets out no white list. The Commission and national competition authorities (which can show within their territory the characteristics of a distinct geographic market) may withdraw the benefits of exemption in a particular case where a vertical agreement falling within the regulation nevertheless produces effects incompatible with Article 81(3);[139] the Commission may do so with blanket effect, by regulation and without showing incompatibility with Article 81(3), where parallel networks of similar vertical restraints cover more than 50 per cent of a relevant market.[140] And, as is the case with some block exemption regulations, the application of Article 82 is expressly saved.[141] The regulation will, says the Commission, create a 'safe harbour' for vertical agreements,[142] especially for parties which are small and medium-sized undertakings, and allow for a greater degree of suppleness, lessening the 'straightjacket' effect of present block exemptions, without sacrificing legal certainty.[143]

4.7 Comfort letters

Formal exemption or negative clearance for a notified agreement can be granted only by a Commission decision. In practice such decisions are rare, and response to a notification often consists in a 'comfort letter' (or 'administrative letter'). The vast majority of cases (about 95 per cent)[144] are now resolved by 'closing the file' in this way; Form A/B asks whether the applicant(s) would be satisfied with a comfort letter in lieu of a formal decision, and warns that a procedure will be terminated with the issue of a comfort letter 'except in cases of particular legal, economic or political importance' (exemption) or 'only where an important problem of interpretation has to be solved' (negative clearance).[145] A comfort letter is issued by the Competition Directorate-General, not by the Commission proper, where it is satisfied upon the information before it that the agreement does not infringe Article 81(1), or, if it does, that it would qualify for an exemption. It states that the Commission takes the view that there is no reason to intervene in the matter or to proceed to a final decision. Before issuing a

---

[138] arts 4(c), (d) and 5(c).

[139] arts 6, 7.

[140] art 8.

[141] Recital 16.

[142] Guidelines on vertical restraints attached to the draft regulation, OJ 1999 C270/12, Chap III.1.

[143] Commission proposal for a Council Regulation amending Regulation No 19/65, COM (98) 546 final, Explanatory Memorandum.

[144] Tabulated from data for 1993–98 supplied in EC Commission, *XXVIIIth Report on Competition Policy* (1998), p 59.

[145] Form A/B, headings II.2 and II.1.

comfort letter the Commission may publish a notice consisting of a summary of the contents of a notified agreement in the *Official Journal* and invite interested parties to submit observations,[146] after which it may issue a more formal comfort letter with 'enhanced' value.

Comfort letters are a product of the Commission's inability adequately to cope with its workload, but they are not a happy solution to it. A comfort letter, which can be issued only in respect of a properly notified agreement, does *not* constitute exemption or negative clearance.[147] The agreement is and continues to be immune from Commission fines as it remains notified, unless the Commission reopens the file (as latterly it expressly reserves the right to do) and alters its views where new information comes to light, there has been a material change in circumstances or the comfort letter was based upon incomplete or incorrect information.[148] But it does not bind national courts, which are 'perfectly free to reach a different decision'[149] and not precluded from holding that Articles 81(1) or 82 apply and that the agreement or conduct is illegal. A comfort letter 'constitutes a factor'[150] or a 'factual element',[151] or 'merely constitutes an element of fact of which the national courts may take account'[152] or are 'entirely at liberty to take into account'[153] in determining whether this is so; greater weight may be attached to a comfort letter following publication in the *Official Journal*. However, as comfort letters are not required to be published it may be that a national judge does not know if submissions were made to the Commission or of the market conditions and facts which underpinned its reasoning. Worst of all, the terms of a comfort letter issued in response to notification for exemption (as opposed to notification for

---

[146] See Reg 17, art 19(3). Care should be taken as third parties are frequently afforded very short notice to submit observations.

[147] Cases 253/78 & 1–3/79 *Procureur de la République* v *Giry et Guerlain* [1980] ECR 2327; Case 99/79 *Lancôme* v *Etos* [1980] ECR 2511; Case 37/79 *Marty* v *Lauder* [1980] ECR 2481 (the Perfume Cases); Case 31/80 *L'Oréal* v *de Nieuwe* [1980] ECR 3775.

[148] Case 31/80 *L'Oréal, ibid, per* A–G Reischl at 3803; Case 107/82 *AEG-Telefunken* v *Commission* [1983] ECR 3151; Case T-7/93 *Langnese-Iglo* v *Commission* [1995] ECR II-1533 and Case T-9/93 *Schöller* v *Commission* [1995] ECR II-1611, the former upheld on appeal as Case C-279/95P *Langnese-Iglo* v *Commission* [1998] ECR I-5609. It appears that the Commission must justify a decision to reopen an investigation by reference to these criteria: Case T-241/97 *Stork Amsterdam* v *Commission*, judgment of 17 February 2000, not yet reported.

[149] Case 31/80 *L'Oréal, ibid per* A-G Reischl at 3802; also Case T-241/97 *Stork Amsterdam, ibid*.

[150] Case 37/79 *Marty* v *Lauder* [1980] ECR 2481 at 2499; Case T-241/97 *Stork Amsterdam, ibid* at para 84.

[151] Notice on co-operation between national courts and the Commission in applying Articles 85 and 86 of the EEC Treaty, OJ 1993 C39/6, para 25.

[152] Case 31/80 *L'Oréal* v *de Nieuwe* [1980] ECR 3775 at 3790.

[153] Case T-241/97 *Stork Amsterdam* v *Commission*, judgment of 17 February 2000, not yet reported, at para 85.

negative clearance – sometimes referred to as 'soft negative clearance') may be such as to imply that the agreement is *prima facie* inconsistent with Article 81(1) (a 'discomfort letter' in the jargon), and so, absent the formal exemption, may be of the nature of a poisoned chalice. The Commission may, but apparently need not, re-open consideration of a notification for exemption if the matter becomes the subject of national litigation.[154]

4.8 Judicial review of exemption decisions

A Commission decision granting[155] or refusing[156] exemption is a decision within the meaning of Article 249 (ex Article 189) of the Treaty and so subject to judicial review by the Court of First Instance or the Court of Justice under Article 230 (ex Article 173) of the Treaty (the action of annulment). Proceedings are normally brought by a disgruntled undertaking refused an exemption (and sometimes an undertaking granted exemption but disgruntled by terms attached thereto)[157] – that is, the addressee of the decision, and so entitled as of right to challenge it.[158] Third (private) parties wishing to challenge a decision must show that it affects them directly and individually,[159] tests for title and interest being generally very difficult to meet.[160] Review of a Commission decision raised by a private person goes, since its creation in 1989, to the Court of First Instance, from which there is appeal to the Court of Justice on a point of law only.[161]

A Commission (and generally a Community) act is liable to judicial review only if it is definitive and it is not provisional as a step in an ongoing administrative procedure.[162] A decision granting or refusing exemption clearly falls within this category. But the Court of Justice has held that a

---

[154] See Chap 6.

[155] eg, Case T-19/92 *Leclerc* v *Commission* [1996] ECR II-1851; Case T-87/92 *Kruidvat* v *Commission* [1996] ECR II-1931; Cases T-528 etc/93 *Métropole Télévision* v *Commission* [1996] ECR II-649.

[156] Case C-360/92P *Publishers Association* v *Commission* [1995] ECR I-23; Case T-34/92 *Fiatagri & New Holland Ford* v *Commission* [1994] ECR II-905 and Case T-35/92 *John Deere* v *Commission* [1994] ECR II-957, both upheld on appeal as Case C-7/95P *John Deere* v *Commission* [1998] ECR I-3111 and Case C-8/95P *New Holland Ford* v *Commission* [1998] ECR I-3175; Cases T-213/95 & 18/96 *Stichting Certificatie Kraanverhuurbedrijf* v *Commission* [1997] ECR II-1739.

[157] eg, Cases T-374 etc/94 *European Night Services* v *Commission* [1998] ECR II-3141.

[158] EC Treaty, Art 230(4).

[159] *Ibid.*

[160] See pp 189–90 *infra.*

[161] EC Treaty, Art 225 (ex Art 168a); Decision 88/591 (establishing the Court of First Instance) as amended, OJ 1993 L144/21.

[162] See pp 188–9 *infra.*

comfort letter is a provisional act and so does not.[163] It appears that a decision granting negative clearance does not change the legal situation or adversely affect the interests of the addressee, but it does affect the interests of third parties[164] – the (arguably) perverse result of which is that such a decision may be challenged by third parties (provided they can show sufficient standing) but not by the addressee. The matter is again before the Court of First Instance.[165]

The grounds for review are provided in the Treaty.[166] The Court will annul a decision granting or refusing exemption where the Commission has failed to comply with an essential procedural requirement, where the decision is insufficiently reasoned, or where it disagrees with the Commission's assessment or interpretation of the facts or of the law, or both.[167]

It is possible that a question on the validity of a Commission decision granting (but not refusing) exemption could arise in civil proceedings before a national court,[168] although some parties to those proceedings may be estopped from raising it.[169] Were this to occur, the court would be bound by any decision of the Court of First Instance or the Court of Justice, either as *res judicata* or in order to obviate an abuse of process.[170] If proceedings had not been taken to either court (or had been by a third party but declared inadmissible for lack of title and interest),[171] the national court would have the option of finding the decision unobjectionable; but if it was minded to agree with the argument that the decision was legally flawed, it would be obliged to refer the question of its validity to

---

[163] Cases 253/78 & 1–3/79 *Procureur de la République* v *Giry et Guerlain* [1981] ECR 2327; Case 99/79 *Lancôme* v *Etos* [1980] ECR 2511; Case 37/79 *Marty* v *Lauder* [1980] ECR 2481 (the Perfume Cases); Case 31/80 *L'Oréal* v *de Nieuwe* [1980] ECR 3775.

[164] Implicit in Case 26/76 *Metro-SB-Großmärkte* v *Commission* (No 1) [1977] ECR 1875; express consideration of the issue in Case T-138/89 *Nederlandse Bankiersvereniging* v *Commission* [1992] ECR II-2181.

[165] Case T-112/99 *Métropole Télévision* v *Commission*, pending.

[166] EC Treaty, Art 230(1); see pp 190–91 *infra*.

[167] Case C-260/92P *Publishers Association* v *Commission* [1995] ECR I-23; Cases T-528 etc/93 *Métropole Télévision* v *Commission* [1996] ECR II-649; Cases T-374 etc/94 *European Night Services* v *Commission* [1998] ECR II-3141. For more detailed consideration of judicial control of the Commission see Chap 6.

[168] Recognised *obiter* in Case T-87/92 *Kruidvat* v *Commission* [1996] ECR II-1931, upheld on appeal as Case C-70/97P *Kruidvat* v *Commission* [1998] ECR I-7183.

[169] Applying Case C-188/92 *TWD Textilwerke Deggendorf* v *Germany* [1994] ECR I-833 by analogy, only parties without clear standing to raise annulment proceedings directly before the Court of First Instance under Art 230 (so excluding at the least any addressee of a Commission decision) would be entitled to plead the illegality of a decision in civil proceedings: applied in *Iberian UK Ltd* v *BPB Industries* [1997] EuLR 1 (Ch).

[170] *Iberian UK Ltd, ibid.*

[171] eg, Case T-87/92 *Kruidvat* v *Commission* [1996] ECR II-1931, upheld on appeal as Case C-70/97P *Kruidvat* v *Commission* [1998] ECR I-7183.

the Court of Justice for a preliminary ruling under Article 234 (ex Article 177), for only the Court of Justice and the Court of First Instance have jurisdiction to invalidate (Article 234) or annul (Article 230) a Community act.[172]

4.9 Reform

In April 1999 the Commission produced a White Paper proposing reform to the enforcement of the competition rules,[173] amongst which are significant changes to the application of Article 81(3). This was a bold step not only in the breadth of possible reform, but also in that it was produced by a Commission which had resigned *en masse* a month earlier and remained in office discharging what on one view ought to be caretaker functions only.[174] The meaning of Article 81(1) cannot of course be altered by the Community institutions; only the authorities competent to amend the Treaty (the '*Herren der Vertrag*')[175] can do that. But the *application* of Article 81(1) through the device of the exemption power of Article 81(3), which is given effect by Regulation 17 which *is* a creation of the institutions, is, at least insofar as the parameters set by Article 81(3) so permit, up for grabs (although the changes proposed will probably also require amendment to the EEA Agreement, so vesting, ironically, non-member states with a veto which individual Community member states do not enjoy[176]). According to the White Paper the Commission monopoly on the power of exemption, and the consequent plethora of notifications to it, has been justified in order to enable the Commission to establish the uniform meaning and parameters of Article 81(1) – 'to build up a coherent body of precedent cases, and to ensure that the competition rules are applied consistently throughout the Member States'.[177] Now, however, following more than 35 years of Commission activity (and case law of the Court of Justice)

---

[172] Case 314/85 *Foto-Frost* v *Hauptzollamt Lübeck-Ost* [1987] ECR 4199.

[173] White Paper on Modernisation of the Rules Implementing Articles 85 and 86 of the EC Treaty, Commission Programme No 99/027.

[174] The Commission resigned in March 1999 owing to a damning 'Wise Men' report on corruption and maladministration (First Report by the Committee of Independent Experts on allegations of fraud, mismanagement and nepotism in the European Commission, 15 March 1999). Article 215 (ex Art 159) of the Treaty provides that a Commission which is censured by the Parliament and/or resigns stays in office until replaced, which in the event did not occur until six months later.

[175] See Chap 2, n 16.

[176] As a matter of Community law Reg 17 may be amended by qualified majority vote in the Council (EC Treaty, Art 83(1) (ex Art 87(1))) but the consent also of the EEA Joint Committee, which requires the consent of the EFTA states 'speaking with one voice' (EEA Agreement, Art 93(2)), would probably be necessary; see p *295 infra*.

[177] White Paper, para 76.

the law is 'clarified' and 'more predictable',[178] it consists of a 'set of clear rules'[179] and the conditions for exemption under Article 81(3) 'have been largely clarified by case-law and decision-making practice and are known to undertakings'.[180] The centralised system of Regulation 17 is therefore 'cumbersome, inefficient and impose[s] excessive burdens on economic operators'[181] and is 'no longer consistent with the effective supervision of competition'.[182] After canvassing a number of options for reform the White Paper appears to come down in support of the adoption of a 'directly applicable exemption system' (*exception légale*) and '*ex post* control'[183] whereby legislation adopted under Article 83 (ex Article 87) would scrap the notification system (except for partial function production joint ventures, at present subject to Article 81 but which will be absorbed into the Merger Regulation[184]) and require that all national competition authorities and all national courts before which Article 81(1) was raised also apply Article 81(3). The whole of Article 81, sundered by Regulation 17, would therefore be reunited, parties could rely directly upon Article 81(3), and restrictive practices prohibited by Article 81(1) but which meet the criteria of Article 81(3) would be valid and enforceable from the time they were concluded without need of a prior decision to that effect. Similarly, restrictive practices which meet the criteria of Article 81(3) and so are valid *ab initio* would cease to be valid if, and at the point at which, the conditions for exemption were no longer fulfilled. In other words, Article 81(3) would become directly effective.

This is a bold turn indeed – 'a lifelong devout Catholic suddenly converting him/herself to Protestantism'.[185] It may even verge upon unconstitutionality, for in providing in Article 81(3) that '[t]he provisions of paragraph 1 may ... *be declared* inapplicable' the Treaty may necessarily countenance a declaratory legislative/administrative scheme such as that which obtains at present, and a directly effective Article 81(3) – one which confers this declaratory power upon the courts in the course of private litigation – would be inconsistent with it. This is the view at least of the German[186] and Austrian[187] governments. But assuming that authority to

---

[178] para 48.

[179] para 51.

[180] para 78.

[181] para 42.

[182] para 9.

[183] paras 69 *et seq*.

[184] paras 79–81; as to the Merger Regulation see Chap 8.

[185] J. Nazerali & D. Cowan, 'Modernising the Enforcement of EU Competition Rules – Can the Commission Claim to be Preaching to the Converted?' [1999] ECLR 422 at 422.

[186] Stellungnahme der Bundesregierung zum Weissbuch der Europäischen Kommission über die Modernisierung der Vorschriften zur Anwendung der Artikel 81 und 82 EGV, 29. Oktober 1999.

[187] Österreichische Position zum Weissbuch der Europäischen Kommission über die Modernisierung der Anwendung der Art. 81 und 82 EG-V, undated.

make this change falls properly within the competence of the Council 'to lay down detailed rules for the application of Article 81(3)'[188] it is nonetheless a radical proposal. If it is followed up it will free the Commission from its present onerous task of processing notifications and so allow it to concentrate its resources in other areas as it sees fit. But it will also self evidently mark a far-reaching change to the enforcement of Article 81. Much of what has been discussed in this chapter – notification, article 4(2) of Regulation 17 and provisional validity – will become redundant. It will have a wider impact upon the law generally. The rule of reason, for example, at present an (elusive) aspect of the interpretation of Article 81(1) *simpliciter*, would also become redundant by, or become homogenised with, directly effective consideration of the Article 81(3) criteria. Other aspects will change out of all recognition. The concurrent reform of the block exemption system, for example, which is stated to be a complement to the White Paper proposals, *prima facie* makes no sense if Article 81(3) is to become directly effective. The Commission view is that it has a utility as a means of defining more precisely the scope of Article 81(3); but it is inevitable that there will be disharmony between the Commission view of Article 81(3) and that of various national authorities and courts. The proposals will necessarily bring about fundamental problems of regulating the relationship amongst the Commission, national competition authorities and national courts and possibly imperil the uniform application of the law. These issues will be considered in Chapter 6.

---

[188] EC Treaty, Art 83(2)(b).

CHAPTER 5

Article 82

5.1 General

Whilst Article 81 (ex Article 85) is concerned with distortion to competition which is the product of collaboration between or amongst undertakings, Article 82 (ex Article 86) is concerned more with the unilateral conduct of single undertakings which alone enjoy such market power that they are not bound by the discipline of competitive forces which (ought to) mark the play of the market. The natural target for regulation such as that laid down by Article 82 is the monopoly. But it casts its nets wider than this, so bringing other undertakings within its discipline.

There are a number of ways that monopolies may be addressed by competition rules. One of course is to ignore them, and allow them to carry on as they will unhindered. Another is to ban them outright: that the market power of the monopolist is inherently and intolerably incompatible to even workable competition, and they ought not to be allowed to persist. This is in part the approach of American antitrust law under section 2 of the Sherman Act, the text of which addresses the acquisition of monopoly power and not its exploitation, and is the reason why, for example, Standard Oil was broken up in 1911, American Telephone and Telegraph in 1984, and Microsoft is currently waging mortal battle in the American courts on its monopoly on access to the Internet.[1] A third approach is that they are not necessarily undesirable, or at least that the imbalance they bring to the market is outweighed by other factors – that statutory monopolies are economically and socially efficient, that some markets even without statutory regulation will evolve into natural monopolies, that only monopolies, or at least powerful undertakings, will enjoy the resources and security necessary to pursue and risk adventurous research and develop-

---

[1] For the text of s 2 see p 16 *supra*. Even under the Sherman Act acquisition of monopoly power is prohibited only if it is 'wilful' and not if it is a product of 'growth or development as a consequence of a superior product, business acumen or historic accident': *United States v Grinnell Corp* 384 US 563 (1966).

ment[2] – but that care must be taken to ensure that they do not, or cannot, take unfair advantage of their privileged market position. This latter approach is the one adopted by the Treaty. And, as will be seen, Article 82 is concerned not solely with the conduct of monopolies but also with undertakings enjoying less than monopolistic, yet still substantial, market power.

Article 82 reads:

Any abuse by one or more undertakings of a dominant position within the common market or in a substantial part of it shall be prohibited as incompatible with the common market in so far as it may affect trade between Member States.

Such abuse may, in particular, consist in:

(a) directly or indirectly imposing unfair purchase or selling prices or other unfair trading conditions;

(b) limiting production, markets or technical development to the prejudice of consumers;

(c) applying dissimilar conditions to equivalent transactions with other trading parties, thereby placing them at a comparative disadvantage;

(d) making the conclusion of contracts subject to acceptance by the other parties of supplementary obligations which, by their nature or according to commercial usage, have no connection with the subject of such contracts.

So Article 82 addresses expressly not monopolies, but rather undertakings in a 'dominant position'. It does not outlaw monopolies as such: there is no 'recrimination' (*reproche*) attached to the existence of market dominance,[3] even monopolistic dominance. Rather it prohibits 'any abuse ... of a dominant position'. Most other language versions of the Treaty refer instead to 'the abusive exploitation of a dominant position'.[4] In any event, the concepts are difficult to define. Like Article 81(1), a series of examples of prohibited conduct is provided, and it will be seen that, save for agreements envisaging the sharing of markets or sources of supply,[5] the examples of abusive conduct are identical *mutatis mutandis* to the examples of agreements proscribed by Article 81(1). Equally so, the list is exemplicative ('abuse may, *in particular*, consist in:'), not exhaustive, and a host of infringements of Article 82 have been found to exist beyond the examples given. It is also worth recalling that whilst there is no possibility of exemption from the prohibition of Article 82 analogous to that of Article 81(3), an undertaking which is, or may be, in a dominant position and which proposes to follow a course of conduct which may, or may not

---

[2] *Per contra* the argument that dominant undertakings will tend to absorb smaller firms which are responsible for much innovation.

[3] Case 322/81 *Michelin* v *Commission* [1983] ECR 3461 at 3511.

[4] eg, in the original language versions, 'd'exploiter de façon abusive une position dominante'; 'die mißbräuchliche Ausnutzung einer beherrschenden Stellung'; 'lo sfruttamento abusivo ... di una posizione dominante'; but *cf.* 'misbruik ... van een machtspositie', which is closer to the English.

[5] EC Treaty, Art 81(1)(c).

be, abusive may notify the Commission seeking negative clearance.[6]

Abuse of a dominant position therefore has two consecutive components: market dominance, which is not prohibited, and abusive exploitation of that dominance, which is. A third hurdle necessary to bring Article 82 into play is that the abusive conduct may affect trade between member states. For this the tests to be applied are essentially the same as those which apply to Article 81, that is that it must be possible to foresee with a sufficient degree of probability and on the basis of objective factors of law or fact that abuse of a dominant position may have an influence, direct or indirect, actual or potential, on the pattern of trade between member states such as might prejudice the realisation of the aim of a single market.[7] As with Article 81, it does not mean that the abuse must actually have affected trade; rather it is sufficient to establish only that the conduct is capable of having such an effect.[8] And it does not matter that the conduct is confined to a single member state so long as it is capable of affecting interstate patterns of trade and competition;[9] given the ease with which a dominant undertaking, even by its very existence, may obstruct access to the market, this is not a difficult test to meet. It is important to note that whilst most of the case law on Article 82 has concerned dominance (and abuse thereof) in the manufacture, production, distribution and sale of goods, its prohibition applies equally – and recently with vigour – to the provision of services, and it has now seen tentative application to rules which inhibit the free movement of persons. It also applies – although this has seen virtually no play – to dominance on the demand side, in the purchase of goods and services.[10]

Article 82 prohibits abuse by one 'or more' undertakings of a dominant position. It is only recently that the Commission has turned its guns on abusive conduct of undertakings which together enjoy joint or collective dominance. This will be considered in Chapter 8. The present chapter addresses only situations in which one undertaking alone enjoys dominance.

5.1.1 Co-application of Articles 81 and 82

Since collaboration between or amongst undertakings is a *sine qua non* for the application of Article 81, whilst Article 82 is concerned primarily with

---

[6] See pp 123–5 *supra*.

[7] Cases T-24 etc/93 *Compagnie Maritime Belge* v *Commission* [1996] ECR II-1201 at 1266, upheld for the most part in Cases C-395 & 396/96P *Compagnie Maritime Belge* v *Commission*, judgment of 16 March 2000, not yet reported.

[8] Case C-41/90 *Höfner* v *Macrotron* [1991] ECR I-1979; Cases C-241 & 242/91P *RTE & ITP* v *Commission* [1995] ECR I-743.

[9] Case 322/81 *Michelin* v *Commission* [1983] ECR 3461; Case T-65/89 *BPB Industries and British Gypsum* v *Commission* [1991] ECR II-389.

[10] See eg Decision 2000/74 (*British Airways*) OJ 2000 L30/1 (under review as Case T-219/99 *British Airways* v *Commission*, pending).

unilateral conduct, it was argued that they addressed discrete fields of activity and could not apply coterminously to the same set of circumstances. As the Court of Justice said in an early *dictum*:

Article 85 concerns agreements between undertakings, decisions of associations of undertakings and concerted practices, while Article 86 concerns unilateral activity of one or more undertakings. Articles 85 and 86 seek to achieve the same end on different levels, *viz.* the maintenance of effective competition within the Common Market.[11]

Following later consideration *obiter* by the Court of Justice,[12] the Court of First Instance subsequently confirmed in *Tetra Pak I*:

Articles 85 and 86 are complementary inasmuch as they pursue a common general objective, set out in Article 3[(1)(g)] of the Treaty, which provides that the activities of the Community are to include 'the institution of a system of ensuring that competition in the common market is not distorted'. But they none the less constitute, in the scheme of the Treaty, two independent legal instruments addressing different situations.[13]

Nevertheless, the Court found that they could apply to the same set of circumstances. In that case, an undertaking had acquired an exclusive licence to work a patent – which was therefore an agreement (exempted, in the event, by a block exemption) falling within Article 81. However, the very fact of the acquisition of the licence – the 'anti-competitive effect of its being acquired'[14] – by a dominant undertaking (enjoying about 90 per cent of the relevant market) was libelled by the Commission as an abuse of its dominance,[15] and the Court of First Instance agreed.[16] The Commission has applied both Articles 81 and 82 coterminously in a number of cases since,[17] and has been supported by the Court of First Instance and the

---

[11] Case 6/72 *Europembellage Continental Can* v *Commission* [1973] ECR 215 at 244.

[12] Case 85/76 *Hoffmann-La Roche* v *Commission* [1979] ECR 461; Case 66/86 *Ahmed Saeed Flugreisen* v *Zentrale zur Bekämpfung unlauteren Wettbewerbs* [1989] ECR 803.

[13] Case T-51/89 *Tetra Pak Rausing* v *Commission* [1990] ECR II-309 at 356.

[14] at 357.

[15] Decision 88/501 (*Tetra Pak*) OJ 1988 L272/27.

[16] The judgment in *Tetra Pak I* was not appealed to the Court of Justice, and so now may be taken as good law.

[17] Decision 89/93 (*Flat Glass*) OJ 1989 L33/44; Decisions 91/297–300 (*Soda Ash*) OJ 1991 L152/1, 16, 21, 40; Decision 93/82 (*Cewal*) OJ 1993 L34/20; Decision 93/252 (*Gillette/Wilkinson Sword*) OJ 1993 L116/21; Decision 94/210 (*HOV-SVZ/MCN*) OJ 1994 L104/34; Decision 98/531 (*van den Bergh Foods*) OJ 1998 L246/1; Decision 1999/243 (*Transatlantic Conference Agreement*) OJ 1999 L95/1; Decision 1999/329 (*P& I Clubs*) OJ 1999 L125/12.

Court of Justice.[18] It is also worth noting that there has been in recent Commission decisions a degree of haemorrhaging of principles between the two Articles: considerations of collusive market conduct derived from Article 81 now find a place in determination of dominance shared between or amongst undertakings ('collective dominance') and so subject to Article 82,[19] whilst, in the other direction, in both *Bayer/Adalat*[20] and *Volkswagen*[21] the Commission considered as germane to infractions of Article 81 instances of reduction of supplies, threatening conduct and pressure brought to bear upon independent wholesalers/dealers which were to a degree economically dependent upon a (non-dominant) manufacturer, considerations which stem from, and fall more traditionally within the context of, Article 82.

5.2 Dominance

A dominant position within the meaning of Article 82 is, put concisely:

> a position of economic strength enjoyed by an undertaking which enables it to prevent effective competition being maintained [hinder the maintenance of effective competition] on the relevant market by affording it the power [allowing it] to behave to an appreciable extent independently of its competitors, its customers and ultimately of consumers.

> Such a position does not preclude some competition, which it does where there is a monopoly or quasi-monopoly, but enables the undertaking which profits by it, if not to determine, at least to have an appreciable influence on the conditions under which that competition will develop, and in any case to act largely in disregard of it so long as such conduct does not operate to its detriment.[22]

---

[18] Cases T-68, 77 & 78/89 *Società Italiano Vetro* v *Commission* (Flat Glass) [1992] ECR II-1403; Cases T-24 etc/93 *Compagnie Maritime Belge* v *Commission* [1996] ECR II-1201, upheld for the most part on appeal in Cases C-395 & 396/96P, *Compagnie Maritime Belge* v *Commission*, judgment of 16 March 2000, not yet reported; Case T-224/94 *Deutsche Bahn* v *Commission* [1997] ECR II-1689, upheld on appeal in Case C-436/97P *Deutsche Bahn* v *Commission* [1999] ECR I-2387. The *Soda Ash* decisions were annulled for procedural flaws in Cases T-30 etc/91 *Solvay* v *Commission* [1995] ECR II-1775, 1821, 1825 and Cases T-36 & 37/91 *ICI* v *Commission* [1995] ECR II-1847, 1901, upheld on appeal in Cases C-286 etc/95P *Commission* v *ICI* and Cases C-287 & 288/95P *Commission* v *Solvay*, judgments of 6 April 2000, not yet reported.

[19] See Chap 8.

[20] Decision 96/478, OJ 1996 L201/1 (under review as Case T-41/96 *Bayer* v *Commission*, pending); see pp 63–6 *supra*.

[21] Decision 98/273, OJ 1998 L124/60 (under review as Case T-62/98 *Volkswagen* v *Commission*, pending).

[22] Case 85/76 *Hoffmann-La Roche* v *Commission* [1979] ECR 461 at 520. The words in square parentheses are used in the subsequent formulation of the first paragraph in Case 322/81 *Michelin* v *Commission* [1983] ECR 3461 at 3503.

Dominance is, in other words, a position of market power in which an undertaking is not constrained in its conduct by competitive forces. Further,

> [t]he power to exclude effective competition is not however in all cases coterminous with independence from competitive factors but may also involve the ability to eliminate or seriously weaken existing competitors or to prevent potential competitors from entering the market.[23]

It may also therefore exist in the power an undertaking may exert not only in the market but upon the structure of the market. In order to determine whether an undertaking occupies a dominant position it is necessary to apply a two-stage test: first, to identify the relevant market and second, to assess the market strength of an undertaking alleged to be dominant therein.

5.2.1 Relevant market

The relevant market is defined essentially by identification of a product/service market and a geographic market. The means for doing so, and the economic tests to be applied of substitutability or interchangeability and cross-elasticity of demand, are considered above.[24] But it ought to be emphasised that whilst the Commission (or any party seeking to establish dominance) is sometimes cavalier in its market analysis under Article 81, it has no such latitude under Article 82; definition, and an economically correct definition, of the relevant market is absolutely essential – 'a necessary precondition'[25] – to determination of a breach of Article 82, for dominance cannot be assessed in the absence of market definition. This is borne out by repeated *dicta* of the Court:

> [T]he definition of the relevant market is of essential significance, for the possibilities of competition can only be judged in relation to those characteristics of the products in question by virtue of which those products are particularly apt to satisfy an inelastic need and are only to a limited extent interchangeable with other products.[26]

The economic considerations of interchangeability are stressed repeatedly by the Court:

> The concept of the relevant market in fact implies that there can be effective competition between the products which form part of it and this presupposes

---

[23] Decision 85/609 (*AKZO*) OJ 1985 L374/1 at para 67, upheld on review as Case 62/86 *AKZO v Commission* [1991] ECR I-3359.

[24] at pp 7–12.

[25] Cases T-66, 77 & 78/89 *Società Italiano Vetro v Commission* (Flat Glass) [1992] ECR II-1403 at 1463.

[26] Case 6/72 *Europemballage & Continental Can v Commission* [1973] ECR 215 at 247.

that there is a sufficient degree of interchangeability between all the products forming part of the same market in so far as the specific use of such products is concerned.[27]

According to the Court of First Instance,

in order to be considered the subject of a sufficiently distinct market, it must be possible to distinguish the service or goods in question by virtue of specific characteristics differentiating them from other services or goods to such an extent that they are not interchangeable with those alternatives and are affected only to an insignificant degree by competition from them .... In that context, the degree of interchangeability between products must be assessed in terms of their objective characteristics and of the structure of supply, demand on the market and competitive conditions.[28]

The test admits of a degree of flexibility of interchangeability, but not much:

[F]or the purposes of applying Article 86 of the Treaty, the market for the product or service in question comprises all the products or services which in view of their characteristics are particularly suited to satisfy constant needs and are only to a limited extent interchangeable with other products or services.[29]

Hence the 1997 Commission stab at summing up the relevant considerations:

A relevant product market comprises all those products and/or services which are regarded as interchangeable or substitutable by the consumer, by reason of the products' characteristics, their price and their intended use.[30]

Although Article 82 is frequently applied to the larger undertakings it is important to note that the relevant product/service market need not be a large one. A relevant product market has been identified to be spare parts for a particular make of cash register[31] and cartridges and nails (two distinct product markets) compatible with a single manufacturer's nail gun,[32] buyers having been 'locked in' by their original purchase even if the manufacturer was not dominant in that market. All that is necessary is that there be a distinct market in which the substitution of one product or service for

---

[27] Case 85/765 *Hoffmann-La Roche* v *Commission* [1979] ECR 461 at 516.

[28] Case T-229/94 *Deutsche Bahn* v *Commission* [1997] ECR II-1689 at 1713, upheld on appeal as Case C-436/97P *Deutsche Bahn* v *Commission* [1999] ECR I-2387.

[29] Case C-7/97 *Oscar Bronner* v *Mediaprint* [1998] ECR I-7791 at 7829; see also Case T-65/96 *Kish Glass* v *Commission*, judgment of 20 March 2000, not yet reported.

[30] Notice of definition of the relevant market for the purposes of Community competition law, OJ 1997 C372/5, para 7.

[31] Case 22/78 *Hugin Kassaregister* v *Commission* [1979] ECR 1869.

[32] Case T-30/89 *Hilti* v *Commission* [1991] ECR II-1439, upheld on appeal as Case C-53/92P *Hilti* v *Commission* [1994] ECR I-667.

another is more burdensome or less attractive, for whatever reason, to the customer. It is also important to bear in mind the possibility of supply side substitution, although it is usually a test secondary to demand side considerations. As a general rule, of course, a party libelling an abuse of a dominant position will seek to define the product market as narrowly as possible, whilst the undertaking so libelled will seek to define it as broadly as possible in order to minimise its position in it and so escape the burdens of Article 82.

The second limb of the tests to be applied in identifying the relevant market is that of the geographic market. To the Court of Justice the relevant geographic market is

> a clearly defined geographic area in which [the product or service] is marketed and where the conditions of competition are sufficiently homogenous for the effect of the economic power of the undertaking concerned to be able to be evaluated.[33]

To the Commission it

> comprises the area in which the undertakings concerned are involved in the supply and demand of products or services, in which the conditions of competition are sufficiently homogenous and which can be distinguished from neighbouring areas because the conditions of competition are appreciably different in those area [*sic*].[34]

The relevant geographic market therefore turns on questions of market homogeneity, which is discussed above.[35] It does not require the objective conditions of competition to be perfectly homogenous; it is sufficient that they are 'similar' or 'sufficiently homogenous', and only those territories in which the objective conditions of competition are 'heterogenous' may not be considered to constitute a uniform market.[36] Depending upon the product or service in question, it may be a global market: for example, owing to the fact that they are fungible assets, easily transported, are refined to the same purity standards throughout the world and are readily traded without tariff barriers, the Commission identified the relevant geographic market for platinum group metals as the world;[37] the fluidity of the inter-

---

[33] Case 27/76 *United Brands* v *Commission* [1978] ECR 207 at 270.

[34] Notice of definition of the relevant market for the purposes of Community competition law, OJ 1997 C372/5, para 8.

[35] at pp 11–12.

[36] Case 27/76 *United Brands* v *Commission* [1978] ECR 207; Case T-83/91 *Tetra Pak* v *Commission* [1994] ECR II-755; Case T-229/94 *Deutsche Bahn* v *Commission* [1997] ECR II-1689.

[37] Decision 97/26 (*Gencor/Lonrho*) OJ 1997 L11/30, upheld on review as Case T-102/96 *Gencor* v *Commission* [1999] ECR II-753. The decision was taken under the Merger Regulation, to which the same reasoning applies; see Chap 8.

national market for protection and indemnity insurance in the shipping sector[38] and that of jet engines for wide-bodied commercial aircraft[39] produce the same result. The relevant geographic market may be the whole of Europe, or the whole of the Community, if those areas constitute a geographically homogenous area for the availability of the product or service in question. It may be narrower where the product or service is not available, or is available in limited quantities or at irregular intervals, in parts of the Community, or where the nature of the product or service restricts mobility, or where there are other barriers, physical, legal or financial (for example, freight or transport costs), to entry into particular markets. Article 82 does, however, require that dominance exists within the common market 'or in a substantial part of it'. 'Substantial' ought not to be taken as too high a hurdle, and ought not to be confused with proportions of the overall Community market. Where the relevant geographic market was the island of Ireland – that is, the entire territory of one member state and part of the territory of another – it was 'undeniably' a substantial part of the common market without it being necessary to consider the share of the Community market in the relevant product represented by the Irish market.[40] Luxembourg taken alone might even qualify as a substantial part of the common market.[41] Frequently, owing to statutory monopolies, to intellectual property rights, to linguistic barriers, to simple geography and to residual barriers to the movement of products and services which are a product of Community (for agricultural products) or national regulation, of market conduct, of distribution infrastructure and networks, of currency considerations, of consumer choice or of some other factor, the relevant geographic market is in fact the territory of a member state.[42] It may in certain circumstances be part of a member state, so long as the

---

[38] Decision 1999/329 (*P & I Clubs*) OJ 1999 L125/12.

[39] Decision 2000/182 (*General Electric/Pratt & Whitney*), OJ 2000 L58/16.

[40] Case T-69/89 *Radio Telefis Eireann* v *Commission* [1991] ECR II-485, upheld on appeal as Cases C-241 & 242/91P *RTE & ITP* v *Commission* [1995] ECR I-743.

[41] See the *dictum* of A-G Warner in Case 77/77 *BP* v *Commission* [1978] ECR 1513 at 1537: 'The population of Luxembourg is, I believe, 0.23% of the population of the whole Community. I would however shrink from saying that one who has a monopoly, or near monopoly, of the Luxembourg market for a particular product, was exempt from the application of Article 86'.

[42] eg, Case 127/73 *Belgische Radio en Televisie* v *SABAM* [1974] ECR 51; Case 322/81 *Michelin* v *Commission* [1983] ECR 3461; Cases T-68, 77 & 78/89 *Società Italiano Vetro* v *Commission* (Flat Glass) [1992] ECR II-1403; Case T-7/93 *Langnese-Iglo* v *Commission* [1995] ECR II-1533 and Case T-9/93 *Schöller* v *Commission* [1995] ECR II-1611; Case C-7/97 *Oscar Bronner* v *Mediaprint* [1998] ECR I-7791; Case T-228/97 *Irish Sugar* v *Commission*, [1999] ECR II-2969 (under appeal as Case C-497/99P *Irish Sugar* v *Commission*, pending); Decision 98/531 (*van den Bergh Foods*) OJ 1998 L246/1 (under review as Case T-65/98 *van den Bergh Foods* v *Commission*, pending).

territory is substantial.[43] Individual ports may constitute a substantial part of the common market owing to the amount of traffic, freight and travellers passing through them en route to substantial parts of a member state.[44] The commune of Copenhagen may be a substantial part of the common market for purposes of recycling non-hazardous waste.[45]

It should be noted that the Commission is on occasion less meticulous in defining geographic market than it is product/service market. In some instances it seems to detect an abuse and presume therefrom a distinct geographic territory without considering competitive forces outwith that territory. In *Michelin*,[46] for example, it identified and defined a relevant geographic market for heavy vehicle replacement tyres as the Netherlands without taking account of whether Dutch buyers were able to secure supplies from other member states – which should go to definition of the relevant geographic market – and then found Michelin to be dominant in that market. This is putting the cart before the horse, yet the decision passed muster with the Court of Justice.[47] The Court of First Instance has shown itself to be less complacent in the face of less than rigorous Commission reasoning.

Whilst product/service market and geographic market are the primary variables of relevant market there may on occasion be a subsidiary temporal factor to be taken into account. Product markets may change over time with technological innovation, the introduction of new products and

---

[43] eg, Cases 40 etc/73 *Coöperatieve Vereniging 'Suiker Unie' v Commission* [1975] ECR 1663 (Bavaria, Baden-Württemberg and part of Hesse in the sugar market); Case 30/87 *Bodson v Pompes Funèbres des Régions Libérées* [1988] ECR 2479 (a number of French communes in the market for funeral services).

[44] Case C-179/90 *Merci Convenzionali Porto di Genova v Siderurgica Gabrielli* [1991] ECR I-5889 and Case C-18/93 *Corsica Ferries Italia v Corpo dei Piloti del Porto di Genova* [1994] ECR I-1783 (freight facilities in the port of Genoa); Case C-242/95 *GT-Link v De Danske Statsbaner* [1997] ECR I-4449 (ferry facilities in the port of Gedser); Case C-163/96 *Criminal Proceedings against Silvano Raso* [1998] ECR I-533 (container freight in the port of La Spezia); Decision 94/19 (*Sea Containers/Stena Sealink*) OJ 1994 L15/8 (ferry services in the port of Holyhead); Decision 98/190 (*Flughafen Frankfurt/Main*) OJ 1998 L72/30 (airport facilities at Frankfurt Airport); Decision 98/513 (*Alpha Flight Services/Aéroports de Paris*) OJ 1998 L230/10 (groundhandling services at Orly and Charles de Gaulle airports); Decision 1999/198 (*Ilmailulaitos/Luftfartsverket*) OJ 1999 L69/24 (discriminatory landing charges at Finnish airports; under review as Case T-116/99 *Ilmailulaitos v Commission*, pending); Decision 1999/199 (*Portuguese Airports*) OJ 1999 L69/31 (discounts on landing charges at Lisbon, Oporto and Faro airports; under review as Case C-163/99 *Portugal v Commission*, pending).

[45] Case C-209/98 *Entreprenørforeningens Affalds/Miljøsektion v Københavns Kommune*, judgment of 23 May 2000, not yet reported.

[46] Decision 81/969, OJ 1981 L353/33.

[47] Case 322/81 *Michelin v Commission* [1983] ECR 3461.

change in consumer habits.[48] Markets may be altered by temporary crisis, as during the oil shortages of 1973/74.[49] Currency fluctuations may alter geographic markets, opening up supply from sources hitherto too costly. And markets for agricultural products[50] and package holidays[51] may vary with seasonal change. But it is legitimate, according to the Commission, to construe temporal considerations (if applicable) narrowly, for abuse may occur even during short periods of time.[52]

5.2.2 Market strength

Having identified the relevant market – both product or service market and geographic market – the next step is to determine the strength in that market of an undertaking alleged to be dominant. Market strength constitutive of dominance within the meaning of Article 82 can be as elusive as the product market. It turns upon a number of indicators, no one of which may necessarily be determinative;[53] but the most obvious test is market share. As the Court of Justice said in *Hoffmann-La Roche*:

> The existence of a dominant position may derive from several factors which, taken separately, are not necessarily determinative but among these factors a highly important one is the existence of very large market shares.[54]

Where there is a monopoly – whether by virtue of statutory privilege[55] or of simple absolute market dominance – there is by definition no competition, and so necessarily dominance. Shy of monopoly, a very high market share – more than 85 per cent – is determinative of itself of a dominant position except in wholly exceptional circumstances.[56] A market share of

---

[48] Decision 92/163 (*Tetra Pak II*) OJ 1992 L72/1.

[49] Decision 77/327 (*Aardolie Belangen Gemeenschap*) OJ 1977 L117/1, annulled in Case 77/77 *BP* v *Commission* [1978] ECR 1513 on different grounds.

[50] Case 27/76 *United Brands* v *Commission* [1978] ECR 207.

[51] Decision 2000/276 (*Airtours/First Choice*) OJ 2000 L93/1 (under review as Case T-342/99 *Airtours* v *Commission*, pending).

[52] Decision 92/163 (*Tetra Pak II*) OJ 1992 L72/1, at para 94.

[53] Case 85/76 *Hoffmann-La Roche* v *Commission* [1979] ECR 461; Cases T-24 etc/93 *Compagnie Maritime Belge* v *Commission* [1996] ECR II-1439.

[54] at 520.

[55] eg, Case 127/73 *Belgische Radio en Televisie* v *SABAM* [1974] ECR 51; Case C-260/89 *Elliniki Radiophonia Tileorasi* v *Dimotiki Etairia Pliroforissis* [1991] ECR I-2925; Case C-41/90 *Höfner* v *Macrotron* [1991] ECR I-1979; Case C-230/91 *Criminal Proceedings against Paul Corbeau* [1993] ECR I-2533. This may apply also to a statutory monopoly in only part of a member state: Case 30/87 *Bodson* v *Pompe Funèbres des Régions Libérées* [1988] ECR 2479; Case C-179/90 *Merci Convenzionali Porto di Genova* v *Siderurgica Gabrielli* [1991] ECR I-5889. As to specific rules relating to state monopolies see Chap 7.

[56] Case 85/75 *Hoffmann-La Roche* v *Commission* [1979] ECR 461; Case T-83/91 *Tetra Pak* v *Commission* (Tetra Pak II) [1994] ECR II-755; Case T-228/97 *Irish Sugar* v

70 to 80 per cent is 'in itself, a clear indication of the existence of a dominant position',[57] and a market share of 50 per cent constitutes a dominant position except in exceptional circumstances.[58] Whether dominance can exist with a lesser market share depends upon the respective shares of the undertaking and its competitors: in *United Brands* a market share of 40 to 45 per cent was held to constitute dominance where the competition was highly fragmented, the next largest undertaking enjoying 15 to 20 per cent of the market, the rest significantly less;[59] and dominance was found in *British Airways* with a market share of just under 40 per cent, being 2.2 times the share of its four largest rivals combined.[60] There are no instances of lower market shares having been held to constitute dominance, but it cannot be ruled out. A market share of 10 per cent has been confirmed by the Court of Justice as too small to constitute dominance in the absence of exceptional circumstances.[61]

Whilst market share is the most straightforward test of dominance, other considerations frequently come into play. The overall size and strength of the undertaking, its financial and technical resources, its distribution networks, its ancillary services, its ownership of intellectual property rights – all of which may constitute barriers to market entry – and its very conduct on the market may all have a bearing. Latterly the Commission has placed increasing emphasis upon barriers to market entry as an independent and determinative test of dominance.[62] The fact that an undertaking operates at a loss is not inconsistent with dominance.[63] Given that the various criteria are nebulous and potentially arbitrary, the most reliable indicator of dominance, notwithstanding its element of circularity, probably remains the *Michelin* test: a position of economic strength which enables an undertaking to hinder the maintenance of effective competition on the relevant market by allowing it to behave to an appreciable extent independently of its competitors and customers and ultimately of consumers.[64] Further, or

---

Commission, [1999] ECR II-2696. In Decision 91/535 (*Tetra Pak/Alfa-Laval*) OJ 1991 L290/35 the Commission said that a market share as high as 90 per cent, whilst a very strong indicator of the existence of a dominant position, may nevertheless not be constitutive of dominance in certain rare circumstances.

[57] Case T-30/89 *Hilti* v *Commission* [1991] ECR II-1439 at 1481.

[58] Case 62/86 *AKZO* v *Commission* [1991] ECR I-3359.

[59] Case 27/76 *United Brands* v *Commission* [1978] ECR 207.

[60] Decision 2000/74 (*British Airways*) OJ 2000 L30/1 (under review as Case T-219/99 *British Airways* v *Commission*, pending).

[61] Case 75/84 *Metro-SB-Großmärkte* v *Commission* (No 2) [1986] ECR 3021.

[62] See eg Decision 98/531 (*van den Bergh Foods*) OJ 1998 L246/1 (under review as Case T-65/98 *van den Bergh Foods* v *Commission*, pending).

[63] Case 322/81 *Michelin* v *Commission* [1983] ECR 3461; Case T-228/97 *Irish Sugar* v *Commission*, [1999] ECR II-2696 (under appeal as Case C-497/99P *Irish Sugar* v *Commission*, pending).

[64] Case 322/81 *Michelin*, *ibid*; see n 22 *supra* and accompanying text.

alternatively, an undertaking holds a dominant position when it is able to hinder the emergence of any effective competition because actual or potential competitors are in a position of economic dependence upon it.[65]

5.3 Abuse

Having established the existence of a dominant position, the next question is whether an undertaking has abused that dominance. It is a supple concept and is permitted by the Court to have a wide application. As will be seen, it imposes upon dominant undertakings burdens not shared by other undertakings, for whilst a dominant undertaking is not to be reproached for its dominance, 'irrespective of the reasons for which it has such a dominant position, [it] has a special responsibility not to allow its conduct to impair genuine undistorted competition on the common market'.[66] But this can be a fine line. Dominance as a general principle cannot and should not deprive an undertaking of the right/obligation vigorously to compete in the marketplace:

> Although it is true ... that the fact that an undertaking is in a dominant position cannot disentitle it from protecting its own commercial interests if they are attacked, and that such an undertaking must be conceded the right to take such reasonable steps as it deems appropriate to protect its said interests, such behaviour cannot be countenanced if its actual purpose is to strengthen this dominant position and abuse it.[67]

Put another way, abuse of a dominant position is

> an objective concept relating to the behaviour of an undertaking in a dominant position which is such as to influence the structure of the market where, as a result of the very presence of the undertaking in question, the degree of competition is weakened and which, through recourse to methods different from those which condition normal competition in products or services on the basis of the transactions of commercial operators, has the effect of hindering the maintenance of the degree of competition still existing in the market or the growth of that competition.[68]

Whilst the language of Article 82 ('abuse of ... a dominant position') suggests that there must be a cause and effect between the dominant posi-

---

[65] Cases T-69, 70 & 76/89 *RTE, BBC & ITP* v *Commission* [1991] ECR II-485, 535, 575, upheld on appeal as Cases C-241 & 242/91P *RTE & ITP* v *Commission* [1995] ECR I-743; Case T-229/94 *Deutsche Bahn* v *Commission* [1997] ECR II-1689.

[66] Case 322/81 *Michelin* v *Commission* [1983] ECR 3461 at 3511.

[67] Case 27/76 *United Brands* v *Commission* [1978] ECR 207 at 293; to much the same effect Case T-83/91 *Tetra Pak* v *Commission* (Tetra Pak II) [1994] ECR II-755 at 826; Case T-228/97 *Irish Sugar* v *Commission* [1999] ECR II-2969 at 3021.

[68] Case 85/76 *Hoffmann-La Roche* v *Commission* [1979] ECR 461 at 541.

tion and its abusive exploitation – in the words of the Court of Justice, 'Article 86 presupposes a link between the dominant position and the alleged abusive conduct'[69] – it provides no guidance as to where in the market an abuse occurs. Abuse will occur most frequently directly in the product market in which the undertaking is dominant, but it need not do so in order to be caught by Article 82. Where there is abusive conduct in a market distinct from the market in which the undertaking enjoys dominance – for example, cross-subsidisation of or exclusion from the former by the latter – there will be a breach of Article 82 in 'special circumstances',[70] that is, if the two markets are linked. Whether or not this is so must be considered in the light of the specific circumstances of each case. A necessary link between dominated market and 'associated market' will be present where an undertaking uses market strength, a function of dominance in one market, in order to reserve a complementary, ancillary or dependent activity in a neighbouring but distinct associated market in which it is not dominant,[71] where the associated market is a sub-market of the dominated market[72] or where an undertaking is dominant in one market, has a leading position in the associated market and customers in the former are also customers, or potential customers, in the latter.[73] In service markets questions of associated and sub-markets become easier to circumscribe and raise issues of access to infrastructure facilities which are 'essential' to a service provider; this is discussed below.

Some abusive conduct to which a dominant undertaking might incline – unfair prices, limitation of production to keep prices artificially high, discriminatory dealing – is self-evident, and are the subject of the examples provided in Article 82, but which are exemplicative and not exhaustive.[74] Abusive conduct may be of the nature of 'exploitative' abuse, simple exploitation of consumers in the relevant market, 'exclusionary' abuse, the use of dominance to prevent or hinder competition from other undertakings, or both. It is unnecessary to show that abuse affects the structure of

---

[69] Case C-333/94P *Tetra Pak* v *Commission* (Tetra Pak II) [1996] ECR I-5951 at 6008.

[70] Case C-333/94P *Tetra Pak II, ibid.*

[71] Cases 6–7/73 *Commercial Solvents* v *Commission* [1974] ECR 223; Case 311/84 *CBEM* v *CLT & IPB* (Télémarketing) [1985] ECR 3261; Decision 98/190 (*Flughafen Frankfurt/Main*) OJ 1998 L72/30.

[72] Case 62/86 *AKZO* v *Commission* [1991] ECR I-3359; Cases T-69, 70 & 76/89 *RTE, BBC & ITP* v *Commission* [1991] ECR II-485, 535 and 575, upheld on appeal as Cases C-241 & 242/91P *RTE & ITP* v *Commission* [1995] ECR I-743.

[73] Case T-69/89 *BPB Industries and British Gypsum* v *Commission* [1993] ECR II-389, upheld on appeal as Case C-310/93P *BPB Industries and British Gypsum* v *Commission* [1995] ECR I-865; Case C-333/94P *Tetra Pak* v *Commission* (Tetra Pak II) [1996] ECR I-5951; Case T-228/97 *Irish Sugar* v *Commission* [1999] ECR II-2969.

[74] Case 6/72 *Europemballage & Continental Can* v *Commission* [1973] ECR 215.

competition or that it produces financial or competitive advantage to the dominant undertaking, prejudice to the interests of the consumer being sufficient.[75] The concept of abuse is an objective one, so that conduct of a dominant undertaking may be abusive even in the absence of any fault.[76] Whilst it is important to bear in mind that the innovation with which dominant undertakings may seek further to entrench their market position and see off existing or prospective competition is virtually limitless, so that the *Michelin* and *Hoffmann-La Roche* tests of, respectively, 'special responsibility not to allow [their] conduct to impair genuine undistorted competition on the common market'[77] and 'behaviour ... which, through recourse to methods different from those which condition normal competition ..., has the effect of hindering the maintenance of the degree of competition still existing in the market or the growth of that competition'[78] remain the most reliable, common examples of abusive conduct are as follows.

5.3.1 Pricing

Price lies of course at the heart of competition and is the medium through which it is normally waged. Yet dominance may enable an undertaking to have recourse to means other than those of competition on its merits, so that not all competition on price can be considered legitimate.[79] If by (one) definition a dominant undertaking is one which can behave to an appreciable extent independently of its competitors,[80] its pricing policy is unconstrained by normal market forces, and it is not unreasonable to assume that it may therefore incline towards charging excessively high prices for its goods or services. Hence, Article 82(a) expressly provides that abuse may consist in 'directly or indirectly imposing unfair purchase or selling prices'; but supracompetitive prices are not the only such abuse. Any attempt artificially to sustain high prices by reducing output would fall under the Article 82(b) rubric of 'limiting production ... to the prejudice of consumers'.

Excessive pricing

Surprisingly there has been only one case in which the Commission libelled the existence of excessive pricing *simpliciter*,[81] and this finding was

---

[75] Decision 2000/12 (*Comité Français d'Organisation de la Coupe du Monde*) OJ 2000 L5/55.

[76] Case 85/76 *Hoffmann-La Roche* v *Commission* [1979] ECR 461; Case T-65/89 *BPB Industries* v *Commission* [1993] ECR II-389.

[77] Case 322/81 *Michelin* v *Commission* [1983] ECR 3461 at 3511.

[78] Case 85/76 *Hoffmann-La Roche* v *Commission* [1979] ECR 461 at 541.

[79] Case 62/86 *AKZO* v *Commission* [1991] ECR I-3359.

[80] Case 322/81 *Michelin* v *Commission* [1983] ECR 3461.

[81] Decision 76/353 (*Chiquita*) OJ 1976 L95/1.

annulled by the Court of Justice.[82] The Court added *obiter* that 'charging a price which is excessive because it has no reasonable relation to the economic value of the product supplied is ... an abuse',[83] but supplied no indication as to what might constitute an 'excessive' profit margin or a fair price, which would require to be the product of a construction of the price obtainable under conditions of normal competition. The question was raised again in *Danske Statsbaner*,[84] but as the case was a reference under Article 177 (now Article 234) the question of whether prices were excessive was left to the referring national court with no guidance as to how it ought to be determined.

Predatory pricing

With the wherewithal to sustain losses at least in the short term, a dominant undertaking may charge prices lower than the production cost of a good or service in order to drive lesser, more vulnerable, competitors from the market.[85] In *AKZO*[86] the Court of Justice supplied a working definition of predatory pricing as prices set lower than average variable cost. This definition was reapplied subsequently in *Tetra Pak II*,[87] in which the Court added that predatory pricing was always abusive conduct, for it had 'no conceivable economic purpose other than elimination of a competitor'.[88] Prices above average variable cost but lower than average total cost are abusive only if it can be shown that the intention was to eliminate or inhibit competition.[89] There was concern voiced in Parliament as to whether, and if so how, the Competition Act 1998 ought to proscribe predatory pricing in the media, and specific provisions designed for that purpose were introduced by the House of Lords but opposed successfully by the government.[90] It is nevertheless entirely possible that the pricing policies pursued by *The Times* from time to time, which earned a rebuke from the Director General of Fair Trading for sailing close to the wind under the Fair Trading Act 1973,[91] is already caught by Article 82, although no one appears to have seen fit to challenge it on that ground.[92]

---

[82] Case 27/76 *United Brands* v *Commission* [1978] ECR 207.

[83] at 310.

[84] Case C-242/95 *GT-Link* v *De Danske Statsbaner* [1997] ECR I-4449.

[85] See eg Case 85/76 *Hoffmann-La Roche* v *Commission* [1979] ECR 461.

[86] Case 62/86 *AKZO* v *Commission* [1991] ECR I-3359.

[87] Case C-333/94P *Tetra Pak* v *Commission* [1996] ECR I-5951.

[88] at 6012.

[89] *Ibid.*

[90] See s 19 of the draft Bill as amended on Report.

[91] OFT Press Release PN 17/99 of 21 May 1999.

[92] Although *The Times* may not itself be dominant (applying the market share test) in the national broadsheet newspaper market, the latter may well be a sub or associated market of News Corporation's general dominance. This presumes a distinct product market in

Discriminatory pricing

In the real world producers frequently charge different prices for the same product or service. This is a function of a variety of market and commercial considerations. But for a dominant undertaking there is a danger that differing prices may fall foul of the Article 82(c) rubric of 'applying dissimilar conditions to equivalent transactions with other trading parties, thereby placing them at a competitive disadvantage'.[93] It is generally accepted that Article 82 does not impose upon dominant undertakings a duty to charge identical prices for all transactions. Quantity discounts are, for example, normally unobjectionable. However, any artificial price differences,[94] and certainly price discrimination based upon nationality of the buyer, is abusive conduct unless it can be objectively justified by, for example, variation in the conditions of marketing and intensity of competition.[95] Attempts further to seal off the home market by offering lower prices in border areas where imports might be more attractive to buyers is equally abusive,[96] as is a policy of 'export rebates' whereby rebates are offered to buyers intending to export their final product[97] and is a differential tariff structure offered by a rail carrier so as to distort freight movement to its advantage.[98] A policy of selective offering of lower prices to buyers who purchase or might purchase from other producers in order to dissuade them from so doing is unfair both to the other suppliers and other buyers to whom the offer is not made, and so is abusive.[99] But there may be a thin line here, as lowering prices in order to match those offered by a competitor may simply be intelligent adaptation to competitive forces. It appears that selective price cutting in order to match that of a competitor, assuming prices are not predatory, is abusive only if its purpose (or its effect?) is to eliminate the competitor from the market.[100]

---

national broadsheet newspapers; if there is a narrower market of the rightwing national broadsheets, there is a probably a duopoly, with *The Daily Telegraph* holding a dominant position. As to effect upon trade between member states, the Irish market for these newspapers would suffice.

[93] See eg Case 27/76 *United Brands* v *Commission* [1978] ECR 207; Case T-222/97 *Irish Sugar* v *Commission* [1999] ECR II-2969 (under appeal as Case C-497/99P *Irish Sugar* v *Commission*, pending); Decision 2000/74 (*British Airways*) OJ 2000 L30/1 (under review as Case T-219/99 *British Airways* v *Commission*, pending).

[94] Case T-83/91 *Tetra Pak* v *Commission* (Tetra Pak II) [1994] ECR II-755; Decision 98/513 (*Alpha Flight Services/Aéroports de Paris*) OJ 1998 L230/10.

[95] Case 27/76 *United Brands* v *Commission* [1978] ECR 207; Case T-83/91 *Tetra Pak II*, *ibid*.

[96] Case T-222/97 *Irish Sugar* v *Commission* [1999] ECR II-2969.

[97] Case T-228/97 *Irish Sugar*, *ibid*.

[98] Case T-229/94 *Deutsche Bahn* v *Commission* [1997] ECR II-1689, upheld on appeal as Case C-436/97P *Deutsche Bahn* v *Commission* [1999] ECR I-2387.

[99] Case 62/86 *AKZO* v *Commission* [1991] ECR I-3359; Case T-228/97 *Irish Sugar* v *Commission* [1999] ECR II-2969.

[100] Cases C-395 & 396/96P *Compagnie Maritime Belge* v *Commission*, judgment of 16 March 2000, not yet reported.

5.3.2 Loyalty or fidelity rebates

Closely associated with discriminatory pricing are loyalty or fidelity rebates, whereby a dominant undertaking offers price rebates, bonuses or other form of payment in return for an undertaking from a buyer (or a group of buyers)[101] or agents[102] not to purchase from the former's competitors.[103] Unless it is one which is related to efficiencies (where, for example, greater volumes are in fact cheaper to produce and/or supply and the saving is passed on to the buyer) a rebate is not a quantity discount but is designed to secure loyalty (or 'tie' the buyer) at the expense of competing suppliers.[104] In the face of a discount system from a dominant undertaking it is therefore necessary

> to investigate whether, in providing an advantage not based on any economic service justifying it, the discounts tend to remove or restrict the buyer's freedom to choose his sources of supply, to bar competitors from access to the market, to apply dissimilar conditions to equivalent transactions with other trading parties or to strengthen the dominant position by distorting competition.[105]

It applies equally to turnover or target-related rebates and discounts, which will dissuade buyers from seeking alternative suppliers,[106] and applies if the rebates or discounts are offered only on purchases beyond the buyer's 'core' demands ('top-slicing').[107] It is irrelevant that the rebate or discount was granted at the buyer's request.[108]

'English clauses' or 'competition clauses', whereby a buyer may secure supplies from competing suppliers without losing the benefits of a fidelity rebate but only in circumstances in which the competing supplier offers more attractive terms which the dominant undertaking does not wish to

---

[101] Decision 88/518 (*Napier Brown/British Sugar*) OJ 1988 L284/41.

[102] Decision 2000/74 (*British Airways*) OJ 2000 L30/1.

[103] Cases 40 etc/73 *Coöperatieve Vereniging 'Suiker Unie' v Commission* [1975] ECR 1663; Case 85/76 *Hoffmann-La Roche v Commission* [1979] ECR 461; Case 322/81 *Michelin v Commission* [1983] ECR 3461; Case T-65/89 *BPB Industries v Commission* [1993] ECR II-389, upheld on appeal as Case C-310/93P *BPB Industries v Commission* [1995] ECR I-865.

[104] Cases 40 etc/73 *Suiker Unie*, ibid; Decision 91/299 (*Soda Ash/Solvay*) OJ 1991 L152/21 and Decision 91/300 (*Soda Ash/ICI*) OJ 1991 L152/40, both annulled in Cases T-32/91 *Solvay v Commission* [1995] ECR II-1825 and T-37/91 *ICI v Commission* [1995] ECR II-1901, upheld on appeal as Case C-286/95P *Commission v ICI* and Cases C-287 & 288/95P *Commission v Solvay*, judgments of 6 April 2000, not yet reported.

[105] Case 322/81 *Michelin v Commission* [1983] ECR 3461 at 3515.

[106] Case 322/81 *Michelin*, ibid; Case T-228/97 *Irish Sugar v Commission* [1999] ECR II-2969; Decision 2000/74 (*British Airways*) OJ 2000 L30/1.

[107] Decision 91/299 (*Soda Ash/Solvay*) OJ 1991 L152/21; Decision 91/300 (*Soda Ash/ICI*) OJ 1991 L152/40.

[108] Case 85/76 *Hoffmann-La Roche v Commission* [1979] ECR 461.

meet, are less restrictive of competition than a fidelity rebate *simpliciter*, but are nonetheless abusive.[109]

Loyalty secured even by means other than rebates or discounts can fall foul of Article 82. Where a dominant undertaking insists upon long-term and exclusive supply contracts with its customers – perfectly reasonable and commonplace practice in the context of Article 81 – it can be abusive if the effect is such as to hinder the emergence and development of competing suppliers.[110]

5.3.3 Refusal to deal or supply

There is a presumption that an undertaking whose business it is to sell goods or services will do so whenever a willing buyer presents it with the opportunity. An undertaking refusing to do so must have a reason. Under Article 81 freedom of contract is the general rule, but Article 82 limits that freedom to an extent as part of the price of dominance in the market. To illustrate, a dominant undertaking may have happily sold goods to a downstream manufacturer over the course of a number of years. If, however, the dominant undertaking were subsequently to set itself up, directly or through a subsidiary, as a manufacturer at the same level of production, it makes no commercial sense to continue to supply its erstwhile customer and so assist an undertaking with which it is now in direct competition. But if the buyer cannot, or cannot easily, obtain the goods for manufacture from another supplier, the buyer is in a position of 'economic dependence' upon the dominant supplier (which goes to defining its dominance),[111] and it is an abuse for the latter to refuse to sell. This is so *a fortiori* where the buyer has previously been a regular customer.[112] As the Court of Justice said in *United Brands*:

> [An] undertaking in a dominant position for the purposes of marketing a product ... cannot stop supplying a long standing customer who abides by regular commercial practice, if orders placed by that customer are in no way out of the ordinary.[113]

---

[109] Case 85/76 *Hoffmann-La Roche, ibid.*

[110] *IRE/Nordion*, discussed in Commission press release IP (98) 647 (suspension of a procedure under Art 86 following undertakings given by Nordion).

[111] Cases T-69, 70 & 76/89 *RTE, BBC & ITP v Commission* [1991] ECR II-485, 535 and 575, upheld on appeal as Cases C-241 & 242/91P *RTE & ITP v Commission* [1995] ECR I-743.

[112] Cases 6 & 7/73 *Commercial Solvents v Commission* [1974] ECR 223; Case 27/76 *United Brands v Commission* [1978] ECR 207; Decision 78/68 (*Lipton/Hugin*) OJ 1978 L22/23, annulled on other grounds in Case 22/78 *Hugin v Commission* [1979] ECR 1869.

[113] at 292.

But it may apply also to a potential buyer with no previous links[114] and to a new competitor seeking to enter the market.[115]

In service markets in particular (but not exclusively), Article 82 may impose a duty upon dominant undertakings through what is sometimes called the 'essential facilities' (or sometimes in the United States, 'bottle-neck') doctrine: where an undertaking controls (and so enjoys a dominant position in the provision of) an essential facility – that is, a facility or infra-structure without access to which competitors cannot or cannot without difficulty provide complementary or ancillary services in a neighbouring or sub-market – it may be abusive to refuse competitors access to that facility. This of course cuts across a principle of competition law which generally seeks to inhibit cooperation between or amongst undertakings, which pro-vides succour to competitors. In this context the Court of Justice has said:

> an abuse within the meaning of Article 86 is committed where, without any objective necessity, an undertaking holding a dominant position on a particular market reserves to itself or to an undertaking belonging to the same group an ancillary activity which might be carried out by another undertaking as part of its activities on a neighbouring but separate market, with the possibility of elimi-nating all competition from such undertaking.[116]

A tailor-made test case involved a long-running battle of wills between the Commission and International Business Machines (IBM), the former taking a preliminary view that IBM was abusing its dominance in the data processing (hardware) market by, in part, refusing to supply sufficient technical information to its 'plug compatible' competitors in order to enable them to compete in the associated market for interconnected (soft-ware) equipment[117] (a course of conduct which is not objectionable in American antitrust law),[118] but the matter was settled before coming to a formal decision.[119] In any event, care must be taken with the essential

---

[114] Decision 94/19 (*Sea Containers/Stena Sealink*) (Sealink I) OJ 1994 L15/8.

[115] Cases T-69, 70 & 76/89 *RTE, BBC & ITP v Commission* [1991] ECR II-485, 535 and 575, upheld on appeal as Cases C-241 & 242/91P *RTE & ITP v Commission* [1995] ECR I-743.

[116] Case 311/84 *CBEM v CLT & IPB* (Télémarketing) [1985] ECR 3261 at 3278; Case 18/88 *Régie des Télégraphes et des Téléphones v GB-Inno-BM* [1991] ECR I-5941 at 5979–80 (except omitting the words 'or to an undertaking belonging to the same group'); see also Decision 94/19 (*Sea Containers/Stena Sealink*) (Sealink I) OJ 1994 L15/8; Decision 94/119 (*Rødby Port*) OJ 1994 L55/52; Decision 98/190 (*Flughafen Frankfurt/Main*) OJ 1998 L72/30.

[117] See Case 60/81 *IBM v Commission* [1981] ECR 2639 (unsuccessful attempt to annul the decision to initiate a procedure under Reg 17). The Commission also took the view that IBM was 'bundling' (as to which see *infra*) its main memory function to the central pro-cessing unit.

[118] *California Computer Products v IBM* 613 F 2d 727 (9th Cir 1979).

[119] See *Fourteenth Report on Competition Policy* (1984), pp 77–9.

facilities doctrine lest it become too accessible a remedy for neutralising a legitimate advantage enjoyed by a (dominant) competitor or justification for seeking access to an infrastructure in which it may have invested heavily (and perhaps at high risk) to create. It has its origins in American antitrust law,[120] has been incorporated expressly into the competition law of some member states,[121] and has been deployed expressly by the Commission,[122] but it appears to curry less favour with the Court, which has never referred to it directly.[123] Freedom of contract is the general rule even under Article 82, and ought to be limited only in exceptional circumstances.[124] The zenith of an implicit (the Court, probably intentionally, did not use the term) essential facilities doctrine was *Magill*,[125] in which undertakings dominant (owing to copyright) in the supply of television listings were required by Article 82 to license third party competitors.[126] However, the Court of First Instance said subsequently that a service is necessary (or essential) only if there is no real or potential substitute,[127] and in its most

---

[120] See the discussion of A–G Jacobs in Case C-7/97 *Oscar Bronner* v *Mediaprint* [1998] ECR I-7791 at 7807–08.

[121] eg, (Greek) Law 703/1977, ΦΕΚ 278/Α/26.9.1977, art 2α; Decreto-Lei nᵒ 371/93, art 4ᵒ; Konkurrenceloven, § 11(4); § 19 IV Nr. 4 GWB. It is interesting, and ironic, to note in the latter case that § 19 IV Nr. 4 GWB came into force in 1999, and the official commentary to the bill (Bundestags-Drucksache 13/9720, Se 36 *et seq.*) expressly cited as part justification for it the development of an essential facilities (*wesentliche Einrichtungen*) doctrine in Community law, from which the Court of Justice has now stepped back.

[122] *B&I Line/Sealink Harbours & Sealink Stena* (Sealink I), decision of 11 June 1992, not published; Decision 94/19 (*Sea Containers/Stena Sealink*) (Sealink II) OJ 1994 L15/8; Decision 94/119 (*Rødby Port*) OJ 1994 L55/52; *Irish Continental/CCI Morlaix*, decision of 16 May 1995, not published. See also the earlier but less articulate Commission efforts in the same direction in Decision 88/589 *London European Airways/Sabena* OJ 1988 L317/47 and Decision 92/213 (*British Midlands/Aer Lingus*) OJ 1992 L96/34. It is also implicit in subsequent decisions involving access to airport facilities, eg Decision 98/190 (*Flughafen Frankfurt/Main*) OJ 1998 L72/30.

[123] The Court of First Instance has referred to it *obiter* thus: 'a product or service cannot be considered necessary or essential unless there is no real or potential substitute'; Cases T-374 etc/94 *European Night Services* v *Commission* [1998] ECR II-3141 at 3223. However, this is semantics: the French text (English and French being the authentic languages of the case) reads 'essentiel ou indispensable'. In Case C-7/97 *Oscar Bronner* v *Mediaprint* [1998] ECR I-7791 the Court of Justice let slip the word 'essential', again *obiter*, thus (at 7830): 'it would need to be determined whether ... such refusal deprives the competitor of a means of distribution judged essential ...'.

[124] Cases C-241–2/91P *RTE & ITP* v *Commission* [1995] ECR I-743.

[125] *Ibid.*

[126] See Chap 10.

[127] Case T-504/93 *Tiercé Ladbroke* v *Commission* [1997] ECR II-923 (under appeal as Case C-300/97P *Tiercé Ladbroke* v *Commission*, pending).

recent consideration of an implicit essential facilities doctrine in *Oscar Bronner* the Court of Justice said that an undertaking which controlled a very large share of the daily newspaper market and also the only nation-wide home delivery system for newspapers in a member state could not be compelled by Article 82 to provide access to the system to a competitor because of the existence of other distribution systems (post, shops, kiosks) and the possibility of the competitor setting up its own home delivery scheme.[128] The test therefore seems to be that access to the facility must be indispensable – according to the Court, 'inasmuch as there is no actual or potential substitute in existence',[129] or, according to Advocate-General Jacobs, the dominant undertaking has a 'genuine stranglehold' on the related market;[130] there are no objective grounds, for example lack of spare capacity[131] or insufficient technical ability of the undertaking seeking access, for refusal; and without it all effective competition would be eliminated.

Related to refusal to deal is dealing or supplying on less favourable[132] or discriminatory[133] terms. These fall within the rubrics of 'unfair trading conditions' (Article 82(b)) or 'applying dissimilar conditions to equivalent transactions' (Article 82(c)), and are prohibited. It applies equally to terms for access to essential facilities.[134] Dealing on discriminatory terms based upon nationality (or residence) is a clear breach of Article 82, and this is why the French organisers of the 1998 World Cup incurred the wrath of, if eventually only a slap on the wrist (a fine of €1000) from, the Commission for the manner in which it allocated ticket sales.[135]

The Court of Justice accepts that a dominant undertaking may refuse to deal or may discriminate amongst buyers where it can furnish objective justification for so doing. A genuine shortage – in which case the dominant supplier owes a greater loyalty to established, rather than occasional, buyers – can justify a reduction in supplies.[136] Presumably even an essential

---

[128] Case C-7/97 *Oscar Bronner* v *Mediaprint* [1998] ECR I-7791.

[129] at 7831.

[130] at 7813.

[131] This is expressly recognised in a directive on airport groundhandling facilities (Directive 96/67, OJ 1996 L272/36) which permits, with Commission authorisation, a (dominant) airport administration to refuse access to the (sub-) groundhandling market on grounds of limited space or capacity.

[132] Case C-260/89 *Elliniki Radiophonia Tileorasi* v *Dimotiki Etairia Pliroforissis* [1991] ECR I-2925.

[133] Case 311/84 *CBEM* v *CLT & IPB* (Télémarketing) [1985] ECR 3261; Case T-228/97 *Irish Sugar* v *Commission* [1999] ECR II-2969.

[134] eg, Case C-242/95 *GT-Link* v *De Danske Statsbaner* [1997] ECR I-4449.

[135] Decision 2000/12 (*Comité Français d'Organisation de la Coupe du Monde*) OJ 2000 L5/55.

[136] Case 77/77 *BP* v *Commission* [1978] ECR 1513.

service provider is not bound to supply if it would exceed the natural capacity of the system or undermine working security or consumer protection. And there would be no compulsion to sell to a buyer who is notoriously slow at payment or who was unlikely to make payment at all.[137] But any protection of commercial interests must be justified by 'objective necessity'[138] and must be fair and proportionate.[139] The Court has not been generous in recognising justification.

5.3.4 Tying

Related in turn to refusal to deal is tying, or bundling, by which a dominant undertaking will supply a dependent buyer only if the buyer agrees also to buy another product or service (the 'tied' product or service) which the latter might otherwise be disinclined to do. This type of conduct is caught by Article 82(d), which prohibits 'making the conclusion of contracts subject to acceptance of supplementary obligations which, by their nature or according to commercial usage, have no connection with the subject of such contracts'. So, if a dominant undertaking refuses to supply the tying product without purchases of the tied product,[140] or otherwise ties buyers, even if it does so at the latter's request, by an obligation or promise to purchase all or most of their requirements from the former, it is abusive.[141] It is not uncommon for the sale of non-patented (or non-patentable) goods to be tied to the sale of patented goods;[142] if the seller has a dominant position by virtue of ownership of the patent (or of some other reason), it is abusive. A tying arrangement may be a more subtle form of inducement: a dominant manufacturer of ice cream abuses its dominance if it offers retailers free freezer cabinets and free maintenance thereof conditional upon exclusivity of supply of ice cream products.[143] Notwithstanding the language of Article 82(d), even where tied sales of two products are in accordance with normal commercial conduct or there is a natural link between the two products, tying is abusive, as usage which is acceptable in a competitive market ought not to be permitted in the case of a market in which competition is already restricted by the existence of a

---

[137] See eg *Leyland DAF* v *Automotive Products* [1994] 1 BCLC 245 (CA).

[138] Case 311/84 *CBEM* v *CLT & IPB* (Télémarketing) [1985] ECR 3261 at 3278.

[139] Case 27/76 *United Brands* v *Commission* [1978] ECR 207.

[140] Case T-30/89 *Hilti* v *Commission* [1991] ECR II-1439, upheld on appeal as Case C-53/92P *Hilti* v *Commission* [1994] ECR I-667.

[141] Case 85/76 *Hoffmann-La Roche* v *Commission* [1979] ECR 461; Case 62/86 *AKZO* v *Commission* [1991] ECR I-3359.

[142] eg Case 193/83 *Windsurfing International* v *Commission* [1996] ECR 611; see Chap 10.

[143] Decision 98/531 (*van den Bergh Foods*) OJ 1998 L246/1 (under review as Case T-65/98 *van den Bergh Foods* v *Commission*, pending).

dominant undertaking.[144] The Commission has even condemned a practice by a dominant undertaking of insisting upon delivery rather than ex-factory prices for its goods, as this reserved to it the ancillary activity of transport which might otherwise be provided by another undertaking.[145] Closer to home, subscriptions to the L and C series of the *Official Journal* are available (at increasing cost) from the Community's Office for Official Publications only as a package: in other words, each is tied to the other, and subscription to the L series (or to the C series) cannot be had singly. Also, subscription to offset copies of individual judgments and opinions of the Court of Justice (which are issued promptly) is available only to subscribers to the bound European Court Reports (which are not). Neither of these transparent breaches of Article 82 has yet been challenged. Tying may be permitted where it is objectively justified, but even then the tying clauses must be proportionate and cannot be intended to strengthen dominance by reinforcing economic dependence upon the dominant undertaking.[146]

5.3.5 Cross buying

Although it is not common owing to the cost involved, the purchase by a dominant undertaking of a competitor's products[147] or the exchange with wholesalers or retailers of the competitor's products with its own ('product swaps'),[148] which will remove the competing products from the market and so consolidate the dominant undertaking's position therein, is abusive where it has as its object or effect the restriction or elimination of competition from a new entrant on the market.

5.3.6 Mergers

An abuse of a dominant position may consist in a dominant undertaking acquiring, or merging with, a competitor. This is discussed in Chapter 8.

5.3.7 Intellectual property rights

In certain circumstances the exercise of an intellectual property right by a dominant undertaking may infringe Article 82. This is discussed in Chapter 10.

5.3.8 'Bullying'

Threats issued to, or general bullying of, competitors or customers by a

---

[144] Case T-83/91 *Tetra Pak* v *Commission* (Tetra Pak II) [1994] ECR II-755, upheld on appeal as Case C-333/94P *Tetra Pak* v *Commission* [1996] ECR I-5951.

[145] Decision 88/518 (*Napier Brown/British Sugar*) OJ 1988 L284/41.

[146] Case T-83/91 *Tetra Pak* v *Commission* (Tetra Pak II) [1994] ECR II-755.

[147] Decision 92/163 (*Tetra Pak II*) OJ 1992 L72/1.

[148] Case T-228/97 *Irish Sugar* v *Commission* [1999] ECR II-2969.

dominant undertaking as a means of imposing discipline is abusive, irrespective of whether the threats are carried out, or indeed can be carried out. So, threats of general or selective undercutting of a smaller competitor's prices with the aim of eliminating the latter from the market[149] and pressure brought to bear upon a carrier to stop transporting competing products under pain of withdrawal of business[150] will breach Article 82. In the view of the Commission, vexatious litigation launched by a dominant undertaking the sole purpose of which is to harass another undertaking and being a function of a plan intended to eliminate competition may also – but 'only in wholly exceptional circumstances' – amount to an abuse.[151] A 'dirty tricks' campaign waged by an airline against another, which may include hacking by the former into the latter's computers and rubbishing the latter's reputation, would breach Article 82 if it could be shown that the former had dominance over competing routes and there was an effect upon air transport between member states. In some member states such conduct may have civil and even criminal consequences irrespective of abuse of dominance, and irrespective of Community law.[152]

5.3.9 Indolence and morality

It may be that a dominant undertaking engages in conduct which is generally considered to constitute an infringement of Article 82 – for example, a refusal to deal or supply – simply because it lacks the wherewithal to meet market demand. Is this 'limiting production' proscribed by Article 82(b)? And if it fails to meet market demand, so perhaps maintaining or generating higher prices, is it 'unfair purchase or selling prices' proscribed by Article 82(a)? In other words, does Article 82 require a dominant undertaking to maximise efficiency and output? It may be difficult to envisage an indolent undertaking which nonetheless occupies a dominant position. But it is possible in a new market in which there are high barriers to entry, and it is entirely possible where dominance is a product of, for example, a statutory monopoly or ownership of important intellectual property rights. The Court of Justice has condemned as breaches of Article 82 a port authority which failed to use modern technology, so increasing costs and producing delays,[153] and statutory German and Italian employment agencies which were insufficiently staffed properly to discharge their duties and satisfy demand for their services.[154] It has also said that the (dominant)

---

[149] Case 62/86 *AKZO* v *Commission* [1991] ECR I-3359.
[150] Case T-222/97 *Irish Sugar* v *Commission* [1999] ECR II-2969.
[151] Case T-111/96 *ITT Promedia* v *Commission* [1998] ECR I-2937.
[152] eg, it would be contrary to 'good morals' (*gute Sitten*) and so prohibited by the UWG.
[153] Case C-179/90 *Merci Convenzionale Porto di Genova* v *Siderurgica Gabrielli* [1991] ECR I-5889.
[154] Case C-41/90 *Höfner* v *Macrotron* [1991] ECR I-1979; Case C-55/96 *Job Centre Coop* [1997] ECR I-7119.

proprietor of a copyright infringes Article 82 if it uses copyright as a means of preventing the emergence of a new product for which there is consumer demand[155] and, *obiter*, that it would be abusive for the proprietor of a registered design to cease production of the protected product where there continued to be a market for it.[156] What is by no means clear is whether Article 82 applies to conduct of a dominant undertaking which is a function of purely non-commercial considerations. Must a dominant undertaking, for example, sell to an economically dependent buyer where it (or its shareholders) objects on moral or ethical grounds to the (lawful) use to which the product or service is put? Can a dominant purchaser require that its suppliers meet higher environmental standards in their manufacturing processes than the law requires? May a Channel ferry service for which there is no satisfactory substitute refuse to transport live animals to the continent? The issue has never been considered by the Court of Justice.

---

[155] Cases C-241–2/91P *RTE & ITP* v *Commission* [1995] ECR I-743; see Chap 10.
[156] Case 238/87 *Volvo* v *Veng* [1988] ECR 6211; see Chap 10.

CHAPTER 6

Enforcement

6.1. General

The EC Treaty laid down mechanisms for the provisional enforcement of Articles 81 and 82 (ex Articles 85 and 86) by national competition authorities[1] and by the Commission[2] pending the adoption of 'appropriate regulations or directives to give effect to the principles' set out therein.[3] An appropriate measure was adopted by the Council in 1962 in the form of Regulation 17,[4] the principal regulation implementing Articles 81 and 82, leaving the transitional measures largely (but not entirely) spent.

In 1974 the Court of Justice declared both Articles 81(1) and 82 to be directly effective;[5] that is, they create rights which are enforceable in national courts.[6] In British terminology, a Community right which is directly effective is an 'enforceable Community right' which is 'without further enactment to be ... recognised and available in law and be enforced, allowed and followed accordingly'.[7] Unlike many Treaty articles, Articles 81 and 82 are 'horizontally' directly effective. This means that they address obligations to, and so create rights enforceable against, not only public authorities but also natural and legal persons. This is only reasonable, as the clear subjects of the competition rules are not the member states (as is the case with most Treaty provisions) but 'undertakings'.[8] In the event, a finding of direct effect of both Articles of themselves was not strictly accurate. The Court said subsequently that, whilst Article 82 was sufficiently clear and precise to create an unconditional obligation, and so

---

[1] EC Treaty, Art 84 (ex Art 88).
[2] Art 85 (ex Art 89).
[3] Art 83 (ex Art 87).
[4] Reg 17/62, JO 1962, 204.
[5] Case 127/73 *Belgische Radio en Televisie* v *SABAM* [1974] ECR 51.
[6] See Chap 2, n 15.
[7] European Communities Act 1972, s 2(1).
[8] As to the meaning of 'undertaking' see pp 33–8 *supra*.

of itself be directly effective, Article 81 was required to be viewed as the whole of its parts, and so long as no decision on a particular case had been taken under direct Treaty authority – by a competent national authority under Article 84 (ex Article 88) or by the Commission under Article 85 (ex Article 89) – or, more generally, no implementing rules had been adopted in order to provide the machinery for giving effect to the exemption power of Article 81(3) (ex Article 85(3)),[9] Article 81(1) was not of itself directly effective.[10] The adoption, by authority of Article 83 (ex Article 87), of Regulation 17 (and equivalent implementing regulations) supplied this machinery (amongst other things), so completing the edifice and rendering Article 81(1) thereafter directly effective.

At the same time Regulation 17 conferred upon the Commission autonomous and formidable powers of investigation and enforcement of the competition rules, and it is this which, alongside the exclusive power of exemption under Article 81(3),[11] endows the Commission with pre-eminence in shaping the direction of Community competition policy. Articles 81 and 82 are therefore enforced coterminously by the Commission on the one hand and by national authorities, primarily national courts, on the other. In a number of respects it is not an entirely happy marriage.

6.2 Enforcement by the Commission

Under the transitional regime of Article 85 (ex Article 89) the Commission was charged with 'ensur[ing] the application of the principles laid down in Articles 81 and 82'.[12] To this end it had a duty to investigate suspected infringements and to propose measures appropriate to bring them to an end,[13] and thereafter to authorise member states to adopt appropriate remedial action.[14] Article 85 therefore endowed the Commission with little power other than that of investigation and recommendation. Predominant enforcement authority remained with the (competent authorities of the) member states: they alone enjoyed powers of coercion, and by authority of Article 84 (ex Article 88) they could grant an exemption under Article 81(3), which power the Commission did not enjoy under Article 85.[15]

---

[9] See Chap 4.

[10] Cases 209 etc/84 *Ministère Public* v *Asjes* (Nouvelles Frontières) [1986] ECR 1425; Case 66/86 *Ahmed Saeed Flugreisen* v *Zentrale zur Bekämpfung unlauteren Wettbewerbs* [1989] ECR 803.

[11] See Chap 4.

[12] EC Treaty, Art 85(1) (ex Art 89(1)).

[13] *Ibid.*

[14] Art 85(2) (ex Art 89(2)).

[15] Cases 209 etc/84 *Ministère Public* v *Asjes* (Nouvelles Frontières) [1986] ECR 1425.

All changed utterly with the adoption of Regulation 17. Not only did the power of exemption pass exclusively to the Commission,[16] Regulation 17 conferred upon it wide powers of investigation of apprehended infractions of the competition rules and of prohibition and sanction where an infraction is found to exist. Article 85 is still recognised as a specific expression of the supervisory role of the Commission in the field of competition from which principles adhering to that duty may be derived,[17] but it continues to have direct relevance for the application of Articles 81 and 82 only in those (very few) areas which are not yet governed by Regulation 17 or any other implementing regulation, and the Commission has (very infrequent) recourse to it for that purpose.[18] As Regulation 17 is of general application, whilst other, equivalent regulations apply in, or moderate the application of Regulation 17 to, certain specific economic sectors,[19] in what follows primary reference will be made to Regulation 17 with only passing reference to the other implementing sectoral regulations.

6.2.1 Enforcement of the prohibitions
Complaint

The Commission may, upon its own initiative or upon a complaint ('application') from a member state or a natural or legal person who can show a legitimate interest, launch an investigation of an alleged infraction of Articles 81 or 82.[20] A special form ('Form C') has been prepared by the Commission for the lodging of a complaint,[21] but its use is not obligatory. When a complaint is made, the Commission has a duty carefully and diligently to consider the issues raised in order to determine whether there

---

[16] Reg 17, art 9(1).

[17] Cases 100–03/80 *Musique Diffusion Française* v *Commission* (Pioneer) [1983] ECR 1825; Case T-77/92 *Parker Pen* v *Commission* [1994] ECR II-549; Case T-77/95 *Syndicat Français de l'Express International* v *Commission* [1997] ECR II-1.

[18] See, for example, the notices in OJ 1996 C289/6 and 8 on the opening of a procedure under Art 89 (now Art 85) concerning commercial air transport from Community airports to a third country, and the subsequent notices on proposed measures to bring infringements of Arts 85 and 86 to an end: OJ 1998 C239/5 and 10. The general investigatory powers conferred upon the Commission by Reg 17 (see *infra*) apply also under Art 85: Reg 17, arts 11(1) and 14(1).

[19] See Chap 4, n 7.

[20] Reg 17, art 3. Owing to workload and understaffing the Commission has become increasingly reactive: from 1993 to 1999 'own initiative' proceedings accounted for only 14 per cent of investigations: tabulated from EC Commission, *XXVIIIth Report on Competition Policy* (1998), p 45.

[21] Reg 3666/93 OJ 1993 L336/1. A different form ('Form TR') is used under the transport regulations: Reg 2843/98, OJ 1998 L354/22.

exists conduct liable to distort competition and so which infringes the competition rules.[22] Failure to do so may be the subject of proceedings against the Commission under Article 232 (ex Article 175) of the Treaty for failure to act.[23] Beyond that, there is no duty to adopt a decision regarding the existence or otherwise of a breach of Articles 81 or 82 and no duty to pursue the complaint by means of an investigation; the Commission need only give reasons for not doing so.[24] Legitimate reasons may include other priorities (and the Commission enjoys a discretion to apply different degrees of priority to complaints and to concentrate its scarce resources where it sees fit),[25] in particular insufficient 'Community interest' (the ambit of which is still developing)[26] and the adequacy of

---

[22] Case 210/81 *Demo-Studio Schmidt* v *Commission* [1983] ECR 3045; Case 298/83 *CICCE* v *Commission* [1985] ECR 1105; Case C-19/93P *Rendo* v *Commission* [1995] ECR I-3319. A duty to act is more expressly stated in the implementing regulations in the transport sector.

[23] Case T-28/90 *Asia Motor France* v *Commission* [1992] ECR II-2285; Case C-282/95P *Guérin Automobiles* v *Commission* [1997] ECR I-1503; Case T-127/98 *UPS Europe* v *Commission* [1999] ECR II-2633.

[24] Case 125/75 *GEMA* v *Commission* [1979] ECR 3173; Case T-24/90 *Automec* v *Commission* (Automec II) [1992] ECR II-2223; Case T-186/94 *Guérin Automobiles* v *Commission* [1995] ECR II-1753, upheld in Case C-282/95P *Guérin Automobiles* v *Commission* [1997] ECR I-1503; Case T-575/93 *Koelman* v *Commission* [1996] ECR II-1, upheld in Case C-59/96P *Koelman* v *Commission* [1997] ECR I-4809; Case T-387/94 *Asia Motor France* v *Commission* [1996] ECR II-961. This is not so if a complaint is lodged by a member state, in which event the Commission has a duty to initiate an investigation: EC Treaty, Art 85(1) (ex Art 89(1)) and Case T-24/90 *Automec II* at 2275. There is also a duty to initiate an investigation where a complaint is lodged under the transport regulations. For the administrative procedure to be followed in examining a complaint see Case T-64/89 *Automec* v *Commission* (Automec I) [1990] ECR II-367 at 382–3.

[25] Case T-24/90 *Automec II*, *ibid*; Cases T-213/95 & 18/96 *Stichting Certificatie Kraanverhuurbedrijf* v *Commission* [1997] ECR II-1739; Cases T-189/95 & 39 & 123/96 *Service pour Groupement d'Aquisitions* v *Commission* [1999] ECR II-3587.

[26] Case T-24/90 *Automec II*, *ibid*; Case T-114/92 *BEMIM* v *Commission* [1995] ECR II-147; Case T-5/93 *Tremblay* v *Commission* [1995] ECR II-185; Case T-110/95 *International Express Carriers Conference* v *Commission* [1998] ECR II-3605 (under appeal as Case C-449/98P *International Express Carriers Conference* v *Commission*, pending); Cases T-133 & 204/95 *International Express Carriers Conference* v *Commission* [1998] ECR II-3645, upheld in Case C-428/98P *Deutsche Post* v *International Express Carriers Conference & Commission*, order of 11 May 2000, not yet reported; Cases T-185, 189 & 190/96 *Riviera Auto Service* v *Commission* [1999] ECR II-93. The discretion enjoyed by the Commission in determining 'sufficient Community interest' was pared back in Case C-119/97P *Union Française de l'Express* v *Commission* [1999] ECR I-1341, the Court of Justice stressing a duty to assess the gravity and the persistence of the consequences of alleged anti-competitive conduct; see now Case T-77/95 *Union Française de l'Express* v *Commission*, judgment of 25 May 2000, not yet reported. In its 1997 notice on agreements of minor importance (see pp 72–5 *supra*) the Commission said that it will not institute proceedings, either upon its own initiative or upon a complaint, to an agreement or conduct falling within the notice or to agreements between small and medium-ized undertakings except in exceptional circumstances: see paras 5, 11, 19 and 20 of the notice.

alternative relief available from national authorities and courts.[27] A complainant is entitled to a response from the Commission within a reasonable period of time[28] and at the least an 'article 6 letter'[29] informing him of the Commission's reasons for not proceeding and allowing him a reasonable period of time to respond with further comments. It has been Commission practice thereafter to give a definitive decision on rejection or acceptance of the complaint. The Court of First Instance implied,[30] and the Court of Justice subsequently confirmed,[31] that provided the complainant has submitted written observations by way of response to the article 6 letter, the Commission is under a duty to adopt, within a further reasonable period of time, a final and definitive decision not to proceed. This is important because it is only then that the decision becomes justiciable and amenable to judicial review.[32] The Commission must therefore disclose with sufficient clarity the reasons for which the complaint was rejected, so enabling the complainant to defend his rights before the Court of First Instance in reviewing the legality of the decision.[33] In the event of review proceedings of a definitive decision rejecting a complaint the Court cannot substitute its own reasoning for that of the Commission but must ensure that there were no legal defects in the provisional stages leading up to its adoption[34] and that it was not based upon a materially incorrect appreciation or assessment of the facts or vitiated by an error of law, insufficient reasoning, a

---

[27] Case T-24/90 *Automec II, ibid.* The Commission may sometimes be overly sanguine in asserting the availability of national remedies, but it appears that it is for the complainant to show that they are inadequate: *Automec II* at 2279–80; Cases T-189/95 & 39 & 123/96 *Service pour le Groupement d'Aquisitions* v *Commission* [1999] ECR II-3587.

[28] Case C-282/95P *Guérin Automobiles* v *Commission* [1997] ECR I-1503; Cases T-213/95 & 18/96 *Stichting Certificatie Kraanverhuurbedrijf* v *Commission* [1997] ECR II-1739; Case T-127/98 *UPS Europe* v *Commission* [1999] ECR II-2633.

[29] Reg 2842/98, OJ 1998 L354/18 (repealing and replacing Reg 99/63, JO 1963, 2268), art 6; see Case 125/78 *GEMA* v *Commission* [1979] ECR 3173.

[30] Case T-24/90 *Automec* v *Commission* (Automec II) [1992] ECR II-2223; Case T-74/92 *Ladbroke* v *Commission* [1995] ECR II-115.

[31] Case C-282/95P *Guérin Automobiles* v *Commission* [1997] ECR I-1503.

[32] Case T-64/89 *Automec* v *Commission* (Automec I) [1990] ECR II-367; Case T-37/92 *Bureau Européen des Unions de Consummateurs* v *Commission* [1994] ECR II-285; on judicial review see pp 187–94 *infra.*

[33] Case C-360/92P *Publishers Association* v *Commission* [1995] ECR I-23; Case T-5/93 *Tremblay* v *Commission* [1995] ECR II-185; Case T-387/94 *Asia Motors France* v *Commission* [1996] ECR II-961; Case T-49/95 *van Megen Sports* v *Commission* [1996] ECR II-1799; Cases T-70–1/92 *Florimex* v *Commission* [1997] ECR II-693; Case T-504/93 *Tiercé Ladbroke* v *Commission* [1997] ECR II-923; Case T-241/97 *Stork Amsterdam* v *Commission*, judgment of 17 February 2000, not yet reported.

[34] Case C-282/95P *Guérin Automobiles* v *Commission* [1997] ECR I-1503.

manifest error of appraisal or misuse of powers.[35] Where the Commission initiates an investigation in response to a complaint it must conduct it with 'requisite care, seriousness and diligence' so as to be able properly to assess the factual and legal issues, the substance of the complaint;[36] where an investigation is initiated, but subsequently terminated, that is also a final, reviewable act to which the same criteria apply.[37]

Investigation

Request for information

Having elected to proceed with an investigation, article 11 of Regulation 17 authorises the Commission to seek to obtain all 'necessary information' from the undertakings under investigation, from third parties, and from national competition authorities.[38] Information is 'necessary' where it might enable the Commission to investigate the putative infringement which underpins the conduct of the inquiry.[39] There is a compulsory two-stage procedure: first, a simple request for information to which the addressee may, but need not, respond;[40] and second, a request by way of formal decision.[41] In both cases the Commission is required to state the legal basis and the purpose of the request.[42] A request for information by way of formal decision imposes upon an undertaking a duty of 'active

---

[35] Case T-24/90 *Automec v Commission* (Automec II) [1992] ECR II-2223; Case T-37/92 *Bureau Européen des Unions des Consummateurs v Commission* [1994] ECR II-285; *BEMIM v Commission* [1995] ECR II-147; Cases T-70–1/92 *Florimex v Commission* [1997] ECR II-693, upheld on appeal in Case C-265/97P *Coöperatieve Vereniging de Verenigde Bloemenvielingen Aalsmeer v Florimex & Commission*, judgment of 30 March 2000, not yet reported; Cases C-359 & 379/95P *Commission and France v Ladbroke Racing* [1997] ECR I-6265; Case T-111/96 *ITT Promedia v Commission* [1998] ECR II-2937; Case T-17/96 *Télévision Française 1 v Commission* [1999] ECR II-1757; Cases T-189/95 & 39 & 123/96 *Service pour le Groupement d'Aquisitions v Commission* [1999] ECR II-3587 (under appeal as Case C-39/00P *Service pour le Groupement d'Aquisitions v Commission*, pending); Case T-198/98 *Micro Leaders Business v Commission* [1999] ECR II-3989.

[36] Case T-7/92 *Asia Motor France v Commission* [1993] ECR II-669 at 684.

[37] Case 156/84 *BAT & Reynolds v Commission* (Philip Morris) [1987] ECR 4487; Case C-39/93P *Syndicat Français de l'Express International v Commission* [1994] ECR I-2681; Case C-19/93P *Rendo v Commission* [1995] ECR I-3319.

[38] Reg 17, art 11(1).

[39] Case T-39/90 *Samenwerkende Elektriciteits-produktiebedrijven v Commission* [1991] ECR II-1497.

[40] Reg 17, art 11(2); Case T-30/89 *Hilti v Commission* [1991] ECR II-1439; Cases T-305 etc/94 *Limburgse Vinyl Maatschappij v Commission* [1999] ECR II-931.

[41] art 11(5).

[42] art 11(3) and (5).

cooperation' with the Commission,[43] and failure to respond or supplying incorrect information may result in a fine.[44]

Whilst this power of investigation is very broad it is not limitless. The request for information, both simple and formal, must be proportionate to the purpose of the investigation,[45] and the general principle of privilege against self-incrimination has been applied to the effect that an undertaking cannot be compelled to respond to leading questions the answers to which would constitute an admission of unlawful conduct, that being for the Commission to establish.[46] These considerations apply logically only to a formal request for information, for there is no obligation to respond to the informal request; however, should an undertaking elect to respond to an informal request and provide incorrect information, the Commission may impose a fine.[47] 'Incorrect' information embraces information which is incomplete, misleading or which provides a distorted picture of the true facts being sought.[48] Any information gleaned by the Commission in a request for information may be used only 'for the purpose of the relevant request'[49] and so cannot be used by the Commission in order to make out another infraction different from that envisaged in the request (although the Commission may start a new investigation afresh)[50] and it cannot be used by national competition authorities as evidence of an infringement of

---

[43] Case 374/87 *Orkem* v *Commission* [1989] ECR 3283; Case T-34/93 *Société Générale* v *Commission* [1995] ECR II-545.

[44] Reg 17, art 15(1)(b). The current maximum fine is €5,000; in its 1999 White Paper (see pp 219–23 *infra*) the Commission proposes that it be increased to €50,000.

[45] Case T-39/90 *Samenwerkende Elektriciteits-produktiebedrijven* v *Commission* [1991] ECR II-1497.

[46] Case 374/87 *Orkem* v *Commission* [1989] ECR 3283. Nor may the Commission use information uncovered in national civil proceedings which would offend the *Orkem* rule in order to establish an infringement of Arts 81 or 82 or as evidence justifying the initiation of an investigation: Case C-60/92 *Otto* v *Postbank* [1993] ECR I-5683. Implicitly it may use information which would not be barred by *Orkem*. Subsequent judgments of the European Court of Human Rights (in unrelated cases) are thought to imply that parts of the *Orkem* judgment are inconsistent with the requirements of the European Convention on Human Rights: see *Funke* v *France* (1993) 16 EHRR 297 and *Saunders* v *United Kingdom* (1997) 23 EHRR 313.

[47] Reg 17, art 15(1)(b). See eg Decision 2000/146 (*Anheuser-Busch/Scottish & Newcastle*) OJ 2000 L49/37.

[48] Decision 82/124 (*Telos*) OJ 1982 L58/19.

[49] Reg 17, art 20(1).

[50] Case 85/87 *Dow Benelux* v *Commission* [1989] ECR 3137.

national competition rules.[51] It is also privileged insofar as it is 'covered by the obligation of professional secrecy'.[52]

Investigation

Distinct and independent from but complementary to the power to require information,[53] the Commission is further empowered by article 14 of Regulation 17 to authorise its officials to enter the premises of any undertaking, examine books and business records (in any medium), take copies therefrom, and ask for oral explanations on the spot.[54] An investigation may be ordered by written authorisation ('the mandate')[55] or by formal decision.[56] As with requests for information, an undertaking is required to comply only if the investigation is ordered by formal decision.[57] But unlike the former there is no need for a preliminary request: having consulted the competition authorities in the member state(s) in which it is to take place (a mandatory procedural requirement),[58] the Commission may proceed directly to investigation, either by mandate or by decision,[59] and need provide no advance warning.[60] So as not to alert undertakings to its interest, and because it is an independent procedure, an investigation under article 14 may precede any request for information under article 11. The Commission may,[61] in some circumstances must,[62] and in all cases invariably does, seek assistance from and cooperate with the appropriate national authorities – in the United Kingdom, the Office of Fair Trading –

---

[51] Case C-67/91 *Dirreción General de Defensa de la Competencia* v *Asociación Española de Banca Privada* [1992] ECR I-4785.

[52] Reg 17, art 20(2), which is an expression of a more general duty imposed upon Community institutions by Art 287 (ex Art 214) of the Treaty.

[53] Case 136/79 *National Panasonic* v *Commission* [1980] ECR 2033; Case 387/87 *Orkem* v *Commission* [1989] ECR 3283.

[54] Reg 17, art 14(1).

[55] art 14(2).

[56] art 14(3).

[57] This option to refuse consent to a mandate investigation may not buy the undertaking much time, for a formal decision is in practice adopted in the name of the Commission by the Commissioner for competition under delegated authority and so may be adopted very speedily. Being an 'administrative or management' matter, the Court of Justice has not objected to this practice: Case 5/85 *AKZO* v *Commission* [1986] ECR 2585. As with a request for information, if an undertaking submits to an Art 14(2) investigation but supplies incomplete books or records the Commission may impose a fine: Reg 17, art 15(1)(c).

[58] Reg 17, art 14(4). The consultation may be informal: Case 5/85 *AKZO, ibid.*

[59] Case 136/79 *National Panasonic* v *Commission* [1980] ECR 2033.

[60] Case 136/79 *National Panasonic* v *Commission* [1980] ECR 2033; Case 5/85 *AKZO* v *Commission* [1986] ECR 2585.

[61] Reg 17, art 14(4)–(5).

[62] Cases 46/87 & 227/88 *Hoechst* v *Commission* [1989] ECR 2859.

which have a duty to cooperate to the extent necessary to make the investigation effective.[63]

An undertaking is bound to 'submit' to an investigation ordered by formal decision – so-called on-the-spot investigations[64] or 'dawn raids' – but exactly how far that duty extends is not yet clear. Both mandates and formal decisions must specify their subject matter and purpose[65] and the Commission is under an obligation to state clearly the alleged facts it seeks to verify.[66] The documents and records liable to examination and any oral explanations demanded are restricted thereto. Nevertheless it is the Commission which frames the subject matter of the investigation, and it is allowed a wide latitude.[67] As to the conduct of the investigation, the Court of Justice has said that the premises of an undertaking cannot, as a general principle of law, be subjected to arbitrary or disproportionate intervention by the Commission, and in some circumstances the assistance of national authorities and compliance with national procedural safeguards on inviolability of property may be required.[68] For this latter reason, in 10 of the 15 member states (those other than Italy, the Netherlands, Austria, Finland and Sweden) prior judicial authorisation is required (and is required to be granted).[69] Written communications between an undertaking and outside (but not in-house) lawyers are, as a general principle of law, privileged and so protected from disclosure insofar as they are instrumental to the under-

---

[63] Reg 17, art 14(6); Cases 46/87 & 227/88, *Hoechst, ibid*.

[64] art 14(3).

[65] art 14(2)–(3).

[66] Cases 46/87 & 227/88 *Hoechst* v *Commission* [1989] ECR 2859.

[67] See eg Case 85/87 *Dow Benelux* v *Commission* [1989] ECR 3137.

[68] Cases 46/87 & 227/88 *Hoechst* v *Commission* [1989] ECR 2859. The Court found that Art 8(1) of the European Convention on Human Rights (which provides that '[e]veryone has the right to respect for his private and family life, his home and his correspondence') extended fully only to private premises and not to business premises. It also noted that there had been no case law of the European Court of Human Rights on the subject. There has now been such case law (*Chappell* v *United Kingdom* (1990) 12 EHRR 1; *Niemitz* v *Germany* (1993) 16 EHRR 97) which suggests that the Court of Justice was wrong in its narrow interpretation of Art 8(1).

[69] According to *Hoechst* a national judge cannot question the need for the investigation which is a matter exclusively for the Commission and subject to the control of the Court of Justice only, but he may require to satisfy himself that the measures of constraint envisaged are not arbitrary or excessive. If no warrant is sought, the obligation imposed upon national authorities by art 14(6) of Reg 17 to cooperate with the Commission would extend to a duty of national courts to pronounce an *ex parte* injunction or an order for specific performance compelling an undertaking which had refused to cooperate with an investigation to do so, and the High Court in England has so ordered on one occasion: *DTI* v *UKWAL*, order of 28 June 1989, unreported. Express authority for the issue of warrants in this context, following application by the Director-General of Fair Trading, is now provided by the Competition Act 1998, ss 62–65.

taking's rights of defence.[70] Generally the rights of defence must be adhered to throughout.[71] The authorisation now carries an 'explanatory memorandum'[72] defining – cursorily – the inspectors' powers and the undertaking's rights: for example, a right to have counsel present (so long as the investigation is not unduly delayed as a result) and a right to an inventory of copies taken and a copy of any minutes drawn up resulting from oral explanations. Particular records and documents to be scrutinised need not be identified beforehand so long as they can be said to fall within the subject matter of the investigation, and whilst the Commission holds an undertaking responsible positively to assist its inspectors,[73] an investigation ought not to degenerate into a fishing expedition. It is not unknown for the Commission to ask questions not directly related to documents found, but it is not yet clear whether there is an obligation to answer. What is least clear is which individual(s) within the company may be required to provide an on-the-spot explanation. As a result of these grey areas a cottage industry has sprung up in instructions on how best to cope with a Commission dawn raid. This is not surprising, for it would be difficult to overemphasise the importance of this power of investigation by which, especially in the context of a covert cartel, the Commission is able to lay hands on any 'smoking documents'. Refusal to cooperate with any lawful aspect of an investigation and/or supplying incomplete books or records may result in a fine and/or a periodic penalty payment.[74] As with requests for information, any information uncovered in the course of an investigation may be used only 'for the purpose of the relevant ... investigation',[75] cannot be used in other proceedings[76] and is privileged by rules of professional secrecy.[77] Whilst an undertaking may have recourse to Article 230 (ex Article 173) in order to force review of a decision to require information or to authorise an investigation,[78] it cannot challenge the legality of the manner in which an investigation is carried out in that context; that

---

[70] Case 155/79 *AM & S Europe* v *Commission* [1982] ECR 1575.

[71] Case 85/87 *Dow Benelux* v *Commission* [1989] ECR 3137; see *infra*.

[72] See European Commission, *Thirteenth Report on Competition Policy* (1983), Annex, pp 270–2.

[73] Decision 80/334 (*Fabbrica Pisana*) OJ 1980 L75/30.

[74] Reg 17, arts 15(1)(c), 16(1)(d); see eg Decision 92/237 (*UKWAL*) OJ 1992 L121/45; Decision 94/735 (*AKZO*) OJ 1994 L294/31. The ceilings are as those for requests for information: n 44 *supra*. As to periodic penalty payments see *infra*.

[75] art 20(1); see also Case 85/87 *Dow Benelux* v *Commission* [1989] ECR 3137.

[76] See nn 50 and 51 *supra*.

[77] Reg 17, art 20(2).

[78] *Ibid*, arts 11(5) and 14(3); but this option may afford an aggrieved undertaking little comfort, for a Community act (including a Commission decision) is presumed to be valid, and

may be raised only in the context of review of any final decision to which the investigation may lead.[79]

Termination and fines

Termination

Having completed its fact finding and/or investigation, the Commission may proceed to the formal establishment of a breach of Article 81(1) or of Article 82. Before it does so it must comply with a number of procedural rights of defence intended to safeguard the interests of the party under investigation,[80] and must in any event act within a 'reasonable' period of time;[81] the latter has now hardened into a general principle of Community law,[82] although the Court of First Instance adopts a fairly generous view as to what is reasonable.[83] Where the Commission finds that a breach has occurred 'it may by decision require the undertakings or associations of undertakings concerned to bring such infringement to an end'.[84] This consists usually in an order compelling undertakings simply to stop doing whatever they were doing which constituted the infringement, but it includes the power to specify the extent of the obligation necessary to bring the infringement to an end, provided that obligation is appropriate and necessary to do so,[85] and to prohibit repetition of, or adoption of similar, offending conduct in the future.[86] 'Similar' conduct is not yet clearly

---

so must be complied with, until set aside or suspended by the Court of Justice (Case 46/87R *Hoechst* v *Commission* [1987] ECR 1549; Cases 46/87 & 227/88 *Hoechst* v *Commission* [1989] ECR 2859; Cases C-137/92P *Commission* v *BASF* [1994] ECR I-2555), and in any event, so broad is Commission discretion here that it would be unlikely to be set aside, except perhaps on grounds of procedural impropriety. Presumably should such a challenge prove successful, information secured by means of the investigation would be inadmissible as a means of establishing a breach of Arts 81 or 82. On judicial control of the Commission see pp 187–94. *infra.*

[79] Case 85/87 *Dow Benelux* v *Commission* [1989] ECR 3137; Case T-9/97 *Elf Atochem* v *Commission* [1997] ECR II-909; Cases T-305 etc/94 *Limburgse Vinyl Maatschappij* v *Commission* [1999] ECR II-931 (under appeal as Cases C-238 etc/99P *Limburgse Vinyl Maatschappij* v *Commission*, pending).

[80] See pp 184–7 *infra.*

[81] Cases T-213/95 & 18/96 *Stichting Certificatie Kraanverhuurbedrijf* v *Commission* [1997] ECR II-1739.

[82] Case C-185/95P *Baustahlgewebe* v *Commission* [1998] ECR I-8417; Cases T-305 etc/94 *Limburgse Vinyl Maatschappij* v *Commission* [1999] ECR II-931 (under appeal as Cases C-238 etc/99P *Limburgse Vinyl Maatschappij* v *Commission*, pending).

[83] Cases T-305 etc/94 *Limburgse Vinyl Maatschappij*, *ibid*; Case T-228/97 *Irish Sugar* v *Commission* [1999] ECR II-2969.

[84] Reg 17, art 3(1).

[85] Case T-311/94 *BPB de Eendracht* v *Commission* [1998] ECR II-1129; Case T-334/94 *Sarrió* v *Commission* [1998] ECR II-1439; Case T-352/94 *Mo och Domsjö* v *Commission* [1998] ECR II-1989 (all *Cartonboard* cases).

[86] Case T-83/91 *Tetra Pak* v *Commission* [1994] ECR II-755.

circumscribed; the Court of First Instance has recently adverted to the prohibition of previous infringements in the future or adoption of 'any measure having equivalent effect',[87] and found nothing objectionable in a Commission formulation of a general future prohibition which related back to specific infringements found. Yet the Commission cannot order an undertaking, the purchasing agreements of which it has found to infringe Article 81(1), to refrain from concluding new agreements of that kind in the future,[88] and it must in any event show that any future conduct it prohibits would have anticompetitive effects.[89] Whether it has the power to prohibit an anticipated infringement of Articles 81 or 82, as opposed to ordering termination and non-repetition of an infringement formally found, seems unlikely.[90]

The Commission may also order any remedial positive action necessary to cure the breach of Articles 81(1) or 82.[91] The power of positive compulsion, although not fully explored, is limited to the extent appropriate and necessary to restore compliance with the rule infringed.[92] It is most appropriate where an undertaking has infringed Article 82; the Commission has in principle no power to order a party to enter into a contractual agreement in order to cure a breach of Article 81(1)[93] – although it has in that context frequently ordered undertakings to comply with certain positive obligations as regards existing contractual relations, such as notifying contracting partners that certain terms of a contract found by the Commission to infringe Article 81(1) are void.

The Commission may, and frequently does, issue a decision declaring the existence of an infraction, even if it has already been brought to an end, in order to establish its existence or to clarify a point of law and so prevent future infractions; this practice has been endorsed by the Court of Justice.[94]

---

[87] Case T-228/97 *Irish Sugar* v *Commission* [1999] ECR II-2969 at 3082.

[88] Case T-7/93 *Langnese-Iglo* v *Commission* [1995] ECR II-1533; cross appeal on that point was ruled inadmissible: Case C-279/95P *Langnese-Iglo* v *Commission* [1998] ECR I-5609.

[89] Cases T-311/94 etc *Cartonboard*, cited n 85 *supra*.

[90] Applying Case T-34/92 *Fiatagri UK & New Holland Ford* v *Commission* [1994] ECR II-905, upheld tacitly on appeal as Case C-8/95P *New Holland Ford* v *Commission* [1995] ECR I-3175, by analogy.

[91] Cases 6 & 7/72 *Commercial Solvents* v *Commission* [1974] ECR 223; Cases T-69, 70 & 76/89 *RTE, BBC & ITP* v *Commission* [1991] ECR II-485, 535 and 575.

[92] Cases C-241–2/91P *RTE & ITP* v *Commission* [1995] ECR I-743.

[93] Case T-24/90 *Automec* v *Commission* (Automec II) [1992] ECR II-2223.

[94] Case 7/82 *Gesellschaft zur Verwertung von Leistungsschutzrechten* v *Commission* [1983] ECR 483.

Fines

If it finds that the breach was intentional or negligent, the Commission may impose a fine of up to €1 million or 10 per cent of an undertaking's worldwide annual turnover, whichever is the higher.[95] 'Intentional' does not require that an undertaking knew it was infringing the competition rules; rather it requires only that it could not have been unaware that its conduct would result in a distortion of competition.[96] So, a plea that an undertaking was ignorant of the very existence of such a thing as competition law is irrelevant.[97] Calculation of a fine is a function of the gravity and duration of the infringement.[98] There is no distinction to be drawn amongst agreements, decisions of associations of undertakings or concerted practices in imposing fines for infringement of Article 81(1),[99] although the higher individual fines tend to fall under Article 82 and the Commission sometimes declines to fine undertakings party to agreements procured under duress.[100] The fact that a fine is unprecedented – for example, none had previously been imposed in the particular sector – cannot be argued as a ground for its unfairness or reduction provided that the gravity of the infringement and the resulting restriction of competition are undisputed.[101] The Commission must be allowed a margin of discretion in fixing the amount of a fine,[102] and deterrence in both senses of ensuring effective penalty and *pour encourager les autres*, especially when pursuing general and important policy matters, are legitimate considerations.[103] It

---

[95] Reg 17, art 15(2). Under the ECSC Treaty the limit is twice the turnover on the products which were the subject of the agreement or 10 per cent of the undertaking's turnover: Art 65(5).

[96] Case 19/77 *Miller* v *Commission* [1978] ECR 131 (in which the Court said that the opinion of a legal adviser upon which an undertaking has relied is not a mitigating factor): Case T-83/91 *Tetra Pak* v *Commission* [1994] ECR II-755.

[97] Decision 87/406 (*Tipp-Ex*) OJ 1987 L222/1, upheld in Case 279/87 *Tipp-Ex* v *Commission* [1990] ECR I-261.

[98] Reg 17, art 15(2).

[99] Cases T-213/95 & 18/96 *Stichting Certificatie Kraanverhuurbedrijf* v *Commission* [1997] ECR II-1739.

[100] eg, Decision 96/478 (*Bayer/Adalat*) OJ 1996 L201/1 (under review as Case T-41/96 *Bayer* v *Commission*, pending); Decision 98/273 (*Volkswagen*) OJ 1998 L124/60 (under review as Case T-62/98 *Volkswagen* v *Commission*, pending).

[101] Case T-83/91 *Tetra Pak* v *Commission* [1994] ECR II-755, upheld as Case C-333/94P *Tetra Pak* v *Commission* [1996] ECR I-5951; Case T-229/94 *Deutsche Bahn* v *Commission* [1997] ECR II-1689, upheld as Case C-436/97P *Deutsche Bahn* v *Commission* [1999] ECR I-2387.

[102] Case T-49/95 *van Megen Sports* v *Commission* [1996] ECR II-1799.

[103] Cases 100–03/80 *Musique Diffusion Française* v *Commission* (Pioneer) [1983] ECR 1825; Case T-13/89 *ICI* v *Commission* [1992] ECR II-1021; Case T-334/94 *Sarrió* v *Commission* (Cartonboard) [1998] ECR II-1439.

was fairly gentle in the early years, girding its loins to impose substantial fines for the first time in 1979, for a concerted practice inhibiting parallel imports, in *Pioneer*.[104] Since then fines have grown progressively steeper. To date the highest fine imposed has been 273 million ECUs (about £175 million), upon 15 parties to a liner conference found to have infringed both Articles 81(1) and 82;[105] the highest fine visited upon a single undertaking is 102 million ECUs (£70 million) imposed upon Volkswagen for, through a series of agreements with its dealers, sealing off the German and Austrian markets from parallel imports of its motorcars from the Italian market.[106] The Court of First Instance said (for the first time, surprisingly, only in 1995) that it is 'desirable' for the method used in calculating a fine to be ascertainable from the decision so as to enable an undertaking to challenge its fairness.[107] Notwithstanding long commitment to the principle that uncertainty as to the amount of a fine is a legitimate element of its deterrent effect (which also allowed it a very wide – arbitrary? – discretion), in 1998 the Commission published a notice detailing various tariffs it uses and the consideration it will give to gravity ('minor', 'serious' and 'very serious' infractions), duration and aggravating and attenuating circumstances.[108] The probative value of the notice is unknown; in several of the *Cartonboard* cases (decided some four months after publication of the notice) the Court of First Instance said that 'no binding or exhaustive list of the criteria which must be applied [to the calculation of fines] has been drawn up',[109] and in *Thyssen Stahl* (decided over a year later) it said 'there being no binding or exhaustive list of criteria which must be applied'.[110]

In order to ensure prompt(ish) compliance with a decision the

---

[104] Decision 80/256, OJ 1980 L60/21. The fines against three exclusive dealers and the Japanese parent's subsidiary European importer totalled almost 7 million u.a., reduced on review to 3.2 million u.a.: Cases 100–03/80 *Musique Diffusion Française, ibid.*

[105] Decision 1999/243 (*Transatlantic Conference Agreement*) OJ 1999 L95/1 (under review as Cases T-191 etc/98 *Atlantic Container Line* v *Commission*, pending).

[106] Decision 98/273 (*Volkswagen*) OJ 1998 L124/60 (under review as Case T-62/98 *Volkswagen* v *Commission*, pending. The previous highest fine was 75 million ECUs (£50 million) imposed in Decision 92/163 (*Tetra Pak II*) OJ 1992 L72/1 for serious, persistent and deliberate breach of Art 82; upheld by the Court of First Instance in Case T-83/91 *Tetra Pak* v *Commission* [1994] ECR II-755 and, on appeal, by the Court of Justice in Case C-333/94P *Tetra Pak* v *Commission* [1996] ECR I-5951.

[107] Case T-148/89 *Tréfilunion* v *Commission* [1995] ECR II-1063.

[108] Guidelines on the method of setting fines pursuant to article 15(2) of Regulation No 17 and Article 65(5) of the ECSC Treaty: OJ 1998 C9/3.

[109] eg, Case T-295/94 *Buchmann* v *Commission* [1998] ECR II-813 at 862; Case T-334/94 *Sarrió* v *Commission* [1998] ECR II-1439 at 1541.

[110] Case T-141/94 *Thyssen Stahl* v *Commission* [1999] ECR II-347 at 556 (under appeal as Case C-194/99P *Thyssen Stahl* v *Commission*, pending).

Commission may also impose a liquidate penalty ('periodic penalty payment') of up to €1000 per day for each day on which an undertaking, having been ordered to do so, fails to put an end to an infringement, fails to comply with a formal request for information, or refuses to submit to a formal investigation.[111] Commission fines are subject to a prescription period of three years in respect of infringements concerning notification, requests for information and the carrying out of investigations, and of five years for all other infringements.[112]

It is sometimes queried whether these fines constitute deterrence sufficient and appropriate to ensure compliance with the competition rules. The liability lies only with the undertaking and not individuals within it, and the Commission can award no damages to injured third parties. Compare the recent (and record) fine of $500 million (£312 million) imposed upon Hoffmann-La Roche by the American Department of Justice for monopolistic price fixing,[113] personal fines ($150,000 and $100,000) and terms of imprisonment (five and four months) visited upon two executives of the company (both Swiss citizens and residents)[114] and the availability there of treble damages in civil litigation.[115] Nevertheless the Commission has recently pronounced itself satisfied with its present powers of sanction (they have 'proved appropriate') and proposes no change.[116]

---

[111] Reg 17, art 16. This may not of itself seem dissuasive, for an ongoing fine of €1,000 per day represents the salary of one higher-ranking executive in larger undertakings; however, as Commission decisions are subject to civil process (see *infra*) it could be enforced in national courts, if necessary through contempt proceedings. To add teeth, in its 1999 White Paper (pp 219–23 *infra*) the Commission proposes that this sum be increased to €25,000.

[112] Reg 2988/74, OJ 1974 L319/1, art 1(1). In the event of a continuing or repeated infringement, time runs from when the infringement ceased (art 1(2)); any action taken by the Commission (eg, initiating an investigation) causes time to begin afresh (art 2(3)).

[113] *Unites States* v *Hoffmann-La Roche*, consent decree in the US District Court, Dallas of 20 May 1999. Hoffmann-La Roche was also fined C$51 million (£20 million) out of total fines of C$88.4 million, the largest in Canadian history, for offences arising in the same circumstances under the Competition Act; see *R* v *Hoffmann-La Roche*, judgment of the Federal Court (Trial Div) of 22 September 1999, not yet reported.

[114] *United States* v *Sommer* and *United States* v *Brönnimann*, consent decrees in the US District Court, Dallas of 20 May 1999 and 19 August 1999. Dr Brönnimann was let off rather lightly by the Americans, being also fined C$250,000 for offences under the Competition Act; *R* v *Brönnimann*, judgment of the Ontario Superior Court of 25 October 1999, unreported.

[115] § 4 Clayton Act 15 USC § 15.

[116] White Paper on Modernisation of the Rules Implementing Articles 85 and 86 of the EC Treaty, Programme No 99/027, para 123.

Fines and periodic penalty payments are, in the view of Community law, administrative, not criminal, penalties.[117] This is in part because, generally, the Community enjoys no power under the Treaty in the area of criminal law[118] and it has importance in two respects: first, in a number of member states the distinction between administrative and criminal penalties is closely circumscribed, and a criminal record, even if imposed against a body corporate, may seriously affect the right to pursue economic activities; and second, were they criminal sanctions, a raft of procedural safeguards for the protection of the individual, required by national law and by the European Convention on Human Rights, would come into play. However, it is not yet clear that the European Court of Human Rights would take a view as benign as the Court of Justice. Of particular importance to Strasbourg in the context is Article 6(1) of the Convention, which ensures in both civil and criminal matters the right to a fair and public hearing within a reasonable time by an independent and impartial tribunal established by law but is recognised by the Court of Human Rights as imposing a higher burden in proceedings in which a 'criminal charge' – criminal charge having an autonomous Convention meaning[119] – is at issue.[120] According to its earlier case law the Court of Justice found the Commission not to be a 'tribunal' within the meaning of Article 6(1) and so not subject in its workings and procedure to its restraint.[121] However, the European Commission of Human Rights found a fine imposed by the French Minister of Finance (who *was* a tribunal for purposes of Article 6(1)) deploying powers of sanction similar to those enjoyed by the Commission under Regulation 17 to be a criminal charge,[122] and the Court of Justice now seems to be moving gingerly in that direction. According to (acting) Advocate-General Vesterdorf in 1991:

---

[117] Reg 17, art 15(4), confirmed by the Court of Justice in Case 45/69 *Boehringer Mannheim v Commission* [1970] ECR 769.

[118] See eg Case C-299/95 *Kremzow v Austria* [1997] ECR I-2629.

[119] *Engel v Netherlands* (1976) 1 EHRR 647.

[120] eg, *Funke v France* (1993) 16 EHRR 297.

[121] Cases 209–15 & 218/78 *van Landewyck v Commission* (FEDETAB) [1980] ECR 3125; Cases 100–03/80 *Musique Diffusion Française v Commission* (Pioneer) [1983] ECR 1825; Case T-11/89 *Shell v Commission* (Polypropylene) [1992] ECR II-757.

[122] See *Société Stenuit v France* (1992) 14 EHRR 509, in which the Commission unanimously found an infringement (*infraction*) established by the French competition authorities to be of a criminal law nature and so subject to the protection of Art 6(1), but the case was withdrawn before reaching the Court; for similar, although only indirectly related, consideration by the Court of Human Rights see *Öztürk v Germany* (1984) 6 EHRR 409; but *cf.* the decision of the Commission of Human Rights in Case No 13258/87 *M & Co v Germany*, unreported decision of 9 February 1990.

the fines which may be imposed on undertakings pursuant to Article 15 of Regulation 17/62 do in fact, notwithstanding what is stated in Article 15(4), have a criminal law character, [so] it is vitally important that the Court should seek to bring about a state of legal affairs not susceptible of any justified criticism with reference to the European Convention for the Protection of Human Rights. At all events, within the framework formed by the existing body of rules and the judgments handed down hitherto it must therefore be sought to ensure that legal protection within the Community meets the standard otherwise regarded as reasonable in Europe.[123]

And according to Advocate-General Darmon in 1993, whilst a regulation of general application need not be reasoned in great detail,

[a] Commission decision in the field of competition is another matter entirely, particularly where it orders a trader to pay a fine *and is therefore manifestly of a penal nature*.[124]

Most recently Advocate-General Léger said in *Baustahlgewebe* (1998):

Article 6 of the Convention enshrines the right of any person to a 'fair ... hearing within a reasonable time', which is available where a court is required to determine 'his civil rights and obligations or ... any criminal charge against him'. It cannot be disputed – and the Commission does not dispute – that, in the light of the case law of the European Court of Human Rights and the opinions of the European Commission of Human Rights, the present case involves a 'criminal charge'.[125]

As for the Court, it has identified a general principle of Community law, 'inspired' by Article 6(1), that every person is entitled to fair legal process.[126] A number of the *Cartonboard* cases included pleas relating to the applicability of Article 6(1) but they were dismissed as having been improperly raised.[127] The Court applied Article 6(1) (again, indirectly, as a general principle of Community law inspired by it) for the first time in *Baustahlgewebe*, reducing a Commission fine (marginally, knocking 50,000 ECUs off a 3 million ECU fine) as 'reasonable satisfaction' for the excessive duration of proceedings before the Court of First Instance.[128]

---

[123] Case T-1/89 *Rhône-Poulenc* v *Commission* (Polypropylene) [1991] ECR II-867 at 885–6.

[124] Cases 89 etc/85 *Åhlström* v *Commission* (Woodpulp) [1993] ECR I-1307 at 1551; emphasis added.

[125] Case C-185/95P *Baustahlgewebe* v *Commission* [1998] ECR I-8417 at 8431.

[126] Opinion 2/94 *re Accession to the European Convention on Human Rights* [1996] ECR I-1759; Case C-299/95 *Kremzow* v *Austria* [1997] ECR I-2629.

[127] Case T-311/94 *BPB de Eendracht* v *Commission* [1998] ECR II-1129; Case T-352/94 *Mo och Domsjö* v *Commission* [1998] ECR II-1989.

[128] Case C-185/95P *Baustahlgewebe* v *Commission* [1998] ECR I-8417.

The Court of First Instance itself subsequently considered the issue of whether Commission proceedings had been prosecuted within a reasonable period of time but deploying a variety of reasons found it, rather generously, not to be excessive.[129] Whatever the shifting nature of the criminal quality of the Commission's powers under Regulation 17, various safeguards of the rights of defence apply,[130] and the Court has a duty in reviewing the conduct of the Commission to be vigilant to ensure that this is so.[131]

The 1997 notice on agreements of minor importance provides that if an agreement covered by it nevertheless falls foul of Article 81(1), and was not notified[132] because the parties assumed in good faith that the notice applied, the Commission will not 'consider imposing fines'.[133] In order better to detect and combat (or corrode) cartels, and inspired in part by the corporate leniency programme introduced by the American Justice Department in 1978 and 1993, the Commission has adopted another notice (the 'leniency' or 'whistleblowers' notice) by which it has undertaken to impose no fine upon an undertaking participating in a cartel which shops the cartel to the Commission, provided that undertaking was not a 'ringleader' in, or originator of, the cartel, and to grant 'very substantial reductions' in a fine where an undertaking cooperates fully with an investigation already initiated by the Commission.[134] It is probably now estopped from imposing fines contrary to the terms of these undertak-

---

[129] Cases T-305 etc/94 *Limburgse Vinyl Maatschappij* v *Commission* [1999] ECR II-931 (under appeal as Cases C-238 etc/99P *Limburgse Vinyl Maatschappij* v *Commission*, pending).

[130] See *infra*.

[131] On judicial review of the Commission see pp 187–94 *infra*.

[132] As to notification, see Chap 4.

[133] Commission notice on agreements of minor importance which do not fall within the meaning of Article 85(1), OJ 1997 C372/13, para 5. On the notice, see pp 72–5 *supra*.

[134] Commission notice on the non-imposition or the mitigation of fines in cartel cases, OJ 1996 C207/4. This is codification of occasional Commission practice given a preliminary nudge by the Court of First Instance in Case T-13/89 *ICI* v *Commission* (Polypropylene) [1992] ECR II-1021 and first expressly seen in Decision 94/601 (*Cartonboard*) OJ 1994 L243/1, in which it noted (at para 171) that, even after the launch of an investigation, a cartel ringleader's 'spontaneous admission of the infringement and the detailed evidence which it provided to the Commission has contributed materially to the establishment of the truth, reduced the need to rely upon circumstantial evidence and no doubt influenced other producers who might otherwise have continued to deny all wrongdoing', and so reduced the fine imposed upon the (perhaps not universally popular) ringleading undertaking by two-thirds. For express application of the notice by the Commission see Decision 1999/60 (*Pre-Insulated Pipe Cartel*) OJ 1999 L24/1; Decision 1999/210 (*British Sugar/Tate & Lyle/Napier Brown/James Budgett*) OJ 1999 L76/1; Decision 1999/271 (*Greek Ferries*) OJ 1999 L109/24.

ings.[135] The Court of First Instance has said that a reduction in fines owing to cooperation during the administrative procedure is justified only if it enables the Commission more easily to establish the infringement and bring it to an end, and an express statement declining to contest the factual allegations upon which the Commission has made its case falls within that category;[136] neither cooperation during the administrative phase which does not go beyond the legal obligations of Regulation 17, irreproachable conduct following a decision, nor the fact an undertaking is a newcomer to the market can serve as mitigating circumstances justifying a reduction in fines.[137] There are arguments that the reductions indicated in the whistle-blowers notice are unfair in that they may result in two parties being penalised differently for the same material infraction and so offend the general principle of equal treatment, they may inhibit a party from exercising its right of mounting a robust defence to a Commission decision,[138] they may induce a party, through financial incentive, to an admission of unlawful conduct contrary to *Orkem* principles of privilege against self-incrimination,[139] and they may result in over-enthusiastic (and so un-reliable) admissions from undertakings eager to curry favour with the Commission and/or to damage competitors in terms of reputation and the impact of any fine; but the Court of First Instance seems not to be impressed by them.[140] It could, for sake of completeness, be added that the Commission does not have an unblemished record as regards individual whistleblowers.[141]

---

[135] The whistleblowers notice (para E.3) expressly accepts that the Commission 'is aware that this notice will create legitimate expectations on which enterprises may rely ...'.

[136] Case T-13/89 *ICI* v *Commission* (Polypropylene) [1992] ECR II-1021; Case T-352/94 *Mo och Domsjö* v *Commission* [1998] ECR II-1989 (Cartonboard).

[137] Cases T-305 etc/94 *Limburgse Vinyl Maatschappij* v *Commission* [1999] ECR II-931 (under appeal as Cases T-238 etc/99P *Limburgse Vinyl Maatschappij* v *Commission*, pending).

[138] See the judgments of the European Court of Human Rights in *Deweer* v *Belgium* (1980) 2 EHRR 439 and *Funke* v *France* (1993) 16 EHRR 297 which provide authority that pressure to refrain from challenging a criminal charge in return for a reduction in a fine is a breach of Art 6 of the ECHR.

[139] Case 374/87 *Orkem* v *Commission* [1989] ECR 3283; see n 46 *supra* and accompanying text.

[140] Case T-311/94 *BPB de Eendrecht* v *Commission* [1998] ECR II-1129; Case T-347/94 *Mayr-Melnhof Kartongesellschaft* v *Commission* [1998] ECR II-1751; Case T-352/94 *Mo och Domsjö* v *Commission* [1998] ECR II-1989 (all *Cartonboard* cases).

[141] In 1973 a disgruntled employee of Hoffmann-La Roche (based in Basel) informed against the latter to the Commission for a number of infringements of Art 82. He was inadver-tently identified to Hoffmann-La Roche by the Commission and as a result was convicted of 'economic espionage' and gaoled under the Swiss Penal Code. The Commission was ordered to pay him substantial damages under Art 215(2) (now Art 288(2)) of the Treaty

The legal person to which the Commission addresses a decision imposing a fine (or any decision) may in some circumstances give rise to problems. Where an infringement is attributed to an association of undertakings but the association has no legal personality, it is legitimate to impose fines upon the individual undertakings rather than the association itself.[142] Although the lack of legal personality ought in principle to be immaterial,[143] in some circumstances it may as a practical matter be necessary, for recovery of a fine may involve recourse to national enforcement proceedings and that may require legal personality as a matter of national law.[144] If an association is fined there is no provision for the joint and several liability of its members, but in its 1999 White Paper[145] the Commission proposes amendment to Regulation 17 to make it so. In all events the identity of the addressee undertaking must be absolutely clear from the decision[146] and, in the interests of the rights of defence, must be clear prior to that, in the Commission's statement of objections.[147] Subject to that, according to the economic entity doctrine conduct of a subsidiary undertaking which carries out 'in all material respects' the policies of its parent undertaking may be attributed to the parent,[148] so that a fine may be imposed either upon the parent or upon the parent and subsidiary, in which case the liability may be joint and several.[149] According to the Commission it is appropriate to address a decision to the parent where more than one undertaking in the group participated in the (alleged) infringement and/or where there is express evidence implicating the parent

---

for failing in a duty of confidentiality: Case 145/83 *Adams* v *Commission* [1985] ECR 3539. Further, the Commission whistleblower who went public with the information regarding maladministration and corruption which led to the resignation of the Commission in 1999 was suspended without pay, subsequently reinstated but severely reprimanded for his pains.

[142] Cases T-24 etc/93 *Compagnie Maritime Belge* v *Commission* [1996] ECR II-1201, upheld for the most part as Cases C-395 & 396/96P *Compagnie Maritime Belge* v *Commission*, judgment of 16 March 2000, not yet reported.

[143] Cases C-395 & 396/96P *Compagnie Maritime Belge, ibid* at para 144.

[144] Decision 1999/60 (*Pre-Insulated Pipes*) OJ 1999 L24/48 (under review as Cases T-9 etc/99 *HFB Holding für Fernwärmetechnik Beteiligungsgesellschaft* v *Commission*, pending).

[145] See pp 219–23 *infra*.

[146] Case T-38/92 *All Weather Sports Benelux* v *Commission* [1994] ECR II-211.

[147] Cases C-395 & 396/96P *Compagnie Maritime Belge* v *Commission*, judgment of 16 March 2000, not yet reported; as to rights of defence see *infra*.

[148] Case 48/69 *ICI* v *Commission* (Dyestuffs) [1972] ECR 619; Case 107/82 *AEG-Telefunken* v *Commission* [1983] ECR 3151.

[149] Case T-65/89 *BPB Industries and British Gypsum* v *Commission* [1993] ECR II-389, upheld tacitly on appeal as Case C-310/93P *BPB Industries and British Gypsum* v *Commission* [1995] ECR I-865.

company in the conduct of its subsidiary showing the latter acted under the direction or with the knowledge of the parent.[150] The fact that the product which is the subject of a cartel is only one of many in which the parent or group is involved within the corporate structure and is the responsibility of a subsidiary is not decisive.[151] But because the liability of the parent for the subsidiary is a function of the latter being deemed to adhere to the commercial policy laid down by the former, it would be inappropriate to stretch the economic entity doctrine in order to impose a fine upon a subsidiary where it played no part in the anticompetitive conduct of the parent – however attractive a course this may be as a means of exerting jurisdiction over parent undertakings outwith the Community.[152] Related to this is a problem of succession: where one undertaking acquires another the former generally succeeds to the liabilities in competition law of the latter. An infringement of the competition rules must be attributed to the legal person responsible for the operation (*exploitation*; *Betrieb*) of the undertaking at the time of the infringement[153] and a change in legal form does not create a new undertaking free of liability for the anticompetitive conduct of the predecessor undertaking when, from an economic point of view, the two are identical.[154] According to the Commission, rights of action against a body corporate are generally not extinguished when control passes, it would be contrary to public policy to make an exception for competition law, it is to be determined as a matter of Community law, and the appropriate test is the functional and economic continuity of the successor undertaking.[155] But the Commission must provide a clear statement of reasons justifying the imputation to the successor undertaking of the (unlawful) activities of its predecessor,[156] which must be

---

[150] Decision 88/138 (*Hilti*) OJ 1988 L65/19; Decision 94/601 (*Cartonboard*) OJ 1994 L243/1.

[151] Decision 1999/60 (*Pre-Insulated Pipes*) OJ 1999 L24/1 (under review as Cases T-9 etc/99 *HFB Holding für Fernwärmtechnik Beteiligungsgesellschaft* v *Commission*, pending).

[152] See Chap 9.

[153] Case T-6/89 *Enichem Anic* v *Commission* (Polypropylene) [1991] ECR II-1623 at 1695.

[154] Cases 29-30/83 *Compagnie Royale Asturienne des Mines* v *Commission* [1984] ECR 1679; Case T-134/94 *NMH Stahlwerke* v *Commission* [1999] ECR II-239.

[155] Decision 84/405 (*Zinc Producer Group*) OJ 1984 L220/27; Decision 85/206 (*Aluminium Imports from Eastern Europe*) OJ 1985 L92/1; Decision 86/398 (*Polypropylene*) OJ 1986 L230/1; Decision 89/190 (*PVC*) OJ 1989 L74/1; Decision 89/515 (*Welded Steel Mesh*) OJ 1989 L260/1; Decision 94/601 (*Cartonboard*) OJ 1994 L243/1; Decision 1999/210 (*British Sugar/Tate & Lyle/Napier Brown/James Budgett*) OJ 1999 L76/1.

[156] Case T-38/92 *All Weather Sports Benelux* v *Commission* [1994] ECR II-211; Case T-327/94 *SCA Holding Ltd* v *Commission* [1998] ECR II-1373 and Case T-354/94 *Stora Kopparbergs Bergslags* v *Commission* [1998] ECR II-2111 (both *Cartonboard* cases).

especially detailed if these had been contested at the administrative stage.[157]

A final problem arises where a decision imposing a fine is addressed to an undertaking which is an arm of the state, or, put another way, (an organ of) a member state acting in its capacity as an undertaking,[158] for the Treaty provides that '[d]ecisions of the ... Commission which impose a pecuniary obligation *on persons other than States*, shall be enforceable'.[159] However, the Commission has fined an arm of the Italian Ministry of Finance, the state having a single legal personality in Italian constitutional law, saying simply that 'whilst not having a legal personality as such, [it] is an undertaking within the meaning of Article 86 of the Treaty' and so liable to a fine;[160] the authority has challenged the decision but not directly on that ground.[161]

A Commission decision imposing a financial penalty is enforced by civil process.[162] In the United Kingdom it is registered by the High Court or the Court of Session as a 'European Community judgment'[163] and enforced in accordance with specific rules of court.[164] The Commission may (but need not)[165] agree – and frequently offers – to defer enforcing payment of a fine pending any judicial review of the decision upon condition that the undertaking will pay default interest if the action for review fails and provides bank guarantees as to eventual payment of principal, interest and any increase in the fine.

Rights of defence
Regulation 17 provides that, prior to the adoption of a decision on termi-

---

[157] Case T-38/92 *All Weather Sports Benelux, ibid.*

[158] See pp 36–38 *supra.*

[159] Art 256 (ex Art 192); emphasis added. Thus it is in part that the power introduced by the Maastricht Treaty and contained in Art 228(2) (ex Art 171(2)) of the EC Treaty to fine a member state which fails to comply with an Art 226 (ex Art 169) judgment of the Court of Justice was granted not to the Commission (and so would be unenforceable absent amendment of Art 256) but to the Court of Justice.

[160] Decision 98/538 (*Amministrazione Autonoma dei Monopoli di Stato*) OJ 1998 L352/47 at para 62.

[161] Case T-139/98 *Amministrazione Autonoma dei Monopoli di Stato* v *Commission*, pending, in which the AAMS is arguing in part not that it, as an undertaking, is immune from fines, but that it is not an undertaking in the terms identified by the Commission.

[162] EC Treaty, Art 256 (ex Art 192).

[163] European Communities (Enforcement of Community Judgments) Order 1972, SI 1972/1590.

[164] RSC, Ord 71, rr 15–24 (England and Wales), RCS, rr 62.18–62.25 (Scotland).

[165] eg, Case T-191/98R *DSR-Senator Lines* v *Commission*, order of 21 June 1999 [1999] ECR II-2531, upheld on appeal as Case C-364/99P(R) *DSR-Senator Lines* v *Commission* [1999] ECR I-8733.

nation of an infraction, fines or periodic penalty payments, the undertakings concerned have a right 'of being heard on the matters to which the Commission has taken objection'.[166] This requires at least the exercise of two basic principles: first, the Commission is under an obligation to make known its case; and second, the undertaking has a right to reply.[167] The right to be heard in any proceedings likely to culminate in a measure adversely affecting a particular person is of particular importance, and is guaranteed even in the absence of any rules governing a procedure as a fundamental principle of Community law.[168]

Detailed provisions to give effect to these rights are set out by regulation.[169] The Commission must inform the undertaking(s) in writing of its 'objections' (the 'statement of objections') and set a (reasonable) time limit for a reply.[170] The statement of objections, which consists of two parts – one on fact, the other the legal assessment – need not be in great detail and at length but must set forth 'clearly, albeit succinctly' the case against.[171] Any subsequent decision is limited to the subject matter of the statement of objections, and only those upon which the undertakings have had the opportunity of replying.[172] 'Concerned' undertakings – those whose conduct is the subject of the proceedings and to whom a decision may be addressed – have a right to be heard.[173] The Commission may hear representation from any other party it considers necessary;[174] third parties have a right to be heard if they apply to do so and they can show a 'sufficient interest'.[175]

In preparing a defence, access to the Commission file is 'one of the procedural safeguards intended to protect the rights of the defence' as it 'enable[s] the addressees of statements of objections to examine evidence in the Commission's file so that they are in a position effectively to express

---

[166] Reg 17, art 19(1).

[167] Cases 56 & 58/64 *Consten & Grundig v EEC Commission* [1966] ECR 299; Case T-1/89 *Rhône-Poulenc v Commission* (Polypropylene) [1991] ECR II-867.

[168] Case 113/77 *NTN Toyo Bearings v Council* [1979] ECR 1185 *per* Advocate-General Warner at 1261; Case 85/76 *Hoffmann-La Roche v Commission* [1979] ECR 461; Cases 48 & 66/90 *Netherlands v Commission* [1992] ECR I-565; Case T-450/93 *Lisestral v Commission* [1994] ECR II-1177, upheld on appeal as Case C-32/95P *Commission v Lisestral* [1996] ECR I-5373.

[169] Reg 2842/98, OJ 1998 L354/18 (repealing and replacing Reg 99/63, JO 1963, 2268).

[170] *Ibid*, arts 2(1), 3(4).

[171] Cases 41, 44–5/69 *ACF Chemifarma v Commission* (Quinine) [1970] ECR 661 at 684; also Case 48/69 *ICI v Commission* (Dyestuffs) [1972] ECR 619.

[172] Reg 2842/98, art 2(2).

[173] Reg 17, art 19(1).

[174] *Ibid*, art 19(2).

[175] *Ibid*, art 19(2); Reg 2842/98, art 9.

their views on the conclusions reached by the Commission in its statement of objections on the basis of that evidence'.[176] Whilst there was no positive rule that the Commission was under an obligation to disclose the contents of the file,[177] in 1982 the Commission decided[178] that thenceforward any undertaking 'involved in the procedure' would be entitled to inspect the full file, excluding confidential information, business secrets[179] and internal Commission documents (which exclusion cannot be permitted to frustrate the rights of defence), and the Commission seems now to be estopped from departing from it.[180] It recently created for itself a more express duty to 'make appropriate arrangements for allowing access to the file'[181] and has issued a notice on procedure for gaining access to it.[182] Owing to this general principle of 'equality of arms', if the Commission fails to disclose certain documents it cannot rely upon them in a subsequent decision if they alone form the basis of its reasoning.[183]

The reply is in the first instance in writing, in which the undertaking may challenge the accuracy of fact in the statement of objections as well as the economic and legal analysis of the Commission case. Thereafter there are closed oral hearings, before a hearings officer.[184] In accordance with the principle of good administration, the Commission must give due consideration to the arguments of the undertakings. Settlement may be, and

---

[176] Case T-30/91 *Solvay* v *Commission* (Soda Ash) [1995] ECR II-1775 at 1802; Case C-51/92P *Hercules Chemicals* v *Commission* (Polypropylene) [1999] ECR I-4235 at 4274 (using virtually identical wording).

[177] Case 62/86 *AKZO* v *Commission* [1991] ECR I-3359.

[178] EC Commission, *Twelfth Report on Competition Policy* (1982), point 34.

[179] It is for the Commission to determine what is a business secret; but so sensitive is the area that the Court of Justice has said that if the Commission elects to release what may fall into that category, it must first inform the undertaking, await a reply, then adopt a reasoned decision subject to judicial review and wait until a legal challenge is lost or time barred before releasing it: Case 53/85 *AKZO* v *Commission* [1986] ECR 1965; Case T-353/94 *Postbank* v *Commission* [1996] ECR II-921.

[180] Case T-1/89 *Rhône-Poulenc* v *Commission* (Polypropylene) [1991] ECR II-867; Decision 94/815 (*Cement*) OJ 1994 L343/1 at para 38; Case T-30/91 *Solvay* v *Commission* (Soda Ash) [1995] ECR II-1775.

[181] Reg 2842/98, art 13(1).

[182] Notice on internal rules of procedure for processing requests for access to the file, OJ 1997 C23/3.

[183] Case T-30/91 *Solvay* v *Commission* (Soda Ash) [1995] ECR II-1775. This right is objective in nature and does not depend upon whether the Commission acts in good or in bad faith.

[184] Reg 2842/98, arts 10–12. The terms of reference of the hearings officer and the conduct of hearings are laid down in Decision 94/810, OJ 1994 L330/67. As the report of the hearings officer is an internal Commission document the rights of defence do not extend to a right of access to and comment upon it: Case T-2/69 *Petrofina* v *Commission* [1991] ECR II-1087; Case T-13/89 *ICI* v *Commission* [1992] ECR II-1021.

frequently is, reached, especially where undertakings are prepared to moderate their existing agreements or conduct. The Commission may then proceed to a formal decision; if it is one declaring an infringement of Articles 81(1) or 82 or imposing a fine or a periodic penalty payment it must first consult the Advisory Committee on Restrictive Practices and Monopolies.[185] Various infringements by various parties of Articles 81 and 82 may be – and invariably are in the event of a cartel – covered in a single decision provided that it provides adequate reasoning with respect to each of the addressees and permits each to obtain a clear picture of the unlawful conduct of which it is libelled.[186]

Interim measures

Although the power was not expressly conferred by Regulation 17,[187] the Commission asserted, and the Court of Justice accepted, that in the course of an investigation the Commission may order appropriate interim remedial measures, either positive or negative, where there is a *prima facie* breach of Articles 81(1) or 82, urgency, and either a likelihood of serious and irreparable injury or a situation intolerable to the public interest.[188] Although they may be and are deployed in the context of Article 81,[189] interim measures are more likely to be adopted, and justified, in cases involving injury through abuse of a dominant position.[190] The Commission may, and frequently does, accept an undertaking rather than pronounce a formal order.[191] It will in appropriate cases require the lodging of a cross undertaking or caution in damages.

6.2.2 Judicial control of the Commission

Any decision adopted by the Commission under the authority granted it by Regulation 17, including decisions refusing to launch an investigation,[192]

---

[185] Reg 17, arts 10(3), 10(5).

[186] Cases 40 etc/73 *Coöperatieve Vereniging 'Suiker Unie'* v *Commission* [1975] ECR 1663; Cases 209–15 & 218/78 *van Landewyck* v *Commission* (FEDETAB) [1980] ECR 3125; Case T-38/92 *All Weather Sports Benelux* v *Commission* [1994] ECR II-211; Case T-227/95 *AssiDomän Kraft Products* v *Commission* [1997] ECR II-1185, set aside on appeal as Case C-310/97P *Commission* v *AssiDomän Kraft Products* [1999] ECR I-5363 but not on that ground.

[187] *cf.* the position under the ECSC Treaty, Art 66(5) and Case 109/75R *National Carbonising Co* v *Commission* [1975] ECR 1193.

[188] Case 792/79R *Camera Care* v *Commission* [1980] ECR 119; Case T-44/90 *La Cinq* v *Commission* [1992] ECR II-1.

[189] See eg *Mars/Langnese & Schöller*, decision of 25 March 1992, unpublished.

[190] See eg Decision 83/462 (*ECS/AKZO*) OJ 1983 L252/13.

[191] See eg Decision 87/500 (*BBI/Boosey & Hawkes*) OJ 1987 L286/36; Decision 94/19 (*Sea Containers/Stena Sealink*) OJ 1994 L15/8.

[192] See pp 165–8 *supra*.

formally requesting information or launching an article 14 investigation,[193] granting or refusing exemption,[194] imposing financial penalties,[195] adopting or refusing to adopt interim measures,[196] or even electing to release certain documents in a file,[197] is a decision within the meaning of Article 249 (ex Article 189) of the Treaty and so subject to judicial review by the Court of First Instance or the Court of Justice under Article 230 (ex Article 173) of the Treaty (the action of annulment). However, a Commission (and generally a Community) act is liable to judicial review only if it is definitive – that is, immediately and irreversibly affecting the legal position of the applicant – and not provisional as a step in an ongoing administrative procedure.[198] So, for example, neither the initiation of a procedure,[199] the statement of objections,[200] an 'article 6 letter',[201] a report containing a summary of oral explanations provided in the course of an article 14 investigation,[202] a refusal of the Commission to allow access to certain documents in a case file,[203] nor a comfort letter,[204] all being provi-

---

[193] Reg 17, arts 11(5) and 14(3); see pp 170–3 *supra*.

[194] See pp 132–4 *supra*.

[195] EC Treaty, Art 229 (ex Art 172); Reg 17, art 17; see p 192 *infra*.

[196] Cases 228–9/82 *Ford Werke* v *Commission* [1984] ECR 1129; Case T-23/90 *Automobiles Peugeot* v *Commission* [1991] ECR II-653; Case T-44/90 *La Cinq* v *Commission* [1992] ECR II-1; Cases T-24 & 28/92R *Langnese-Iglo & Schöller Lebensmittel* v *Commission* [1992] ECR II-1839.

[197] See n 179 *supra*.

[198] See, in the present context, Case 60/81 *IBM* v *Commission* [1981] ECR 2639; Case T-64/89 *Automec* v *Commission* (Automec I) [1990] ECR II-367; Case T-116/89 *Prodiforma* v *Commission* [1990] ECR II-843; Case T-138/89 *Nederlandse Bankverening* v *Commission* [1992] ECR II-2181; Case T-28/90 *Asia Motor France* v *Commission* [1992] ECR II-2285; Cases T-10–12 & 15/92 *Cimenteries CBR* v *Commission* [1992] ECR II-2667; Case T-37/92 *Bureau Européen des Consommateurs* v *Commission* [1994] ECR II-285; Case C-19/93P *Rendo* v *Commission* [1995] ECR I-3319; Case T-186/94 *Guérin Automobiles* v *Commission* [1995] ECR II-1753, upheld in Case C-282/95P *Guérin Automobiles* v *Commission* [1997] ECR I-1503; Cases C-68/94 & 30/95 *France & SCPA & EMC* v *Commission* [1998] ECR I-1375.

[199] Case 60/81 *IBM*, *ibid*; Cases T-10–12 & 15/92 *Cimenteries CBR*, *ibid*.

[200] Case 60/81 *IBM*, *ibid*; Cases T-10–12 & 15/92 *Cimenteries CBR*, *ibid*.

[201] Case T-64/89 *Automec* v *Commission* (Automec I) [1990] ECR II-367; Case T-114/92 *BEMIM* v *Commission* [1995] ECR II-147; Case T-5/93 *Tremblay* v *Commission* [1995] ECR II-185; Case C-282/95P *Guérin Automobiles* v *Commission* [1997] ECR I-1503. As to 'art 6' letters, see p 167 *supra*.

[202] Case T-9/97 *Elf-Autochem* v *Commission* [1997] ECR II-909.

[203] Cases T-10–12 & 15/92 *Cimenteries CBR* v *Commission* [1992] ECR II-2667. However, it may be fatal to the legality of any subsequent decision if certain documents are not disclosed: Case T-30/91 *Solvay* v *Commission* (Soda Ash) [1995] ECR II-1775, upheld on appeal in Cases C-287 & 288/95P *Commission* v *Solvay*, judgment of 6 April 2000, not yet reported.

[204] See pp 130–2 *supra*.

sional, is an act susceptible to judicial review. Under present rules if an action of annulment is raised by a member state or a Community institution – a rare (but not unknown) occurrence in the context of Commission enforcement of the competition rules – it falls within the jurisdiction of the Court of Justice; if raised by a natural or legal person – usually a disgruntled addressee of a Commission decision – it falls, since its creation in 1989, within that of the Court of First Instance. If the same act is competently challenged before both courts the Court of First Instance may stay/sist proceedings and await the judgment of the Court of Justice or decline jurisdiction and have both cases joined before the latter.[205] Appeal of a judgment of the Court of First Instance lies to the Court of Justice on points of law only.[206] Much of the case law on procedural aspects of the competition rules is therefore fashioned now by the Court of First Instance. On substance, it shares honours with the Court of Justice, both through the latter's appellate jurisdiction and in its exclusive jurisdiction in references from national courts under Article 234 (ex Article 177) of the Treaty.

If the addressee of a decision fails to seek judicial review under Article 230 within the (two-month) time limit allowed by Article 230(5) it becomes definitive for and binding upon him, even if it is subsequently annulled in proceedings raised by another party.[207] Third (private) parties wishing to challenge a Commission decision must satisfy the tests laid down by Article 230(4) that the decision affects them directly and individually. These, and especially the test of individual concern, are normally applied very stringently, so restricting significantly access to judicial review. However, the Court of Justice has been more lenient in recognising individual concern in the competition field than in more general areas of Community activity, so that a complainant, an undertaking participating or playing a significant role in a Commission investigation, and sometimes others so long as they are appreciably affected, are recognised as being individually concerned by a Commission decision and so enjoy standing to

---

[205] Statute of the Court of Justice, Art 47(3).

[206] EC Treaty, Art 225 (ex Art 168a); Decision 88/591 (establishing the Court of First Instance) as amended, OJ 1993 L144/21.

[207] Case C-310/97P *Commission* v *AssiDomän Kraft Products* [1999] ECR I-5363, reversing the Court of First Instance which had said (Case T-227/95 *AssiDomän Kraft Products* v *Commission* [1997] ECR II-1185) that Art 233 (ex Art 176) of the Treaty and the principle of good administration required the Commission to reconsider the decision as it applied to undertakings which had not challenged it in the light of the reasoning by which it had been annulled.

raise an action seeking its annulment.[208] Third parties may intervene in cases before the Court but only by leave and if they can show sufficient interest, and only in support of one or the other party to the action.[209] Whilst a question on the legality of a Commission decision granting exemption could quite conceivably arise in civil proceedings before a national court,[210] the circumstances in which any other type of decision under Regulation 17 could do so and which would not be an abuse of process in the *Textilwerke Deggendorf* sense[211] are remote, and the jurisdiction of the Community courts may be taken as privitive.

The grounds for annulment of a Community act, modelled upon French administrative law, are: lack of competence, infringement of an essential procedural requirement, infringement of the Treaty or of any rule of law relating to its application, and misuse of powers.[212] So, specific to the field of competition, the Court will annul a Commission decision where it fails to comply with an essential procedural requirement, including not only those prescribed by Regulations 17 and 2842/98 but also those laid down in the Commission's rules of procedure[213] and those deriving from general principles of Community law,[214] or with any material aspect of a party's right of defence;[215] where it improperly rejects a complaint lodged under

---

[208] See eg Case 26/76 *Metro* v *Commission (No 1)* [1977] ECR 1875; Case 75/84 *Metro* v *Commission (No 2)* [1986] ECR 3021; Case T-19/92 *Leclerc* v *Commission* [1996] ECR II-1851; Cases T-528 etc/93 *Métropole Télévision* v *Commission* [1996] ECR II-649; but *cf.* Case T-87/92 *Kruidvat* v *Commission* [1996] ECR II-1931, upheld on appeal as Case C-70/97P *Kruidvat* v *Commission* [1998] ECR I-7183.

[209] Statute of the Court of Justice, Art 37. An intervening party may use arguments different from those of the party litigant so long as it is supporting the latter's submissions: Case C-150/94 *United Kingdom* v *Council* [1998] ECR I-7235.

[210] See pp 133–4 *supra*.

[211] Case C-188/92 *TWD Textilwerke Deggendorf* v *Germany* [1994] ECR I-833; see p 133 *supra*.

[212] EC Treaty, Art 230(1).

[213] Case C-137/92 *Commission* v *BASF* (PVC) [1994] ECR I-2555; Cases T-31 & 32/91 *Solvay* v *Commission* (Soda Ash) [1995] ECR II-1821 and 1825, both upheld on appeal in Cases C-287 & 288/95P *Commission* v *Solvay*, judgment of 6 April 2000, not yet reported; Case T-37/91 *ICI* v *Commission* (Soda Ash) [1995] ECR II-1901, upheld on appeal in Case C-286/95P *Commission* v *ICI*, judgment of 6 April 2000, not yet reported); Case T-141/94 *Thyssen Stahl* v *Commission* [1999] ECR II-347 (under appeal as Case C-194/99P *Thyssen Stahl* v *Commission*, pending). For the current Commission Rules of Procedure see OJ 1999 L252/41; they are binding and contrary practice does not cause them to fall into desuetude: Case C-137/92P *PVC*.

[214] Case 17/74 *Transocean Marine Paint Association* v *Commission* [1974] ECR 1063.

[215] eg, Cases T-30/91 *Solvay* v *Commission* [1995] ECR II-1775 and T-36/91 *ICI* v *Commission* [1995] ECR II-1847 (Soda Ash); Case T-353/94 *Postbank* v *Commission* [1996] ECR II-921.

article 3 of Regulation 17;[216] where it is insufficiently reasoned;[217] where the legal identity of the addressee of a decision is not absolutely clear;[218] where the Commission has failed to adduce sufficient evidence to the requisite standard of proof,[219] it bearing the burden of showing the existence of an infringement;[220] or where the Court disagrees with the Commission's assessment or interpretation of the facts or of the law, or both.[221] The Court of First Instance has generally been more rigorous than the Court of Justice in scrutiny of both the Commission's economic reasoning[222] and

---

[216] See pp 165–8 *supra*.

[217] Cases 8–11/66 *Cimenteries CBR* v *Commission* [1967] ECR 75; Cases 89 etc/85 *Åhlström* v *Commission* (Woodpulp) [1993] ECR I-1307; Case C-360/92P *Publishers Association* v *Commission* [1995] ECR I-23; Cases T-374 etc/94 *European Night Services* v *Commission* [1998] ECR II-3141. The requirement of sufficient reasoning derives from both Art 253 (ex Art 190) of the Treaty and the rights of defence. The 'statement of reasons' must be contained in the decision itself and cannot be put forward subsequently except in exceptional circumstances (Case T-61/89 *Dansk Pelsdyravlerforening* v *Commission* [1992] ECR II-1931; Case T-334/94 *Sarrió* v *Commission* (Cartonboard) [1998] ECR II-1439; Cases T-374 etc/94 *European Night Services, supra*), which is why a typical Commission decision in the field will consist of many pages of preambular economic and legal analysis followed by only a handful of operative articles. If the anticompetitive effects are obvious the Commission need not provide lengthy reasoning: Case 272/85 *ANTIB* v *Commission* [1987] ECR 2201. If the Commission is breaking new ground, the reasoning will require to be more extensive: Case 73/74 *Groupment des Fabricants des Papiers Peints de Belgique* v *Commission* [1975] ECR 1491; Cases T-70–1/92 *Florimex* v *Commission* [1995] ECR II-693.

[218] Case T-38/92 *All Weather Sports Benelux* v *Commission* [1994] ECR II-211; see also Case T-327/94 *SCA Holding Ltd* v *Commission* [1998] ECR II-1373 and Case T-354/94 *Stora Kopparbergs Bergslags* v *Commission* [1998] ECR II-2111 (both *Cartonboard* cases).

[219] Cases 41, 44–5/69 *ACF Chemifarma* v *Commission* (Quinine) [1970] ECR 665; Case 6/72 *Europemballage & Continental Can* v *Commission* [1973] ECR 215; Cases 40 etc/73 *Coöperatieve Vereniging 'Suiker Unie'* v *Commission* [1975] ECR 1663; Cases T-68, 77–8/91 *Società Italiano Vetro* v *Commission* (Flat Glass) [1992] ECR II-1403; Case T-337/94 *Enso-Gutzeit* v *Commission* (Cartonboard) [1998] ECR II-1571.

[220] Case C-185/95P *Baustahlgewebe* v *Commission* [1998] ECR I-8417.

[221] Case 26/75 *General Motors* v *Commission* [1975] ECR 1367; Case 258/78 *Nungesser* v *Commission* (Maize Seeds) [1982] ECR 2015; Cases T-68 & 77–8/89 *Società Italiano Vetro* v *Commission* (Flat Glass) [1992] ECR II-1403; Cases 89 etc/85 *Åhlström* v *Commission* (Woodpulp) [1993] ECR I-1307; Case T-77/94 *Vereniging van Groothandelaren in Bloemkwekerijprodukten* v *Commission* [1997] ECR II-759; Cases T-374 etc/94 *European Night Services* v *Commission* [1998] ECR II-3141; Cases T-133 & 204/95 *International Express Carriers Conference* v *Commission* [1998] ECR II-3645, upheld in Case C-428/98P *Deutsche Post* v *International Express Carriers Conferences & Commission*, order of 11 May 2000, not yet reported.

[222] eg Cases T-68 & 77–8/89 *Flat Glass* and Case T-77/94 *Vereniging van Groothandelaren in Bloemkwekerijprodukten, ibid*.

procedural irregularities.[223] A judgment of the Court of First Instance may be set aside by the Court of Justice on appeal only if the former erred in law.[224] Appeal of a Court of First Instance judgment annulling a Commission decision has no suspensory effect.[225]

The Court may also, by express Treaty authority, cancel or vary the amount of a Commission fine.[226] Whilst the Commission enjoys a margin of discretion in fixing fines, it is 'desirable' for the method used in their calculation be ascertainable from a decision,[227] and the Court is bound to consider whether the amount is proportionate to the gravity and duration of the infraction, taking into account all relevant factors of the case.[228] The Court of First Instance seems disinclined to take note of the 1998 Commission Notice on the setting of fines as a function of review of the quantum of a fine.[229] In the event of an appeal from the Court of First Instance on the matter of fines, the Court of Justice cannot substitute its own appraisal for that of the Court of First Instance,[230] but it may consider whether the Court of First Instance has responded to a sufficient legal standard to the arguments raised for having the fine cancelled or reduced.[231]

---

[223] In Cases T-79 etc/89 *BASF* v *Commission* (PVC) [1992] ECR II-315 the Court of First Instance found Commission procedure to be such a shambles that it declared a purported decision to be 'non-existent', an extraordinary finding deriving from French and German administrative law; on appeal (Case C-137/92P *Commission* v *BASF* [1994] ECR I-2555) the Court of Justice said a finding of non-existence could apply to only very extreme situations and so overturned it, but annulled the decision for its procedural flaws. For related and similar judicial impatience with the Commission's cavalier approach to procedure see Cases T-31/91 and T-32/91 *Solvay* v *Commission* [1995] ECR II-1821 and 1825 and Case T-37/91 *ICI* v *Commission* [1995] ECR II-1901, all upheld on appeal in Case C-286/95P *Commission* v *ICI* and Cases C-287 & 288/95P *Commission* v *Solvay*, judgments of 6 April 2000, not yet reported.

[224] EC Treaty, Art 225 (ex Art 168a); Decision 88/591, OJ 1993 L144/21, art 51.

[225] *cf.* annulment by the Court of First Instance of a regulation, which takes effect only when an appeal becomes time barred or is dismissed: Statute of the Court of Justice, art 53.

[226] EC Treaty, Art 229 (ex Art 172); also Reg 17, art 17, under which the Court enjoys 'unlimited jurisdiction' to cancel, reduce or increase Commission fines. It has never increased a fine.

[227] Case T-148/89 *Tréfilunion* v *Commission* [1995] ECR II-1063.

[228] Case T-49/95 *van Megen Sports* v *Commission* [1996] ECR II-1799; Case T-229/94 *Deutsche Bahn* v *Commission* [1997] ECR II-1689. For extensive and close consideration of the fairness of Commission fines see a number of the *Cartonboard* judgments: Case T-295/94 *Buchmann* v *Commission* [1998] ECR II-813; Case T-327/94 *SCA Holding Ltd* v *Commission* [1998] ECR II-1373; Case T-334/94 *Sarrió* v *Commission* [1998] ECR II-1439; Case T-352/94 *Mo och Domsjö* v *Commission* [1998] ECR II-1989; and Case T-354/94 *Stora Kopparbergs Bergslags* v *Commission* [1998] ECR II-2111.

[229] See p 176 *supra*.

[230] Case C-320/92P *Finsider* v *Commission* [1994] ECR I-5697; Case C-310/93P *BPB Industries and British Gypsum* v *Commission* [1995] ECR I-865.

[231] Case C-219/95P *Ferriere Nord* v *Commission* [1997] ECR I-4411.

Other than varying the amount of a fine, the jurisdiction of the Court is limited to annulment of the contested decision; it cannot in principle issue positive directions to the Commission,[232] although the latter is bound by Article 233 (ex Article 176) of the Treaty to take the necessary measures to comply with the judgment. If it fails to do so an action may be raised against it under Article 232 (ex Article 175) for failure to act.[233] Only those aspects vitiated by illegality will be annulled, provided they can be severed from the whole of the decision.[234] Where a decision is annulled on procedural grounds or on grounds of insufficiency of reasoning or of proof, there is, other than the five-year time bar for the imposition of fines,[235] nothing to prevent the Commission, its nose having been bloodied by the Court, from re-initiating proceedings. Indeed, following the annulment of the infamous 1988 *PVC* decision for gross procedural flaws,[236] the Commission speedily (six weeks later) adopted a fresh decision libelling essentially the same breaches of Article 81 and imposing identical fines,[237] and the Court of First Instance said that this was not improper in terms of *res judicata* or of *non bis in idem*, that neither a rule of prescription, as time had not run during the previous proceedings before it and the Court of Justice, nor the rights of defence had been transgressed, and that as the original decision was annulled for flaws at the final stage of its adoption the Commission was entitled to recycle in the second decision measures and procedures preparatory to the first.[238] The judgment has been appealed,[239] and the Court of Justice may take a less generous view of Commission procedural liberties.

---

[232] Case 53/85 *AKZO* v *Commission* [1986] ECR 1965; Cases 142 & 156/84 *BAT & Reynolds* v *Commission* (Philip Morris) [1987] ECR 4487; Case T-74/92 *Ladbroke Racing* v *Commission* [1995] ECR II-115; Case T-504/93 *Tiercé Ladbroke* v *Commission* [1997] ECR II-923; Case T-227/95 *AssiDomän Kraft Products* v *Commission* [1997] ECR II-1185. The Court may, and in some circumstances must, order the Commission to produce documents specifically requested and alleged by the applicant to be instrumental to a question of proof: Case C-119/97P *Union Française de l'Express* v *Commission* [1999] ECR I-1341.

[233] eg, although not directly in point, Case T-220/97 *H & R Ecroyd Holdings* v *Commission* [1999] ECR II-1677.

[234] Cases 56 & 58/64 *Consten & Grundig* v *EEC Commission* [1966] ECR 299. This applies also to the annulment of conditions imposed by the Commission, which may be severed provided it does not alter the substance of the decision: Case 37/71 *Jamet* v *Commission* [1972] ECR 483; Case 17/74 *Transocean Marine Paint* v *Commission* [1974] ECR 1063; Cases C-68/94 & 30/95 *France & SCPA & EMC* v *Commission* [1998] ECR I-1375.

[235] n 112 *supra*.

[236] Case C-137/92P *Commission* v *BASF* [1994] ECR I-2555.

[237] Decision 94/599 (*PVC*) OJ 1994 L239/14.

[238] Cases T-305 etc/94 *Limburgse Vinyl Maatschappij* v *Commission* [1999] ECR II-931.

[239] Cases C-238 etc/99P *Limburgse Vinyl Maatschappij* v *Commission*, pending.

Interim remedies in the Court

Whilst the initiation of proceedings before the Court of Justice or the Court of First Instance has no automatic suspensory effect, the Court may, upon application from a party to a case before it and 'if it considers that circumstances so require', suspend the operation of a contested decision.[240] An application for interim relief can therefore be made only within the context of substantive proceedings (the 'main action') pending before the Court. An application for interim order is by way of summary procedure, and may be, and usually is, heard by the President sitting alone.[241] The Court may by reasoned order suspend the operation of a Commission decision (or of any Community act) at issue in the main action where there is a *prima facie* case, urgency and a likelihood of serious and irreparable injury by the continued application of the decision;[242] the tests are cumulative.[243] The grant of interim relief cannot prejudice the outcome of the main action;[244] and the Court may order the lodging of an appropriate security or caution.[245] It is often unnecessary to seek interim suspension of a fine owing to Commission willingness to forego enforcement pending appeal if certain undertakings are entered into.[246]

6.3 Enforcement by national authorities

6.3.1 National competition authorities

As indicated above, Article 84 (ex Article 88) of the Treaty confers upon national competition authorities the power to 'rule on the admissibility' of agreements, decisions and concerted practices and of abuse of a dominant

---

[240] EC Treaty, Art 242 (ex Art 185). It may also, in any action, order 'any necessary interim measures': Art 243 (ex Art 186).

[241] Statute of the Court of Justice, art 36; Rules of Procedure of the Court of Justice, arts 83–89; Rules of Procedure of the Court of First Instance, arts 104–110.

[242] Rules of Procedure of the Court of Justice, art 83(2); Rules of Procedure of the Court of First Instance, art 104(1). See eg Case T-395/94R *Atlantic Container Line* v *Commission* [1995] ECR II-595, appealed unsuccessfully as Case C-149/95P(R) *Commission* v *Atlantic Container Line* [1995] ECR I-2163; Case T-41/96R *Bayer* v *Commission* [1996] ECR II-381; Case C-393/96P(R) *Antonissen* v *Council and Commission* [1997] ECR I-441; Case T-65/98R *van den Bergh Foods* v *Commission* [1998] ECR II-2641.

[243] Case C-268/96P(R) *Stichting Certificatie Kraanverhuurbedrijf* v *Commission* [1996] ECR I-4971.

[244] Rules of Procedure of the Court of Justice, art 86(4); Rules of Procedure of the Court of First Instance, art 107(4); Cases T-24 & 28/92R *Langnese-Iglo & Schöller Lebensmittel* v *Commission* [1992] ECR II-1839; more generally, Case C-180/96R *United Kingdom* v *Commission* [1996] ECR I-3903.

[245] Rules of Procedure of the Court of Justice, art 86(2); Rules of Procedure of the Court of First Instance, art 107(2).

[246] See p 184 *supra*.

position in accordance with national law and with Articles 81 (including 81(3)) and 82. National authorities also have a duty to cooperate with the Commission in any investigation launched by the latter by authority of Article 85 (ex Article 89)[247] and may adopt measures remedying a breach of Articles 81 or 82 if invited to do so by the Commission within that framework.[248] The Commission is keen to 'farm out' some of its responsibilities to national competition authorities, and has adopted a notice on cooperation with them which addresses *inter alia* the proper 'allocation' of cases between the Commission (acting under, primarily, Regulation 17) and national authorities (acting under Article 84 and applicable national procedural rules).[249] National authorities are (and are required to be) notified of any complaint lodged with the Commission.[250]

Both Articles 84 and 85 were intended to be transitional measures pending the adoption of implementing measures under Article 83 (ex Article 87). Such implementing rules may have the effect of pre-empting the exercise by national authorities of these powers. Regulation 17 did so insofar as it disabled them of, and reserves exclusively to the Commission, the power of exemption under Article 81(3). But otherwise it (and the analogous sectoral implementing regulations) did not do so; quite the reverse, it provides expressly that national authorities remain competent to apply Articles 81(1) (but no longer 81(3)) and 82 in accordance with Article 84 so long as the Commission has not 'initiated any procedure' as to negative clearance, exemption or termination,[251] and only thereafter is national jurisdiction excluded. 'Initiated any procedure' means the existence of an authoritative act of the Commission evidencing an intention of taking a decision.[252] There is an argument that this provision of Regulation 17 is unlawful as national authorities may apply the prohibition of Article 81(1) but have no power to exempt under Article 81(3), so unbundling the 'indivisible whole' of Article 81, and the question was raised before the Court of Justice in a reference from the Kammergericht Berlin, but the order for reference was subsequently recalled.[253] In some cases, particularly in

---

[247] EC Treaty, Art 85(1) (ex Art 89(1)).

[248] Art 85(2) (ex Art 89(2)).

[249] Notice on cooperation between national competition authorities and the Commission in handling cases falling within the scope of Articles 85 or 86, OJ 1997 C313/3.

[250] Reg 17, art 10(1).

[251] art 9(3). There are equivalent provisions in the three implementing regulations in the transport sector, but national competence in the field of Community merger control has been significantly pre-empted; see Chap 8.

[252] Case 48/72 *Brasserie de Haecht v Wilkin-Janssen* [1973] ECR 77.

[253] Case C-365/96 *Ruhrgas & Thyssengas v Bundeskartellant* (see OJ 1997 C9/12), removed from the register by order of 26 March 1998.

Germany where the *Bundeskartellamt* wields formidable powers, it has resulted in notifications for exemption or negative clearance designed to block investigation by national authorities ('dilatory notifications').

The 'authorities in Member States' under Article 84 are administrative authorities which enforce national competition law, which excludes national courts[254] unless they are courts to which the task of applying national competition rules has been 'especially entrusted'.[255] This goes to the jurisdiction of various courts in a number of member states; it does not apply in the United Kingdom, with the possible exception of the Competition Commission Appeal Tribunals. Article 84 is an important power in member states where there is such an authority enjoying comprehensive powers and accustomed to wielding them with vigour, such as the *Bundeskartellamt*. But generally there is limited enthusiasm amongst national authorities to pursue infringements of the Treaty rather than of national law, for which they were designed (in some cases involving statutory duties), at which they are skilled and to which they are accustomed. Even where enthusiasm surfaces they can be gazumped by the Commission if it initiates a procedure under Regulation 17. In the United Kingdom there is no body with express statutory authority analogous to that enjoyed by the *Bundeskartellamt*[256] to require termination of conduct prohibited by Articles 81 and 82, and although the Court of Justice has said that such authority derives directly from Article 84[257] so that statutory authority could be said to reside in section 2(1) of the European Communities Act 1972, there are no procedural rules in British law for exercising it, and it is in practice a power which is not wielded in the UK or in five other member states;[258] indeed, two of the five (Luxembourg and Austria) have no administrative competition authorities distinct from and independent of the courts. British regulations were adopted in 1996[259] authorising the Secretary of State to cause an investigation (carried out by the Director-General of Fair Trading, with or without the assistance of the Competition Commission) of suspected infractions of Articles 81 and 82 and, if satisfied that an infraction exists, to make orders requiring its ter-

---

[254] Case 127/73 *Belgische Radio en Televisie* v *SABAM* [1974] ECR 51; *cf.* the earlier judgment in Case 43/69 *Bilger* v *Jehle* [1970] ECR 127.

[255] Cases 209 etc/94 *Ministère Public* v *Asjes* (Nouvelles Frontières) [1986] ECR 1425.

[256] § 50 GWB.

[257] Case 127/73 *Belgische Radio en Televisie* v *SABAM* [1974] ECR 51.

[258] ie, Ireland, Luxembourg, Austria, Finland and Sweden. Enabling legislation enters into force in Denmark in October 2000; lov nr. 416 af 31. maj 2000 (Lov om ændring af konkurrenceloven); Koncurrenceloven, § 23a.

[259] EC Competition Law (Articles 88 and 89) Enforcement Regulations 1996, SI 1996/2199; by authority of the European Communities Act 1972, s 2(2).

mination. However, the regulations provide throughout that they apply only where the Secretary of State apprehends a duty to act under Article 84. Since such a duty exists, if at all, only until the entry into force of implementing Community regulations, the Secretary of State may act only in those areas still unregulated by Regulation 17 and the analogous regulations or if requested to assist by the Commission in one of its (very rare) forays under Article 85.[260] For these reasons the 1996 regulations have not provided Article 84 with a new lease of life in the United Kingdom.

6.3.2 National courts

As a general rule and a function of judicial autonomy (or subsidiarity), the enforcement of Community rights and obligations is a matter left to the jurisdictional and procedural rules of the courts of the member states.[261] There is an added proviso that such rules and procedures must be no less favourable than those which apply to analogous domestic claims and that they are not such as to make it impossible or excessively difficult to obtain redress.[262] There is therefore a presumption that there exist national remedies which will be sufficient effectively to protect Community rights. If such remedies do not exist, they must be fashioned by the courts, irrespective of national rules to the contrary.[263] As indicated above, Articles 81(1) and 82 are directly effective. National courts are therefore required to apply the panoply of civil remedies, and maybe more, in order to give full and effective protection to any rights created by them.

The direct effect of Articles 81(1) and 82 has two civil consequences:

---

[260] In fact, the regulations were adopted in order to enable the Secretary of State to respond to anticipated requests for assistance against a background of Commission investigations into trans-Atlantic airline alliances (and in particular for the OFT an alliance between British Airways and American Airlines), civil aviation to non-Community airports remaining one of the few areas not governed by implementing regulations.

[261] eg, generally Case 33/76 *Rewe-Zentralfinanz and Rewe-Zentral* v *Landwirtschaftskammer für das Saarland* [1976] ECR 1989; Case 45/76 *Comet* v *Produktschap voor Siergewassen* [1976] ECR 2043; confirmed in the context of the competition rules in Case C-60/92 *Otto* v *Postbank* [1993] ECR I-5683.

[262] This is an established formula used consistently to describe the minimum standard required for the protection of Community rights in national courts: see eg Case 199/92 *Amministrazione delle Finanze dello Stato* v *San Giorgio* [1983] ECR 3595; Cases C-6 & 9/90 *Francovich & Bonifaci* v *Italy* [1991] ECR I-5357; Case C-208/90 *Emmott* v *Minister for Social Welfare and Attorney General* [1991] ECR I-4269; Case C-312/93 *Peterbroeck* v *Belgium* [1995] ECR I-4599; Cases C-430-1/93 *van Schijndel* v *Stichting Pensioenfonds voor Fysiotherapeuten* [1995] ECR I-4705; Case C-261/95 *Palmisani* v *Instituto Nazionale della Previdenza Sociale* [1997] ECR I-4025.

[263] See eg Case 213/89 *R* v *Secretary of State for Transport, ex parte Factortame* (Factortame I) [1990] ECR I-2433.

■ First, an agreement or a decision of an association of undertakings which is prohibited by Article 81(1) (and provided, of course, it does not benefit from an exemption granted by authority of Article 81(3)) is, by virtue of Article 81(2), 'automatically void' – not voidable, but void; unlike the scheme adopted in the competition law of some member states, 'no prior decision to that effect [is] required'.[264] Presumably, although it is yet to be tested,[265] this is so even if the proper law of the contract is that of a non-member state, upon the basis that Article 81(1) is a mandatory provision which would be contrary to public policy to escape by means of choice of (foreign) law. Equally, a court in a third country considering a contract the proper law of which is that of a member state ought to apply the prohibition, although it is on its own in determining the existence of the breach: not being a court 'of a Member State' it is not competent to seek a preliminary ruling from the Court of Justice under Article 234 (ex Article 177). Article 82 contains no provision equivalent to Article 81(2), but its prohibition is absolute, again 'no prior decision to that effect being required',[266] and conduct infringing it cannot give rise to rights enforceable by the defaulting party – although the rights of other parties may be protected.[267]

■ Second, breach of Articles 81 and 82 is a tort/delict, and so third parties affected or injured by a prohibited agreement, decision, concerted practice or abusive conduct may be entitled to other civil remedies, such as declaratory relief, injunctive relief and/or damages. It is worth noting, by comparison, that the equivalent provisions of the ECSC Treaty are not directly effective, for they require the positive intervention of the Commission, so that a national court cannot entertain an action for damages in the absence of that intervention.[268]

An agreement prohibited by Article 81(1) is automatically void (*nul de plein droit*). But there is precious little direction from the Court of Justice as to what exactly this ought to mean. It has said only that the nullity is

---

[264] Reg 17, art 1. This provision, made before the development of the principles of direct effect, is probably declaratory only. However, it was required early on to withstand a challenge from Italy that it was inconsistent with the scheme of Arts 81 and 83: Case 32/65 *Italy* v *EEC Council and Commission* [1966] ECR 389.

[265] But see Case C-381/98 *Ingmar GB Ltd* v *Eaton Leonard Technologies*, pending, which raises the issue in a related context.

[266] Reg 17, art 1.

[267] See Case 22/79 *Greenwich Film Production* v *SACEM* [1979] ECR 3275 *per* A-G Warner at 3296: '[I]n the case of an abuse of a dominant position, it would be unthinkable that Article 86 should be held indiscriminately to avoid contracts in a manner detrimental to the victims of the abuse or to third parties'.

[268] Case C-128/92 *Banks* v *British Coal Corporation* [1994] ECR I-1209.

'absolute'[269] and

> [s]ince the nullity referred to in Article 85(2) is absolute, an agreement which is null and void by virtue of this provision has no effect as between the contracting parties and cannot be set up against [*n'est pas opposable aux*] third parties.[270]

Article 81(2) therefore requires at the least that the offending provisions of an (unexempted) agreement breaching Article 81(1) cannot be enforced as between the parties and cannot be relied upon by them as against third parties, and that any relief sought by them which would have that purpose or effect must be declined.[271] According to the English Court of Appeal this is a necessary consequence of, and so adds nothing to, Article 81(1):

> On a proper reading of the passage which I have set out [from *Kerpen & Kerpen*] ..., as a matter of Community law, the nullity imposed by Art. 85(2) is an exact reflection of the prohibition imposed by Art. 85(1).[272]

It is otherwise for national courts to determine the legal consequences of its nullity in accordance with national law.[273] When asked expressly in *Kerpen & Kerpen* what they ought to be the Court declined to set a Community standard:

> [T]he automatic nullity decreed by Article 85(2) of the Treaty applies only to those contractual provisions which are incompatible with Article 85(1). The consequences of such nullity for other parts of the agreement, and for any orders or deliveries made on the basis of the agreement, and the resulting financial obligations, are not a matter for Community law. Those consequences are to be determined by the national court according to its own law.[274]

This is surprising for, according to Advocate-General van Gerven, it 'entails serious risks for the uniform and effective application of Community law'[275] and, according to the English Court of Appeal, marks 'a possible tension between two well-established principles', the principles being the direct effect of the competition rules and the fact that the remedy lies in the fashioning of national law.[276] Proceedings normally arise where

---

[269] Case 22/71 *Béguelin v GL Import/Export* [1971] ECR 949 at 961; Case 319/82 *Société de Vente de Ciments et Bétons de l'Est v Kerpen & Kerpen* [1983] ECR 4173 at 5184.

[270] Case 22/71 *Béguelin, ibid,* at 961–2.

[271] See eg *Philips Electronics v Ingman* [1998] EuLR 666 (Ch).

[272] *Passmore v Morland* [1999] EuLR 501 *per* Chadwick LJ at 514.

[273] Case 56/65 *Société Technique Minière v Maschinenbau Ulm* [1966] ECR 235; Case 319/82 *Société de Vente de Ciments et Bétons de l'Est v Kerpen & Kerpen* [1983] ECR 4173; Case C-230/96 *Cabour v Arnor 'SOCO'* [1998] ECR I-2055; Cases T-185 & 190/96 *Riviera Auto Service v Commission* [1999] ECR I-93.

[274] Case 319/82, *ibid,* at 4184.

[275] Case C-128/92 *Banks v British Coal Corporation* [1994] ECR I-1209 at 1252.

[276] *Crehan v Courage* [1999] EuLR 834 at 851.

a party to a contract becomes disillusioned with it, ceases to comply with it or fails to perform for some other reason, and the other party raises an action seeking specific performance/implement and/or damages. Alternatively, a party may seek a declaration/declarator that a contract into which it has entered is void. If the contract is prohibited by Article 81(1) performance cannot be compelled and damages cannot as a general principle be awarded. Part performance may give rise to a restitutionary claim in unjust(ified) enrichment, unless a contract infringing Article 81(1) is not only void but illegal. Recent indications from the Court of Appeal in England suggest that in English law this is in fact the case.[277] In *Gibbs Mew* v *Gemmell* it said that Article 81(1) (unlike Article 82) is designed to protect only third party competitors and not parties to the agreement who are the cause, not the victim, of the distortion, restriction or prevention of competition, so that

> English law does not allow a party to an illegal agreement to claim damages from the other party for loss caused to him by being a party to the illegal agreement. This is so whether the claim is for restitution or damages.[278]

It may be that *Gibbs Mew* requires reconsideration in the light of the subsequent reformulation by the House of Lords of the law of restitution in *Kleinwort Benson*.[279] In any event it is still not settled in English law the extent to which, if at all, a party *non in pari delicto* – for example, one (but not the other) party to a contract, inevitably the weaker of the two, who did not know and could not reasonably have known that it breached Article 81(1) and/or had no effective voice in its terms (as, for example, with non-negotiable standard form contracts) – may overcome the illegality bar for purposes of a right of action in restitution and even in reparation. Scots law by comparison would be less likely to take the view that a contract in breach of Article 81(1) is an illegal contract,[280] and it is clearer that even if it did so, whilst recognising no contractual remedy, it may well afford to the party *non in pari delicto* a remedy in restitution for unjustified enrichment,[281] but the law is underdeveloped. The question arose again before the Court of Appeal in *Crehan* v *Courage*,[282] and owing

---

[277] *Gibbs Mew* v *Gemmell* [1998] EuLR 588; *Trent Taverns* v *Sykes* [1999] EuLR 492; *Crehan* v *Courage, ibid.*

[278] *per* Peter Gibson LJ at 606.

[279] *Kleinwort Benson* v *Lincoln City Council* [1998] 4 All ER 513.

[280] *Cuthbertson* v *Lowes* (1870) 8 M 1073 (1st Div).

[281] The authorities are not clear; *cf. Cuthbertson* v *Lowes, ibid*, and *Jamieson* v *Watt's Trustee* 1950 SC 265 (2nd Div); see also W.M. Gloag, *The Law of Contract* (2nd edn, W Green & Son, Edinburgh, 1929), pp 586 *et seq*; W.W. McBryde, *The Law of Contract in Scotland* (W Green & Son, Edinburgh, 1987), pp 628–34.

[282] [1999] EuLR 834.

to the uncertainty it submitted the point to the Court of Justice in a reference under Article 234 (ex Article 177);[283] it is anticipated the Court may be more forthcoming with guidance than it was in *Kerpen & Kerpen*. It is not clear whether third party rights created by a contract (the *jus quaesitum tertio*) found to be void could be recoverable.

The entire contract does not necessarily fall. The Court of Justice early on gave its blessing to the doctrine of severance[284] and subsequently recognised that this too is a matter for national, not Community, law.[285] So, if national law permits the offending provisions of a contract to be severed by application of a 'blue pencil' test, as do both English and Scots law, the remaining, inoffensive, provisions will be enforceable.[286] Care must therefore be taken in drafting, for a blue pencil may leave an enforceable contract and a party facing significant burdens with fewer of the benefits anticipated following severance; it might in some circumstances be prudent to make express provision that if certain clauses of a contract are found to breach Article 81(1) the rest ceases to be binding. In English law the automatic nullity of Article 81(2) is of a temporaneous or transient character: a contract which is void for breach of Article 81(1), even if void at its formation, is nevertheless not void *ab initio*, and so if owing to a change in circumstances the prohibition ceases to apply to the contract (*in casu* the transfer of a tied house tenancy to a new landlord with a smaller, inappreciable market share) it will cease to be void and becomes valid and enforceable.[287] It is unlikely that Scots law could entertain the same conclusion. A judicial finding that an agreement (or part of an agreement) is void is the exclusive preserve of the national courts; the Community Courts have no jurisdiction to annul an agreement concluded by a natural or legal person at the behest of one of the parties.[288] If a contract provides for, and goes to, arbitration and national law provides for the judicial annulment of an arbitration award which is contrary to public policy, such

---

[283] Case C-453/99 *Crehan* v *Courage*, pending.

[284] Cases 56 & 58/64 *Consten & Grundig* v *EEC Commission* [1966] ECR 299; Case 56/65 *Société Technique Minière* v *Maschinenbau Ulm* [1966] ECR 235.

[285] Case 319/82 *Société de Vente de Ciments et Bétons de l'Est* v *Kerpen and Kerpen* [1983] ECR 4172.

[286] See eg, in English law, *Chemidus Wavin* v *Société pour la Transformation et l'Exploitation des Résines Industrielles* [1978] 3 CMLR 514 (CA); *Inntrepreneur Estates* v *Mason* [1993] 2 CMLR 293 (QBD); *Parkes* v *Esso Petroleum Company* [1999] 1 CMLR 455 (Ch).

[287] *Passmore* v *Morland* [1999] EuLR 501 (CA).

[288] Case T-56/92R *Koelman* v *Commission* [1993] ECR II-1267. A national court may of course seek the interpretative assistance of the Court of Justice under Art 234 (ex Art 177), but the jurisdiction to hold an agreement void belongs to it alone.

a remedy must be available for awards granted for breach of a contract prohibited by Article 81(1).[289]

Third parties injured by the operation of a prohibited agreement, decision or concerted practice or abusive conduct from a dominant undertaking have a remedy in declaratory relief, injunction/interdict[290] or damages. English courts will grant interlocutory relief where a plaintiff can show that there is unlikely to be an adequate remedy in damages,[291] and have granted interim injunctions at the instance of third parties restraining undertakings from giving effect to agreements likely to be found contrary to Article 81(1)[292] and restraining an alleged abuse of a dominant position;[293] the Court of Session refused a motion for interim interdict to prevent an alleged breach of Article 82 but for lack of a *prima facie* case and on the balance of convenience rather than for want of jurisdiction.[294] The normal rules governing injunction/interdict generally apply.[295] This can give rise to constitutional difficulties in Scotland where breach of the competition rules is attributable to a branch of government acting as an undertaking,[296] for, unlike in England,[297] the Crown still enjoys immunity from interim interdict.[298] However, the Court of Session recently consid-

---

[289] Case C-126/97 *Eco Swiss China Time* v *Benetton International* [1999] ECR I-3055. It should be noted that this is an important judgment in other of its aspects, those relating to time bars, which have caused the referring national court (the Dutch Hoge Raad) significant difficulties in applying.

[290] In Scotland, where, unlike England, interdict cannot be mandatory (*Grosvenor Developments (Scotland)* v *Argyll Stores* 1987 SLT 738 (Extra Div)), the remedy for a positive order (absent any contract to be enforced by specific implement) is probably a petition for an order requiring the specific performance of a statutory duty under the Court of Session Act 1988, s 45(b).

[291] *R* v *Secretary of State for Transport, ex parte Factortame* [1991] 1 AC 603 (HL) *per* Lord Goff at 672.

[292] *Cutsforth* v *Mansfield Inns* [1986] 1 All ER 577 (QBD); *Holleran* v *Thwaites* [1989] 2 CMLR 917 (Ch); but *cf. Fyffes* v *Chiquita* [1993] FSR 83 (Ch); *Scottish and Newcastle* v *Bond*, judgment of 25 March 1997 (QBD), unreported; *Greenalls Management Ltd* v *Canavan* [1998] EuLR 507 (CA); *Trent Taverns* v *Sykes* [1999] EuLR 492 (CA).

[293] *Budgett* v *British Sugar Corporation*, order of 16 February 1979 (QBD), unreported; *Engineering and Chemical Supplies* v *AKZO*, order of 6 December 1979 (QBD), unreported; *Garden Cottage Foods* v *Milk Marketing Board* [1983] 2 All ER 292 (CA), overturned by the House of Lords; see *infra*.

[294] *Argyll Group* v *Distillers* 1987 SLT 514; see to the same effect *Leyland DAF* v *Automotive Products* [1994] 1 BCLC 245 (CA); *Potato Marketing Board* v *Hampden-Smith* [1997] EuLR 435 (CA); *EasyJet* v *British Airways* [1998] EuLR 350 (QBD).

[295] ie, those of *American Cyanamid* v *Ethicon* [1975] AC 396 (HL).

[296] See p 197 *supra*.

[297] *M* v *Home Office* [1994] 1 AC 377 (HL).

[298] *McDonald* v *Secretary of State for Scotland* 1994 SC 234 (2nd Div), holding that interdict and interim interdict were incompetent by virtue of s 21(1) of the Crown Proceedings Act 1947.

ered the *Factortame* rule[299] requiring the setting aside of national bars to the effective protection of Community rights, and in a petition for judicial review pronounced an interim order *ad factum praestandum* against a Crown servant under the Court of Session Act 1988 where it was claimed that the latter might infringe Article 82, and implied that an interim interdict might be appropriate if necessary to prevent the putative breach.[300] Whilst interim orders have been granted in order to preserve rights under Articles 81 and 82 pending trial, there is, owing to a pronounced inclination to settle, yet to be an injunction/interdict ordered in a final judgment in a UK court.

As for damages, the remedy generally preferred by the English courts,[301] there is nothing in Community law which expressly requires that damages be available to parties injured by infringements of the competition rules. In light of the series of judgments which have now established a right in reparation from a member state which has deprived a natural or legal person of a Community law right,[302] it would be a natural consequence for the Court of Justice so to hold. Advocate-General van Gerven urged such a course in *Banks* v *British Coal Corporation*,[303] but the Court did not address the question and it is at the moment still a matter for national law; and given the marked reluctance of English and Scottish courts to award damages for pure economic loss it is a remedy for which more fertile

---

[299] Case 213/89 *R* v *Secretary of State for Transport, ex parte Factortame* (Factortame I) [1990] ECR I-2433.

[300] *Millar & Bryce* v *Keeper of the Registers of Scotland* 1997 SLT 1000 (OH).

[301] See most recently *Co-operative Insurance Society* v *Argyll Stores (Holdings)* [1998] AC 1 (HL); but *cf. Sockel* v *Body Shop International* [2000] EuLR 276 (Ch).

[302] Cases C-6 & 9/90 *Francovich and Bonifaci* v *Italy* [1991] ECR I-5357; Cases C-46 & 48/93 *Brasserie du Pêcheur* v *Germany* and *R* v *Secretary of State for Transport, ex parte Factortame* (No 3) [1996] ECR I-1029; Case C-392/93 *R* v *HM Treasury, ex parte British Telecommunications* [1996] ECR I-1631; Case C-5/94 *R* v *Ministry of Agriculture, Fisheries and Food, ex parte Hedley Lomas* [1996] ECR I-2553; Cases C-178 etc/94 *Dillenkofer* v *Germany* [1996] ECR I-4845; Cases 283 & 291–2/94 *Denkavit Internationaal* v *Bundesamt für Finanzen* [1996] ECR I-5063; Case C-140/97 *Rechberger* v *Austria* [1999] ECR I-3499.

[303] Case C-128/92 [1994] ECR I-1209, wherein he proposed (at 1250 and 1260) that a right in reparation existed as a matter of Community law:

[A] right to obtain reparation constitutes a logical conclusion of the horizontal direct effect of the [competition] rules .... The only effective method whereby the national court can in those circumstances fully safeguard the directly effective provisions of Community law which have been infringed is by restoring the rights of the injured party by the award of damages ....

[EC competition law is] aimed at safeguarding undistorted competition and freedom of competition for undertakings operating in the common market, with the result that a breach of that system must be made good in full.

ground could be expected on the continent. The leading English case is *Garden Cottage Foods*,[304] in which the House of Lords held that a breach of Article 82 (and presumably also of Article 81(1), at least for injured third parties[305]) could give rise to a cause of action, but (by a 4–1 majority) discharged an interlocutory injunction granted by the Court of Appeal[306] because damages would be an available and preferable remedy. The point was not authoritatively established as the parties settled before trial. *Garden Cottage Foods* was subsequently cited by Parker LJ as 'clear authority that a private law action for breach of article 86 against an undertaking sounds in damages'.[307] The House of Lords characterised the issue not as a common law restraint of trade, rather underpinning the remedy as a cause of action for breach of statutory duty.[308] Surprisingly, there is yet to be a successful final judgment awarding damages for breach of the competition rules in a British court, and precious few in the courts of other member states. In fact, given the powers they have clearly had at their disposal since, at the latest, *BRT v SABAM*,[309] the enforcement of Articles 81 and 82 before national courts is still astonishingly underdeveloped.

6.4 Problems of co-enforcement

As the Court of Justice noted,

> the Commission does not have exclusive competence to apply Articles 85 and 86. It shares that competence with the national courts.[310]

But each has fundamentally different goals and the jurisdiction of each is of a fundamentally different quality.

> The actions of competition authorities, at both national and Community level, are guided by considerations of public policy in the economic sphere; unlike the national courts, they do not set out to decide disputes between parties, but rather

---

He therefore supported *restitutio in integrum* which applies also to the liability in reparation of the member states but did not discuss (in part because *Banks* predated) the 'sufficiently serious' test laid down in *Brasserie du Pêcheur* and *Factortame III* necessary to determine the existence of liability.

[304] *Garden Cottage Foods* v *Milk Marketing Board* [1984] AC 130.
[305] *cf. Gibbs Mew* v *Gemmell* [1998] EuLR 588 (CA) and p .... *supra*.
[306] [1983] 2 All ER 292.
[307] *Bourgoin* v *Minister for Agriculture, Fisheries and Food* [1985] 1 All ER 585 (CA) at 631; recognised *obiter* also in *Scots law: Argyll* v *Distillers* 1987 SLT 514 (OH).
[308] *per* Lord Diplock at 141; *cf.* the view of Denning MR in *Application des Gaz* v *Falks Veritas* [1974] Ch 381 at 396 that breaches of Arts 81(1) and 82 constitute 'new torts or wrongs'.
[309] Case 127/73 *Belgische Radio en Televisie* v *SABAM* [1974] ECR 51.
[310] Case C-234/89 *Delimitis* v *Henninger Bräu* [1991] ECR I-935 at 992.

to guarantee the maintenance of a system ensuring that competition is not distorted.[311]

One is an administrative authority, the other an exercise of the civil jurisdiction of the courts.[312] They may operate in tandem to the same set of circumstances: although the initiation of Commission proceedings can pre-empt the intervention of national (administrative) competition authorities, it does not and cannot have the same effect over judicial proceedings,[313] whilst at the same time ongoing civil litigation does not prevent the intervention of the Commission under Regulation 17. Neither is subservient to the other. They ought in principle to function, each in their own way, concurrently and in parallel which produces a compatible result. In practice they do not always work together in perfect harmony.

To the undertaking wishing action to be taken against a competitor in order to enforce the competition rules there are, when the two are compared, both advantages and disadvantages in pursuing civil remedies before national courts and enforcement through the intermediary of the Commission. As mentioned above, the Commission is under no duty to pursue a complaint lodged by a disgruntled undertaking; it is required only to justify electing not to do so. Lacking the resources adequately to discharge its duties under Regulation 17, it has pursued a policy of 'decentralisation' of enforcement of Articles 81 and 82, not only urging national competition authorities to lend a hand[314] but actively encouraging undertakings to pursue civil remedies in national courts,[315] taking the view that there will not normally be a 'sufficient Community interest' justifying Commission intervention where a complainant is able to secure adequate protection of his rights from a national court.[316] It also indicated in its 1997 notice on agreements of minor importance that in the event of agreements falling within the terms of the notice or those involving small and medium-sized undertakings, it is 'in the first instance ... for the authorities

---

[311] European Commission, White Paper on Modernisation of the Rules Implementing Articles 85 and 86 of the EC Treaty, Programme No 99/027, para 91.

[312] The courts may also exercise administrative jurisdiction in this context where there is application of Arts 81 and 82 by national competition authorities. In some member states the courts also exercise criminal jurisdiction in the competition field generally, but not in the context of the enforcement of Community rules.

[313] Case 127/73 *Belgische Radio en Televisie* v *SABAM* [1974] ECR 51.

[314] Notice on cooperation between national competition authorities and the Commission in handling cases falling within the scope of Articles 85 or 86, OJ 1997 C313/3.

[315] EC Commission, *Fifteenth Report on Competition Policy* (1985), point 38; Notice on cooperation between national courts and the Commission in applying Articles 85 and 86 of the EEC Treaty, OJ 1993 C39/6 (hereinafter '1993 Cooperation Notice'), paras 14–16.

[316] Case T-24/90 *Automec* v *Commission* [1992] ECR II-2223; 1993 Cooperation Notice, *ibid.* Nor is the Commission under a duty to intervene where there is divergent national case law on Arts 81 and 82, for 'it falls first to the national courts' to ensure the uniform

and courts of the Member States to take action', and it will institute proceedings, either upon its own initiative or upon a complaint, only exceptionally.[317] The national court, on the other hand, must respond to a competently raised action. This goes back to the 'vigilance of the individual' cited in *van Gend en Loos*,[318] the handmaiden of direct effect, for the aggrieved undertaking is surely likely to be more robust in seeking to protect its interests than will a public authority. In a number of cases it will be the only option. In order to assist national courts (and national competition authorities) the Commission has, as part of its policy of decentralisation, now adopted a number of notices, most notably on cooperation with the Commission,[319] on agreements of minor importance[320] and on the definition of relevant markets.[321] Whether or not these soft law instruments and the increasing reliance upon them is prudent or will lead to greater efficiency in enforcement remains fairly to be assessed, but for the present the entrails are not good.[322]

If the Commission can be persuaded to intervene it has an advantage over national courts in a number of respects. It has undoubted expertise, certainly when compared to a civil judge who may know nothing of competition law (but who may on questions of law seek the assistance of the Court of Justice through an Article 234 (ex Article 177) preliminary reference). The unfamiliarity, to put it gently, of some national judges with competition law and with the comprehensive economic analysis which necessarily attends it, and of some advocates in leading evidence which is in large measure of that quality, is a practical difficulty which ought not to be

---

application of Community law: Case T-5/93 *Tremblay* v *Commission* [1995] ECR II-185 at 215. The Court of First Instance has recognised that the Commission may lessen the priority given to a complaint if an alleged infringement has been ordered to be stopped by a national court through civil proceedings: Cases T-213/95 & 18/96 *Stichting Certificatie Kraanverhuurbedrijf* v *Commission* [1997] ECR II-1739.

[317] Notice on agreements of minor importance which do not fall within the meaning of Article 85(1), OJ 1997 C372/13, paras 5, 11, 19, 20; see pp 72–5 *supra*.

[318] Case 26/62 *Algemene Transport Onderneming van Gend en Loos* v *Nederlandse Administratie der Belastingen* [1963] ECR 1.

[319] 1993 Cooperation Notice. For cooperation between competition authorities and the Commission, see the 1997 notice cited n 314 *supra*.

[320] Notice on agreements of minor importance which do not fall within the meaning of Article 85(1), OJ 1997 C372/13.

[321] Notice on definition of the relevant market for the purposes of Community competition law, OJ 1997 C372/5.

[322] See eg *Gibbs Mew* v *Gemmell* [1998] EuLR 588 in which the English Court of Appeal expressly ignored a Commission Notice (OJ 1984 C101/2) on the interpretation of block exemption 1984/83 on exclusive purchasing agreements (OJ 1983 L173/5) on the ground that, as a mere notice, it was insufficiently persuasive.

underestimated; one useful by-product of the introduction into national law, such as in the Competition Act 1998, of principles akin to Articles 81 and 82 will be to familiarise national courts and judges with the field, and from this base of better understanding to become less reticent and better skilled to wield their powers. Practitioners will both lead and necessarily follow in their wake. The Commission further has significant powers of investigation. This is especially important in cases where there are cross-border elements to an investigation; the Commission can, and frequently does, mount simultaneous 'dawn raids' in a number of member states. The power of national courts to order discovery of documents, on the other hand, is confined to the territorial jurisdiction of the court. By the same token the Commission may order remedial action effective (and enforceable by civil process) throughout the Community whilst the judgment of a national court may encounter *de facto* difficulties of enforcement outwith its jurisdiction, although the problem is moderated by the existence of the Brussels and Lugano Conventions. On the other side of the ledger, there is no *Orkem* privilege,[323] at least as a matter of Community law, in national civil proceedings; as it is intended to protect persons against the conduct of public authorities, it does not apply to inhibit disclosure of information in civil proceedings which cannot lead, directly or indirectly, to the imposition of a penalty by a public authority.[324] And if the Commission takes up the baton it is free (save for the – possibly considerable – costs of participation in an investigation); this is a significant benefit given the huge costs of going to litigation, which acts as a serious impediment to the small or medium-sized undertaking injured by breach of the competition rules. Measured against that, however, is the possibility of the successful litigant recovering all costs in a civil action. Finally, there is a general sentiment abroad, which is very difficult to quantify and measure, that the Commission is simply more minded to identify a breach of the competition rules than are the courts of (most) member states; a rudimentary indication of this can be had from the saga of the Irish ice cream war.[325]

Civil action can have advantages over Commission action. The Commission is notoriously slow, civil proceedings invariably much speedier. Injunctive relief is far more quickly to be obtained from a national judge; indeed, the High Court in England has recognised the Commission's workload as a factor to be taken into account in granting interlocutory relief.[326] The sole sanction at its disposal is the power to impose an

---

[323] Case 374/87 *Orkem* v *Commission* [1989] ECR 3283; see p 169 *supra*.
[324] Case C-60/92 *Otto* v *Postbank* [1993] ECR I-5683.
[325] *Infra.*
[326] *Holleran* v *Thwaites* [1989] 2 CMLR 917 (Ch).

'administrative' fine upon an undertaking. It can award no damages to an injured third party. This compares poorly with the right in civil courts to damages, sometimes exemplary,[327] and, in some member states, the imposition of criminal penalties upon an undertaking and/or individuals within the undertaking. Again, the two mechanisms of enforcement are not mutually exclusive: an undertaking may be fined by the Commission and remain liable to civil remedies, the purpose of which is not deterrence and punishment but reparation for loss.

There may be variations in the standard of proof required to show a breach of Articles 81 and 82. Notwithstanding the qualitative difference between Commission enforcement proceedings and civil action (for which the Court of Justice has supplied no guidelines), if it varied too widely it would produce unfairness. The standard of proof imposed by the Court of Justice upon the Commission in review proceedings under Article 230 (ex Article 173) is discussed above.[328] In the one English authority in which it was expressly considered the High Court said that it ought to apply 'a standard known to our courts if it is consistent with those tests', and given the liability to penalties (albeit in distinct, Commission proceedings) the correct standard was therefore 'a high degree of probability, but less than the standard of proof in criminal matters'.[329] In interlocutory proceedings balance of convenience remains the appropriate test.[330]

The most obvious problem with the co-enforcement of Articles 81 and 82 is that the two agents of enforcement – the Commission and a national court – may in considering the same substantive matter come to different conclusions. It may happen for perfectly legitimate reasons – the two applying different standards of proof or different evidence being led before and considered by them – or a more straightforward reason – the national court (or the Commission) simply getting it wrong. Where such a possibility arises, there is terse advice from the Court of Justice in *BRT v SABAM*:

> [I]f the Commission initiates a procedure ... a [national] court may, if it considers it necessary for reasons of legal certainty, stay the proceedings before it while awaiting the outcome of the Commission's action.

---

[327] (Irish) Competition Act, 1991, s 6(3)(b). The Act provides for the availability of exemplary damages for breach of Irish competition law; as the relief applies to Irish matters it must also be available for breach of Arts 81 and 82; Cases C-46 & 48/93 *Brasserie du Pêcheur v Germany* and *R v Secretary of State for Transport, ex parte Factortame (No 3)* [1996] ECR I-1029.

[328] at pp 55–60.

[329] *Sheason Lehman Hutton v Maclaine Watson* [1989] 3 CMLR 429 (QBD) at 443.

[330] eg, *Argyll Group v Distillers* 1987 SLT 514 (OH); *Leyland DAF v Automotive Products* [1994] 1 BCLC 245 (CA); *EasyJet v British Airways* [1998] EuLR 350 (QBD).

On the other hand, the national court should generally allow proceedings before it to continue when it decides either that the behaviour in dispute is clearly not capable of having any appreciable effect on competition or on trade between Member States, or that there is not doubt of the incompatibility of that behaviour with Article 86.[331]

This has been read very broadly by the English courts as an invitation to deference to the role of the Commission. Bingham MR has said:

[T]he material rulings of the European Court of Justice are, as I understand them, based on the extreme undesirability of inconsistent decisions as between the Commission, on one side, and national courts on the other. It is not hard to understand the undesirability of such inconsistency which undermines legal certainty, leaving parties in doubt as to where they stand, and infringes the integrity of the Community legal order ....

It seems to me that the effect of [*BRT v SABAM*] is that the national court should generally stay proceedings pending a decision by the Commission in the interests of legal certainty unless the answer to the complaint is clear.[332]

Stay of proceedings has therefore been granted by the High Court even in the absence of the initiation of Commission action, where a party had made an 'informal complaint' to the Commission and met a 'not discouraging reception',[333] where even that stage had not been reached, the stay granted on condition that the party lodge a serious complaint with the Commission and prosecute it diligently,[334] and where a *functionnaire* in the Commission had indicated informally that 'there is a case to answer'.[335] In any event this will lead to significant delay: the Commission may turn a deaf ear, in which case an aggrieved complainant may challenge its decision not to intervene. It may initiate a procedure, in the fullness of time adopt a formal decision, which may then be challenged before the Court of First Instance, and again on appeal to the Court of Justice. This sits ill with the general admonition from the Court of Justice that judicial protection of a directly effective Community law right be effective and prompt, and the time factor must be a serious consideration for a national court invited to stay a case. But should a party take the Commission at faith and resort to national remedies, and should the national court elect to proceed with its jurisdiction, it may give rise to further problems of confusion and delay. To illustrate: in Ireland the High Court granted a

---

[331] Case 127/73 *Belgische Radio en Televisie v SABAM* [1974] ECR 51 at 63.
[332] *MTV Europe v BMG Records* [1997] EuLR 100 (CA) at 105, 106.
[333] *Philips Electronics v Ingman* [1998] EuLR 666 (Ch).
[334] *British Leyland v Wyatt Interpart* [1979] FSR 583 (Ch).
[335] *Williams & Cardiff RFC v Welsh Rugby Union* [1999] EuLR 195 (QBD).

permanent injunction sought by an ice cream manufacturer restraining the defendant competitor from wrongful interference with the former's contractual rights *vis-à-vis* its retailers, the defendant alleging (unsuccessfully) both that the contracts infringed Article 81(1) and that the manufacturer was abusing a dominant position.[336] Following an interim injunction ordered by the High Court[337] but prior to final judgment the defendant had lodged a complaint with the Commission, in response to which the Commission launched an investigation, seemed originally to adopt an emollient view[338] but changed its mind and in due season (six years after the High Court granted the permanent injunction) came to the contrary conclusion and adopted a decision declaring the manufacturer to have infringed both Articles 81 and 82.[339] As for the problems of this difference in opinion, the Commission's laconic observation was that

> [i]t is not inconsistent with the principles governing the concurrent powers of the national courts and the Commission in the application of Article 85(1) and Article 86 of the Treaty, for the Commission to take a decision which differs from a judgment delivered by a national court ....
>
> As to [the manufacturer]'s concern with the existence of conflicting decisions, and with the legal uncertainty allegedly resulting from this, it should be pointed out that it is for the Court of Justice to give a final interpretation of the Treaty Articles involved.[340]

The manufacturer immediately raised annulment proceedings against the Commission decision before the Court of First Instance under Article 173 (now Article 230)[341] and also secured its interim suspension;[342] were it otherwise the parties would be placed in the difficult position of being required to comply with two mandatory but mutually inconsistent orders – the High Court injunction and the Commission decision. The original defendant then appealed against the permanent injunction granted by the High Court (raising questions of time bars), and the Supreme Court has in turn submitted an Article 177 (now Article 234) reference to the Court of Justice asking a number of questions of substance but also whether it is in the meanwhile barred from upholding the High Court judgment, which it appears to be minded to do, and whether it has a duty to stay the appeal

---

[336] *HB Ice Cream v Masterfoods*, order of 28 May 1992, unreported.

[337] *HB Ice Cream v Masterfoods* [1990] 2 IR 463.

[338] See its Reg 17, art 19(3) notice in OJ 1995 C211/4.

[339] Decision 98/531 (*van den Bergh Foods*) OJ 1998 L246/1.

[340] paras 279, 280.

[341] Case T-65/98 *van den Bergh Foods v Commission*, pending.

[342] Case T-65/98R *van den Bergh Foods v Commission* [1998] ECR II-2641. On interim suspension of a Commission decision, see p 194 *supra*.

pending the outcome of the proceedings before the Court of First Instance[343] – which have themselves been stayed pending judgment of the Court of Justice in the reference from the Supreme Court.[344] We therefore have a minor Irish ice cream donnybrook which started in 1989 in which there is still deadlock between the Irish courts and the Commission which will not be resolved until well into the new millennium.

An even more intractable problem is the possibility of conflict which arises essentially in the presence of one set of circumstances. That is, the correct course for a national court to follow when seised of a question involving an agreement which appears to be prohibited by Article 81(1), which does not fall within the terms of a block exemption, which has been notified to the Commission, and so which may be, but has not yet been, granted an individual exemption.[345] In *Delimitis*[346] the Court of Justice said where these circumstances arise,[347] a national court ought to proceed as follows. First it ought to determine, in the light of case law and of previous Commission decisions, whether Article 81(1) applies at all. If the conditions for application of the prohibition are clearly not joined, the court should set Article 81 aside and consider otherwise the legality of the agreement.[348] If it satisfies itself that the agreement falls or may fall foul of Article 81(1), the court ought then to determine, in the light of the exemption regulations and previous Commission decisions, whether the agreement is *unlikely* to be granted an exemption.[349] If it so concludes, it should proceed to exercise its power under Article 81(2). But if it concludes that exemption of the agreement is a possibility, it ought to stay or sist proceedings, supplying any appropriate national interim remedy, until such time as the Commission has reached a decision. Meanwhile, the Commission has a duty under Article 10 (ex Article 5) of the Treaty of 'sin-

---

[343] Case C-344/98 *Masterfoods v HB Ice Cream*, pending.

[344] Case T-65/98R *van den Bergh Foods v Commission*, order of 28 April 1999, unreported.

[345] As to notification and exemption, see Chap 4.

[346] Case C-234/89 *Delimitis v Henninger Bräu* [1991] ECR I-935; *cf.* the earlier judgment in Case 48/72 *Brasserie de Haecht v Wilkin-Janssen (No 2)* [1973] ECR 77.

[347] Implicit in *Delimitis* is that the following considerations apply not only where an agreement has been notified, but also where it was not required to be notified – ie, an agreement falling within art 4(2) of Reg 17. With the amendment of art 4(2) in 1999 and the resulting explosion in the number of agreements which now fall within it (see pp 121–2 *supra*) the *Delimitis* tests acquire significantly greater practical application and importance.

[348] Affirmed, in greater detail, in Case C-250/92 *Gøttrup-Klim v Dansk Landbrugs Grovvarselskab* [1994] ECR I-5641.

[349] The Court imposes a strict test here: the national court must satisfy itself that the agreement may 'on no account' (*keinesfalls*; *ne peut en aucun cas*) become the subject of an exemption decision under Art 81(3); *Delimitis* at 993.

cere cooperation' with the national court by, for example, informing it of the state of play with the notification, whether any procedure has been initiated, giving priority to it and providing any relevant information on factual data (statistics, market studies and economic analysis) and law. The Commission cannot prohibit the disclosure in civil proceedings of documents received by a party in the course of an investigation, and has a duty to produce 'such economic and legal information as it may be able to supply' if requested to do so by a national court, leaving to the court the responsibility of protecting confidential information and business secrets; owing to Community legislation on public access to Commission documents[350] the Commission may refuse to disclose information it has supplied to a national court to third parties only if such disclosure would be contrary to the law of the jurisdiction of the referring court.[351] In England, the Court of Appeal has said that national courts are 'obliged loyally to give effect' to the *Delimitis* principles, and so in an action for damages refused to grant a stay of proceedings pending Commission determination of a notification for negative clearance and/or exemption but upon the understanding that only preparation for trial could proceed and no judgment should be rendered prior to the Commission taking a decision.[352] The *Delimitis* considerations were subsequently set out, and essentially codified, by the Commission in the 1993 Cooperation Notice. They (alongside comfort letters) have been criticised by the High Court in England for the state of limbo in which they leave civil proceedings and the national judge.[353] Even the Commission has recognised that if civil proceedings can in practice be halted simply by a party lodging a notification with it, it is a 'major obstacle' to more extensive application of Article 81 by national courts.[354] Surprisingly, since the adoption of the 1993 Notice there have been fewer than 20 instances of national courts seeking Commission assistance under it. However changes are now afoot which may remove, or at least alter, the problem.[355]

---

[350] Decision 94/90, OJ 1994 L46/58.

[351] Cases C-174 & 189/98P *Netherlands & van der Wal v Commission*, judgment of 11 January 2000, not yet reported. See also Case T-353/94 *Postbank v Commission* [1996] ECR II-921. In this the Commission is limited only by Art 287 (ex Art 214) of the Treaty, for, as cooperation between the Commission and national courts falls outwith Reg 17, art 20(1) and (2) of that regulation do not apply.

[352] *MTV Europe v BMG Records* [1997] EuLR 100. See also, to much the same effect, *Harrison v Matthew Brown*, judgment of 30 October 1997 (CA), unreported.

[353] *Inntrepreneur Estates v Mason* [1993] 2 CMLR 293 (QBD) at 305–06.

[354] White Paper on Modernisation of the Rules Implementing Articles 85 and 86 of the EC Treaty, Programme No 99/027, para 100.

[355] See *infra*.

6.5 Co-application of Community law and national law

There is another, only tangentially related problem which can lead to discord between the Commission and national enforcement authorities, and that is the co-application of the Community competition rules and the substantive and procedural provisions of national competition law.[356] It is trite to say, but nonetheless bears saying because of the confusion to which it seems sometimes to give rise, that the powers conferred upon national authorities by Article 84 (ex Article 88) and the pre-emption of those powers by Commission intervention in accordance with article 9(3) of Regulation 17 refer to circumstances in which national authorities apply *Community* rules; they say nothing about their right and duty to apply *national* rules. In theory Community law is concerned with anticompetitive practices which affect trade between member states, whilst national rules are concerned with considerations peculiar to each member state and with practices in that context alone. But the two are not hermetically sealed, and can overlap. The problem has tended to arise in Germany owing to the existence there of a comprehensive body of competition law (the GWB) which pre-dates the Community rules and in some measure diverges from them, and in part through the enforcement procedures of the *Bundeskartellamt* and frequent intervention of a robust (private) association (the *Zentrale zur Bekämpfung unlauteren Wettbewerbs*) which pursues infringements of the GWB in the public interest. As more and more member states come to adopt competition rules the problem is likely to become more widespread. For the United Kingdom it has become a serious issue with the entry into force of the Competition Act 1998, but in this respect the Act is noteworthy as 'Community friendly': British courts determining a question arising under national competition law are under a statutory duty to

act ... with a view to securing that there is no inconsistency between —
(a) the principles applied, and decisions reached, by the court in determining that question; and
(b) the principles laid down by the Treaty and the European Court, and any relevant decision of that Court, as applicable at the time in determining any corresponding question arising in Community law.[357]

This is of significant importance in the interpretation of national competi-

---

[356] The problem could also arise in the same manner in the context of the co-application of the competition rules of the EEA Agreement and those of the EC Treaty, although care has been taken to minimise this risk; see p 292 *infra*.
[357] Competition Act 1998, s 60(2).

tion law by British courts. But it will not solve the problem entirely.

The primacy of Community law was recognised by the Court of Justice in 1964 in *Costa* v *ENEL*.[358] The application of the principle in the field of competition was first explored in 1969 in *Wilhelm* v *Bundeskartellamt*;[359] the Court said that so long as legislation adopted by authority of Article 83 (ex Article 87) of the Treaty did not seek to pre-empt or exclude national jurisdiction (which it may do, but no legislation outwith the fields of coal and steel – governed exclusively by the competition rules of the ECSC Treaty – and merger control does so),

> national authorities may take action against an agreement in accordance with their national law, even when an examination of the agreement from the point of view of its compatibility with Community law is pending before the Commission, subject however to the condition that the application of national law may not prejudice the full and uniform application of Community law or the effects of measures taken to implement it.[360]

And subsequently:

> Community law and national law on competition consider restrictive practices from different points of view. Whereas Articles 85 and 86 regard them in the light of obstacles which may result from trade between Member States, national law proceeds on the basis of the considerations peculiar to it and considers restrictive practices only in that context. It follows that national authorities may also take action in regard to situations which are capable of forming the subject-matter of a decision by the Commission.
>
> However, ... parallel application of national competition law can only be permitted in so far as it does not prejudice the uniform application, throughout the common market, of the Community rules on cartels or the full effects of the measures adopted in implementation of those rules.[361]

The test is therefore that national rules apply so long as they do not imperil the 'full and uniform application' of the Community rules. It is a principle the ambit of which is not yet clear. The following situations may arise:

(a) an agreement or practice is not caught by Articles 81(1) and/or 82: this may occur where the conduct falls entirely outwith the field of application of the Treaty rules, or where it falls within that field but escapes the

---

[358] Case 6/64 [1964] ECR 585.
[359] Case 14/68 [1969] ECR 1.
[360] Case 14/68 *Wilhelm* v *Bundeskartellamt* [1969] ECR 1 at 15.
[361] Cases 253/78 & 1–3/79 *Procureur de la République* v *Giry et Guerlain* (Perfume) [1980] ECR 2327 at 2374–5.

prohibition by virtue of application of the *de minimis* rule or the rule of reason. In either event there is a presumption that the agreement or conduct is such as to affect only the national market, the Community regime is not compromised, and national rules, if any, may be applied in their entirety without reference to Community law.

> The fact that a practice has been held by the Commission not to fall within the ambit of the prohibition contained Article 85(1) and (2) [*sic*], the scope of which is limited to agreements capable of affecting trade between Member States, in no way prevents that practice from being considered by the national authorities from the point of view of the restrictive effects which it may produce nationally.[362]

This is entirely consistent with the principle of subsidiarity.

(b) an agreement or practice is caught by Articles 81(1) and/or 82 but not by a national prohibition: in this event the principle of primacy applies and the Community rules prevail, irrespective of national rules ignoring, permitting, or even encouraging – but not requiring[363] – contrary conduct.[364] So, for example, neither express exemption from the Resale Prices Act 1976 by the Restrictive Practices Court[365] nor express approval from the *Bundeskartellamt* for the establishment of a structural crisis cartel[366] can save participating undertakings from the application of Article 81(1).[367]

(c) an agreement or practice is caught both by Articles 81 and/or 82 and by national rules: the Community rules prevail equally. However, because national rules are not pre-empted the national prohibition may operate concurrently, and penalties provided by national law may apply.[368] This, of course, gives rise to problems of *non bis in idem*, recognised to be a general principle of Community law. The Court therefore said in *Wilhelm*:

> If, however, the possibility of two procedures being conducted separately were to

---

[362] Cases 253/78 & 1–3/79 *Giry et Guerlain, ibid*, at 2375.

[363] See pp 40–2 *supra*.

[364] Case 229/83 *Leclerc* v *Au Blé Vert* [1985] ECR 1; Case 45/85 *Verband der Sachversicherer* v *Commission* [1987] ECR 405; Cases 89 etc/85 *Åhlström* v *Commission* (Woodpulp) [1988] ECR 5193 (in which the national law at issue was that of a non-member state); Case T-7/92 *Asia Motor France* v *Commission* [1993] ECR II-669; Case T-37/92 *Bureau Européen des Unions de Consummateurs* v *Commission* [1994] ECR II-285.

[365] *Re Net Book Agreements, 1957* [1962] 3 All ER 751.

[366] See § 6 GWB.

[367] Decision 89/44 (*Net Book Agreements*) OJ 1989 OJ L22/12, upheld in Case T-66/89 *Publishers Association* v *Commission* [1992] ECR II-1995, overturned on other grounds in Case C-360/92P *Publishers Association* v *Commission* [1995] ECR I-23; Decision 89/515 (*Welded Steel Mesh*) 1989 OJ L260/1, upheld essentially in Case T-145/89 *Baustahlgewebe* v *Commission* [1995] ECR II-987 and on appeal in Case C-185/95P *Baustahlgewebe* v *Commission* [1998] ECR I-8417.

[368] Case 14/68 *Wilhelm* v *Bundeskartellamt* [1969] ECR 1.

lead to the imposition of consecutive sanctions, a general requirement of natural justice ... demands that any previous punitive decision be taken into account in determining any sanction which is to be imposed.[369]

This is perhaps easily enough done where the two sanctions are of a similar character; it is not so easy when the Community sanction is a Commission fine and the national sanction, say, a criminal penalty. The Commission is not bound by any assessment or conclusions reached by national competition authorities applying national law,[370] but may be required at least to consider them if put forward by a party seeking exemption as evidence of the benefits of an agreement and justify departing from their logic.[371] In the United Kingdom the Director-General of Fair Trading and appeal tribunals and courts are statutorily bound to take account of penalties or fines imposed by the Commission or by authorities in other member states when imposing a penalty under the Competition Act.[372]

(d) an agreement or practice is caught by Article 81(1) and by national rules but enjoys exemption under Article 81(3):[373] this is where the greatest difficulties arise, and is an area in which the reconciliation of national rules and the primacy of Community law is, according to Advocate-General Tesauro, 'a desperate undertaking, even a diabolical one'.[374] The logical question to ask is whether exemption from the prohibition of Article 81(1) is permissive only, or whether it is a device which actively encourages the implementation of Community competition policy – for example, market interpenetration.[375] If the first obtains, national rules ought to be applicable notwithstanding the exemption – in other words, exemption is permissible but not indispensable: it lifts (or 'waives')[376] only the Community barrier to the enforceability of an agreement (that is, Article 81(1)), leaving unimpaired the application of national prohibitions (the 'double barrier' theory, or *Zweischrankentheorie*). If the latter

---

[369] at 15. See also Case 7/72 *Boehringer* v *Commission* [1972] ECR 1281. For an example of the application by the Commission of this principle see Decision 89/515 (*Welded Steel Mesh*) OJ 1989 L260/1.

[370] Case T-149/89 *Sotralentz* v *Commission* [1995] ECR II-1127.

[371] Case C-360/92P *Publishers Association* v *Commission* [1995] ECR I-23.

[372] Competition Act 1998, s 38(9).

[373] See Chap 4.

[374] Case C-70/93 *Bayerische Motorenwerke* v *ALD Auto-Leasing* [1995] ECR I-3439 at 3455.

[375] Supporters of the latter view take comfort from an observation *obiter* of the Court in *Wilhelm* (at 14): the Treaty 'permits the Community authorities to carry out certain positive, though indirect, action with a view to promoting a harmonious development of economic activities within the whole Community'.

[376] Case 14/68 *Wilhelm* v *Bundeskartellamt* [1969] ECR 1 *per* A–G Roemer at 23.

obtains, an exemption is both permissible and indispensable, and ought to pre-empt the application of the national rule. There is then a corollary question of whether the same answer applies irrespective of whether the exemption is the fruit of an individual decision (and so the product of active deliberation of, leading to a positive administrative/quasi-judicial act from, the Commission) or of a block exemption. There is little authority generally here. The Commission, not surprisingly, rejects the double barrier theory and takes the view that the *Wilhelm* test of 'full and uniform application' of Community law requires that the benefit of (any) exemption will occupy the field and render national rules inapplicable to the exempted agreement,[377] but this is a generous (if not necessarily invalid) interpretation of *Wilhelm*. As for case law, the Court of Justice has said that the issue by the Commission of a comfort letter cannot have the effect of displacing the application of national competition rules which are more rigorous than the Community prohibition, but was silent as to the possible effects of an exemption.[378] Advocate-General Tesauro subsequently said that a block exemption must have the effect of setting aside the application of inconsistent national law, but the issue was not addressed in the judgment.[379] Most recently the Court said that neither Article 81(3) nor a block exemption into which an agreement fell has the effect of displacing national case law on unfair competition which imposes more stringent criteria than those of the block exemption for the agreement to be valid;[380] however, it must be noted that the block exemption in question expressly envisaged the application of national prohibitive rules to agreements falling within the block exemption.[381] It may be that the problem is resolved by legislative intervention: in its 1999 White Paper[382] the Commission has now proposed that the authority provided by Article 83(1)(e) (ex Article 87(1)(e)), whereby Community legislation may deter-

---

[377] See, eg, EC Commission, *Fourth Report on Competition Policy* (1974), point 45. In Case C-266/93 *Bundeskartellamt* v *Volkswagen* [1995] ECR I-3477 the Commission argued that any national prohibition of an agreement enjoying the benefits of a block exemption would frustrate the uniform application of Community law and disregard the effectiveness of the block exemption, but the Court was not required to address the question as it found the agreements in question to fall outwith the relevant block exemption.

[378] Cases 253/78 & 1–3/79 *Procureur de la République* v *Giry et Guerlain* (Perfume) [1980] ECR 2327. Implicit in the case was that, following alteration to the agreements (on exclusive distribution), the comfort letters issued were based upon considerations of negative clearance, so taking the agreements into category (*a*) above.

[379] Case C-70/93 *Bayerische Motorenwerke* v *ALD Auto-Leasing* [1995] ECR I-3439.

[380] Case C-41/96 *VAG-Händlerbereit* v *SYD-Consult* [1997] ECR I-3123.

[381] Reg 123/85, OJ 1985 L15/16 (now repealed and replaced by Reg 1475/95, OJ 1995 L145/25), recital 29; this was also the block exemption at issue in Case C-70/93 *BMW*, n 379 *supra*.

[382] See *infra*.

mine the relationship between Articles 81 and 82 and national law, be deployed in order that block exemptions provide expressly that agreements falling within their ambit be exempted from the application of contrary national competition law. It has already, by stealth, had a first stab at this: the original draft of the new block exemption regulation on vertical agreements[383] contained a preambular recital providing 'Whereas national laws on competition cannot be applied to vertical agreements which fall within Article 81(1) and are exempted by this Regulation'.[384] In the event cooler heads prevailed and the terms of the recital were progressively watered down[385] so that the version appearing in the regulation as adopted is the anodyne

> [w]hereas ... In accordance with the principle of the primacy of Community law, no measure taken pursuant to national laws on competition should prejudice the uniform application throughout the common market of the Community competition rules or the full effect of any measures adopted in implementation of those rules, including this Regulation.[386]

Even if this may be taken to mean what the Commission wants it to mean, it is a preambular reference only, it is not addressed in the operative part, and it very likely exceeds Commission competence, absent express authority from the Council (which does not exist in the enabling regulation[387]), so to require. Pending action by the Council many of the answers are simply not yet known, and further case law will be required to supply them.[388] One by-product of the uncertainty is that the Commission receives a number of notifications from German undertakings – for exemption, very carefully *not* for negative clearance – in order to secure an exemption in

---

[383] See pp 128–30 *supra*.

[384] Commission proposal for a regulation on the application of Article 81(3) to categories of vertical agreements, unpublished, recital 18.

[385] See the penultimate draft (OJ 1999 C270/7), recital 18: 'Whereas ... In accordance with the principle of primacy of Community law, this Regulation prevails over any decision taken in application of national laws on competition'.

[386] Reg 2790/1999, OJ 1999 L336/21, recital 17.

[387] Reg 19/65, JO 1965, 533 as amended.

[388] A good place to start would be the Supply of Beer (Tied Estates) Order 1989, SI 1989/2390, which imposes more onerous requirements on the purchase of beer supplies than those laid down (expressly for beer) in the exclusive purchasing block exemption, Reg 1984/83, OJ 1983 L193/5. However, the Commission stated in response to a Parliamentary question that 'it has always considered that national regulations which are more stringent than block-exemption regulations ... are compatible with them, provided they do not affect the essential conditions of such exemptions' and that the British regulations were therefore not inconsistent with Reg 1984/83: EP Debates No 3–416/192–3. Similarly, s 44 of the Patents Act 1977 (now repealed; Competition Act 1998, s 70) provided conditions for patent licensing which were narrower than those permitted by the technology transfer block exemption: Reg 240/96, OJ 1996 L31/2.

the hopes of circumventing the prohibitions of German competition law. Whether or not this *Taschenspieltrick* will prove effective remains properly to be tested. In the United Kingdom (and in four other member states[389]) the uncertainty is circumvented by the device of 'parallel exemption', whereby an agreement is exempt from the Chapter I prohibition (the equivalent of Article 81(1)) of the Competition Act 1998 if it is exempt from Article 81(1) by virtue of a Commission decision or of a regulation (and so a block exemption)[390] – although the (parallel) exemption may be cancelled by the Director-General of Fair Trading.[391] Even more generously, parallel exemption will apply to a Chapter I prohibition if the agreement falls within the criteria of a (block exemption) regulation but does not affect trade between member states[392] – which takes the agreement beyond the application of Article 81, allowing national law to apply in its full vigour as in *(a)* above, but nevertheless incorporating wholesale into British law the thinking and techniques of the block exemptions. It may be that their application to wholly British agreements – for which they were not designed and are in some ways ill-suited – emasculates some of the force of the Chapter I prohibition.[393] Whatever the result, it gives the Commission significant influence over the direction of purely British law, for as block exemptions change and evolve to suit Community purposes – as they are currently[394] – so will the application of the Competition Act.

6.6 Reform of Regulation 17

In 1999 the Commission produced its White Paper on reform of Regulation 17.[395] The focus is upon surrender of the Commission monopoly over the power of exemption under Article 81(3), and is discussed above.[396] However, should any of it come to pass it will have a significant knock-on effect for the enforcement of Article 81 and, to a lesser extent, Article 82 more generally.

---

[389] Belgium (loi du 5 août 1991, art 32) Denmark (Konkurrenceloven, § 4); Spain, but block exemptions only (Real decreto 157/1992 de 2 de febrero de 1992, BOE núm 52 de 29 de febrero de 1992, art 1º); and the Netherlands (Mededingingswet, artt 12, 14).

[390] Competition Act 1998, s 10. This does not apply to a finding of incompatibility with Art 81 by the Secretary of State under authority of Art 84 (ex Art 88) of the Treaty: s 11(1).

[391] *Ibid*, s 10(5).

[392] *Ibid*, s 10(2).

[393] See Chap 12.

[394] See pp 128–30 *supra*.

[395] White Paper on Modernisation of the Rules Implementing Articles 85 and 86 of the EC Treaty, Programme 99/027.

[396] at pp 134–6.

To recap the central proposition of the White Paper, the exclusive authority to grant exemption was once justified in order to enable the Commission to establish the uniform meaning, parameters and application of Article 81. Now the law and the conditions for exemption under Article 81(3) are clarified and predictable, so that the centralised system of Regulation 17 is inefficient, unwieldy and no longer necessary. The present notification system ought therefore to be scrapped and all national competition authorities and all national courts before which Article 81(1) is raised be given the authority directly to apply Article 81(3). Article 81 would be reunited, parties could rely upon a directly effective Article 81(3), and restrictive practices prohibited by Article 81(1) but which meet the criteria of Article 81(3) would be valid and enforceable from the time they were concluded without need of a prior decision to that effect.

Whilst national courts already have the wherewithal (if not necessarily the expertise) to assume these responsibilities, national competition authorities do not. Or rather, some do not have the authority, and many do not have the habit. If they are to be competent to wield powers upon a footing more equal with that of the Commission as to prohibition of restrictive practices and abusive conduct, they must be given the powers necessary to do so. The seven member states in which there is no statutory authority to move against breaches of Articles 81 or 82, which include the United Kingdom,[397] must therefore adopt it,[398] and if they do not they may be compelled to do so by a directive adopted under Article 83 (ex Article 87). This is in itself no guarantee they will actually use the power, so express duties could be laid down by directive. As for the Commission, it will continue to adopt prohibition decisions in (serious) individual cases – for example, those which raise new legal issues and, because of political sensitivity and potential for bias, cases involving the application of Article 86 (ex Article 90) of the Treaty[399] – and to this end it wants both its powers of investigation[400] and the penalties it can impose[401] beefed up. It also wants the authority to adopt a new type of individual decision whereby commitments given by undertakings in the course of a Commission investigation, which at present may lead to the termination of proceedings but no

---

[397] The existing EC Competition Law (Articles 88 and 89) Enforcement Regulations 1996, SI 1996/2199 are insufficient to this task; see pp 196–7 *supra*. The choice is therefore to amend these considerably or make appropriate amendments to the Competition Act 1998.

[398] White Paper, para 94.

[399] White Paper, para 59; as to Art 86 see Chap 7.

[400] White Paper, paras 109–16.

[401] *Ibid*, paras 123–8.

more, would be adopted formally by decision, the commitments then binding, breach of which would lead to fines.[402] As for exemption, the need of which ought logically to disappear, the Commission will continue to adopt (new type) block exemptions as a means of clarifying the scope and application of Article 81(3) which will be binding upon both national competition authorities and national courts and proposes that, for certainty, a regulation be adopted in accordance with Article 83(2)(e) (ex Article 87(2)(e)) providing expressly that such exemption override contrary national law. Whilst it will no longer adopt individual exemption decisions, it proposes to adopt 'positive decisions' from time to time finding an agreement to be compatible with Article 81 as a whole, either because it falls outwith Article 81(1) or because it satisfies the criteria of Article 81(3). It will do so in exceptional cases only, for guidance and in the general interest. A positive decision will be declaratory in nature and have the same legal effect as negative clearance at present.[403]

It is not clear why the Commission is prepared now to surrender its long jealously guarded monopoly over exemption. The White Paper must be read as an admission – according to the (then) president of the *Bundeskartellamt* it 'comes close to capitulation'[404] – that the Commission is unequal to the task of administering the present system. But its confidence as to the clarity and maturity of the system which enables it to abandon its monopoly may be questioned. The benefits in terms of efficiency (no notification, no *Delimitis* problems, rare pre-emption by the Commission, relatively speedy resolution of disputes) are self evident. It would also free up the now overstretched Court of First Instance from the onerous jurisdiction of review of the bulk of Commission decisions in the field, although doubtless this would result, swings and roundabouts, in a new flood of references to the Court of Justice from national courts under Article 234 (ex Article 177) involving both civil litigation and judicial supervision of national competition authorities. But the pitfalls are many. The first, logically, is the diligence and enthusiasm national competition authorities may bring to the task. Will they simply be bothered to expend time and resources which upon a national view might be better directed elsewhere? Will they be vigorous in pursuing anticompetitive practices or conduct which may confer an advantage upon domestic industry in the Community market? Has the historical cultural affinity in some member

---

[402] *Ibid*, para 90.
[403] *Ibid*, paras 88–9.
[404] Dr D. Wolf, 'Perspektiven des Europäischen Kartellrechts', a position paper delivered to the Frankfurter Institut – Stiftung Marktwirtschaft und Politik on 8 July 1999.

states to cartels been wholly overcome? Even assuming good faith, how will they exercise the discretion now enjoyed by the Commission to reject a complaint upon grounds of insufficient importance? And will the different penalties they may impose (unless harmonised) not lead to forum shopping? Second, and probably more serious, there is the likelihood – or racing certainty – of an even greater degree than at present of divergent interpretation of Articles 81 and 82 by the Commission on the one hand and the re-invigorated national authorities (both administrative authorities and the courts) on the other. The problem would no longer be limited to Article 81(1): with a directly effective Article 81(3) fissures will appear as to when the criteria of Article 81(3) are, or are not, satisfied. And as national authorities, administrative and judicial, are in no way bound by the determinations of those in other member states it will almost inevitably lead to divergences amongst the member states and thence to even more forum shopping. It was precisely for these reasons that the Commission has long justified its monopoly under Regulation 17. There remains, finally, in the context of enforcement of Article 81 by national courts the fundamental and arguable proposition that Article 81(3) necessarily raises questions of economic judgment and balancing tests which are simply not the proper province of judges.

In order to minimise the problems the White Paper proposes a number of safeguards. At present the Commission must inform national authorities of proceedings before it;[405] this should be mirrored by an obligation for the latter, when applying Articles 81 and 82, to inform the Commission and, implicitly, allow it to state a view.[406] They ought also to inform the Commission if they intend to use the power which they have enjoyed since 1999[407] to withdraw the benefit of a Commission block exemption. It must become possible – which at present it is not[408] – for files, including confidential information, to be passed both ways and used by either (whichever is more appropriate in the circumstances, perhaps upon the basis of a still to be developed 'centre of gravity' (*Schwerpunkttheorie*) test[409]) in order to show an infringement of Articles 81 or 82.[410] Equally national courts should inform the Commission of any relevant litigation before them and allow it, by leave, to intervene as *amicus curiae*,[411] as it

---

[405] Reg 17, art 10.

[406] White Paper, para 105; this is already the case under German law, § 50 III GWB.

[407] See p 126 *supra*.

[408] Reg 17, art 20; Case C-67/91 *Dirección General de Defensa de la Competencia* v *Asociación Española de Banca Privada* [1992] ECR I-4785; see pp 169–70 *supra*.

[409] White Paper, paras 59–61.

[410] *Ibid*, paras 96–8.

[411] *Ibid*, para 107.

does now before the Court of Justice in cases referred under Article 234 (ex Article 177)[412] and as the *Bundeskartellamt* does in analogous cases, and to frequently persuasive effect, before German courts.[413] But these are all vertical arrangements: the White Paper does not address questions of transfrontier collaboration between different national authorities, in which area legislation is probably *ultra vires* the Community under Article 83 (ex Article 87) and so would require a convention amongst the member states. Otherwise these safeguards ought all to be codified in Regulation 17 (or a replacement thereto) and in the 1993 (national courts) and 1997 (administrative authorities) cooperation notices. The Commission also envisages the adoption of a raft of new notices as the system develops and finds its feet. Whether upon sober reflection all this is seen by the Commission and by the Council – the German government has already expressed serious reservations[414] – to be sufficient to justify letting the genie out of the bottle remains to be seen.

---

[412] Statute of the Court of Justice, art 20.

[413] §§ 90 I, 96 GWB.

[414] Stellungnahme der Bundesregierung zum Weissbuch der Europäischen Kommission über die Modernisierung der Vorschriften zur Anwendung der Artikel 81 und 82 EGV, 29. Oktober 1999.

CHAPTER 7

Public and privileged undertakings

The framers of the Treaty recognised that some undertakings would be in public ownership within each of the member states and that they, or other undertakings in private ownership, might be charged with special rights and duties in the public interest. The duties usually include the universal provision of goods or services throughout the whole or defined parts of the territory of the member state, the rights various privileges – usually monopoly privileges and so a captive market, and immunity from competition – in order to enable them properly or effectively to discharge their duties. In all events they are subject to significant state intervention, such as price controls and sometimes (massive) subsidies. Such undertakings are seen frequently to serve a desirable social function, for left to market forces undertakings would cream off profitable sectors (by service market or geographically) and leave others unsupplied or suppliable only at prohibitive cost. They are also seen to be more reliable in matters of public safety as they are less likely than the private sector to cut corners. They include first and foremost undertakings in the supply of utility, communications and transport services, but may extend into other areas as the state sees fit.

Governments might be disinclined to be scrupulously fair in the matter of undertakings in which they have a direct stake and, because of this and the conferral upon them or upon a favoured private undertaking of monopoly or related privileges and attendant regulation of both, they pose a threat to the application of the competition rules. Put at its simplest, could undertakings in Germany and France expect to compete on equal footing in, say, the Italian market with a state-owned enterprise there? The Treaty could therefore address the issues in a number of ways. At opposite ends of the spectrum it could, first, leave to the member states absolute discretion in relation to both public ownership and the creation of legal monopolies and their privileges, and provide them with immunity from Treaty rules (the 'absolute sovereignty approach') or, second, prohibit their very creation or existence, for their ownership and/or privileges will inevitably result in anticompetitive conduct (the 'absolute competition approach'). The first option would lead to gross distortion in conditions of competition within and between member states depending upon whether the state was inclined to public ownership and/or statutory monopolies; the second would deprive the member states of a legitimate medium for the direction of economic and social policies. Not surprisingly, the Treaty therefore pursues a course which is somewhere in between.

Article 86 (ex Article 90) of the Treaty provides:

1. In the case of public undertakings and undertakings to which Member States grant special or exclusive rights, Member States shall neither enact nor maintain in force any measure contrary to the rules contained in this Treaty, in particular to those rules provided for in Article 12 and Articles 81 to 89.
2. Undertakings entrusted with the operation of services of general economic interest or having the character of a revenue-producing monopoly shall be subject to the rules contained in this Treaty, in particular to the rules on competition, insofar as the application of such rules does not obstruct the performance, in law or in fact, of the particular tasks assigned to them. The development of trade must not be affected to such an extent as would be contrary to the interests of the Community.
3. The Commission shall ensure the application of the provisions of this Article and shall, where necessary, address appropriate directives or decisions to Member States.

It will be observed that Article 86(1) addresses 'public undertakings' and undertakings, public or private, which enjoy special or exclusive rights conferred by the state, whilst Article 86(2) applies to certain classes of undertakings, which again may be public or private, and which because of special duties with which they are entrusted enjoy the privilege of immunity from Treaty rules in limited circumstances. Article 86(3) provides the Treaty base for legislation to ensure the application of Article 86 (1) and (2) – one of the very few Treaty articles which confers autonomous legislative authority directly upon the Commission. It will also be observed that Article 86 lays down no substantive provisions of its own; rather it defines the manner in which *other* Treaty provisions – including those governing the four freedoms but primarily ('in particular') the rules on competition – are to be applied to undertakings which fall within its ambit. The three paragraphs will be considered in turn.

7.1 Article 86(1)

Article 86(1) admits of the state ownership of undertakings. Community law cannot do otherwise, the Treaty reserving to the member states the rules governing the system of property ownership.[1] The taste for public ownership varies with time: nationalisation was in greater vogue when the Treaty was drafted but for the last 15 years the tendency has been in the other direction across the Community. Like 'undertaking', public undertakings are not defined in the Treaty. They are however defined in legislation – a 1980 directive (the 'transparency directive')[2] adopted with a view to increased transparency of the financial relationship between public undertakings and the state. A public undertaking is

> any undertaking over which the public authorities may exercise directly or indirectly a dominant influence by virtue of their ownership of it, their financial participation therein, or the rules which govern it.[3]

'Public authorities' are the state and regional or local authorities, and they exercise a dominant influence over an undertaking where they hold the major part of its subscribed capital, control the majority of votes attached to shares issued or approve more than half the members of its administrative, managerial or supervisory body.[4] As for undertakings to which member states grant 'special or exclusive rights', they are defined by legislation for purposes of the telecommunications sector (but applicable elsewhere) as

> the rights granted by a Member State or a public authority to one or more public or private bodies through any legal, regulatory or administrative instrument reserving them the right to provide a service or undertake an activity.[5]

The grant of an 'exclusive' (monopoly) right is straightforward; the grant of 'special rights' is less so, but appears to apply to rights granted to more than one undertaking operating in the same market where their number is limited and they are chosen upon discriminatory and subjective criteria.[6] The two categories (public undertakings and undertakings granted special or exclusive rights) are not mutually exclusive[7] and either category may, or may not, fall for consideration also under Article 86(2): a public undertaking or an undertaking granted special or exclusive rights may, but does not necessarily, operate a service of general economic interest.

---

[1] Art 295 (ex Art 222). For further consideration of Art 295 see Chap 10.
[2] Directive 80/723, OJ 1980 L195/35; see *infra*.
[3] art 2.
[4] *Ibid.*
[5] Directive 90/388, OJ 1990 L233/19, art 1.
[6] Cases C-271, 281 & 289/90 *Spain* v *Commission* [1992] ECR I-5833, *per* A-G Jacobs at 5856.
[7] eg, Case 155/73 *Giuseppe Sacchi* [1974] ECR 409.

Unlike Article 86(2), Article 86(1) provides no privileges or derogations from Treaty rules. Quite the opposite, it prohibits the introduction or maintenance of rules governing public undertakings or undertakings granted exclusive rights which are contrary to the requirements of the Treaty. It addresses not those undertakings themselves but the member states; it is concerned not directly with the conduct of undertakings which distorts competition but with the legislation or regulation through which the member state permits, encourages or compels them to do so. This is a function of the 'autonomous conduct of undertakings' required in order for Articles 81 and 82 to be joined:[8] in the absence of public law regulation undertakings have no shield against the full application of Articles 81 and 82; and in the absence of public law regulation Article 86 has nothing to say. It should be noted in this context that there existed a degree of tension in the application of Article 86(1) to the exercise by the state of true public law functions. This has now been circumvented by the recent case law of the Court on the meaning of undertaking. So, in *Poucet et Pistre*,[9] *Eurocontrol*,[10] and *Diego Calì e Figli*[11] (respectively operation by social security offices of a compulsory social security scheme, maintenance and improvement of safety in air navigation, and anti-pollution surveillance in an Italian port) the Court did not consider whether these authorities were compelled to infringe the competition rules because it found that owing to the public nature of the duties they discharged they were not undertakings at all.[12] This relieves them of the application of Articles 81 and 82 and so necessary consideration of Article 86. Article 86(1) appears to have as its object national legislation which addresses directly the regulation of the undertakings and not legislation of general application; this is clearer from other language versions of the Treaty.[13]

The first target of Article 86(1) is national rules regulating public under-takings. Owing to the sometimes opaque financial relationship between the state *qua* public authority and the state *qua* undertaking (and hence the utility of and necessity for the transparency directive), it is frequently in the context of compliance with Articles 87 to 89 (ex Articles 92 to 94) on state aids that they fall for consideration under Article 86(1). As for undertak-

---

[8] Cases C-359 & 379/95P *Commission and France v Ladbroke Racing* [1997] ECR I-6265; see pp 40–42 *supra*.

[9] Cases C-159–60/91 *Poucet v Assurances Générales de France* [1993] ECR I-637.

[10] Case C-364/92 *SAT Fluggesellschaft v Eurocontrol* [1994] ECR I-43.

[11] Case C-343/95 *Diego Calì e Figli v Servizi Ecologici Porto di Genova* [1997] ECR I-1547.

[12] See p 38 *supra*.

[13] 'Les États membres, *en ci qui concerne* les entreprises publiques ...'; 'die Mitgliedstaaten werden *in bezug auf* öffentliche Unternehmen ...'; 'de Lid-Staten ... *met betrekking tot* de openbare bedrijven ...' emphasis added.

ings granted monopoly rights, because a member state is frequently a substantial part of the common market and a statutory monopoly within it necessarily precludes all competition, they usually enjoy a dominant position[14] and the point of tangency is therefore frequently Article 82. (Where special, as opposed to exclusive, rights are granted considerations of collective dominance may arise.[15]) It will be recalled that under Article 82 there is no reproach in the existence of a dominant position and so there can be no reproach to the creation and existence of a statutory monopoly. The Court is always quick to recognise this:

> [T]he simple fact of creating a dominant position ... by granting an exclusive right within the meaning of Article 90(1) is not as such incompatible with Article 86 of the Treaty.[16]

But it is equally quick to add immediately that

> [a] Member State is in breach of [contravenes] the prohibition contained in those two provisions only if the undertaking in question, merely by exercising the exclusive right granted to it, cannot avoid abusing its dominant position.[17]

And so

> any measure adopted by a Member State which maintains in force a statutory provision that creates a situation in which a[n undertaking] cannot avoid infringing Article 86 is incompatible with the rules of the Treaty.[18]

The Court has also used the formulae 'led to infringe',[19] 'induced to commit',[20] 'led to commit'[21] and 'led necessarily to commit'[22] a breach of Article 82.

---

[14] First recognised in Case 311/84 *CBEM* v *CLT & IPB* (Télémarketing) [1985] ECR 3261.

[15] eg, Case C-323/92 *Société Civile Agricole du Centre d'Insémination de la Crespelle* v *Coopérative d'Élevage et d'Insémination Artificielle du Département de la Mayenne* [1994] ECR I-5077. As to collective dominance see Chap 8.

[16] eg, Case C-41/90 *Höfner* v *Macrotron* [1991] ECR I-1979 at 2018; Case C-179/90 *Merci Convenzionali Porto di Genova* v *Siderurgica Gabrielli* [1991] ECR I-5889 at 5928; Case C-323/92 *La Crespelle, ibid* at 5104; Case C-55/96 *Job Centre Coop* [1997] ECR I-7119 at 7149.

[17] *Ibid.* The word in square parantheses appears in the latter two judgments.

[18] Case C-41/90 *Höfner* at 2017; repeated essentially *verbatim* in Case C-323/92 *La Crespelle* at 5104 and in Case C-55/96 *Job Centre* at 7148.

[19] Case C-260/89 *Elliniki Radiophonia Tileorassi* v *Dimotiki Etairia Pliroforissis* [1991] ECR I-2925 at 2962.

[20] Case C-179/90 *Merci Convenzionali Porto di Genova* v *Siderurgica Gabrielli* [1991] ECR I-5889 at 5928.

[21] Case C-163/96 *Criminal Proceedings against Silvano Raso* [1998] ECR I-533 at 579.

[22] Case C-266/96 *Corsica Ferries France* v *Gruppo Antichi Ormeggiatori del Porto di Genova* [1998] ECR I-3949 at 3995. 'Led necessarily to commit a breach' is closest to the French formulation ('serait nécessairement amené à contrevenir') normally used.

There is an uncommonly fine line between a lawful grant of monopoly rights and a breach of the Treaty under the combined provisions of Articles 82 and 86(1). In *Höfner*[23] and *Job Centre*[24] the creation of German and Italian statutory monopolies in public employment procurement led necessarily to a breach of Articles 82 and 86(1) where both monopolies were insufficiently staffed to meet market demand,[25] as did Italian legislation in *Siderurgica Gabrielli*[26] which induced a port authority to refuse to use modern technology which resulted in inefficiency. Even more telling, Greek legislation conferring upon a public broadcasting organisation a monopoly in the broadcast of its own programmes and reception and retransmission of foreign broadcasting,[27] Belgian legislation conferring upon the telephone monopoly the power to lay down technical standards and check conformity with those standards,[28] and Italian legislation conferring upon dockers' companies a monopoly in supplying labour to authorised operators with which they competed,[29] all created such a conflict of interest that they led necessarily to a breach of Article 82. In all of these cases it was the possibility (or inevitability), not the fact, of abuse of the dominant position which constituted the breach. This is very close to finding that the grant of exclusive rights is *per se* an infringement. It is not to be read that *all* exclusive rights enjoyed by monopolies will infringe Article 86(1) (in concert with Article 82), for it is only the more egregiously anticompetitive which have hitherto been challenged – frequently the reservation to the monopoly of ancillary activities remote from the legitimate services they may provide or blatant price/access discrimination. But it can be taken to indicate that the Court interprets the requirements of Article 90(1) very strictly.

Article 86(1) is enforced in two different ways. First, the Commission may by decision adopted by authority of Article 86(3) order the member state to repeal or amend the offending legislation.[30] Secondly, Article 86(1) is directly effective[31] – although necessarily in concert with some other

---

[23] Case C-41/90 *Höfner v Macrotron* [1991] ECR I-1979.

[24] Case C-55/96 *Job Centre Coop* [1997] ECR I-7119.

[25] See p 161 *supra*.

[26] C-179/90 *Merci Convenzionali Porto di Genova v Siderurgica Gabrielli* [1991] ECR I-5889.

[27] Case C-260/89 *Elliniki Radiophonia Tileorassi v Dimotiki Etairia Pliroforissis* [1991] ECR I-2925 at 2962.

[28] Case 18/88 *Régie des Télégraphes et des Téléphones v GB-Inno-BM* [1991] ECR I-5941.

[29] Case C-163/96 *Criminal Proceedings against Silvano Raso* [1998] ECR I-533 at 579.

[30] See *infra*.

[31] eg, Case C-260/89 *Elliniki Radiophonia Tileorassi v Dimotiki Etairia Pliroforissis* [1991] ECR I-2925; Case C-41/90 *Höfner v Macrotron* [1991] ECR I-1979; C-179/90 *Merci Convenzionali Porto di Genova v Siderurgica Gabrielli* [1991] ECR I-5889.

Treaty provision which the (compulsory) conduct of an undertaking offends, and so the normal formula is 'Article 86(1), in conjunction with Article X'. There is a problem here in that the direct effect of Article 86(1) may not have the finesse of the Commission decision. Where there is a comprehensive statutory regime creating and governing a public monopoly, there seems to be a presumption that its offending provisions can be severed. But if they cannot, presumably Article 86(1) requires the whole law to be set aside, and this could in some circumstances create a serious legal vacuum. The problem has not been addressed by the Court.

The Treaty does not address Community rules which produce effects analogous to those of the member states which are the target of Article 86(1). However, since all Community institutions derive their authority from the Treaty, Community legislation which leads necessarily to a breach of Articles 81 or 82 is probably an infringement of the Treaty within the meaning of Article 230 (ex Article 173) and so void/invalid, although the means by which such legislation may be challenged is circumscribed.[32]

Article 86(1) prohibits national law which induces an undertaking to breach the Treaty. But there is no breach of the Treaty if the privileged undertaking can successfully plead the exceptional circumstances of Article 86(2).

7.2 Article 86(2)

Whilst Article 86(1) addresses the member states, Article 86(2) addresses undertakings themselves and provides to them a degree of immunity from Treaty rules, 'in particular ... the rules on competition', where the application of those rules would obstruct the performance of their tasks. It applies to two categories of undertakings. The first is revenue-producing state monopolies, which used to be more prevalent on the continent and still exist to a limited extent; the most widely recognised is probably *Systembolaget* in Sweden.[33] None exists in the United Kingdom. They are specifically addressed by Article 31 (ex Article 37), found in the Title on the free movement of goods, and it is normally in relation to immunity from Article 31 (if a monopoly involving the provision of goods) that they arise for consideration under Article 86(2). Second, Article 86(2) applies to undertakings, public or private, which are 'entrusted with the operation of services of general economic interest'. Since such undertakings are fre-

---

[32] See pp 42–3 *supra*.

[33] On the rules governing *Systembolaget* and their compatibility with the Treaty see Case C-189/95 *Criminal Proceedings against Harry Franzén* [1997] ECR I-5909.

quently statutory monopolies it is usually in the context of immunity from Article 82 that they fall to be considered. This is a more complex construction than revenue-producing monopolies, and there are several preliminary points to be observed:

■ The 'operation' of services with which an undertaking is entrusted refers more accurately to its management or administration (*gestion des services*; *gestione di servizi*; *beheer van diensten*), and 'services' within the meaning of Article 86(2) is different from the meaning of services in its normal Treaty context under Articles 49 to 55 (ex Articles 59 to 66); it may, for example, include an undertaking concerned with the distribution of goods.

■ 'General economic interest', a concept which is capable of extremely broad application,[34] is not a term of law known to any of the member states and is a creation and construct of the Treaty. Presumably 'economic' interest was thought to be dissociable from other, non-economic (moral, social and cultural for example) interests, and this was a distinction drawn in the early days,[35] but the interpretation given more recently by the Court to the meaning of undertaking[36] has rendered it unnecessary. So, as with Article 86(1), some conduct of a member state need not be tested against the general economic interest because the authorities which discharge it are not undertakings. But having properly identified an undertaking, the determination of whether the service it discharges is of general economic interest is a function neither of the nature of the undertaking providing it nor of whether it is entrusted with exclusive rights; rather it is the essence of the service deemed to be of general economic interest and the special characteristics of this interest which distinguish it from the general economic interest of other economic activities.[37] Services recognised hitherto to be in the general economic interest have included the utilities (public water,[38] gas[39] and electricity[40] supply), the postal

---

[34] Case 10/71 *Ministère Public* v *Muller* [1971] ECR 723, *per* A-G Dutheillet de Lamothe at 739.

[35] eg, Decision 71/224 (*GEMA*) JO 1971 L134/15 at paras III.2 and III.3; Case 155/73 *Guiseppe Sacchi* [1974] ECR 409.

[36] See p 38 *supra*.

[37] Case C-179/90 *Merci Convenzionali Porto di Genova* v *Siderurgica Gabrielli* [1991] ECR I-5889; Case C-266/96 *Corsica Ferries France* v *Gruppo Antichi Ormeggiatori del Porto di Genova* [1998] ECR I-3949.

[38] Cases 96 etc/82 *IAZ International Belgium* v *Commission* [1983] ECR 3369.

[39] Case C-159/94 *Commission* v *France* [1997] ECR I-5815.

[40] Case C-393/92 *Gemeente Almelo* v *Energiebedrijf IJsselmij* [1994] ECR I-1477; Case C-157/94 *Commission* v *Netherlands* [1997] ECR I-5699; Decision 91/50 (*IJsselcentrale*) OJ 1991 L28/32.

service,[41] a public telephone system (but not the provision of telephone equipment)[42] and other telecommunications services,[43] national public broadcasting (television) services,[44] certain activities (mooring[45] and, probably, piloting[46] services) of port authorities, maintaining the navigability of a member state's most important (*in casu*, only) waterway,[47] maintaining non-commercially viable air routes,[48] 'external' funeral services,[49] public employment procurement,[50] supplementary pension schemes,[51] and the recovery and management of (non-hazardous) waste.[52] The provision of railway services has arisen only in the context of services within a port[53] and health services have never been considered, but railways and other forms of universal public transport and health and related services[54]

---

[41] Cases C-48 & 66/90 *Netherlands & Koninklijke PTT v Commission* [1992] ECR I-565; Case C-230/91 *Criminal Proceedings against Paul Corbeau* [1993] ECR I-2533; Cases C-147 & 148/97 *Deutsche Post v Gesellschaft für Zahlungssysteme*, judgment of 10 February 2000, not yet reported. The Commission has published a notice on the application of the competition rules to the postal sector, OJ 1998 C39/2.

[42] Case 18/88 *Régie des Télégraphes et Téléphones v GB-Inno-BM* [1991] ECR I-5941.

[43] Decision 82/861 (*British Telecommunications*) OJ 1982 L360/36, upheld on review as Case 41/83 *Italy v Commission* [1985] ECR 873.

[44] Case 155/73 *Giuseppe Sacchi* [1974] ECR 409; Case 260/89 *Elliniki Radiophonia Tileorassi v Dimotiki Etairia Pliroforissis* [1991] ECR I-2925; Case T-69/89 *Radio Telefis Éireann v Commission* [1991] ECR II-485; Cases T-258 etc/93 *Métropole Télévision v Commission* [1996] ECR II-649. The Amsterdam Treaty appended a new 'interpretative' protocol (Protocol on the System of Public Broadcasting in the Member States) to the EC Treaty which provides that the Treaty is to be 'without prejudice to the competence of the Member States to provide for the funding of public service broadcasting ... for fulfilment of the public service remit as conferred, defined and organised by each Member State'.

[45] Case C-266/96 *Corsica Ferries France v Gruppo Antichi Ormeggiatori del Porto di Genova* [1998] ECR I-3949.

[46] Decision 97/745 (*Port of Genoa*) OJ 1997 L301/27.

[47] Case 10/71 *Ministère Public v Muller* [1971] ECR 723.

[48] Case 66/88 *Ahmed Saeed Flugreisen v Zentrale zur Bekämpfung unlauteren Wettbewerbs* [1989] ECR 803.

[49] Case 30/87 *Bodson v Pompes Funèbres des Régions Liberées* [1988] ECR 2479, *per* A-G da Cruz Vilaça.

[50] Case C-41/90 *Höfner v Macrotron* [1991] ECR I-1979; Case C-55/96 *Job Centre Coop* [1997] ECR I-7119.

[51] Case C-67/96 *Albany International v Stichting Bedrijfspensioenfonds Textielindustrie* [1999] ECR I-5751.

[52] Case C-209/98 *Entreprenørforeningens Affalds/Miljøsektion v Københavns Kommune*, judgment of 23 May 2000, not yet reported.

[53] Decision 94/119 (*Rødby Port*) OJ 1994 L55/52.

[54] The question of the compatibility with Art 86(2) of a statutory monopoly in the provision of ambulance services is currently before the Court: Case C-575/99 *Ambulanz Glöckner v Landkreis Südwestpfalz*, pending.

doubtless meet the necessary test. It does not apply to banking services,[55] to the services of authors' rights societies,[56] to the co-financing by a public undertaking of public services[57] or (probably) to dock work within a port.[58]

■ In order for Article 86(2) to be joined it is necessary that an undertaking be 'entrusted' with the operation of services. This requires a specific act of a public authority (although not necessarily a legislative act) which imposes express public service obligations upon identifiable undertakings;[59] it is not enough to be subject to obligations created by law which apply generally to all undertakings active (or potentially active) in a sector,[60] nor even if a service originating amongst private undertakings operates with the knowledge and express approval of public authorities.[61] In the United Kingdom it would normally be the product of an Act of Parliament setting out statutory duties for named (or to be prescribed or licensed) undertakings.

■ Article 86(2) is directly effective. The Court seemed originally to imply that whilst a national court could find the conditions for the application of Article 86(2) not joined, it could not satisfy itself that they were met and so set aside the application of Treaty rules in the absence of Commission action under Article 86(3).[62] This was also the stated (and unsurprising) view of the Commission itself.[63] But the Court has since confirmed the full direct effect of Article 86(2) and so the competence of a national court to

---

[55] Case 172/80 *Zückner* v *Bayerische Vereinsbank* [1980] ECR 2021. However, in Case E-4/97 *Norwegian Bankers' Association* v *EFTA Surveillance Authority* [1999] EFTA CR 1, the EFTA Court found a Norwegian state-owned bank which lends to certain categories of housing and related projects on advantageous terms, loans being available throughout the country to everyone on equal terms, to be providing a service in the general economic interest.

[56] Case 127/73 *Belgische Radio en Televisie* v *SABAM* [1974] ECR 313.

[57] Case C-108/98 *RI.SAN* v *Comune di Ischia* [1999] ECR I-5219.

[58] Case C-179/90 *Merci Convenzionali Porto di Genova* v *Siderurgica Gabrielli* [1991] ECR I-5889; Case C-242/95 *GT-Link* v *De Danske Statsbaner* [1997] ECR I-4449; Case C-163/96 *Criminal Proceedings against Silvano Raso* [1998] ECR I-533; Decision 97/744 (*Italian Ports*) OJ 1997 L301/17.

[59] Case 127/73 *Belgische Radio en Televisie* v *SABAM* [1974] ECR 313; Case 172/80 *Zückner* v *Beyerische Vereinsbank* [1980] ECR 2021.

[60] Decision 71/224 (*GEMA*) JO 1971 L134/15; Decision 98/190 (*Flughafen Frankfurt/Main*) OJ 1998 L72/30.

[61] Decision 85/77 (*Uniform Eurocheques*) OJ 1985 L35/43.

[62] Case 10/71 *Ministère Public* v *Muller* [1971] ECR 821; Case 155/73 *Giuseppe Sacchi* [1974] ECR 409 *per* A-G Reischl.

[63] Guidelines on the application of EEC competition rules in the telecommunications sector, OJ 1991 C233/2 at para 23.

apply it in its entirety.[64] This does not give rise to the problem of severance which adheres to the direct effect of Article 86(1): the conduct of an entrusted undertaking which offends the Treaty and cannot be saved by recourse to Article 86(2) may be severed, but if it is unseverable from conduct which is saved then it may stand.

■ There is no procedure or necessity for notification and authorisation under Article 86(2), and if its criteria are met any or all other Treaty provisions may be set aside. This has greater direct importance for the competition rules, for other Treaty freedoms are subject to limitation by virtue of specific derogation clauses in the interests of, for example, public policy,[65] whilst the competition rules (except for Article 81(3)) are not. So, for example, abuse of a dominant position is tolerated – Article 86(2) therefore constituting the one means of exemption from the strictures of Article 82 – and there is in principle no requirement to notify and seek approval from the Commission for state aids necessary to subvent undertakings falling within it, although in practice the procedures of Articles 88 (ex Article 93) are invariably complied with.[66] But because it represents an exception to the application of fundamental Treaty rules Article 86(2) is strictly interpreted.[67]

Assuming these preconditions to be met, Article 86(2) then imposes two concurrent tests: the competition rules are kept at bay if and insofar as they would obstruct the performance by the undertaking of its entrusted task, and the development of trade must not be affected to an extent contrary to the interests of the Community. Article 86(2) therefore

> seeks to reconcile the Member States' interests in using certain undertakings, in particular in the public sector, as an instrument of economic or fiscal policy with the Community's interest in ensuring compliance with the rules on competition and the preservation of the unity of the Common Market[68]

and represents 'a situation in which conflicting interests are delicately

---

[64] Case 260/89 *Elliniki Radiophonia Tileorassi v Dimotiki Etairia Pliroforissis* [1991] ECR I-2925; Case C-230/91 *Criminal Proceedings against Paul Corbeau* [1993] ECR I-2533; Case C-393/92 *Gemeente Almelo v Energiebedrijf IJsselmij* [1994] ECR I-1477.

[65] eg, Art 30 (ex Art 36) (free movement of goods); Art 39(3) (ex Art 48(3)) (workers); Art 46 (ex Art 56) (establishment); Art 55 (ex Art 66) (services).

[66] See Chap 11.

[67] Case 127/73 *Belgische Radio en Televisie v SABAM* [1974] ECR 313; Case C-179/90 *Merci Convenzionali Porto di Genova v Siderurgica Gabrielli* [1991] ECR I-5889; Case 18/88 *Régie des Télégraphes et des Téléphones v GB-Inno-BM* [1991] ECR I-5941; Case C-157/94 *Commission v Netherlands* [1997] ECR I-5699.

[68] Case 202/88 *France v Commission* (Telecommunications Terminals Equipment) [1991] ECR I-1223 at 1263.

poised'.[69] Both criteria therefore necessarily require a balancing test. They will be considered in turn.

7.2.1 Obstruction of the performance of the entrusted task

The rules on competition apply to privileged undertakings 'in so far as the application of such rules does not obstruct the performance, in law or in fact, of the particular tasks assigned to them'. For 'obstruct' other language texts read 'hinder' (*verhindern*; *ostare*; *verhinderen*) but the French suggests a test which is closer in meaning to defeating or rendering impossible ('... où l'application des ces règles ne fait pas échec à l'accomplisement ... de la mission particulière'), and this is closer to the manner in which the Article was originally construed. According to the Commission,

> [i]t is not sufficient ... that compliance with the provisions of the Treaty makes the performance of the particular task more complicated. A possible limitation of the application of the rules on competition can be envisaged [n'entre en ligne de compte] only in the event that the undertaking concerned has no other technically or economically feasible means of performing its particular task.[70]

The formulation was subsequently cited with approval by Advocate-General da Cruz Vilaça.[71] As a result there was for a long time no instance in which the Court of Justice found the conditions of Article 86(2) to be satisfied (although it had in the context of the Article 177 (now Article 234) preliminary ruling procedure enunciated the test and left it to be applied by the referring national court[72]). However, there has been a sea change in Article 86(2). The Court began to moderate its language in *Höfner* (1991):[73] a privileged undertaking is subject to the competition rules 'unless and to the extent to which it is shown that their application is *incompatible* with the discharge of its duties'.[74] Incompatibility was taken

---

[69] Case 41/83 *Italy v Commission* [1985] ECR 873 at 888.

[70] Decision 82/371 (*Anseau/Navewa*) OJ 1982 L167/39 at para 66, upheld implicitly on review as Cases 96 etc/82 *IAZ International Belgium v Commission* [1983] ECR 3369; see also Decision 82/861 (*British Telecommunications*) OJ 1982 L360/36, upheld on review as Case 41/83 *Italy v Commission* [1985] ECR 873.

[71] Case 30/87 *Bodson v Pompes Funèbres des Régions Liberées* [1988] ECR 2479 at 2499–500.

[72] Case 66/88 *Ahmed Saeed Flugreisen v Zentrale zur Bekämpfung unlauteren Wettbewerbs* [1989] ECR 803; Case 260/89 *Elliniki Radiophonia Tileorassi v Dimotiki Etairia Pliroforissis* [1991] ECR I-2925; Case C-230/91 *Criminal Proceedings against Paul Corbeau* [1993] ECR I-2533; C-393/92 *Gemeente Almelo v Energiebedrijf IJsselmij* [1994] ECR I-1477.

[73] Case C-41/90 *Höfner v Macrotron* [1991] ECR I-1979.

[74] at 2017; emphasis added. The formula was also used in Case 155/73 *Giuseppe Sacchi* [1974] ECR 409 at 430 but *Höfner* marks a resuscitation.

further in *Corbeau* (1993).[75] In Belgium the Régie des Postes, a legal person governed by public law, enjoyed an absolute monopoly within the Kingdom in the collection, carrying, distribution and delivery of all correspondence of whatever nature. Mr Corbeau began an express postal delivery service within the city and area of Liège, and was accordingly charged with an offence under the Belgian legislation. The Court said Article 86(2)

> permits the Member States to confer on undertakings to which they entrust the operation of services of general economic interest, exclusive rights which may hinder the application of rules of the Treaty on competition in so far as restrictions on competition, or even the exclusion of all competition, by other economic operators are necessary to ensure the performance of the particular tasks assigned to the undertakings possessed of the exclusive rights.[76]

The Régie des Postes was clearly ('it cannot be disputed') entrusted with a service of general economic interest. The question therefore to be applied was

> the extent to which a restriction on competition or even the exclusion of all competition from other economic operators is necessary in order to allow the holder of the exclusive right to perform its task of general interest *and in particular to have the benefit of economically acceptable conditions.*[77]

It then went on to discuss the risks to the Régie des Postes of creaming off by competitors offering a specific service and said:

> the exclusion of competition is not justified as regards special services dissociable from the service of general interest which meets special needs of economic operators and which call for certain additional services not offered by the traditional postal service ... in so far as such specific services ... *do not compromise the economic equilibrium* of the service of general economic interest performed by the holder of the exclusive right.[78]

Whether or not the test was met was left to be determined by the referring national court, which it never did because in the event the prosecution was abandoned for unconnected reasons.

The present definitive view of the Court of Article 86(2) is to be had now from the 1997 *Electricity Supply* judgments,[79] the result of proceedings

---

[75] Case C-320/91 *Criminal Proceedings against Paul Corbeau* [1993] ECR I-2533.

[76] at 2568.

[77] at 2569; emphasis added.

[78] *Ibid*; emphasis added.

[79] Case C-157/94 *Commission* v *Netherlands* [1997] ECR I-5699; Case C-158/94 *Commission* v *Italy* [1997] ECR I-5789; Case C-159/94 *Commission* v *France* [1997] ECR I-5815 (involving also importation of gas); Case C-160/94 *Commission* v *Spain* [1997] ECR I-5851 (the Electricity Supplies cases).

raised by the Commission under Article 169 (now Article 230) against four member states (the Netherlands, Italy, France and Spain) seeking a declaration that the monopoly right provided by law in each for the importation of electricity for public distribution (and the Commission had limited its challenge to the monopoly on importation and not other monopoly rights such as transmission and distribution) contravened Articles 30 and 37 (now Articles 28 and 31) of the Treaty, electricity being a good and exclusive right of importation a breach of Article 37.[80] The Court found that electricity distribution throughout a defined territory to all consumers at uniform tariff rates is a task of general economic interest within the meaning of Article 86(2), then went on to consider whether exclusive importation rights could be justified. It is worth citing a judgment at some length in order to understand the Court's now established approach to Article 86(2):

> [F]or the Treaty rules not to be applicable to an undertaking entrusted with a service of general economic interest under Article 90(2) of the Treaty, it is sufficient that the application of those rules obstruct the performance, in law or in fact, of the special obligations incumbent upon that undertaking. It is not necessary that the survival of the undertaking itself be threatened ....
>
> [I]t is not necessary ... that the financial balance or economic viability of the undertaking ... should be threatened. It is sufficient that, in the absence of the rights at issue, it would not be possible for the undertaking to perform the particular tasks entrusted to it, defined by reference to the obligations and constraints to which it is subject.
>
> Moreover ... the conditions for the application of Article 90(2) are fulfilled in particular if maintenance of those rights is necessary to enable the holder to perform the tasks of general economic interest assigned to it under economically acceptable conditions ....
>
> [The] burden of proof cannot be so extensive as to require the Member State, when setting out in detail the reasons for which, in the event of the elimination of the contested measures, the performance, under economically acceptable conditions, of the tasks of general economic interest which it has entrusted to the undertaking would, in its view, be jeopardized, to go even further and prove, positively, that no other conceivable measure, which by definition would be hypothetical, could enable those tasks to be performed under the same conditions.[81]

The Commission failed to rebut the arguments for justification under

---

[80] Case *59/75 Pubblico Ministero* v *Manghera* [1976] ECR 91.
[81] Case C-157/94 *Commission* v *Netherlands* [1997] ECR I-5699 at 5780–4. The formulation was similar in the other three judgments.

Article 86(2) and the actions were dismissed.[82] And in a subsequent reference from an Italian court the Court of Justice took it upon itself to answer the question of fact (a reliable indication of an intention more firmly to establish the application of principles) and held that mooring operations in Italian ports are services of general economic interest, the enjoyment of an exclusive right conferred upon local groups of operators which provide a universal mooring service is justified on grounds of safety in port waters and public security, and so, for the first time, held the criteria of Article 86(2) to be satisfied.[83] Subsequently in *Albany International* it held a monopoly on the provision of a sectoral supplementary pension scheme to be justified in order to spread the risk, otherwise, because of creaming off, the removal of the exclusive right 'might' imperil the performance of its tasks under economically acceptable conditions and threaten its financial equilibrium.[84] Most recently it declared Deutsche Post, upon the same reasoning, to enjoy a degree of immunity from Article 82 in the manner in which it charged for the delivery of international post,[85] and found the recovery and management scheme for (non-hazardous) waste within the commune of Copenhagen, although restricted to three undertakings, justified on grounds of recycling efficiency.[86]

This is an altogether more gentle line of reasoning than previously. Mr Corbeau was unlikely to bring the Régie des Postes to its knees and monopoly rights in transmission and distribution enjoyed by the electricity operators had not been impugned; but deprived of aspects of their monopoly may have rendered their public duties more burdensome. The judgments speak not of defeating but of 'jeopardising' the operation of services by the entrusted undertaking and of justification for derogation 'in particular' if necessary for the 'economically acceptable conditions' and 'economic equilibrium' in which it operates. This lowers the bar significantly from earlier *dicta*, more closely approximates standard objective

---

[82] Ironically an association of Dutch electricity producers was subsequently found to have abused a dominant position by refusing to transmit imported electricity over its grids and so to have breached the Mededingingswet, was not saved by its art 25 (partial equivalent to Art 86(2) of the Treaty) and was fined 14 million guilders: NMa-besluit nr 650/52 (*Samenwerkende Elektriciteits-Produktiebedrijven*), 26 augustus 1999.

[83] Case C-266/96 *Corsica Ferries France v Gruppo Antichi Ormeggiatori del Porto di Genova* [1998] ECR I-3949.

[84] Case C-67/96 *Albany International v Stichting Bedrijfspensioenfonds Textielindustrie* [1999] ECR I-5751 at 5894–5. The English reads 'might make it impossible', reverting in part to older language, but the (authentic) Dutch reads that the performance of its tasks 'could be imperilled' ('dit ertoe zou konnen leiden … in gevaar komt').

[85] Cases C-147 & 148/97 *Deutsche Post v Gesellschaft für Zahlungssysteme*, judgment of 10 February 2000, not yet reported.

[86] Case C-209/98 *Entreprenørforeningens Affalds/Miljøsektion v Københavns Kommune*, judgment of 23 May 2000, not yet reported.

necessity and proportionality tests, and seems to mark a greater tolerance of state monopolies. There is another case in the pipeline (*Wouters*) addressing universally binding rules imposed by a Bar Council in order to safeguard the professional standards of advocates which may shed further light on the matter.[87]

In any event the application of Article 86(2) will be marked by a degree of transience, for two reasons. The first is technological change. The Belgian legislation at issue in *Corbeau*, for example, had been adopted in 1956 and 1971,[88] long before express courier delivery had been envisaged. It was not long ago that post and telephone services were in common, public, ownership throughout the Community (the 'PTTs', in the United Kingdom the old GPO), the telegraph, under the same ownership, was at the cutting edge of international communications, and telephone lines were used simply for what is now apparently called 'voice telephony', never mind faxes or the Internet. This has all changed. What is in the general economic interest today and what is justified in ring fencing the provider may be different next year. According to the Commission 'the goalposts are constantly moving',[89] and the Court may say in *GB-Inno* that the provision of telephone services is in the general economic interest 'at the present stage of development of the Community'.[90] There is a second reason, again a function of time, which is both the pendulum swinging back against the rush to privatisation and a contemporaneous function of the common/internal market timetable: whilst it may have been appropriate to adopt a stringent construction during the earlier periods of integration and dismantling of state intervention, with much of the work complete it may now be possible to ease off and allow a degree of variation in the melody. Perhaps for this reason the Treaty was amended at Amsterdam, adding a new Article 16 to Part I (the Principles) which reads:

> Without prejudice to Articles 73, 86 and 87, and given the place occupied by services of general economic interest in the shared values of the Union as well as their role in promoting social and territorial cohesion, the Community and the Member States, each within their respective powers and within the scope of application of this Treaty, shall take care [*veillent*; *Sorge tragen*] that such serv-

---

[87] Case C-309/99 *Wouters* v *Algemene Raad van de Nederlandse Orde van Advocaten*, pending.

[88] Loi du 26 décembre 1956 sur le service des postes, Moniteur Belge du 30–31 décembre 1956; Loi du 6 juillet 1971 portant création de la Régie des postes, Moniteur Belge du 14 août 1971.

[89] Notice on the application of the competition rules to the postal sector, OJ 1998 C39/2 at 3.

[90] Case 18/88 *Régie des Télégraphes et des Téléphones* v *GB-Inno-BM* [1991] ECR I-5941 at 5979.

ices operate on the basis of principles and conditions which enable them to fulfil their missions [*missions; Aufgaben*].

Aside from the immediate observation that it is drafted in inexcusably lazy English,[91] Article 16 looks likely at the least to bring a change of emphasis. The thrust of Article 86(2) is inimical to statutory monopolies: they enjoy limited derogation and only in exceptional circumstances. Now the Treaty, through Article 16 (in the light of which Article 86(2) must now be construed), stresses that they be enabled to fulfil their tasks/missions. Exactly what this means waits upon the Court of Justice.

7.2.2 The Community interest

The second balancing test required is that 'the development trade must not be affected to such an extent that it would be contrary to the interests of the Community'. There is virtually no case law on this; indeed, it is a test which seems in many cases to be overlooked.[92] It was the primary reason, in the early days, for the refusal to recognise the direct effect of Article 86(2), for there is a policy argument that this is a matter which cannot be adequately determined by a national court and so must be left to Commission intervention under Article 86(3).[93] However, the subsequent finding by the Court of direct effect must embrace the Community interest test as well. But it is still not clear what it means. In *Corsica Ferries France*[94] the Court said it was one of two tests which required to be applied, considered at some length (and confirmed) that the exclusivity at issue was justified in safeguarding the service of general economic interest, and then, without reasoning, said simply 'the other conditions for applying the derogation from application of the Treaty rules which is laid down in the provision are satisfied'.[95] Nor was the point considered by the

---

[91] The French uses *veiller* in both Art 86(3) ('La Commission veille l'application des dispositions du présent article …') and Art 16, the English uses 'ensure' in Art 86(3) but 'take care' in Art 16. The French and German use *missions* and *Aufgaben* in Art 16, *mission particulière* and *besondere Aufgabe* for 'particular tasks' in Art 86(2) and also *mission* and *Aufgabe* in defining the 'task' of the Community in Art 2, yet the English which is content with 'task(s)' in Arts 86(2) and 2 resorts in Art 16 to the 'missions' of services in the general economic interest. This is not only feeble English in itself but slapdash and confusing in the Treaty context.

[92] *cf.* Case E-4/97 *Norwegian Bankers' Association v EFTA Surveillance Authority* [1999] EFTA CR 1 in which the EFTA Court annulled a decision of the EFTA Surveillance Authority for failure sufficiently to consider whether an impugned practice was contrary to the interests of the EEA.

[93] Case 10/71 *Ministère Public v Muller* [1971] ECR 723.

[94] Case C-266/96 *Corsica Ferries France v Gruppo Antichi Ormeggiatori del Porto di Genova* [1998] ECR I-3949.

[95] at 3997.

Advocate-General. The only recent substantial consideration is that of Advocate-General Cosmas who ventured in the *Electricity Supply* cases that for recourse to Article 86(2) to be excluded it would be necessary not only that trade was affected potentially but had also been affected *in practice* (*en fait*; στην πραξη),[96] that is, in the present, this implication not present in the English text but clearer in some other language versions,[97] and 'the restrictive effects being so great that intra-Community trade in the sector in question is practically non-existent'.[98] This is consistent with the subsequent judgment of the Court, which noted that the Commission had failed to demonstrate that as a function of the exclusive import right the development of intra-Community trade 'has been and continues to be affected'.[99] If this is an accurate formulation of the test it is not unduly burdensome. And now that the Treaty in Article 16 recognises that services in the general economic interest are part of the 'shared values of the Union', and by implication consistent with the Community interest, it may become even less so.

7.3 Article 86(3)

Article 86(3) provides a legal base for the Commission to adopt directives and decisions 'where necessary' to ensure compliance with Article 86. This is a more specific enunciation of its general duty as guardian of the Treaty to ensure its application, both generally (Article 211 (ex Article 155)) and in the field of competition (Article 85 (ex Article 89)), and is different to and more specific than the power conferred upon the Council by Article 83 (ex Article 87).[100] In the narrower context of Article 86 the Commission may adopt both legislative measures (directives) and administrative/quasi-judicial measures (decisions). They must in both cases be addressed to the member states – directives because they are necessarily so and decisions because given the tenor and purpose of Article 86, Article 86(3) expressly so provides. Because Article 86 addresses public undertakings and state monopolies and so trenches upon sensitive issues of national economic and social policy, Article 86(3) is perhaps a power to be wielded with care. The

---

[96] Case C-157/94 *Commission v Netherlands* [1997] ECR I-5699 at 5765; emphasis in original.

[97] The development of trade 'ne doit pas être affecté', 'darf nicht ... beeinträchtigt werden', 'mag niet worden beïnvloed'.

[98] Case C-157/94 *Commission v Netherlands* [1997] ECR I-5699 at 5765; referring to the opinion of A-G Rozès in Case 78/82 *Commission v Italy* [1983] ECR 1955.

[99] at 5786.

[100] Case 202/88 *France v Commission* (Telecommunications Terminal Equipment) [1991] ECR I-1223.

sensitivity is best illustrated by the fact that, should all the proposals for reform envisaged in the 1999 White Paper come to pass, the power to adopt decisions under Article 86(3) will remain reserved to the Commission.[101] Having said that, the vested interests and political pressures at issue are such that had the matter been left to the Council we should probably have seen no legislation at all. The Commission cannot be compelled to adopt legislation under Article 86(3) but as with complaints lodged under Regulation 17 must reason and justify a refusal to do so,[102] and a refusal to act may be challenged only in exceptional circumstances.[103]

The fruits of the power to adopt directives are essentially two. First, the Commission adopted the transparency directive.[104] The concern here was the difficulty in applying the provisions of the Treaty on state aids to public undertakings. The directive therefore requires the member states in effect to open their books on publicly owned undertakings. Second, the Commission has adopted a number of directives geared towards liberalisation of the telecommunications sector by which exclusive rights conferred by national law are pared away.[105]

The adoption of decisions under Article 86(3), by which the Commission identifies and orders rectification of a breach of Article 86(1), has been more common. In keeping with the tenor of Article 86(1) the power is restricted to breaches occasioned by public law measures concerning public undertakings or state monopolies;[106] it cannot therefore be used to order termination of anticompetitive conduct of the undertakings themselves, which is a matter for the enforcement procedures of Articles 81 and 82. Examples include decisions to adjust the monopoly provisions governing compulsory public sector insurance in Greece,[107] telecommunications ter-

---

[101] White Paper on Modernisation of the Rules Implementing Articles 85 and 86 of the EC Treaty, Programme 99/027, paras 109–116.

[102] Cases C-359 & 379/95P *Commission and France v Ladbroke Racing* [1997] ECR I-6265; see pp 165–8 *supra*.

[103] Case C-107/95P *Bundesverband der Bilanzbuchhalter v Commission* [1997] ECR I-947; Case T-17/96 *Télévision Française 1 v Commission* [1999] ECR II-1757.

[104] Directive 80/723, OJ 1980 L195/35. The directive successfully withstood a challenge on the ground that it was *ultra vires*: Cases 188–90/80 *France, Italy and the United Kingdom v Commission* [1982] ECR 2545.

[105] Directive 90/388, OJ 1990 L233/19. The directive was also challenged (unsuccessfully) in Cases C-271, 281 & 289/90 *Spain, Belgium and Italy v Commission* [1992] ECR I-5833. It has been amended (in order to expand its application) a number of times, most recently by Directive 1999/64, OJ 1999 L175/39.

[106] Case 202/88 *France v Commission* (Telecommunications Terminal Equipment) [1991] ECR I-1223.

[107] Decision 85/276 (*Greek Insurance*) OJ 1985 L152/25.

minal equipment in France,[108] courier services in the Netherlands[109] and in Spain,[110] commercial television in Flanders,[111] access to facilities in Danish ports,[112] freeing up of port handling operations[113] and piloting tariffs[114] in Italian ports, and discriminatory handling charges laid down by law governing the operation of Belgian and Portuguese airports.[115]

Although it is not provided in Article 86(3), because a decision adopted under it may directly affect legal rights both the member state, its addressee and undertakings the direct beneficiary of the state measure have a right, as a general principle of Community law, to be heard prior to its adoption.[116] If a member state wishes to challenge an Article 86(3) decision it must, as with decisions generally, do so directly under Article 230 (ex Article 173); it is barred from arguing subsequently in other proceedings that the decision was unlawful.[117] This will in most cases apply also to the undertaking(s) concerned.[118] If the member state fails to comply with it the remedy is enforcement proceedings raised by the Commission under Article 226 (ex Article 169).[119]

---

[108] Decision 88/301, OJ 1988 L131/73, partially annulled on review as Case 202/88 *France* v *Commission* (Telecommunications Terminal Equipment) [1991] ECR I-1223.

[109] Decision 90/16 (*Dutch Couriers*) OJ 1990 L10/47; annulled on procedural grounds in Cases C-48 & 66/90 *Netherlands* v *Commission* [1992] ECR I-565.

[110] Decision 90/456 (*Spanish Express Courier Service*) OJ 1990 L233/19.

[111] Decision 97/606 (*Vlaamse Televisie*) OJ 1997 L244/18, upheld on review in Case T-266/97 *Vlaamse Televisie Maatschappij* v *Commission* [1999] ECR II–2329.

[112] Decision 94/119 (*Rødby Port*) OJ 1994 L55/52.

[113] Decision 97/744 (*Italian Ports*) OJ 1997 L301/17.

[114] Decision 97/745 (*Port of Genoa*) OJ 1997 L301/27.

[115] Decision 95/364 (*Zaventem Airport*) OJ 1995 L216/8; Decision 1999/199 (*Aeroportos e Navigaçao Aerea*) OJ 1999 L69/31 (under review as Case C-163/99 *Portugal* v *Commission*, pending).

[116] Cases C-48 & 66/90 *Netherlands* v *Commission* [1992] ECR I-565.

[117] Case 226/87 *Commission* v *Greece* [1988] ECR 3611.

[118] Applying Case C-188/92 *TWD Textilwerke Deggendorf* v *Germany* [1994] ECR I-833 by analogy.

[119] eg, Case 226/87 *Commission* v *Greece* [1988] ECR 3611 (failure to comply with Decision 85/276, n 107 *supra*).

CHAPTER 8

Oligopolies and mergers

As discussed above, liberal economists will identify control of oligopolistic markets and mergers as legitimate and necessary components of a competition law regime. But whilst both phenomena have been recognised for some decades as a proper concern of competition law, it is only recently that competition authorities in Europe have begun seriously to come to terms with them. They are not expressly countenanced in the competition rules of the EC Treaty, which are ill-fitted to deal with them for two reasons: first, Articles 81 and 82 (ex Articles 85 and 86) are addressed primarily to cartels and monopolies respectively; and second, oligopolies and mergers raise problems less of market conduct, with which Articles 81 and 82 are concerned, than of market structure. The Community is therefore faced with two options: either adopt new legislation under Article 83 (ex Article 87) 'to give effect to the principles set out in Articles 81 and 82' which is designed specifically to address the problems of oligopolies and mergers, or attempt to shoe-horn them into the existing rules. It has opted for the former course for mergers, but is left only with the latter for oligopolies.

8.1 Oligopolies

An oligopolistic market is a market for goods or services marked by the presence of a small number of undertakings, no one of which is dominant, but which between or amongst them control the market or a large part of it. There may, or may not, be a 'fringe' of smaller firms surrounding the oligopoly. Reference ought also to be made to oligopsonistic markets, which are marked by control of the demand side shared amongst a small number of purchasers,[1] and to which the same considerations apply. Oligopolies may be created and maintained by statutory privileges, such as the post-privatisation utilities in the UK (although many of these are more

---

[1] Purchase of food for retail in the UK, for example, could be characterised as an oligopsonistic market, and one which is coming under increasing fire for anticompetitive conduct.

of the nature of regional monopolies); others exist or evolve naturally. It is a broad church, ranging from duopoly to a larger number of undertakings (but how many?), and there is a wide variety of markets which may fall within the rubric. Even in homogenous, non-differentiated markets, which oligopolies tend to be, there may be situations ranging from one end of the oligopoly spectrum which is marked by free competition yet with a number of undertakings ahead of the herd, to another towards the opposite end in which one undertaking comes very close to dominance yet still competes with a small number of other operators ('asymmetric oligopoly'). It is also a growing church: industrial concentration in Europe over the last decades has produced an increasing number of markets with oligopolistic tendencies, and the trend is likely to continue.

The problem for competition regulation springs from the theory of 'oligopolistic interdependence'. Much of the motive force of competition is the uncertainty as to the manner in which competitors will behave. This is well and good where conditions of effective competition operate. But an oligopolistic market is marked by a number of characteristics: product homogeneity, low demand growth, low price sensitivity of demand, substantial barriers to entry, and first and foremost because it is shared between or amongst a small number of operators, a high degree of transparency, for both buyers and sellers. A price rise imposed or a price reduction offered by an oligopolist is detected straightaway and has an immediate impact upon the market, the one causing buyers to desert the oligopolist, the other causing them to desert its competitors. In the latter case, all competitors must respond immediately with their own reductions or go under. The natural state of an oligopolistic market – and it is all the truer the narrower the oligopoly, and most pronounced in a duopolistic market – is therefore one in which an interdependence is generated between or amongst undertakings such that they will tend not to compete with each other on price. And without price competition, prices rise inexorably to supracompetitive levels. Further, they will have little incentive to compete in other ways. The very stability of the market – one might say lethargy – does little to encourage efficiency or innovation; an oligopolistic market is naturally inefficient. In short, market power settles naturally but jointly upon oligopolists and the competitive forces which ought to motivate undertakings and compel them to act in ways which produce all the benefits of competition are simply not there. Whilst the theory of oligopolistic interdependence is not without its critics,[2] and there are some oligopolistic markets which are marked by fierce competition, this remains the basic premise.

The question facing a competition regime is what to do about oligopo-

---

[2] See generally R. Whish, *Competition Law* (Butterworths, London, 1993), p 469 *et seq*; R.H. Bork *The Antitrust Paradox: A Policy at War with Itself* (Basic Books, New York, 1978), Chap 8.

lies. Since it is the very structure of the market which works to the disadvantage of the consumer, one option is to prevent their formation and compel the dismantling, or 'deconcentration', of existing oligopolies. But this would presuppose that, as with one view of monopolies, oligopolistic markets are always and necessarily undesirable. German law, for example, allows the *Bundeskartellamt* to prevent mergers, and until recently to order the dissolution of completed mergers, which produce or strengthen not only single 'market dominating' (*marktbeherrschend*) undertakings but also groups of undertakings which are jointly (*in ihrer Gesamtheit*) market dominating,[3] and it is required to do so unless the merger is authorised by the government because the parties can show that it will result in improvements to competitive conditions which outweigh the disadvantages of market domination.[4] In the United Kingdom the Secretary of State, following an investigation by and recommendation of the Competition Commission, has powers to prevent the creation of, and order divestiture or compulsory deconcentration in, any 'monopoly situation', including oligopolies, under the Fair Trading Act 1973;[5] but in the UK, unlike Germany, it is a discretionary rather than a mandatory procedure, and one rarely deployed. Second, certain conduct of oligopolists may be expressly prohibited.[6] A third, more supple, option is monitoring and direct regulation either of the market or of oligopolistic undertakings within it in order to inhibit potential abuse.[7] A fourth option is, of course, to do nothing.

It is the fourth option that the Community has pursued. Or rather, it has not elected to adopt legislation under Article 83 of the Treaty specifically to address the problems of oligopolies. The only course is therefore to apply the existing rules – Articles 81 and 82 – to undertakings in oligopolistic markets. Again, this is a task for which they were not designed and are ill-suited, each in their own way.

8.1.1 Article 81

Article 81(1) prohibits agreements or concerted practices between or amongst undertakings which prevent, restrict or distort competition. Primary amongst the targets of Article 81(1) is the cartel, to which oligopolies are all too prone, for the small number of competitors make

---

3   §§ 22 II, 23a II, 24 (pre-1999) GWB. However, the 1998 amendments to the GWB (in force 1999) abandoned *ex post facto* control of mergers but beefed up considerably the machinery for their prior authorisation; see now §§ 19 II(2), (3) and 35 *et seq* ('new version') GWB.
4   §§ 36 I, 42 GWB.
5   ss 6(2), 7(2), 56, 73 and Sched 8.
6   §§ 19–23 GWB.
7   See § 22 II, V (pre-1999) GWB; the provisions of the Fair Trading Act 1973 cited in n 5 *supra*.

concertation and imposition of cartel discipline all the easier. The problem is showing it. A concerted practice consists in 'a form of coordination between undertakings which ... knowingly substitutes practical cooperation between them for the risks of competition'.[8] Price parallelism in the relevant market is a prime indicator of its existence. Again, the Court in *Dyestuffs*:

> Although parallel behaviour may not of itself be identified with a concerted practice, it may however amount to strong evidence of such a practice if it leads to conditions of competition which do not correspond to the normal conditions of the market.... This is especially the case if the parallel conduct is such as to enable those concerned to stabilize prices at a level different from that to which competition would have led.[9]

A case could therefore be made that the price parallelism which marks an oligopolistic market falls within this definition and is conscious conduct, even absent other evidence of collusion, and conduct which could be strengthened by an apparent disinclination to compete in other ways, and so be caught by the prohibition of Article 81(1).

This, however, ignores other criteria necessary to find a concerted practice. The Court of Justice has stressed that the prohibition of concerted practices does not deprive economic operators of the right to adapt themselves intelligently to existing and anticipated conduct of their competitors,[10] and this applies no less in an oligopolistic market.[11] In a transparent, oligopolistic market, this is precisely what occurs, even absent the contact, however desultory, amongst undertakings which is another prerequisite for a concerted practice,[12] owing to the simple fact that, because of the transparency of an oligopolistic market, much of the advantage normally gleaned from contact and, say, exchanges of information, is unnecessary. Moreover, implicitly in earlier cases and expressly in *Woodpulp*,[13] price parallelism is no proof of the concertation necessary for a concerted practice unless it is the only plausible explanation for such conduct. What is required is conduct which 'leads to conditions of competition which do not correspond to the normal conditions of the market'. But accepting the theory of oligopolistic interdependence, price parallelism *is* the normal condition of the market. And *this* is a plausible explanation for market conduct.

---

[8] Case 48/69 *ICI* v *Commission* (Dyestuffs) [1972] ECR 619 at 655; see pp 53–60 *supra*.

[9] *Ibid.*

[10] Cases 40 etc/73 *Coöperatieve Vereniging 'Suiker Unie'* v *Commission* [1975] ECR 1663 at 1942; Case T-1/89 *Rhône-Poulenc* v *Commission* (Polypropylene) [1991] ECR II-867 at 1068; see pp 55–6 *supra*.

[11] Cases 89 etc/85 *Åhlström* v *Commission* (Woodpulp) [1993] ECR I-1307 at 1601.

[12] Case T-1/89 *Rhône-Poulenc* v *Commission* (Polypropylene) [1991] ECR II-867.

[13] Cases 89 etc/85 *Åhlström* v *Commission* [1993] ECR I-1307.

So, the Commission is shorn of one of its prime indicators for collusive conduct. It is sensitive to this lacuna, citing the danger of undertakings seeking to defeat 'any investigation into their pricing conduct by the competition authorities by invoking the defence of oligopolistic interdependence', and so a burden upon it to show price uniformity so striking that the inference of prior collusion is almost inescapable.[14] It is therefore especially vigilant in oligopolistic markets to seek out corroboration – which undertakings will go to some lengths to conceal[15] – through other conduct which may go to concertation, such as contact and exchanges of information, and so build a case on grounds other than parallel conduct. It also recognises and imposes lower thresholds to conduct which may distort competition: information exchange systems which do not concern prices may be beneficial in a competitive market and so fall well beyond the reach of Article 81(1), but they will distort competition 'on a highly concentrated oligopolistic market ... on which competition is as a result already greatly reduced'.[16] Of course, if the Commission can find the existence of an *agreement* by which oligopolists have shared markets, fixed prices or set production quotas, then a breach of Article 81(1) can fairly be found. When it does, it is disinclined to be gentle with the offenders.[17] Thus it is that detection of agreements amongst oligopolists is expected to be one of the fruits of the 'leniency notice' to encourage whistleblowers.[18] It is also one of the reasons behind the Commission's increasing tendency to blur the distinction between agreements and concerted practices, libelling the existence of one and/or the other.[19] Nevertheless, as the law now stands, collusion, however rudimentary, is a necessary component of a breach of Article 81(1). The Commission (or in civil proceedings the party libelling it) bears the burden of showing collusion, and absent an agreement the Court of First Instance subjects the Commission's findings on market structure and conduct, by which it claims to find it, to closer scrutiny and analysis than did the Court of Justice.[20] Article 81, like Article 82, addresses market behaviour: it prohibits collusion, even contact, but it does not address the structural problem of interdependence which forms the basis of an oligopolistic mar-

---

[14] Decision 94/601 (*Cartonboard*) OJ 1994 L234/1 at para 73.

[15] *Ibid.*

[16] Case T-34/92 *Fiatagri & New Holland Ford* v *Commission* [1994] ECR II-905 at 949 and Case T-35/92 *John Deere* v *Commission* [1994] ECR II-957 at 987, both upheld on appeal as Case C-7/95P *John Deere* v *Commission* [1998] ECR I-3111 and Case C-8/95P *New Holland Ford* v *Commission* [1998] ECR I-3175.

[17] See eg Decision 1999/210 (*British Sugar/Tate & Lyle/Napier Brown/James Budgett*) OJ 1999 L76/1 (under review as Cases T-202 & 207/98 *Tate & Lyle and Napier Brown* v *Commission*, pending).

[18] See p 180 *supra*.

[19] See pp 61–2 *supra*.

[20] See eg Cases 89 etc/85 *Åhlström* v *Commission* (Woodpulp) [1993] ECR I-1307.

ket. As a result, it is impotent in significant measure for the control of oligopolies.

8.1.2 Article 82

It will be recalled that Article 82 prohibits abuse 'by one *or more* undertakings' of a dominant position. The wording may owe its existence to nothing more than an attempt expressly to contemplate and accommodate the economic entity doctrine.[21] The Court of Justice seemed to suggest that the problems presented by oligopolistic markets could not fall under Article 82 owing to the construct (of its own making) that dominance is defined as a function of an ability to act independently of market forces:

> A dominant position must also be distinguished from parallel courses of conduct which are peculiar to oligopolies in that in an oligopoly the courses of conduct interact, while in the case of an undertaking occupying a dominant position the conduct of the undertaking which derives profits from that position is to a great extent determined unilaterally.[22]

So for some time the application of Article 82 to oligopolistic markets, in which no one undertaking could be shown to be dominant, was in some doubt. Even if it were to apply, there would be problems in differentiating the general principles built up around Article 82: conduct deemed abusive from an individually dominant undertaking – price cutting, for example – might actually be pro-competitive in an oligopolistic market. However, it may have been that the Commission was simply biding its time waiting for the right case to come along – which it eventually did, in the shape of *Flat Glass*.[23]

Flat Glass was virtually a laboratory test tube oligopoly: narrow, homogenous product markets (automotive flat glass and other flat glass), a distinct geographic market (Italy) effectively protected by typography (the Alps and the Mediterranean, across which large sheets of glass are not easily transported)[24] and cost barriers to market entry (starting up costs being very high), and three undertakings, no one of which was dominant within the meaning of Article 82, but which amongst them accounted for 95 per cent and 79 per cent of the market (automotive glass and other glass

---

[21] See pp 43–5 *supra*.

[22] Case 85/76 *Hoffmann-La Roche* v *Commission* [1979] ECR 461 at 520.

[23] Decision 89/93 OJ 1989 L33/44. Earlier considerations of the nature of the application of Art 82 to oligopolistic markets may be said to be provided in the judgment of the Court in Case 30/87 *Bodson* v *Pompes Funèbres des Régions Libérées* [1988] ECR 2479, but very inarticulately.

[24] But for a more generous view of the geographic market for flat glass (the Commission refusing to define Ireland as a distinct market) see Case T-65/96 *Kish Glass* v *Commission*, judgment of 30 March 2000, not yet reported.

respectively).[25] The Commission found evidence of agreements and practices amongst them by which they shared information on prices and discounts, allocated quotas, exchanged products and ensured agreed prices with wholesalers. It therefore libelled several breaches of Article 81(1), ordered that they be terminated and imposed heavy fines.[26] But at the same time the Commission also claimed that the three undertakings represented themselves on the market as a single entity and therefore held a 'collective dominant position' falling within Article 82 which they abused by depriving customers of getting the suppliers to compete on prices and terms of sale and by limiting outlets through setting quotas[27] and ordered that this breach be terminated, although it imposed no fines for the breach of Article 82 owing to the novelty of collective dominant position.[28]

On review of the decision, the Court of First Instance did not follow the Commission's 'single entity' construct, and annulled that part of the decision because the Commission had not made out the case, having simply 'recycled' the Article 81(1) points without providing the proper market analysis – ie, close identification of the relevant markets – which is required by Article 82.[29] Nevertheless, the Court said:

> There is nothing, in principle, to prevent two or more independent economic operators from being, on a specific market, united by such economic links that, by virtue of that fact, *together they hold a dominant position* vis-à-vis the other operators on the same market.[30]

So, finally, the imprimatur of the Court[31] to the application of Article 82 to oligopoly markets, so long as the undertakings taken together hold what came to be called a 'joint dominant position'. The concept was circumscribed: because there is no reproach in the existence of dominance under Article 82, there can be no reproach in the existence of joint dominance. And rejecting the Commission's market structure analysis, the Court of First Instance further required (*obiter*) that there be some sort of relationship ('united by economic links') between or amongst the parties. Nevertheless, whatever that was meant to mean, it was a breakthrough, for it imposes upon the individual conduct of undertakings, no one of which is dominant but together can be shown to enjoy joint dominance, the discipline of Article 82.

---

[25] It was actually an asymmetric oligopoly, as two of the three undertakings accounted for 80 per cent of the automotive glass market.

[26] Decision 89/93, arts 1, 3, 4.

[27] art 2.

[28] para 84(a).

[29] Cases T-68, 77 & 78/89 *Società Italiano Vetro* v *Commission* (Flat Glass) [1992] ECR II-1403.

[30] at 1548; emphasis added.

[31] ie, the Court of First Instance; the judgment was not appealed to the Court of Justice so may be taken as good law.

Thus emboldened, the Commission set out to apply the new doctrine with enthusiasm. In *Cewal*,[32] involving liner shipping conferences, it found distinct breaches of both Articles 81(1) (non-competitive agreements) and 82 (participating in implementation of the agreements, modifying rates and loyalty contracts), this time imposed a fine for the breach of Article 82 (but not that of Article 81(1)), and, mindful of the *dictum* of the Court of First Instance in *Flat Glass*, said, very carefully:

> The dominant position is held jointly by the members of Cewal given that they are linked to each other by the conference agreement, which creates very close economic links between them.[33]

Whilst *Cewal* was under review before the Court of First Instance, the Court of Justice intervened courtesy of references from national courts brought before it directly under Article 177 (now Article 234). In *Gemeente Almelo* it held that an electricity distributor enjoying a statutory non-exclusive concession for part of the Netherlands was prohibited from applying an exclusive purchasing clause in its conditions of sale by Article 81 *and* that such a tying clause was also an abuse of a dominant position under Article 82 if the undertaking imposing it

> belongs to a group of undertakings enjoying a collective dominant position.
> However, in order for such a collective dominant position to exist, the undertakings in the group must be linked in such a way that they adopt the same conduct on the market.[34]

Whether or not there were such links, and whether they were 'sufficiently strong'[35] to constitute a collective dominant position, was left to the national court to determine, with, it must be said, absolutely no guidance as to how it ought to do so. Shortly thereafter in *La Crespelle*,[36] a case involving one (of 51) artificial insemination centres enjoying a regional monopoly under French statute and alleged to be charging excessive prices, the Court found that a contiguous series of monopolies together covering the entire territory of a member state constituted a dominant position (what has been called a 'shared dominant position'), and so the centres were precluded 'in the independent exercise of their economic activity' from abusing it.[37] In three subsequent cases arising in Italy the Court of

---

[32] Decision 93/82 OJ 1993 L34/20; see also Decision 92/262 (*French West-African Shipowners' Committees*) OJ 1992 L134/1.

[33] para 61.

[34] Case C-393/92 *Gemeente Almelo v Energiebedrijf IJsselmij* [1994] ECR I-1477 at 1519–20.

[35] at 1520.

[36] Case C-323/93 *Société Civile Agricole du Centre d'Insémination de la Crespelle v Coopérative d'Elevage et d'Insémination Artificielle du Département de la Mayenne* [1994] ECR I-5077.

[37] at 5106.

Justice reiterated the *Almelo* formula, although was more helpful as to its application.[38] And in *Bosman* Advocate-General Lenz argued that professional football clubs enjoy a collective dominant position,[39] but the Court did not take up the point. The Court of First Instance was therefore able to uphold the Commission in *Cewal*, saying:

> [I]t is settled case-law ... that Article 86 is capable of applying to situations in which several undertakings together hold a dominant position on the relevant market ....
>
> In order for such a collective dominant position to exist, the undertakings in question must be linked in such a way that they adopt the same conduct on the market.[40]

The question was raised again before the Court of First Instance, inconclusively, in *Tiercé Ladbroke*.[41] In a subsequent case under the Merger Regulation which, it was alleged, produced collective dominance,[42] the Court of Justice rearticulated the test to 'undertakings which together, in particular because of correlative factors which exist between them, are able to adopt a common policy on the market and act to a considerable extent independently of their competitors'[43] and applied it to the 'cluster of structural links' present in the case;[44] however, this may be language which is peculiar to the field of mergers, and it is an area in which the Court of First Instance seems to take a more lenient line.[45] In the subsequent appeal judgment in *Cewal*, being the most recent statement from the Court of Justice on the matter, the Court settled for a requirement of economic links *or* other factors:

> In terms of Article 86 of the Treaty, a dominant position may be held by several 'undertakings'. The Court of Justice has held, on many occasions, that the concept of 'undertaking' in the chapter of the Treaty devoted to the rules on competition presupposes the economic independence of the entity concerned.
>
> It follows that the expression 'one or more undertakings' in Article 86 of the Treaty implies that a dominant position may be held by two or more economic entities legally independent of each other, provided that from an economic point

---

[38] Case C-96/94 *Centro Servizi Spediporto v Spedizioni Marittima del Golfo* [1995] ECR I-2883; Cases C-140–2/94 *DIP v Comuni del Bassano del Grappa e del Chioggia* [1995] ECR I-3257; Case C-70/95 *Sodemare v Regione Lombardia* [1997] ECR I-3395.

[39] Case C-415/93 *Union Royale Belge des Sociétés de Football Association v Bosman* [1995] ECR I-4921 at 5038.

[40] Cases T-24 etc/93 *Compagnie Maritime Belge v Commission* [1996] ECR II-1201 at 1230.

[41] Case T-504/93 *Tiercé Ladbroke v Commission* [1997] ECR II-923, in which the Court of First Instance addressed a claim of 'joint dominant position' (which the Commission contested), but avoided discussion of it by leapfrogging to, and finding no, abusive conduct.

[42] Cases C-68/94 & 30/95 *France & SCPA & EMC v Commission* [1998] ECR I-1375; see pp 268–9 *infra*.

[43] at 1519.

[44] at 1522.

[45] See pp 269–70 *infra*.

of view they present themselves or act together on a particular market as a collective entity. This is how the expression 'collective dominant position' ... should be understood ....

In order to establish the existence of a collective entity as defined above, it is necessary to examine the economic links or factors which give rise to a connection between the undertakings concerned.

In particular, it must be ascertained whether economic links exist between the undertakings which enable them to act together independently of their competitors, their customers and consumers ....

Nevertheless, the existence of an agreement or other links in law is not indispensable to a finding of collective dominant position; such a finding may be based on other connecting factors and would depend on an economic assessment and, in particular, on an assessment of the structure of the market in question.[46]

Whether 'other connecting factors' which depend 'in particular, on an assessment of the structure of the market in question' may exist in mere oligopolistic interdependence will require further elaboration from the Court.

Building upon these decisions, the Commission most recently found in *TACA* two abuses of a joint dominant position within a liner conference upon reasoning similar to that of *Cewal* – 'the members of the TACA collectively enjoy a dominant position by reason of the fact that they are bound together by a considerable number of economic links which has led to a significant diminution of their ability to act independently of each other';[47] and in *P & I Clubs* it found a number of shipping insurers to hold together a dominant position by virtue of a claim sharing arrangement which 'creates strong economic links between them' and agreement as to common conditions, so 'adopt[ing] a uniform line of action in the market'.[48] The most recent judicial pronouncement from the Court of First Instance is *Irish Sugar*, in which the Commission found a joint dominant position held by an Irish dominant undertaking and its sole Irish distributor where the two were linked by the former's equity interest in and representation on the board of the latter and the variety of economic ties between them[49] – also noteworthy as the first and only case which libels the existence of joint dominance as a function of vertical, not horizontal, links. On review, the Court of First Instance upheld the Commission in all essentials, reiterating the earlier case law thus:

[T]wo independent economic entities may hold a joint dominant position on the market .... [T]here must be close links between the two entities, and ... those

---

[46] Cases C-395 & 396/96P *Compagnie Maritime Belge* v *Commission*, judgment of 16 March 2000, not yet reported, at paras 35, 36, 41, 42 and 45.

[47] Decision 1999/243 (*Transatlantic Conference Agreement*) OJ 1999 L95/1 at para 525 (under review as Cases T-191 etc/98 *Atlantic Container Line* v *Commission*, pending).

[48] Decision 1999/329, OJ 1999 L125/12 at para 122.

[49] Decision 97/624, OJ 1997 L258/32.

links must be such as to be capable of leading to the adoption of the same conduct and policy on the market in question ....

[A] joint dominant position consists in a number of undertakings being able together, in particular because of factors giving rise to a connection between them, to adopt a common policy on the market and act to a considerable extent independently of their competitors, their customers, and ultimately consumers.[50]

The fact of a vertical, and not horizontal, relationship was immaterial:

[U]nless one supposes there to be a lacuna in the application of Article 86 of the Treaty, it cannot be accepted that undertakings in a vertical relationship, without however being integrated to the extent of constituting one and the same undertaking, should be able abusively to exploit a joint dominant position.[51]

And that is where matters stand.

A number of issues are raised. First, there is probably nothing in the terminology. The English texts cited above use 'joint' and 'collective' dominance interchangeably, but the French texts rely almost uniformly upon the term 'collective dominant position' (*position dominante collective*),[52] and doubtless the 'shared dominance' attributed to *La Crespelle* means the same thing. Second, the 'links' – be they the 'economic links' of *Flat Glass* and *Compagnie Maritime Belge*, the 'links' (*suffisament liées*) of *Almelo*, the 'correlative factors' of *France* v *Commission*, the 'close links' of *Irish Sugar* or the (open ended) 'other connecting factors' of *Compagnie Maritime Belge* – by which the undertakings adopt the 'same conduct' on the market is a reasonable and laudable test (or tests) to be applied, allowing greater suppleness in the application of Article 82 (accommodating and exempting, for example, pro-competitive conduct which would be abusive if pursued by an individually dominant undertaking) and adapted to the peculiarities of an oligopolistic market. But what links/factors are necessary, and when do they produce the same conduct on the market? The judgments cited include three in which the test was met (*Compagnie Maritime Belge*, member undertakings complying with decisions adopted by a liner conference; *La Crespelle*, authorisation required, and exclusive rights conferred, by statute; *Irish Sugar*, equity interest, representation on the board, contractual purchasing commitments); three where it was not (*Centro Servizi Spediporto*, legislation fixing road haulage tariffs; *DIP*, legislation requiring a licence to open a shop and limiting the number of

---

[50] Case T-228/97 *Irish Sugar* v *Commission* [1999] ECR II-2969 at 2993 (under appeal as Case C-497/99P *Irish Sugar* v *Commission*, pending).

[51] at 3005.

[52] There are exceptions; in *Flat Glass* the undertakings 'détiennent ensemble' a dominant position, and in the Commission decision in *Cewal* the dominant position was 'tenu conjointement'.

shops within a municipality; *Sodemare*, legislation on authorisation of firms providing residential care and a prohibition of profit making); and one in which the matter was left to the national court (*Almelo*, contractual relations of non-exclusive concession holders with purchasers set by model general terms and conditions).[53] There may well have been such sufficient links/factors and similarity of conduct in *Flat Glass* and in *France* v *Commission* had the Commission taken the effort to show them, and in the former the Court of First Instance supplied an example of two or more undertakings jointly having, through agreements or licences, a technological lead affording them the power to behave independently of market forces.[54] Advocate-General Fennelly thinks this is in fact one, not two, tests:

> It seems to me that the two-fold test – the existence of sufficient economic links to lead to an effective single market entity – is in substance one and that the latter is the predominant element.[55]

What is clear is that the test is more burdensome than the existence and conditions of simple oligopolistic interdependence, unless the 'other connecting factors' of *Compagnie Maritime Belge*[56] can be stretched that far. A statutory (*Almelo*; *La Crespelle*), contractual (*Compagnie Maritime Belge*) or other relationship which governs their activities seems to be required which induces or encourages the undertakings to act in a similar fashion.[57] It is submitted that the legislative and regulatory framework now governing many UK utilities would meet this test, although some effect upon trade between member states would have to be shown. But further questions remain still to be answered. Can an undertaking which is collectively (but not individually) dominant abuse that position unilaterally or does exploitative abuse arise only in joint conduct? Put another way, is joint conduct constitutive of dominance alone, or is it a necessary component also of abuse? The *Almelo* criteria are ambiguous, but *La Crespelle* would seem to imply the former. Is conduct abusive only when a function of the link/correlative factors amongst them, or, once the link establishes

---

[53] In the event, the referring Dutch court found that both Arts 85 and 86 (now Arts 81 and 82) applied to the exclusive purchasing contracts, but with scant reasoning on the point of collective dominance, that the contracts could not be saved by an Art 90(2) (now Art 86(2)) exemption (see Chapter 7), and ordered the parties to negotiate a settlement: *Gemeente Almelo v Energiebedrijf IJsselmij*, Gerechtshof Arnhem, Arrest van 22 oktober 1996, unreported.

[54] Cases T-68, 77 & 78/89 *Società Italiano Vetro v Commission* (Flat Glass) [1992] ECR II-1403 at 1548.

[55] Cases C-395 & 396/96P *Compagnie Maritime Belge v Commission*, judgment of 16 March 2000, not yet reported, per A-G Fennelly at para 28 of his opinion.

[56] Cases C-395 & 396/96P *Compagnie Maritime Belge, ibid* at para 45.

[57] So, A-G Lenz argued in *Bosman* that association football clubs are 'united by such economic links' simply because they are dependent upon each other if they wish to be successful – what he described as a virtually unique 'natural community of interests'.

collective dominance, is it all conduct of the undertaking(s) subject to Article 82? A provisional answer to both these questions may be found in *Irish Sugar*:

> Whilst the existence of a joint dominant position may be deduced from the position which the economic entities concerned together hold on the market in question, the abuse does not necessarily have to be the action of all the undertakings in question. It only has to be capable of being identified as one of the manifestations of such a joint dominant position being held. Therefore, undertakings occupying a joint dominant position may engage in joint or individual abusive conduct. It is enough for the abusive conduct to relate to the exploitation of the joint dominant position which the undertakings hold on the market.[58]

As a general principle this must, however, be treated with caution. The joint dominance aspects of *Irish Sugar* (there were others in which it was not at issue) were established by a vertical relationship between producer and distributor. But since a vertical relationship will be entered into only for mutual advantage it is much easier to find pursuit of a common policy which is a function ('one of the manifestations') of the joint dominance within that context. It will be more difficult to show where joint dominance and abuse thereof exists on the horizontal plane. For that, further elucidation from the Court(s) is required.

Third, however, it is an important development. Recognition of collective dominance between or amongst oligopolists extends the reach of the competition rules significantly beyond what is possible under Article 81. And once (collective) dominance is shown, the burdens of Article 82 are heavy. Supracompetitive prices, for example, which escape the prohibition of Article 81 absent collusion may well amount to abuse of collective dominance, as will refusal to deal or dealing in a discriminatory manner. The Treaty still does not address the phenomenon of oligopolistic markets coherently or comprehensively; but it is no longer toothless.

Oligopolies may also fall for consideration as an aspect of Community control of mergers. To which we now turn.

8.2 Mergers

Like oligopoly, there is nothing in the EC Treaty specifically addressing mergers. This was no oversight, as the ECSC Treaty did provide comprehensive rules governing mergers and takeovers ('concentrations') of undertakings in the coal and steel sectors.[59] Rather it is likely to be simply a product of predominant economic thought of the 1950s, that owing to concerns of postwar reconstruction and the fragmentation of European

---

[58] Case T-228/97 *Irish Sugar* v *Commission* [1999] ECR II-2969 at 3006.
[59] ECSC Treaty, Art 66.

industry generally, concentration was a good thing which ought perhaps to be encouraged, and certainly not impeded. Regulation of mergers and takeovers was slow in coming, but the pace has now quickened: relevant law came into force for the first time, for example, in 1957 in Germany (the GWB), in 1965 in the UK (the Monopolies and Mergers Act, now displaced by the Fair Trading Act 1973), in 1998 in the Netherlands, and in Finland[60] and in 2000 in Denmark.[61] By 1989 only four member states (Germany, France, Ireland and the UK) had merger control legislation of any substance; by June 2000 only Luxembourg does not.

Mergers produce greater economic efficiency, primarily through increase in economies of scale, but also through increased operative efficiency (as in vertical mergers and takeovers), management efficiency (fear of takeover) and improved dissemination of new technology. In the purely Community context, they lead to integration, more rationalised market interpenetration and generally the unification of the single market. On the other side of the ledger, they can be said to diminish competition. Put simply, if one undertaking acquires another, that is one fewer competitor in the market. This is, of course, more harmful in the case of horizontal mergers, and more harmful still in oligopolistic markets than in others. It also raises concerns over conglomeration (the primary reason for the birth of antitrust law in America in the 1890s and its adoption in Germany after the war), asset stripping, unemployment, regional policy and loss of indigenously controlled industry. It touches the heart of competition policy in the Community, but not only there, and the perennial problem of weighing the balance between ensuring Community undertakings compete amongst themselves whilst not emasculating them of their ability to compete globally.

Notwithstanding the lack of express provision, the application of the existing competition rules of the Treaty to mergers proved less fraught than in the case of oligopolies. It was first recognised in *Continental Can*. There the Commission found that an undertaking which held a dominant position in the markets for packaging of preserved foodstuffs and metal caps for glass jars had abused that dominance by acquiring control of its main competitor, with the result that competition in those products was practically eliminated.[62] The Court of Justice annulled the decision, but because the Commission had failed properly to define the product market; it gave its express blessing to the Commission proposition that mergers fall within the ambit of Article 82:

> By providing for the establishment of a system that will protect competition within the Common Market from distortion, Article 3(f) [now Article 3(1)(g)] demands *a fortiori* that competition must not be eliminated ....

[60] Mededingingswet, in force 1 January 1998, artt 26 *et seq*; Laki Kilpailunrajoituksista 11–11 i § (303/1998), in force 1 October 1998.

[61] Lov nr. 416 af 31. maj 2000 (Lov om ændring af Konkurrenceloven); Konkurrenceloven, §§ 12–12g, in force 1 October 2000.

[62] Decision 72/21 (*Continental Can*) JO 1972 L7/25.

There may therefore be abusive behaviour if an undertaking in a dominant position strengthens that dominant position so that the degree of control achieved substantially obstructs competition, *i.e.*, so that the only undertakings left in the market are those which are dependent on the dominant undertaking with regard to their market behaviour.[63]

So, mergers are caught by Article 82, but only insofar as an undertaking which is *already* dominant abuses that dominance by acquiring a competitor in the market in which it is dominant. This is fairly rudimentary merger control, but as dominance itself is not prohibited by Article 82, merging of non-dominant undertakings *into* dominance is not proscribed, and Article 82 can be stretched no further.

As for Article 81, it was long thought – not least by the Commission[64] – that it had no application to mergers. This was a function essentially of the logic that the net product of a merger is a single undertaking, and the conduct of a single undertaking is not subject to the constraints of Article 81. Quite why an agreement to merge – as opposed to a hostile takeover – could not fall within Article 81 was never canvassed. In any event, speculation was overtaken by the Court of Justice, which ruled in the *Philip Morris* case in 1987 that certain aspects of concentration between undertakings which remain independent – here, a company acquiring an equity interest in, and so a degree of control of the operations of, a competitor – could in some circumstances fall within the prohibition of Article 81(1).[65]

The parameters of the *Philip Morris* judgment have not yet been fully explored.[66] But it, combined with the pending completion of the internal market programme in 1992, led to pressure from industry for the adoption of comprehensive, clear and reliable rules on the regulation of mergers and acquisitions. This inspired the Commission to dust off a draft regulation, first proposed in 1973,[67] and breathe new life into it. It was finally adopted by the Council as Regulation 4064/89 in 1989,[68] which entered into force in 1990, and was significantly overhauled in 1998.[69] Unlike control of oligopolistic market conduct, the Regulation marks a serious

---

[63] Case 6/72 *Europemballage Continental Can* v *Commission* [1973] ECR 215 at 244–5. The text presented is taken from the CMLR report of the case ([1973] CMLR 199 at 223, 225) as the ECR version is in virtually unintelligible English.

[64] EC Commission, *Memorandum on the Problems of Concentration in the Common Market*, Competition Series, Study No 3 (Brussels, 1966) and *Fifteenth Report on Competition Policy* (1985), para 26.

[65] Cases 142 & 156/84 *BAT and Reynolds* v *Commission* [1987] ECR 4487.

[66] They have been further considered by the Commission in *Hudson's Bay/Dansk Peldyravlerforening*, Commission Press Release IP(88)810 of 15 December 1988, and especially in Decision 93/252 (*Gillette/Wilkinson Sword*) OJ 1993 L116/21.

[67] OJ 1973 C92/1.

[68] Reg 4064/89, OJ 1989 L395/1; revised text in OJ 1990 L257/13.

[69] Reg 1310/97, OJ 1997 L180/1, which entered into force in March 1998.

attempt at legislative consolidation of Treaty rules, and it now occupies much, but not all, of the field of merger control, at least at Community level.

8.2.1 The Merger Regulation

Regulation 4064/89 applies to 'concentrations' between or amongst undertakings. A concentration arises where

(a) two or more previously independent undertakings merge, or
(b) one or more persons already controlling at least one undertaking, or one or more undertakings acquire, whether by purchase of securities or assets, by contract or by any other means, direct or indirect control of the whole or parts of one or more other undertakings.[70]

A concentration falling short of a merger requires that one undertaking acquire, at the least, 'decisive influence' (*influence déterminante*) over the commercial conduct of another.[71] A concentration may also exist in certain joint ventures.[72] Notwithstanding its application to concentrations of lesser degrees of integration than mergers, Regulation 4064/89 is universally known as the Merger Regulation. It forms a 'composite whole' with Articles 81 and 82 in pursuing the aims of Article 3(1)(g) of the Treaty and so is to be interpreted in a manner consistently with them.[73] It does not apply to concentrations in the coal and steel sectors, which continue to be governed directly by rules laid down in the ECSC Treaty.[74]

The Regulation further applies only to concentrations which have a 'Community dimension'. Prior to March 1998, a concentration had a Community dimension if

(a) the combined aggregate worldwide turnover of all undertakings involved exceeded 5 thousand million ECUs;
(b) the aggregate Community-wide turnover of each of at least two of the undertakings exceeded 250 million ECUs; and
(c) the undertakings did not generate two-thirds of their turnover in a single member state.[75]

The means of calculating turnover are provided.[76]

It will be observed that 'Community dimension' was an attempt, first, to limit the application of the Regulation to large scale concentrations. The 5

---

[70] Reg 4064/89, art 3(1).
[71] art 3(3)(b).
[72] art 3(2); see *infra*.
[73] Case T-22/97 *Kesko* v *Commission* [1999] ECR II-3775 at 3811.
[74] ECSC Treaty, Art 66.
[75] Reg 4064/89, art 1(2).
[76] art 5.

thousand million ECU (about £3.5 thousand million) threshold is a very high one: according to the Commission, only 152 companies in the Community and the EFTA member states themselves enjoyed a worldwide turnover in 1993 in excess of that figure[77] – although, of course, applying the economic entity doctrine, if a subsidiary is involved the turnover of the parent, if it effectively controls the former, is taken into account.[78] In the first three years after its entry into force the Regulation applied to about 60 concentrations per year, rising to around 100 in 1994 and in 1995, 130 in 1996 and 170 in 1997.[79] Second, a concentration must involve at least two substantial undertakings within the Community; so, the takeover by an existing dominant undertaking of a second undertaking fell outwith the Regulation if the latter's Community-wide turnover was less than 250 million ECUs[80] – although Article 82 may still apply.[81] Third, it will not apply even to large scale concentrations which involve undertakings and economic activity essentially or primarily outwith the territory of the Community – although the 250 million ECU threshold for Community turnover was not a particularly high one.[82] And fourth, consistent with the principle of subsidiarity, the Regulation recognises that a concentration which otherwise has a Community dimension but the preponderant impact of which is restricted to one member state (the 'two-thirds rule') ought to fall for consideration to the competition authorities of that state.

The Regulation required the Council to review the thresholds by the end of 1994.[83] Following significant delay (and a degree of natural erosion of the thresholds by inflation), amendments were finally adopted in 1997,[84] with the result that, since March 1998, a concentration which does not meet the above thresholds nevertheless has a Community dimension if:

---

[77] EC Commission, Community Merger Control: Green Paper on the review of the Merger Regulation, COM (96) 19 final, p 14.

[78] See art 5(4) of the Merger Regulation for circumstances in which this is appropriate.

[79] EC Commission, D-G IV-B, Statistics on Mergers (from the Internet).

[80] For example, a concentration between British Airways and Dan Air did not have a Community dimension because only the two undertakings were involved and Dan Air's holding company enjoyed a Community-wide turnover of less than 250 million ECUs; see Case T-3/93 *Air France* v *Commission* [1994] ECR II-121. Ironically, had the merger in Decision 91/619 (*Aérospatiale-Alenia/de Havilland*) OJ 1991 L334/42, the first merger prohibited under the Regulation (see *infra*) and the most politically sensitive to date, been structured as a takeover of de Havilland not by Aérospatiale and Alenia jointly but by their subsidiary ATR it would have fallen outwith the Regulation, de Havilland's Community turnover being less than 250 million ECUs, by virtue of art 1(2).

[81] See *infra*.

[82] So an increasing number of mergers in third countries fall within the scope and jurisdiction of the Merger Regulation even if their 'centre of gravity' lies well outside the Community. These cases raise difficult questions of the extraterritorial application of Community competition rules; see Chap 9.

[83] Reg 4064/89, art 1(3); now repealed.

[84] Reg 1310/97, OJ 1997 L180/1.

(a) the combined aggregate worldwide turnover of all undertakings involved exceeds €2500 million;

(b the combined aggregate turnover of all undertakings concerned exceeds €100 million in at least three member states;

(c) in each of the member states covered by (b), the aggregate turnover of each of at least two undertakings involved exceeds €25 million; and

(d) the undertakings do not generate two-thirds of their turnover in a single member state.[85]

The new thresholds ('supplementary turnover thresholds') do not displace the old ones; rather the two sets coexist and apply coterminously to what may be different situations. They mark a recognition that the previous threshold excluded a considerable number of concentrations with significant Community and cross-border effects, and so a policy decision to broaden the application of the Regulation and bring a significantly greater number of concentrations within its scope – the number of notifications rising in 1998 to 235 and in 1999 to 292[86] – but only where there is an impact in at least three member states. So, where a concentration falls beneath the worldwide €5 thousand million threshold but exceeds the new €2.5 thousand million threshold, it will have a Community dimension provided that combined turnover in at least three member states exceeds €100 million and that of at least two of them exceeds a (low) €25 million threshold in each. This too is consistent with the principle of subsidiarity. The two-thirds rule applies as with the first set of thresholds. The new thresholds were to be reviewed again by July 2000.[87]

The scheme of the Merger Regulation is that a concentration with a Community dimension falls exclusively within Community competence, pre-empting the application of national law,[88] and will be permitted only with the prior authorisation of the Commission. Such a concentration is therefore required to be notified by the parties to it within a week from the conclusion of the agreement;[89] failure to notify or supplying incomplete or misleading information may result in a fine.[90] As with Regulation 17, the procedure for notification, the forms ('Form CO'), guidance as to their use and the rules regulating time limits and hearings are laid down in an imple-

---

[85] Reg 4064/89, art 1(3).

[86] Further contributing factors are the advent of EMU and the growth of concentrations in the telecommunications field following the deadline for full implementation of liberalisation and free competition laid down in Directive 96/19, OJ 1996 L74/13 on 1 January 1998.

[87] Reg 4064/89, art 1(4), (5).

[88] But see *infra*.

[89] art 4(1). Notification must be made jointly by the parties to a merger or by the undertaking acquiring joint control: art 4(2).

[90] art 14(1)(a), (b); see n 117 *infra*.

menting regulation,[91] and the Commission has adopted (and re-adopted) five guidance notices on the manner in which it is likely to interpret various provisions of the Regulation – ie, restrictions ancillary to concentrations,[92] the concept of a full function joint venture,[93] the notion of a concentration,[94] the notion of concerned undertakings[95] and the calculation of turnover.[96] If the concentration falls within the scope of the Regulation, the Commission must publish the fact of notification.[97] It is required to examine the notification immediately it is received,[98] the purpose of which is to determine whether or not the concentration is 'compatible with the common market'.[99] The Commission is required therefore to respond in the first instance in one of three ways:

(a) conclude that the concentration does not fall within the scope of the Regulation, and adopt a decision to that effect (article 6(1)(a));
(b) conclude that, although the concentration does fall within the scope of the Regulation, it does not raise serious doubts as to its compatibility with the common market, and adopt a decision to that effect (article 6(1)(b)); or
(c) find that the concentration falls within the scope of the Regulation and does raise serious doubts as to its compatibility with the common market, and so decide to initiate proceedings – 'phase two' proceedings (article 6(1)(c)).

Throughout the proceedings stage an accommodation may be reached with the Commission, and in the light of any subsequent modification by the parties to remove the perceived incompatibility in the sense of article 6(1)(c), the Commission may by decision declare a concentration compatible with the common market as in article 6(1)(b).[100] It may attach conditions to a declaration of compatibility and/or to ensure compliance with any commitments agreed.[101] A decision adopted in the context of article 6(1)(a) and (b) may be revoked by the Commission if it is based upon incorrect information for which one of the notifying undertakings is responsible or which was obtained by deceit, or where undertakings breach an obligation attached to a decision permitting a concentration to

---

91 Reg 447/98, OJ 1998 L61/1 (replacing Reg 3384/94, OJ 1994 L377/1).
92 OJ 1990 C203/5.
93 OJ 1998 C66/1 (replacing an earlier notice on the distinction between concentrative and cooperative joint ventures at OJ 1994 C385/1); see *infra*.
94 OJ 1998 C66/5 (replacing an earlier notice at OJ 1994 C385/5).
95 OJ 1998 C66/14 (replacing an earlier notice at OJ 1994 C385/12).
96 OJ 1998 C66/25 (replacing an earlier notice at OJ 1994 C385/21).
97 Reg 4064/89, art 4(3).
98 art 6(1).
99 art 2(1); see *infra*.
100 Arts 6(1a), 8(2).
101 *Ibid*.

proceed;[102] a decision under article 6(1)(b) may be revoked upon these grounds without limit of time.[103] To give an idea of the data:[104] as of 1 June 2000 the Commission had received 1353 notifications under the Regulation, of which 48 per cent involved joint ventures, 38 per cent acquisition of majority shareholding, 8 per cent outright takeovers and 6 per cent others. It adopted 1138 final phase one decisions, of which 52 were article 6(1)(a) decisions and 1086 article 6(1)(b) decisions, 58 with conditions attached. Phase two proceedings under article 6(1)(c) were initiated in 77 cases, following which the concentration was found to be compatible with the common market in 54 cases, 43 with conditions attached. Concentrations have been vetoed outright on only 12 occasions.[105]

No concentration with a Community dimension may be put into effect before notification[106] and until the Commission has acted,[107] although the Commission may grant a derogation from this rule.[108] Deliberations are

---

[102] art 6(1b); see eg Case M.1497 (*Sanofi/Synthélabo*), decision of 23 April 1999, not yet published.

[103] art 6(1c).

[104] Source: EC Commission, D-G Competition, Statistics on Mergers (from the Internet); any apparent arithmetical flaw in the data is due to notifications withdrawn and/or mergers aborted or phase two investigations still in train. There is a problem with sources, as the Commission is required to publish only decisions taken under art 8 of the Regulation (art 20(1)) – although it elects to publish some others – in full in the *Official Journal*; the rest are available (only in the authentic language(s) of the decision) through the Office of Official Publications of the European Communities and on Celex database.

[105] Decision 91/619 (*Aérospatiale-Alenia/De Havilland*) OJ 1991 L334/42; Decision 94/922 (*MSG Media Service*) OJ 1994 L364/1; Decision 96/177 (*Nordic Satellite Distribution*) OJ 1996 L53/20; Decision 96/346 (*RTL/Veronica/Endemol*) OJ 1996 L134/32 (upheld in Case T-221/95 *Endemol* v *Commission* [1999] ECR II-1299; a significantly restructured concentration amongst the same undertakings was subsequently approved: Decision 96/649, OJ 1996 L294/4); Decision 97/26 (*Gencor/Lonrho*) OJ 1997 L11/30 (upheld in Case T-102/96 *Gencor* v *Commission* [1999] ECR II-753); Decision 97/277 (*Kesko/Tuko*) OJ 1997 L110/53 (upheld in Case T-22/97 *Kesko* v *Commission* [1999] ECR II-3775; Decision 97/610 (*Saint Gobain/Wacker Chemie/NOM*) OJ 1997 L247/1; Decision 98/663 (*Blokker/Toys 'R' Us*) OJ 1998 L316/1; Decision 1999/153 (*Bertelsmann/Kirch/Premiere*) OJ 1999 L53/1; Decision 1999/154 (*Deutsche Telekom/BetaResearch*) OJ 1999 L53/31; Decision 2000/276 (*Airtours/First Choice*) OJ 2000 L93/1 (under review as Case T-342/99 *Airtours* v *Commission*, pending); Case M.1672 (*Volvo/Scania*), decision of 15 March 2000, not yet published.

[106] A concentration lacking a Community dimension falls outwith the Regulation and so need not be notified, but notification of a peripheral concentration may nonetheless be prudent in case the parties have incorrectly applied the criteria of Community dimension.

[107] Reg 4064/89, art 7(1). A concentration which has been implemented may be ordered by decision to be dissolved, a party may be ordered to divest, or the parties may be ordered to comply with any other order so as to restore conditions of effective competition (art 8(4)); this has happened twice (Decision 97/409 (*Kesko/Tuko*) OJ 1997 L174/47; Decision 98/663 (*Blokker/Toys 'R' Us*) OJ 1998 L316/1), in each case upon a referral from a member state under art 22(3); see *infra*.

[108] art 7(3).

carried out by the Merger Task Force, a newly established Directorate within the Competition D-G, but any final decision is taken by the college of Commissioners. However, in the interests of expediency – for severe time constraints usually attend matters of mergers and acquisitions – and legal certainty, and comparing favourably to the situation which obtains under Regulation 17, very short time limits apply. A phase one decision must be taken within a month.[109] Following initiation of phase two proceedings, a decision declaring a concentration incompatible with the common market must be adopted within four months.[110] If the Commission fails to meet either of these deadlines, the concentration is deemed to be compatible with the common market[111] and so may proceed. If a Commission decision is annulled by the Court of First Instance or the Court of Justice, time starts afresh from the date of judgment.[112]

The criteria to be considered in determining compatibility with the common market are purely competition based: the need to maintain and develop effective competition and the market position of the undertakings concerned.[113] This compares with UK law which applies a general public interest test,[114] although the government is now proposing change.[115] In order properly to consider the matter, the Commission is granted powers analogous to, but independent of, Regulation 17 to request information, carry out investigations, liaise with the competent national authorities, hear the parties and third parties,[116] consult an Advisory Committee on Concentrations, and impose fines.[117] A concentration which does not 'cre-

---

[109] art 10(1). The period may be extended to six weeks at the request of a member state or where a notified concentration is modified by the parties.

[110] art 10(3). The period may be extended exceptionally where an undertaking is responsible for delay.

[111] art 10(6).

[112] art 10(5).

[113] art 2(1).

[114] Fair Trading Act 1973, s 84; in practice competition considerations are paramount.

[115] Chap 12, p 44.

[116] On the rights of third parties see Case T-96/92 *Comité Central d'Entreprise de la Société Générale des Grandes Sources* v *Commission* [1995] ECR II-1213; Case T-12/93 *Comité Central d'Entreprise de la Société Anonyme Vittel* v *Commission* [1995] ECR II-1247; Case T-290/94 *Kaysersberg* v *Commission* [1997] ECR II-2137.

[117] Reg 4064/89, arts 11–19. Fines have been imposed five times under the Regulation, for unintentional (Decision 1999/594 (*Samsung/AST Research Inc*) OJ 1999 L225/12) and 'grossly negligent' (Decision 1999/459 (*A.P. Møller*) OJ 1999 L183/29) failure to notify and nonetheless proceed with concentrations, and for supplying incomplete information in a notification or in response to requests for further information Decision 2000/291 (*Sanofi/Synthélabo*. OJ 2000 L95/34, *Deutsche Post* and *Koninklijke Luchtvaart Maatschappij*, decisions of 28 July 1999, 14 December 1999, not yet published; the *Deutsche Post* decision is under review as Case T-29/00 *Deutsche Post* v *Commission*, pending). As with Reg 17, the Court of First Instance and the Court of Justice are afforded unlimited jurisdiction to cancel, reduce or increase fines imposed by the Commission: art 16.

ate or strengthen a dominant position as a result of which competition would be significantly impeded within the common market or a substantial part of it' is to be declared compatible with the common market;[118] a concentration which does so is to be declared incompatible.[119] If the Commission so concludes it *must* prohibit the concentration; it cannot accept undertakings that the dominant position will not be abused, and so can impose and accept only commitments which remove that incompatibility.[120] Any decision adopted under the Merger Regulation is subject to review before the Court of First Instance or the Court of Justice; a merger decision was annulled for the first time in 1998.[121] Whilst partial annulment of a decision is expressly envisaged in the Regulation,[122] an attempt to have conditions imposed by the Commission annulled has little chance of success, as they are likely to be unseverable from the whole.[123] A decision approving a concentration may not be challenged by an undertaking which had notified it but which is dissatisfied with some of the Commission reasoning (owing to the precedential value it may have in other proceedings) in order that that reasoning be drawn from it.[124]

A number of observations are to be made. First, there are two consecutive but distinct limbs to the test of whether a concentration is compatible with the common market. The first is whether it creates or strengthens a dominant position. For this, the Commission borrows wholesale the market analysis techniques which apply in the context of abuse of a dominant position under Article 82.[125] There must be a causal link between the concentration and the creation or strengthening of a dominant position; if no such link exists, the concentration must be approved without obligation or condition.[126] And as a corollary, there must be a link between markets; so, the Commission will not, indeed cannot, oppose a concentration between an undertaking which enjoys a virtual monopoly in one product market and another undertaking which has a very high share of another market without being dominant where there is no significant overlap in the two

---

[118] art 2(2).

[119] art 2(3).

[120] Case T-102/96 *Gencor v Commission* [1999] ECR II-753.

[121] Cases C-68/94 & 30/95 *France & SCPA & EMC v Commission* [1998] ECR I-1375.

[122] Reg 4064/89, art 10(5).

[123] Cases C-68/94 & 30/95 *France & SCPA & EMC v Commission* [1998] ECR I-1375.

[124] Cases T-125 & 127/97 *Coca-Cola v Commission*, judgment of 22 March 2000, not yet reported.

[125] See Chapter 5. Form CO provides (sections 6.I and 6.II) definitions of relevant product and geographic markets which are essentially identical to those of the Commission notice on definition of the relevant market for purposes of Community competition law, OJ 1997 C372/5.

[126] Cases C-68/94 & 30/95 *France & SCPA & EMC v Commission* [1998] ECR I-1375.

product markets.[127] The second limb is whether the result is one by which competition is 'significantly impeded'. This addresses market structure, not behaviour, and has no equivalent in Article 82. The question is whether the very existence of the concentration – which is not a consideration under, for it is not proscribed by, Article 82 – is detrimental to competition. As the Regulation provides that '[a] concentration which does not create or strengthen a dominant position *as a result of which* effective competition would be significantly impeded ... shall be declared compatible with the common market',[128] there must be a further causal link between the creation or strengthening of a dominant position and the significant impediment to effective competition. And it necessarily requires prospective market analysis.[129] The Commission is to take into account:

(a) the need to maintain and develop effective competition within the Common Market in view of, among other things, the structure of all the markets concerned and the actual or potential competition from undertakings located either within or outwith the Community;

(b) the market position of the undertakings concerned and their economic and financial power, the alternatives available to suppliers and users, their access to suppliers or markets, any legal or other barriers to entry, supply and demand trends for the relevant goods and services, the interests of the intermediate and ultimate consumers, and the development of technical and economic progress provided that it is to consumers' advantage and does not form an obstacle to competition.[130]

The Commission therefore enjoys a 'discretionary margin [of appraisal] implicit in the provisions of an economic nature which form part of the rules on concentrations',[131] and a number of considerations apply. The most obvious is the degree of market share acquired. The preamble of the Regulation provides that a concentration between or amongst undertakings with a combined market share of less than 25 per cent may be presumed to be compatible with the common market,[132] and although this is a presumption only ('is given purely by way of guidance')[133] and is not incorporated into the body of the Regulation, the Commission has cleared all such concentrations hitherto. Nonetheless, concentrations which produce control of a higher market share – as high as 80 per cent[134] – have

---

[127] Decision 91/535 (*Tetra Pak/Alfa-Laval*) OJ 1991 L290/35.

[128] Reg 4064/89, art 2(2); emphasis added.

[129] Case T-22/97 *Kesko* v *Commission* [1999] ECR II-3775.

[130] Reg 4064/89, art 2(1).

[131] Cases C-68/94 & 30/95 *France & SCPA & EMC* v *Commission* [1998] ECR I-1375 at 1520; Case T-102/96 *Gencor* v *Commission* [1999] ECR II-753 at 805; Case T-22/97 *Kesko* v *Commission* [1999] ECR II-3775 at 3824; the words in square parentheses appear only in *Kesko*.

[132] recital 15.

[133] Case T-102/96 *Gencor* v *Commission* [1999] ECR II-753 at 796.

[134] Decision 91/251 (*Alcatel/Telettra*) OJ 1991 L122/48.

been declared compatible when taking into account other criteria. The Commission puts significant store by market entry, so that a concentration which creates a dominant position is not incompatible with the common market where there is 'strong evidence' that the dominance is temporary and likely to be quickly eroded owing to a 'high probability' of competitors entering the market.[135] Other factors include effective competition from outside the Community, alternative (if not directly substitutable) products, and the restructuring of the market generally. What is not clear is the extent to which the Commission may consider other, non-purely competition issues, such as industrial, social, employment, regional and environmental concerns. The first decision declaring a concentration incompatible with the common market, *Aérospatiale-Alenia/De Havilland*,[136] attracted the obloquy of the French and Italian governments for, according to the former, taking no account of industrial policy and employment considerations in a region of high unemployment. The preamble to the Regulation provides that the Commission 'must place its appraisal within the general framework of the achievement of the fundamental objectives referred to in Article 2 of the Treaty, including that of strengthening the Community's economic and social cohesion, referred to in Article 130a [now Article 158]',[137] but there is no further reference to this in the body proper of the Regulation. In response to *Aérospatiale-Alenia/De Havilland* the European Parliament adopted a resolution that the Merger Regulation be amended to require the Commission to take account of the likely industrial, social, regional and environmental consequences of a concentration,[138] but it remains blithely silent on these concerns. Notwithstanding, the Court of First Instance has said that, whilst it is properly concerned primarily with questions of competition, that does not preclude the Commission from taking into account the social effects of a concentration if it is liable adversely to affect the social objectives referred to in Article 2 of the Treaty and liable to have consequences, even if only indirectly, upon the level or conditions of employment within the Community or a significant part of it.[139]

It should be self-evident, but bears mentioning, that even if a concentration results in a dominant position which is declared to be compatible with

---

[135] Decision 91/619 (*Aérospatiale-Alenia/De Havilland*) OJ 1991 L334/42.

[136] *Ibid.*

[137] Reg 4064/89, recital 13. For an example of the application of this principle see Decision 94/449 (*Kali + Salz/Mitteldeutsche Kali/Treuhand*) OJ 1994 L186/38, para 95. The Treaty also incorporates other 'integration clauses' (see Chap 4, n 21) which could be, but never have been, considered by the Commission in its reasoning.

[138] OJ 1991 C280/140.

[139] Case T-96/92 *Comité Central d'Entreprise de la Société Générale des Grandes Sources* v *Commission* [1995] ECR II-1213 at 1229; Case T-12/93 *Comité Central d'Entreprise de la Société Anonyme Vittel* v *Commission* [1995] ECR II-1247 at 1267.

the common market, it then becomes subject to the discipline of Article 82.

Another consideration is that, unlike Article 82, the Merger Regulation applies not only to the strengthening, but also to the creation, of a dominant position.[140] This borrows directly from German law[141] and, again, is a function of the concern of the Regulation with market structure rather than market behaviour. In *Nestlé/Perrier* this was stretched further by the Commission asserting jurisdiction to apply the Regulation to the creation of joint dominance.[142] There is further clear borrowing here from the thinking in German competition law, in which there is a (rebuttable) presumption that concentration in an oligopolistic market leads to the strengthening of market dominance,[143] and the recently developed case law on Article 82 on joint dominance,[144] but whether or not this was competent within the Regulation[145] was not tested in *Nestlé/Perrier* before the Court of First Instance, in part because the Commission offered conditions so sweet that it would have been madness for the parties to the concentration to challenge it.[146] Since then it has applied the Regulation in a number of instances to concentrations resulting in oligopolistic, and particularly duopolistic, collective dominance.[147] But in *Kali + Salz/Mitteldeutsche Kali/Treuhand*[148] it pushed the boat out further, holding that the Regulation applied where a takeover produced a collective dominant position shared by the new, post-takeover undertaking on the one hand and another undertaking unconnected with the takeover on the other. This time there was a vigorous challenge from both France and the unconnected undertaking.[149] The Court of Justice held, first, that if the Regulation were

---

[140] Reg 4064/89, art 2(2), (3).

[141] § 36 I GWB.

[142] Decision 92/553 (*Nestlé/Perrier*) OJ 1993 L356/1. The Commission had addressed the question in previous decisions (Case M.165 (*Alcatel/AEG-Kabel*) OJ 1992 C6/23; Case M.202 (*Thorn EMI/Virgin*) OJ 1992 C120/30) but expressly left it open.

[143] §§ 19 II(2) and 35 *et seq* GWB.

[144] See pp 249–56 *supra*.

[145] *cf*. the wording of Art 82 ('abuse by one *or more* undertakings of a dominant position') from which the principles of joint dominance were developed (see *supra*) with that of art 2(2) and (3) of the Merger Regulation ('a concentration which [does not] create[s] or strengthen[s] a dominant position').

[146] The decision was challenged by a number of competitors' works councils, employees' representatives and trade unions, but they were held to have standing to challenge only infringement of the procedural guarantees afforded them in the administrative stage, and not the substance of the decision: Case T-96/92 *Comité Central d'Entreprise de la Société Générale des Grandes Sources* v *Commission* [1995] ECR II-1213 and Case T-12/93 *Comité Central d'Entreprise de la Société Anonyme Vittel* v *Commission* [1995] ECR II-1247.

[147] eg, Decision 94/208 (*Mannesmann/Vallourec/Ilva*) OJ 1994 L102/15; Case M.399 (*Rhône Poulenc-SNIA/Nordfaser*) OJ 1994 C42/13; Decision 97/26 (*Gencor/Lonrho*) OJ 1997 L11/30.

[148] Decision 94/449, OJ 1994 L186/38.

[149] Cases C-68/94 & 30/95 *France & SCPA & EMC* v *Commission* [1998] ECR I-1375.

to apply only to the creation or strengthening of a dominant position on the part of the parties to a concentration, its purpose would be 'partially frustrated';[150] and second, and of more general importance, the creation of a collective dominant position did fall within the scope of the Regulation. However, as with collective dominance under Article 82, it was necessary to show, *inter alia* and if necessarily prospectively, that the jointly dominant undertakings 'together, in particular because of correlative factors which exist between them, are able to adopt a common policy on the market ...'.[151] This the Commission had failed to show, and the decision was annulled. In the subsequent review of *Gencor/Lonrho*, in which the Commission found that a proposed concentration would produce a dominant duopoly (in the medium to long term) and so prohibited it,[152] the Court of First Instance said that specific reasoning justifying the application of the Merger Regulation to the creation of a collective dominant position was not necessary as the Commission 'had already expressed its view on that subject ... in other concentration cases, including the Nestlé-Perrier decision',[153] that the Commission had shown the necessary 'structural links' in appointment and voting rights of directors, cross control of marketing and sales and similar cost structures,[154] and so sustained the Commission.

It must be noted, however, that the Court of First Instance seems here to break ranks with the Court of Justice. In the *Gencor/Lonrho* decision the Commission showed the existence of structural links but also argued implicitly that it was unnecessary to do so, the requisite links subsisting merely in the interdependent nature of an oligopolistic market:

> Similar negative effects which arise from a dominant position held by one firm arise from a dominant position held by an oligopoly. Such a situation can occur where a mere adaptation by members of the oligopoly to market conditions causes anti-competitive parallel behaviour whereby the oligopoly becomes dominant. Active collusion would therefore not be required for the members of the oligopoly to become dominant and to behave to an appreciable extent independently of their remaining competitors, their customers and, ultimately, the consumers.[155]

The Court of First Instance agreed, finding market structure alone to satisfy the 'economic links' test:

> [T]here is no reason whatsoever in legal or economic terms to exclude from the notion of economic links the relationship of interdependence existing between the parties to a tight oligopoly within which, in a market with the appropriate

---

[150] at 1502.
[151] at 1519.
[152] Decision 97/26, OJ 1997 L11/30.
[153] Case T-102/96 *Gencor v Commission* [1999] ECR II-753 at 802.
[154] at paras 280–4.
[155] Decision 97/26 at para 140.

characteristics, in particular in terms of market concentration, transparency and product homogeneity, those parties are in a position to anticipate one another's behaviour and are therefore strongly encouraged to align their conduct in the market, in particular in such a way as to maximise their joint profits by restricting production with a view to increasing prices.[156]

If the Court of First Instance is right the test for joint dominance is a lower hurdle under the Merger Regulation than under Article 82. This may be possible and fair, for the former addresses market structure rather than market behaviour, and the reasoning 'is all the more pertinent with regard to the control of concentrations, whose objective is to prevent anti-competitive market structures from arising or being strengthened'.[157] Subsequently the Commission prohibited another merger and cited as the 'strong economic links' merely the 'mutual dependency' of undertakings in a tightly oligopolistic market.[158] Therefore

> [i]t is sufficient that the merger makes it rational for the oligopolists, in adapting themselves to market conditions, to act, individually, in ways which will substantially reduce competition between them ....[159]

The decision has been challenged by one of the parties to the merger.[160] The Court of First Instance may well agree with the Commission. Whether the Court of Justice will do so is another matter.

In any event, now emboldened by the question of jurisdiction of the Merger Regulation having been settled, the Commission will doubtless return to the creation or strengthening of collective dominance/oligopoly with vigour.

Finally, it ought to be mentioned at this point that the Commission has significant powers of enforcement of merger control not only within the Community but also at EEA-wide level. This will be discussed in Chapter 9.

Joint ventures

The application of Article 81 to joint ventures has been discussed above.[161] However, they are of a hybrid character, in that by definition they create one or more new undertakings which the parents endow with the resources necessary to carry out their purpose. The relationship between and amongst the parents and the joint venture may properly fall for consideration under Article 81 (and perhaps Article 82). But the creation of the new undertaking(s) may further have the character of a concentration. In fact,

---

[156] Case T-102/96 *Gencor*, at 838.
[157] at 838.
[158] Decision 2000/276 (*Airtours/First Choice*) OJ 2000 L93/1 at paras 142 *et seq.*
[159] at para 54.
[160] Case T-342/99 *Airtours v Commission*, pending.
[161] at pp 89–91 *supra*.

joint ventures have comprised about half of the concentrations considered under the Merger Regulation. The provisions applying to joint ventures were significantly amended in 1998.[162]

According to the Merger Regulation,

> The creation of a joint venture performing on a lasting basis all the functions of an autonomous economic entity shall constitute a concentration within the meaning of [the Regulation].[163]

For a joint venture to be concentrative it must be jointly controlled.[164] Joint control exists where decisions concerning the activities of the joint venture require the agreement of the parents. So, if one parent can alone determine these activities (through, eg, control of a majority of share capital or of appointment to the board) there is no joint control.[165] The qualities of an enduring and autonomous economic entity require that the joint venture be full-function[166] – that it has the human, material and financial resources necessary to function and to function independently, not merely in an ancillary manner to the commercial activities of its parents, and that it must be intended to operate upon a lasting basis.[167]

Prior to 1998, a joint venture was cooperative if it had as its object or effect the coordination of competitive behaviour between or amongst independent undertakings, particularly between or amongst the parents or between them and the joint venture,[168] and a cooperative joint venture was not a concentration within the meaning of the Merger Regulation but fell for consideration under Articles 81 and/or 82 *simpliciter*. This was an unsupple arrangement; it meant that concentrative joint ventures were governed wholly by the Merger Regulation, but a cooperative joint venture which fell just on the wrong side of the cooperative/concentrative divide was required to resort to the procedures of Regulation 17, so (notwithstanding the 'fast track' procedure introduced in 1993)[169] losing the

---

[162] Reg 1310/97, OJ 1987 L180/1.

[163] Reg 4064/89, art 3(2). Prior to March 1998 the words 'which does not give rise to coordination of the competitive behaviour of the parties amongst themselves or between them and the joint venture' were interposed between 'entity' and 'shall'.

[164] Notice on the distinction between concentrative and cooperative joint ventures under Regulation 4064/89, OJ 1994 C385/1 (hereinafter 'the concentrative/cooperative notice'), para 11. Some of the provisions of this notice have been rendered unreliable by the 1998 amendments to the Merger Regulation; see now OJ 1998 C66/1.

[165] See the Commission notice on the notion of concentration, OJ 1994 C385/5, paras 18–39.

[166] Reg 4064/89, recital 23; see the notice on the concept of a full function joint venture, OJ 1998 C66/1. However, in its 1999 White Paper the Commission has now proposed that the Merger Regulation be extended to embrace also partial function production joint ventures.

[167] See the concentrative/cooperative notice, paras 12–16; Case T-87/96 *Assicurazioni Generali & Unicredito* v *Commission* [1999] ECR II-203.

[168] Reg 4064/89, art 3(2), now repealed and replaced.

[169] See p 91 *supra*.

former's advantages of quick response and resolution which are at a premium in these matters. This is therefore no longer so: a joint venture now need meet only the joint control and enduring and full-function tests in order to be concentrative. They must of course also meet the thresholds in order for the Merger Regulation to apply. However, to the extent that a concentrative joint venture has as its object or effect the coordination of the competitive conduct of undertakings which remain independent, Article 81 will apply to it.[170] If the effect of a joint venture is primarily structural, Article 81(1) will not normally apply.[171] However, where two or more parents retain significant economic activities in the same market or in an upstream, downstream or closely neighbouring market as the joint venture,[172] Article 81(1) may well apply. In this event and to that extent, the Commission is to consider a notified concentrative joint venture in the context of Article 81(1) and (3) – in effect, as if it were in that respect also a notification for exemption under Article 81(3). So, a joint venture may fall to be considered upon two distinct but related tests: the concentrative aspects fall within the criteria of the Merger Regulation, the cooperative aspects (if any) within those of Article 81(1) and (3). If in the latter context, if the criteria of Article 81(3) are not satisfied – which is likely to be the case where the creation of the joint venture results in coordination which affords the relevant undertakings the possibility of substantial elimination of competition[173] – the (entire) concentration is to be declared incompatible with the common market.[174] From the entry into force of the 1998 amendments to 1 June 2000, 45 decisions addressing joint ventures have included an appraisal under Article 81 criteria and 17 required approval by Article 81(3) criteria; in no case was it refused. It is worth noting that various arrangements common to joint ventures fall within a number of block exemptions;[175] but as the benefits of block exemption can be set aside by the Commission, and as the cooperative aspects of a notified joint venture must be autonomously considered and approved by the Commission, this will be of minimal benefit to the parties. Presumably, if the Commission fails to meet the deadlines required by the Merger Regulation the concentration may proceed, and its cooperative aspects are

---

[170] Reg 4064/89, art 2(4); see the Commission notice concerning the assessment of cooperative joint ventures pursuant to Article 85 of the EEC Treaty, OJ 1993 C43/2. On the assessment of the concentrative and cooperative aspects of a joint venture, which is a function less of legal form than of economic and factual considerations, see the concentrative/cooperative notice.

[171] recital 23.

[172] art 2(4).

[173] *Ibid.*

[174] art 8(3).

[175] eg, Reg 417/85 OJ 1985, L53/1 (specialisation agreements); Reg 418/85, OJ 1985 L53/5 (R & D); Reg 240/96, OJ 1996, L31/2 (technology transfer).

deemed to be exempted from the prohibition of Article 81(1); for how long is entirely unclear. Implicitly the application of national competition rules to the cooperative aspects of a joint venture is pre-empted, provided it has a Community dimension, by the system of the one-stop shop.

The 'one-stop shop'

One of the aims of the Merger Regulation was to bring about a degree of legal certainty and efficiency in merger control. Given the transnational elements of a number of concentrations, undertakings might otherwise be required to deal with 14 different national competition authorities.[176] The implementation of any sort of 'one-stop shop' is therefore of huge benefit to economic operators. In principle, if a concentration has a Community dimension it ought to be regulated exclusively by the Regulation; if it does not, it ought to fall to the relevant national competition authorities. This was part of the reasoning that led to new thresholds for smaller undertakings but which spanned three or more member states. The Regulation therefore provides that '[t]his Regulation alone shall apply to concentrations as defined in Article 3',[177] national competition law is not to be applied to concentrations with a Community dimension,[178] and the Commission has sole jurisdiction to adopt decisions under the Regulation,[179] thereby seeking to pre-empt national rules, occupy the field and institute a system of a 'one-stop shop'. But the clarity of the system is blurred by a number of features.

A first lacuna is that the Regulation provides that it, and it alone, applies to concentrations as defined in the Regulation. But the Regulation in turn applies only to such concentrations which fall within the definition *and* which have a Community dimension. This means that concentrations lacking a Community dimension fall outwith the Regulation. The application of national competition rules to concentrations with a Community dimension is expressly excluded; implicitly as well as logically they do apply to sub-threshold concentrations. But does the Regulation pre-empt the application of any other Community control of concentrations within the meaning of the Regulation with no Community dimension?

The Commission itself has said it is concerned only with concentrations with a Community dimension, and will wash its hands of lesser ventures.[180] But it is not the Commission alone which enforces the Treaty. It is

---

[176] There is no merger control regulation in Luxembourg.

[177] Reg 4064/89, art 22(1).

[178] art 21(2); Case T-102/96 *Gencor v Commission* [1999] ECR II-753. The text of art 21(2) published in the *Official Journal* actually reads 'considerations' rather than concentrations, but logic and comparison with other language texts make it clear that concentrations is what is meant.

[179] art 21(1).

[180] See European Commission, *Merger Control Law in the European Union* (1995), 'Notes on Council Regulation (EEC) 4064/89', 're Article 22': 'The Commission states that it does not normally intend to apply Articles 85 and 86 ... to concentrations as defined in Article 3 other than by means of this regulation'.

trite law to say that the Council cannot, by adopting the Regulation, set aside the application of any Treaty rule. So Articles 81 and 82 continue to apply to merger control, rudimentary though the manner of that may be, and they may be invoked in civil proceedings in national courts. The application of Article 82 is not problematic, for it is a directly effective Treaty provision,[181] and there could be a large number of takeovers by dominant undertakings of a competitor in markets which fall below the thresholds supplied in the Regulation but which are still caught, by virtue of the *Continental Can* rule,[182] by Article 82. Article 81 is more difficult. As discussed in Chapter 6, Article 81(1) is not of itself directly effective; it was made so only with the adoption of the implementing legislation of Regulation 17 or the equivalent provisions of the sectoral implementing regulations. However, the Merger Regulation expressly 'disapplies' these regulations to concentrations as it defines them.[183] The purpose of this was to ensure the exclusive application of the investigative and enforcement machinery of the Regulation and obviate any possible confusion or overlap with that of Regulation 17. But it is possible also to have had the effect of disabling the direct effect of Article 81(1), and the automatic nullity of Article 81(2), as regards concentrations to which it does not apply – that is, those lacking a Community dimension.[184]

Second, the Merger Regulation itself envisaged a sharing of competences with national authorities, in four ways:

■ First, the Germans were concerned that certain concentrations, notwithstanding the two-thirds rule, might have a Community dimension and so fall within the ambit of the Regulation yet nevertheless have a preponderant effect within one member state, in which circumstances (of 'mainly national impact') even according to the Commission it is better dealt with at national level[185] and ought to be governed by national competition rules. Implicit in this was a German fear that such a concentration would escape the application of the (generally perceived) more sophisticated burdens and more stringent control of the GWB. As a result, article 9 (the 'German clause') provides that, upon a request from a member state which can show the characteristics of a 'distinct market' for the goods or services

---

[181] See pp 163–4 *supra*.

[182] Case 6/72 *Europemballage Continental Can* v *Commission* [1973] ECR 215; see pp 257–8 *supra*.

[183] Reg 4064/89, art 22(1); since March 1998 they are expressly saved in relation to cooperative joint ventures which do not have a Community dimension.

[184] It could be argued that the direct effect of Art 81(1), brought about by the adoption of Reg 17 and similar implementing regulations, formed part of the *acquis communautaire* and beyond the power of the Council to recall, so that Reg 4064/89 is illegal insofar as Art 22(1) purports to disapply Reg 17 to concentrations which do not have a Community dimension. But this has not been tested before the Court of Justice. It is conversely possible that the disapplication of Reg 17 resuscitates the enforcement procedures of Arts 84 and 85 (ex Arts 88 and 89) to sub-threshold concentrations.

[185] Green Paper on the review of the Merger Regulation, COM (96) 19 at para 92.

in question,[186] the Commission may, or must,[187] refer a notified concentration, even if it has a Community dimension, to the competition authorities of that state for determination in accordance with national competition law. Whilst not clear from the wording of article 9 that it had authority to do so, the Commission has latterly referred certain aspects of a concentration to national authorities whilst retaining other aspects for its own consideration ('partial referrals', as compared to 'total' or 'full' referrals).[188]

■ Second, the Dutch, having had no merger control law of their own,[189] were concerned that a concentration which does not have a Community dimension but which nevertheless impedes competition within the territory of a member state would escape regulation altogether. Article 22(3) (the 'Dutch clause') therefore provides that a member state[190] may request that such a concentration, provided that there is an effect upon trade between member states, be considered by the Commission in the context of the Regulation as if, in effect, it did have a Community dimension.[191] A con-

---

[186] Reg 4064/89, art 9(2), (3). Article 9 does not actually provide that a member state must make the request, but since the procedure is set in train only after it 'informs' the Commission of its concerns, that is read as 'request'. 'Member state' is understood to mean the government of a member state and not its competition authorities.

[187] Since March 1998 if the member state does not constitute a substantial part of the common market the Commission must accede to the request: Reg 4064/89, art 9(2)(b) & (3). If it does, the Commission has a discretion to refer: art 9(3)(a). See, eg Decision 94/922 (*MSG Media Service*) OJ 1994 L364/1, in which the Commission refused a German request for referral under Art 9 on grounds of Community interest, and went on to declare the concentration incompatible with the common market.

[188] The Merger Regulation provided that the Commission may 'refer *the case* to the competent [national] authorities' (art 9(3)(b)); this was cured by the 1998 amendments, art 9(3)(b) now reading: it may 'refer the whole or part of the case to the competent [national] authorities'. Of the 12 partial referrals to date, most occurred prior to amendment of art 9(3)(b).

[189] This is no longer so with the entry into force of the Mededingingswet in 1998.

[190] Art 22(3) provides for 'request[s] of a Member State' but the Court of First Instance held admissible a request from the competition authorities of a state, even where there were serious questions in constitutional law as to the competence of the authority to make the request; Case T-22/97 *Kesko* v *Commission* [1999] ECR II-3775. Since March 1998 a request may be made by two or more member states jointly (the 'Scandinavian clause').

[191] It should be noted that whilst the thinking behind Art 22(3) was that referrals would come from member states in which the concentration was to take place but which had insufficient merger control regulation of their own, this is not necessarily the case; its first use involved a concentration between British Airways and Dan Air (Case M.278, OJ 1993 C68/5) which fell below the (then) 250 million ECU turnover threshold and so outwith the regulation, but which was referred to the Commission – which in the event did not oppose it – by Belgium. However, this gives rise to an ancillary problem, in that the Commission may consider the effects of a concentration, and adopt measures necessary to maintain or (re)store (the English text reads 'store' but means restore) effective competition, only within the territory of the referring member state(s): art 22(3), (5). Hence the utility of the Scandinavian clause.

centration already in train must be suspended with effect from the date the Commission informs the parties of the request,[192] and if it subsequently opposes the concentration it may order the parties to divest.[193] Once referred, the matter is entirely in the hands of the Commission; the member state may not purport to direct or control its conduct or deliberations.[194] Where the Commission intervenes, it does not prevent other member states from applying national competition rules.

To 1 June 2000 there have been 23 referrals (11 total, 12 partial) from the Commission under article 9[195] and four to the Commission under article 22(3). The Dutch clause was originally intended to be dropped once the Regulation thresholds had been reviewed[196] but in the event was not, although with the entry into force of merger control legislation in the Netherlands and in Finland (which were between them responsible for the only referrals since the 1992 Belgian referral in *British Airways/Dan Air*[197]) in 1998 and in Denmark in 2000, further recourse to it is likely to be rare. The German clause was itself to be reviewed[198] but it underwent no substantial change, and the number of requests for a referral under it is likely to increase with the lower thresholds introduced in 1998; given the three member states rule, the Commission is unlikely to be accommodating.

■ Third, notwithstanding the exclusive application of the Merger Regulation to concentrations with a Community dimension, member states may seek to apply national law to them where justified in order to protect 'legitimate interests other than those taken into consideration by [the] Regulation', such as public security, plurality of the media and prudential rules.[199] For other legitimate interests the Commission must be notified and must approve.[200] In the absence of approval, and *a fortiori* notifica-

---

[192] Reg 4064/89, art 22(4).

[193] arts 22(4), 8(4); see Decision 97/409 (*Kesko/Tuko*) OJ 1997 L174/47; Decision 98/663 (*Blokker/Toys 'R' Us*) OJ 1998 L316/1.

[194] Case T-221/95 *Endemol* v *Commission* [1999] ECR II-1299.

[195] Four of the 23 (Case M.180 (*Steetley/Tarmac*) OJ 1992 C50/25; Case M.716 (*Gehe/Lloyds Chemists*), decision of 22 March 1996; Case M.1779 (*Anglo American/Tarmac*), decision of 13 January 2000; Case M.1825 (*Hanson/Pioneer*), decision of 24 March 2000) were made to the Monopolies and Mergers Commission/ Competition Commission; of the remaining 19, 11 were made to the *Bundeskartellamt*, four to the French *Conseil de la Concurrence*, one each to the competent Dutch, Italian and Spanish authorities, and one (Case M.1030 (*Redland/Lafarge*), decision of 16 December 1997, not published) to both the MMC and the *Conseil de la Concurrence*.

[196] Reg 4064/89, art 22(6), now repealed.

[197] n 191 *supra*.

[198] Reg 4064/89, art 9(10), now replaced with a commitment for review by July 2000.

[199] art 21(3).

[200] *Ibid*; see, eg, Case M.567 (*Lyonnaise des Eaux/Northumbrian Water*) OJ 1995 C94/2, in which the UK successfully invoked safeguarding the provision of a vital service and protection of the consumer in the water sector as legitimate public interests.

tion, national authorities may not act and the Commission may suspend any attempt to do so.[201] Where the Commission accepts the justification, it will not oppose the concentration and national law falls to be applied. This provision has been invoked successfully on three occasions, twice by the United Kingdom.[202]

■ Fourth and finally, the Treaty itself provides that member states may take the measures necessary to protect their essential security interests connected with the production of and trade in arms, munitions and war materials, so long as such measures do not adversely affect competition in the markets for products not intended for specific military purposes.[203] This too, if accepted by the Commission, will cause the Regulation to be disapplied to those aspects of a concentration.[204]

---

[201] See, eg, Case M.1616 (*Banco Santander Centro Hispano/Champalimaud*), decision of 20 July 1999, not yet published, suspending the purported blocking of a concentration by the Portuguese government; the concentration was approved by the Commission by decision of 3 August 1999, not yet published. The Commission decision was challenged by Portugal and the Commission raised enforcement proceedings against Portugal for breach of its obligations under Community law (ie, the Merger Regulation) under Art 226 (ex Art 169) of the Treaty. Both were subsequently dropped in the light of a friendly settlement.

[202] Case M. 567 (*Lyonnaise des Eaux/Northumbrian Water*), n 200 *supra* and Case M.759 (*Sun Alliance/Royal Insurance*) OJ 1996 C225/12, on grounds of legitimate interests with regard to prudential supervision of the insurance market.

[203] EC Treaty, Art 296(1)(b) (ex Art 223(1)(b)).

[204] See, eg Case M.724 (*GEC/Thomson-CSF (II)*) OJ 1996 C186/2; Case M.820 (*British Aerospace/Lagardère*) OJ 1997 C22/6; Case M.1438 (*British Aerospace/GEC Marconi*),

CHAPTER 9

Extraterritoriality

9.1 Introduction

One of the thorniest issues confronting public international law is the extraterritorial application of law promulgated by the state. If the state is sovereign – and this is the cornerstone of international law – then it ought not to interfere in the affairs of other states and ought to brook no interference in its own. But conflicts of jurisdiction between and amongst states are inevitable and commonplace. To put it at its simplest, authority wielded by the state by virtue of even the two bases of its jurisdiction undisputed in international law – territoriality and nationality[1] – will result in concurrent jurisdiction and overlap, for the conduct of a national of state X within the territory of state Y will fall within the jurisdiction of both states. In reality, of course, the problems are much more complex. In the economic sphere, the increasing globalisation of industry and markets make for geometric complexity. It is an area in which the Community assumes the qualities of a state and acts on the international plane, like a state, in accordance with the rules of international law.

Public international law traditionally recognises the assertion of the jurisdiction of the state upon two bases:

- *territoriality*: this is the basis for state jurisdiction and a bedrock of state sovereignty: the state enjoys unimpeded sovereign jurisdiction over all matters within its territory, unless and until it disables itself (by treaty) or is disabled (by customary rules of international law) of that jurisdiction – for example, traditionally conventional or customary rules on diplomatic and consular protection or of military bases of foreign states, and more recently serious limitations upon the way the state conducts itself even as regards its own nationals, such as the European Convention on Human Rights;

- *nationality*: states are recognised as enjoying jurisdiction over their own

---

[1] See, eg, R. Higgins, 'The Legal Bases of Jurisdiction', in C.J. Olmstead (ed), *Extra-territorial Application of Laws and Responses Thereto* (ESC Publishing, Oxford, 1983); B.H. Oxman, 'Jurisdiction of States', in R. Bernhardt (ed), (1987) 10 *Encyclopedia of Public International Law* 277.

nationals (including juristic persons), wherever they may be. This may be subdivided into active and, more controversially, passive nationality, the former addressing the nationality of the author, the latter that of the victim, of a rule infringed.[2]

The nationality principle will clearly accommodate the extraterritorial assertion of jurisdiction by the state, but so too will the territorial principle. Authority for this can be traced back to the 1927 judgment in *The Lotus*,[3] in which the Permanent Court of International Justice held (by a razor thin majority) that the assertion of jurisdiction requires no permissive rule in international law, is rather an exercise of the panoply of sovereignty (unless proscribed by international law), and does not prohibit a state 'from exercising jurisdiction in its own territory, in respect of any case which relates to acts which have taken place abroad'.[4] The Court went on to consider the territorial limitations normally placed upon criminal law, and said that it is nevertheless invariably interpreted to cover offences, even if committed elsewhere, 'if one of the constituent elements of the offence, and more especially its effects, have taken place [within the state]';[5] the 'two elements [the commission and its effects] are, legally, entirely inseparable'.[6] From this derives two distinct subsets of the territorial principle: *subjective* territoriality, whereby a state has jurisdiction over matters originating within its territory, even in cases where the matter is directed beyond its frontiers, and *objective* territoriality, whereby a state has jurisdiction over matters which originate outwith, but culminate within, its territory.

So, states are competent in international law to assert jurisdiction within their territory over events which occur elsewhere. With no limits upon this jurisdiction (except insofar as it is proscribed by international law or limited voluntarily by treaty), its exercise is one which states, in the exercise of their sovereignty, reserve to themselves. It may be tempered by application

---

2   There are other bases of jurisdiction which have developed recently and are still the subject of some dispute. For example, it is claimed that states may assert jurisdiction over events outwith the state which pose a threat to the fundamental order of the state – for example, insurrection against the state fomented within the territory of another state, or counterfeiting of currency or forgery of passports or the use of either (the protective principle); and it is now recognised that all states enjoy jurisdiction to apprehend and submit to criminal process any person commissioning an international crime (eg genocide, slavery, piracy, hijacking, possibly drug trafficking), irrespective of the nationality of the perpetrator or where the offence took place (the universality principle). But even accepting their existence, these have no application in the present context.

3   [1927] PCIJ Ser A, No 9; see also the separate opinion of Sir Gerald Fitzmaurice in *Barcelona Traction* [1970] ICJ Rep 3 at 65 *et seq*.

4   at 19.

5   at 23.

6   at 30.

of the principle of comity, whereby states claiming to have jurisdiction over matters beyond their frontiers nevertheless decline to exercise it. But there is no uniformity here, and increasingly states adopt legislation which may have – and sometimes expressly has – extraterritorial application. Some do so with robust enthusiasm. The adoption in 1996 of the Iran and Libya Sanctions (D'Amato) Act and the Cuban Liberty and Democratic Solidarity (Libertad) (Helms-Burton) Act,[7] by which the United States asserts jurisdiction to confiscate within the United States the property of companies in third states which deal with Iran, Libya or Cuba and, in the case of the Helms-Burton Act, ban company directors and their families from entry into the US and subject them to imprisonment should they be so bold as to try, is only the most recent of many examples of strongarm tactics in the sphere. And it frequently leads to 'blocking statutes', by which states (and, now, the Community) compel persons within their territory to act in defiance of foreign law,[8] which may lead in turn to tit for tat escalation and threats of trade war. It is not an area given to harmony in relations amongst states.

9.1.1 Competition law

If international law permits states to assert jurisdiction extraterritorially, it follows that the state may adopt competition rules to be applied within the state but to instances of anticompetitive conduct occurring outwith the state. In this sphere the lead on the extraterritorial reach of national law has been taken by United States courts in developing the application of the 'effects doctrine' in antitrust law. In its postwar incarnation, the effects doctrine is a wide-ranging assertion of jurisdiction over the economic conduct of companies in third countries. In 1945 the Federal Court of Appeal said:

> It is settled law ... that any State may impose liabilities, even upon persons not within its allegiance, for conduct outside its borders which has consequences within its borders which the State reprehends; and these liabilities other States will ordinarily recognize.[9]

---

[7] 22 USC § 6021 ff.

[8] See, eg, the Protection of Trading Interests Act 1980, adopted in response to American legislation purporting to prohibit companies from engaging in contract work on the Siberian pipeline, which empowered the Secretary of State to compel UK companies to act in defiance of the American law under pain of criminal sanctions and UK courts to order the recovery of any damages awarded against them by a foreign court. In direct response to the D'Amato and Helms-Burton Acts, the Council adopted Reg 2271/96, OJ 1996 L309/1 which cites that they 'violate international law' (recital 7) and provides that no judgment of a court made thereunder is to be enforced within the Community and that persons injured by their application may recover damages.

[9] *United States* v *Aluminum Company of America* (Alcoa) 148 F 2d 416 (2d Cir 1945) at 443.

Thus any anticompetitive conduct taking place outwith the United States may fall nonetheless within the strictures of the Sherman Act and the jurisdiction of the American civil and criminal courts so long as it created effects there, even if they were incidental or secondary.[10]

The effects doctrine is, taken to its widest amplitude, either an extreme manifestation of the objective territorial principle recognised in *The Lotus*, or it goes beyond it. In either case it has caused significant disquiet and given rise to near universal obloquy in other countries, although it has found fertile ground for a gentler application elsewhere, for example in German law.[11] It has been applied by American courts with an ebb and flow, and has on occasion descended into farce.[12] More recent formulations have tended to temper its application by applying a balancing and reasonableness test derived from comity (a 'jurisdictional rule of reason')[13] and requiring that effects of anticompetitive conduct be not only intended but direct, substantial and foreseeable.[14] Nevertheless, the 'long arm' of American antitrust law and the liberality with which it is applied by the American government and courts, not least because of the swingeing penalties imposed (a fine of $500 million recently)[15] and a civil remedy of

---

[10] A rich irony here is that American law (the United States Export Trade (Webb Pomerene) Act 1918 15 USC § 62) exempts from prohibitions of the Sherman Act American cartels for the purpose of export trade, so long as their conduct does not restrain trade within the United States. However, it must be said that the Americans are not uniquely at fault here: the competition laws of a number of member states provide likewise (eg, § 6 II ÖKG; (Greek) Law 703/1977, ΦEK 278/A/26.9.1977, art 6; Laki Kilpailunrajoituksista 2 § (447/1994)) and Art 81 will tolerate an export cartel within the Community provided it does not produce a knock-on effect upon trade between member states.

[11] See § 130 II GWB; BGH, 12. Juli 1973, BGHSt 25, 208 (*Ölfeldrohren*).

[12] The most notorious application of the effects doctrine was *United States* v *Watchmakers of Switzerland Information Center* 1963 Trade Cases No 70,600 (SDNY 1962), in which a New York district court held that a series of agreements made by the Swiss Federation of Watch Makers with a number of undertakings fell within the Sherman Act, ordered Switzerland to annul certain Swiss contracts (which were in conformity with Swiss law) and to put an end to all restrictions on exports to the US (again in conformity with Swiss law), ordered that various clauses of intra-European contracts be annulled and ordered the Swiss Federation of Watch Makers to forbid its members from doing anything prohibited by the court on pain of fines. In effect, the American court ordered Switzerland to restructure its watch industry.

[13] *Timberlane Lumber Co* v *Bank of America* 549 F 2d 597 (9th Cir 1976); *Mannington Mills* v *Congoleum Corporation* 595 F 2d 1287 (3d Cir 1979). It should be noted that whilst several Courts of Appeals now recognise the jurisdictional rules of reason, they continue to assert American jurisdiction in virtually all cases: see eg *Laker Airways* v *Sabena* 731 F 2d 921 (DC Cir 1984); also *Hartford Fire Insurance Co* v *California* 509 US 764 (1993).

[14] This requirement ('direct, substantial and reasonably foreseeable') was codified in 1982 by the Foreign Trade Antitrust Improvements Act 1982; § 7 Sherman Act 15 USC § 6a.

[15] See p 177 *supra*.

treble damages available for breach of the Sherman Act,[16] is treated with great circumspection further abroad. However, it should be understood that the extraterritorial application of competition law does not work in one direction only: in 1997 the Commission subjected to close scrutiny under the Merger Regulation, and so delayed for some time, a takeover of MacDonnell Douglas by Boeing, an assertion of jurisdiction which raised eyebrows, and some ire, in the United States.[17]

A final problem facing the extraterritorial application of competition rules, as with law generally, is their practical effectiveness outwith the territorial jurisdiction, and so the powers of coercion, of their author: even if international law tolerates the assertion of state jurisdiction to events beyond its frontiers as a function of subject matter (subject matter or prescriptive jurisdiction: *jurisdictio*), it is another matter entirely whether that jurisdiction can be enforced (enforcement jurisdiction: *imperium*) – for, as the Permanent Court of International Justice said in *The Lotus*, 'failing the existence of a permissive rule to the contrary [the state] may not exercise its power in any form in the territory of another State'.[18]

9.2 Extraterritorial application of Community competition rules

Against this background, what of the Community competition rules? The first question is how the Community comes to be regulated by international law. Classical international law shied away from attributing to any person other than the state the privileges and duties of statehood; the state, and the state alone, was the subject of international law, all other legal persons merely objects. But in 1949 the International Court of Justice recognised that an international organisation could be a subject of international law, provided that its constituent documents so intended and provided.[19] The EC Treaty provides expressly that 'the Community shall have legal personality'[20] and confers upon it treaty-making power.[21] In external trade and commercial matters generally, the exercise of Community authority has now supplanted that of the member states.[22] As a matter of Community constitutional law, the Community clearly enjoys international personality (although the European Union does not), this personality is now universally recognised by third states, and so it is an actor subject to the rules of public international law – which, being essen-

---

[16] § 4 Clayton Act 15 USC § 15.

[17] Decision 97/816 (*Boeing/MacDonnell Douglas*) OJ 1997 L336/16; see *infra*.

[18] [1927] PCIJ Ser A, No 9, at p 18.

[19] *Reparations for Injuries Suffered in the Service of the United Nations* [1949] ICJ Rep 174.

[20] Art 281 (ex Art 210).

[21] Art 310 (ex Art 238).

[22] See, eg, Opinion 1/94 *Re the World Trade Organisation* [1994] ECR I-5267.

tially a monist system, is expressly recognised by the Court of Justice.[23] As for Community competition rules, in an important constitutional judgment in 1971, the Court of Justice established that in any sphere in which the Community enjoys competence within the Community, it also enjoys competence externally.[24] The question is then whether the competition rules of the Treaty were intended to have, or admit of having, extraterritorial effect.

Articles 81 and 82 (ex Articles 85 and 86) contain no express reference as to their (extra)territorial application; they merely proscribe anticompetitive conduct 'within the common market' which 'may affect trade between Member States'. In accordance with general principles the object or effect must be appreciable, but it may be direct or indirect.[25] In some circumstances, where an agreement or concerted practice exists between or amongst Community undertakings but has some extraterritorial element(s), the issues are relatively straightforward, and Community jurisdiction, founded upon either the territorial or the nationality principle, is undisputed. An agreement between or amongst undertakings within the Community, or even between or amongst Community undertakings and their competitors in third countries, intended to reduce the supply, within the Community, of goods or services originating in third countries is liable, at least potentially, of affecting trade and distorting competition between member states and so will fall foul of Article 81(1),[26] unless it can be shown that the effects are confined to one member state or to trade between one member state and one or more non-member states.[27] Agreements and concerted practices producing even *per se* distortion of competition in third country markets fall in principle beyond the reach of Article 81(1). Thus an agreement between a Community supplier and a Community distributor by which the latter is awarded an exclusive contract territory, with absolute territorial protection (normally a cardinal infringement), of three non-Community countries and agrees to a re-export ban (another cardinal infraction) 'cannot be contrary, by [its] very nature, to Article 85(1)' and the restrictive territorial provisions 'do not, by their very nature, have as their object the prevention, restriction or distortion of competition within the common market within the meaning of Article 85(1)'.[28] However, whilst such is not their object, it may be their effect.

---

[23] Case C-286/90 *Anklagemyndigheden* v *Poulsen* [1992] ECR I-6019.

[24] Case 22/70 *Commission* v *Council* (ERTA) [1971] ECR 263.

[25] See pp 68–71 *supra*.

[26] Case 22/71 *Béguelin* v *GL Import/Export* [1971] ECR 949; Case 71/74 *Frubo* v *Commission* [1975] ECR 563; Case 51/75 *EMI* v *CBS* [1976] ECR 811; Cases T-24 etc/93 *Compagnie Maritime Belge* v *Commission* [1996] ECR II-1201.

[27] Case 28/77 *Tepea* v *Commission* [1978] ECR 1391; Case 22/78 *Hugin* v *Commission* [1979] ECR 1869; Case 174/84 *Bulk Oil* v *Sun International* [1986] ECR 559.

[28] Case C-306/96 *Javico International* v *Yves Saint Laurent Parfums* [1998] ECR I-1983 at 2004–05.

Whether or not there is such effect is a measure essentially of the likelihood, absent the restrictive provisions in the agreement, of re-export to the Community. Appraisal of the likelihood ought to include consideration of the economic and legal context (a perennial consideration), the structure of the Community market for the goods or services, price differences between the Community and the (third country) contract territories, customs duties and transport costs, a (requisite) effect upon trade between member states, and appreciability.[29] The effect is the more likely to be present if the third country has entered into an association agreement with the Community which diminishes or prohibits customs duties and other barriers to trade and so increases the fluidity of markets and the likelihood of traders seeking to supply the Community market from outwith the Community.[30]

So much for the easy answers. The serious difficulties begin where there is anticompetitive practice or conduct which may produce effects within the Community, but some or all of its authors are established, and its centre of gravity lies, beyond the Community's frontiers.

For some time the Court of Justice dealt with the problem of the extraterritorial application of the competition rules through the device of the economic entity doctrine – which, indeed, seemed almost to be developed for that purpose. In 1969 the Commission libelled the existence of a concerted practice in the dyestuffs market, ordered its termination and imposed fines upon a number of participating undertakings, including one British and two Swiss companies.[31] The three challenged the decision *inter alia* on the ground that the Commission had no jurisdiction over an undertaking in the (pre-accession) UK or in Switzerland. The Court of Justice skirted the question by finding that the British and Swiss parents directly controlled their subsidiaries within the Community (this finding, it must be said, on virtually non-existent evidence before it), that the latter had no autonomy, that 'the formal separation between these companies, resulting from their separate legal personality, cannot outweigh the unity of their conduct on the market for the purposes of applying the rules on competition', and so attributed the conduct of the subsidiary undertakings – over which it had clear jurisdiction – to their parents.[32] The Commission relied upon the economic entity doctrine in order to assert jurisdiction over undertakings outwith the Community subsequently, and in this it was supported by the Court of Justice.[33] A variation of the doctrine would

---

[29] Case C-306/96 *Javico International*, *ibid*.

[30] See the Opinion of A-G Tesauro in Case C-306/96 *Javico International*, *ibid*.

[31] Decision 69/243 (*Dyestuffs*) JO 1969 L195/11.

[32] Case 48/69 *ICI* v *Commission* [1972] ECR 619 at 663; Case 52/69 *Geigy* v *Commission* [1972] ECR 787; Case 53/69 *Sandoz* v *Commission* [1972] ECR 845 (the *Dyestuffs* cases).

[33] eg Decision 72/21 (*Continental Can*) JO 1972 L7/25; Decision 72/457 (*Commercial Solvents*) JO 1972 L299/51, upheld in Cases 6–7/73 *Commercial Solvents* v *Commission*

probably serve to assert Community jurisdiction over the conduct of the Union of European Football Associations (UEFA), a private person in Swiss law, by virtue of the allegiance owed it by national football associations within the Community.[34]

The test case came with *Woodpulp*.[35] *Woodpulp* involved an (alleged) concerted practice amongst 41 producers of bleached sulphate woodpulp, all of them – principally Swedish, Finnish, Canadian and American, plus one each from Norway, Portugal and Spain – then outwith the Community. The Commission libelled an infraction of Article 81(1), ordered its termination and imposed fines upon 36 of the undertakings.[36] Eighteen challenged the decision *inter alia* on the ground that the Commission had no jurisdiction over them. As some of the undertakings had subsidiaries within the Community, but others did not, the Court could not attribute jurisdiction over all of them to the economic entity doctrine. It was therefore required to face the issue of the extraterritorial reach of the competition rules head-on. It set aside the substance of the case in order first expressly to do so.[37]

Advocate-General Darmon embarked upon a lengthy discussion of the rules of public international law and the effects doctrine, and came down recommending essentially the adoption of a qualified effects doctrine: that the Community was competent in international law to assert jurisdiction in competition matters over undertakings outwith the Community provided that the anticompetitive conduct in question produced effects within the territory of the Community which were direct, substantial and

---

[1974] ECR 223; Decision 76/353 (*Chiquita*) OJ 1976 L95/1, upheld in Case 27/76 *United Brands* v *Commission* [1978] ECR 207; Decision 88/138 (*Hilti*) OJ 1988 L65/19, upheld in Case T-30/89 *Hilti* v *Commission* [1991] ECR II-1429 and on appeal as Case C-53/92P *Hilti* v *Commission* [1994] ECR I-667.

[34] See Case C-415/93 *Union Royale Belge des Sociétés de Football Association* v *Bosman* [1995] I-4921, in which A-G Lenz discussed the application of EC competition rules to association football; although the Court of Justice decided the case on other grounds, the question is very likely to resurface.

[35] Arguably the Court implicitly recognised the effects doctrine in an earlier case ('the fact that one of the undertakings which are parties to the agreement is situated in a third country does not prevent application of [Article 81] since the agreement is operative [*produit ses effets*] on the territory of the common market': Case 22/71 *Béguelin* v *GL Import/Export* [1971] ECR 949 at 959), but it involved contracts between undertakings one of which was established within the Community, and so the effects doctrine was not determinative.

[36] Decision 85/202 (*Woodpulp*) OJ 1985 L85/1.

[37] Cases 89 etc/85 *Åhlström* v *Commission* (Woodpulp) [1988] ECR 5193. The decision was eventually annulled almost in its entirety because the Commission had failed to show the existence of a concerted practice: Cases 89 etc/85 *Åhlström* v *Commission* (Woodpulp) [1993] ECR I-1307; see pp 56–7 *supra*.

foreseeable.[38] This was entirely to the liking of the Commission, which had long supported the incorporation of the effects doctrine, and which had clearly motivated its reasoning in a number of competition decisions.[39] The Court did not follow either. Rather it shied away from, and made no mention of, the effects doctrine, and cleaved to the territorial principle:

> It should be observed that an infringement of Article 85, such as the conclusion of an agreement which has had the effect of restricting competition within the common market, consists of conduct made up of two elements, the formation of the agreement, decision or concerted practice and the implementation thereof. If the applicability of prohibitions laid down under competition law were made to depend on the place where the agreement, decision or concerted practice was formed, the result would obviously be to give undertakings an easy means of evading those prohibitions. The decisive factor is therefore the place where it is implemented.
>
> The producers in this case implemented their pricing agreement within the common market. It is immaterial in that respect whether or not they had recourse to subsidiaries, agents, sub-agents, or branches within the Community in order to make their contacts with purchasers within the Community. Accordingly the Community's jurisdiction to apply its competition rules to such conduct is covered by the territoriality principle as universally recognized in public international law.[40]

The Court went on to consider, and reject, arguments based upon the principle of non-interference and comity.[41]

So, a variation of the territorial principle derived from the *Lotus* case, that of objective territoriality. An agreement may be formed or a concerted practice exist outwith the Community, but so long as its object or effect is one which distorts intra-Community trade – again, a general requirement to be caught by Article 81 – and is 'implemented' (*mis en oeuvre*; *durchgeführt*) within the Community – which it was in *Woodpulp* by sale of the product directly to buyers within the Community – the Court claims to draw upon the non-contentious territorial principle in order to found Community jurisdiction and need not venture into deeper waters. Since *Woodpulp* the Commission has adopted decisions ordering termination of agreements/concerted practices and fining undertakings outwith the territory of the Community for breach of Article 81(1) 'in so far as the

---

38 at 5226–7. This was similar to the Opinion of A-G Mayras in the *Dyestuffs* cases.

39 eg, the *Dyestuffs* and *Woodpulp* decisions themselves; Decision 85/206 (*Aluminium Imports from Eastern Europe*) OJ 1985 L92/1, in which the Commission also considered, but declined to exercise, self restraint in the exercise of its jurisdiction.

40 Cases 89 etc/85 *Woodpulp* at 5243.

41 at 5244. See also, to much the same effect, Case T-102/96 *Gencor v Commission* [1999] ECR II-753 at 788–9.

agreements were implemented inside the Community',[42] where they 'carried out the bulk of their business inside the Community' and 'to the extent they supplied the product inside the Community',[43] or, in the cases of an American export cartel seeking to break into the Community market[44] and a pan-European cement cartel,[45] with no territorial justification whatsoever. In keeping with general principles, the distortion to intra-Community competition must also be appreciable.[46] By logical extension of *Woodpulp*, the abusive conduct of a dominant undertaking outwith the Community which is implemented within the Community in a manner which has an appreciable effect upon intra-Community trade is equally made subject to Article 82.[47] In a 1997 decision taken under the Merger Regulation[48] the Commission declared incompatible with the common market a concentration involving essentially mining interests in South Africa and was sustained by the Court of First Instance by application of *Woodpulp* reasoning.[49] In one passage the Court used language which might be taken as implicit recognition of an effects doctrine – the preambular recitations in the Merger Regulation 'in no way exclude from the Regulation's field of

---

[42] Decision 89/190 (*PVC*) OJ 1989 L74/1, para 40; Decision 89/191 (*LdPE*) OJ 1989 L74/21, para 48. Both were annulled for procedural irregularities: Case C-137/92P *Commission* v *BASF* [1994] ECR I-2555; Cases T-80 etc/89 *BASF* v *Commission* [1995] ECR II-729. A re-adopted *PVC* decision (Decision 94/599, OJ 1994 L239/14) was addressed to Community undertakings only. It should be noted that in *LdPE* the Commission applied Art 81 to the conduct of a (pre-accession) Spanish undertaking in language ('[t]o the extent that its involvement in the cartel affected competition within the Community, EEC competition rules applied to [it]': para 48) that comes very close to an effects doctrine, but the Court of First Instance did not consider the point.

[43] Decision 94/601 (*Cartonboard*) OJ 1994 L243/1, para 139.

[44] Decision 91/301 (*Ansac*) OJ 1991 L152/54.

[45] Decision 94/815 (*Cement*) OJ 1994 L343/1, upheld in this particular in Cases T-25 etc/95 *Cimenteries CBR* v *Commission*, judgment of 15 March 2000, not yet reported.

[46] But see Decision 91/301 (*Ansac*), *ibid*, in which the Commission refused negative clearance (and exemption) to a proposed American export cartel which was predicted (by the Americans) to be able to supply less than 5 per cent of the Community market. The Commission has also said that even if the conduct of a single undertaking party to a cartel does not itself appreciably affect trade within the Community, the small scale of its participation will not exculpate it if the effect of the cartel as a whole is appreciable: Decision 85/206 (*Aluminium Imports from Eastern Europe*) OJ 1985 L92/1.

[47] The Commission has imposed fines upon a number of undertakings outwith the Community for breaches of Art 82, but the decisions were reasoned upon the economic entity doctrine (Decision 72/21 (*Continental Can*) JO 1972 L7/25; Decision 72/457 (*Commercial Solvents*) JO 1972 L299/51; Decision 76/353 (*Chiquita*) OJ 1976 L95/1; Decision 88/138 (*Hilti*) OJ 1988 L65/19), upon abusive conduct occasioned by unfair contract terms with undertakings within the Community (Decision 76/248 (*Hoffmann-La Roche*) OJ 1976 L51/7), or, following *Woodpulp*, with no express territorial justification (Decision 92/163 (*Tetra Pak II*) OJ 1992 L72/1).

[48] Decision 97/26 (*Gencor/Lonrho*) OJ 1997 L11/30.

[49] Case T-102/96 *Gencor* v *Commission* [1999] ECR II-753.

application concentrations which, while relating to ... activities outside the Community, *have the effect* of creating or strengthening a dominant position as a result of which effective competition in the Common Market is significantly impeded'[50] – but this would probably be to attribute too much to a chance formulation, the judgment otherwise being on all fours with *Woodpulp*. The Court added that in order to comply with international law the criteria of immediate, substantial and foreseeable effect within the Community were required to be satisfied.[51]

It is therefore still an open question whether Community law recognises an effects doctrine. There is also the question of whether there is any practical difference between the effects doctrine and the objective territorial principle. The former, in its modern formulation, requires an effect upon trade which is intended, direct, substantial and foreseeable. Substantial, or at least 'appreciable', is already a necessary component of breaches of Articles 81 and 82, and foreseeability ('intentional or negligent') necessary for liability to Commission fines. Articles 81 and 82 also catch a restrictive practice or conduct which is unintentional ('object or effect') and one affects trade not only directly but also indirectly, so arguably, ironically, bringing within the objective territorial rule practices which may escape the effects doctrine – although this is probably obviated if 'implemented within the Community' can be equated with 'direct'; this might be supported by an earlier decision in which the Commission said that Article 81 applies only to those parties to a cartel 'which were directly involved in the manipulation of competition within the Community'.[52] And considerations of comity and self restraint apply equally irrespective of which of the two bases of jurisdiction are deployed. In any event, the objective territorial principle of *Woodpulp* will serve as a satisfactory basis of jurisdiction in most cases. Nevertheless, there are lacunae – instances which would be caught by the former but (probably) not the latter. A number of examples spring to mind. First, would it have made any difference if all contracts of sale in *Woodpulp* (by which the alleged concerted practice had been implemented within the Community) had stipulated that the buyer acquires title to and takes possession of the goods before they leave the territory of the exporting state? Probably not. What if the producers had sold to Community buyers only via middlemen all situated outwith the Community? Would their conduct be caught by the territorial principle which the Court stressed applied because its implementation lay in direct sales into the Community? Quite possibly no. Second, a more sophisticated

---

[50] at 783; emphasis added.
[51] at 785–8.
[52] Decision 84/405 (*Zinc Producer Group*) OJ 1984 L220/27, para 84. The English text here reads 'indirectly', the French, German and Dutch (the other authentic language versions) *directement*, *mittelbar* and *rechtstreeks*; with a two/two linguistic split and a direct contradiction, 'directly' seems from the context to be correct.

variation: assume a raw commodity produced entirely outwith the Community and processed, again, entirely outwith the Community. The commodity is not sold within the Community because there are no processors and so no market there, but the finished product is. Assume further that there is a cartel amongst the commodity producers, which engage in gross anticompetitive conduct, but not amongst the processors. The price of the finished product is, presumably, higher within the Community owing to the conduct of the cartel and so it produces effects there, but is the anticompetitive conduct 'implemented' within the Community when the product the subject of the anticompetitive conduct (the commodity) is not sold in the Community? Third, assume any product produced outwith the Community, the producers of which agree a collective boycott of Community buyers; alternatively, a collective boycott of Community producers by non-Community buyers. Both effects, clearly; but is it implementation? Until such (admittedly unlikely) events come to pass and so force the Court's hand, we shall probably not know.

There remains the problem of how far the Community, or any state, can enforce its will in this context. The Community is competent to proscribe conduct outwith – provided it is 'implemented' within – its frontiers and to impose penalties upon those engaging in that conduct; this is subject matter or prescriptive jurisdiction. But it remains powerless to enforce the proscription or the penalty. Here the economic entity doctrine was clearly of greater utility: conduct could be attributed to the parent (outwith the Community) but could be enforced against the subsidiary (within the Community) by civil process. Beyond the economic entity doctrine, there is no enforcement jurisdiction, no power of compulsion. If the Commission seeks to carry out an investigation under Regulation 17 or the Merger Regulation of an undertaking outwith the Community it is free to request information under article 11 or knock on the front door demanding entry and answers under article 14, but the undertaking is equally free to ignore it unless the authorities in that state assist.[53] As we shall see, the Community has now entered into a number of agreements with third states for just such mutual assistance upon a reciprocal basis. But lacking such an agreement, the competent authorities of third states (unlike those of the member states by virtue of Regulation 17) have no duty to assist, and are markedly unenthusiastic to do so; indeed, as a function of protection of territorial sovereignty a number of states prohibit the furnishing of documents, and some make it a criminal offence simply to supply information, to authorities outwith the state.[54] And certainly any attempt to fine an

---

[53] A recent Commission ploy has been to seek information from an undertaking in a third state by addressing the request care of a Community subsidiary, but it is unlikely that this creates an enforceable obligation for the parent to respond.

[54] See Case 145/83 *Adams v Commission* [1985] ECR 3539.

undertaking outwith the Community cannot be enforced, for this would be the 'exercise [of] its power ... in the territory of another State', proscribed in *The Lotus*.[55] However, it is consistent with the territorial principle that any property or assets within the Community of a third country undertaking upon which a fine has been imposed would be liable to seizure. This then is the only sanction, but one which has hitherto proved effective: undertakings in third states pay up, or play the Commission game generally, because the Community market is too important to abandon. Thus, when a merger between two Canadian banks,[56] between two American aircraft manufacturers[57] or between two companies jockeying for control of oilfields in the North Slope of Alaska[58] falls within the Merger Regulation the parties to it will notify the Commission and comply with any conditions imposed by it. By the same token South African mining interests seeking to merge complied with a Commission decision blocking them even though the merger had been approved by the South African Competition Board.[59] And the first fine (of five to date) imposed under the Regulation was for the quite innocent failure of a Korean firm to notify, and nonetheless proceed with, the acquisition of an American firm.[60] An exception is when the shoe is on the other foot. In application of the objective territorial principle, the Commission would be free to impose massive fines upon the various members of OPEC for gross cartellisation of the world oil market. It has not done so, and were it to do so there is every likelihood that it would be ignored.[61] This is a rare case in which the Community market needs the suppliers rather than the other way around.

9.3 Agreements with third states

As mentioned above, the EC Treaty confers treaty-making power upon the Community, and in exercise of this power the Community has entered into a number of agreements with third states. The Community's treaty-making power is restricted essentially to the commercial sphere, so that a number of agreements which go beyond the merely commercial are negotiated,

---

55 [1927] PCIJ Ser A, No 9, at p 18.
56 Case M.1138 (*Royal Bank/Bank of Montréal*) OJ 1998 C74/32. In the event, the merger was blocked by the Canadian Competition Bureau; decision of 11 December 1998, unpublished.
57 Decision 97/816 (*Boeing/MacDonnell Douglas*) OJ 1997 L336/16; see *infra*.
58 Case M.1532 (*BP Amoco/Atlantic Richfield*), decision of 29 September 1999, not yet published.
59 Decision 97/26 (*Gencor/Lonrho*) OJ 1997 L11/30, upheld in Case T-102/96 *Gencor v Commission* [1999] ECR II-753.
60 Decision 1999/594 (*Samsung/AST Research Inc*) OJ 1999 L225/12.
61 It is interesting to note that many of OPEC's offices were relocated from Vienna to Geneva following Austrian accession to the European Union.

signed and ratified by both the Community and its member states ('mixed agreements'). Some of them contain competition rules in varying degrees. Whilst not addressing the extraterritorial application of Community rules directly, they do have some relevance for it.

9.3.1 European Economic Area

In January 1994 the Treaty between the Community and its member states on the one part and each of the European Free Trade Area (EFTA) states of Iceland, Liechtenstein, Norway, Austria, Finland and Sweden on the other, establishing the European Economic Area (EEA), entered into force.[62] Prior to that, relations between the Community and the EFTA states were governed by a number of free trade agreements signed with each EFTA state in 1972 and 1973. Switzerland (an EFTA member state) had signed the EEA Agreement but, following a negative vote in a referendum, declined to ratify it.[63] The accession of Austria, Finland and Sweden to the European Union in January 1995 took much of the steam out of the EEA, leaving behind an even more imbalanced structure with a 15-state strong Community on one side and Iceland, Liechtenstein and Norway on the other. Its interest, however, lies not only in the present EEA but also the likelihood that it will serve as a model for future association with the Community, either for its own sake or as a transitional step on the road to accession.[64]

The purpose of the EEA is

> to promote a continuous and balanced strengthening of trade and economic relations between the Contracting Parties with equal conditions of competition, and the respect of the same rules, with a view to creating a homogenous European Economic Area ....[65]

It is not otherwise defined in the Agreement, and its nature is difficult to define. Essentially it is a sophisticated free trade area (that is, the rules on free movement of goods apply only to goods originating within the territory of the EEA)[66] with elements of a common market, or, in other words, an experiment in economic integration less profound than that of the Community but deeper than that of the EFTA. The *acquis communautaire*

---

[62] For the text see OJ 1994 L1/3.

[63] Community/Swiss relations are therefore now still governed by their 1972 Free Trade Agreement (for the text see JO 1972 L300/189); a series of agreements addressing closer cooperation in a number of spheres is in the offing: see COM (99) 229 final. Owing to the close economic links between Switzerland and Liechtenstein, the latter enjoyed a temporary transitional status within the EEA, becoming fully integrated into it in May 1995.

[64] The EEA has been dubbed by a number of wags the 'European waiting room', from EWR, the German name (*Europäischer Wirtschaftsraum*) for the EEA.

[65] EEA Agreement, Art 1.

[66] Art 8(2).

(as at the date of the signing of the Agreement) is incorporated into the EEA.[67] The Treaty creates EEA institutions competent to oversee the running of the EEA and further requires the EFTA member states to create other institutions to enforce the Agreement within their territory.

Article 53 of the EEA Agreement is identical *mutatis mutandis* to Article 81 of the EC Treaty, prohibiting restrictive practices 'between Contracting Parties' which distort competition 'within the territory covered by [the EEA] Agreement'. The block exemptions adopted by the Commission and existing prior to the signing of the Treaty apply to Article 53;[68] subsequent block exemptions have been incorporated into EEA law by the EEA Joint Committee.[69] Agreements exempted by authority of Article 81(3) of the EC Treaty prior to the entry into force of the EEA Treaty are exempted under Article 53(3) until exemption expires or is withdrawn.[70] The Agreement also directs enforcement authorities to 'take due account' of the various Commission notices (then) adopted in the field;[71] subsequent notices have been echoed in notices fashioned and adopted by the EFTA Surveillance Authority (as to which see *infra*) where it considers them to have EEA relevance.[72] Article 54 of the EEA Agreement is identical to Article 82 of the EC Treaty except that it applies to a dominant undertaking 'within the territory covered by this Agreement' insofar as it may affect trade 'between Contracting Parties'. Restrictive practices and potentially abusive conduct within the Community but with wider effects are therefore to be assessed in the light of Articles 81 and 82 of the EC Treaty *and* of Articles 53 and 54 of the EEA Agreement, so increasing the territorial scope in which (essentially the same) anticompetitive conduct is proscribed. The Agreement provides further rules governing public undertakings and state aids analogous to Articles 86 (ex Article 90) and 87–89 (ex Articles 92–94) of the EC Treaty.[73]

The competition rules of the EEA are enforced by the Commission within the territory of the Community[74] and by the EFTA Surveillance

---

[67] Art 6.

[68] Art 60 and Annex XIV, the latter which adopts them as 'acts' for these purposes.

[69] The Committee is competent to amend Annex XIV of the Agreement by virtue of Art 98; so, see eg Decision 46/96, OJ 1996 L291/39 and Decision 12/97, OJ 1997 L182/42, adopting block exemption Regs 1475/95 and 240/96 respectively into EEA law.

[70] EEA Agreement, Protocol 21, Art 13.

[71] Annex XIV.

[72] See, eg, Decision (of the EFTA Surveillance Authority) 46/98, OJ 1998 L200/46, which adapts and incorporates for purposes of its enforcement of the EEA Agreement the Commission notice on the definition of the relevant market (OJ 1997 C372/5) and the Commission notice on agreements of minor importance (OJ 1997 C372/13).

[73] EEA Agreement, Arts 59, 61–64.

[74] Appropriate amendments were made to existing regulations so as to enable the Commission to discharge this task: Reg 3666/93, OJ 1993 L336/1.

Authority[75] within the territory of the EFTA states, where the latter enjoys 'equivalent powers and similar functions to those of the EC Commission, at the time of the signature of the Agreement, for the application of the competition rules of the EEC Treaty'.[76] This bicephalous enforcement was necessitated after the Court of Justice held that the original EEA Agreement, which purported to create autonomous EEA enforcement authorities, was inconsistent with the EEC Treaty.[77] Nevertheless, the Agreement establishes a 'one-stop shop' in competition enforcement. The two institutions are required to cooperate closely,[78] and there are rules governing which of them ought to be competent to determine situations which fall within the territorial jurisdiction of both ('mixed' cases).[79] Parties wishing to notify a restrictive agreement or conduct in the context of a mixed case are required to determine (for which guidance is now provided in Form A/B) which of the two is, by virtue of these rules, the 'competent surveillance authority'; if the wrong authority has been notified it is required to transfer the case 'without delay' to the other.[80] Each is required to carry out investigations within its territory at the request of the other and transmit to it the results,[81] and both may impose pecuniary sanctions enforceable by civil process throughout the territory of the EEA.[82] A decision of the EFTA Surveillance Authority is subject to judicial review by the EFTA Court.[83] As Articles 53 and 54 of the EEA Agreement are identical *mutatis mutandis* to Articles 81 and 82 of the EC Treaty and the *acquis communautaire* is part of EEA law, they ought to be interpreted in the same manner and ought to have direct effect within the territory of the EEA and so be enforceable in national courts.[84] So, assuming this to be so,

---

[75] On the creation of the EFTA Surveillance Authority, see Agreement of 2 May 1992 establishing a Surveillance Authority and an EFTA Court of Justice: [1992] 1 *Commercial Laws of Europe* 277.

[76] EEA Agreement, Protocol 21, Art 1; for the detail see the EFTA Surveillance Agreement, Protocol 4.

[77] Opinion 1/91 *re the EEA Agreement (No 1)* [1991] ECR I-6079.

[78] EEA Agreement, Art 58 and Protocols 23 and 24.

[79] Art 56.

[80] Protocol 23, Art 10.

[81] Protocol 23, Art 8(3), (5); Protocol 24, Art 8(4) for concentrations.

[82] Art 110; transposed into UK law by the European Economic Area Act 1993, s 4(b).

[83] Established by the Agreement of 2 May 1992 establishing a Surveillance Authority and an EFTA Court of Justice, cited n 75 *supra*.

[84] Some provisions of the EEA Treaty have been considered, and recognised as directly effective, by both the Court of First Instance (Case T-115/94 *Opel Austria* v *Council* [1997] ECR II-39) and the EFTA Court (eg Case E-1/94 *Ravintoloitsijain Liiton Kustannus Restamark* v *Helsingen Piiritullikamari* [1994–95] EFTA CR 15); the Community Courts have yet to rule on Arts 53 and 54, but the EFTA Court implied that Art 53 is directly effective in Case E-3/97 *Jan og Kristian Jæger* v *Opel Norge* [1998] EFTA CR 1). This compares with the 1972/73 Free Trade Agreements between the Community and the EFTA states which the courts of some EFTA states found not to be directly effective.

an unexempted anticompetitive agreement between, say, a British and a Norwegian firm may escape the strictures of Article 81 because it does not appreciably affect trade between Community member states, but it is still subject in a British (or a Norwegian) court to a declaration of nullity by virtue of Article 53(2) of the EEA Agreement.

The Commission enjoys legal as well as actual enforcement pre-eminence over the EFTA Surveillance Authority in one area, that of concentrations. The Merger Regulation applies – the thresholds intact[85] but 'adapted' for purposes of the EEA Agreement so that turnover includes EEA-wide turnover – to concentrations with a 'Community or EFTA dimension'.[86] The Commission has 'sole competence' so long as the concentration is caught by the Merger Regulation.[87] It may therefore veto a concentration even if it creates or strengthens a dominant position within the territory of the EFTA and not within that of the Community. The EFTA Surveillance Authority has jurisdiction only where a concentration falls outwith the Merger Regulation – where, for example, only one party to it enjoys a turnover of more than €100 million within three Community member states[88] – but meets the thresholds provided by the Regulation within the territory of the EFTA.[89] Concentrations meeting these criteria are unlikely to be common. Where a concentration does fall within the jurisdiction of the EFTA Surveillance Authority, it does not prevent the application of national rules on merger control within the Community[90] – this being the one overt exception to the principle of the one-stop shop instituted by the Merger Regulation.

The EEA marks a significant step towards international competition regulation and cooperation. Control of anticompetitive conduct within it has become homogenised, and the one-stop shop minimises problems of co-application and enforcement. This was not the case under the competition provisions of the 1972/73 Free Trade Agreements between the Community and the EFTA states, in which context Articles 81 and 82 could be applied notwithstanding autonomous enforcement procedures provided by those agreements.[91] And the provisions on cooperation in investigation and enforcement of pecuniary sanctions overcome the problem of the bar in international law to the extraterritorial exercise of enforcement jurisdic-

---

[85] The original 1989 thresholds were those in force at the entry into force of the EEA Agreement; the new, additional thresholds introduced within the Community in 1998 (see Chapter 8) were adopted into EEA law by a decision of the EEA Joint Committee (Decision 27/98 OJ 1998 L310/9) with effect from April 1998.

[86] EEA Agreement, Art 57 and Annex XIV.

[87] Art 57(2)(a).

[88] Reg 4064/89, OJ 1990 L395/1 art 1(3), as amended.

[89] EEA Agreement, Art 57(2)(b) and Annex XIV.

[90] Art 57(2)(b).

[91] Cases 89 etc/85 *Åhlström* v *Commission* (Woodpulp) [1988] ECR 5193.

tion. It should be noted that the entire structure rests upon a complex contractual *modus vivendi* between the Community and the EFTA states and one into which the reform of Regulation 17 now mooted by the Commission[92] could throw a spanner. Given the presumption of the EEA Agreement of the present notification and authorisation system essentially intact and the creation of an EEA *acquis* it is unlikely that such reform could proceed without adjustment to various EEA protocols, which requires a decision of the EEA Joint Committee.[93]

9.3.2 Europe Agreements

Following the collapse of the old regimes in Eastern Europe, a number of bilateral Free Trade Agreements were entered into between the Community and various middle and eastern European countries.[94] Shortly thereafter these were upgraded into the 'Europe Agreements' between the Community and its member states on the one hand and the same middle and eastern European countries on the other – Bulgaria, the Czech Republic, Estonia, Hungary, Latvia, Lithuania, Poland, Romania, Slovakia and Slovenia.[95] The Europe Agreements cover commercial matters, including limited free movement of persons and services, but also matters such as political dialogue and cultural cooperation. They are considered, and formally expressed, to be a first step towards 'gradual' accession to the European Union.[96]

Each Europe Agreement contains competition provisions which are identical. They declare as incompatible with the agreement insofar as they affect trade between the contracting parties

(i)   all agreements between undertakings, decisions by associations of undertakings and concerted practices between undertakings which have as their object or effect the prevention, restriction or distortion of competition;
(ii) abuse by one or more undertakings of a dominant position in the territories of the Community or of [the other contracting party] as a whole or in a substantial part thereof;
(iii) any public aid which distorts or threatens to distort competition by favouring certain undertakings or the production of certain goods.[97]

They go on to provide that 'any practice contrary to this Article shall be assessed on the basis of criteria arising from the application of the rules of

---

[92] See pp 134–6 *supra*.
[93] EEA Agreement, Art 98.
[94] See, eg, the Free Trade Agreement between the Community and Estonia, OJ 1994 L373/2.
[95] See, eg, the Europe Agreement with Estonia, OJ 1998 L68/3.
[96] *Ibid*, Art 1(2).
[97] *Ibid*, Art 63(1).

Articles 85, 86 and 92 [now Articles 81, 82 and 87] of the Treaty establishing the European Community'.[98] There is no provision for exemption. Unlike Articles 81 and 82 of the EC Treaty and Articles 53 and 54 of the EEA Treaty, such practice or conduct is not 'prohibited'; it is 'incompatible' with the agreement. The language is drawn directly from the 1972/73 Free Trade Agreements between the Community and the EFTA states, and it is submitted that the same considerations will apply – that is, they will not be read as being of themselves directly effective. However, each Europe Agreement created an Association Council competent *inter alia* to adopt the rules necessary to give effect to the competition provisions,[99] and where such rules have been adopted (as they have been for most of the Europe Agreements)[100] it may be, although it is yet to be tested in either Community or Eastern European courts, that the Agreement provisions cross the threshold into direct effect. Articles 81 and 82 nevertheless continue to be of application insofar as anticompetitive practices or conduct within Eastern Europe are implemented within the Community. It remains to be seen if the European Agreement countries will graduate to EEA status on the road to accession.

9.3.3 The Community/North American Agreements

In 1991 the Commission and the United States government entered into an agreement, the first such for the Community, designed to promote cooperation and coordination in the application of their respective competition laws.[101] It was dealt a temporary blow when the Court of Justice found that the Commission had exceeded its powers (as a matter of Community constitutional law) in adopting the act by which it purported to conclude it,[102] and so in 1995 a joint decision was adopted by the Council and the Commission which brought the agreement into force with effect retroactive to the date of signature.[103] A virtually identical agreement with Canada entered into force in 1999.[104] The implementing rules adopted by the Europe Agreement Association Councils bear some of the characteristics of the Community/US and Community/Canada agreements.

The purpose of the agreements is 'to promote cooperation and coordina-

---

[98] *Ibid*, Art 63(2).

[99] *Ibid*, Art 63(3).

[100] eg, Decision 1/1999 of the Community/Estonia Association Council adopting implementing rules for competition provisions applicable to undertakings, OJ 1999 L144/16.

[101] Agreement between the Commission of the European Communities and the Government of the United States of America regarding the application of their competition laws, OJ 1995 L95/47.

[102] Case C-327/91 *France v Commission* [1994] ECR I-3641.

[103] Decision 95/145, OJ 1995 L95/45.

[104] Agreement between the European Communities and the Government of Canada regarding the application of their competition laws, OJ 1999 L175/50.

tion and lessen the possibility or impact of differences between the parties in the application of their competition laws'.[105] They require both respective parties to notify one another in the event that enforcement activities of either affects important interests of the other;[106] to exchange information, subject to a requirement of confidentiality;[107] to cooperate where both pursue enforcement of related situations, where enforcement by one may adversely affect important interests of the other, and where anti-competitive conduct within the territory of one may have adverse consequences for the other;[108] to coordinate enforcement activities in situations in which they are both concerned;[109] to seek accommodation of their competing interests (comity);[110] and to consult at the request of the other party.[111] The Community/US agreement, but not (yet) the Community/Canada agreement, has been supplemented by a subsequent agreement on the application of principles of 'positive comity' to the mutual enforcement of competition rules.[112]

The agreements are essentially statements of intent. They do not integrate the application of competition rules or of their enforcement as does the EEA Treaty; it is not clear that either side will be prepared to carry out the other's investigative work or entrust the other to do so; and the confidentiality provisions prevent the exchange of much useful information. On the American side the Community/US agreement is not a 'treaty', for the Senate never approved it; rather it is an executive agreement, which cannot be enforced in the American courts. Nor has the Canadian agreement been incorporated into Canadian law by Act of Parliament. Whether or not the agreements are directly effective within Community courts depends upon their terms, and it is submitted that they are not. As for the American agreement (the Canadian agreement is too recent to have borne fruit) the

---

[105] art I(1) of both agreements. The Canadian agreement adds the words 'between the competition authorities of the Parties and to' between 'coordination' and 'lessen'. 'Competition laws' are defined in art I(2) for the Community as Arts 85, 86, 89 and 90 (now Arts 81, 82, 85 and 86) of the EC Treaty (and so not the state aids provisions of Arts 87–89 (ex Arts 92–94)), the Merger Regulation and Arts 65 and 66 of the ECSC Treaty. Article 90 (now Art 86) does not appear in the Canadian agreement owing to the privileged position afforded Crown monopolies in Canada and so to reciprocity considerations.

[106] art II. Notification of a proposed concentration under the Merger Regulation rates special mention: art II(3) (US) and art II(4) & (6)(a) (Canada).

[107] arts III, VIII (US); arts VII, X (Canada). Exchanges of information take place at biannual meetings or by request.

[108] arts IV, V.

[109] art IV.

[110] art VI.

[111] art VII (US); art III (Canada).

[112] Agreement between the European Communities and the United States of America on the application of positive comity principles in the enforcement of their competition laws, OJ

Commission has hitherto seemed to resort to it with slightly greater enthusiasm than its American counterparts.[113] Its most noteworthy application has been the Boeing acquisition of MacDonnell Douglas, both American aircraft, defence and aerospace undertakings, and, after *Aérospatiale-Alenia/de Havilland*,[114] probably the most politically sensitive merger decision to date. The Commission found the acquisition to be a concentration with a Community dimension, originally opposed it as it would strengthen Boeing's already dominant position, and permitted it to proceed only after extracting a number of undertakings from Boeing.[115] The acquisition was also considered by the American Federal Trade Commission, which elected not to oppose it. Notification required by the Community/US agreement was duly complied with. But concerns voiced by the US government as to the harmful effects of Commission opposition to important American interests (in the defence sector) and, apparently without conscious irony, a plea that it would lead to serious loss of employment in America were met with a laconic '[t]he Commission took the above concerns into consideration to the extent consistent with Community law',[116] which, other than restricting the scope of the decision to the civil side of the takeover, gave no further (express) consideration to American interests and proceeded to test it against the criteria of the Merger Regulation. Of course, it could be argued that the Commission was overgenerous in allowing the acquisition to proceed at all – it was after all a concentration between the first (which was itself already dominant) and third largest competitors in a market of three[117] – and that the undertakings given by Boeing were not that onerous, so that the extraterritorial dimension of the acquisition, and the political pressure brought to bear, tacitly coloured the Commission's assessment. But it did nothing to ease concern over the long arm of competition rules, this time exercised in a less common direction. At the time of writing the Commission has initiated phase 2 proceedings involving a concentration between Boeing and Hughes,[118] which could renew frictions.

---

[113] To 1999 the Commission made 338 notifications, 190 of them merger related, to the American authorities whilst the latter (both the Federal Trade Commission and the Department of Justice) made 282 notifications, 184 merger related, to the Commission; EC Commission, *XXVIIIth Report on Competition Policy*, 1998, p 319. The American authorities may, and do, also notify national competition authorities within the framework of OECD recommendations.

[114] Decision 91/619, OJ 1991 L443/42.

[115] Decision 97/816 (*Boeing/MacDonnell Douglas*) OJ 1997 L336/16.

[116] para 12.

[117] The product market, being large commercial jet aircraft, was shared amongst Boeing (64 per cent), Airbus Industrie (30 per cent) and MacDonnell Douglas (6 per cent).

[118] Case M.1879 (*Boeing/Hughes*).

9.3.4 Other agreements

The Community has entered into bilateral agreements with a large number of third states addressing various stages of economic integration between the parties. In 1995 a customs union between the Community and Turkey entered into force and there are provided competition provisions identical to Articles 53 and 54 of the EEA Agreement.[119] Considerations which apply to the EEA Agreement ought to apply equally here except that the Association Council was required by 1998 to adopt rules to give effect to their implementation[120] and none has yet been adopted. Other agreements contain competition provisions, some analogous to those of the Europe Agreements[121] but none more comprehensive, and no greater legal effect is created thereby. The largest multilateral treaty to which the Community is party, the Lomé Agreement with 72 states (including South Africa and Cuba, which were granted, respectively, qualified membership and observer status in 1997 and 1998) of the African, Caribbean and Pacific (ACP) regions, most of them erstwhile colonies of the present member states,[122] addresses commercial relations between the parties, development assistance and human rights. But it contains no provisions on competition and nothing which could alter or limit the general application of Articles 81 and 82.

---

[119] Decision 1/95 of the EC–Turkey Association Council, OJ 1996 L35/1, arts 32–33.

[120] art 37.

[121] eg, Agreement on Trade, Development and Cooperation between the European Community and the Republic of South Africa, OJ 1999 L311/3, art 35: anticompetitive practices are 'incompatible with the proper functioning' of the agreement.

[122] For the most recent Lomé text see the Fourth ACP–EC Convention of Lomé (Lomé IV) as revised by the Mauritius text of 4 November 1995, *The Courier*, No 155, January/February 1996.

CHAPTER 10

Intellectual property

10.1 General

Intellectual property rights[1] encompass the rights conferred by patents, copyright and trade marks, the three most common and visible forms of intellectual property, but extends also to include industrial designs, plant breeders' rights, trade secrets, confidential information, 'know-how' and a range of related, similar rights. They are recognised, in varying degrees and in varying ways, in the laws of all countries.

A basic tension exists in competition law with the creation, recognition and enforcement of intellectual property rights. Such rights exist, or are conferred,[2] for the purpose of encouraging innovation: a presumption that the creator or inventor of a new product, process, or simply 'thing', will not expend the time, effort and (sometimes vast) cost[3] of doing so unless he enjoys a degree of monopoly in the commercial exploitation of whatever is produced. But the very existence of a monopoly right is inimical with free competition, which presupposes the free exchange of, and adaptation to, new information and ideas. A balance is always to be drawn between on the one hand the exclusive right conferred by an intellectual property right, which is a private law right but one, in order to encourage innovation, recognised to be in the public interest, and on the other the freedom of competition, which is also in the public interest.

---

[1] Traditionally reference is made to 'industrial' property (eg, the Paris Convention of 1883 for the Protection of Industrial Property, 828 UNTS 306), but the term intellectual property (describing all property the fruit of intellect) is now more commonly used in order to be all-embracing and accommodate other forms of recognised property rights (eg, copyright) which may have no industrial application.

[2] Some intellectual property rights (copyright, trade marks) come into being simply with the creation or use of the protected work or mark (although they may, for certainty, be registered), others (patents) only by conferral by a public authority.

[3] For example, in 1996, according to its trade association, average R & D expenditure upon a new pharmaceutical product which reaches the market was 400 million ECU: European Federation of Pharmaceutical Industries and Associations, *The Pharmaceutical Industry in Figures* (1998), p 10.

Although the field is expanding and developing sophistication and complexity at a rapid (some would say alarming) rate, intellectual property law has a venerable tradition. Its early development in Europe goes back to the fifteenth century, and there were significant developments at the global level on minimum standards and recognition of intellectual property rights dating back to the last century.[4] More recently, intellectual property falls within the umbrella of the World Intellectual Property Organisation (WIPO), a specialised agency of the United Nations based in Geneva, and which has promulgated a number of instruments in the field.[5] And most importantly, one of the four pillars of the World Trade Organisation created in 1994 is the Trade Related Aspects of Intellectual Property Rights (TRIPS) Agreement,[6] which brings an altogether higher degree of engagement to the field and provides for the contracting parties a high standard of protection, mutual recognition and, through the plurilateral agreement, access to GATT dispute settlement procedures and so the teeth hitherto lacking, and which forms part of Community law.[7] But whilst these are signal achievements, they address only a degree of coordination and mutual recognition of rights; the creation, recognition and enforcement of intellectual property and rights accruing to it remain almost entirely[8] within the gift of national law.

10.2 Intellectual property and the Community

The problems created by intellectual property law are particularly acute in the Community. The first is that shared by any legal system – the accommodation of the anticompetitive effects which are a necessary product of the very existence and exercise of intellectual property rights. But it is compounded by the fact that within the Community – a primary purpose of which is the creation of a single market as closely as possible replicating the conditions of a unified national market – their creation and enforcement remains essentially a matter of national law, so resulting in the

---

[4] See, eg, the Paris Union Convention of 1883 for the Protection of Industrial Property, 828 UNTS 306; the Berne Convention of 1886 for the Protection of Literary and Artistic Works, 828 UNTS 221; the Madrid Agreement of 1891 concerning the International Registration of Marks, 828 UNTS 389.

[5] See, eg, the WIPO Copyright Treaty 1996 (1997) 36 ILM 65 and the WIPO Performances and Phonograms Treaty 1996 (1997) 36 ILM 76, ratified for the Community by Council Decision 2000/ 278, OJ 2000 L89/6.

[6] Cmnd 3046.

[7] Ratified by Council Decision 94/800 OJ 1994 L336/1; see Case C-53/96 *Hermès International* v *FHT Marketing Choice* [1998] ECR I-3603.

[8] There are a very few exceptions. There is, for example, a single trade mark for the Benelux states created by the Convention Benelux en Matière de Marques de Produits, *Bulletin Benelux* 1962–2, p 57, and there is now, alongside national trade marks, a single Community trade mark; see *infra*.

coterminous application of 15, in some respects disparate, legal systems. So, national rules which reserve to the proprietor exclusive right to the exploitation of a protected process or article within its territory will also confer, expressly[9] or implicitly,[10] the right to oppose the importation of a good enjoying an identical or similar right in another member state. Thus, it is anticompetitive within the member state, but also anticompetitive in a manner which affects trade between member states and so may provoke the application of Articles 81 and/or 82 (ex Articles 85 and 86). As will be discussed, it also brings into play the Treaty rules on the free movement of goods.

A partial solution to the problem of impediments to trade created by intellectual property rights, at least within the Community, is, of course, to harmonise at Community level: to create a single Community patent, copyright, trade mark and the rest, registered centrally, uniform and recognised throughout the Community. However, this course has proved exceptionally difficult to prosecute. Notwithstanding harmonisation at international level and common legal traditions, there remain significant disparities amongst the laws of the member states regarding intellectual property. The German and Roman Dutch law systems, for example, confront serious difficulties simply in recognising a property right vested in intangibles, a fate spared Scots law only by the incursion of British statutory regulation. The moral rights (*droit moral*) of an author are well developed in the copyright law of most of the 'romance' member states, but they were recognised in the UK for the first time, and then only feebly, with the Copyright, Designs and Patents Act 1988. In some member states a trade mark, with all its attendant goodwill, may be assigned (ie, sold) independently of its proprietor undertaking – for example, Volkswagen acquired Rolls Royce in 1998,[11] but the Rolls Royce 'marque' was assigned separately to BMW – whilst in others this would be impermissible. Enforcement varies widely: whilst infringement of an intellectual property right is viewed in a number of member states as a delictual invasion of property, enforcement of the right may fall within the property or other provisions of the Civil Code, within specific or general statute law, or within various combinations thereof.[12] There is a further, built-in, problem in that Article 295 (ex Article 222) of the Treaty provides that:

---

[9] eg, in the UK, the Patents Act 1977, s 60; the Copyright, Designs and Patents Act 1988, ss 22 and 227.

[10] Trade Marks Act 1994, s 10.

[11] Case M.1283 (*Volkswagen/Rolls Royce/Cosworth*), decision of 24 August 1998.

[12] In Germany, for example, the substance, and some aspects of the protection, of an intellectual property right are laid down in statutes specific to the various rights, but their enforcement falls also under the Bürgerliches Gesetzbuch, §§ 812 I Nr. 2, 823 I and the UWG.

The Treaty shall in no way prejudice the rules in Member States governing the system of property ownership.

Neither 'property' nor the scope or breadth of national rules which is in no way prejudiced (or is 'left untouched': *läßt unberührt*) is defined, although other language versions (*le régime de la propriété*; *Eigentumsordnung*) suggest a wider rather than a narrower scope. It may be that the sole purpose of Article 295 was to reserve to the member states sovereignty in the narrow area of ownership and transfer of immovable or heritable property. Alternatively, it may have been to ensure national autonomy in determining those undertakings which would be in public ownership and which ought to be left to the private sector.[13] But whatever its intention, taken to its fullest ambit it could exempt from the application of the Treaty anything to do with intellectual property rights. At the least, Article 295 poses constitutional problems for any Community legislation in the field.

There has been some progress, both alongside and within the Community. By virtue of the European Patent Convention of 1973[14] a patent may be secured from the European Patent Office, based in Munich. This Convention is open to ratification by all European – not just Community – states. However, whilst the Convention does contain some harmonisation measures, this is not an independent European patent; rather the European Patent Office acts in effect as agent for the various national patent offices, granting individual or baskets of national patents, the property in which remains based in, and exercisable in accordance with, national patent law. A single patent, valid for the whole of the territory of the Community, is envisaged by the Community Patent Conventions of 1975 and 1989.[15] Although applying to Community member states, because these Conventions are independent of the EC Treaty, the constitutional difficulties of Article 295 are circumvented. However, both Conventions require ratification by all member states; the 1975 Convention was not ratified by some owing to constitutional difficulties, and the replacement 1989 version remains unratified, and so is not yet in force. Owing to this inertia, the Commission has now produced a Green Paper on the Community Patent[16] which proposes an approach similar to that of the Community trade mark, but it has not been met with universal enthusiasm.

---

[13] See, eg, the arguments of the French government in Case 202/88 *France v Commission* [1991] ECR I-1223. On public undertakings see Chap 7.

[14] Convention on the Grant of European Patents, TS 16 (1982).

[15] Convention for the European Patent for the Common Market, OJ 1976 L17/1; supplemented and replaced by the Luxembourg Agreement relating to Community Patents, OJ 1989 L401/9.

[16] COM (97) 314 final.

The most noteworthy and ambitious Community initiative lies in the 1994 Regulation on the Community Trade Mark,[17] by which a single trade mark (the 'Community trade mark') may be registered at the Office for Harmonisation in the Internal Market (Trade Marks and Designs),[18] based in Alicante, and is thereafter valid throughout the territory of the Community.[19] The regulation is a self-contained trade mark regime, providing rules governing definition, capacity, property rights, assignation and rights *in rem*, application, registration, duration, renewal, alteration, surrender, revocation, enforcement and settlement of disputes.[20] The Community trade mark does not replace its national counterparts – it exists alongside them – and it is this which allows it to side-step the Treaty imperative of Article 295. The question of constitutional *vires* appears to have been settled incidentally by the Court of Justice in 1994:

> The Community is competent, in the field of intellectual property, to harmonize national laws pursuant to Articles 100 and 100a [now Articles 94 and 95] and may use Article 235 [now Article 308] as the basis for creating new rights superimposed on national laws, as it did in [the trade mark regulation].[21]

A Community trade mark is created by registration only and not by use, and it cannot be registered in the face of an existing identical or potentially confusing registered trade mark in a member state, but because this is a relative, not absolute, ground for refusal, an opposition procedure must be taken by the registered proprietor.[22]

---

[17] Reg 40/94, OJ 1994 L11/1; necessary implementing legislation adopted in the UK by the Trade Marks Act 1994. See also the three implementing Commission regulations: Reg 2868/95, OJ 1995 L303/1 (the implementing regulation); Reg 2869/95, OJ 1995 L303/33 (the fees regulation); and Reg 216/96, OJ 1996 L28/11 (the Board of Appeals regulation).

[18] On the Office see Reg 40/94, arts 2, 111–39. A trade mark or design may be filed in any official language of the Community, but correspondence with the Office may be conducted only in one of its languages – English, French, German, Italian and Spanish (art 115). The lawfulness of this linguistic discrimination was challenged directly by a Dutch lawyer/trade mark agent, but she was held to have no standing to do so (Case T-107/94 *Kik* v *Council and Commission* [1995] ECR II-1717, upheld on appeal as Case C-270/95P *Kik* v *Council and Commission* [1996] ECR I-1987); she now has returned, indirectly, for another bite at the cherry: Case T-120/99 *Kik* v *Office for Harmonisation in the Internal Market*, pending.

[19] art 1(2).

[20] Any decision of the Office may be challenged before the Board of Appeal of the Community Trade Mark Office, from which appeal/review lies to the Court of First Instance (Reg 40/94, art 63). There is very real fear that actions raised under this new jurisdiction, the first of which was lodged in 1998 (Case T-163/98 *Proctor & Gamble* v *Office for Harmonisation in the Internal Market* [1999] ECR II-2383; under appeal as Case C-383/99P *Proctor & Gamble* v *Office for Harmonisation in the Internal Market*, pending) will come to flood the Court.

[21] Opinion 1/94 *re the World Trade Organisation* [1994] ECR I-5267 at 5405.

[22] Reg 40/94, art 6, art 8.

A regime similar to the Community Trade Mark has been established for plant variety rights.[23] Otherwise the achievements of harmonisation have been modest. For copyright, the duration has been rounded up to 70 years *post mortem auctoris* by a 1993 directive,[24] and certain neighbouring rights relating to rental and lending have been harmonised,[25] as have been designs[26] and national trade marks[27] in part, along with preliminary steps in legal protection in the fields of biotechnological inventions,[28] design rights in semiconductor topographies,[29] computer programs,[30] databases[31] and copyright and cable retransmission of satellite broadcasting.[32] But even these instruments address only partial harmonisation of national law, which in any event remains the source of the right. And so long as rights derive from national law, their use, such as the simple exercise of their subject matter, independently or through licences, may have the object or effect of distorting trade between member states and so fall within the prohibitions of Articles 81 and 82. It may also fall within the Treaty rules on the free movement of goods, and it is necessary to understand why this is so in order better to understand the application of the competition rules.

10.3 Intellectual property rights and the free movement of goods

Amongst the Treaty rules governing the free movement of goods is a prohibition of quantitative restrictions and any measure having an equivalent

---

[23] Reg 2100/94, OJ 1994 L227/1.

[24] Dir 93/98, OJ 1993 L290/9 (the 'duration directive'); performers' rights and those of producers of phonograms were rounded up to 50 years; implemented in the UK by the Duration in Copyright and Rights in Performance Regulations 1995, SI 1995/3297.

[25] Dir 92/100, OJ 1992 L346/61; implemented in the UK by the Copyright and Related Rights Regulations 1996, SI 1996/2967. The validity of this directive was challenged unsuccessfully in Case C-200/96 *Metronome Musik* v *Music Point Hokamp* [1998] ECR I-1953, but on grounds of compatibility with Community fundamental rights, and not of constitutionality. The Commission has proposed the adoption of a directive harmonising further certain aspects of copyright and neighbouring rights: see COM (97) 628 final.

[26] Dir 98/71, OJ 1998 L289/28.

[27] Dir 89/104, OJ 1989 L40/1, which also codifies much of the case law of the Court of Justice; implemented in the UK by the Trade Marks Act 1994. The anticipated flood of actions under the trade mark regulation regarding the definition of 'likelihood of confusion' to the consumer and related, undefined principles has already begun to make itself felt under this directive: see, eg, Case C-251/95 *Sabel* v *Puma* [1997] ECR I-6191; Case C-39/97 *Canon* v *Metro-Goldwyn-Meyer* [1998] ECR I-5507; Case C-342/97 *Lloyd Schuhfabrik* v *Klijsen* [1999] ECR I-3819; Case C-375/97 *General Motors* v *Yplon* [1999] ECR I-5421.

[28] Dir 98/44, OJ 1998 L213/13.

[29] Dir 87/54, OJ 1987 L24/36.

[30] Dir 91/250, OJ 1991 L122/42.

[31] Dir 96/9, OJ 1996 L77/20.

[32] Dir 93/83, OJ 1993 L248/15.

effect upon imports (Article 28, ex Article 30) and exports (Article 29, ex Article 34). Measures having effect equivalent to a quantitative restriction within the meaning of Article 28 are defined very broadly and cut very deeply into national rules regulating markets, including, as in the so-called *Dassonville* formula:

> [a]ll trading rules enacted by Member States which are capable of hindering, directly or indirectly, actually or potentially, intra-Community trade.[33]

Whilst they are property, intellectual property rights are not themselves goods; rather they have a character *sui generis* which can have the effect of hindering the free movement of goods (and of other Treaty freedoms).[34] The *Dassonville* formula therefore extends to embrace the opposition of imports by means of the exercise of an intellectual property right.

There is a fundamental question here which has never been properly addressed, let alone answered. Article 28 is addressed to the member states, and imposes upon public authorities – but only public authorities, albeit read very broadly – an obligation to do nothing which hinders the free movement of goods. It has never, at least to date, been recognised as creating obligations for private persons; in other words, it has no horizontal effect. The one exception is intellectual property. Quite why the exercise by a natural or legal person of an intellectual property right – a private law right – should be held to fall within the prohibition of Article 28 has never been adequately explained or considered; in *Deutsche Grammophon*,[35] the first case in which the question arose, it was simply presumed, without reasoning or justification – and in fact without being asked[36] – to be so. The Court said simply:

> [T]he essential purpose of the Treaty, which is to unite national markets into a single market … could not be attained if, under [*en vertu de*; *aufgrund*] the various legal systems of the Member States, nationals of those States were able to partition the market and bring about arbitrary discrimination or disguised restrictions on trade between Member States.[37]

True enough, but the means by which 'nationals of those States [are] able to partition the market' is addressed by Articles 81 and 82, not Article 28. The issue was raised in a subsequent case,[38] but not satisfactorily considered by the Court, although it fashioned a Delphic judgment in terms of

---

[33] Case 8/74 *Procureur du Roi* v *Dassonville* [1974] ECR 837 at 852.

[34] Cases C-92 & 326 *Phil Collins* v *Imtrat* [1993] ECR I-5145.

[35] Case 78/70 *Deutsche Grammophon* v *Metro-SB-Großmärkte* [1971] ECR 487.

[36] The questions put by the referring Hamburg court were restricted to interpretation of Arts 5, 85(1) and 86 (now Arts 10, 81(1) and 82) of the Treaty; there was no reference to Art 30 (now Art 28), which the Court took it upon itself to consider.

[37] at 500.

[38] Case 15/74 *Centrafarm* v *Sterling Drug* [1974] ECR 1147.

the exercise of an intellectual property right 'which [the proprietor] enjoys under the legislation of a Member State'.[39] The justification seems to be that it is not the exercise of the private law right which triggers the application of Article 28, but rather the necessary reliance upon the national statute which creates it and provides the monopoly right – so bringing into the measure which inhibits the free movement of goods the imprimatur and the exercise of state power;[40] this is (marginally) clearer from other language texts.[41] But it is nevertheless sophistry, for all private law rights are created by, and subject to, the legislation of a member state; it is not significantly more disingenuous to say that the conduct of bodies corporate fall within the strictures of Article 28, for they too rely upon national legislation for their existence, so that the exercise by them of any private law right – say, the right to enter into contracts – which partitions the Community market ought to fall within Article 28. Which it does not. It is submitted that it is a distortion of Article 28 to stretch the prohibition to embrace the exercise by a natural or legal person of a property right. At the least, it is inconsistent with all other existing case law on Article 28. Be that as it may, it is now well established by the Court of Justice that it does so.

In any event, the prohibition of Article 28 is not absolute. Article 30 (ex Article 36), which contains virtually the only reference in the Treaty other than Article 295 to property rights,[42] reads:

> The provisions of Articles 28 and 29 shall not preclude prohibitions or restrictions in imports, exports or goods in transit justified on grounds of ... the protection of industrial or commercial property. Such prohibitions or restrictions shall not, however, constitute a means of arbitrary discrimination or a disguised restriction on trade between Member States.

This is the one compelling argument for finding the exercise of an intellectual property right to fall within Article 28: otherwise what is the purpose of the inclusion of 'the protection of industrial or commercial property' in the derogation provision of Article 30? Being an exception to a fundamental Treaty right (Article 28), Article 30 is interpreted restrictively. The questions first confronting the Court in the context of intellectual property and the free movement of goods were therefore (a) the extent to which

---

[39] at 1163.

[40] *cf.* the Commission argument rehearsed in *Centrafarm* (at 1157–8) that it is not the attempt by the proprietor to exercise the right afforded by national law which infringes Art 28 but the judgment of a national court which gives effect to it.

[41] *cf.* the English, French and German texts in *Deutsche Grammophon* quoted above; where the English text in *Centrafarm* reads 'the exercise ... of the right which [the proprietor] enjoys under the legislation of a Member State' the French text reads 'que ... l'exercise ... du droit qui lui confère la législation d'un État membre', the Dutch (the language of the case) 'de uitoefening ... van het hem bij de wetgeving van een Lid-Staat verleende recht'.

[42] A new Art 133(4) introduced by the Amsterdam Treaty extends the application of the common commercial policy expressly to cover intellectual property.

Article 295 reserved the field to the member states, and, assuming the Treaty has some application, (b) the extent to which 'the protection of industrial or commercial property' serves to temper the prohibition of Article 28.

Both questions were answered in *Deutsche Grammophon*. There a German manufacturer of gramophone records sought to enforce the exclusive right of which it was the proprietor under German copyright law[43] in order to oppose the importation into Germany by a third party of records manufactured and sold under licence in France by its wholly owned French subsidiary. Article 81 did not apply to the licensing agreement because manufacturer and subsidiary fell within the economic entity doctrine, and the Court implied that Deutsche Grammophon did not enjoy a dominant position, so sidestepping Article 82. It therefore turned – uninvited – to consideration of Article 28. The Court said, first, that whilst Article 295 reserved to the member states authority to create and define the subject matter of an intellectual property right (the *existence* of the right), the *exercise* of the right nevertheless falls within the field of the application of the Treaty, and this existence/exercise dichotomy, whilst perhaps facile and questionable, has been echoed faithfully by the Court since. Its ramifications were best stated subsequently by the Court thus:

> Article 222 [now Article 295] cannot be interpreted as reserving to the national legislature, in relation to industrial and commercial property, the power to adopt measures which would adversely affect the principle of the free movement of goods within the common market as provided for and regulated by the Treaty.[44]

Second, the Court said that Article 30 does shield the exercise of an intellectual property right from the full vigour of Article 28, but only insofar as it is necessary for the protection of the 'specific subject matter' of the right. Beyond that the right is 'exhausted', and cannot be relied upon in a manner which inhibits the free movement of goods. This, then, is the trade off between the mutually incompatible interests of protection of rights and the free movement of goods: the proprietor continues to enjoy certain of the privileges accruing to the former, but the principle of exhaustion of rights cuts into the monopoly profits which he was previously able to wield in various member states to his maximum advantage.

The specific subject matter – the pith and substance, the essence of the right, which justifies its anticompetitive effects which are tolerated by Community law as in national law – therefore lies at the heart of the pro-

---

[43] Gesetz über Urheberrecht und verwandte Schutzrechte vom 9. September 1965 (the Urheberrechtgesetz, or URG), 1965 BGBl. I, S 1273, § 85.
[44] Case C-30/90 *Commission v United Kingdom* (Compulsory Patent Licences) [1992] ECR I-829 at 865; see also Cases C-92 & 326/92 *Phil Collins v Imtrat* [1993] ECR I-5145.

tection of intellectual property rights in Community law. It varies some-what from right to right, depending upon the subject matter. For a patent, for example, the specific subject matter is the reward of creative effort, through a guarantee to the patentee of the exclusive right to use the patented invention as a means of producing goods with a view to its com-mercial exploitation.[45] As for copyright, it was not clear that it fell within 'industrial and commercial property' at all, for in some member states it falls within a separate category of intellectual and artistic property, and so may not have been addressed by Article 30; even then it may have included simply the moral right (if recognised in national law) to claim authorship and protect a work from distortion, mutilation or alteration. Copyright is also distinct from other rights in that it does not require use in order to survive. However, the Court of Justice confirmed that industrial and com-mercial property includes the protection secured by copyright, 'notably the right to exploit commercially the marketing of the protected work',[46] and including any neighbouring right recognised in national law.[47] This is also consistent with the existence/exercise dichotomy, since the recognition or creation of copyright goes to the existence of the right (reserved to the member states), and it is only through its commercial exploitation (its exercise) that it could offend the Treaty. For trade marks, the purpose of which is to guarantee to the consumer that all products which bear it have been manufactured under the control of an undertaking to which responsi-bility for its quality may be attributed,[48] it is the guarantee that the proprietor has the exclusive right to use it, and may protect himself against competitors wishing to take advantage of its reputation or status by mar-keting goods (or services) illegally bearing it.[49] It is interesting to note that at one time the Court of Justice ventured into 'grading' various intellectual property rights and sought to relegate trade marks to the second division, saying in 1971:

> a trade-mark right is distinguishable in this context from other rights of indus-trial and commercial property, inasmuch as the interests protected by the latter are usually more important, and merit a higher degree of protection, than the interests protected by an ordinary trade-mark.[50]

But it did so without reasoning or justification, and has long since aban-doned the exercise. Having said that, there is a qualitative difference

---

[45] Case 15/74 *Centrafarm v Sterling Drug* [1974] ECR 1147.
[46] Cases 55 & 57/80 *Musik-Vertrieb v GEMA* [1981] ECR 147 at 162.
[47] Case 158/86 *Warner Brothers v Christiansen* [1988] ECR 2605.
[48] Case C-10/89 *CNL-Sucal v Hag GF* (Hag II) [1990] ECR I-3711; Cases C-427, 429 & 436/93 *Bristol-Meyers Squibb v Paranova* [1996] ECR I-3457.
[49] Case 16/74 *Centrafarm v Winthrop* [1974] ECR 1183; Case 102/77 *Hoffmann-La Roche v Centrafarm* [1978] ECR 1139; Case C-10/89, *Hag II, ibid*; Cases C-427, 429 & 436/93 *Bristol-Meyers Squibb, ibid.*
[50] Case 40/70 *Sirena v Eda* [1971] ECR 69 at 82; see also the Opinion of A-G Dutheillet de Lamothe at 87.

between the specific subject matter of, on the one hand, patents and copyright (to ensure reward for creative effort) and, on the other, trade marks (to ensure for the consumer the identity and to protect the goodwill of the proprietor)[51] which may justify differing treatment under Articles 28 and 30. This will be discussed below.

Notwithstanding these differences, most of the applicable principles are common to all intellectual property rights. The specific subject matter embraces the essence of the right, the monopoly right to the process, the article, the work or the mark in question. These are either not touched by Article 28, or, insofar as they are, they are saved by Article 30 as part of their specific subject matter. Article 28 comes into play only when the proprietor seeks commercially to exploit the protected article through sale or trade. Even then, the specific subject matter of the right has been held by the Court to extend, across all forms of intellectual property, to conferring upon the proprietor the exclusive right to place the product on a market where the right exists *for the first time* – the right of first marketing. It is then, and only then, that the right is exhausted.

So to illustrate: a proprietor applies for, and is granted, patents for a process in, say, the UK, Ireland and Denmark. British, Irish and Danish law confer the patents, define the subject matter of the right and grant to the patentee the exclusive right to exploit the process in each jurisdiction. He then begins so to do ('works' the patent) in each, or works the patent in one member state and supplies the markets in others from there. Having done so, the monopoly right in each to produce goods by means of the patented process continues to subsist; this survives as part of its specific subject matter. He also enjoys a monopoly right to introduce the goods into the market of each. But once having done so, he has exhausted his exclusive marketing right, and may no longer exercise the right provided in the legislation of each to oppose the importation – for example, by a third party buying up supplies in one of the three markets where prices are lower for purposes of re-export – of protected goods from any one of those territories. Nor, of course, may he oppose the export of the goods by a third party to a member state in which no protection exists. But he may oppose the importation from *another* territory – a fourth member state where the patent exists but the proprietor of which is a distinct and unrelated undertaking, and so by definition he has not exhausted his right there. So, Article 30 permits the exercise of intellectual property rights to partition the Community market, but not as between or amongst member states in which the proprietor of the right is the same undertaking or group of undertakings (in the sense of the economic entity doctrine). And it bears emphasising here that whilst exercise of the right in this manner may

---

[51] See, eg, the discussion of Laddie J in *Zino Davidoff* v *A & G Imports* [1999] 3 All ER 711 (Ch).

escape the prohibition of Article 28, it does not mean that it escapes the prohibitions of Articles 81 and/or 82.

This has a number of permutations and ramifications. First, exhaustion of the right applies to those goods which have been marketed by the proprietor within those Community member states where the right exists. The marketing by the proprietor within the Community of, for example, a batch of goods protected by his trade mark exhausts his marketing rights in respect of that batch but not in respect of an identically marked batch marketed by him in a non-Community country, importation of which he may continue to oppose.[52] Second, from the beginning the Court has stressed that the specific subject matter of the right is exhausted following first marketing by the proprietor *or with his consent*. So, Article 28 cannot be circumvented by licensing: if the process is worked or the product marketed in any member state by licence from the proprietor, even where the licensee is an unconnected, independent undertaking, the right is as exhausted as if he had done so himself. This principle came subsequently to be refined by the Court to require that it be the proprietor's *free* consent. So, if, as in the above illustration for example, the proprietor of the British, Irish and Danish patents declines to work the patent or sell products made by it in the UK for a period of more than three years (which he may do, for example, as a commercial choice if given the nature and circumstances of the good and the market, British prices would be significantly lower than those obtaining in Ireland and Denmark, which prices could not be sustained in the face of parallel imports from the UK) the Comptroller of Patents may grant to another party a compulsory licence to work the patent.[53] However, in these circumstances the proprietor has not consented freely to the exhaustion of his British right, and may continue to assert his Irish and Danish rights to oppose the importation of goods produced in the UK under the compulsory licence.[54] This

---

[52] Case C-173/98 *Sebago* v *GB-Unic* [1999] ECR I-4103; see *infra*.

[53] Patents Act 1977, ss 48–50. However, the power of the Comptroller to grant a compulsory licence on the ground of insufficiency of exploitation within the UK (s 48(3)) has been declared by the Court of Justice to be a breach of Art 30 (now Art 28) where demand may be met by imports from other member states: Case C-30/90 *Commission* v *United Kingdom* [1992] ECR I-829. Similar Italian legislation (Decreto reale 1127 del 29 giugno 1934, 1939 GURI N° 189, artt 52, 53) met the same fate: Case C-235/89 *Commission* v *Italy* [1992] ECR I-777.

[54] Case 19/84 *Pharmon* v *Hoechst* [1985] ECR 2281. This also applies if the proprietor works the patent in the UK but only to an extent insufficient to supply the market, in which case the Comptroller may grant a compulsory licence for insufficiency of exploitation (subject to Case C-30/90 *Commission* v *United Kingdom, ibid*). The proprietor may no longer oppose the importation into Ireland or Denmark of goods he has produced in the UK, but may do so for goods produced under the compulsory licence. A compulsory licence will therefore help stabilise the home market in member states in which the protected goods are relatively cheap and so much of the demand is from parallel traders seeking to supply export markets.

applies equally to the opposition of imports from a member state where the proprietor markets the goods owing to any legal obligation to do so;[55] but there must be a genuine legal obligation: marketing by virtue of a perceived ethical obligation (for example, to keep a market sufficiently supplied with an important pharmaceutical product) is not enough.[56]

Having said that, the principle of exhaustion applies as regards imports from a member state in which the proprietor has marketed his goods but in which no intellectual property protection is granted or recognised – and so, strictly speaking, no right has been exhausted because none there exists. This has arisen primarily in the context of sale of pharmaceutical products in the Mediterranean member states which, until recently and for public policy reasons, did not grant patent protection to them. Where the proprietor of a right in another member state nevertheless elects freely, and in full knowledge of all relevant circumstances, to market the protected goods in the unprotected market, he must accept the consequences and cannot oppose the re-importation of those goods[57] – although he can oppose the importation of goods marketed there, unhindered as he is, by another party proprietor of an analogous right in another member state or by a domestic manufacturer.[58] But it is important to distinguish the rights which have been exhausted. This has particular resonance in the (remaining) disparity of protection given neighbouring rights in copyright amongst the member states. So, where a proprietor of a Danish copyright markets video cassettes in another member state (the United Kingdom) in which there is no protection for the hiring out of the cassette – that is, a purchaser may hire it out without the proprietor's consent – he may no longer oppose the importation from the UK into Denmark of the cassette for marketing, but he may continue to assert the neighbouring right provided in Danish law[59] to oppose its hiring out without his consent;[60] and additional royalties provided by French law[61] for the public performance of sound recordings may be imposed even if the sound recordings were imported from a member

---

[55] Cases C-297–8/95 *Merck* v *Primecrown* (Merck II) [1996] ECR I-6285.

[56] Cases C-297–8/95, *Merck II, ibid.*

[57] Case 187/80 *Merck* v *Stephar* (Merck I) [1981] ECR 2063. The English High Court subsequently urged the Court of Justice to reconsider the *ratio* in *Merck I*, but the Court declined to do so: Cases C-267–8/95, *Merck II, ibid.*

[58] Case 24/67 *Park, Davis* v *Probel* [1968] ECR 55.

[59] Lov nr. 158 af 31. maj 1961 (Lov om ophavsret), §§ 2, 23.

[60] Case 158/86 *Warner Brothers* v *Christiansen* [1988] ECR 2605; see also Case C-61/97 *Foreningen af danske Videogramdistributorer* v *Laserdisken* [1998] ECR I-5171. Partial protection is now afforded in UK law by virtue of the Copyright, Designs and Patents Act 1988, ss 16–18.

[61] Loi n° 57–298 du 11 mars 1957 sur la propriété littéraire et artistique, JORF du 14 mars 1957, arts 30, 31.

state where no such royalty is exigible.[62] In all events, rules of fair marketing continue to apply.[63]

Thus, so long as a proprietor holds a right in a number of member states, he is seriously constrained by the exhaustion doctrine in the exercise of traditional rights in the marketing of the protected goods. Not assisted by licensing, the only way he can avoid this is assignment/assignation of the right. Even this was not always so. In *Hag I*,[64] the proprietor of a Benelux trade mark sought to oppose the importation into Belgium and Luxembourg from Germany of goods bearing an identical mark. In other circumstances this would have been a lawful exercise of the trade mark right, as the Belgian proprietor and the German proprietor/exporter were wholly distinct and independent undertakings. However, the Belgian proprietor had acquired title to the Belgian/Luxembourg, and subsequently Benelux, mark only after it had been sequestrated after the war as enemy property. The Court held that even though the identical marks were owned by distinct undertakings, the fact that they had once been in common ownership – even if before the entry into force of the Treaty – meant that the proprietor no longer enjoyed the right to oppose importation of the marked goods. This 'common origin principle' may have been an attempt to pre-empt undertakings from skirting the prohibition of Article 28 by the device of assigning the right; but the Court supplied no reasoning to justify it,[65] it flies in the face of the specific subject matter of a trade mark, and was roundly criticised, not least in a blistering opinion of Advocate-General Jacobs in its follow-up case, *Hag II*.[66] In *Hag II* the reverse situation obtained: the German proprietor sought to oppose the importation from Belgium of marked goods sold there by the (successor to the) Benelux proprietor of the trade mark. The Court considered the specific subject matter of a trade mark, for the first time expressly overruled a previous judgment ('the Court deems it necessary to reconsider the interpretation given in [*Hag I*]')[67] and reversed itself. It did not in *Hag II* overtly abandon the common origin principle; rather it limited its reasoning to the fact that the German proprietor had not freely consented to the assignment of the right. The *coup de grâce* was delivered in a subsequent case in which a trade mark had been freely assigned to an independent undertaking.[68] Thus the common origin principle, which in any event was never applied outwith the area of trade marks, is dead. So, a proprietor

---

[62] Case 402/85 *Basset* v *SACEM* [1977] ECR 1745.

[63] Case 58/80 *Dansk Supermarked* v *Imerco* [1981] ECR 181.

[64] Case 192/72 *van Zuylen Frères* v *Hag* [1974] ECR 731.

[65] It sought to do so subsequently, with only partial success, in Case 119/75 *Terrapin* v *Terranova* [1976] ECR 1039.

[66] Case C-10/89 *CNL Sucal* v *HAG AG* [1990] ECR I-3711.

[67] at 3757.

[68] Case C-9/93 *IHT Internationale Heiztechnik* v *Ideal Standard* [1994] ECR I-2789.

may re-erect barriers to trade and reacquire a right of opposition by the assignment of the right in another member state. Or more accurately, he may do so without infringing Article 28. Assignment may well result in an infringement of Article 81.

There remain two problems unique to trade marks. First, the importation of goods bearing an identical mark in two member states may be opposed by the (independent) proprietors in each in order to protect the specific subject matter of their rights. A difficult problem arises as to whether the proprietor may also oppose the importation of goods marketed in one member state under a mark which is not identical but is, perhaps quite innocently, similar. He may do so, subject to the test, which in English and Scots law would fall within the common law of passing off, of a likelihood of confusion amongst consumers.[69] This gives rise to some disequilibrium, as Community law does not require a strict interpretation of the risk of confusion;[70] it is a question of fact, and what is confusingly similar may vary from member state to member state owing to differences in language and tradition. There is no better example than that cited by Advocate-General Jacobs in his Opinion in *Hag II*, in which the Bundespatentgericht found a likelihood of confusion between the marks 'Lucky Whip' and 'Schöller-Nucki'[71] – 'a decision that seems to postulate a body of consumers afflicted with an acute form of dyslexia'.[72] So it may be that where two similar but not identical marks exist in two member states, the proprietor of one could oppose importation of the marked goods because he could show a likelihood of confusion amongst consumers, but the proprietor of the other could not because he could show no such likelihood. This is perhaps not fair, but it is the present law. The second problem is that of repackaging or relabelling. A parallel trader may wish to buy up goods marked and marketed by the proprietor of a trade mark in one member state in order to undercut the price offered by the latter in another member state. But in order to do so he may be required, or wish, to repackage or relabel the goods, either because he must do so by virtue of

---

[69] Case 119/75 *Terrapin* v *Terranova* [1976] ECR 1039; Case C-317/91 *Deutsche Renault* v *Audi* [1993] ECR I-6227; Case C-251/95 *Sabel* v *Puma* [1997] ECR I-6191; Case C-255/97 *Pfeiffer Großhandel* v *Löwa Warenhandel* [1999] ECR I-2835. The likelihood of confusion varies with the similarity of the marks and the similarity of the goods to which they are affixed. The test has been adopted for the opposition of a trade mark in both national law (by virtue of Dir 89/104, OJ 1989 L40/1) and in the Community Trade Mark Regulation (Reg 40/94, OJ 1994 L11/1, art 8).

[70] Case C-317/91, *Deutsche Renault, ibid.*

[71] Beschluß vom 28. März 1973, GRUR 1975, S 74.

[72] Case C-10/89 *CNL Sucal* v *HAG AG* [1990] ECR I-3711 at 3740. It is fairer and more accurate to read into a judgment such as this not that German consumers are not discerning, but, given the priority which German law attaches to consumer protection, a statutory direction to German judges to deem them not to be.

national law – simply a requirement, for example, that any external instructions be in the language(s) of the member state – or he may see some advantage in doing so from his view of the attractiveness of the packaging to the consumer. Yet if the purpose (and specific subject matter) of a trade mark is to guarantee to the consumer that all products which bear it have been manufactured under the control of an undertaking to which responsibility for its quality may be attributed, does its specific subject matter extend to the appearance of the product in the shop? The Court of Justice has held that the proprietor may oppose any use of the trade mark which is liable to impair the guarantee of origin;[73] where this is not the case repackaging and/or relabelling by a third party is permissible, even to the extent of replacing the trade mark used in the member state of export with that used in the member state of import if it is objectively necessary in order to be marketed in the latter,[74] but only under restricted conditions.[75] A third party reseller may also use the trade mark freely for purposes of advertising the availability of the marked goods unless it would seriously damage the reputation of the mark or of the goods,[76] and a service provider (a garage business) may without consent use a motor manufacturer's trade mark to advertise the availability of repair services unless it would create the false impression that there is a commercial connection between the garage and the trade mark proprietor.[77]

A final point in the context of Article 28 is that, by its text, it requires an impediment to the free movement of goods 'between Member States'. Therefore the exercise of an intellectual property right to oppose the importation of a protected good into a Community member state from a non-member state, even if the right is in common ownership and it has been exhausted in each, will not infringe Article 28,[78] and the Court of Justice said in *Silhouette* that it is contrary to the requirements of Community law, at least for trade marks, for a member state to provide otherwise (that is, for national law to recognise the 'international exhaustion' of the right).[79] The judgment turned solely upon the interpretation of

---

[73] Case 102/77 *Hoffmann-La Roche v Centrafarm* [1978] ECR 1139; Cases C-427, 429 & 436/93 *Bristol-Meyers Squibb v Paranova* [1996] ECR I-3457.

[74] Case C-379/97 *Pharmacia & Upjohn v Paranova* [1999] ECR I-6927.

[75] eg, Case 1/81 *Pfizer v Eurim-Pharm* [1981] ECR 2913; Case C-232/94 *MPA Pharma v Rhône-Poulenc Pharma* [1996] ECR I-3671; Case C-349/95 *Frits Loendersloot v Ballantine & Son* [1997] ECR I-6227; Case C-379/97 *Pharmacia & Upjohn*, ibid.

[76] Case C-337/95 *Christian Dior v Evora* [1997] ECR I-6013.

[77] Case C-63/97 *Bayerische Motorenwerke v Deenik* [1999] ECR I-905, this by virtue of the trade mark directive, Dir 89/104, OJ 1989 L40/1.

[78] Case 51/75 *EMI v CBS* [1976] ECR 811; Case C-355/96 *Silhouette International Schmied v Hartlauer* [1998] ECR I-4799; Case C-173/98 *Sebago v GB-Unic* [1999] ECR I-4103.

[79] Case C-355/96 *Silhouette*, ibid, affirmed in Case C-173/98 *Sebago*, ibid.

a provision of the trade marks directive,[80] for international exhaustion does not compromise the specific subject matter of a trade mark. Indeed, according to Mr Justice Laddie in the English High Court, *Silhouette*

> has bestowed on a trade mark owner a parasitic right to interfere with the distribution of goods which bears little or no relationship to the proper function of a trade mark right.[81]

It was not a complete surprise, as the Bundesgerichtshof had earlier reached the same conclusion as to the correct interpretation of the German law giving effect to the directive, contrary to established German principles of international exhaustion.[82] *Silhouette* nevertheless engendered a voluble collective sigh of relief from proprietors of internationally recognised branded goods, for it abruptly curtailed the growing grey market of goods imported from (much) cheaper third countries into those member states which did recognise international exhaustion and then leaking into other member states. The 'Community exhaustion' rule applies even where the non-member state has concluded a free trade association with the Community.[83] The exception is the EEA, for Article 11 of the EEA Agreement is identical *mutatis mutandis* to Article 28, the *acquis communautaire* at the time of the signing of the Agreement was expressly incorporated into EEA law,[84] and a protocol to the Agreement extends exhaustion of rights throughout the territory of the EEA.[85] The exhaustion principle therefore now doubtless applies in the case of imports into a Community member state from an EFTA member state party to the EEA Agreement, and vice-versa, but it has not yet been definitively tested before either the Court of Justice or the EFTA Court.[86] A small crack in the importation of grey markets goods has therefore already opened up here, for whilst the Court of Justice said in *Silhouette*[87] that Community member states may not adopt a rule of international exhaustion, the EFTA Court said in *Mag Instruments*[88] (decided prior to *Silhouette*) that EFTA

---

[80] Dir 89/104, OJ 1989 L40/1, art 7.

[81] *Zino Davidoff* v *A & G Imports* [1999] 3 All ER 711 (Ch) at 724.

[82] BGH, 14. Dezember 1995, BGHZ 131, 308 (*Internationale Erschöpfung des Zeichenrechts*).

[83] Case 270/80 *Polydor* v *Harlequin Records* [1982] ECR 329.

[84] EEA Agreement, art 6.

[85] Protocol 28, art 2.

[86] It was affirmed *obiter* in Case C-355/96 *Silhouette International Schmied* v *Hartlauer* [1998] ECR I-4799 and Case C-173/98 *Sebago* v *GB-Unic* [1999] ECR I-4103, in particular in the opinions of A-G Jacobs, and in Case E-2/97 *Mag Instrument Inc* v *California Trading Co Norway, Ulsteen* [1997] EFTA CR 127 and Case E-1/98 *Norway* v *Astra Norge* [1998] EFTA CR 140. As to the EEA Agreement, see p 291–5 *supra*.

[87] Case C-355/96 *Silhouette, ibid.*

[88] Case E-2/97 *Mag Instrument Inc* v *California Trading Co Norway, Ulsteen* [1997] EFTA CR 127.

member states may do so. However, as the EEA Treaty applies only to goods which have their origin within the EEA[89] this does little to force the door open. A potentially much larger crack has developed as a result of the judgment of the English High Court in *Zino Davidoff*,[90] in which it said that where a proprietor markets protected goods in a third country (Singapore) the law of which allows restrictions to be imposed upon the further marketing or use of the goods but the proprietor imposes no such restrictions, this may be taken as consent to marketing in any country, including Community member states, and as a result the right to oppose importation is exhausted. As this is, to put it at its lowest, an iconoclastic view of consent, the question has been referred to the Court of Justice for a preliminary ruling under Article 234 of the Treaty.[91] An ancillary attack on *Silhouette* has been engineered by the sale of grey market Levi jeans by Tesco supermarkets.[92]

10.4 The competition rules

The points of tangency between Community law and the exercise of intellectual property rights first fell for consideration by the Court of Justice in the context of Articles 81 and 82. This was simply because the competition rules were fully effective from the early 1960s whilst the prohibition in Article 28 of measures having equivalent effect to a quantitative restriction was effective only from the end of the final transition period (1970).[93] However, there has been a significant degree of cross fertilisation between Articles 28/30 on the one hand and Articles 81/82 on the other. In particular, the Court has come to rely upon the principles of specific subject matter, developed primarily in the context of the former, as an aid to the interpretation of the latter. Thus,

> Article 36 [now Article 30], although it appears in the Chapter of the Treaty dealing with quantitative restrictions on trade between Member States, is based on a principle equally applicable to the question of competition.[94]

And

> [u]nder Article 36, as it has been interpreted by the Court of Justice in the light of the objectives pursued by Articles 85 and 86 ..., only those restrictions on

---

[89] EEA Agreement, art 8(2).
[90] *Zino Davidoff* v *A & G Imports* [1999] 3 All ER 711 (Ch).
[91] Case C-414/99 *Zino Davidoff* v *A & G Imports*, pending.
[92] Cases C-415 & 416/99 *Levi Strauss* v *Tesco*, pending.
[93] Case 74/76 *Ianelli* v *Meroni* [1977] ECR 557.
[94] Case 40/70 *Sirena* v *Eda* [1971] ECR 69 at 81.

freedom of competition … which are inherent in the protection of the actual sub-stance of the intellectual property right are permitted in Community law.[95]

In other words, the exercise of an intellectual property right in a manner which affects competition will not infringe Articles 81 and 82 if it falls within the specific subject matter of the right. Beyond that, it may do so. So, the exercise of an intellectual property right in a manner which is not saved by the specific subject matter test will fall foul of Article 28, and may *also* fall foul of Articles 81 and/or 82. At the same time, there are circum-stances in which the exercise of the right may skirt the prohibition of Article 28 and fall to be considered in the context of Articles 81 and 82 alone. There are two important points to bear in mind in the application of these two prohibitions: first, whilst Articles 28, 81 and 82 are all directly effective and so rights arising therefrom may be enforced before a national court, infringements of Articles 81 and 82 may also be pursued by the Commission under powers conferred upon it by Regulation 17; it has no equivalent power directly to pursue an infringement of Article 28 in the context of the exercise by an undertaking of an intellectual property right. Second, the application of Articles 81 and 82 is subject to relatively supple principles of *de minimis* and the rule of reason and, in the case of Article 81, the possibility of exemption, which do not apply in the context of Article 28.[96] It is also important to bear in mind that Article 28 will fre-quently apply to situations in which third parties seek to trade in protected goods marketed by the proprietor or with his consent, whilst Articles 81 and 82 will often apply to the manner in which, and restrictions upon, which, the proprietor markets and/or distributes the goods. It does a paral-lel trader seeking to undercut an 'official' distribution network little good to have the right to trade in the goods if he cannot acquire them from a supplier in the first place.

10.4.1 Article 81

The application of the competition rules to intellectual property rights was first considered in *Consten & Grundig*.[97] There, it will be recalled, a con-tract sought to secure to a French distributor (Consten) absolute territorial protection for the distribution of a German manufacturer's (Grundig) products in France. It did so by means of express terms and (re-)export

---

[95] Case T-69/89 *RTE* v *Commission* [1991] ECR II-485 at 518–19; Case T-70/89 *BBC* v *Commission* [1991] ECR II-535 at 562–3; Case T-76/89 *ITP* v *Commission* [1991] ECR II-575 at 601.

[96] There *is* what is sometimes called a rule of reason in Art 28 deriving from the principles of Case 120/78 *Rewe Zentrale* v *Bundesmonopolverwaltung für Branntwein* (Cassis de Dijon) [1979] ECR 649, but as it applies only to indistinctly applicable measures it cannot apply to the exercise of an intellectual property right.

[97] Cases 56 & 58/64 *Consten & Grundig* v *EEC Commission* [1966] ECR 299.

bans imposed upon Grundig's distributors and wholesalers elsewhere; but it did so also by means of a licence which authorised the exclusive use by Consten of Grundig's trade mark in France.[98] The Commission condemned this as a breach of Article 81(1),[99] and both parties sought the annulment of the Commission decision. The Court considered Article 295 (ex Article 222) and set it aside by reasoning which was to become the existence–exercise dichotomy enunciated subsequently in *Deutsche Grammophon*[100] thus:

> The injunction contained in ... the contested decision to refrain from using rights in national trade-mark law in order to set an obstacle in the way of parallel imports does not affect the grant of those rights but only limits their exercise to the extent necessary to give effect to the prohibition under Article 85(1).[101]

The Court considered the licensing of the trade mark a material factor in the attempt to ensure for Consten absolute territorial exclusivity, which is what caused the agreement to fall foul of Article 81(1):

> [T]he registration in France by Consten of the ... trade mark ... is intended to increase the protection inherent in the disputed agreement, against the risk of parallel imports into France of Grundig products, by adding the protection deriving from the law on industrial property rights ....
>
> Consten's right under the contract to the exclusive user [*sic*] in France of the ... trade mark ... is intended to make it possible to keep under surveillance and to place an obstacle in the way of parallel imports. Thus, the agreement by which Grundig ... authorized Consten to register it in France in its own name tends to restrict competition ....
>
> That agreement therefore is one which may be caught by the prohibition in Article 85(1). The prohibition would be ineffective if Consten could continue to use the trade-mark to achieve the same object as that pursued by the agreement which has been held to be unlawful.[102]

---

[98] Technically it was not a licensing agreement but temporary assignment of an international trade mark recognised in France, by which Grundig agreed to allow Consten to register the trade mark in its own name, and Consten agreed to transfer the mark to Grundig or cancel its registration upon ceasing to be its exclusive French distributor.

[99] Directive (*sic*) 64/566, JO 1964, 2545; see Chapter 3, n 262.

[100] Case 78/70 *Deutsche Grammophon* v *Metro-SB-Großmärkte* [1971] ECR 487; see p 306 *supra*.

[101] Cases 56 & 58/64 *Consten & Grundig* at 345. The existence–exercise dichotomy was more fully absorbed in the context of the competition rules in Case 40/70 *Sirena* v *Eda* [1971] ECR 69 at 81:

> [E]ven if the rights recognized by the legislation of a Member State on the subject of industrial and commercial property are not affected, so far as their existence is concerned, by Articles 85 and 86 of the Treaty, their exercise may still fall under the prohibitions imposed by those provisions.

[102] at 343, 345.

Consten & Grundig was, of course, a vertical arrangement between manufacturer and distributor. So it was established from the start that a licensing agreement – which would come subsequently to attract the exhaustion of rights doctrine (first marketing by a proprietor or 'with his consent') and so the application of Article 28 – could fall within the prohibition of Article 81(1), vertical though it may be. This is in keeping with the general principles of Article 81. But it may also apply to horizontal agreements or concerted practices the subjects of which are intellectual property rights, and some which may not be caught by Article 28.

It will be recalled that the proprietor of an intellectual property right may oppose the importation of protected goods from a member state in which he has not exhausted his right – where, normally, the right is owned and exercised by an unconnected proprietor – without infringing Article 28. With the unlamented passing of the common origin principle, a proprietor may also exercise that right to oppose the importation of the protected goods from another member state in which he was proprietor but in which he has assigned the right to an independent third party, again without infringing Article 28. But in such circumstances there is a likelihood that he may infringe Article 81(1). The Court of Justice said in *Sirena* v *Eda*:

> [T]he exercise of that [trade mark] right might fall within the ambit of the prohibitions contained in the Treaty each time it manifests itself as the subject, the means or the result of a restrictive practice ....
>
> Such situations may in particular arise from restrictive agreements between proprietors of trade-marks or their successors in title enabling them to prevent imports from other Member States. If the combination of assignments to different users of national trade-marks protecting the same product has the result of re-enacting impenetrable frontiers between the Member States, such practice may well affect trade between Member States, and distort competition in the Common Market ....
>
> Article 85(1), therefore, is applicable to the extent to which trade-mark rights are invoked so as to prevent imports of products which originate in different Member States, which bear the same trade-mark by virtue of the fact that the proprietors have acquired it, or the right to use it, whether by agreements between themselves or by agreements with third parties.[103]

The *Sirena* formula of the exercise of an intellectual property right as 'the subject [or object or purpose], the means or the result [or consequence] of a[n agreement or] restrictive practice' has been used repeatedly by the Court.[104] *Sirena* involved the assignment of a trade mark long before the

---

[103] Case 40/70 [1971] ECR 69 at 82–3.

[104] eg, Case 15/74 *Centrafarm* v *Sterling Drug* [1974] ECR 1147 at 1167; Case 51/75 *EMI* v *CBS* [1976] ECR 811 at 848; Case 258/78 *Nungesser* v *Commission* (Maize Seeds) [1982] ECR 2015 at 2061; Case 144/81 *Keurkoop* v *Nancy Kean Gifts* [1982] ECR 2853 at 2873.

entry into force of the Treaty, and so could not possibly have had the object or purpose of circumventing it, yet the prohibition of Article 81(1) applied so long as 'they [the restrictive practices] continue to produce their effects'.[105] It also confirmed by necessary implication that assignment of a right is an agreement within the meaning of Article 81. If it can be shown that the purpose of assignment was to resuscitate the right to partition the market, there is a strong likelihood that an attempt to do so may infringe Article 81(1). Equally, if independent undertakings simultaneously or successively file for an identical or similar intellectual property right in various member states there is the whiff of an agreement or concerted practice the object, purpose and effect of which is to partition markets.[106] However, the mere exercise of the right is not enough to infringe Article 81(1): it is further necessary to show an intention, by agreement or concerted practice, between the parties to do so.[107] As the Court said early on:

> [T]he exercise of [intellectual property] rights cannot of itself fall ... under Article 85(1), in the absence of any agreement, decision or concerted practice prohibited by that provision.[108]

And subsequently, in the context of voluntary assignment of a trade mark:

> [W]here undertakings independent of each other make trade-mark assignments following a market-sharing agreement, the prohibition of anti-competitive agreements under Article 85 applies and assignments which give effect to that agreement are consequently void. However, ... that rule and the accompanying sanction cannot be applied mechanically to every assignment. Before a trade-mark assignment can be treated as giving effect to an agreement prohibited under Article 85, it is necessary to analyse the context, the commitments underlying the agreement, the intention of the parties and the consideration for the assignment.[109]

So, the standard analysis of the restrictive effects of agreements and concerted practices applies.[110] The difficulty here is that if the object (or effect) of a contract by which a trade mark is assigned is found to be contrary to Article 81(1), the contract is, in accordance with Article 81(2), void. This could have serious repercussions for recovery of or restitution in property or assets which passed with the (purported) contract.

Article 81 may also apply to agreements, the subject of which is the exercise of intellectual property rights, between Community and

---

[105] at 83. See also Case 51/75 *EMI* v *CBS, ibid.*
[106] Case 144/81 *Keurkoop* v *Nancy Kean Gifts* [1982] ECR 2853.
[107] Case 51/75 *EMI* v *CBS* [1976] ECR 811.
[108] Case 24/67 *Park, Davis* v *Probel* [1968] ECR 55 at 72.
[109] Case C-9/93 *IHT Internationale Heiztechnik* v *Ideal Standard* [1994] ECR I-2789 at 2855.
[110] See generally Chap 3.

non-Community undertakings which fall outwith the prohibition of Article 28 because they do not affect trade between member states. This is particularly so where such an agreement isolates the Community market and reduces the supply of imports of the protected goods, producing a knock-on effect in intra-Community trade;[111] such effect is more likely to be present if the third country has entered into an association agreement with the Community which diminishes or prohibits customs duties and other barriers to trade and so increases the fluidity of markets and the likelihood of traders seeking to supply the Community market from outwith the Community.[112] But in keeping with general principles, the effect upon intra-Community trade must be appreciable.[113] Thus, a licensing agreement between a German patentee and a Japanese company which contained an export prohibition did not offend Article 81(1) because even in the absence of the prohibition there was no real likelihood of the protected goods being exported to the Community.[114] But a prohibition of active sales outwith the contract territory contained in a trade mark and know-how licensing agreement between a Canadian brewer and a British licensee did, at least in the view of the Commission, offend Article 81(1), for the large production capacity of the latter would otherwise enable it to supply other Community markets to an appreciable extent.[115] However, the application of Article 81 and not only of Article 28 took a serious knock when the Court found in *Silhouette*[116] that Community law does not permit national law to recognise international exhaustion of a trade mark. So, hitherto the thriving grey market in imported branded goods required producers to risk restrictive distribution agreements in order to staunch the flow. Following *Silhouette*, and more recently *Sebago*,[117] they may rely simply upon the specific subject matter of the right to oppose imports and need no longer resort to such agreements to achieve the same end. In this context *Silhouette* therefore not only neutered Article 28 but made Article 81 in large measure redundant.

Finally, whilst repackaging or relabelling of trade marked goods may lawfully be opposed in order to protect the specific subject matter of the right under Article 30, the competition rules may nevertheless apply if it

---

[111] Case 51/75 *EMI* v *CBS* [1976] ECR 811.

[112] Although not an intellectual property case, see discussion of the issue in the opinion of A-G Tesauro in Case C-306/96 *Javico International* v *Yves Saint Laurent Parfums* [1998] ECR I-1983.

[113] Case 28/77 *Tepea* v *Commission* [1978] ECR 1391; Case 27/87 *Erauw-Jacquery* v *La Hesbignonne* [1988] ECR 1919.

[114] Decision 72/238 (*Raymond/Nagoya*) JO 1972 L143/39 (negative clearance granted); *cf.* Decision 88/541 (*BBC Brown Boveri/NGK Insulators*) OJ 1988 L301/68.

[115] Decision 90/186 (*Moosehead/Whitbread*) OJ 1990 L100/32.

[116] Case C-355/96 *Silhouette International Schmied* v *Hartlauer* [1998] ECR I-4799.

[117] Case C-173/98 *Sebago* v *GB-Unic* [1999] ECR I-4103.

can be shown that the proprietor does so in order to partition markets – for example, to assist in the identification of suppliers to parallel traders in order to combat parallel imports.[118]

Licensing

The most common type of vertical agreement addressing the exercise of intellectual property rights is a licensing agreement, whereby the proprietor (the licensor) confers upon another party (the licensee) some or all of the rights accruing to the right – usually the monopoly right to produce the protected product and market it within a contract territory. Common to the field of patents, licensing agreements are also used to govern transfer of know-how and the use of trade marks, design rights and copyright. Generally, patent licensing agreements are pro-competitive: they permit the licensee to do something which would otherwise be unlawful, they allow the proprietor a reasonable return on his right whilst at the same time improving the efficiency of the manufacture and distribution of the protected good – and so new technology and/or new products – throughout a number of states and so promote market integration. But some conditions imposed by such an agreement may be objectionable. Some aspects of a standard licensing agreement – generally the payment of royalties, quality control, confidentiality provisions, a prohibition of sublicensing, obligations upon the licensee to inform and assist the licensor in the event of infringement, marking of the goods, post-termination restraints where an intellectual property right remains in force, for example – do not fall within the prohibition of Article 81(1) because they do not distort competition within the meaning of Article 81(1). Others may do but are saved as falling within the specific subject matter of the right: a prohibition of sale or export contained in a licence from a proprietor of a plant breeder's right addressing propagation only, not marketing, of basic seeds, for example, is doubtless a distortion of competition but falls outwith the prohibition of Article 81(1) as being an integral part of the breeder's right.[119] Still others may go beyond that, but are exempted by block exemption. It is only beyond that point that a licensing agreement (absent an individual exemption)[120] risks being found to be void. In *Windsurfing*,[121] for example, the Court of Justice found a number of provisions contained in a licensing

---

[118] Case C-349/95 *Frits Loendersloot v Ballantine & Son* [1997] ECR I-6227.

[119] Case 27/87 *Erauw-Jacquery v La Hesbignonne* [1988] ECR 1919.

[120] art 4(2) of Reg 17 exempts from the requirement of notification provisions of a licensing agreement which impose restrictions upon the methods of exploitation of an intellectual property right (see p 12 *supra*). However, this is otiose, as such restrictions probably fall within the specific subject matter of the right (Reg 17 having been adopted before the development of the case law on specific subject matter) and so require no exemption.

[121] Case 193/83 *Windsurfing International v Commission* [1986] ECR 611.

agreement – tying unpatented goods to the patented good, royalties computed on the basis of sales of final assembled (unpatented and patented) products, fixing of patent attribution and logo on unpatented goods, termination in the event of manufacture by a licensee in a territory not covered by the patent, and a no challenge clause – to be ancillary restraints beyond the specific subject matter of the right and so, no block exemption then having been adopted (which in any event would not have saved many of these provisions), prohibited by Article 81(1).

The principal judgment of the Court of Justice involving territorial restrictions in licensing is that in the *Nungesser*, or *Maize Seeds*, case.[122] A French institute had developed certain varieties of maize seeds for which it held plant breeders' rights in French and German law.[123] By a series of agreements the German rights were partly assigned and partly licensed to a German undertaking, with whom the French institute undertook to ensure absolute territorial exclusivity for the production and sale of the seeds in Germany. The Commission found the agreements to offend Article 81(1) insofar as they restrained the French institute (or any of its other licensees) from (a) licensing another German undertaking, (b) producing or marketing the seeds in Germany themselves, and (c) exporting to Germany without authorisation of the German licensee.[124] On review, the Court of Justice annulled the Commission's decision on points (a) and (b), but not on (c). It distinguished between exclusive licensing agreements which purport to ensure for the licensee absolute territorial protection, and 'open' exclusive licensing agreements, which do not ('a licence which does not affect the position of third parties such as parallel importers and licensees for other territories'),[125] took the view that without the minimum protection of the latter a licensee would be deterred from accepting the risk of manufacturing and marketing a newly developed product, and so such an open agreement falls outwith the prohibition of Article 81(1). This is entirely consistent with and analogous to the rule of reason approach adopted in *Technique Minière*.[126] It is apparent that considerations of the benefits of the dissemination of new technology coloured the judgment, but the extent of it is not clear: the agreements in issue dated back to 1960, the Commission decision was adopted in 1978, which seems a generous amount of lead in time. Of course a provision of a licensing agreement which purported, expressly or implicitly, to authorise the licensee to

---

[122] Case 258/78 *Nungesser* v *Commission* (Maize Seeds) [1982] ECR 2015.

[123] Loi nº 70–489 du 11 juin 1970 relative à la protection des obtentions végétales, JORF du 12 Juin 1970, Art 3; Sortenschutzgesetz vom 20. Mai 1968, 1968 BGBl. I, S 429, § 15 I. The UK equivalent is the Plant Varieties and Seeds Act 1964.

[124] Decision 78/823 (*Breeders' Rights–Maize Seed*) OJ 1978 L286/23.

[125] Case 258/78 *Nungesser*, n 122, at 2069.

[126] Case 56/65 *Société Technique Minière* v *Maschinenbau Ulm* [1966] ECR 235; see pp 97–101 *supra*.

oppose parallel imports from other licensed territories would be unenforceable owing to the exhaustion of rights doctrine and so the application of Article 28; but its very existence could nevertheless be caught by Article 81(1) as one having as its object (even if not its effect) the distortion of competition, and no licensee would be bound by it. In addition, even if not bound, an attempt to abide by and give effect to it – by, for example, refusing without justification to respond to unsolicited orders from outwith the contract territory or limiting sales to parallel traders within the territory – would equally breach Article 81(1). Although *Nungesser* involved plant breeders' rights, it may be read more widely to apply to patent and similar licensing generally.[127]

In the light of various provisions of a licensing agreement which are beneficial, yet, notwithstanding *Nungesser*, may fall foul of Article 81(1), the Commission adopted a block exemption regulation governing patent licensing agreements in 1984.[128] In 1996 it was merged with the 1989 block exemption regulation on know-how licensing agreements[129] into a single block exemption governing technology transfer.[130] It applies to pure or mixed patent licensing or know-how licensing agreements, including those addressing utility models, topographies and semiconductors, and plant breeders' rights,[131] between two parties.[132] It codified the *Nungesser* principles and provides a number of further territorial restraints – including a prohibition of passive sales outwith the contract territory for a period of five years following first marketing anywhere in the Community – which an agreement may impose (the 'white list');[133] for certainty, it provides a list of other provisions of a standard licensing agreement 'which are generally not restrictive of competition' but will be exempted should they be found to be so in the particular circumstances of a case;[134] it provides a number of contractual restraints – limitations on research and development, production or distribution, price, quantity and some export and post-termination restraints – which will take a licensing agreement outwith the block exemption (the 'black list');[135] and it provides for an opposition

---

[127] Recognised implicitly by the Commission in block exemption Reg 240/96, OJ 1996 L31/2 (as to which see *infra*), recital 10. See also the observation of the Court in *Nungesser* (at 2065) that '[i]t is therefore not correct to consider that breeders' rights are a species of commercial or industrial property with characteristics of so special a nature as to require, in relation to the competition rules, a different treatment from other commercial or industrial property rights'.

[128] Reg 2349/84, OJ 1984 L219/15.

[129] Reg 556/89, OJ 1989 L61/1.

[130] Reg 240/96, OJ 1996 L31/2; on the nature of block exemptions generally, see Chap 4.

[131] art 8.

[132] art 1(1).

[133] art 1.

[134] art 2.

[135] art 3.

procedure to be mounted by the Commission for matters not addressed by the regulation (the 'grey list'), should a licensing agreement be notified, within a (shorter than normal) period of four months.[136] The benefits of the block exemption may be withdrawn by the Commission should it find the criteria of Article 81(3) not met in a particular case.[137]

Some aspects of trade mark licensing and know-how transfer may be addressed by franchising agreements. Until June 2000 they are governed by a separate block exemption on franchising[138] which then lapses and is replaced by the block exemption on vertical agreements.[139] Under the new regulation the assignment or licensing of an intellectual property right directly related to the use, sale or resale of the contract goods or services by the buyer and ancillary to a vertical agreement which otherwise falls within the regulation is exempt from Article 81(1).[140]

10.4.2 Article 82

As title to an intellectual property right confers upon the proprietor a monopoly within the territory of a member state, and a member state may comprise a substantial part of the common market within the meaning of Article 82,[141] it may be that the proprietor is in a dominant position and so subject to the constraints of Article 82.

However, the proprietor of a right 'does not enjoy a "dominant position" within the meaning of Article 82 merely because he is in a position to prevent third parties from putting into circulation, on the territory of a Member State, products [protected by the right]';[142] '[s]o far as dominant position is concerned … mere ownership of an intellectual property right cannot confer such a position'.[143] There are straightforward reasons, consistent with the manner in which Article 82 has been developed and applied, why this ought to be so. A patentee, for example, enjoys the exclusive right to use the patented process, but it may be that goods may be produced by other processes which form part of the same product market, so that there is no dominance; the proprietor of a trade mark for washing powder competes with other washing powder producers unless there is something so extraordinary about his washing powder that it forms a distinct market. Thus,

---

[136] art 4.
[137] art 7; for an example see Decision 88/501 (*Elopak/Tetra Pak*) 1988 L272/27.
[138] Reg 4087/88, OJ 1988 L359/46.
[139] Reg 2790/1999, OJ 1999 L336/21.
[140] *Ibid*, art 2(3).
[141] See generally Chap 4.
[142] Case 40/70 *Sirena* v *Eda* [1971] ECR 69 at 83.
[143] Cases C-241–2/91P *RTE & ITP* v *Commission* [1995] ECR I-743 at 822.

it is also necessary that the proprietor should have the power to impede the maintenance of effective competition over a considerable part of the relevant market, having regard in particular to the existence and position of any distributors who may be marketing similar goods or goods which may be substituted for them.[144]

Given the market privileges which ownership of an intellectual property right brings, it may of course be a material – and in some cases determinative – consideration in the identification of a dominant position, but the fuller, standard analysis of Article 82 dominance must be deployed. The question which then arises is, even given a dominant position, when does the proprietor abuse it? A fairly straightforward example is that of *Tetra Pak I*, in which the Commission found that an undertaking already dominant in the production and supply of antiseptic packaging machines infringed Article 82 by acquiring another undertaking which held an exclusive patent licence in a (potentially) competing process, the abuse consisting in strengthening an already considerable dominance and preventing, or considerably delaying, the emergence of new technology and a new competitor;[145] another is *Hilti*, in which an undertaking abused its dominance by protracting negotiations with third parties for the grant of licences of right by making manifestly excessive demands for royalties.[146] But better understanding may be gleaned by a comparison of two important judgments in the field, those in *Volvo* v *Veng* and the *Magill TV Guide* cases.

In *Volvo* v *Veng*[147] a supplier of spare motorcar parts (Veng) imported into the United Kingdom consignments of front wings to a make of motorcar, the motorcar manufacturer (Volvo) being the proprietor of a UK registered industrial design for the wing.[148] The wings were manufactured in other member states, or in third states and imported into the Community, by undertakings independent of Volvo – which had therefore not exhausted its right so as to make opposition of imports a breach of Article 28. Volvo commenced proceedings in the English courts for infringement of its design right. Veng argued that the refusal of Volvo to grant a licence, for a reasonable royalty, to import and supply the parts

---

[144] Case 40/70 *Sirena* v *Eda* [1971] ECR 69 at 83.
[145] Decision 88/501 (*Elopak/Tetra Pak*) OJ 1988 L272/27. The Commission was upheld by the Court of First Instance in Case T-51/89 *Tetra Pak Rausing* v *Commission* [1990] ECR II-309, the sole ground of review being that a breach of Art 82 could not be found in conduct which was expressly permitted by the (then) block exemption on patent licensing; see Chap 4, n 105 *supra*.
[146] Decision 88/138, OJ 1988 L65/19; upheld in Case T-30/89 *Hilti* v *Commission* [1991] ECR II-1439 and on appeal as Case C-53/92P *Hilti* v *Commission* [1994] ECR I-667.
[147] Case 238/87 [1988] ECR 6211; see also the similar Case 53/87 *CICRA* v *Renault* [1988] ECR 6039.
[148] Under the Registered Designs Act 1949.

constituted an abuse of Volvo's dominant position and so a breach of Article 82. Without considering whether Volvo did in fact enjoy a dominant position by virtue of its design right,[149] the Court of Justice said that

> the right of the proprietor to a protected design to prevent third parties from manufacturing and selling or importing, without its consent, products incorporating the design constitutes the very subject-matter of his exclusive right. It follows that an obligation imposed upon the proprietor of a protected design to grant to third parties, even in return for a reasonable royalty, a licence for the supply of products incorporating the design would lead to the proprietor thereof being deprived of the substance of his exclusive right, and that a refusal to grant such a licence cannot in itself constitute an abuse of a dominant position.[150]

The Court went on to give examples of conduct which could be abusive in the context, such as arbitrary refusal to supply spare parts to independent repairers, unfair fixing of prices or halting production of spare parts for which there was still a market. But shy of that, *Volvo v Veng* defines the specific subject matter of an intellectual property right for purposes of Article 82 and does so fairly widely.

The *Magill* cases were at first blush not so very different, but produced the diametrically opposite result. Under (then in force) British and Irish law, weekly schedules for television programmes were entitled to copyright protection as literary works.[151] Radio Telefís Éireann, the BBC and Independent Television Publications (owned by the various ITV franchisees) each published weekly guides containing only their programme schedules, and through copyright prevented their reproduction by third parties. An Irish company began producing a weekly guide (*Magill TV Guide*), which provided comprehensive schedules for all three services, which was marketed throughout Ireland, north and south; RTE, BBC and ITP secured an order from the Irish High Court restraining its publication for breach of copyright,[152] and its publication ceased. But in the meanwhile Magill had lodged a complaint with the Commission under Regulation 17, which initiated an investigation and found that RTE, BBC and ITP each held a monopoly and so a dominant position in the relevant markets (their respective programme listings) and had abused their dominance by reserving for themselves the derivative market of weekly listings

---

[149] Which point was considered by A-G Mischo, who determined that Volvo did enjoy a dominant position.

[150] Case 238/87 *Volvo v Veng* [1988] ECR 6211 at 6235.

[151] Respectively the Copyright Act 1956, confirmed in *ITP & BBC v Time Out* [1984] FSR 64 (Ch) (affirming *BBC v Wireless League Gazette Publishing Co* [1926] Ch 433), and the Copyright Act 1963 (Act No 10 of 1963), confirmed in *RTE v Magill* [1990] ILRM 534 (HC). The Broadcasting Act 1990, s 176, now imposes a duty upon UK proprietors to make their schedules available to any person wishing to publish them.

[152] *RTE v Magill, ibid.*

and so preventing the emergence of a new product – a comprehensive weekly guide – for which there was a clear demand.[153] This, said the Commission, allowed the three to

> use copyright as an instrument of the abuse, in a manner which falls outside the scope of the specific subject-matter of that intellectual property right,[154]

and so ordered them to supply each other and third parties on request and upon a non-discriminatory basis the relevant programme information and to permit reproduction of those listings by third parties in exchange for reasonable royalties.

Annulment of the decision was sought by RTE, BBC and ITP, essentially on *Volvo* v *Veng* grounds that the exclusive right of reproduction falls within the specific subject matter of copyright, there is no obligation to license, their conduct was not abusive in the mere exercise of the right, and the fact that this may prevent the emergence of a new product was therefore irrelevant.[155] The Court of First Instance said that

> while it is plain that the exercise of the exclusive right to reproduce a protected work is not itself an abuse, that does not apply when, in the light of the details of each individual case, it is apparent that the right is exercised in such ways as in fact to pursue an aim manifestly contrary to the objectives of Article 86. In that event, the copyright is no longer exercised in a manner which corresponds to its essential function, within the meaning of Article 36 of the Treaty .... In that case, the primacy of Community law, particularly as regards principles as fundamental as those of the free movement of goods and the freedom of competition, prevails over any use of a rule of national intellectual property law in a manner contrary to those principles.[156]

It then distinguished *Volvo* v *Veng* as follows:

> [Each] applicant, by reserving the exclusive right to publish its weekly television programme listings, was preventing the emergence on the market of a new product, namely a general television magazine likely to compete with its own magazine, the [*RTE Guide/Radio Times/TV Times*]. The applicant was thus using its copyright in the programme listings which it produced as part of its broadcasting activity in order to secure a monopoly in the derivative market of weekly television guides ....
>
> Conduct of that type – characterized by preventing the production and mar-

---

[153] Decision 89/205 (*Magill TV Guide*) OJ 1989 L78/43.

[154] para 23.

[155] They also sought, and were granted, an interim order suspending the Commission decision on the ground that compliance with it would cause serious and irreparable injury should they be proved right: Cases 76, 77 & 91/89R *RTE, BBC & ITP* v *Commission* [1989] ECR 1141.

[156] Case T-69/89 *RTE* v *Commission* [1991] ECR II-485 at 519–20; Case T-70/89 *BBC* v *Commission* [1991] ECR II-535 at 563–4; Case T-76/89 *ITP* v *Commission* [1991] ECR II-575 at 601–02.

keting of a new product, for which there is potential consumer demand, on the ancillary market of television magazines and thereby excluding all competition from that market solely in order to secure the applicant's monopoly – clearly goes beyond what is necessary to fulfil the essential function of the copyright as permitted in Community law.[157]

The proper analogy, said the Court, was that of an arbitrary refusal by a motor manufacturer to supply spare parts to an independent repairer in the derivative market of motor maintenance and repair, and, by stifling the emergence of a new product and so 'fail[ing] to take consumer needs into consideration', of a refusal to supply spare parts for existing motorcars for which there was still consumer demand.[158] On appeal by RTE and ITP, the Court of Justice said that the mere exercise by a proprietor enjoying a dominant position of an intellectual property may constitute abuse 'in exceptional circumstances', found such exceptional circumstances to exist here in the prevention of the emergence of a new product, the absence of justification for it, and the reservation to themselves of the derivative market, and so upheld the Court of First Instance.[159]

The dividing line between *Volvo* v *Veng* and the *Magill* cases may appear a thin one, but the differences are pivotal. The Commission was clearly contemptuous that copyright ought to subsist in television listings and argued that such right ought not to be recognised.[160] The Court of First Instance rightly demurred and cleaved to the established rule that the existence of the right was a matter exclusively for national law. But doubtless the very triteness of the right coloured the Court's judgment, which, combined with the abusive (in both its Article 82 and its wider sense) behaviour of the proprietors, took their refusal to license 'clearly ... beyond what is necessary to fulfil the essential function of the copyright as permitted in Community law'; the very exercise of the right, normally part of its specific subject matter (*Volvo* v *Veng*), was the instrument of abuse, in a manner which falls outside the scope of the specific subject matter. The judgment was clad in raiment addressing the inhibition of the emergence of a new product in a derivative market. In a subsequent case, the Court of First Instance both tightened and loosened the screws, saying that a refusal to license will be abusive only if it concerns a product or service which is essential for the exercise of an ancillary activity (and so a variation of the essential facilities doctrine)[161] or if it prevents the introduction of a new

---

[157] Case T-69/89 *RTE* v *Commission* at 520–1; Case T-70/89 *BBC* v *Commission* at 564–5; Case T-76/89 *ITP* v *Commission* at 602–03.

[158] *Ibid*, at 521, 565 and 603.

[159] Cases C-241–2/91P *RTE & ITP* v *Commission* [1995] ECR I-743.

[160] Case T-69/89 *RTE* v *Commission* at 510; Case T-70/89 *BBC* v *Commission* at 552–3; Case T-76/89 *ITP* v *Commission* at 591 (full citations at n 156).

[161] See pp 156–8 *supra*.

product or service despite 'specific, constant and regular potential demand on the part of consumers', which will not be the case where the new product or service, although additional and suitable, is not in itself indispensable to consumer choice.[162] Otherwise, how the 'exceptional circumstances' of *Magill* – unless *Magill* is a freak to be confined to its facts – will be found to exist in future, similar situations and involving intellectual property rights less hackneyed than television listings, remains to be seen.[163]

It ought finally to be noted that whilst as a general principle there is no obligation to license the exploitation of an intellectual property right to third parties, the Commission will sometimes impose such a duty as a condition for approval of a concentration under the Merger Regulation.[164]

---

[162] Case T-504/93 *Tiercé Ladbroke* v *Commission* [1997] ECR II-923 at 969.

[163] An answer may come (in the fullness of time) following Case T-198/98 *Micro Leaders Business* v *Commission* [1999] ECR II-3989, in which the Court of First Instance annulled the Commission rejection of a complaint involving the exercise by Microsoft of copyright to prevent the parallel importation into France of its French language software from Canada because the Commission, finding Microsoft's conduct unobjectionable as falling within the specific subject matter of its copyright, made a manifest error of appraisal by not properly having considered whether it met *Magill* exceptional circumstances and so constituted an infringement of Art 82.

[164] eg, Decision 98/526 (*Hoffmann-La Roche/Boehringer Mannheim*) OJ 1998 L234/14.

CHAPTER 11

State aids

Amongst the rules on competition in the Treaty, but forming a distinct section in the chapter and a *lex specialis*, are rules governing 'Aids granted by States', addressed in Articles 87 to 89 (ex Articles 92 to 94). That they are necessary is self-evident: any subvention granted by a member state to an undertaking gives that undertaking a comparative advantage over its competitors. Subvention is legion notwithstanding various governments claiming to set their faces against it; and it is not only the member states – the Community itself plays the same game, awarding significant financial assistance through agricultural guidance spending and regional aid.[1] The need increases with Community integration, the Treaty depriving member states of the tools with which they would traditionally combat foreign subvention (countervailing duties), and gathers even greater pace with the advent of economic and monetary union. That the rules are different is equally apparent: they address not the anticompetitive conduct of undertakings but the financial intervention of member states (which are not undertakings in this context) in the market.

Given that the rules on state aids are different a body of law has been developed by the Commission and the Court of Justice distinct to Articles 87 to 89 both in substance and procedure. It is an important, highly sensitive and complex area of competition law, tightly bound up with industrial and regional policies (both national and Community), and raises fundamental economic questions of the viability and desirability of public services and, for example, public support for crisis industry, 'sunset' industries and remote industry – whether without permanent subvention undertakings in the Algarve and the Altmark can ever compete with those in the 'golden crescent'. It is also an issue very much to the fore in international deliberations in the World Trade Organisation. They will be

---

[1] The Community, however, is exempt from the strictures of Arts 87–89, which apply only to aid 'granted by a Member State'.

addressed in another book in this series, so what follows is a very superficial consideration of the applicable rules.

11.1 The Treaty scheme

Article 87(1) provides:

> Save as otherwise provided in this Treaty, any aid granted by a Member State or through State resources in any form whatsoever which distorts or threatens to distort competition by favouring certain undertakings or the production of certain goods shall, insofar as it affects trade between Member States, be incompatible with the common market.

Article 87(2) then goes on to list by way of exception state aids which are compatible with the common market (those having a social character granted to individual consumers, those to make good damage caused by natural disasters or exceptional occurrences and those granted by Germany in order to compensate for economic disadvantages caused by the division of Germany[2]) and Article 87(3) lists those which *may* be compatible with the common market, that is:

- aids promoting the development of economically disadvantaged regions;
- aids promoting the execution of important projects of common European interest or remedying a serious disturbance in the economy of a member state;
- aids facilitating the development of certain economic activities or regions;
- aids promoting culture and heritage conservation; and
- such other categories of aid to be determined by the Council.

Article 87(2) thus constitutes exceptions to the general prohibition (alongside state aids necessary to support services in the general economic interest which are excepted from the prohibition by Article 86(2) (ex Article 90(2))),[3] Article 87(3) the possibility, across much broader categories of activity, of exemption from it. Article 88 vests the Commission with the duty of supervision of state aids to ensure compliance with Article 87 and confers upon it sole power of exemption of Article 87(3) aids.

---

[2] The Commission takes the view that this exceptional derogation lapsed with German (re)unification (*XXth Report on Competition Policy, 1990*, p 131), although it was not repealed in the Treaty of Amsterdam spring clean of the Treaty, and aids granted in border areas and in the former territories of the DDR are subject now to the general rules on regional aid; the Court of First Instance implicitly disagrees: Cases T-132 & 143/96 *Freistaat Sachsen and Volkswagen v Commission* [1999] ECR II-3663.

[3] See Chap 7.

Article 89 provides the Council with authority to adopt regulations to give effect to the application of Articles 87 and 88. This is similar to the Treaty base in Article 83 (ex Article 87), but unlike Article 83, Article 89 saw first action only in 1998, the Commission until then relying largely upon soft law devices.

11.2 The prohibition

Like Article 81, the general approach of the Treaty is that state aids are *prima facie* incompatible with the common market. Although they are 'incompatible' with the common market and not 'prohibited', as are breaches of Articles 81 and 82, it has been construed by the Court to amount effectively to the same thing. According to Article 87(1), state aid is 'any aid granted by a Member State or through State resources *in any form whatsoever* which distorts or threatens to distort competition'; it is not further defined in the Treaty. The Court of Justice established early on (in a case under the ECSC Treaty, to which the same considerations apply) that Article 87 therefore addresses not only subsidies but much wider state subvention:

> A subsidy is normally defined as a payment in cash or in kind made in support of an undertaking other than the payment by the purchaser or consumer for the goods or services which it produces. An aid is a very similar concept, which, however, places emphasis on its purpose and seems especially devised for a particular objective which cannot normally be achieved without outside help. The concept of aid is nevertheless wider than that of a subsidy because it embraces not only positive benefits, such as subsidies themselves, but also intervention which, in various forms, mitigate the charges which are normally included in the budget of an undertaking and which, without, therefore, being subsidies in the strict meaning of the word, are similar in character and have the same effect.[4]

Article 87 therefore embraces subvention which is not only direct subsidies but investment grants, free or reduced rental of premises, concessions on tax (exemption, reduced rate, rebates, deferment of payment) or national insurance/social security employer contributions, 'sweeteners' to attract a buyer, bonuses to attract new employees, preferential interest rates on loans, donations, lower energy prices, preferential conditions on the supply of goods or services or the award of contracts, various guarantees (cover for operating losses, export credits or exchange risks, dividend guaran-

---

[4] Case 30/59 *Gezamenlijke Steenkolenmijnen in Limburg* v *High Authority* [1961] ECR 1 at 19.

tees), debt write-offs and, in some circumstances, the acquisition of a holding in capital. Generally the breadth of state aids is very wide.[5]

Thereafter there are four cumulative elements in order for Article 87 to be joined: the aid be granted by a member state or through state resources, it confers an advantage upon ('favours') the assisted undertaking(s), it distorts (or threatens to distort) competition and it affects trade between member states. An aid is granted by a member state if it comes from any public source – national, provincial or local and any public agency acting under their authority.[6] Aids are sometimes hidden (intentionally or otherwise) and difficult to detect, particularly so with publicly owned undertakings; as a result the Commission adopted a directive in 1980 (the 'transparency directive')[7] requiring member states to make the books of those undertakings available to Commission inspection. The tests of advantage and effect upon trade between member states are not difficult to meet. As with Articles 81 and 82 it is necessary to show only a potential effect: it must be real but need not be appreciable.[8] So, aid granted to an undertaking which is not an exporter may be caught because exporters from other member states may be disadvantaged in supplying its home market.[9] There is necessarily an inarticulated remoteness test for public works and general economic measures, otherwise, for example, a road building programme assists undertakings which will use those roads, subvention for ferry services to the Western Isles (even if excepted by Article 86(2)) both assists Caledonian MacBrayne to the exclusion of Greek ferry operators who might wish to provide those services and arguably assists Lewis sheep farmers in exporting to the continent, and a currency devaluation (an option open now only to three member states) assists all exporters.

---

[5] For an example of one of the few exceptions see Cases C-72 & 73/91 *Sloman Neptun Schiffahrts v Seebetriebsrat Bodo Ziesemer* [1993] ECR I-887, in which the Court of Justice found that the German scheme whereby seafarers on German registered ships not Community nationals and not resident in Germany were by law excluded from various employment rights, including those regulating wages, was *not* a state aid notwithstanding arguments put forward by the Commission that the loss of German tax revenues was a tax relief which conferred an advantage upon German shipping.

[6] Case 323/82 *Intermills v Commission* [1984] ECR 3809; Case 248/84 *Germany v Commission* [1987] ECR 4013; Cases 67, 68 & 70/85 *Kwekerij Gebroeders van der Kooy v Commission* [1988] ECR 219.

[7] Directive 80/723, OJ 1980 L195/35.

[8] See eg Case 323/82 *Intermills v Commission*, n 6 *supra*; Cases 296 & 318/82 *Netherlands & Leeuwarder Papierwarenfabriek v Commission* [1985] ECR 809; Case 102/87 *France v Commission* [1988] ECR 4067; Case 142/87 *Belgium v Commission* [1990] ECR I-959.

[9] eg, Case 102/87 *France v Commission*, *ibid*; Cases C-278–80/92 *Spain v Commission* [1994] ECR I-4103; Case C-75/97 *Belgium v Commission* [1999] ECR I-3671.

However, Article 87 lays down no *de minimis* rule, and the Court of Justice has declined to grant its imprimatur to *de minimis* considerations as a means of avoiding the prohibition of Article 87 as it has for that of Article 81.[10] By contrast, the Commission has since 1990 operated a *de minimis* principle as part of its reasoning on compatibility.[11] In 1998 the Council adopted a regulation authorising the Commission to adopt, in effect, block exemption regulations declaring state aids to be compatible with the common market without need of notification upon *de minimis* grounds and in the subject areas of small and medium-sized undertakings, research and development, environmental protection, employment and training, and aid to poorer regions.[12] The Commission has now proposed a draft regulation exempting from the prohibition and the notification requirements aid granted to any one undertaking which does not exceed €100,000 over any three years;[13] aid to small and medium-sized undertakings (as defined by Community law[14]) is the subject of a separate draft regulation,[15] as is training aid.[16] The Commission has also adopted decisions (under the ECSC Treaty) or guidelines from time to time relative to aids in the specific sectors of coal and steel, motorcars, textiles, shipbuilding, transport and agriculture and fisheries.[17]

11.3 Supervision of state aids

Article 88 of the Treaty imposes upon the Commission the (Augean) task of supervision of state aids to ensure compliance with the requirements of

---

[10] eg, Case 730/79 *Philip Morris* v *Commission* [1980] ECR 2671; Case 310/85 *Deufil* v *Commission* [1987] ECR 901; Case 142/87 *Belgium* v *Commission*, n 8 *supra*; Case 303/88 *Italy* v *Commission* [1991] ECR I-1433; Case 305/89 *Italy* v *Commission* [1991] ECR I-1603; Cases C-329/93 & 62 & 63/95 *Germany* v *Commission* [1996] ECR I-5202.

[11] Notice of an aid scheme of minor importance, OJ 1990 C40/2, replaced by guidelines on state aid for small and medium-sized enterprises (*sic*), OJ 1992 C213/2 and notice of the *de minimis* rule for State aids, OJ 1996 C68/9.

[12] Reg 994/98, OJ 1998 L142/1.

[13] Draft Regulation on the application of Articles 87 and 88 of the EC Treaty to *de minimis* aid, OJ 2000 C89/6, art 2(2).

[14] Commission Recommendation 96/280, OJ 1996 L107/4; see Chap 3, n 121.

[15] Draft Regulation on the application of Articles 87 and 88 of the EC Treaty to State aid to small and medium-sized enterprises (*sic*), OJ 2000 C89/15. Generally investment aid is exempted where the 'gross aid intensity' does not exceed 15 per cent for small undertakings and 7.5 per cent for medium-sized undertakings (art 4(2)), whilst higher thresholds are provided if the investment occurs in areas qualifying for regional aid (art 4(3)); consultancy and other service activities may be subvented up to 50 per cent of their cost (art 5); there is a ceiling of €50 million in total project aid (art 6).

[16] Draft Regulation on the application of Articles 87 and 88 of the EC Treaty to training aid, OJ 2000 C89/8.

[17] See, eg, most recently, guidelines on State aid in the agriculture sector, OJ 2000 C28/2.

Article 87. There is distinct treatment of 'new aids', in which the Commission exercises *a priori* control, and 'existing aids', those lawfully introduced prior to the entry into force of the Treaty or accession or in accordance with the procedures of Article 88, where control is *ex post*. Alteration of an existing aid is a new aid.[18] Rules applicable to the process of supervision developed over time through Commission procedure and case law of the Court of Justice; they were eventually codified and given greater precision in a 1999 Council regulation ('Regulation 659').[19]

11.3.1 New aids

Article 88(3) provides:

> The Commission shall be informed, in sufficient time to enable it to submit its comments, of any plan to grant or alter aid. If it considers that any such plan is not compatible with the common market having regard to Article 87, it shall without delay initiate the procedure provided for in paragraph 2. The Member State concerned shall not put its proposed measures into effect until this procedure has resulted in a final decision.

There is therefore a 'standstill' clause, which is directly effective,[20] prohibiting the introduction of a new aid without the consent of the Commission.[21] However, the Commission is required to respond to a proper notification with a preliminary examination 'with due expedition [*diligence*]' and within 'an appropriate period', set by the Court at two months, after which absent a response Commission consent is deemed[22] and the Commission is barred from acting against it as a new aid.[23] This was codified in Regulation 659[24] which further provides, mimicking the procedures of the Merger Regulation,[25] that the Commission must within two months of notification respond with a decision which (a) finds the notified measure not to constitute aid, (b) finds the measure to be compatible with the common market in accordance with Article 87(3), or (c) if there are doubts as to its compatibility with the common market, initiate a 'formal investigation procedure'.[26] The formal investigation procedure has

---

[18] EC Treaty, Art 88(3), referring to 'plans to grant or alter aid'.

[19] Reg 659/1999, OJ 1999 L83/1.

[20] See *infra*.

[21] EC Treaty, Art 88(3), final sentence; Reg 659/1999, art 2.

[22] Case 84/82 *Germany* v *Commission* [1984] ECR 1451 at 1488; also Case 120/73 *Lorenz* v *Germany* [1973] ECR 1471. The member state must inform the Commission of its intention to proceed.

[23] Case C-312/90 *Spain* v *Commission* [1992] ECR I-4117.

[24] art 4(5)–(6).

[25] See p 262 *supra*.

[26] Reg 659/1999, art 4.

developed through Commission practice and includes publication of the
notification in the *Official Journal* with an invitation to third parties to
comment, the gathering of information,[27] and as a general principle of
Community law a right of interested parties to be heard.[28] The procedure
is terminated by a decision (a) that the measure does not constitute aid; (b)
that, with or without modification, the aid is compatible with the common
market ('positive decision'), which may have monitoring conditions
imposed ('conditional decision'); or (c) that the aid is incompatible with
the common market ('negative decision').[29] The Commission should (must
'as far as possible endeavour') take the decision within a period of 18
months from the opening of the procedure,[30] and must, should the relevant
member state so request, take a decision within two months thereafter,
although should the information available to the Commission be insufficient to establish compatibility, there is a presumption of a negative
decision.[31] As to determination of compatibility with the common market,
the Commission set out its stall and the criteria upon which it relies in
1983:[32]

(a) the aid ought to promote development which is in the interests of the
Community as a whole; the promotion of national interest, which state
aids generally subvent, is not enough to justify approval;
(b) the aid is necessary to achieve that development, and without it the
measure in question would not be realised; for example, funds would
be unlikely to be raised on the private capital markets (the 'market
economy investor principle');
(c) the 'modalities' of the aid, its intensity, duration, displacement, the
degree of distortion to competition, must be commensurate with the
importance of the objective of the aid.

However, determination of compatibility with the common market
requires examination and appraisal of economic facts and circumstances
which may be complex and liable to rapid change, so the Commission necessarily enjoys a broad discretion.[33]

---

[27] *Ibid*, art 5.
[28] Cases 234/84 & 40/85 *Belgium* v *Commission* [1986] ECR 2263; Case 259/85 *France* v
Commission [1987] ECR 4393; Case C-294/90 *British Aerospace* v *Commission* [1992]
ECR I-493; codified in Reg 659/1999, arts 6, 20.
[29] Reg 659/1999, art 7(1)–(5).
[30] art 7(6).
[31] art 7(7).
[32] *Twelfth Report on Competition Policy* (1982), pp 110–11.
[33] eg, Case 730/79 *Philip Morris* v *Commission* [1980] ECR 2671; Case C-301/87 *France* v
Commission (Boussac) [1990] ECR I-307.

Failure to notify a new aid and proceeding with its introduction pending (timeous) preliminary examination or formal investigation by the Commission is a breach of Article 88(3) irrespective of its merits[34] and renders the aid 'unlawful'.[35] It is not clear whether state aids falling within Article 87(2) and which are thus compatible with the common market (or, equally, state aids excepted from the prohibition of Article 87 by recourse to Article 86(2)[36]) are required to be notified, for in practice they invariably are. The Commission may order the suspension of an unauthorised (and so unlawful) aid ('suspension injunction')[37] and may in cases of urgency order its recovery ('recovery injunction').[38] If the member state fails to comply the Commission may use a 'fast track' procedure seeking a declaration from the Court of Justice that the failure constitutes an infringement of the Treaty.[39] If the Court agrees, the Commission may pursue penalties against the defaulting member state in accordance with the procedures of Article 228 (ex Article 171) of the Treaty.[40]

The normal rule is that unlawful aid is required to be repaid by the recipient,[41] it being the logical consequence of a finding that it was unlawful as it allows the *status quo ante* to be restored.[42] Prior to the adoption of Regulation 659 the Commission would normally order repayment, to be effected through national law and procedures.[43] Now it is required to do so: where an unlawful aid is disbursed in the face of a negative decision the Commission must order the member state to take 'all necessary measures' to recover it ('recovery decision') unless 'it would be contrary to a general principle of Community law'[44] – that is, the legitimate expectation of the recipient, and therefore a plea open only to the recipient and not to the subventing member state.[45] Recovery usually did,[46] and now must,[47]

---

[34] Case 120/73 *Lorenz* v *Germany* [1973] ECR 1471; Case C-39/94 *Syndicat Français de l'Express International* v *La Poste* [1996] ECR I-3547.

[35] Reg 659/1999, art 1(f).

[36] See Chap 7.

[37] Reg 659/1999, art 11(1).

[38] *Ibid*, art 11(2).

[39] EC Treaty, Art 88(2), 2nd para; Reg 659/1999, art 12.

[40] Reg 659/1999, art 23(2).

[41] Case C-74/89 *Commission* v *Belgium* [1990] ECR I-492; Case C-39/94 *Syndicat Français de l'Express International* v *La Poste* [1996] ECR I-3547.

[42] Case 310/85 *Deufil* v *Commission* [1987] ECR 901; Case C-142/87 *Belgium* v *Commission* [1990] ECR I-959; Case C-169/95 *Spain* v *Commission* [1997] ECR I-135.

[43] Case T-459/93 *Siemens* v *Commission* [1995] ECR II-1675.

[44] Reg 659/1999, art 14(1).

[45] See *infra*.

[46] Case T-459/93 *Siemens*, n 43 *supra*.

[47] Reg 659/1999, art 14(2).

include payment of interest; it is by civil process,[48] and is subject to a limitation period of 10 years.[49] If recovery is ordered the aid must be repaid except in cases of 'absolute impossibility'.[50] The administrative difficulties of recovering from a large number of undertakings[51] and the intervening insolvency of some of them[52] does not render recovery impossible.

The standstill provisions of Article 88(3) and Regulation 659 are directly effective, therefore actions of prohibition and recovery may also be taken to national courts.[53]

11.3.2 Existing aids

Article 88(1) imposes upon the Commission a duty

> to keep under constant review all systems of aid existing in [the Member] States. It shall propose to the latter any appropriate measures required by the progressive development or by the functioning of the common market.

It must therefore monitor all existing aids for continuing compatibility with Article 87, including aids excepted under Article 87(2). In order to assist, member states are required to submit annual reports on all exising aid schemes.[54] If the Commission determines that an existing aid no longer meets the criteria for exception or exemption it may recommend its termination[55] or order its termination within a reasonable period of time,[56] failing which it must initiate a formal investigation procedure.[57] As a nod to importance and sensitivity of state aids, the Commission may be overruled by the Council 'if justified by exceptional circumstances' and acting by unanimity.[58]

---

[48] art 14(3).

[49] art 15.

[50] Case 52/84 *Commission* v *Belgium* [1986] ECR 89; Case 301/87 *France* v *Commission* (Boussac) [1990] ECR I-307; Case T-67/94 *Ladbroke Racing* v *Commission* [1998] ECR II-1, upheld on appeal in Case C-83/98P *France* v *Ladbroke Racing & Commission*, judgment of 16 May 2000, not yet reported.

[51] Case C-280/95 *Commission* v *Italy* [1998] ECR I-259; Case C-75/97 *Belgium* v *Commission* [1999] ECR I-3671.

[52] Cases C-278–80/92 *Spain* v *Commission* [1994] ECR I-4103; Case C-75/97 *Belgium* v *Commission, ibid*.

[53] See *infra*.

[54] Reg 659/1999, art 21(1).

[55] EC Treaty, Art 88(1); Reg 659/1999, art 18.

[56] EC Treaty, Art 88(2).

[57] Reg 659/1999, art 19(2). This is new with Reg 659, prior to which the Commission was entitled to proceed directly to the Court of Justice seeking a declaration that the member state was in breach of Treaty obligations: EC Treaty, Art 88(2), 2nd para. Presumably the new procedure is compatible with Art 88(2) as a legitimate use of the Council's power under Art 89.

[58] EC Treaty, Art 88(2), 3rd para. This applies also to new aids. In practice, because it requires Council unanimity, it does not happen.

11.4 Judicial control of the Commission

A decision taken under Article 88 or under Regulation 659 is a decision (addressed always to the relevant member state(s)) within the meaning of Article 249 (ex Article 189) of the Treaty and so subject to review before the Court of First Instance and the Court of Justice under Article 230 (ex Article 173). Whilst the Commission enjoys a broad discretion in its powers, the administrative rules – in particular those on the right to be heard and sufficient (and sound) economic analysis and reasoning – which adhere to Regulation 17[59] apply equally here. Unlike Regulation 17, the initiation of an investigation *is* a reviewable act because it suspends aid disbursement.[60] A Commission decision may be challenged by any member state as of right[61] or by the recipient of the aid, which by virtue of being the recipient is affected directly and individually by the decision;[62] third party competitors (or their trade associations) must show direct and individual concern,[63] which is a less difficult test here than in Community law generally.[64] Recourse to the Court is commonplace: a negative decision will frequently bring the subventing member state and/or the aggrieved (putative) recipient(s) to Luxembourg, a preliminary or positive decision other member states and disgruntled competitors. An action raised by a member state – a not uncommon occurrence in the area of state aids (if sometimes for form rather than conviction) – goes to the Court of Justice, whereas an action raised by an undertaking goes to the Court of First Instance. This gives rise to its own judicial variable geometry, and cases considering the same Commission decision are normally joined before the Court of Justice.

11.5 National courts

National courts have two roles to play in the context of state aids. First, a disgruntled competitor of a recipient of an aid approved by the Commission may lack title and interest to challenge the decision before the Court of First Instance. If it wishes to do so nonetheless, it will require to challenge the disbursement of the aid before a national court and, invalidation of a Community act being the exclusive preserve of the Court of

---

[59] See pp 190–2 *supra*.
[60] Case C-312/90 *Spain* v *Commission* [1992] ECR I-4117.
[61] EC Treaty, Art 230(2).
[62] Case C-188/92 *TWD Textilwerke Deggendorf* v *Germany* [1994] ECR I-833.
[63] EC Treaty, Art 230(4).
[64] eg, Case 323/82 *Intermills* v *Commission* [1984] ECR 3809; Case C-198/91 *William Cook* v *Commission* [1993] ECR I-2487.

Justice,[65] urge the national court to refer a question of the validity of the decision to the Court of Justice under Article 234 (ex Article 177) which will then be competent to entertain the plea.[66] The recipient of an aid is estopped from mounting any such challenge in a national court, it having enjoyed clear standing to seek direct recourse to the Court of First Instance under Article 230 (ex Article 173) and having failed to invoke it; the decision becomes thereafter definitive for it.[67]

Second and more important, whilst the Commission alone enjoys the power to determine whether an Article 87(3) aid is compatible with the common market, the prohibition in Article 88(3) of disbursement of an unauthorised, and *a fortiori* unnotified, aid is directly effective and so triggers the jurisdiction of the national courts which must make available such remedies as exist for the enforcement of equivalent rights in national law (eg, declaration/declarator, prohibition).[68] If a national court is seised of a question of an infringement of Article 88(3) through premature (and so unlawful) disbursement and Commission deliberations under Regulation 659 are in train, the Court of Justice said in *SFEI* v *La Poste* – the state aids equivalent of *Delimitis*[69] – that the national court may proceed with the case even if that means it is second guessing the Commission as to whether or not the instrument at issue is in fact a state aid caught by Article 87(1).[70] It may seek the assistance of the Commission (and the Commission has published a cooperation notice applying in such circumstances[71]) and may or must refer the question to the Court of Justice in accordance with Article 234 (ex Article 177). Any appropriate interim measures may be adopted. The general rule that unlawful aids ought to be repaid applies equally in national courts, and the court ought in principle to make an appropriate order.[72] However, in 'exceptional circumstances' it would be 'inappropriate' to do so.[73] Exceptional circumstances appear to be the legitimate expectation of a recipient which reasonably believed that the aid had been disbursed in accordance with the procedures of Article 88 and so the aid to be lawful. However 'a diligent operator should normally

---

[65] Case 314/85 *Foto-Frost* v *Hauptzollamt Lübeck-Ost* [1987] ECR 4199.

[66] Case T-330/94 *Salt Union* v *Commission* [1996] ECR II-1475.

[67] Case C-188/92 *TWD Textilwerke Deggendorf* v *Germany* [1994] ECR I-833.

[68] For English examples, see *R* v *Attorney-General, ex parte ICI* [1987] 1 CMLR 72 (CA); *R* v *Commissioners of Customs and Excise, ex parte Lunn Poly* [1999] 1 CMLR 1357 (CA).

[69] Case C-234/89 *Delimitis* v *Henninger Bräu* [1991] ECR I-935; see pp 211–12 *supra*.

[70] Case C-39/94 *Syndicat Français de l'Express International* v *La Poste* [1996] ECR I-3547.

[71] Notice on cooperation between national courts and the Commission in the State aid field, OJ 1995 C312/8.

[72] Case C-39/94 *SFEI* v *La Poste*, n 70 *supra*.

[73] Case C-39/94 *SFEI* v *La Poste*, *ibid*, at 3598.

be able to determine whether that procedure has been followed',[74] and even the fact that the Commission declined originally to object (but which decision was successfully challenged by a competitor), 'however regrettable it may be', does not create sufficient legitimate expectation to justify non-repayment.[75] It is a plea available only to the recipient and not to the member state, which would otherwise be relying upon its own unlawful conduct.[76] If an unlawful aid has been disbursed a competitor might conceivably have a claim in damages against the subvented undertaking[77] or against the member state applying a *Brasserie du Pêcheur* rule.[78] Stretching credulity even further, it might have a claim against the Commission under Articles 235 and 288(2) (ex Articles 178 and 215(2)) if the aid was disbursed by authority of a rogue Commission decision subsequently found to be unlawful.

11.6 European Economic Area

It should be noted that because the free trade arrangements within the European Economic Area echo (if less resoundingly) the concerns of the Community competition rules,[79] provisions similar to Articles 87 and 88 exist at EEA level. Article 61 of the EEA Agreement effectively replicates Article 87 of the Treaty; Article 62 is similar to Article 88. The Commission enforces the EEA rules within the territory of the Community,[80] the EFTA Surveillance Authority within the territory of the EFTA,[81] their determinations then binding for the whole of the EEA (subject to judicial control of the Court of Justice and the EFTA Court of Justice). Both are required to consult and cooperate closely in order to ensure uniform application of the rules.[82]

---

[74] Case C-169/95 *Spain v Commission* [1997] ECR I-135 at 163.

[75] *Ibid*, at 163.

[76] *Ibid*, Case T-459/93 *Siemens v Commission* [1995] ECR II-1675.

[77] See Case C-39/94 *Syndicat Français de l'Express International v La Poste* [1996] ECR I-3547.

[78] Cases C-46 & 48/93 *Brasserie du Pêcheur v Germany* and *R v Secretary of State for Transport, ex parte Factortame (No 3)* [1996] ECR I-1029; see Chap 6, n 302 and accompanying text.

[79] See Chap 9.

[80] EEA Agreement, art 62(1)(a).

[81] *Ibid*, art 62(1)(b); Protocol 26; Agreement establishing a Surveillance Authority and an EFTA Court of Justice, art 24; for the Surveillance Authority's procedural and substantive rules see OJ 1994 L231/1.

[82] EEA Agreement, art 62(2); Protocol 27.

CHAPTER 12

The Competition Act 1998

In November 1998 the Competition Act 1998 was given royal assent. Other than a very few supplemental and transitional provisions,[1] none of it entered into force as a result. The Act provides that the rest was to come into force on such day or days as the Secretary of State may by order appoint,[2] and whilst a number of enabling sections and transitional measures were in the intervening time given effect, the bulk and heart of it became law on 1 March 2000.[3]

The Competition Act marks a radical departure from (and repeals most of) the existing spatchcock of UK competition law (although it does nothing to amend its polycephalous administration). Following the initiative of other countries, if coming rather late in the queue, a 1988 Green Paper[4] and a 1989 White Paper,[5] a lengthy gestation period in the Department of Trade and Industry and a minor battle of wills between the government and the Lords,[6] it has adopted wholesale into British law the approach of the EC Treaty. Various provisions of the Act have been mentioned in the preceding text. However, it is useful to present a brief overview of the Act in order to mark its origins and the new (national) competition environment in which British undertakings are now required to act – and the challenges the courts will face. An important by-product of the 1998 Act is that, having acquired a taste for a competition regime by virtue of the Act, British judges may well come to take a more robust view of their jurisdiction to give effect to Community rules.

---

[1] Competition Act 1998, s 76(2).
[2] s 76(3).
[3] Competition Act 1998 (Commencement No 5) Order 2000, SI 2000/344.
[4] Review of Restrictive Trade Practices Policy, Cmnd 331.
[5] Opening Markets: A New Policy on Restrictive Trade Practices, Cmnd 727.
[6] The House of Lords voted for an amendment providing for a 'press diversity prohibition' applying special rules to 'national newspapers' seeking to underpin diversity of media ownership (see the draft Bill as amended on report, s 19), but it was deleted at government insistence.

Section 2 of the Act provides:

(1) Subject to [excluded agreements[7]], agreements between undertakings, decisions by associations of undertakings or concerted practices which –

    (a) may affect trade within the United Kingdom, and

    (b) have as their object or effect the prevention, restriction or distortion of competition within the United Kingdom,

are prohibited unless they are exempt in accordance with the provisions of this Part.

(2) Subsection (1) applies, in particular, to agreements, decisions or practices which –

    (a) directly or indirectly fix purchase or selling prices or any other trading condition;

    (b) limit or control production, markets, technical development or investment;

    (c) share markets or sources of supply;

    (d) apply dissimilar conditions to equivalent transactions with other trading parties, thereby placing them at a competitive disadvantage;

    (e) make the conclusion of contracts subject to acceptance by the other parties of supplementary obligations which, by their nature or according to commercial usage, have no connection with subjects of such contracts.

(3) Subsection (1) applies only if the agreement, decision or practice is, or is intended to be, implemented in the United Kingdom.

(4) Any agreement or decision which is prohibited by subsection (1) is void.

...

(8) The prohibition imposed by subsection (1) is referred to in this Act as 'the Chapter I prohibition'.

The Director-General of Fair Trading ('the Director') may grant an exemption ('individual exemption') to a prohibited agreement or concerted practice upon a request ('application') by any party to it;[8] the grounds for exemption are *verbatim* those of Article 81(3).[9] A party may also apply seeking 'guidance' from the Director to whether or not, in his view, an agreement is likely to infringe the Chapter I prohibition[10] – in effect, for negative clearance. Rules ('Director's Rules') governing application have now been adopted;[11] a substantial fee (£5000 for guidance, £13,000 for

---

[7] See *infra*.
[8] Competition Act 1998, ss 4, 12 and 14; Sch 5.
[9] s 9.
[10] ss 12–16; Sch 5.
[11] Competition Act 1998 (Director's Rules) Order 2000, SI 2000/293.

individual exemption) is exigible.[12] As with Regulation 17, no penalty may be imposed by the Director following application and prior to its determination;[13] an agreement notified to the (European) Commission under Regulation 17 is also immune from penalties under the Act until such time as the Commission determines the issue or withdraws the immunity.[14] The Secretary of State may by order, upon a recommendation from the Director, adopt block exemptions ('block exemption orders') for categories of agreements which meet the criteria for exemption.[15] An agreement which falls within a Community block exemption or has been individually exempted by the Commission under Regulation 17 is automatically exempted from the Chapter I prohibition ('parallel exemption').[16] This is so even if the agreement does not affect trade between member states.[17]

Section 18 of the Act provides:

(1) Subject to [excluded cases[18]], any conduct on the part of one or more undertakings which amounts to the abuse of a dominant position in a market is prohibited if it may affect trade within the United Kingdom.

(2) Conduct may, in particular, constitute such abuse if it consists in –

(a) directly or indirectly imposing unfair purchase or selling prices or other unfair trading conditions;

(b) limiting production, markets or technical development to the prejudice of consumers;

(c) applying dissimilar conditions to equivalent transactions with other trading parties, thereby placing them at a competitive disadvantage;

(d) making the conclusion of contracts subject to acceptance by the other parties of supplementary obligations which, by their nature or according to commercial usage, have no connection with the subject of the contracts.

...

---

[12] *Ibid*, rule 6 and Annex 2.

[13] Competition Act 1998 ('1998 Act'), s 14(4).

[14] s 41. This refers to the Commission power under art 15(6) of Reg 17 to withdraw after a preliminary examination what the Act calls the 'provisional immunity from penalties': see the Competition Act 1998 (Provisional Immunity from Penalties) Regulations 1999, SI 1999/2281.

[15] s 6.

[16] s 10.

[17] s 10(2). The Act refers here to 'an agreement [which] does not affect trade between Member States but otherwise falls within a category of agreement which is exempt from the Community prohibition by virtue of a Regulation' – ie, a block exemption. Exemption by individual Commission decision is not mentioned because an agreement which does not affect trade between member states falls outwith the prohibition of Art 81(1) and so need not be and ought not to be granted exemption.

[18] See *infra*.

(4) The prohibition imposed by subsection (1) is referred to in this Act as 'the Chapter II prohibition'.

There is no possibility of exemption from the Chapter II prohibition. An undertaking engaged in conduct which may infringe the Chapter II prohibition may apply to the Director for guidance (again, negative clearance) as to whether, in his view, it does or does not do so, either because there is no dominance and/or abuse or the matter at issue falls within an excluded area.[19]

It does not require forensic skills of the highest order to detect the inspiration of Articles 81 and 82 in this. The wording is virtually identical. The clear intention and outcome of the Act is that competition law in the Community becomes competition law within the United Kingdom *mutatis mutandis*. Powers of enforcement ('Chapter III powers') also borrow heavily from Community experience. The Director is given powers of investigation ('Director's investigation') of suspected infractions ('if there are reasonable grounds for suspecting' infringement) of Chapters I and II prohibitions analogous to those enjoyed by the Commission under Regulation 17.[20] Implicitly an investigation may be launched in response to a notification or upon the Director's own initiative;[21] unlike Regulation 17 there is no express provision for lodging a complaint, and although the present Director is on record that he welcomes complaints as a source of information[22] he is under no duty to act upon them. Authorised OFT officials have a right to enter premises for purposes of an investigation with or without a warrant: if they have no warrant they are required to give notice; if they have a warrant their powers are more extensive.[23] Interim measures may be adopted in the course of an investigation where urgency so requires.[24] It is an offence to refuse to comply with or to obstruct the requirements of an investigation, to destroy or falsify documents or to supply false or misleading information;[25] individuals may be charged under these provisions and are liable to fines and a term of imprisonment of up to two years.[26] Professional legal advice is privileged and need not be dis-

---

[19] 1998 Act, ss 20–22 and Sch 6.

[20] ss 25–31. Although there is scant mention of the Office of Fair Trading in the Act, it will be officials of the OFT working under the authority of the Director who carry out investigations.

[21] See ss 32(2) and 33(2).

[22] OFT 400, paras 8.1 *et seq.*

[23] 1998 Act, ss 27, 28.

[24] s 35.

[25] ss 42–44.

[26] *Ibid.*

closed;[27] as this will apply to in-house counsel it is the one major difference from Commission investigations, the latter recognising privilege only in accordance with the *A M & S* rule.[28] Following an investigation, the Director may 'give such directions as he considers appropriate to bring the infringement to an end'.[29] Should a party fail to comply with such directions he may apply to the court for an order to enforce compliance.[30] He may also require the payment of a penalty, to be paid into the Consolidated Fund, of up to 10 per cent of an undertaking's turnover,[31] the term to be defined by the Secretary of State,[32] who has now set 'turnover' as UK-wide turnover of up to a three year period.[33] Penalties are recoverable through normal civil procedure.[34] As with Regulation 17, an undertaking is liable to a fine only if the infraction was intentional or negligent.[35] Parties to 'small agreements' (Chapter I prohibition; excepting price-fixing agreements) and a party engaged in 'conduct of minor significance' (Chapter II prohibition) enjoy immunity from penalties unless it is expressly withdrawn;[36] the meaning of the terms was to be prescribed, and small agreements are now defined as those amongst undertakings the combined annual turnover of which is less than £20 million, conduct of minor significance as that of an undertaking the annual turnover of which is less than £50 million.[37] The Director has published 'guidance' as to how he is minded to deploy his power to fine,[38] which incorporate equivalents of the Commission's notice on the method of setting fines and the whistleblowers notice.[39] Any decision of the Director may be appealed to the Competition

---

[27] s 30.

[28] Case 155/79 *A M & S Europe* v *Commission* [1982] ECR 1575; see pp 171–2 *supra*.

[29] 1998 Act, s 32(1) (Chapter I prohibition), s 33(1) (Chapter II prohibition).

[30] s 34.

[31] s 36.

[32] s 36(8).

[33] Competition Act 1998 (Determination of Turnover for Penalties) Order 2000, SI 2000/309.

[34] 1998 Act, s 37.

[35] s 36(3). There may be a minor difference here between Reg 17 and the Act, in that under the former liability to a fine turns upon whether the infraction was intentional or negligent, whilst under the latter it turns upon whether the Director is satisfied that the infraction was committed intentionally or negligently. This may imply a more objective test under Reg 17, and that a decision of the Director can be set aside only if he has acted (*Wednesbury?*) unreasonably.

[36] ss 39, 40; see *infra*.

[37] Competition Act 1998 (Small Agreements and Conduct of Minor Significance) Regulations 2000, SI 2000/262.

[38] OFT 423.

[39] See p 176 and p 180 *supra*.

Commission Appeal Tribunals,[40] from which further appeal lies on points of law and determination of the amount of a penalty to the Court of Appeal or the Court of Session.[41]

The Act further provides for procedures to assist the (European) Commission in its powers of investigation under Regulation 17 ('Commission investigation'),[42] amendments to the Fair Trading Act 1973 which will continue to regulate merger control in the United Kingdom[43] (although the government has recently published a consultation document proposing significant change to the Act in this respect, replacing the current public interest test with a competition-based test such as that used in the Merger Regulation and in most other member states),[44] and the creation of the Competition Commission which replaced and absorbed the powers of the Monopolies and Mergers Commission in 1999[45] and is given further powers to assist the Director in discharging his responsibilities under the Act.[46]

It ought to be noted that the Competition Act gives rise to no direct constitutional issues in the context of devolution: competition law is a reserved matter in terms of the Scotland and Northern Ireland Acts,[47] and the rules and regime established by the Act cannot be altered by Holyrood or Stormont, although there may be a degree of trenching by *intra vires* legislation there, regulating, for example, public and/or privileged undertakings or simply the law of contract.

So closely does the UK scheme follow the Community model that it is easier to point out the differences between the two than it is the similarities. They may be adumbrated as follows.

- The Act is of course restricted, for both prohibitions, to conduct which distorts competition 'within the United Kingdom',[48] and so does not incorporate the (gentle) test required by Articles 81 and 82 of showing an effect upon interstate trade. Section 2(3) provides that the Chapter I prohibition applies only to restrictive practices which are, or are intended to be,

---

[40] 1998 Act, ss 46–48. For the Rules of the Appeal Tribunals, which are modelled upon the Rules of Procedure of the Court of First Instance, see the Competition Commission Appeal Tribunal Rules 2000, SI 2000/261.
[41] s 49.
[42] ss 61–65.
[43] ss 66–68.
[44] DTI, *Merger Consultation Document: Proposals for Reform*, July 1999.
[45] Competition Act 1998 (Commencement No 3) Order 1999, SI 1999/505.
[46] 1998 Act, s 45; Sch 7.
[47] Sch 5, Part II, Section C3 and Sch 3, para 26 respectively.
[48] 1998 Act, ss 2(1)(a), 18(1).

'implemented' in the UK, so both incorporating the *Woodpulp* rule on extraterritoriality[49] and presumably exempting a purely export cartel. There is no express equivalent in section 18 to the Article 82 prohibition of abuse of a dominant position in 'a substantial part of the common market', as there is in the national law of some other, even small, member states;[50] it refers instead to abuse of a dominant position 'in a market'. Whether this means that the relevant geographic market for purposes of the Chapter II prohibition can be no smaller than that of the UK falls to be determined by the courts.[51]

■ A number of subject areas are expressly excluded (*not* exempted) from the prohibitions: these are mergers and concentrations (both Chapter I and Chapter II prohibitions),[52] reserved to the Fair Trading Act 1973, and planning obligations[53] and 'designated professional rules'[54] (Chapter I only). The application of the Act is also expressly moderated in the case of competition scrutiny under other statutes (the Financial Services Act 1986, the Companies Act 1989, the Broadcasting Act 1990 and the Environment Act 1995);[55] this is suppleness (or complexity) which is not permitted under the broad strokes of Community rules. There are special provisions for agriculture,[56] as there are in the competition law of some member states[57] and in Community law,[58] and, echoing Article 86(2) (ex Article 90(2)) virtually *verbatim*, neither prohibition applies to

> an undertaking entrusted with the operation of services of general economic interest or having the character of a revenue-producing monopoly in so far as the prohibition would obstruct the performance, in law or in fact, of the particular tasks assigned to that undertaking.[59]

---

[49] Cases 89 etc/85 *Åhlström v Commission* [1988] ECR 5193; see Chap 9. Given the extent of Community integration it is entirely possible that a significant number of agreements the centre of gravity of which fall outwith the United Kingdom will therefore be caught by s 2.

[50] See, eg, the (Irish) Competition Act, 1991, s 5(1) ('in the State or in a substantial part of the State'); the Konkurrenceloven, § 11(1) ('på det danske marked eller en del heraf').

[51] See *infra*.

[52] 1998 Act, ss 3(1), 19(1); Sch 1.

[53] s 3(1); Sch 3, para 1.

[54] s 3(1); Sch 4. For application for designation see the Competition Act 1998 (Application for Designation of Professional Rules) Regulations 1999, SI 1999/2546.

[55] s 3(1); Sch 2.

[56] s 3(1); Sch 3, para 9.

[57] eg, Greece (Law 703/1977, Art 5(β)); Finland (Laki Kilpailunrajoituksista 2 § (908/1995)); Sweden (Konkurrenslaget 18a–18c § (1993:20)).

[58] EC Treaty, Art 36 (ex Art 42); Reg 26/62, JO 1962, 993.

[59] 1998 Act, Sch 3, para 4. There is no equivalent to the second (public interest) test prescribed by Art 86(2).

Otherwise they apply fully to the (recently privatised) telecommunications, gas, electricity, water and rail sectors, powers of enforcement of the Act, including the power to impose penalties, falling concurrently to the director-general/regulator of each and the Director;[60] as this could give rise to parallel, perhaps conflicting, enforcement proceedings, rules (the 'concurrency' regulations) have been drawn up to coordinate the enforcement activities of these authorities and to authorise the Secretary of State, should conflict arise, to determine the most appropriate enforcement authority (the 'competent person') in a particular case.[61] Also excluded from the prohibitions are agreements made and conduct engaged in (*sic*) 'in order to comply with a legal requirement'.[62] This is a statutory enunciation of the case law of the Court of Justice bearing upon 'the autonomous conduct of undertakings' which exempts them from compliance with Articles 81 and 82 where they respond to statutory compulsion,[63] and it gives rise to two issues. The first is whether the courts will view an express legal privilege as a legal requirement: whether, for example, tied public houses will be able to circumvent the Act by reliance upon the guest beer rule.[64] The case law of the Court of Justice, which the British courts are bound to apply,[65] would suggest not. The second and more important is the absence in the Act of an equivalent of Article 86(1) (ex Article 90(1)) in order to prohibit statutory or regulatory rules which compel anticompetitive conduct. Unless the courts read such provision into the Act rules adopted by a host of regulatory bodies, so long as they are not themselves undertakings, will escape its application.[66]

■ The Secretary of State is authorised to adopt, by order, specific rules excluding or exempting from the prohibitions or otherwise modifying their application to vertical agreements or land agreements, the terms to have

---

[60] s 54; Sch 10. The director/regulator applies specific competition rules under each relevant Act but 'shall regard his functions under ... the Competition Act 1998 as paramount': Telecommunications Act 1984, s 3(3B); Gas Act 1986, s 4(3A); Electricity Act 1989, s 3(6A); Water Industry Act 1991, s 2(6A); Railways Act 1993, s 4(7A). The exception is the Channel Tunnel, enforcement power being reserved for the most part to the Director-General: Channel Tunnel Rail Link Act 1996, s 22(3).

[61] Competition Act 1998 (Concurrency) Regulations 2000, SI 2000/260.

[62] 1998 Act, Sch 3, para 5.

[63] See pp 40–42 *supra*.

[64] Supply of Beer (Tied Estates) Order 1989, SI 1989/2390.

[65] See *infra*.

[66] The contrary argument is the exclusion from the application of the Act of designated professional rules (s 3(1); Sch 4) which implies professional bodies are otherwise intended to be caught. But it is submitted that much of their activities – for example, those discharged by the Law Societies – are of a nature not of (an association of) undertakings but of public law regulation which absent an equivalent of Art 86(1) appears to escape the Act.

such meaning as may be prescribed.[67] Land agreements are now prescribed as agreements which create, alter, transfer or terminate an interest in land,[68] and an agreement is now excluded (*sic*) from the Chapter I prohibition 'to the extent that it is a land agreement';[69] vertical agreements are

> agreement[s] between undertakings, each of which operates, for the purposes of the agreement, at a different level of the production or distribution chain, and relating to the conditions under which parties may purchase, sell or resell certain goods or services and includes provisions contained in such agreements which relate to the assignment to the buyer or use by the buyer of intellectual property rights, provided that those provisions do not constitute the primary object of the agreement and are directly related to the use, sale or resale of goods or services by the buyer or its customers.[70]

An agreement, to the extent that it is a vertical agreement, and provided it does not directly or indirectly, in isolation or in combination with other factors, impose fixed or minimum sales prices,[71] is also excluded.[72] This mirrors to an extent the Commission's own new approach to vertical agreements[73] but is even more generously disposed to them, providing no turnover thresholds. The Director may withdraw from a given agreement the benefit of exclusion.[74] The Secretary of State may also add to, amend or delete all exclusion/moderating provisions by order.[75]

- The Director will enjoy a much wider degree of latitude ('he *may* grant an exemption',[76] he '*may* conduct an investigation',[77] he '*may* give ... such directions *as he considers appropriate* to bring [an] infringement to an end'[78]) in the enforcement of the Act than does the Commission in the enforcement of the Community rules. Whilst it may well be that a rampant Director will pursue infringements with the same or greater doggedness and tenacity as the Commission, the terms of the Act appear not to impose a statutory duty upon him to do so, and it seems unlikely that he may be subjected to judicial proceedings to compel him to act.

- The powers of the Director are subject to appeal to the Competition

---

[67] 1998 Act, s 50.
[68] Competition Act 1998 (Land and Vertical Agreements Exclusion) Order 2000, SI 2000/310, art 2.
[69] art 5.
[70] art 2.
[71] art 4.
[72] art 3.
[73] See pp 104–5 *supra*.
[74] SI 2000/310, art 7.
[75] 1998 Act, ss 3(3), 19(2)–(4).
[76] s 4(1).
[77] s 25.
[78] ss 32(1), 33(1).

Commission Appeal Tribunals. Being a right of appeal and not judicial review, it will allow a full re-hearing of the case on its merits and so allow the Tribunals greater power and a greater latitude than that enjoyed by the Court of Justice in (essentially review) proceedings raised under Article 230 (ex Article 173).

■ The Act is silent as to state aids. Competition may be distorted by public subvention within a member state as it may be between member states. In the UK the potential to do so has increased with the tax varying powers devolved to the Scottish parliament; but it is a matter unaddressed by the Act and left to the wisdom of governments.

Whilst the Director enjoys substantial powers of enforcement analogous to those of the Commission, the greater importance, on which it is strangely silent, will lie in whether the Competition Act creates, in Community language, horizontal directly effective rights. Some national competition laws provide expressly for a tortious/delictual right of action in the event of a breach of their prohibitions.[79] So in fact did immediately pre-existing British legislation;[80] but the Competition Act does not (and nor of course, in pre-direct effect days, did the Treaty). This is a problem which Hobhouse LJ in the English Court of Appeal recently observed:

> It has been a matter of judicial comment now for over 50 years that Parliament causes unnecessary uncertainty by enacting provisions which prohibit or render unlawful activities or action without saying at the same time what is to be the effect (if any) on the validity or enforceability of the transactions referred to. In recent years parliamentary draftsmen seem to have heeded this advice ....[81]

Other than section 2(4) (Chapter I prohibited agreements or decisions are 'void') it went unheeded by the draftsmen of the Competition Act. The government took the view that the 'clear intention' of the Act is that '[t]hird party rights of action under the domestic regime are to be the same as those under Articles 85 and 86', and that express provision of this in the

---

[79] eg the (Irish) Competition Act, 1991, s 6; § 33 GWB.

[80] The Restrictive Trade Practices Act 1976 (repealed with the entry into force of the Competition Act) provided (s 35(1)(b)) that it was 'unlawful' for any party to an agreement required to be, but not, registered with the Director (a requirement of the 1976 Act not replicated in the Competition Act) to give effect to it or to enforce or purport to enforce it, and (s 35(2)):

the obligation to comply with [s 35(1)(b)] is a duty owed to any person who may be affected by the contravention of it and any breach of that duty is actionable accordingly subject to the defences and any other incidents applying to actions for breach of statutory duty.

[81] *Fuji Finance v Aetna Life Insurance Co* [1997] Ch 173 at 199.

Act was unnecessary.[82] This could of course be immediately countered with the argument that with principles and precedents of express provision so readily to hand, the fact that the Act is silent must be taken to mean that Parliament did not intend it. This is compounded by the fact that, should the courts be minded to elect breach of statutory duty to be the cause of action upon which to found a right in damages as the House of Lords did for breach of Article 82,[83] there is a strong presumption in English statutory construction that where an Act contains its own form of sanction (provided here in Chapter III penalties) it cannot have been the intention of Parliament to create a right in damages for breach of statutory duty.[84]

Whether the necessary cause of action identified by the courts is breach of statutory duty or some other tort (for example, unlawful interference) which would circumvent the damages problem, it is submitted that breach of the Chapters I and II prohibitions will be actionable, for three reasons. First, the very language of the Act is one which creates statutory duties for the undertakings which are its addressees. If section 2(4) provides that pro- hibited agreements or decisions are 'void' – language which mirrors that of Article 81(2) – and sections 2(1) and 18 provide that certain practices and conduct are 'prohibited', the duty to refrain from either is clear and the right of a third party to elicit the assistance of the courts to that end would seem to flow therefrom inexorably. Certainly an express provision that performance of prohibited agreements or conduct is 'unlawful' and the obligation to refrain from it is 'a duty owed to any person' (the Restrictive Trade Practices Act 1976) would place the issue beyond question, but it is submitted that it is necessarily to be implied. Second, the House of Lords characterised an infringement of Article 82 as a breach of statutory duty,[85] the statute being the European Communities Act 1972. This was a device to found a cause of action in English law for third parties injured by con- duct prohibited by Community competition rules, a necessary step to make Community rights effective but one not entirely comfortable – according to Lord Wilberforce (dissenting) 'a conclusionary statement concealing a vital and unexpressed step'[86] – and one maybe unnecessary within a purely UK context. But it would nonetheless be surprising if the courts refused to

---

[82] *Hansard* (HL), Vol 583, No 68, 25 November 1997, cols 955–6.

[83] *Garden Cottage Foods v Milk Marketing Board* [1984] AC 130; see pp 203–4. *supra*.

[84] *Cutler v Wandsworth Stadium* [1949] AC 398 (HL); *R v Deputy Governor of Parkhurst Prison, ex parte Hague* [1992] 1 AC 58 (HL); *cf. R v HM Treasury, ex parte Petch*, judg- ment of the High Court (QBD) of 24 February 1989, unreported.

[85] *Garden Cottage Foods*, n 83 *supra*.

adopt the far less tortuous reasoning necessary to construe an infringement of Chapters I or II prohibitions as a breach of statutory duty. Third, and most remarkable, is the direction given to both the Director and the courts by section 60 of the Act:

(1) The purpose of this section is to ensure that so far as is possible (having regard to any relevant differences between the provisions concerned), questions arising under this Part in relation to competition within the United Kingdom are dealt with in a manner which is consistent with the treatment of corresponding questions arising in Community law in relation to competition within the Community.

(2) At any time when the court determines a question arising under this Part, it must act (so far as is compatible with the provisions of this Part and whether or not it would otherwise be required to do so) with a view to securing that there is no inconsistency between –
   (a) the principles applied, and decisions reached, by the court in determining that question; and
   (b) the principles laid down by the Treaty and the European Court, and any relevant decision of that Court, as applicable at that time in determining any corresponding question arising in Community law.

(3) The court must, in addition, have regard to any relevant decision or statement of the Commission.

(4) Subsections (2) and (3) also apply to –
   (a) the Director; and
   (b) any person acting on behalf of the Director, in connection with any matter arising under this Part.

(5) In subsections (2) and (3), 'court' means any court or Tribunal.

(6) In subsections (2)(b) and (3), 'decision' includes a decision as to –
   (a) the interpretation of any provision of Community law;
   (b) the civil liability of an undertaking for harm caused by its infringement of Community law.

The purpose of section 60, already dubbed the 'Europrinciples clause', is, as stated, to ensure that British competition law is construed consistently, and is therefore as compatible as possible, with that of Community law. Whilst it has the advantage of expediting the development of British law by incorporating into the Act an established body of competition law, it is also 'Community friendly' in the extreme, ensuring for undertakings a coherence between the two tiers of competition regulation, and for this reason it is laudable. It also surely means that, in discharging their statutory duty under section 60(2) of ensuring that there is no inconsistency with 'the principles laid down by ... and any relevant decision of [the]

---

[86] *Ibid*, at 151.

Court', British courts will take notice of *BRT* v *SABAM*[87] and subsequent case law in order to make sections 2(1) and 18 'directly effective'. But it is still not clear what exactly this entails. Section 60(6)(b), a provision added to the Bill only after committee stage, requires a British court to ensure consistency with any 'decision' of the Court of Justice as to the civil liability of undertakings for harm caused by infringement of Community law (and adds weight to the argument that Parliament intended the availability of civil redress), but it cannot do so when, as discussed above,[88] no such decision exists. Nevertheless it seems more than likely that the courts will weld the 'direct effect' of sections 2(1) and 18 to breach of statutory duty and so activate the host of civil remedies available for breach thereof, and therefore it will be less the Director than disgruntled competitors that will come to stretch the Act. Assuming the competence of civil action, *Delimitis*-type problems[89] will necessarily arise, although it is likely the Director will be able to discharge his part with greater expedience than does the Commission.

A primary advantage of section 60 is that, in transposing Community principles into UK law, it makes what would otherwise be a formidable interpretative task easier. The irony is that it voluntarily nails the direction of purely British law to the Community mast, to the independent development and evolution of law directed from Brussels and Luxembourg to Community ends, and this in a member state from certain quarters of which there is perennial grousing about overbearing European interference in national affairs. The serious peril here is that the Act introduces the Community system of prohibition/*ex post* administrative exemption at just the time the Commission may be abandoning it;[90] if it does so the intended compatibility and convergence of the two systems will necessarily suffer. A less fraught but still telling example: it is now established that in English law the automatic nullity of Article 81(2) is of a temporaneous or transient character[91] and that a contract prohibited by Article 81(1) is illegal, so barring any claim for loss by a party to it in damages or in restitution.[92] Presumably this is also an accurate statement of the law which will attend an agreement which is void for breach of the Chapter I prohibition. Should the Court of Justice take a different view in the reference in *Crehan* v *Courage*,[93] British courts will of course require to apply Article 81(2)

---

[87] Case 127/73 *Belgische Radio en Televisie* v *SABAM* [1974] ECR 313.
[88] at pp 198–200.
[89] Case C-234/89 *Delimitis* v *Henninger Bräu* [1991] ECR I-935; see pp 211–12 *supra*.
[90] See pp 134–6 *supra*.
[91] *Passmore* v *Morland* [1999] EuLR 501 (CA).
[92] *Gibbs Mew* v *Gemmell* [1998] EuLR 588 (CA); *Crehan* v *Courage* [1999] EuLR 838 (CA).

accordingly. But will they also follow suit in the purely UK context and attribute the same meaning and effects to section 2(4)? They may do so by statutory obligation, because section 60(6)(b) of the Act instructs them to do so, or they may elect to do so because if they do not a gap in remedies will open up depending upon whether a British or a Community right is at issue (such as that which persuaded the House of Lords in *M v Home Office*[94] to alter the English rules on Crown immunity from interim injunction following *Factortame I*[95]) and there would be huge difficulty in disentangling the result of an agreement prohibited by both section 2 and Article 81, it being void under both provisions but the civil consequences of the two breaches being different.

Much will turn upon the extent to which, or suppleness with which, the courts read their interpretative duty 'so far as is possible'[96] and 'so far as is compatible with the provisions of [the Act]'[97] as one desirable and appropriate. To illustrate: the term 'undertaking' is introduced for the first time (indigenously) into British law but is not defined in the Act; clearly its Community law meaning is intended to become its British law meaning. This could be said equally for the bedrock notions of 'agreement', 'concerted practice' and 'abuse of a dominant position'. Other, only slightly less fundamental terms of the Act may also borrow just as easily: identification of undertakings entrusted with services in the 'general economic interest' and what obstructs the performance of their tasks can cannibalise Article 86(2) (ex Article 90(2)) case law (although there are good policy arguments for applying the principles with a broader brush than does Community law), a working definition of predatory pricing can conveniently be borrowed from *AKZO*[98] and the principle of collective dominance from the developing case law in that area. These are reasonable and uncontroversial, and will positively assist in the judicial development of the Act. Others Community principles may be borrowed and may acquire a life of their own: British courts will, for example, be required to apply the rule of reason, a task which would be made easier if it had greater clarity or precision. But it *may* be absorbed by them and fashioned into something which comes to provide it.

However, in cleaving to Community principles there are ambiguities and potential risks, and British courts may find some less easy to transplant.

---

[93] Case C-453/99, pending; see pp 200–1 *supra*.
[94] [1994] 1 AC 377.
[95] C-213/89 R v *Secretary of State for Transport, ex parte Factortame* [1990] ECR I-2433.
[96] 1998 Act, s 60(1).
[97] s 60(2).
[98] Case 62/86 *AKZO v Commission* [1991] ECR I-3359.

This is not simply the question of the purposive canons of interpretation adopted by the Court of Justice as sitting uncomfortably with British tradition and practice. The Court of Justice has itself recognised and emphasised that legal texts are to be interpreted in the light of their objectives and purpose in their context, so that even identically worded texts in different instruments ought not necessarily to be accorded the same interpretation,[99] the most recent example being the diametrically opposed interpretations accorded the same instrument (the trade mark directive)[100] by the EFTA Court in the EEA context[101] and by the Court of Justice in the Community context.[102] The context of the EC Treaty is one in which a primary goal is market integration; but this is *not* the context of the Competition Act, the UK having become a legislative, economic and monetary union and a common market in 1707 (at the time by far the largest in the world) and 1801 and not requiring competition rules to prise markets open as they have in the Community context. With no integration goals, to which purpose much of the application of Articles 81 and 82 has been bent, it is not clear how far sections 2 and 18 can, or should, be interpreted in the same way.

In terms of substance the greatest importance is likely to be geography and relevant market. Sections 2 and 18 allude only obliquely to geographic application of the prohibitions: they apply 'within the United Kingdom' and United Kingdom 'means, in relation to an agreement which operates ... only in a part of the United Kingdom, that part'[103] (Chapter I prohibition) and 'means the United Kingdom or any part of it'[104] (Chapter II prohibition). Otherwise section 2 (like Article 81) makes no direct reference to markets; section 18 prohibits abuse of a dominant position 'in a market'. Absent more specific statutory guidance, British courts will, and will be required by section 60, to take notice of and apply the case law of the Court and 'have regard to' the Commission notice on the definition of relevant market.[105] But much of this was fashioned to suit and to assist the purpose and ambit of Articles 81 and 82 and the attendant requirements of the internal market and has been interpreted in that light. The relevant

---

[99] Case 270/80 *Polydor v Harlequin Records* [1982] ECR 329.

[100] Directive 89/104, OJ 1989 L40/1.

[101] Case E-2/97 *Mag Instrument Inc v California Trading Co Norway, Ulsteen* [1997] EFTA CR 127.

[102] Case C-355/96 *Silhouette International Schmied v Hartlauer* [1998] ECR I-4799.

[103] 1998 Act, s 2(7).

[104] s 18(3).

[105] Notice on definition of the relevant market for the purposes of Community competition law, OJ 1997 C372/5. On the OFT's preliminary views of market definition see OFT 403.

geographic market 'comprises the area ... which can be distinguished from other neighbouring areas because the conditions of competition are appreciably different' there.[106] With the Competition Act bringing the Treaty scheme down to scale, will the market be narrowed accordingly? It is analogous to increasing the magnification of a microscope, so necessitating greater precision and focus, which is maybe reflected in the Act in the Chapter II prohibition – abuse of dominance – again, not within a substantial part of the market (Article 82) but 'in a market'. Competition can be distorted at the local level. This is especially so for retail markets, which enjoy a relatively light touch under Community rules. The Treaty does not concern itself with restrictive practices or abuse of dominance which produce effects solely within Glasgow or Gateshead or Godalming; but there is no reason why the Competition Act should not. By the same token, product market can be, and is likely to be, defined with greater precision, taking greater account of UK market characteristics. Hitherto, for example, the Commission has on several occasions taken notice of a market in 'beer' but never one narrower; surely there are within the UK distinct markets for proper beer and the chemical soup which is also marketed under that generic name. Where the line is to be drawn – between licensed and off-licensed sales, bitter/heavy and lager, draught and bottled, cask conditioned and keg conditioned – is for the courts, but in the more specific UK (or local?) context they are likely to draw it with greater sensitivity than does Community law.

Whatever the determination of the relevant markets, what then of competition within them? British courts are instructed to take notice of the *de minimis* defence and various Commission notices amplifying it; but a number of the notices adopt not only market share but also threshold criteria which were drafted from a Community perspective and cannot translate to a market only 15 per cent of the size of that for which they were designed. For example, agreements between or amongst small and medium-sized enterprises as defined by Community law[107] are 'rarely capable' of distorting competition appreciably within the meaning of Article 81.[108] But surely a company with an annual turnover of £25 million and 240 employees – an SME to the Community – is of a size quite capable, certainly in concert with others of like size, of appreciably distorting competition within even the UK-wide market. It is instructive to consider the express provisions of

---

[106] *Ibid*, para 8.

[107] Recommendation 96/280, OJ 1996 L107/4.

[108] Notice on agreements of minor importance which do not fall within the meaning of Article 85(1), OJ 1997 C372/13, para 19; see p 73 *supra*.

the law in other member states emulating the Treaty and providing thresholds: in Denmark (admittedly with a much smaller population) an anticompetitive agreement produces inappreciable effects if the *combined* annual turnover of all parties to it is less than £12 million (150 million kroner);[109] for the Netherlands it is only £600,000 (2 million guilders).[110] Others provide differing scales depending upon geographic market definition: in Austria an agreement produces inappreciable effects (the splendidly named *Bagatellkartell*) if the parties have a 5 per cent share of the national market but rising to 25 per cent if it is a local (*örtlich*) market.[111] On all of this the Competition Act remains silent. The immunity from fines provided to parties to 'small agreements' and a party engaged in 'conduct of minor significance'[112] appears to be an attempt to incorporate principles of appreciability into the Act, but if so it is inarticulate in the extreme. Efforts during passage of the Bill to construct a test and/or thresholds to be embodied expressly in it were rebuffed by the government,[113] which indicated in the House of Lords its own views as to what are small agreements and conduct of minor significance.[114] But these are quite irrelevant unless *Pepper* v *Hart*[115] tests can be brought to play which, it is submitted, they cannot. The Director has indicated that he views a margin of appreciability (excluding market sharing or price-fixing agreements) at 25 per cent of the combined market share of the parties,[116] which is consistent with the Commission's growing emphasis upon market share rather than size of an undertaking. He may do so, and may be estopped thereby from otherwise exercising his own powers, but the Commission notice on agreements of minor importance sets a much lower threshold (5 and 10 per cent for horizontal and vertical agreements respectively). The Act exempts small agreements and conduct of minor significance, now defined by the Secretary of State (and not using market share criteria),[117] from liability to Chapter III penalties only; it does *not* exempt them from the Chapters I and II prohibitions. In civil litigation in which the Director plays no part

---

[109] Konkurrenceloven, § 7(1)(2); or Kr 1000 million (£80 million) if together they account for less than 10 per cent of the relevant market: § 7(1)(1).

[110] Mededingingswet, art 7(1)(b)(2); or ƒ10 million (£3 million) if amongst distributors: art 7(1)(b)(1). In both cases the agreement must be amongst eight or fewer undertakings: art 7(1)(a).

[111] §§ 16, 18 ÖKG.

[112] 1998 Act, ss 39, 40.

[113] *Hansard* (HL), Vol 583, No 63, 13 November 1997, cols 256–9.

[114] *Hansard* (HL), Vol 583, No 64, 17 November 1997, col 434.

[115] [1993] AC 593 (HL).

[116] Assessment of Market Power, OFT 415, para 2.3.

[117] Competition Act 1998 (Small Agreements and Conduct of Minor Significance) Regulations 2000, SI 2000/262.

British courts are bound by section 60 to take notice of and apply the Community tests; and it is important to emphasise that it is a task which is likely to fall primarily to them.[118] Just as the Commission repels complaints for insufficient Community interest, the Director is likely to have too burgeoning an in-tray involving, say, the motor trade or the utilities to concern himself with the availability or price of a pint of real ale in Nether Wallop, where many of the preliminary, at least, skirmishes under the Act may be fought.

The most contentious issue may well come to be whether the Director's Chapter III powers of investigation and enforcement is on all fours with the Human Rights Act: whether the penalties provided are 'criminal charges' within the meaning of Article 6(1) of the European Convention on Human Rights and, if so, whether powers of investigation offend the Convention rules on presumption of innocence (Article 6(2)), self-incrimination (Article 6(1)) and/or inviolability of premises (Article 8(1)). Hitherto the Court of Justice has taken a benign view of the compatibility of Regulation 17 with the Convention.[119] Now it is finally to be incorporated by the Human Rights Act 1998 it will fall to the British courts (in the first instance to the Competition Commission Appeal Tribunals) to ensure that the Director, deploying powers under the Competition Act analogous to those of the Commission under Regulation 17, meets the prescribed standards. They may be tempted to incorporate the Court's case law on Regulation 17 into UK law via the interpretative obligation of section 60, so allowing the Competition Act to 'trump' the interpretative obligation of the Human Rights Act, but it is unlikely. The United Kingdom ratified the Convention before it did the Treaty, so that even Community law accepts that a (prior) Convention right trumps ('shall not be affected by') a Treaty right.[120] And it is clear from the Strasbourg judgment in *Matthews* v *United Kingdom*[121] that the UK cannot plead a 'Euro defence' to justify a

---

[118] It should also be noted that the courts are in principle unable to seek assistance in the interpretation of the Act, it being a wholly UK statute, from the Court of Justice under Article 234 (ex Article 177): Case C-346/94 *City of Glasgow District Council* v *Kleinwort Benson* [1995] ECR I-615. However, more likely is the contrary argument to be derived from Cases C-297/88 & 197/89 *Dzodzi* v *Belgium* [1990] ECR I-3763 and Case C-130/95 *Giloy* v *Hauptzollamt Frankfurt am Main-Ost* [1997] ECR I-4291 that, because Treaty provisions are expressly incorporated into the Act, the Court of Justice will have jurisdiction to render preliminary rulings on the interpretation not of the Act itself but of the provisions of Community law relevant to its interpretation. The reference in Case C-7/97 *Oscar Bronner* v *Mediaprint* [1998] ECR I-7791 could be said to have been a device adopted by the referring Austrian court for the interpretation of purely (but very similar) Austrian law, and the reference was admissible.

[119] See pp 178–80 *supra*.

[120] EC Treaty, Art 307 (ex Art 234).

[121] (1999) 28 EHRR 361.

breach of the Convention. Earliest indications from Scottish courts (where the Human Rights Act first became effective, in matters relative to the Scotland Act 1998) are of a robust view of Article 6 of the Convention.[122] Unlike litigation involving Regulation 17 which is played out largely in Luxembourg, there *is* recourse to Strasbourg from the British courts which will give effect to the Competition Act. It would be an irony indeed if by the incursion of European (Convention) law British authorities exercising powers under a British statute within the United Kingdom in order to bring British companies to book fall subject to more stringent procedural safeguards than when the Commission seeks to do the same under Community legislation; and it would be no service to consumer welfare if the OFT expends much of its time not pursuing infringements of the Competition Act but defending its practices in the courts.

---

[122] *Starrs* v *Ruxton (PF Linlithgow)* 2000 SC 208 (J) (*cf. Clancy* v *Caird* 2000 SLT 546 (Ex Div)); *Brown* v *Stott (PF Dunfermline)* 2000 SC 328 (J).

SELECT BIBLIOGRAPHY

Primary materials

The most reliable source of Commission decisions in the field of competition is a trawl through the Official Journal, in which a large number of decisions are published; the time lag between adoption and publication of a decision is sometimes considerable. More efficient but less reliable is *Reports of Commission Decisions relating to Competition*, comprising the most important decisions taken directly from the Official Journal and bound up from time to time; at present these are in seven volumes from 1973 to the end of 1998.

The Commission publishes annually a *Report on Competition Policy* which includes a survey of relevant case law of the Courts and its own decisions. From time to time it also contains a number of important policy statements as to the manner in which it intends to apply its powers of enforcement.

Since 1988 the Common Market Law Reports (CMLR) has published the '*CMLR Antitrust Reports*' (from 1988 to 1991 the '*CMLR Antitrust Supplement*') monthly, which become volumes 4 and 5 of the CMLR general reports. It reports selected recent judgments of the Court of Justice and the Court of First Instance (usually long before they are reported in the ECR), Commission decisions, legislation and draft legislation, and parliamentary questions and Commission answers in the field of competition.

A very useful compendium of materials necessary for competition law practice is Jones, C., van der Woude, M. and Lewis, X., *EC Competition Law Handbook*, Sweet & Maxwell, London, published annually.

The most up-to-date source is the D-G Competition website, at europa.eu.int/comm/competition. Recent judgments of the Court of Justice and the Court of First Instance are available (from the date of judgment, but not always in all languages) at europa.eu.int/eur-lex.

Secondary materials

There is a huge (and multilingual) literature in EC competition law. The following are only the most comprehensive (and up to date, for Community law books enjoy only a short shelf-life) secondary sources in English.

Bellamy, C. and Child, G. *Common Market Law of Competition* (5th edn, Sweet & Maxwell, London, 2000)

Bishop, S. and Walker, M. *The Economics of EC Competition Law: Concepts, Application and Measurement* (Sweet & Maxwell, London, 1999)

Cook, J. and Kerse, C. *EC Merger Control* (3rd edn, Sweet & Maxwell, London, 1999)

Evans, A. *EC Law of State Aid* (Clarendon Press, Oxford, 1997)

Faull, J. and Nikpay, A. *The EC Law of Competition* (Oxford UP, Oxford, 1999)

Goyder, D.G. *EC Competition Law* (3rd edn, Clarendon Press, Oxford, 1998)

Green, N. and Robertson, A. *Commercial Agreements and Competition Law: Practice and Procedure in the UK and EC* (2nd edn, Kluwer, London, 1997)

Hancher, L., Slot, P.J. and Ottervanger, T. *EC State Aids* (Sweet & Maxwell, London, 1999)

Hawk, B.E. and Huser, H.L. *European Community Merger Control: A Practitioner's Guide* (Kluwer, London, 1996)

Kerse, C. *EC Antitrust Procedure* (4th edn, Sweet & Maxwell, London, 1998)

Korah, V. *An Introductory Guide to EC Competition Law and Practice* (6th edn, Hart, Oxford, 1997)

Maitland-Walker, J. *Competition Laws of Europe* (Butterworths, London, 1995)

Ritter, L., Braun W.D. and Rawlinson, F. *European Competition Law: A Practitioner's Guide* (2nd edn, Kluwer, London, 2000)

Whish, R. *Competition Law* (4th edn, Butterworths, London, 2000)

INDEX

judicial review *see* Judicial review
jurisdiction, 134, 180, 189, 192, 221
Court of Justice
  action of annulment *see* Action of
    annulment
  appeal to, 132, 189, 192
  declaratory judgment from, 42
  European Economic Area and, 293, 343
  jurisdiction, 134, 189, 201n
  merger decision, review of, 265
  references to, for preliminary ruling,
    133–4, 189, 221, 342
  role of, 24, 32, 74
  state aids, review of decision as to, 341
  see also Judicial review
Cross-buying as abusive conduct, 160
Customs agent
  competition rules, application of, to,
    35
Customs duties
  EEC Treaty, aims of, 21–2
Customs union
  creation of, 22
  Turkey, with, 299

Damages, availability of, 42, 177, 203–4,
  208, 343
De minimis defence, 71–3, 75, 101–2,
  121, 124–5, 215, 318
Delimitis principle, 76, 211–12, 221, 356
Denmark
  anticompetition agreements, 360
  competition law in, 31
  EEC, membership of, 21
  ECU and, 25
Design rights *see* Intellectual property
  rights
Diplomatic immunity, 278
Director-General of Fair Trading
  powers of, under Competition Act *see*
    Competition Act
Discount
  joint prohibition of, 84
  maximum, setting, 109
  quantity, as to, 153
Distortion etc. of competition
  article 81(1) and *see* Article 81(1)
Distribution agreement
  exclusive agreement, article 81(1) and,
    102–3, 104–5, 107
  franchising agreement, 104
  motor trade, 127
Dominant position
  abuse of *see* Article 82
  Merger Regulation and, 268–70
Dumping
  meaning, 33

member states, between, 31
third countries, from 33
Duress, agreement obtained by, 52
Dynamic efficiency; meaning, 7

Eastern European Countries
  accession to European Union, 21,
    296
  agreements with, 295–6
  joint ventures in, 89
EC competition rules
  agricultural sector and, 113
  application of
    EC law and national law, 213–19
    generally, 29
  breach of, remedies for, 42
  British judiciary and, 344
  Commission, role of, 46–8
  dumping and, 33
  economic goals, 26–9
  economic entity doctrine *see* Economic
    entity doctrine
  enforcement of *see* Enforcement
  extraterritorial application of, 282–90
  integration goals, 20, 22, 27–9, 94, 96,
    358
  intellectual property rights and *see*
    Intellectual property rights
  monopolies and, 137–8
  national competition rules and, 32
  public and privileged undertakings, as to
    see Public and private undertakings
  relevant market *see* Relevant market
  transport sector, application to, 113,
    114
  Treaty scheme, 20, 29–33
  role of, 82
  undertakings, scope of *see* Undertakings
EC law
  primacy of, 41, 214, 215, 216, 221
  supranational character of, 24
Economic and monetary union, 25, 26,
  358
Economic democracy, 15
Economic entity doctrine, 43–5, 65, 94,
  182, 249, 260, 284–5, 289, 308
Economists
  Chicago school of, 12, 15
  Harvard school of, 12
ECSC *see* European Coal and Steel
  Community
EEA *see* European Economic Area
EEC *see* European Economic Community
EFTA *see* European Free Trade Area
Electronics
  selective distribution system, 106–8
Employment, protection of, 15